MANAGEMENT OF ORGANIZATIONAL BEHAVIOR

MANAGEMENT OF ORGANIZATIONAL BEHAVIOR
Utilizing Human Resources
Fifth Edition

Paul Hersey

Graduate School of Applied Behavioral Sciences
California American University
Escondido, California

Kenneth H. Blanchard

University of Massachusetts
Amherst, Massachusetts

PRENTICE HALL, Englewood Cliffs, New Jersey 07632

y of Congress Cataloging-in-Publication Data

y, Paul.
Management of organizational behavior : utilizing human resources
Paul Hersey, Kenneth H. Blanchard. -- 5th ed.
      p.   cm.
  Bibliography: p.
  Includes index.
  ISBN 0-13-551268-9   ISBN 0-13-551250-6 (pbk.)
  1. Organizational behavior. 2. Management. 3. Leadership.
 I. Blanchard, Kenneth H. II. Title.
 HD58.7.H47 1988
 658.3--dc19   87-23064
                                                       CIP

Editorial/production supervision and
   interior design: Eleanor Perz
Cover design: Lundgren Graphics, Ltd.
Manufacturing buyer: Ed O'Dougherty

 © 1988, 1982, 1977, 1972, 1969 by Prentice-Hall, Inc.
A Division of Simon & Schuster
Englewood Cliffs, New Jersey 07632

Printed in the United States of America
10 9 8 7 6 5 4 3 2 1

ISBN 0-13-551268-9   01

Prentice-Hall International (UK) Limited, *London*
Prentice-Hall of Australia Pty. Limited, *Sydney*
Prentice-Hall Canada Inc., *Toronto*
Prentice-Hall Hispanoamericana, S.A., *Mexico*
Prentice-Hall of India Private Limited, *New Delhi*
Prentice-Hall of Japan, Inc., *Tokyo*
Simon & Schuster Asia Pte. Ltd., *Singapore*
Editora Prentice-Hall do Brasil, Ltda., *Rio de Janeiro*

to

RALPH E. HERSEY, SR., a retired telephone pioneer with over fifty patents for Bell Laboratories, whose work made direct distance dialing a reality. In looking back over his thirty-nine years of work with the telephone industry, he once commented that of all his contributions, the most rewarding aspect to him personally was that he became known as a *developer of people*.

and

the REAR ADMIRAL THEODORE BLANCHARD, USNR, former Naval officer who was decorated with two Silver Stars, the Bronze Star, the Presidential Citation, and a Navy Unit Commendation for his courageous and competent World War II leadership in the Pacific. In talking with people who worked for him over the years, he was always described as an inspirational, dedicated, and caring leader who always fought for his people and the "underdog," whether in peace or war time.

CONTENTS

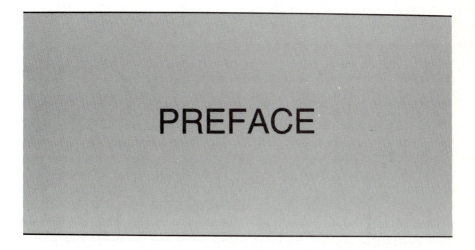

PREFACE

Almost twenty years ago, we introduced our first edition with the following statements which we still believe:

> For a long time management theory has been characterized by a search for universals—a preoccupation with discovering essential elements of all organizations. The discovering of common elements is necessary, but they do not really provide practitioners with "principles" that can be applied with universal success.
>
> In the past decade there has appeared a relative maturity in this field as it begins to focus on "patterned variations"—situational differences. We assume that there are common elements in all organizations, but we also assume differences among them and in particular the managing of their human resources. As the inventory of empirical studies expands, making comparisons and contrasts possible, management theory will continue to emerge. Common elements will be isolated and important variables brought to light.
>
> We believe that management theory is important to all categories of organizations—business, government, military, medicine, education, "voluntary" organizations such as the church, and even the home. We thus have drawn our illustrations and cases from a variety of these organizations and incorporated concepts from many disciplines. Our purpose is to identify a framework which may be helpful in integrating independent approaches from these various disciplines to the understanding of human behavior and management theory.
>
> The focus of this book is on behavior within organizations and not between

organizations. Our belief is that an organization is a unique living organism whose basic component is the individual and this individual is our fundamental unit of study. Thus, our concentration is on the interaction of people, motivation, and leadership.

Though this book is an outgrowth of the insights of many earlier writers, we hope it will make some contribution to management theory.

The response to our first four editions has been very gratifying and encouraging. Individuals and organizations not only in the United States but throughout the world have made use of the behavioral science concepts, tools, and techniques to improve performance. Our goal of writing a concise and easy-to-read book that would make the behaviorial sciences come alive for operating managers, parents, teachers, and students alike appears to have been accomplished through this broad-based acceptance.

In writing this fifth edition, as in the previous editions, we have assumed the serious responsibility of preparing you for the real world through a quality research-based approach to the behavioral sciences. Our purpose is to equip you for the real world, not the fantasy world—a real world, where each of us has to understand the challenges of managing human organizations in a highly competitive environment. This is why our primary emphasis is on practical applied behavioral science concepts, tools, and techniques.

After writing the fourth edition of *Management of Organizational Behavior*, we went our separate ways and crystallized our different approaches to the field of applied behavioral sciences. We are excited about once again working together to produce this new edition of *Management of Organizational Behavior*.

The emphasis of Paul's work and his colleagues at the Center for Leadership Studies has been the refinement of Situational Leadership and the expansion of its applications to various organizational settings as well as to the selling process. These efforts culminated in the writing of *The Situational Leader* and *Situational Selling*, both of which have had a significant impact on many of the changes and improvements found in this edition.

The major thrust of Ken's work and his colleagues at Blanchard Training and Development has been on taking some of the basic concepts associated with performance management and Situational Leadership and organizing them into the One Minute Management system. The international best seller, *The One Minute Manager*, which he co-authored with Spencer Johnson, and the follow-up book, *Putting the One Minute Manager to Work*, written with Bob Lorber, were the result of these efforts. The concepts presented in these books are highlighted in this revision.

As a result of all the new developments in our thinking and the varied research and consulting activities of our respective organizations, this fifth edition is our most extensive revision. Six new chapters have been added. These chapters include Communicating with Rapport, Helping and Hindering Roles in Groups, and four chapters focusing specifically on managing performance. It is in these four chapters that Paul presents his new thinking about the application of Situational Leadership and Ken shares his most recent ideas concerning putting One Minute Management to work.

In addition, each of the remaining chapters has been revised to make the contents practical and useful in today's challenging world. We trust that this fifth edition will make an important contribution to your personal and professional growth and development.

We owe much to colleagues and associates without whose guidance, encouragement, and inspiration the first edition of this book—much less the fifth—would never have been written. In particular, we are indebted to Harry Evarts, Ted Hellebrandt, Norman Martin, Don McCarty, Bob Melendes, Walter Pauk, Warren Ramshaw, and Franklin Williams.

We wish to make special mention of Chris Argyris, William J. Reddin, and Edgar A. Schein. Their contributions to the field of applied behavioral science have been most valuable to us in the course of preparing this book, and we hereby express our appreciation to them.

We also wish to express our special appreciation to our friend and colleague for almost two decades, Dewey E. Johnson, Professor of Management, California State University-Fresno, who assisted us in the preparation of this edition.

Finally, to Suzanne and Margie, our wives, for their continued patience, support, and interest in the progress of our work.

Paul Hersey

Kenneth H. Blanchard

MANAGEMENT OF ORGANIZATIONAL BEHAVIOR

CHAPTER 1

MANAGEMENT:
An Applied Behavioral Sciences Approach

This is a tremendously exciting period for both the understanding and practice of leadership and management. Now, as perhaps never before, there is a growing awareness that the success of our organizations is directly dependent on the effective use of human resources based on the applied behavioral sciences.[1] As we consider the challenging problems in the management of organizations—business, government, not-for-profit, school, and family—we realize that the real test of our abilities as leaders and managers is how effectively we can establish and maintain human organizations.

To meet these challenges we need special tools and the skills to use these tools. This is what this book is all about. It not only presents fundamental behavioral science concepts and theories but also suggests proven simple-to-use tools based on the behavioral sciences.

Some concepts in the behavioral sciences by themselves are well intended but fall short of the mark. They give you good ideas to think about, but they do not always tell you how or when to put these ideas into practice. Woody Allen, the well-known actor and director, says that success in life is ". . . twenty percent timing and eighty percent just showing up:".[2] We have all seen people who just "show up" in leadership and management situations. But we believe that success is much more than just "showing up." We believe it is the knowledge and application of tested behavioral science concepts plus the "timing" skills to get things done. This book will help you not only to acquire the knowledge, but also to help you develop the skills necessary to be a high-performing leader.

Leading, the influencing of the behavior of others, must not be thought of as a single event. Leadership and management are full-time responsibilities that must be practiced every hour of every day. Each minute must be spent wisely. Of course, this is not easy. Leadership and management, because they involve the complexities of people, almost defy description and understanding. We have all known courageous men and women who have provided the vision and energy to make things happen in very difficult situations. But even after decades of research, we are still unable to identify with certainty the specific causal factors that determine managerial success at a specific time and place. This is because real-life situations are never static. They are in a constant state of change, with many factors or variables interacting at the same time. Because of this, the behavioral sciences, unlike the physical sciences, deal in probabilities. Our purpose then is to help increase the odds in your favor, not to suggest rules. In the arena of behavioral sciences, there are no rules.

What has long been needed is an approach to leadership and management that is both conceptually sound and practical in application. We have found through our research and writing, our conversations with thousands of managers throughout the world, our consulting and seminars that most people want an easy-to-grasp approach that is broad enough in scope to permit its application to a number of organizations and situations. Such an approach would promote a common understanding and language that would make it possible for managers to work together and act upon the problems they experience in managing their human resources. In developing these ideas and skills, we wanted to build upon the considerable legacy of the behavioral sciences by using a common language so managers could easily master the key ideas and skills. Situational Leadership provides such a common language to help solve performance problems. It provides a valuable language that can be used on the job, in the home, in every leadership situation. It provides a common language we can use to diagnose leadership problems, adapt behavior to solve these problems, and to communicate solutions.

Rather than reacting to problems in an emotional way, Situational Leadership provides a vehicle for talking about performance problems in a rational way that focuses on the key issues involved. We also wanted to present an approach that has face validity and that is based on empirical evidence. The acceptance that we have received for more than twenty years has indicated to us that this approach is easily understood, accepted, and implemented at all levels of organizations. It is a fundamental approach to the management of organizational behavior.

A LOOK BACK

The transformation of American society since the turn of the century has been breathtaking. We have progressed from a basically agrarian society to a dynamic industrial society, with a higher level of education and standard of living than was ever thought possible. In addition, our scientific and technical advancement staggers the imagination.

This progress has not been without its seamy side. At a time when we should be rejoicing in a golden age of plenty, we find ourselves wallowing in conflict—conflict between nations, conflict between races, conflict between management and workers, even conflict between neighbors. These problems that we face cannot be solved by scientific and technical skills alone; they will require social skills. Many of our most critical problems are not in the world of *things* but in the world of *people*. Our greatest failure as human beings has been the inability to secure cooperation and understanding with others. Shortly after World War II, Elton Mayo recognized this problem when he reflected that "the consequences for society of the unbalance between the development of technical and of social skills have been disastrous."[3]

SUCCESSFUL VERSUS UNSUCCESSFUL SCIENCES

In seeking reasons for this unbalance, Mayo suggested that a significant part of the problem might be traced to the difference between what he called "the successful sciences" (chemistry, physics, and physiology) and "the unsuccessful sciences" (psychology, sociology, and political science). He labeled the former "successful" because in studying these sciences, both theory and practice are provided. Pure knowledge is limited in value unless it can be applied in real situations. The implication of these profound conclusions is that in learning about chemistry or physics, students or practitioners are given direct experience in using their new technical skills in the laboratory, but on the other hand, according to Mayo, the unsuccessful sciences

> do not seem to equip students with a single social skill that is usable in ordinary human situations . . . no continuous and direct contact with the social facts is contrived for the student. He learns from books, spending endless hours in libraries; he reconsiders ancient formulae, uncontrolled by the steady development of experimental skill, the equivalent of the clinic or indeed of the laboratory.[4]

Change

Early contributions in the behavioral sciences, as Mayo suggests, seemed to provide knowledge without effecting changes in behavior. This book will focus on four levels of change in people: (1) knowledge changes, (2) attitud-

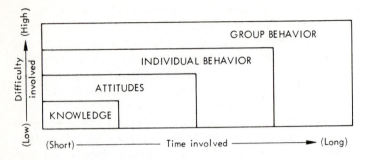

FIGURE 1-1   Time and difficulty involved in making various changes

inal changes, (3) behavioral changes, and (4) group or organizational performance changes.[5] The time relationship and the relative difficulty involved in making each of these levels of change when force or compliance is not a factor is illustrated in Figure 1-1.

Changes in knowledge are the easiest to make, followed by changes in attitudes. Attitude structures differ from knowledge structures in that they are emotionally charged in a positive or a negative way. Changes in behavior are significantly more difficult and time consuming than either of the two previous levels. But the implementation of group or organizational performance change is perhaps the most difficult and time consuming. Our destiny may, in fact, be dependent upon how well the behavioral sciences are able to resolve conflict through understanding and implementing change.

A Problem of Investment

A major obstacle to the practical application of the behavioral sciences has been the small amount of money allocated by government, business, and other agencies for research in these areas. In the United States, only one of every thirty dollars spent on research and development is channeled to behavioral science areas. The remainder is spent for research in the "hard sciences," to be used in developing "things." However, more must be done than just to spend money on research in the behavioral sciences. Funds are also needed to support the practical application of this research. This is especially important since managers, to be effective, regardless of the type of organization in which they operate, need to develop know-how in human skills in addition to their knowledge of the technical aspects of their jobs.

MANAGEMENT DEFINED

It is obvious after a review of the literature that there are almost as many definitions of management as there are writers in the field. A common thread that appears in these definitions is the manager's concern for accomplishing organizational goals or objectives.[6] We shall define management as the process of *working with and through individuals and groups and other resources to accomplish organizational goals.*

This definition, it should be noted, makes no mention of business or industrial organizations. Management, as defined, applies to organizations whether they are businesses, educational institutions, hospitals, political organizations, or even families. To be successful, these organizations require their management personnel to have interpersonal skills. The achievement of organizational objectives through leadership is management. Thus, everyone is a manager in at least certain activities.

Distinction Between Management and Leadership

Management and leadership are often thought of as one and the same thing. We feel, however, that there is an important distinction between the two concepts.

In essence, leadership is a broader concept than management. Management is thought of as a special kind of leadership in which the achievement of organizational goals is paramount. The key difference between the two concepts, therefore, lies in the word *organization*. Leadership occurs any time one attempts to *influence the behavior* of an individual or group, regardless of the reason. It may be for one's own goals or for those of others, and they may or may not be congruent with organizational goals.

THREE COMPETENCIES OF LEADERSHIP

In leading or influencing, there are three general skills or competencies: (a) diagnosing—being able to understand the situation you are trying to influence, (b) adapting—being able to adapt your behavior and the other resources you have available to meet the contingencies of the situation, and (c) communicating—being able to communicate in a way that people can easily understand and accept. We will discuss each of these competencies in greater detail in subsequent chapters, but for now here is a brief summary of each.

- Diagnosing is a *cognitive*—or cerebral—competency. It is understanding what the situation is now and knowing what you can reasonably expect it to be in the future. The discrepancy between the two is the *problem* to be solved. This is what the other competencies are aimed at changing.
- Adapting is a *behavioral* competency. It involves adapting your behaviors and other resources in a way that helps to close the gap between the current situation and what you want to achieve.

■ Communicating is a *process* competency. Even if you are able to understand the situation, even if you are able to adopt behavior and resources to meet the situation, you need to communicate effectively. If you can't communicate in a way that people can understand and accept, the whole process will not have the impact you would like it to have.[7]

MANAGEMENT PROCESS

The managerial functions of *planning, organizing, motivating,* and *controlling* are considered central to a discussion of management by many authors. These functions that comprise the management process—a step-by-step way of doing something—are relevant regardless of the type of organization or level of management with which one is concerned. As Harold Koontz and Cyril O'Donnell have said: "Acting in their managerial capacity, presidents, department heads, foremen, supervisors, college deans, bishops, and heads of governmental agencies all do the same thing. As managers they are all engaged in part in getting things done with and through people. As a manager, each must, at one time or another, carry out all the duties characteristic of managers."[8] Even a well-run household uses these managerial functions, although in many cases they are used intuitively.

Planning involves setting *goals* and *objectives* for the organization and developing "work maps" showing how these goals and objectives are to be accomplished. Once plans have been made, organizing becomes meaningful. This involves bringing together resources—people, capital, and equipment—in the most effective way to accomplish the goals. Organizing, therefore, involves an integration of resources.

Along with planning and organizing, motivating plays a large part in determining the level of performance of employees, which, in turn, influences how effectively the organizational goals will be met. Motivating is sometimes included as part of directing, along with communicating and leading.

In his research on motivation, William James of Harvard found that hourly employees could maintain their jobs (that is, not be fired) by working at approximately 20 to 30 percent of their ability. His study also showed that employees work at close to 80 to 90 percent of their ability if highly motivated. Both the minimum level at which employees might work and yet keep their jobs and the level at which they could be expected to perform with proper motiviation are illustrated in Figure 1-2.

This illustration shows us that if motiviation is low, employees' performance will suffer as much as if ability were low. For this reason, motivating is an extremely important function of management.

Another function of management is controlling. This involves feedback of results and follow-up to compare accomplishments with plans and to make appropriate adjustments where outcomes have deviated from expectations.

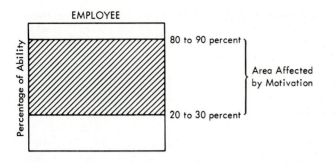

FIGURE 1-2 The potential influence of motivation on performance.

Even though these management functions are stated separately, and as presented seem to have a specific sequence, one must remember that they are interrelated, as illustrated in Figure 1-3. While these functions are interrelated, at any one time one or more may be of primary importance.

SKILLS OF A MANAGER

It is generally agreed that there are at least three areas of skill necessary for carrying out the process of management: technical, human, and conceptual.

- *Technical skill*—Ability to use knowledge, methods, techniques, and equipment necessary for the performance of specific tasks acquired from experience, education, and training.
- *Human skill*—Ability and judgement in working with and through people, including an understanding of motivation and an application of effective leadership.
- *Conceptual skill*—Ability to understand the complexities of the overall organization and where one's own operation fits into the organization. This knowledge permits one to act according to the objectives of the total organization rather than only on the basis of the goals and needs of one's own immediate group.[9]

FIGURE 1-3 Interrelated management functions

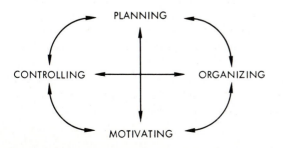

The appropriate mix of these skills varies as an individual advances in management from supervisory to top-management positions. This is illustrated in Figure 1-4.

To be effective, less technical skill tends to be needed as one advances from lower to higher levels in the organization but more conceptual skill is necessary. Supervisors at lower levels need considerable technical skill because they are often required to train and develop technicians and other employees in their sections. At the other extreme, executives in a business organization do not need to know how to perform all the specific tasks at the operational level. However, they should be able to see how all these functions are interrelated in accomplishing the goals of the total organization.

While the amount of technical and conceptual skills needed at these different levels of management varies, *the common denominator that appears to be crucial at all levels is human skill.*

Emphasis on Human Skills

The emphasis on human skills was considered important in the past, but it is of primary importance today. For example, one of the great entrepreneurs, John D. Rockefeller, stated: "I will pay more for the ability to deal with people than any other ability under the sun."[10] These words of Rockefeller are often echoed. According to a report by the American Management Association, an overwhelming majority of the two hundred managers who participated in a survey agreed that the most important single skill of an executive is ability to get along with people.[11] In this survey, management

FIGURE 1-4   Management skills necessary at various levels of an organization

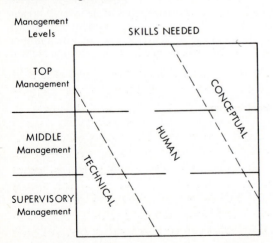

rated this ability more vital than intelligence, decisiveness, knowledge, or job skills.

ORGANIZATIONS AS SOCIAL SYSTEMS

Although the emphasis in this text will be on human skills development, we must recognize that the organizations in which most managers operate are social systems comprised of many interrelated subsystems, only one of which is a human/social system. The others could include an administrative/structural subsystem, an informational/decision-making subsystem, and an economic/technological subsystem.[12]

The focus of the administrative/structural subsystem is on authority, structure, and responsibility within the organization: "who does what for whom" and "who tells whom to do what, when, and why." The informational/decision-making subsystem emphasizes key decisions and their informational needs to keep the system going. The main concern of the economic/technological subsystem is on the work to be done and the cost effectiveness of that work within the specific goals of the organization.

Although the focus of the human/social system is on the motivation and needs of the members of the organization and on the leadership provided or required (the major emphasis of this text), it should be emphasized that within a systems approach there is a clear understanding that changes in one subsystem effect changes in other parts of the total system. As illustrated in Figure 1-5, if the total system is healthy and functioning well, each of its parts or subsystems is effectively interacting with one another. Therefore, an organization over a sustained period of time cannot afford to over-emphasize the importance of one subsystem at the expense of the others. At the same time, the internal management of the organization cannot ignore the needs and pressures from the external environment.

Managerial Roles in a Social System

According to Ichak Adizes,[13] four managerial roles must be performed if an organization is to be run effectively. These four roles are *producing, implementing, innovating,* and *integrating.* Each of these managerial roles is clearly related to one of the four social subsystems of an organization.

A manager in the role of *producing* is expected to achieve results equal to or better than the competition. "The principal qualification for an achiever is the possession of a functional knowledge of his field, whether marketing, engineering, accounting, or any other discipline."[14] The role of producing emphasizes activities in the economic/technological subsystem.

Being individually productive and having technical skills do not necessarily enable a manager to produce results in working with a group of peo-

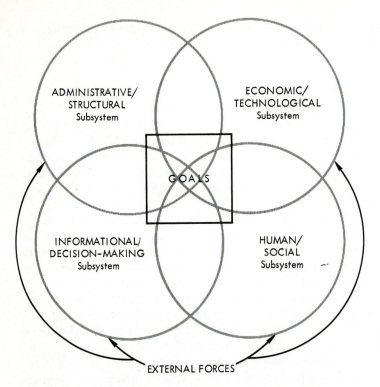

FIGURE 1-5   The interrelated subsystems of an organization

ple. As we stated earlier, a manager should have more than just technical skill. Managers should be more than individual producers. They should be able to administer the people with whom they work and to see that these people also produce results. In this *implementing* role managers schedule, coordinate, control, and discipline. If managers are implementers, they see to it that the system works as it has been designed to work. Implementing emphasizes the administrative/structural subsystem.

While producing and implementing are important, in a changing environment managers must use their judgment and have the discretion to change goals and change the systems by which they are implemented. In this role managers must be organizational entrepreneurs and innovators since, unlike administrators who are given plans to carry out and decisions to implement, entrepreneurs have to generate their own plan of action. They have to be self-starters. This *innovating* role stresses the informational/decision-making subsystem.

According to Adizes, the three roles of producing, implementing, and innovating in combination are insufficient for adequate managerial functioning. He contends, "Many an organization that had been managed by an excellent achiever-administrator-entrepreneur (usually their founder) nosed-ived when this key individual died or for some reason was replaced. For an organization to be continuously successful, an additional role must be performed . . . integrating."[15]

Integrating is the process by which individual strategies are merged into a group strategy; individual risks become group risks; individual goals are harmonized into group goals; ultimately, individual entrepreneurship emerges as group entrepreneurship. "When a group can operate on its own with a clear direction in mind and can choose its own direction over time without depending on any one individual for a successful operation, then we know that the integrating role has been performed adequately. It requires an individual who is sensitive to people's needs. Such an individual unifies the whole organization behind goals and strategies."[16] Integrating emphasizes the human/social system.

Adizes contends that whenever one of the four managerial roles is not performed in an organization, a certain style of mismanagement can be observed. And yet, Adizes argues that

> few managers fill perfectly all four of these roles and thus exhibit no misman-agement style since they are at once excellent technicians, administrators, entrepreneurs, and integrators. Thus, to discuss the role of THE manager, as is done in management literature, is a theoretical mistake. *No one manager can manage alone.* It takes several to perform the process adequately, several people to perform roles which seem to be in conflict but really are complementary. There should be individuals who possess the entrepreneurial and integrating qualities which can guide a united organization to new directions. There should be administrators who can translate these new actions into operative systems which should produce results. And there should be performers who can put the system into action and set an example for efficient operation.[17]

While all the roles seem to be necessary for running an effective organization, Adizes argues that if any one of the four roles can be truly indispensable for any executive, it is integration. If managers do not perform the other roles themselves, there may be others to supply them; but they have to be able to integrate in order to allow the other functions to work in a positive fashion. If this people-part of the managerial role is not fulfilled, the entrepreneur will become a "crisis maker," the administrator a "bureaucrat," and the producer a "loner."

INGREDIENTS FOR EFFECTIVE HUMAN SKILLS

If one accepts the fact that human skill development is important, one may ask what kind of expertise managers and leaders need to be effective in their ability to have an impact on the behavior of other people. We feel that managers need three levels of expertise.

Understanding Past Behavior

First, managers need to understand why people behave as they do. If you are going to get things done through other people, you have to know why other people engage in behavior that is characteristic of them. So, understanding past behavior is the first area that managers need to examine.

What motivates people? What produces the patterns of behavior that are characteristic of individuals or groups? This is where most of the literature focuses. Most of what has been written in the behavioral sciences focuses on why people behave as they do. In both popular and scholarly texts and periodicals, there are literally hundreds of different classifications that are useful in communicating the patterns of behavior that describe individuals and groups interacting with other people. We can say a person is schizophrenic or is paranoid or is a task leader or a team leader, and so on. All these are useful classifications for communicating to others why an individual or group is behaving in certain ways.

Predicting Future Behavior

Although understanding past behavior is important for developing effective human skills, it is not enough by itself. If you are supervising other people, it is essential that you understand why they did what they did yesterday, but perhaps even more important is being able to predict how they are going to behave today, tomorrow, next week, and next month under similar as well as changing environmental conditions. Therefore, the second level of expertise that managers need is predicting future behavior.

Directing, Changing, and Controlling Behavior

If you are going to be effective in your role as a manager or leader, you need to do more than just understand and predict behavior. You need to develop skills in directing, changing, and controlling behavior. You must also accept the responsibility for *influencing* the behavior of others in accomplishing tasks and reaching goals.

These skills determine whether leadership attempts will be successful or unsuccessful, effective or ineffective. Understanding what motivates people, predicting how they will behave in response to your leadership attempts, and directing their behavior are all necessary for effective leadership.

Note that the first two skills are passive in nature. Understanding and predicting do not require actions involving other people. The key to obtaining results is directing, changing and controlling the efforts of people in the accomplishment of organizational goals. That's where the leader translates thoughts and intentions into end results.

Controlling People

People who hear the word *control* often ask, "Does that mean that we have to manipulate others?" Words that suggest control and manipulation sometimes have a negative connotation to many people. However, when you accept the role of leader, you also accept with it the responsibility of having an impact on the behavior of other people—for channeling the behavior of others toward achieving results. That's true whether you're at work striving to gain the commitment of your people or at home attempting to assist your children in developing their basic values.

It's also important to remember that words are simply packages of ideas and, as such, are often misinterpreted. If manipulation means taking unfair advantage, being deceitful, and influencing others for self-interest, then it has a negative connotation. On the other hand, if manipulation means using influence strategies skillfully and managing people fairly for mutually rewarding and productive purposes, it's an appropriate and necessary means for goal accomplishment.

If you are still concerned about words such as *control* or *manipulation*, think instead of training or facilitating. Whatever words you choose, your overall effectiveness depends upon *understanding, predicting,* and *influencing* the behavior of other people.

A Hammer Won't Always Do the Job

For every job there is an appropriate tool. Hammers are great for pounding nails. You could also use a hammer to cut a two by four but it would leave a lot of rough edges. For that particular job there is a better tool. To build effectively you need a variety of tools and the knowledge of what they are designed to accomplish.

The same is true for leadership and management. It is unrealistic to think that a single tool is all that's needed to manage effectively. Many people fall into the trap of relying on the latest fad to solve all their management problems. They seem to develop an unrealistic assumption of what this will do for them. Many useful management tools have developed over the years. But you should know what to expect from them and, just as importantly, what not to expect. You need to understand and be able to use different tools when learning and managing people.[18]

Learning to Apply Behavioral Science Theory

Learning to apply behavioral sciences is much like learning anything; for example, how do you learn to hit a baseball? You learn to hit a baseball by getting up there and attempting to hit—by practice, by doing what you are attempting to learn. There is no way you are going to learn to hit a baseball by merely reading books (even those by people considered to be experts in the field) or by watching (in person or on slow-motion film) great hitters. All that will do is give you conceptual knowledge of how to hit a baseball.

Psychologists define learning as a change in behavior—being able to do something different from what you were able to do before. So, in reading and watching others, all we can get is perhaps a change in our knowledge or a change in our attitude. But if we actually want to learn something, we have to "try on," or practice, that which we want to learn to make it part of our relevant behavior.

Another thing to keep in mind in terms of learning is how you feel about learning something new. How did you feel the first time you ever tried to hit a baseball? If you were like most people, you felt anxious, nervous, and uncomfortable. This is the way most of us feel any time we attempt to do something that is new—something significantly different from the things we are already comfortable doing within our behavioral patterns.

It's the same with learning to use behavioral science. Much of what you read in this book may have an impact on your knowledge and attitudes, but this book becomes relevant only if you are willing to "try on" some new behaviors. If you are, we think you should recognize that the first time you "try on" a new pattern of behavior in terms of attempting to implement behavioral science theory, you are going to feel ill at ease and uncomfortable. It is this "unfreezing" that we have to go through if we want to learn.

Another caution is to be patient—give the new behavior time to work. If you are up at bat attempting to hit a baseball for the first time, what is the probability that you will get a base hit from the first ball the pitcher delivers? The probability is low. It is not any different in learning behavioral science theory. The first time you attempt to behave differently based on theory, we can predict that you probably would have been more effective using your old style of behavior rather than the new (although in the long run the new style may have a higher probability of success). This is why so often practitioners who go through a training experience in which they learn new knowledge as well as attitudes find that in "trying on" some new behavior for the first time, it doesn't work. As a result, they begin to respond negatively to the whole training experience, saying such things as, "How can we accept these things?" "They are not usable." "They do not work in the real world." It is this kind of attitude that has hindered managers from attempting to make behavioral science theory a reality in terms of managing more effectively. All of us have to recognize that just like hitting a baseball, it takes practice. The first few times up, the probability of success is quite low. But the more we practice, the more we attempt to get relevant feedback, the more we can predict that the probability of success will increase.

APPLIED BEHAVIORAL SCIENCES

If managers are able to understand, predict, and direct change and control behavior, they are essentially applied behavioral scientists.

What Is a Behavioral Scientist?

One way to answer this question is to say that a behavioral scientist attempts to bring together, from a variety of disciplines, those concepts, theories, and research that may be useful to people in making decisions about the behavior of individuals and groups. This means that a behavioral scientist integrates concepts and theories and the results of empirical studies from the areas of cultural anthropology, economics, political science, psychology, sociology, and social psychology. At the same time, a behavioral scientist also borrows from other areas such as engineering, physics, quantitative analysis, and statistics. For example, force field analysis, developed by Kurt Lewin, which we will be talking about later in this book, is directly related to concepts in physics. So, perhaps the best way to look at the field is to say that a behavioral scientist attempts to integrate all of those areas or disciplines that can be useful to us as practitioners in better understanding, predicting, and having an impact on the behavior of individuals and groups.

The emphasis in this book will be on the applied behavioral sciences: those concepts from the behavioral sciences that can have an impact on making managers more effective—whether they be managers, supervisors, teachers, or parents. The hope is to apply behavioral science concepts in such a way as to move them from being strictly theoretical and descriptive to being more applied and prescriptive. In doing that, though, it should be remembered that applied behavioral science is not an exact science such as physics, chemistry, and biology. There are no principles or universal truths when it comes to management. People are difficult to predict. All that the behavioral sciences can give you are ways to increase your behavioral batting average. In other words, the behavioral sciences are probability sciences; there aren't any principles of management, only books titled *Principles of Management.*[19]

THE DESIGN OF THIS BOOK

In the chapters that follow, we will attempt to help you better understand the field of applied behavioral science. As we noted in *Organizational Change Through Effective Leadership*, with Robert H. Guest:

> . . . by sharing the insights of those who have studied organizational change and linking their observations, however briefly, to an evolving situation, we hope that managers out on the firing line might come to realize that there are available, in the organizational behavior literature, concepts and frameworks that might help them to do a better job. We believe that these behavioral science contributions might assist managers, in a variety of institutional settings, to sharpen their diagnostic skills and to develop appropriate change strategies. They might, in short, go beyond the intuitive, beyond seat-of-the-pants experience, to sense better the probabilities that one course of action will work and another will not.[20]

Chapters 2 and 3 on motivation are designed to provide information to help you understand and predict the how and why people behave as they do. Chapters 4 through 12 trace the development of modern leadership theory and introduce Situational Leadership. Chapters 13 through 19 focus on applied behavioral science with special attention to One Minute Management and its relationship to Situational Leadership (chapters 17 and 18).

Chapter 20 attempts to integrate all of the concepts on understanding, predicting, and controlling behavior into a common framework that we believe will be helpful to you in increasing organizational productivity. We think you will find the remaining chapters of your journey through this book interesting, informative, and, most important, of practical value.

NOTES

1. J. J. Sullivan, "Human Nature, Organizations, and Management Theory," *Academy of Management Review*, 11 (July 1985), pp. 534−549. See also T. J. Hutton, "Human Resources or Management Resources?" *Personnel Administrator*, 32 (January 1987), pp. 66 ff.; A. Fowler, "When Chief Executives Discover Human Resource Management," *Personnel Management*, 19 (January 1987), p. 3; Randolph M. Hale, "Managing Human Resources," *Enterprise*, June 1985, pp. 6−9; Perry Pascarella, "The New Science of Management," *Industry Week*, January 6, 1986, pp. 45−50.

2. Paul Hersey, *The Situational Leader* (Escondido, Calif.: Center for Leadership Studies, 1984), p. 13.

3. Elton Mayo, *The Social Problems of an Industrial Civilization* (Boston: Harvard Business School, 1945), p. 23.

4. *Ibid.*, p. 20.

5. R. J. House discusses similar concepts in *Management Development: Design, Implementation and Evaluation* (Ann Arbor: Bureau of Industrial Relations, University of Michigan, 1967).

6. See as examples, Harold Koontz and Cyril O'Donnell, *Principles of Management*, 4th ed. (New York: McGraw-Hill, 1968); Harold Koontz and Cyril O'Donnell, *Essentials of Management*, 4th ed. (New York: McGraw-Hill, 1986). See also Kenneth H. Blanchard and Robert Lorber, *Putting the One-Minute Manager to Work* (New York: Berkeley Publishing Group, 1986); John R. Schermerhorn, Jr., *Management for Productivity*, 2nd ed. (New York: Wiley, 1986).

7. Hersey, *The Situational Leader*.

8. Harold Koontz and Cyril O'Donnell, *Principles of Management*, 5th ed. (New York: McGraw-Hill 1972), p. 20.

9. These descriptions were adapted from a classification developed by Robert L. Katz, "Skills of an Effective Administrator," *Harvard Business Review*, January−February 1955, pp. 33−42.

10. John D. Rockefeller as quoted in Garret L. Bergen and William V. Haney, *Organizational Relations and Management Action* (New York: McGraw-Hill, 1966), p. 3.

11. Data as reported in Bergen and Haney, *Organizational Relations and Management Action*.

12. Paul Hersey and Douglas Scott identify these components of an internal social system in "A Systems Approach to Educational Organizations: Do We Manage or Administer?" OCLEA (a publication of the Ontario Council for Leadership in Educational Administration, Toronto, Canada), pp. 3−5. Much of the material for that article was adapted from lectures given by Boris Yavitz, Dean, School of Business Administration, Columbia University.

13. Ichak Adizes, *How to Solve the Mismanagement Crisis* (Los Angeles: MDOR Institute, 1980). Also see Adizes, "Mismanagement Styles," *California Management Review*, 19, No. 2 (Winter 1976).

14. Adizes, "Mismanagement Styles," p. 6.

15. *Ibid.*

16. *Ibid.*

17. *Ibid.*, p. 18.

18. Adapted from Hersey, *The Situational Leader*, pp. 20−22.

19. See as examples, Koontz and O'Donnell, *Essentials of Management*; John M. Ivancerich and Michael Matteson, *Management Classics* (Plano, Tex.: Business Publications, 1986). See also Robert M. Fulmer, *The New Management* (New York: Macmillan, 1987); Louis E. Boone and David L. Kurtz, *Management*, 3rd ed. (New York: Random House, 1987); David H. Holt *Management: Principles and Practices* (Englewood Cliffs, N.J.: Prentice-Hall, 1987).

20. Robert H. Guest, Paul Hersey, and Kenneth H. Blanchard, *Organizational Change Through Effective Leadership* (Englewood Cliffs, N.J.: Prentice-Hall, 1986), p. 222.

CHAPTER 2

MOTIVATION AND BEHAVIOR

The study of motivation and behavior is a search for answers to perplexing questions about human nature. Recognizing the importance of the human element in organizations, we will attempt in this chapter to develop a theoretical framework that may help managers to understand human behavior, not only to determine the "whys" of past behavior but to some extent to predict, to change, and even to control future behavior.

BEHAVIOR

Behavior is basically goal-oriented. In other words, our behavior is generally motivated by a desire to attain some goal. The specific goal is not always consciously known by the individual. All of us may wonder at times, "Why did I do that?" The reason for our action is not always apparent to the conscious mind. The drives that motivate distinctive individual behavioral patterns ("personality") are to a considerable degree subconscious and, therefore, not easily accessible to examination and evaluation.

Sigmund Freund was one of the first to recognize the importance of subconscious motivation. He believed that people are not always aware of everything they want; hence, much of their behavior is affected by subconscious motives or needs. In fact, Freud's research convinced him that an analogy could be drawn between the motivation of most people and the structure of an iceberg. A significant segment of human motivation appears below the surface, where it is not always evident to the individual. Therefore, many times only a small portion of one's motivation is clearly visible or conscious to oneself.[1] This may be due to an individual's lack of effort to gain self-insight. Yet, even with professional help—for example, psychotherapy—understanding oneself may be a difficult process, yielding varying degrees of success.

The basic unit of behavior is an *activity*. In fact, all behavior is a series of activities. As human beings we are always doing something: walking, talking, eating, sleeping, working, and the like. In many instances we are doing more than one activity at a time, such as talking with someone as we walk or drive to work. At any given moment we may decide to change from one activity or combination of activities and begin to do something else. This raises some important questions. Why do people engage in one activity and not another? Why do they change activities? How can we as managers understand, predict, and even control what activity or activities a person may engage in at a given moment? To predict behavior, managers must know which motives or needs of people evoke a certain action at a particular time.

Motives

People differ not only in their ability to do but also in their will to do, or *motivation*. The motivation of people depends on the strength of their motives. *Motives* are sometimes defined as needs, wants, drives, or impulses within the individual. Motives are directed toward goals, which may be conscious or subconscious.

Motives are the "whys" of behavior. They arouse and maintain activity and determine the general direction of the behavior of an individual. In essence, motives or needs are the mainsprings of action. In our discussions we shall use these two terms—*motives* and *needs*—interchangeably. In this context, the term *need* should *not* be associated with urgency or any pressing desire for something. It simply means something within an individual that prompts that person to action.

Goals

Goals are *outside* an individual; they are sometimes referred to as "hoped for" rewards toward which motives are directed. These goals are often called *incentives* by psychologists. However, we prefer not to use this term since many people in our society tend to equate incentives with tangible financial rewards, such as increased pay, and yet most of us would agree that there are many intangible rewards, such as praise or power, which are just as important in evoking behavior. Managers who are successful in motivating employees are often providing an environment in which appropriate goals (incentives) are available for need satisfaction, as seen in Figure 2-1.

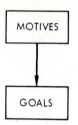

FIGURE 2-1   Motives are directed toward goals

Motive Strength

We have said that motives, or needs, are the reasons underlying behavior. All individuals have many hundreds of needs. All of these needs compete for their behavior. What, then, determines which of these motives a person will attempt to satisfy through activity? The need with the *greatest strength* at a particular moment leads to activity, as illustrated in Figure 2-2. Satisfied needs decrease in strength and normally do not motivate individuals to seek goals to satisfy them.

In Figure 2-2 Motive B is the highest strength need and, therefore, it is this need that determines behavior. What can happen to change this situation?

Changes in Motive Strength

A motive tends to decrease in strength if it is either satisfied or blocked from satisfaction.

FIGURE 2-2   The most prepotent motive determines behavior (Motive B in this illustration)

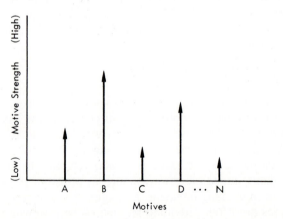

Need satisfaction. When a need is satisfied, according to Abraham Maslow, it is no longer a motivator of behavior.[2] High strength needs that are satisfied are sometimes referred to as "satisficed," that is, the need has been satisfied to the extent that some competing need is now more potent. If a high strength need is thirst, drinking tends to lower the strength of this need, and other needs may now become more important.

Blocking need satisfaction. The satisfaction of a need may be blocked. While a reduction in need strength sometimes follows, it does not always occur initially. Instead, there may be a tendency for the person to engage in *coping behavior*. This is an attempt to overcome the obstacle by trial-and-error problem solving. The person may try a variety of behaviors to find one that will accomplish the goal or will reduce tension created by blockage, as illustrated in Figure 2-3.

Initially, this coping behavior may be quite rational. Perhaps the person may even make several attempts in direction 1 before going to 2, and the same in direction 2 before moving in direction 3, where some degree of success and goal attainment is finally perceived.

If people continue to strive for something without success, they may substitute goals that can satisfy the need. For example, if a boy has a strong desire to play varsity basketball in high school but is continually cut from the squad, he may be willing eventually to settle for playing in the city recreation league.

FIGURE 2-3 Coping behavior when blockage occurs in attempting to accomplish a particular goal

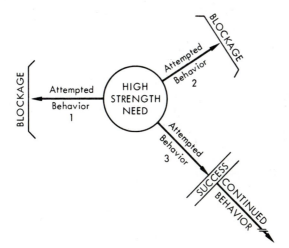

Cognitive dissonance. Blocked motives and continually unsuccessful rational coping behavior may lead to forms of irrational coping behavior. Leon Festinger analyzes this phenomenon.[3] His theory of cognitive dissonance deals primarily with the relationships that exist between perceptions people have about themselves and their environment. When individual perceptions have nothing to do with each other, they are considered irrelevant to each other. If one supports the other, they are said to be in a consonant relationship. Dissonance is created when two perceptions that are relevant to each other are in conflict. This creates tension, which is psychologically uncomfortable and causes the individual to try to modify one of the incompatible knowledges so as to reduce the tension, or dissonance. In a sense, that person engages in coping behavior to regain a condition of consonance, or equilibrium. For example, Festinger has done research that shows that "heavy smokers are less likely to believe that there is a relationship between smoking and lung cancer than nonsmokers."[4] In other words, if they cannot give up smoking they can at least remain skeptical about research that reports harmful effects. The same phenomenon is at work when a person goes out fishing all day, doesn't catch anything, and remarks about the beautiful weather.

Frustration. The blocking or thwarting of goal attainment is referred to as *frustration*. This phenomenon is defined in terms of the condition of the individual, rather than in terms of the external environment. A person may be frustrated by an imaginary barrier and may fail to be frustrated by a real barrier.

As previously discussed, rational coping behavior can lead to alternative goal setting or decreasing need strength. Irrational behavior may occur in several forms when blockage to goal accomplishment continues and frustration develops. Frustration may increase to the extent that the individual engages in aggressive behavior. *Aggression* can lead to destructive behavior such as hostility and striking out. Freud was one of the first to demonstrate that hostility or rage can be exhibited by an individual in a variety of ways.[5] If possible, individuals will direct their hostility against the object or the person that they feel is the cause of frustration. The angry worker may try to hurt her boss or may undermine his job and reputation through gossip and other malicious behavior. Often, however, people cannot attack the cause of their frustration directly, and they may look for a scapegoat as a target for their hostility. For example, a worker may fear his boss because the boss holds his fate in her hands. In this case, "the resentful worker may pick a quarrel with his wife, kick the cat, beat his children, or, more constructively, work off his feelings by chopping wood, by cursing and swearing, or engaging in violent exercises or horseplay of an aggressive nature."[6]

As Norman R.F. Maier has said, aggression is only one way in which frustration can be shown.[7] Other forms of frustrated behavior—such as rationalization, regression, fixation, and resignation—may develop if pressures continue and/or increase.

Rationalization simply means making excuses. For example, an individual might blame someone else for her inability to accomplish a given goal—"It was my boss's fault that I didn't get a raise." Or she talks herself out of the desirability of that particular goal—"I didn't want to do that anyway."

Regression is essentially not acting one's age. "Frustrated people tend to give up constructive attempts at solving their problems and regress to more primitive and childish behavior."[8] A person who cannot start his car and proceeds to kick it is demonstrating regressive behavior; so too is a manager who throws a temper tantrum when he is annoyed and frustrated. Barker, Dembo, and Lewin have shown experimentally that when children are exposed to mild frustration, their play may resemble that of a child two or more years younger.[9]

Fixation occurs when a person continues to exhibit the same behavior pattern over and over again, although experience has shown that it can accomplish nothing. Thus, "frustration can freeze old and habitual responses and prevent the use of new and more effectual ones."[10] Maier has shown that although habits are normally broken when they bring no satisfaction or lead to punishment, a fixation actually becomes stronger under these circumstances.[11] In fact, he argued that it is possible to change a habit into a fixation by too much punishment. This phenomenon is seen in children who blindly continue to behave objectionably after being severely punished. Thus, Maier concluded that punishment can have two effects on behavior: It may either eliminate the undesirable behavior or lead to fixation and other symptoms of frustration as well. It follows that punishment may be a dangerous management tool, since its effects are difficult to predict. According to J.A.C. Brown, common symptoms of fixation in industry are "the inability to accept change, the blind and stubborn refusal to accept new facts when experience has shown the old ones to be untenable, and the type of behavior exemplified by the manager who continues to increase penalties" even when this is only making conditions worse.[12]

Resignation or apathy occurs after prolonged frustration when people lose hope of accomplishing their goal(s) in a particular situation and withdraw from reality and the source of their frustration. This phenomenon is characteristic of people in boring, routine jobs, where often they resign themselves to the fact that there is little hope for improvement within their environments.

A manager should remember that aggression, rationalization, regression, fixation, and resignation are all symptoms of frustration and may be indications that problems exist.

Increasing motive strength.   Behavior may change if an existing need increases in strength to the extent that it is now the high strength motive.

The strength of some needs tends to appear in a cyclical pattern. For example, the need for food tends to recur regardless of how well it has been satisfied at a given moment. One can increase or delay the speed of this cyclical pattern by affecting the environment. For example, a person's need for food may not be high strength unless the immediate environment is changed such that the senses are exposed to the sight and the aroma of tempting food.

People have a variety of needs at any given time They may be hungry, thirsty, and tired, but the need with the highest strength will determine what they do. For example, they may eat, drink, and sleep, in that order, as shown in Figure 2-4.[13] All of these tend to be cyclical over time.

CATEGORIES OF ACTIVITIES

Activities resulting from high strength needs can generally be classified into two categories—goal directed activity and goal activity. These concepts are important to practitioners because of their differing influence on need strength, which can be useful in understanding human behavior.

Goal-directed activity, in essence, is motivated behavior directed at reaching a goal. If one's strongest need at a given moment is hunger, various activities such as looking for a place to eat, buying food, or preparing food would be considered goal-directed activities. On the other hand, *goal activity* is engaging in the goal itself. In the case of hunger, food is the goal and eating, therefore, is the goal activity.

An important distinction between these two classes of activities is their

FIGURE 2-4 Multiple needs

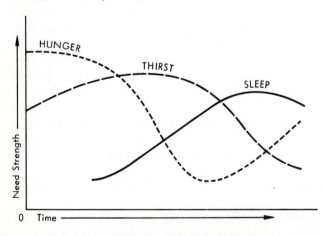

effect on the strength of the need. In goal-directed activity, the strength of the need tends to increase as one engages in the activity until goal behavior is reached or frustration sets in. As discussed earlier, frustration develops when one is continually blocked from reaching a goal. If the frustration becomes intense enough, the strength of the need for that goal may decrease until it is no longer potent enough to affect behavior—a person gives up.

The strength of the need tends to increase as one engages in goal-directed activity; however, once goal activity begins, the strength of the need tends to decrease as one engages in it. For example, as one eats more and more, the strength of the need for food declines for that particular time. At the point when another need becomes more potent than the present need, behavior changes.

On Thanksgiving Day, for example, as food is being prepared all morning (goal-directed activity), the need for food increases to the point of almost not being able to wait until the meal is on the table. As we begin to eat (goal activity), the strength of this need diminishes to the point where other needs become more important. As we leave the table, our need for food seems to be well satisfied. Our activity changes to that of watching football. This need for passive recreation has now become most potent, and we find ourselves in front of the television set. But gradually this need decreases, too. After several games, even though the competition is fierce, the need for passive recreation may also decline to the extent that other needs become more important—perhaps the need for fresh air and a walk or, better still, another piece of pumpkin pie. Several hours before, we had sworn not to eat for a week, but now that pie looks very good. So once again hunger is the strongest need. Thus, it should be remembered that we never completely satiate a need. We satisfy it for only a period of time.

MOTIVATING SITUATION

The relationship between motives, goals, and activity can be shown in a simplified fashion, as illustrated in Figure 2-5.

FIGURE 2-5 A motivating situation

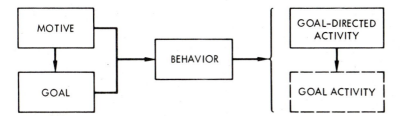

This schematic illustration shows a *motivating situation* in which the motives of an individual are directed toward goal attainment. The strongest motive produces behavior that is either goal-directed or goal activity. Since not all goals are attainable, individuals do not always reach goal activity, regardless of the strength of the motive. Thus, goal activity is indicated by a dashed line.

An example of a tangible goal being used to influence behavior is illustrated in Figure 2-6.

With a broad goal such as food, it should be recognized that the type of food that satisfies the hunger motive varies from situation to situation. If individuals are starving, they may eat anything; at other times, they may realign their goals and only a steak will satisfy their hunger motive.

A similar illustration could be given for an intangible goal. If individuals have a need for recognition—a need to be viewed as contributing, productive people—praise is one incentive that will help satisfy this need. In a work situation, if their need for recognition is strong enough, being praised by their manager or supervisor may be an effective incentive in influencing people to continue to do good work.

In analyzing these two examples, it should be remembered that if you want to influence another person's behavior, you must first understand what motives or needs are most important to that person at that time. A goal, to be effective, must be appropriate to the need structure of the person involved.

A question that may be considered at this point is whether it is better to engage in goal-directed activity or in goal activity. Actually, maintenance at either level exclusively creates problems. If one stays at goal-directed activity too long, frustration will occur to the extent that the person may give up or other patterns of irrational behavior may be evoked. On the other hand, if one engages exclusively in goal activity and the goal is not challenging, a lack of interest and apathy will develop, with motivation again tending to decrease. A more appropriate and effective pattern might be a continuous cycling function between goal-directed activity and goal activity.

FIGURE 2-6 Use of a tangible incentive in a motivating situation

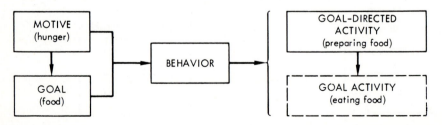

A goal that is appropriate for a six-year-old may not be a meaningful goal for the same child at seven. Once the child becomes proficient in attaining a particular goal, it becomes appropriate for the parent to provide an opportunity for the child to evaluate and set new goals. In the same light, what is an appropriate goal for a new employee may not be meaningful for an employee who has been with a corporation six months or a year. There also may be distinctions between employees who have been with an organization for only a few years and those who have been with it for longer periods of time.

This cycling process between goal-directed activity and goal activity is a continuous challenge for the parent or the manager. As employees increase in their ability to accomplish goals, it is appropriate that the superior reevaluate and provide an environment that allows continual realignment of goals and an opportunity for growth and development. The learning and developing process is not a phenomenon that should be confined to only one stage of a person's life. In this process, the role of managers is not always that of setting goals for their workers. Instead, effectiveness may be increased by providing an environment in which subordinates can play a role in setting their own goals. Research indicates that commitment increases when people are involved in their own goal setting. If individuals are involved, they will tend to engage in much more goal-directed activity before they become frustrated and give up. On the other hand, if their boss sets the goals for them, they are likely to give up more easily because they perceive these as their boss's goals and not as their own.

Goals should be set high enough so that a person has to stretch to reach them but low enough so that they can be attained. Thus, goals must be realistic before a person will make a real effort to achieve them. As J. Sterling-Livingston so aptly states:

> Subordinates will not be motivated to reach high levels of productivity unless they consider the boss' high expectations realistic and achievable. If they are encouraged to strive for unattainable goals, they eventually give up trying and settle for results that are lower than they are capable of achieving. The experience of a large electrical manufacturing company demonstrates this; the company discovered that production actually declined if production quotas were

FIGURE 2-7 Cycling function of goal-directed activity and goal activity

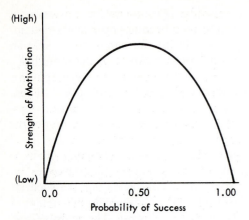

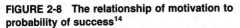

Probability of Success

FIGURE 2-8 The relationship of motivation to probability of success[14]

set too high, because the workers simply stopped trying to meet them. In other words, the practice of "dangling the carrot just beyond the donkey's reach," endorsed by many managers, is not a good motivational device.[15]

David C. McClelland and John W. Atkinson[16] have demonstrated in their research that the degree of motivation and effort rises until the probability of success reaches 50 percent, then begins to fall even though the probability of success continues to increase. This relationship could be depicted in the form of a bell-shaped curve, as illustrated in Figure 2-8.

As Figure 2-8 suggests, people are not highly motivated if a goal is seen as almost impossible or virtually certain to achieve.

Another problem with goals is that so often final goals are set and the person is judged only in terms of success in relation to those terminal goals. For example, a student is doing poorly in school and her parents want her to raise her marks to a *B* average. Suppose that after the first semester she gets only *C's*. The result is usually that her parents reprimand her; if this continues to occur, there is a high probability that she may stop trying. Her grades, instead of improving, may get worse. An alternative for the parents is setting interim goals—realistic goals that move in the direction of the final goals as they are attained. Now with a change in the desired direction, even though only moderate, positive reinforcement may be used rather than reprimand.

EXPECTANCY THEORY

We have already discussed the strength of needs. What additional factors affect the strength of needs? Victor Vroom[17] has suggested an approach in his expectancy theory of motivation that attempts to answer this question. Furthermore, his theory is consistent with our previous assertion that felt needs cause human behavior.

In simplified form, felt needs cause behavior, and this motivated behavior in a work setting is increased if a person perceives a positive relationship between effort and performance. Motivated behavior is further increased if there is a positive relationship between good performance and outcomes or rewards, particularly if the outcomes or rewards are valued. Thus, there are three relationships that enhance motivated behavior: a positive relationship between effort and performance, a positive relationship between good performance and rewards, and the delivery or achievement of valued outcomes or rewards. Let's look at an example. A new manager perceives that a 60-hour workweek is vital to good job performance. Further, the manager also perceives that good job performance will probably result in an early promotion that carries with it a badly needed 10 percent raise. If this sequence of events happens, the manager's willingness to work hard and confidence in the behavior pattern will be reinforced. "Success breeds success!" However, should one or more steps in the sequence be proven wrong—for example, performance does not improve, promotion is denied, or pay raise falls short of expectations—motivation, willingness, and confidence will decline.

This linkage between effort and performance and between performance and valued outcomes is important not only to our understanding of motivation[18] but also to our understanding of a number of leadership theories, especially the Path—Goal Theory discussed in Chapter 5.

EXPECTANCY AND AVAILABILITY

We have already discussed the strength of needs. Two important factors that affect need strength are expectancy and availability. Although these two concepts are interrelated, expectancy tends to affect motives, or needs, and availability tends to affect the perception of goals.

Expectancy is the perceived probability of satisfying a particular need of an individual based on past experience. Although expectancy is the technical term used by psychologists, it refers directly to the sum of the past experience. Experience can be either actual or vicarious. Vicarious experience comes from sources the person considers legitimate, such as parents, peer groups, teachers, and books or periodicals. To illustrate the effect that past experience can have on behavior, let us look at an example. Suppose a boy's father was a basketball star and the boy wants to follow in his footsteps. Initially, his expectancy may be high and, therefore, the strength of the need is high. If he is cut from the eighth-grade team, it is difficult to determine whether this failure will discourage the boy. Since a single failure is usually not enough to discourage a person (in fact, it sometimes results in increased activity), little change in his expectancy is anticipated. But if he continues to get cut from the team year after year, eventually this motive will no longer be as strong or of such high priority. In fact, after enough unsuccessful experiences, he may give up completely on his goal.

Availability reflects the perceived limitations of the environment. It is determined by how accessible the goals that can satisfy a given need are perceived by an individual. For example, if the electricity goes off in a storm, one cannot watch television or read. These goal activities are no longer possible because of the limitations of the environment. One may have a high desire to read, but if there is no suitable substitute for the type of illumination required, that person will soon be frustrated in any attempts to satisfy this desire and will settle for something else, such as sleeping.

Consequently, availability is an environmental variable. Yet it should be stressed that it is not important whether the goals to satisfy a need are really available. It is the perception, or the interpretation of reality, that affects one's actual behavior. In other words, reality is what a person perceives.

An example of how perception can affect behavior was dramatically illustrated in an experiment with a fish. A pike was placed in an aquarium with many minnows swimming around it. After the fish became accustomed to the plentiful supply of food, a sheet of glass was placed between the pike and the minnows. When the pike became hungry, it tried to reach the minnows, but it continually hit its head on the glass. At first, the strength of the need for food increased and the pike tried harder than ever to get the minnows. But finally its repeated failure of goal attainment resulted in enough frustration that the fish no longer attempted to eat the minnows. In fact, when the glass partition was finally removed, the minnows again swam all around the pike, but no further goal-directed activity took place. Eventually, the pike died of starvation while in the midst of plenty of food. In both cases, the fish operated according to the way it perceived reality and not on the basis of reality itself.

The expanded diagram of a motivating situation including expectancy and availability is presented in Figure 2-9.

Motives, needs within an individual, are directed toward goals that are

FIGURE 2-9 Expanded diagram of a motivating situation

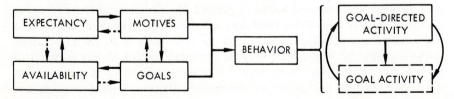

aspirations in the environment. These are interpreted by the individual as being available or unavailable. This affects expectancy. If expectancy is high, motive strength will increase. This tends to be a cyclical pattern moving in the direction of the prominent arrows. But to some extent these are interacting variables indicated by the secondary arrows. For example, experience may affect the way we perceive our feelings of availability. The presence of goals in the environment may affect the given strength of motives and so forth.

PERSONALITY DEVELOPMENT

As individuals mature, they develop habit patterns, or conditioned responses, to various stimuli. The sum of these habit patterns as perceived by others determines their *personality*.

habit *a*, habit *b*, habit *c*, . . . , habit *n* = *personality*

As individuals begin to behave in a similar fashion under similar conditions, this behavior is what others learn to recognize as them—as their personality. They expect and can even predict certain kinds of behavior from these people.

Changing Personality

Many psychologists contend that basic personality structures are developed quite early in life. In fact, some claim that few personality changes can be made after age seven or eight. Using a model similar to the one in Figure 2-9, we can begin to understand why it tends to become more difficult to make changes in personality as people grow older.

Note that in this model we are using *sum of past experience* in place of the term *expectancy* used in the earlier model. These can be used interchangeably.

When an individual behaves in a motivating situation, that behavior becomes a new input to that person's inventory of past experience, as the feedback loop in Figure 2-10 indicates. The earlier in life that this input occurs, the greater its potential effect on future behavior. The reason is that early in life this behavior represents a larger portion of the total past experience of a young person than the same behavior input will later in life. In addition, the longer behavior is reinforced, the more patterned it becomes and the more difficult it is to change. That is why it is easier to make personality changes early in life. The older a person gets, the more time and new experiences are necessary to effect a change in behavior. An illustration might be helpful. Putting one new input, a drop of red coloring, into a

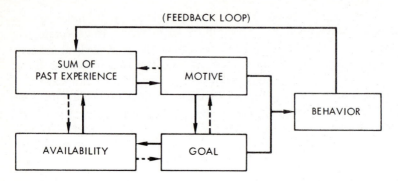

FIGURE 2-10 Feedback model

half-pint bottle of clear liquid may be enough to change drastically the appearance of the total contents. Adding the same input, a drop of red coloring, to a gallon jug may make little, if any, noticeable change in its appearance to others. This example illustrates the relationship between the amount of past experience and the effect of any one new experience.

Although it is possible to change behavior in older people, it will be difficult to accomplish except over a long period of time under conducive conditions. It almost becomes a matter of economics—allocating limited resources in terms of unlimited human wants—how much we are willing to invest in implementing such a change. Not only may it be less expensive in terms of time necessary for training, but the potential payback period for younger people is much greater.

HIERARCHY OF NEEDS

We have argued that the behavior of individuals at a particular moment is usually determined by their strongest need. It would seem significant, therefore, for managers to have some understanding about the needs that are commonly most important to people.

An interesting framework that helps explain the strength of certain needs was developed by Abraham Maslow.[19] According to Maslow, there seems to be a hierarchy into which human needs arrange themselves, as illustrated in Figure 2-11.

The *physiological* needs are shown at the top of the hierarchy because they tend to have the highest strength until they are somewhat satisfied. These are the basic human needs to sustain life itself—food, clothing, shelter. Until these basic needs are satisfied to the degree needed for the sufficient operation of the body, the majority of a person's activity will probably

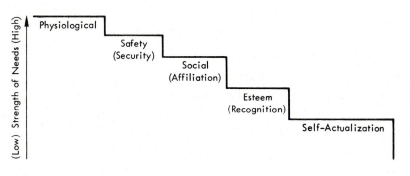

FIGURE 2-11 Maslow's hierarchy of needs

be at this level, and the other needs will provide little motivation.

But what happens to a person's motivation when these basic needs begin to be fulfilled? Instead of physiological needs, other levels of needs become important, and these motivate and dominate the behavior of the individual. And when these needs are somewhat satiated, other needs emerge, and so on down the hierarchy.

Once physiological needs become gratified, the *safety*, or *security*, needs become predominant, as illustrated in Figure 2-12. These needs are essentially the need to be free of the fear of physical danger and deprivation of the basic physiological needs. In other words, this is a need for self-preservation. In addition to the here and now, there is a concern for the future. Will people be able to maintain their property and/or job so they can provide food and shelter tomorrow and the next day? If an individual's safety or security is in danger, other things seem unimportant.

Once physiological and safety needs are fairly well satisfied, *social*, or *affiliation*, will emerge as dominant in the need structure, as illustrated in Figure 2-13. Since people are social beings, they have a need to belong to and be accepted by various groups. When social needs become dominant, a person will strive for meaningful relations with others.

After individuals begin to satisfy their need to belong, they generally want to be more than just a member of their group. They then feel the need

FIGURE 2-12 Safety need when dominant in the need structure

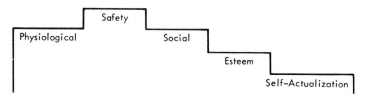

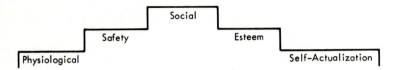

FIGURE 2-13 Social need when dominant in the need structure

for *esteem*—both self-esteem and recognition from others, as seen in Figure 2-14. Most people have a need for a high evaluation of themselves that is firmly based in reality—recognition and respect from others. Satisfaction of these esteem needs produces feelings of self-confidence, prestige, power, and control. People begin to feel that they are useful and have some effect on their environment. There are other occasions, though, when persons are unable to satisfy their need for esteem through constructive behavior. When this need is dominant, an individual may resort to disruptive or immature behavior to satisfy the desire for attention—a child may throw a temper tantrum, employees may engage in work restriction or arguments with their coworkers or boss. Thus, recognition is not always obtained through mature or adaptive behavior. It is sometimes garnered by disruptive and irresponsible actions. In fact, some of the social problems we have today may have their roots in the frustration of esteem needs.

Once esteem needs begin to be adequately satisfied, the *self-actualization* needs become more prepotent, as shown in Figure 2-15. Self-actualization is the need to maximize one's potential, whatever it may be. A musician must play music, a poet must write, a general must win battles, a professor must teach. As Maslow expressed it, "What a man *can* be, he *must* be." Thus, self-actualization is the desire to become what one is capable of becoming. Individuals satisfy this need in different ways. In one person it may be expressed in the desire to be an ideal mother; in another it may be expressed in managing an organization; in another it may be expressed athletically; in still another by playing the piano.

In combat, a soldier may rush a machine-gun nest in an attempt to destroy it, knowing full well that chances for survival are low. This courageous act is not done for affiliation or recognition but rather for what the

FIGURE 2-14 Esteem need when dominant in the need structure

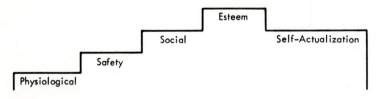

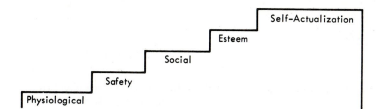

FIGURE 2-15 Self-actualization needs when dominant in the need structure

soldier thinks is important. In this case, you may consider the soldier to have self-actualized—to be maximizing the potential of what is important at this time.

The way self-actualization is expressed can change over the life cycle. For example, a self-actualized athlete may eventually look for other areas in which to maximize potential as physical attributes change over time or as horizons broaden. In addition, the hierarchy does not necessarily follow the pattern described by Maslow. It was not his intent to say that this hierarchy applies universally. Maslow felt this was a *typical* pattern that operates most of the time. He realized, however, that there were numerous exceptions to this general tendency. For example, the Indian leader Mahatma Gandhi frequently sacrificed his physiological and safety needs for the satisfaction of other needs when India was striving for independence from Great Britain. In his historic fasts, Gandhi went weeks without nourishment to protest governmental injustices. He was operating at the self-actualization level while some of his other needs were unsatisfied.

In discussing the preponderance of one category of need over another, we have been careful to speak in such terms as "if one level of needs has been somewhat gratified, then other needs emerge as dominant." This was done because we did not want to give the impression that one level of needs has to be completely satisfied before the next level emerges as the most important. In reality, most people in our society tend to be partially satisfied at each level and partially unsatisfied, with greater satisfaction tending to occur at the physiological and safety levels than at the social, esteem and self-actualization levels. In contrast, people in an emerging society, where much of the behavior engaged in tends to be directed toward satisfying physiological and safety needs, still operate to some extent at other levels. Therefore, Maslow's hierarchy of needs is not intended to be an all-or-none framework but rather one that may be useful in predicting behavior on a high or a low probability basis. Figure 2-16 attempts to portray how people in an emerging nation may be categorized.

Many people in our society today might be characterized by very strong social or affiliation needs, relatively strong esteem and safety needs,

FIGURE 2-16 Need mix when physiological and safety needs are high strength

with self-actualization and physiological needs somewhat less important, as shown in Figure 2-17.

Some people, however, can be characterized as having satisfied to a large extent the physiological, safety, and social needs, and their behavior tends to be dominated by esteem and self-actualizing activities, as shown in Figure 2-18. This will tend to become more characteristic if standards of living and levels of education continue to rise.

These are intended only as examples. For different individuals, varying configurations may be appropriate. In reality, they would fluctuate tremendously from one individual or group to another.

Clare W. Graves[20] has developed a theory that seems to be compatible with Maslow's hierarchy of needs. Graves contends that human beings exist at different "levels of existence." "At any given level, an individual exhibits the behavior and values characteristic of people at that level; a person who is centralized at a lower level cannot even understand people who are at a higher level."[21] According to Graves, "most people have been confined to lower [subsistence] levels of existence where they were motivated by needs shared with other animals. Now, Western man appears ready to move up to a higher [being] level of existence, a distinctly human level. When this happens there will likely be a dramatic transformation of human institutions.[22]

MOTIVATIONAL RESEARCH

Having discussed Maslow's heirarchy of needs, we can now examine what researchers say about some of our motives and the incentives that tend to satisfy them.

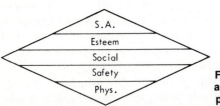

FIGURE 2-17 Need mix when social needs are high strength and self-actualization and physiological needs are less important

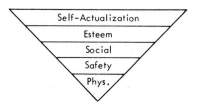

FIGURE 2-18 Need mix when esteem and
self-actualization needs are high strength

Physiological Needs

The satisfaction of physiological needs (shelter, food, clothing) is usually associated in our society with *money*. It is obvious that most people are not interested in dollars as such, but only as a means to be used to satisfy other motives. Thus, it is what money can buy, not money itself, that satisfies one's physiological needs. To suggest that money as a tool is useful *only* to satisfy physiological needs would be shortsighted because money can play a role in the satisfaction of needs at every level. Extensive studies of the impact of money have found that money is so complicated an incentive that it is entangled with all kinds of needs besides physiological ones, and its importance is difficult to ascertain. Consequently, we will discuss the money motive in a separate section later in the chapter. It is clear, however, that the ability of a given amount of money to satisfy *seems* to diminish as one moves from physiological and safety needs to other needs on the hierarchy. In many cases, money can buy the satisfaction of physiological and safety needs and even social needs if, for example, it provides entry into a desired group, such as a country club. But as one becomes concerned about esteem, recognition, and eventually self-actualization, money becomes a less appropriate tool to satisy these needs and, therefore, less effective. The more individuals become involved with esteem and self-actualization needs, the more they will have to earn their satisfaction directly, and thus the less important money will be in their attainment.

Safety (Security) Needs

We mentioned earlier that motives are not always apparent to the individual. Although some motives appear above the surface, many are largely subconscious and are not obvious or easy to identify. According to Saul W. Gellerman, security needs appear in both forms.[23]

The conscious security needs are quite evident and very common among most people. We all have a desire to remain free from the hazards of life—accidents, wars, diseases, and economic instability. Therefore, individuals and organizations are interested in providing some assurance that these catastrophes will be avoided if possible. Gellerman suggests that many organizations tend to overemphasize the security motive by providing elaborate programs of fringe benefits, such as health, accident, and life insurance and retirement plans. Such emphasis on security may make people more docile and predictable, but it does not mean they will be more productive. In fact, if creativity or initiative is necessary in their jobs, an overemphasis on security can thwart desired behavior.

Although concern for security can affect major decisions, such as remaining in or leaving an organization, Gellerman indicates it is not likely to be an individual's dominant motive. Conscious security needs usually play a background role, often inhibiting or restraining impulses rather than initiating outward behavior. For example, if a particular course of action, such as disregarding a rule or expressing an unpopular position, might endanger one's job, then security considerations motivate a person *not* to take this course of action. Organizations can influence these security needs either positively—through pension plans, insurance programs, and the like—or negatively, by arousing fears of being fired or laid off, demoted, or passed over. In both cases, the effect can be to make behavior too cautious and conservative.

Peter F. Drucker suggests that one's attitude toward security is important to consider in choosing a job.[24] He raises some interesting questions: Do you belong in a job calling primarily for faithfulness in the performance of routine work and promising security? Do you find real satisfaction in the precision, order, and system of a clearly laid-out job? Do you prefer the security not only of knowing what your work is today and what it is going to be tomorrow but also security in your job, in your relationship to the people above, below, and next to you? Or do you belong in a job that offers a challenge to imagination and ingenuity—with the attendant penalty for failure? Are you one of those people who tend to grow impatient with anything that looks like a "routine" job? The answers to these questions are not always easy even though we all understand ourselves to some degree. But the answers are involved with how important the security motive is for that particular individual.

To reiterate, security needs can be conscious or subconscious. A strong subconscious orientation toward security is often developed early in childhood. Gellerman discusses several ways in which it can be implanted. A common way is through identification with security-minded parents who are willing to accept whatever fate comes along. This often occurs in depressed economic areas where the prospects for improvement are poor.[25]

The world seems uncertain and uncontrollable to people raised in a security-minded home. As a result, such people may not feel they are competent enough to be able to influence their environment.

The security-minded people we have been describing are often very likable. They are not competitive and, therefore, do not put people on the defensive. Others tend to expect little of them and thus are seldom critical of their work. This combined with the fact that they are pleasant to have around, often enables them to obtain a secure, nonthreatening position in an organization.

Subconscious security motives may also develop in children through interaction with overprotective parents. Such parents are constantly trying to shield their children from heartache, disappointment, or failure. The supportive attitude of these parents in many instances permits their children to have their own way. Conflict is avoided at all costs. As a result, these children are given a distorted picture of reality and gain little insight into what they can expect of other people and what others will expect of them. In some cases, they become unrealistic in their optimism about life. Even in the face of disaster, when they should be threatened, they seem to believe that all is well until it is too late.

When such security-minded people leave home after high school to seek their way in the world, they quickly wake up to reality. Often they find themselves unequipped to handle the hardships of life because they have *not* been permitted the opportunity to develop the capacity to handle frustration, tension, and anxiety. As a result, even a minor setback may throw them for a loop. Drucker suggests that getting fired from their first job might be the best thing that could happen to such young people. He feels that getting fired from the first job is the least painful and least damaging way to learn how to take a setback, and that this is a lesson well worth learning. If people learn how to recover from seeming disaster when they are young, they will be better equipped to handle worse fate as they get older.

To many people, the security motive carries with it a negative connotation. A strong security need is frowned upon, for some reason, as if it were less respectable than other motives. This seems unjust, especially since nearly everyone has some conscious and subconscious security motives. Life is never so simple or clear-cut that one does not maintain some concern for security. In addition, many segments of our society often cater to these needs to the exclusion of such important needs as affiliation and self-actualization. We have already mentioned how industry concentrates on security needs by providing elaborate fringe benefits. Unions have a similar effect with their emphasis on seniority, and the government does much the same thing with welfare and other similar support programs.

Social (Affiliation) Needs

After the physiological and safety needs have become somewhat satisfied, the social needs may become predominant. Since people are social animals, most individuals like to interact and be with others in situations where they feel they belong and are accepted. While this is a common need, it tends to be stronger for some people than for others and stronger in certain situations. In other words, even such a commonplace social need as belongingness is, upon examination, quite complex.

In working toward a better understanding of our need to belong, Stanley Schachter of the University of Minnesota has made a significant contribution.[26] His efforts, in particular, have been directed toward studying the desire to socialize as an end in itself—that is, when people interact simply because they enjoy it. In some of these situations, no apparent reward such as money or protection was gained from this affiliation.

Schachter found that it was not always simply good fellowship that motivated affiliation. In many instances, people seek affiliation because they desire to have their beliefs confirmed. People who have similar beliefs tend to seek each other out, especially if a strongly held belief has been shattered. In this case, they tend to assemble and try to reach some common understanding about what happened and what they should believe (even if it is the same as before). In this instance, the need for affiliation was prompted by a desire to make one's life *seem* a little more under control. When alone, the world seems "out of whack," but if one can find an environment in which others hold the same beliefs, it somehow makes order out of chaos. This attitude hints at some of the problems inherent in any change.

In pursuing this question further, it was found that when people are excited, confused, or unhappy, they do not seek out just anyone—they tend to want to be with others "in the same boat." Misery does not just love company, it loves other miserable company. These conclusions suggest that the strong informal work groups that Elton Mayo found developing in the factory system might have been a reaction to the boredom, insignificance, and lack of competence that the workers felt.[27] As a result, workers congregated because of mutual feelings of being beaten by the system.

In observing loners and rate-busters in similar factory situations, it became apparent that there is not some universal need for affiliation as an end in itself. It was found, however, that these exceptions to the affiliation tendency were special types of people. They tended not to join informal work groups because they felt either suspicious or contemptuous of them or else secure and competent enough to fend for themselves.

Management is often suspicious of informal groups that develop at work because of the potential power these groups have to lower productivity. Schachter found that such work-restricting groups were sometimes formed as a reaction to the insignificance and impotence that workers tend to feel when they have no control over their working environment. Such environments develop when the work is routine, tedious, and oversimplified. This situation is made worse when, at the same time, the workers are closely supervised and controlled but have no clear channels of communication with management.

In this type of environment, workers who cannot tolerate this lack of control over their environment depend on the informal group for support of unfulfilled needs such as affiliation or achievement. Work restriction follows not from an inherent dislike for management but as a means to preserve the identification of individuals within the group and the group itself. Rate-busters are not tolerated because they weaken the group and its power with management, and to weaken the group destroys the only dignity, security, and significance the workers feel they have.

Lowering productivity is not always the result of informal work groups. In fact, informal groups can be a tremendous asset to management if their internal organization is understood and fully utilized. The productivity of a work group seems to depend on how the group members see their own goals in relation to the goals of the organization. For example, if they perceive their own goals as being in conflict with the goals of the organization, then productivity will tend to be low. However, if these workers see their own goals as being the same as the goals of the organization or as being satisfied as a direct result of accomplishing organizational goals, then productivity will tend to be high. Work restriction is therefore not a necessary aspect of informal work groups.

Esteem Needs

The need for esteem or recognition appears in a number of forms. In this section we shall discuss two motives related to esteem—prestige and power.

Prestige.   The prestige motive is becoming more evident in our society today, especially as we move toward a middle-class society. People with a concern for prestige want to "keep up with the Joneses"; in fact, given the choice, they would like to stay ahead of the Joneses. Vance Packard[28] and David Riesman[29] probably had the greatest impact in exposing prestige motivation. Packard wrote about the status seekers and their motives, while Riesman unveiled "other-directed" individuals who were part of "the lonely crowd."

What exactly is prestige? Gellerman describes it as "a sort of unwritten definition of the kinds of conduct that other people are expected to show in one's presence; what degree of respect or disrespect, formality or informality, reserve or frankness."[30] Prestige seems to have an effect on how comfortably or conveniently one can expect to get along in life.

Prestige is something intangible bestowed upon an individual by society. In fact, at birth children inherit the status of their parents. In some cases, this is enough to carry them through life on "a prestige-covered wave." For example, a Rockefeller or a Ford inherits instant prestige with that family background.

People seek prestige throughout their lives in various ways. Many tend to seek only the material symbols of status, while others strive for personal achievement or self-actualization, which might command prestige in itself. Regardless of the way it is expressed, there seems to be a widespread need for people to have their importance clarified and, in fact, set at a level that each feels is deserved. As discussed earlier, people normally want to have a high evaluation of themselves that is firmly based in reality as manifested by the recognition and respect accorded them by others.

The need for prestige is more or less self-limiting. People tend to seek prestige only to a preconceived level. When they feel they have gained this level, the strength of this need tends to decline and prestige becomes a matter of maintenance rather than of further advancement. Some people can become satisfied with their level of importance in their company and community. In their own evaluation, "they have arrived." Only the exceptional seek national or international recognition. Prestige motivation, therefore, often appears in young people who tend not to be satisfied yet with their status in life. Older people tend to have reached a level of prestige that satisfies them, or they become resigned to the fact that they can do little to improve their status.[31]

Power. The resource that enables a person to induce compliance from or to influence others is *power*. It is a person's influence potential. There tend to be two kinds of power—position and personal. Individuals who are able to induce compliance from others because of their position in the organization have *position* power; individuals who derive their influence from their personality and behavior have *personal* power. Some people are endowed with both position and personal power. Others seem to have no power at all.

Alfred Adler, a one-time colleague of Freud, became very interested in this power motive.[32] By power, Adler essentially meant the ability to manipulate or control the activities of others to suit one's own purposes. He found that this ability starts at an early age when children as babies realize that if they cry they influence their parents' behavior. Children's position as babies gives them considerable power over their parents.

According to Adler, this manipulative ability is inherently pleasurable. Children, for example, often have a hard time adjusting to the continuing reduction in their position power. In fact, they might spend a significant amount of time as adults trying to recapture the power they had as children. However, Adler did not feel that children seek power for its own sake as often as they do out of necessity. Power, for children, is often a life-and-death matter because they are helpless and need to count on their parents' availability. Parents are a child's lifeline. Thus, power acquires an importance in children that they somehow never lose, even though they are later able to fend for themselves.

After childhood, the power motive again becomes very potent in individuals who feel somehow inadequate in winning the respect and recognition of others. These people go out of their way to seek attention to overcome this weakness, which is often felt but not recognized. In this connection, Adler introduced two interesting and now well-known concepts in his discussion—*inferiority complex* and *compensation*.

A person with an inferiority complex has underlying fears of inadequacy, which may or may not have some basis in reality. In some cases, individuals compensate for this inferiority complex by exerting extreme efforts to achieve goals or objectives that (they feel) inadequacy would deny.

In many cases, extreme effort seems to be an overcompensation for something not clearly perceived, although felt. Once accurately perceived, the frame of reference can be realigned with reality and can result in more realistic behavior.

Adler found another interesting thing. If children do not encounter too much tension as they mature, their need for power gradually transforms itself into a desire to perfect their social relationships. They want to be able to interact with others without fear or suspicion in an open and trusting atmosphere. Thus, individuals often move from the *task* aspect of power, wanting to structure and manipulate their environment and the people in it, to a concern for *relationships*, developing trust and respect for others. This transformation is often delayed with individuals who have had tension-filled childhoods and have not learned to trust. In these cases, the power motive would not only persist but might even become stronger. Thus, Adler, like Freud, felt that the personality of an individual is developed early in life and is often a result of the kind of past experiences the child had with adults in the world. We will discuss power in much greater detail in Chapter 9.

Self-actualization Needs

Of all the needs discussed by Maslow, the one that social and behavioral scientists know least about is self-actualization. Perhaps this is because people satisfy this need in different ways. Thus, self-actualization is a difficult need to pin down and identify.

Although little research has been done on the concept of self-actualization, extensive research has been done on two motives that we feel are related to it—*competence* and *achievement*.

Competence. According to Robert W. White, one of the mainsprings of action in a human being is a desire for competence.[33] Competence implies control over environmental factors—both physical and social. People with this motive do not wish to wait passively for things to happen; they want to be able to manipulate their environment and make things happen.

The competence motive can be identified in young children as they move from the early stage of wanting to touch and handle everything in reach to the later stage of wanting not only to touch but to take things apart and put them back together again. Children begin to learn their way around their world. They become aware of what they can do and cannot do. This is not in terms of what they are allowed to do but in terms of what they are able to do. During these early years, children develop a feeling of competence.

This feeling of competence is closely related to the concept of expectancy discussed earlier. Whether children have a strong or weak sense of competence depends on their successes and failures in the past. If their successes overshadow their failures, then their feeling of competence will tend to be high. They will have a positive outlook toward life, seeing almost every new situation as an interesting challenge that they can overcome. If, however, their failures carry the day, their outlook will be more negative and their expectancy for satisfying various needs may become low. Since expectancy tends to influence motives, people with low feelings of competence will not often be motivated to seek new challenges or take risks. These people would rather let their environment control them than attempt to change it.

The sense of competence, while established early in life, is not necessarily permanent. White found that unexpected good or bad fortune may influence one's feelings of competence in a positive or negative way. Thus, the competence motive tends to be cumulative. For example, people can get off to a bad start and then develop a strong sense of competence because of new success. There is, however, a point in time when a sense of competence seems to stabilize itself. When this occurs, the sense of competence almost becomes a self-fulfilling prophecy, influencing whether a given experience will be a success or a failure. After people reach a certain age, they seldom achieve more than they think they can, because they do not attempt things they think they cannot achieve.

According to White, the competence motive reveals itself in adults as a desire for job mastery and professional growth. The job is one arena where people can match their ability and skills against their environment in a contest that is challenging but not overwhelming. In jobs where such a contest is possible, the competence motive in an individual can be expressed freely, and significant personal rewards can be gained. But in routine, closely supervised jobs, this contest is often impossible. Such situations make the worker dependent on the system and, therefore, completely frustrate people with high competence needs.

Achievement. Over the years, behavioral scientists have observed that some people have an intense need to achieve; others, perhaps the majority, do not seem to be as concerned about achievement. This phenomenon has fascinated David C. McClelland. For more than twenty years, he and his associates at Harvard University have been studying this urge to achieve.[34]

McClelland's research has led him to believe that the need for achievement is a distinct human motive that can be distinguished from other needs. More important, the achievement motive can be isolated and assessed in any group.

What are some of the characteristics of people with a high need for achievement? McClelland illustrates some of these characteristics in describing a laboratory experiment. Participants were asked to throw rings over a peg from any distance they chose. Most people tended to throw at random—now close, now far away; but individuals with a high need for achievement seemed carefully to measure where they were most likely to get a sense of mastery—not too close to make the task ridiculously easy or too far away to make it impossible. They set moderately difficult but potentially achievable goals. In biology, this is known as the *overload principle.* In weight lifting, for example, strength cannot be increased by tasks that can be performed easily or that cannot be performed without injury to the organism. Strength can be increased by lifting weights that are difficult but realistic enough to stretch the muscles.

Do people with a high need for achievement behave like this all the time? No. Only if they can influence the outcome. Achievement-motivated people are not gamblers. They prefer to work on a problem rather than leave the outcome to chance.

With managers, setting moderately difficult but potentially achievable goals may be translated into an attitude toward risks. Many people tend to be extreme in their attitude toward risks, either favoring wild speculative gambling or minimizing their exposure to losses. Gamblers seem to choose the big risk because the outcome is beyond their power and, therefore, they can easily rationalize away their personal responsibility if they lose. The conservative individual chooses tiny risks where the gain is small but secure, perhaps because there is little danger of anything going wrong for which that person might be blamed. Achievement-motivated people take the middle ground, preferring a moderate degree of risk because they feel their efforts and abilities will probably influence the outcome. In business, this aggressive realism is the mark of the successful entrepreneur.

Another characteristic of achievement-motivated people is that they seem to be more concerned with personal achievement than with the rewards of success. They do not reject rewards but the rewards are not as essential as the accomplishment itself. They get a bigger kick out of winning or solving a difficult problem than they get from any money or praise they receive. Money, to achievement-motivated people, is valuable primarily as a measurement of their performance. It provides them with a means of assessing their progress and comparing their achievements with those of other people. They normally do not seek money for status or economic security.

A desire by people with a high need for achievement to seek situations in which they get concrete feedback on how well they are doing is closely related to this concern for personal accomplishment. Consequently, achievement-motivated people are often found in sales jobs or as owners and managers of their own businesses. In addition to concrete feedback, the nature of the feedback is important to achievement-motivated people. They respond favorably to information about their work. They are not interested in comments about their personal characteristics, such as how cooperative or helpful they are. Affiliation-motivated people might want social or attitudinal feedback. Achievement-motivated people might want task-relevant feedback. They want to know the score.

Why do achievement-motivated people behave as they do? McClelland claims it is because they habitually spend time thinking about doing things better. In fact, he has found that wherever people start to think in achievement terms, things start to happen. Examples can be cited. College students with a high need for achievement will generally get better grades than equally bright students with weaker achievement needs. Achievement-motivated people tend to get more raises and are promoted faster because they are constantly trying to think of better ways of doing things. Companies with many such people grow faster and are more profitable. McClelland has even extended his analysis to countries where he related the presence of a large percentage of achievement-motivated individuals to the national economic growth.

McClelland has found that achievement-motivated people are more likely to be developed in families in which parents hold different expectations for their children than do other parents. More importantly, these parents expect their children to start showing some independence between the ages of six and eight, making choices and doing things without help, such as knowing the way around the neighborhood and taking care of themselves around the house. Other parents tend either to expect this too early, before children are ready, or to smother the development of the personality of these children. One extreme seems to foster passive, defeatist attitudes as children feel unwanted at home and incompetent away from home. They are just not ready for that kind of independence so early. The other extreme yields either overprotected or overdisciplined children. These children become very dependent on their parents and find it difficult to break away and make their own decisions.

Given all we know about the need for achievement, can this motive be taught and developed in people? McClelland is convinced that this can be done. In fact, he has also developed training progams for business people that are designed to increase their achievement motivation. He is also in the process of developing similar programs for other segments of the population. These programs could have tremendous implications for training and developing human resources.

Achievement-motivated people can be the backbone of most organizations, but what can we say about their potential as managers? As we know, people with a high need for achievement get ahead because as individuals they are producers—they get things done. However, when they are promoted—when their success depends not only on their own work but on the activities of others—they may be less effective. Since they are highly task-oriented and work to their capacity, they tend to expect others to do the same. As a result, they sometimes lack the human skills and patience necessary for being effective managers of people who are competent but have a higher need for affiliation than they do. In this situation, their over-emphasis on producing frustrates these people and prevents them from maximizing their own potential. Thus, while achievement-motivated people are needed in organizations, they do not always make the best managers unless they develop their human skills. As was pointed out in Chapter 1, being a good producer is not sufficient to make an effective manager.

Money Motive

As stated earlier, money is a very complicated motive that is entangled in such a way with all kinds of needs besides physiological needs that its importance is often difficult to ascertain. For example, in some cases, money can provide individuals with certain material things, such as fancy sports cars, from which they gain a feeling of affiliation (join a sports car club), recognition (status symbol), and even self-actualization (become outstanding sports car drivers). Consequently, we delayed our discussion of the money motive until other basic concepts were clarified.

From extensive research on incentive pay schemes, William F. Whyte has found that money, the old reliable motivational tool, is not as almighty as it is supposed to be, particularly for production workers.[35] For each of these workers, another key factor, as Mayo discovered, is their work group. Using the ratio of high-producing rate-busters to low-producing restrictors as an index, Whyte estimates that only about 10 percent of the production workers in the United States will ignore group pressure and produce as much as possible in response to an incentive plan. It seems that while workers are interested in advancing their own financial position, there are many other considerations—such as the opinions of their fellow workers, their comfort and enjoyment on the job, and their long-range security—that prevent them from making a direct, automatic, positive response to an incentive plan.

According to Gellerman, the most subtle and most important characteristic of money is its power as a symbol. Its most obvious symbolic power is its market value. It is what money can buy, not money itself, that gives it value. But money's symbolic power is not limited to its market value. Since money has no intrinsic meaning of its own, it can symbolize almost any need an individual wants it to represent. In other words, money can mean whatever people want it to mean.[36]

WHAT DO WORKERS WANT FROM THEIR JOBS?

In talking about motives, it is important to remember that people have many needs, all of which are continually competing for their behavior. No one person has exactly the same mixture or strength of these needs. There are some people who are driven mainly by money, others who are concerned primarily with security, and so on. While we must recognize individual differences, this does not mean that, as managers, we cannot make some predictions about which motives seem to be currently more prominent among our employees than others. According to Maslow, these are prepotent motives—those that are still *not* satisfied. An important question for managers to answer is, what do workers really want from their jobs?

Some interesting research has been conducted among employees in American industry in an attempt to answer this question. In one such study[37] supervisors were asked to try to put themselves in a *worker's* shoes by ranking in order of importance a series of items that describe things workers may want from their jobs. It was emphasized that in ranking the items the supervisors should *not* think in terms of what they want but what they think a worker wants. In addition to the supervisors, the workers themselves were asked to rank these same items in terms of what *they* wanted most from their jobs. The results are given in Table 2-1 (1 = highest and 10 = lowest in importance).

As is evident from the results, the supervisors in this study generally ranked good wages, job security, promotion, and good working conditions as the things workers want most from their jobs. On the other hand, workers felt that what they wanted most was full appreciation for work done, feeling "in" on things, and sympathetic understanding of personal problems —all incentives that seem to be related to affiliation and recognition motives. It is interesting to note that things that workers indicated they wanted most from their jobs were rated by their foremen as least important. This study suggested very little sensitivity by supervisors as to what things were really most important to workers. Supervisors seemed to think that incentives directed to satisfying physiological and safety motives tended to be most important to their workers. Since these supervisors perceived their

TABLE 2-1 What Do Workers Want from Their Jobs?

	Supervisors	Workers
Good working conditions	4	9
Feeling "in" on things	10	2
Tactful disciplining	7	10
Full appreciation for work done	8	1
Management loyalty to workers	6	8
Good wages	1	5
Promotion and growth with company	3	7
Sympathetic understanding of personal problems	9	3
Job security	2	4
Interesting work	5	6

workers as having these motives, they acted, undoubtedly, as if these were their true motives. Therefore, these supervisors probably used the old reliable incentives—money, fringe benefits, and security—to motivate workers.

We have replicated this study periodically over the last several decades as part of management training programs and have found similar results in the perceptions of managers. The only real changes seem to be that workers, over the last five to ten years, were increasing in their desire for "promotion and growth with the company" and "interesting work" (both motivators in Herzberg's framework). We say *were* increasing because with the economic decline of the 1980s, "good wages" and "job security" once again were becoming high-strength needs for workers. It is important that managers know the tremendous discrepancies that seemed to exist in the past between what they thought workers wanted from their jobs and what workers said they actually wanted. It is also important that they realize what effect an economic or other change has on these priorities.

One might generalize at this point that individuals act on the basis of their perceptions or interpretion of reality and *not* on the basis of reality itself. In fact, one of the reasons we study the behavioral sciences is that they give us ways to get our perceptions closer and closer to reality. The closer we get our perceptions to a given reality, the higher the probability that we can have some impact on that particular piece of reality. Therefore, by bringing their perceptions closer and closer to reality—what their people really want—managers can often increase their effectiveness in working with employees. Managers have to know their people to understand what motivates them; they cannot just make assumptions. Even if managers asked employees how they felt about something, this does not necessarily result in relevant feedback. The quality of communications that managers receive from their employees is often based on the rapport that has been established between their people and themselves over a long period of time.

NOTES

1. Sigmund Freud, *The Ego and the Id* (London: Hogarth Press, 1927). See also *New Introductory Lectures on Psychoanalysis* (New York: Norton, 1933).

2. Abraham H. Maslow, *Motivation and Personality* (New York: Harper & Row, 1954). See also Maslow, *Motivation and Personality*, 2nd ed. (New York: Harper & Row, 1970).

3. Leon Festinger, *A Theory of Cognitive Dissonance* (Stanford, Calif.: Stanford University Press, 1957); Stephen Kaplan, *Cognition and Environment: Functioning in an Uncertain World* (New York: Praeger, 1982).

4. *Ibid.*, p. 155.

5. Freud, *The Ego and the Id.*

6. J. A. C. Brown, *The Social Psychology of Industry* (Baltimore: Penguin Books, 1954), p. 249; D. Katz and R. L. Kahn, *The Social Psychology of Organizations*, 2nd ed. (New York: Wiley, 1978).

7. Norman R. F. Maier, *Frustration* (Ann Arbor: University of Michigan Press, 1961).

8. Brown, *The Social Psychology*, p. 252.

9. H. Barker, T. Dembo and K. Lewin, *Frustration and Aggression* (Iowa City: University of Iowa Press, 1942).

10. Brown, *The Social Psychology*, p. 253.

11. Maier, *Frustration*.

12. Brown, *The Social Psychology*, p. 254.

13. Dewey E. Johnson, *Concepts of Air Force Leadership* (Washington, D.C.: Air Force ROTC, 1970), p. 209.

14. This figure was adapted from J. Sterling Livingston, "Pygmalion in Management," *Harvard Business Review*, July–August 1969, p. 89.

15. Livingston, "Pygmalion in Management," pp. 81–89.

16. See John W. Atkinson, "Motivational Determinants of Risk-Taking Behavior, *Psychological Review*, 64, No. 6 (1957), 365; C. N. Cofer and M. H. Appley, *Motivation: Theory and Research* (New York: Wiley, 1964).

17. Victor, H. Vroom, "Leader," in M. D. Dunnette (ed.), *Handbook of Industrial and Organizational Psychology* (Chicago: Rand McNally, 1976), pp. 1527–1551.

18. Martin L. Maehr and Larry A. Braskampt, *The Motivation Factor: A Theory of Personal Investment* (Lexington, Mass.: Heath, 1986).

19. Maslow, *Motivation and Personality*.

20. Clare W. Graves, "Human Nature Prepares for a Momentous Leap," *The Futurist*, April 1974, pp. 72–87.

21. *Ibid.*, p. 72.

22. *Ibid.*

23. Saul W. Gellerman, *Motivation and Productivity* (New York: American Management Association, 1963). See also Gellerman, *Management by Motivation* (New York: American Management Association, 1968); Frederick Herzberg, *Motivating People*, in P. Mali (ed.) *Management Handbook* (New York: Wiley, 1981); Michael LeBoeuf, *The Productivity Challenge: How to Make It Work for America and You* (New York: McGraw-Hill, 1982).

24. Peter F. Drucker, "How to Be an Employee," *Psychology Today*, March 1968, a reprint from *Fortune* magazine; G. J. Gorn and R. N. Kanungo, "Job Involvement and Motivation: Are Intrinsically Motivated Managers More Job Involved?" *Organizational Behavior and Human Performance* 26 (1980), pp. 265–277; W. R. Nord, "Job Satisfaction Reconsidered," *American Psychologist*, 32 (1977), pp. 1026–1035; Craig Pinder, *Work Motivation: Theory, Issues, and Applications* (Glenview, Ill.: Scott, Foresman, 1984).

25. Gellerman, *Motivation and Productivity*, pp. 154–55.

26. Stanley Schachter, *The Psychology of Affiliation* (Stanford, Calif.: Stanford University Press, 1959).

27. Elton Mayo, *The Social Problems of an Industrial Civilization* (Boston: Harvard Business School, 1945); see also Mayo, *The Human Problems of an Industrial Civilization* (New York: Macmillan, 1933).

28. Vance Packard, *The Status Seekers* (New York: David McKay, 1959).

29. David Reisman, *The Lonely Crowd* (New Haven, Conn.: Yale University Press, 1950).

30. Gellerman, *Motivation and Productivity*, p. 151.

31. *Ibid.*, pp. 150–54.

32. Alfred Adler, *Social Interest* (London: Faber & Faber, 1938). See also H. L. Ansbacher and R. R. Ansbacher, eds., *The Individual Psychology of Alfred Adler* (New York: Basic Books, 1956).

33. Robert W. White, "Motivation Reconsidered: The Concept of Competence," *Psychological Review*, No. 5 (1959).

34. David C. McClelland, J. W. Atkinson, R. A. Clark, and E. L. Lowell, *The Achievement Motive* (New York: Appleton-Century-Crofts, 1953); and *The Achieving Society* (Princeton, N.J.: D. Van Nostrand, 1961); John William Atkinson, *Motivation and Achievement* (New York: Halsted Press, 1974). See also Craig Pinder, "Concerning the Application of Human Motivation Theories in Organizational Settings," *Academy of Management Review*, 21 (1977), pp. 384–397.

35. William F. Whyte, ed., *Money and Motivation* (New York: Harper & Row, 1955).

36. Gellerman, *Motivation and Productivity*, pp. 160–69.

37. Lawrence Lindahl, "What Makes a Good Job?" *Personnel*, 25 (January 1949).

CHAPTER 3

MOTIVATING ENVIRONMENT

In 1924 efficiency experts at Hawthorne, Illinois, plant of the Western Electric Company designed a research program to study the effects of illumination on productivity. At first, nothing about this program seemed exceptional enough to arouse any unusual interest. After all, efficiency experts had long been trying to find the ideal mix of physical conditions, working hours, and working methods that would stimulate workers to produce at maximum capacity. Yet by the time these studies were completed (a decade later), there was little doubt that the work at Hawthorne would stand the test of time as one of the most exciting and important research projects ever done in an industrial setting. For it was at Western Electric's Hawthorne plant that the Human Relations Movement began to gather momentum, and one of its early advocates, Elton Mayo of the Harvard Graduate School of Business Administration, gained recognition.[1]

HAWTHORNE STUDIES

Elton Mayo

In the initial study at Hawthorne, efficiency experts assumed that increases in illumination would result in higher output. Two groups of employees were selected: an *experimental*, or *test group*, which worked under varying degrees of light, and a *control group*, which worked under normal illumination conditions in the plant. As lighting power was increased, the output of the test group went up as anticipated. Unexpectedly, however, the output of the control group went up also—without any increase in light.

Determined to explain these and other surprising test results, the efficiency experts decided to expand their research at Hawthorne. They felt that in addition to technical and physical changes, some of the behavioral considerations should be explored, so Mayo and his associates were called in to help.

Mayo and his team started their experiments with a group of women who assembled telephone relays and, like the efficiency experts, the Harvard staff uncovered astonishing results. For more than a year and a half during this experiment, Mayo's researchers improved the working conditions of the women by implementing such innovations as scheduled rest periods, company lunches, and shorter work weeks. Baffled by the results, the researchers suddenly decided to take everything away from the women, returning the working conditions to the exact way they had been at the beginning of the experiment. This radical change was expected to have a tremendous negative psychological impact on the women and to reduce their output. Instead, their output jumped to a new *all-time high*. Why?

The answers to this question were *not* found in the production aspects of the experiment (changes in plant and physical working conditions), but in the *human* aspects. As a result of the attention lavished upon them by experimenters, the women felt that they were an important part of the company. They no longer viewed themselves as isolated individuals, working together only in the sense that they were physically close to each other. Instead, they had become participating members of a congenial, cohesive work group. The relationships that developed elicited feelings of affiliation, competence, and achievement. These needs, which had long gone unsatisfied at the workplace, were now being fulfilled. The women worked harder and more effectively than previously.

Realizing that they had uncovered an interesting phenomenon, the Harvard team extended their research by interviewing more than twenty thousand employees from every department in the company. Interviews were designed to help researchers find out what the workers thought about their jobs, their working conditions, their supervisors, their company, and anything that bothered them, and how these feelings might be related to their productivity. After several interview sessions, Mayo's group found that a structured question-and-answer-type interview was useless for eliciting the information they wanted. Instead, the workers wanted to talk freely about what *they* thought was important. So the predetermined questions were discarded and the interviewer allowed the workers to ramble as they chose.

The interviews proved valuable in a number of ways. First of all, they were therapeutic; the workers got an opportunity to get a lot off their chests. Many felt this was the best thing the company had ever done. The result was a wholesale change in attitude. Since many of their suggestions were being implemented, the workers began to feel that management viewed them as important, both as individuals and as a group; they were now participating in the operation and future of the company and not just performing unchallenging, unappreciated tasks.

Second, the implications of the Hawthorne studies signaled the need for management to study and understand relationships among people. In these studies, as well as in the many that followed, the most significant factor affecting organizational productivity was found to be the interpersonal relationships that are developed on the job, not just pay and working conditions. Mayo found that when informal groups identified with management, as they did at Hawthorne through the interview program, productivity rose. The increased productivity seemed to reflect the workers' feelings of competence—a sense of mastery over the job and work environment. Mayo also discovered that when the group felt that their own goals were in opposition to those of management, as often happened in situations where workers were closely supervised and had no significant control over the job or environment, productivity remained at low levels or was even lowered.

These findings were important because they helped answer many of the questions that had puzzled management about why some groups seemed to be high producers while others hovered at a minimal level of output. The findings also encouraged management to involve workers in planning, organizing, and controlling their own work in an effort to secure their positive cooperation.

Mayo saw the development of informal groups as an indictment of an entire society that treated human beings as insensitive machines that were concerned only with economic self-interest. As a result, workers had been expected to look at work merely as an impersonal exchange of money for labor. Work in American industry meant humiliation—the performance of routine, tedious, and oversimplified tasks in an environment over which one had no control. This environment denied satisfaction of esteem and self-actualization needs on the job. Instead, only physiological and safety needs were satisfied. The lack of avenues for satisfying other needs led to tension, anxiety, and frustration in people. Such feelings of helplessness were called *anomie* by Mayo. This condition was characterized by workers feeling unimportant, confused, and unattached—victims of their own environment.

While anomie was a creation of the total society, Mayo felt its most extreme application was found in industrial settings where management held certain negative assumptions about the nature of people. According to Mayo, too many managers assumed that society consisted of a horde of unorganized individuals whose only concern was self-preservation or self-interest. It was assumed that people were primarily dominated by physiological and safety needs, wanting to make as much money as they could for as little work as possible. Thus, management organized work on the basic assumption that workers, on the whole, were a contemptible lot. Mayo called this assumption the Rabble Hypothesis. He deplored the authoritarian, task-oriented management practices that it created.

THEORY X AND THEORY Y

Douglas McGregor

The work of Mayo and particularly his exposure of the Rabble Hypothesis may have paved the way for the development of the now classic "Theory X-Theory Y" by Douglas McGregor.[2] According to McGregor, the traditional organization—with its centralized decision making, superior-subordinate pyramid, and external control of work—is based upon assumptions about human nature and human motivation. These assumptions are very similar to the view of people defined by Mayo in the Rabble Hypothesis. Theory X assumes that most people prefer to be directed, are not interested in assuming responsibility, and want safety above all. Accompanying this philosophy is the belief that people are motivated by money, fringe benefits, and the threat of punishment.

Managers who accept Theory X assumptions attempt to structure, control, and closely supervise their employees. These managers feel that external control is clearly appropriate for dealing with unreliable, irresponsible, and immature people.

After describing Theory X, McGregor questioned whether this view of human nature is correct and if management practices based upon it are appropriate in many situations today: Are not people in a democratic society, with its increasing level of education and standard of living, capable of more mature behavior? Drawing heavily on Maslow's hierarchy of needs, McGregor concluded that Theory X assumptions about human nature, when universally applied, are often inaccurate and that management approaches that develop from these assumptions may fail to motivate many individuals to work toward organizational goals. Management by direction and control may not succeed, according to McGregor, because it is a questionable method for motivating people whose physiological and safety needs are reasonably satisfied and whose social, esteem, and self-actualization needs are becoming predominant.

McGregor felt that management needed practices based on a more accurate understanding of human nature and motivation. As a result of his feeling, McGregor developed an alternate theory of human behavior called Theory Y. This theory assumes that people are *not*, by nature, lazy and unreliable. It postulates that people *can be* basically self-directed and cre-

TABLE 3-1 List of Assumptions about Human Nature that Underlie McGregor's Theory X and Theory Y

Theory X	Theory Y
1. Work is inherently distasteful to most people.	1. Work is as natural as play, if the conditions are favorable.
2. Most people are not ambitious, have little desire for responsibility, and prefer to be directed.	2. Self-control is often indispensable in achieving organizational goals.
3. Most people have little capacity for creativity in solving organizational problems.	3. The capacity for creativity in solving organizational problems is widely distributed in the population.
4. Motivation occurs only at the physiological and safety levels.	4. Motivation occurs at the social, esteem, and self-actualization levels, as well as at the physiological and security levels.
5. Most people must be closely controlled and often coerced to achieve organizational objectives.	5. People can be self-directed and creative at work if properly motivated.

ative at work if properly motivated. Therefore, it should be an essential task of management to unleash this potential in individuals. Properly motivated people can achieve their own goals *best* by directing *their own* efforts toward accomplishing organizational goals.

The impression that one might get from the discussion of Theory X-Theory Y is that managers who accept Theory X assumptions about human nature usually direct, control, and closely supervise people, while Theory Y managers are supportive and facilitating. We want to caution against drawing that kind of conclusion because it could lead to the trap of thinking that Theory X is "bad" and Theory Y is "good" and that everyone is mature, independent, and self-motivated rather than, as McGregor implies, that most people have the *potential* to be mature and self-motivated. This assumption of the potential self-motivation of people necessitates a recognition of the difference between attitude and behavior. Theory X and Theory Y are attitudes, or predispositions, toward people. Thus, although the "best" assumptions for a manager to have may be Theory Y, it may not be appropriate to behave consistent with those assumptions all the time. Managers may have Theory Y assumptions about human nature, but they may find it necessary to behave in a very directive, controlling manner (as if they had Theory X assumptions) with some people in the short run to help them "grow up" in a developmental sense, until they are truly Theory Y people.

Chris Argyris recognizes the difference between attitude and behavior when he identifies and discusses behavior patterns A and B in addition to Theory X and Y.[3] Pattern A represents the interpersonal behavior, group dynamics, and organizational norms that Argyris has found in his research to be associated with Theory X; pattern B represents the same phenomena found to be associated with Theory Y. In pattern A, individuals do not own up to feelings, are not open, reject experimenting, and do not help others to engage in these behaviors. Their behavior tends to be characterized by close supervision and a high degree of structure. On the other hand, pattern B finds individuals owning up to feelings, open, experimenting, and helping others to engage in these behaviors. Their behavior tends to be more supportive and facilitating. The result is norms of trust, concern, and individuality.

As Argyris emphasizes, "although XA and YB are *usually* associated with each other in everyday life, they do not have to be. Under certain conditions, pattern A could go with Theory Y or pattern B with Theory X."[4] Thus, XA and YB are the most frequent combinations, but some managers at times may be XB or YA. Although XB managers have negative assumptions about people, they seem to behave in supportive and facilitating ways. We have found that this XB combination tends to occur for two reasons. These managers (although they think most people are lazy and unreliable) engage in supportive and facilitating behaviors either because they have been told or have learned from experience that such behavior will increase productivity or that they work for people who have created a supportive environment and if they want to maintain their jobs they are expected to behave accordingly. On the other hand, YA managers (although they think people are generally self-motivated and mature) control and closely supervise people either because they work for controlling people who demand similar behavior from them or they find it necessary to behave in a directive, controlling manner for a period of time. When they use pattern A behavior, these managers usually are attempting to help people develop the skills and abilities necessary for self-direction and thus are creating an environment in which they can become YB managers.

The latter type of Y manager attempts to help employees mature by exposing them to progressively less external control, allowing them to assume more and more self-control. Employees are able to achieve the satisfaction of social, esteem, and self-actualization needs within this kind of environment, often neglected on the job. To the extent that the job does not provide satisfaction at every level, today's employee will usually look elsewhere for significant need satisfaction. This helps explain some of the current problems management is facing in such areas as turnover and absenteeism. McGregor argues that this does not have to be the case.

Management is interested in work, and McGregor feels that work is as natural and can be as satisfying for people as play. After all, both work and play are physical and mental activities; consequently, there is no inherent difference between work and play. In reality, however, particularly under Theory X management, a distinct difference in need satisfaction is discernible. Whereas play is internally controlled by the individuals (they decide what they want to do), work is externally controlled by others (people have no control over their jobs). Thus, management and its assumptions about the nature of people have built in a difference between work and play that seems unnatural. As a result, people are stifled at work and hence look for excuses to spend more and more time away from the job in order to satisfy their esteem and self-actualization needs (provided they have enough money to satisfy their physiological and safety needs). Because of their conditioning to Theory X types of management, most employees consider work a *necessary evil* rather than a source of personal challenge and satisfaction.

Does work really have to be a necessary evil? No—especially in organizations where cohesive work groups have developed and where the goals parallel organizational goals. In such organizations there is high productivity and people come to work gladly because work is inherently satisfying.

HUMAN GROUP

George C. Homans

Management is often suspicious of strong informal work groups because of their potential power to control the behavior of their members and, as a result, the level of productivity. Where do these groups get their power to control behavior? George C. Homans has developed a model of social systems that may be useful to the practitioner trying to answer this question.[5]

There are three elements in a social system. *Activities* are the tasks that people perform. *Interactions* are the behaviors that occur between people in performing these tasks. And *sentiments* are the attitudes that develop between individuals and within groups. Homans argues that while these concepts are separate, they are closely related. In fact, as Figure 3-1 illustrates, they are mutually dependent upon each other.

FIGURE 3-1 The mutual dependence of activities, interactions, and sentiments

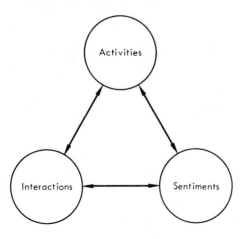

A change in any one of these three elements will produce some change in the other two.

In an organization, certain activities, interactions, and sentiments are essential, or required from its members if it is to survive. In other words, jobs (activities) have to be done that require people to work together (interactions). These jobs must be sufficiently satisfying (sentiments) for people to continue doing them. As people interact on their jobs, they develop sentiments toward each other. As people increase interaction with each other, it is important that positive sentiments be developed. The more positive the sentiment, the more people will tend to interact with each other. It can become a spiraling process until some equilibrium is reached. As this spiraling process continues, there is a tendency for the group members to become more alike in their activities and sentiments—in what they do and how they feel about things. As this happens, the group tends to develop expectations or norms that specify how people in the group "might" tend to behave under specific circumstances. For example, a group of workers might have a norm that "you should not talk to Mary or help her any more than necessary." If the group is cohesive enough—that is, the group is attractive to its members and they are reluctant to leave it—then it will have little trouble in getting members to conform. People who deviate significantly from group norms usually incur sanctions from the group. "The group has at its disposal a variety of penalties, ranging from gentle kidding to harsh ostracism, for pressuring deviant members into line."[6] Group members may react in several ways. They may decide to go ahead and continue to deviate from group norms. If the resulting pressure from their peers becomes too great, they may leave the group.

The influence group pressures can have in achieving conformity in the perceptions and behavior of people is well documented. For example, S. E. Asch conducted a classic experiment in which groups of eight college men were each asked to match the length of a line with one of three unequal lines.[7] Seven members of each group were privately told to give the same incorrect answer. The uninstructed member was the last one asked to give his answer and was thus confronted with the dilemma of either reporting what he saw as being correct or reporting what all the others had said in order to be congruent with the group. Asch reported that "one-third of all the estimates were errors identical with or in the direction of the distorted estimates of the majority."[8] If pressure can cause distorted behavior in this kind of exercise, imagine what peer group pressure can induce with more subjective judgments.

It should be reiterated that strong informal work groups do not have to be a detriment to organizations. In fact, as Mayo discovered at Hawthorne, these groups can become powerful driving forces in accomplishing organizational goals if they see their own goals as being satisfied by working for organizational goals.

INCREASING INTERPERSONAL COMPETENCE

Chris Argyris

Even though management based on the assumptions of Theory X is perhaps no longer widely appropriate, in the opinion of McGregor and others, it is still widely practiced. Consequently, a large majority of the people in the United States today are treated as immature human beings in their working environments. In attempting to analyze this situation, Chris Argyris,[9] has compared bureaucratic/pyramidal values (the organizational counterpart to Theory X assumptions about people) that still dominate most organizations with a more humanistic/democratic value system (the organizational counterpart to Theory Y assumptions about people), as illustrated in Table 3-2.[10]

According to Argyris, following bureaucratic or pyramidal values leads to poor, shallow, and mistrustful relationships. Because these relationships do not permit the natural and free expression of feelings, they are phony or nonauthentic and result in decreased interpersonal competence. "Without interpersonal competence or a 'psychologically safe' environment, the organization is a breeding ground for mistrust, intergroup conflict, rigidity, and so on, which in turn lead to a decrease in organizational success in problem solving."[11]

If, on the other hand, humanistic or democratic values are adhered to in an organization, Argyris claims that trusting, authentic relationships will

TABLE 3-2   Two Different Value Systems as Seen by Chris Argyris

Bureaucratic/Pyramidal Value System	Humanistic/Democratic Value System
1. Important human relationships—the crucial ones—are those related to achieving the organization's objectives, i.e., getting the job done.	1. The important human relationships are not only those related to achieving the organization's objectives but those related to maintaining the organization's internal system and adapting to the environment as well.
2. Effectiveness in human relationships increases as behavior becomes more rational, logical, and clearly communicated; but effectiveness decreases as behavior becomes more emotional.	2. Human relationships increase in effectiveness as *all* the relevant behavior (rational and interpersonal) becomes conscious, discussible, and controllable.
3. Human relationships are most effectively motivated by carefully defined direction, authority, and control, as well as appropriate rewards and penalties that emphasize rational behavior and achievement of the objective.	3. In addition to direction, controls, and rewards and penalties, human relationships are most effectively influenced through authentic relationships, internal commitment, psychological success, and the process of confirmation.

develop among people and will result in increased interpersonal competence, intergroup cooperation, flexibility, and the like and should result in increases in organizational effectiveness. In this kind of environment people are treated as human beings, both organizational members and the organization itself are given an opportunity to develop to the fullest potential, and there is an attempt to make work exciting and challenging. Implicit in "living" these values is "treating each human being as a person with a complex set of needs, *all* of which are important in his work and in his life . . . and providing opportunities for people in organizations to influence the way in which they relate to work, the organization, and the environment."[12]

Immaturity-Maturity Theory

The fact that bureaucratic/pyramidal values still dominate most organizations, according to Argyris, has produced many of our current organizational problems. While at Yale, he examined industrial organizations to determine what effect management practices have had on individual behavior and personal growth within the work environment.[13]

According to Argyris, seven changes should take place in the personality of individuals if they are to develop into mature people over the years.

First, individuals move from a passive state as infants to a state of increasing activity as adults. Second, individuals develop from a state of dependency upon others as infants to a state of relative independence as adults. Third, individuals behave in only a few ways as infants, but as adults they are capable of behaving in many ways. Fourth, individuals have erratic, casual, and shallow interests as infants but develop deeper and stronger interests as adults. Fifth, the time perspective of children is very short, involving only the present, but as they mature, their time perspective increases to include the past and the future. Sixth, individuals as infants are subordinate to everyone, but they move to equal or superior positions with others as adults. Seventh, as children, individuals lack an awareness of a "self," but as adults they are not only aware of, but they are able to control "self." Argyris suggests that these changes reside on a continuum and that the "healthy" personality develops along the continuum from "immaturity" to "maturity" (See Table 3-3).

These changes are only general tendencies, but they give some light on the matter of maturity. Norms of the individual's culture and personality inhibit and limit maximum expression and growth of the adult, yet the tendency is to move toward the "maturity" end of the continuum with age. Argyris would be the first to admit that few, if any, develop to full maturity.

In examining the widespread worker apathy and lack of effort in industry, Argyris questions whether these problems are simply the result of individual laziness. He suggests that this is *not* the case. Argyris contends that, in many cases, when people join the force, they are kept from maturing by the management practices utilized in their organizations. In these organiza-

TABLE 3-3 Immaturity–Maturity Continuum

Immaturity ⟶ *Maturity*

Passive ———————————————————————————— Active
Dependence ———————————————————————— Independence
Behave in a few ways ——————————— Capable of behaving in many ways
Erratic shallow interests ——————————— Deeper and stronger interests
Short time perspective ——————— Long time perspective (past and future)
Subordinate position ————————————— Equal or superordinate position
Lack of awareness of self ——————————— Awareness and control over self

tions, they are given minimal control over their environment and are encouraged to be passive, dependent, and subordinate; therefore, they behave immaturely. The worker in many organizations is expected to act in immature ways rather than as a mature adult. This does not occur only in industrial settings. In fact, one can even see it happening in many school systems, where most high school students are subject to more rules and restrictions and generally treated less maturely than their younger counterparts in elementary school.

According to Argyris, keeping people immature is built into the very nature of the formal organization. He argues that because organizations are usually created to achieve goals or objectives that can best be met collectively, the formal organization is often the architect's conception of how these objectives may be achieved. In this sense, the individual is fitted to the job. The design comes first. This design is based upon four concepts of scientific management: task specialization, chain of command, unity of direction, and span of control. Management tries to increase and enhance organizational and administrative efficiency and productivity by making workers "interchangeable parts."

Basic to these concepts is that power and authority should rest in the hands of a few at the top of the organization, and thus those at the lower end of the chain of command are strictly controlled by their superiors or the system itself. Task specialization often results in the oversimplification of the job so that it becomes repetitive, routine, and unchallenging. This implies directive, task-oriented leadership where decisions about the work are made by the superior, with the workers only carrrying out those decisions. This type of leadership evokes managerial controls such as budgets, some incentive systems, time and motion studies, and standard operating procedures, which can restrict the initiative and creativity of workers.

Theory into Practice

Argyris feels that these concepts of formal organization lead to assumptions about human nature that are incompatible with the proper development of

61

maturity in human personality. He sees a definite incongruity between the needs of a mature personality and the formal organizations as they now exist. Since he implies that the classical theory of management (based on Theory X assumptions) usually prevails, management creates childlike roles for workers that frustrate natural development.

An example of how work is often designed at this extremely low level was dramatically illustrated by the successful use of mentally retarded workers in such jobs. Argyris cites two instances, one in a knitting mill and the other in a radio manufacturing corporation, in which mentally retarded people were successfully employed on unskilled jobs. In both cases, the managers praised these workers for their excellent performance. In fact, a manager in the radio corporation reported that these workers:

> . . . proved to be exceptionally well-behaved, particularly obedient, and strictly honest and trustworthy. They carried out work required of them to such a degree of efficiency that *we were surprised they were classed as subnormals for their age*. Their attendance was good, and their behavior was, if anything, certainly better than that of any other employee of the same age.[14]

Disturbed by what he finds in many organizations, Argyris, as did McGregor, challenges management to provide a work climate in which everyone has a chance to grow and mature as individuals, as members of a group by satisfying their own needs, while working for the success of the organization. Implicit here is the belief that people can be basically self-directed and creative at work if properly motivated, and, therefore, management based on the assumptions of Theory Y will be more profitable for the individual and the organization.

More and more companies are starting to listen to the challenge that Argyris is directing at management. For example, the president of a large company asked Argyris to show him how to better motivate his workers. Together, they went into one of his production plants where a product similar to a radio was being assembled. There were twelve women involved in assembling the product, each doing a small segment of the job, as designed by an industrial engineer. The group also had a foreman, an inspector, and a packer.

Argyris proposed a one-year experiment during which each of the women would assemble the total product in a manner of her own choice. At the same time, each women would inspect, sign her name to the product, pack it, and handle any correspondence involving complaints about it. The women were assured that they would receive no cut in pay if production dropped but would receive more pay if production increased.

Once the experiment began, production dropped 70 percent during the first month. By the end of six weeks it was even worse. The women were upset—morale was down. This continued until the eighth week, when production started to rise. By the end of the fifteenth week production was higher than it had ever been before. And this was without an inspector, a packer, or an industrial engineer. More important than increased productivity, costs due to errors and waste decreased 94 percent; letters of complaint dropped 96 percent.

Experiments such as this are being duplicated in numerous other situations.[15] It is being found over and over again that broadening individual responsibility is beneficial to both the workers and the company. Giving people the opportunity to grow and mature on the job helps them satisfy more than just physiological and safety needs, which in turn motivates them and allows them to use more of their potential in accomplishing organizational goals. Although all workers do *not* want to accept more responsibility or deal with the added problems responsibility inevitably brings, Argyris contends that the number of employees whose motivation can be improved by increasing and upgrading their responsibility is much larger than most managers would suspect.

MOTIVATION-HYGIENE THEORY

Frederick Herzberg

We have noted that needs such as esteem and self-actualization seem to become more important as people mature. One of the most interesting series of studies that concentrates heavily on these areas has been directed by Frederick Herzberg.[16] Out of these studies has developed a theory of work motivation that has broad implications for management and its efforts toward effective utilization of human resources.

Herzberg, in developing his motivation-hygiene theory, seemed to sense that scholars such as McGregor and Argyris were touching on something important. Knowledge about human nature, motives, and needs could be invaluable to organizations and individuals:

> To industry, the payoff for a study of job attitudes would be increased productivity, decreased absenteeism, and smoother working relations. To the individual, an understanding of the forces that lead to improved morale would bring greater happiness and greater self-realization.[17]

Herzberg set out to collect data on job attitudes from which assumptions about human behavior could be made. The motivation-hygiene theory resulted from the analysis of an initial study by Herzberg and his colleagues at the Psychological Service of Pittsburgh. This study involved extensive interviews with some two hundred engineers and accountants from eleven industries in the Pittsburgh area. In the interviews, they were asked about what kinds of things on their job made them unhappy or dissatisfied and what things made them happy or satisfied.

In analyzing the data from these interviews, Herzberg concluded that people have two different categories of needs that are essentially independent of each other and affect behavior in different ways. He found that when people felt dissatisfied with their jobs, they were concerned about the environment in which they were working. On the other hand, when people felt good about their jobs, this had to do with the work itself. Herzberg called the first category of needs *hygiene* or *maintenance* factors: hygiene because they describe people's environment and serve the primary function of preventing job dissatisfaction; maintenance because they are never completely satisfied—they have to continue to be maintained. He called the second category of needs *motivators* since they seemed to be effective in motivating people to superior performance.

Hygiene Factors

Company policies and administration, supervision, working conditions, interpersonal relations, money, status, and security may be thought of as maintenance factors. These are not an intrinsic part of a job, but they are related to the conditions under which a job is performed. Herzberg related his original use of the word *hygiene* to its medical meaning (preventive and environmental). He found that hygiene factors produced no growth in worker output capacity; they only prevented losses in worker performance due to work restriction. This is why, more recently, Herzberg has been calling these maintenance factors.

Motivators

Satisfying factors that involve feelings of achievement, professional growth, and recognition that one can experience in a job that offers challenge and scope are referred to as motivators. Herzberg used this term because these

TABLE 3-4 Motivation and Hygiene Factors

Motivators	Hygiene Factors
The Job Itself	Environment
Achievement	Policies and administration
Recognition for accomplishment	Supervision
Challenging work	Working conditions
Increased responsibility	Interpersonal relations
Growth and development	Money, status, security

factors seem capable of having a positive effect on job satisfaction, often resulting in an increase in one's total output capacity.

In recent years motivation-hygiene research has been extended well beyond scientists and accountants to include every level of an organization, from top management all the way down to hourly employees. For example, in an extensive study at Texas Instruments, Scott Meyers concluded that Herzberg's motivation-hygiene theory "is easily translatable to supervisory action at all levels of responsibility. It is a framework on which supervisors can evaluate and put into perspective the constant barrage of 'helpful hints' to which they are subjected, and hence serves to increase their feelings of competence, self-confidence, and autonomy."[18]

Perhaps an example will further differentiate between hygiene factors and motivators and help explain the reason for classifying needs as Herzberg has done.

Let us assume that a man is highly motivated and is working at 90 percent of capacity. He has a good working relationship with his supervisor, is well satisfied with his pay and working conditions, and is part of a congenial work group. Suppose his supervisor is suddenly transferred and replaced by a person he is unable to work with, or suppose he finds out that someone whose work he feels is inferior to his own is receiving more pay. How will these factors affect this individual's behavior? Since we know performance or productivity depends on both ability and motivation, these unsatisfied hygiene needs (supervision and money) may lead to restriction of output. This decline in productivity may be intentional or he may not be consciously aware that he is holding back. In either case, productivity will be lowered, as illustrated in Figure 3-2.

In our illustration, even if the worker's former supervisor returns and his salary is adjusted well above his expectations, his productivity will probably increase only to its original level.

Conversely, let us take the same person and assume that dissatisfaction has not occurred; he is working at 90 percent capacity. Suppose he is given an opportunity to mature and satisfy his motivational needs in an environ-

FIGURE 3-2   Effect of dissatisfying hygiene factors

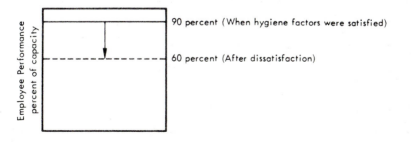

Employee Performance
percent of capacity

90 percent (When hygiene factors were satisfied)

60 percent (After dissatisfaction)

ment where he is free to exercise some initiative and creativity, to make decisions, to handle problems, and to take responsibility. What effect will this situation have on this individual? If he is able to fulfill his supervisor's expectations in performing these new responsibilities, he may still work at 90 percent capacity, but as a person he may have matured and grown in his ability and may be capable now of more productivity, as illustrated in Figure 3-3. His capacity has increased.

Hygiene factors, when satisfied, tend to eliminate dissatisfaction and work restriction, but they do little to motivate an individual to superior performance or increased capacity. Satisfaction of the motivators, however, will permit an individual to grow and develop in a mature way, often implementing an increase in ability. Thus, hygiene factors affect an individual's willingness or motivation and motivators impact an individual's ability.

The Relationship of Herzberg to Maslow

In terms of Hersey and Blanchard's motivating situation framework discussed in Chapter 2, Maslow is helpful in identifying needs or motives and Herzberg provides us with insights into the goals and incentives that tend to satisfy these needs, as illustrated in Figure 3-4.

Thus, in a motivating situation, if you know what are the high strength needs (Maslow) of the individuals you want to influence, then you should be able to determine what goals (Herzberg) you could provide in the environment to motivate those individuals. At the same time, if you know what goals these people want to satisfy, you can predict what their high strength needs are. That is possible because it has been found that money and benefits tend to satisfy needs at the physiological and security levels; interpersonal relations and supervision are examples of hygiene factors that tend to satisfy social needs; increased responsibility, challenging work, and growth and development are motivators that tend to satisfy needs at the esteem and

FIGURE 3-3 Effect of satisfying motivators

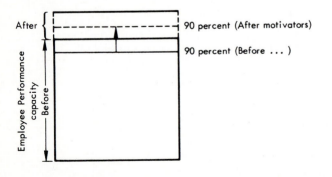

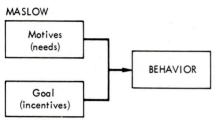

MASLOW

HERZBERG

FIGURE 3-4 The relationship of Maslow and Herzberg to motivation situation

self-actualization levels. Figure 3-5 shows the relationship we feel exists between the Maslow and Herzberg frameworks.

We feel that the physiological, safety, social, and part of the esteem needs are all hygiene factors. The esteem needs are divided because there are some distinct differences between status per se and recognition. Status tends to be a function of the position one occupies. One may have gained this position through family ties or social pressures, and thus this position may not be a reflection of personal achievement or earned recognition. Recognition is gained through competence and achievement. It is earned and granted by others. Consequently, status is classified with physiological, safety, and social needs as a hygiene factor, while recognition is classified with esteem as a motivator.

It appears to us that McClelland's[19] concept of achievement motivation is also related to Herzberg's motivation-hygiene theory. People with high achievement motivation tend to be interested in the motivators (the job itself). Achievement-motivated people want task-relevant feedback. They want to know how well they are doing on their job. On the other hand,

FIGURE 3-5 The relationship between the motivation-hygeine theory and Maslow's hierarchy of needs

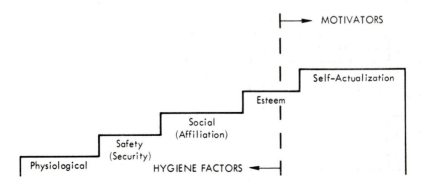

people with low achievement motivation are more concerned about the environment. They want to know how people feel about them rather than how well they are doing.

JOB ENRICHMENT

Prior to Herzberg's work, many other behavioral scientists were concerned with worker motivation. For several years there was an emphasis on what was termed "job enlargement" or "job rotation." This was purported to be an answer to the overspecialization that had characterized many industrial organizations. The assumption was that workers could gain more satisfaction at work if their jobs were enlarged; that is, if the number or variety in which they engaged was increased.

Herzberg makes some astute observations about this trend. He claims that doing a snippet of this and a snippet of that does not necessarily result in motivation. Washing dishes, then silverware, and then pots and pans does no more to satisfy and provide an opportunity to grow than washing only dishes. What we really need to do with work, Herzberg suggests, is to *enrich* the job. By job enrichment is meant the deliberate upgrading of responsibility, scope, and challenge in work.

Example of Job Enrichment

An example of job enrichment may be illustrated by the experience an industrial relations superintendent had with a group of janitors. When the superintendent was transferred to a new plant, he soon found, much to his amazement, that in addition to his duties, fifteen janitors in plant maintenance reported directly to him. There was no foreman over these men. Browsing through the files one day, the superintendent noticed there was a history of complaints about housekeeping around the plant. After talking to others and observing for himself, it took the superintendent little time to confirm the reports. The janitors seemed to be lazy, unreliable, and generally unmotivated. They were walking examples of Theory X assumptions about human nature.

Determined to do something about the behavior of the janitors, the superintendent called a group meeting of all fifteen men. He opened the meeting by saying that he understood there were a number of housekeeping problems in the plant but confessed that he did not know what to do about them. Since he felt they, as janitors, were experts in the housekeeping area, he asked if together they would help him solve these problems. "Does anyone have a suggestion?" he asked. There was a deadly silence. The superintendent sat down and said nothing; the janitors said nothing. This lasted for almost twenty minutes. Finally, one janitor spoke up and related a problem he was having in his area and made a suggestion. Soon others joined in, and suddenly the janitors were involved in a lively discussion while the superintendent listened and jotted down their ideas. At the conclusion of the meeting the suggestions were summarized with tacit acceptance by all, including the superintendent.

After the meeting, the superintendent referred any housekeeping problems to the janitors, individually or as a group. For example, when any cleaning equipment or material salesmen came to the plant, the superintendent did not talk to them—the janitors did. In fact, regular meetings continued to be held in which problems and ideas were discussed.

All of this had a tremendous influence on the behavior of these men. They developed a cohesive productive team that took pride in its work. Even their appearance changed. Once a grubby lot, now they appeared at work in clean, pressed work clothes. All over the plant, people were amazed how clean and well kept everything had become. The superintendent was continually stopped by supervisors in the plant and asked, "What have you done to those lazy, good-for-nothing janitors, given them pep pills?" Even the superintendent could not believe his eyes. It was not uncommon to see one or two janitors running floor tests to see which wax or cleaner did the best job. Since they had to make all the decisions, including committing funds for their supplies, they wanted to know which were the best. Such activities, while taking time, did not detract from their work. In fact, these men worked harder and more efficiently than ever before in their lives.

This example illustrates that even at low levels in an organization, people can respond in responsible and productive ways to a work environment in which they are given an opportunity to grow and mature. People begin to satisfy their esteem and self-actualization needs by participating in the planning, organizing, motivating, and controlling of their own tasks.

A Problem of Placement

It should be pointed out that the problem of motivation is not always a question of enriching jobs. As Chris Argyris dramatically showed in the successful use of mentally retarded workers on the assembly line, some organizations have a tendency to hire people with ability far in excess of the demands of the work.

An example of overhiring happened in the start-up operation of a large plant. As in the case of most new plants, one of the first work groups to be assembled was security. The supervisor of plant security set as hiring criteria a high school education and three years of police or plant protection experience as minimal requirements for applicants. Being the first large industrial plant in a relatively agricultural area, the company was able to hire people not at the minimum level but well over these standards.

When these people began their jobs—which consisted simply of checking badges on the way in and lunch pails on the way out—boredom, apathy, and lack of motivation soon characterized their performance. This resulted in a high rate of turnover. When the problem was reevaluated, the reverse of the hiring procedures was found to be appropriate. Those applicants with a high school education were considered overqualified. Those with police or security experience were also considered overqualified. Rather than experienced workers, applicants with fourth- and fifth-grade educations, and thus lower job expectations, were hired for these positions. Their performance was found to be much superior, and the turnover, absenteeism, and tardiness rates were cut to a minimum. Why? For these workers, a new uniform, a badge, and some power were important, but they also found the job as one incorporating opportunities for more responsibility and challenging work.[20]

TRANSACTIONAL ANALYSIS

Eric Berne

If it is true that we cannot always anticipate the reaction of people to a management intervention, how can we better predict the kind of responses our interventions may evoke from people? *Transactional analysis* (TA) may help us in this area.

TA is a method of analyzing and understanding behavior that was developed by Eric Berne[21] and in more recent years has been popularized in the writings of Thomas Harris,[22] Muriel James and Dorothy Jongeward,[23] and Abe Wagner.[24] In particular, Jongeward[25] and Wagner [26] have shown how the concepts of TA can be applied to organizations and related to the work of other theorists, such as McGregor and Likert. Their work has been very helpful to us in writing this section on transactional analysis.

TA, as we view it, is an outgrowth of earlier Freudian psychology. Sigmund Freud[27] was the first to suggest that there are three sources within the human personality that stimulate, monitor, and control behavior. The Freudian *id, ego,* and *superego* are important concepts, but their definitions are difficult for practitioners to understand or apply without extensive training in psychotherapy. Thus, one of the major contributions of TA theorists is that they have, in a sense, borrowed from Freud but have put some of his concepts into a language that everyone can understand and, without being trained psychiatrists, can use for diagnostic purposes in understanding why people behave as they do.

Ego States

According to TA, a *transaction* is a stimulus plus a response. For example, if you say to one of your staff, "You really did a fine job on that project,

Don." that's a stimulus; if he says, "Thanks," that's a response. Thus, transactions take place between people. They can also take place between the "people" in our heads. If we have a sudden impulse to say something to someone, we may mentally hear a voice telling us not to say it and then a second voice agreeing. These people in our heads are called *ego states*.

The personality of a person is the collection of behavior patterns developed over time that other people begin to recognize as that person. These behavior patterns are evoked in differing degrees from three ego states— Parent, Adult, and Child. These terms are capitalized so as not to be confused with their lower-cased counterparts. Thus, a parent (mother or father) has Parent, Adult, and Child ego states; and a child (son or daughter) also has Parent, Adult, and Child ego states. These ego states have nothing to do with chronological age, only psychological age.

As Berne states, "Although we cannot directly observe these ego states, we can observe behavior and from this infer which of the three ego states is operating at that moment.[28] The three ego states are usually diagrammed as shown in Figure 3-6.

The *Parent* ego state is a result of the "messages" (conditioning) people receive from their parents, older sisters and brothers, school teachers, Sunday school teachers, and other authority figures during their early childhood. These messages can be thought of as recorded on "little cassette tapes" in people's heads. They're in place, stored up, and ready to go. All you have to do is push the right button and you get the message—almost like dialing a number on the telephone. Push another button and you get a different message. After the message is given, the tape is rewound and ready to go again. For instance, if a father's son was eating his dinner and was playing with his food, a common Parent tape such as the following might be played: "Stop playing with your food, Garth, and clean up your plate. People are starving all over the world, so you're going to eat everything." Now where did the father learn to say that? He probably learned it

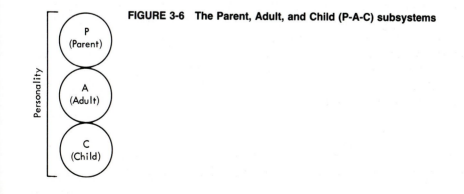

FIGURE 3-6   The Parent, Adult, and Child (P-A-C) subsystems

from his mother and father, who learned it from their parents. And now he's playing it on his kids. This is a Parent tape. Many of us were taught when we were young that it's good to clean our plate and bad to leave food on our plate. In fact, many of us probably still feel guilty today if we leave food on our plate.

Thus, a person is operating from Parent ego state when "old tapes" from childhood are mentally played back. These recordings say such things as "it's right!" "it's wrong!" "it's bad!" "it's good!" "you should!" "you shouldn't!" Thus, our Parent ego state is the *evaluative* part of us that evokes value-laden behavior. But remember, this value-laden behavior is not necessarily "real value"—it's "learned value." In our example with Garth not cleaning his plate, it might have been more appropriate had his father said, "Don't feel you have to eat everything on your plate if you are really not hungry"—particularly if Garth were a little overweight. Thus, cleaning up one's plate is a "learned value" because, in a real sense, whether or not Garth eats all the food on his plate won't impact starving children around the world; it will only impact the size of the garbage.

There are two kinds of Parent ego states: *Nurturing Parent* and *Critical Parent*. The Nurturing Parent is that part of a person that is understanding and caring about other people. While behavior coming from the Nurturing Parent may set limits on and provide direction for people's behavior, it will not put these people down and make them feel not okay as individuals. The Critical Parent makes people feel that they, not just their behavior, are not okay. Thus, Critical Parent behavior attacks people's personalities as well as their behavior. When people are in their Critical Parent ego state, they are very evaluative and judgmental. They are always ready to respond with a "should" or "ought" to almost anything people tell them. People with a heavy Critical Parent ego state "should" on other people as well as "should" on themselves.

The *Adult* ego state evokes behavior that could be described simply as logical, reasonable, rational, and unemotional. Behavior from the Adult ego state is characterized by problem-solving analysis and rational decision making. People operating from the Adult ego state are taking the emotional content of their Child ego state and the value-laden content of their Parent ego state and checking them out in the reality of the external world. These people are examining alternatives, probabilities, and values prior to engaging in behavior.

As suggested, the *Child* ego state is associated with behaviors that appear when a person is responding emotionally. A person's Child contains the "natural" impulses and attitudes learned from child experiences. There are several forms of the Child ego state that various authors discuss.[29] In our work we use two kinds of Child ego states: *Happy Child* and *Destructive Child*.

People behaving from their Happy Child are doing things because they want to, but their behavior is not disruptive to others or destructive to the environment. People in their Destructive Child are also doing things because they feel like it, but their behavior is either disruptive to others or destructive to themselves or their environment. In understanding the difference between these two types of the Child state, it helps to remember that behavior by itself is not happy or destructive. Whether a person's behavior is coming from the Happy Child or the Destructive Child depends on the transaction or feedback from others. For example, if George is a draftsman and is singing while he works, he may be in his Happy Child. But if one of his co-workers, Helen, tells him she's having trouble working because of his singing and he keeps on singing, he has moved from Happy Child to Destructive Child.

One form of the Destructive Child ego state is the *Rebellious Child*. When people are in this ego state, they aren't going to listen to anyone who tells them what to do. They either rebel openly by being very negative or rebel subtly by forgetting, being confused, or putting off doing something that someone wants them to do. Persons behaving from Rebellious Child will not do anything an authority figure asks them to do even if it makes sense.

Another destructive Child ego state is *Compliant Child*. When people are in this ego state, they do what others want. Complying with the wishes of others is okay if the person really wants to or if it makes sense to do it. When that is the case, Compliant Child would be classified as a form of Happy Child because the behavior would not be considered disruptive to others or destructive to themselves or their environment. However, Compliant Child can hurt the development of people who comply unquestionably all the time, even when it makes no sense to them. These people tend to remain dependent instead of becoming independent. When this occurs, Compliant Child becomes a form of Destructive Child.

It is healthy for people to have a functioning Child ego state that is spontaneous, emotional, and sometimes dependent. However, as managers, we want to discourage too much development of our people's Compliant or Rebellious forms of Destructive Child. In later chapters we will talk about when and how people develop a Rebellious or Compliant Child ego state and how to discourage behaviors evoked from these two forms of Child ego state.

Behavior coming from the Adult ego state is very different from behavior evoked from the Child ego state. Child ego state behavior is behavior that's often almost a stimulus-response relationship. Something happens and the person responds almost immediately. What happens is not processed intellectually. It almost goes in one ear, picks up speed, and goes out the other ear. With Adult ego state behavior, when something happens, there is not an immediate response. A response follows only conscious evaluation and thought.

A Healthy Personality

All people behave from these three ego states at different times. A healthy person has a personality that maintains a balance among all three; particularly, according to Abe Wagner,[30] Nurturing *Parent, Adult*, and Happy *Child*. This means that these people are able, at times, to let the Adult ego state take over and think very rationally and engage in problem solving. At other times, these people are able to free the Child ego state and let their hair down, have fun, and be spontaneous and emotional. At still other times, healthy people are able to defer to the Parent ego state and learn from experience; they do not have to reinvent the wheel every time. They develop values that aid in the speed and effectiveness of decision making.

While a balance among all three ego states seems to be most healthy, some people seem dominated at times by one or two ego states. This is especially a problem when the Adult ego state is not in the "executive position" and a person's personality is being dominated by the Critical Parent or the Destructive Child. When this occurs in people, it poses problems for their managers in the world of work.

More specifically, Child-dominated people who are mainly coming from Destructive Child do not engage in much rational problem solving. They learned in their early years that they could get things by screaming, hollering, and being emotional. It's very difficult to reason with them in many situations. Instead of solving their own problems, these people want their managers or some other person to tell them what to do, where to do it, and how to do it—or what's right, what's wrong, what's good, and what's bad.

Parent-dominated people, who are mainly coming from Critical Parent, also do not engage in much rational problem solving because they already know what's right and what's wrong. They seem to have an answer for everything. These people we would characterize with the comment, "Look! Don't confuse me with the facts. I've already made up my mind." It really doesn't matter how much real information anyone brings to these people— they've already decided "it's good," "it's bad," "you should," or "you shouldn't."

Even Adult-dominated people can be troublesome, because they can be very boring people with whom to work. They are often "workaholics." They don't seem to act like other people. They are never able to let down their hair and have fun. Thus, a balance between the three ego states makes for a healthy person.

Life Position

In the process of growing up, people make basic assumptions about their own self-worth, as well as about the worth of significant people in their environment, that may or may not be generalized to other people later in life. Harris[31] calls the combination of an assumption about oneself and another person a *life position*. Life positions tend to be more permanent than ego states. They are learned throughout life by way of reinforcements for, and responses to, expressed needs. These assumptions are described in terms of "okayness." Thus, individuals assume that they are either OK or not OK, or that as people they do not possess value or worth. Further, other individuals are assumed to be either OK or not OK.

Four possible relationships result from these life positions: (1) neither person has value ("I'm not OK, you're not OK"); (2) you have value, but I do not have value ("I'm not OK, you're OK"); (3) I have value, but you do not ("I'm OK, you're not OK"); and (4) we both have value ("I'm OK, you're OK").

"I'm not OK, you're not OK" people tend to feel bad about themselves and see the whole world as miserable. People with this life position usually give up. They don't trust other people and have no confidence in themselves.

People with an *"I'm not OK, you're OK"* life position often come from their Compliant Child ego state. They feel that others are more capable and generally have fewer problems than they themselves do. They tend to think that they always get the short end of the stick. This is the most common life position for people who have a high deference for authority. They see their world as "I don't have any control or much power, but those people (folks with authority or position power) seem to have all the power and rewards and punishments."

People who feel *I'm OK, you're not OK"* often come from their Critical Parent ego state. They tend to be down on other people for at least two reasons. First, they often regard other people as sources of criticism. They feel that if they're not exactly perfect or right, people will be excessively critical of them. Second, they want to break away or rebel from some authority figure and become more independent, but they're either not sure how to go about this or they have had unpleasant experiences in attempting it in the past.

This is a life position in which the person has had a few "zaps" along the road and feels, "I've got a lot of self-confidence and autonomy but I sure don't want to be open, honest, and sharing with others in my environment or I'll get punished." With this life position, listening often tends to stop even when someone is still trying to communicate with this person. Harris found in his work that people with an *"I'm OK, you're not OK"* life position, while acting self-confident and under control, really were hiding "not OK" feelings about themselves. The way they play out their "not OK" feelings often is expressed in the need for power and control.

"I'm OK, you're OK" is suggested as the healthy life position. People with these feelings express confidence in themselves as well as trust and confidence in other people in their environment. Their behavior tends to

come from their Nurturing Parent, Adult, and Happy Child ego states, while seldom being evoked from their Destructive Child or Critical Parent.

Transactions Between People

TA may be used to explain why people behave in specific patterns—patterns that frequently seem to be repeated throughout their lives (life scripts). In this form of analysis, the basic observational unit is called a *transaction*. Transactions are exchanges between people that consist of no less than one stimulus and one response. This analysis enables people to identify patterns of transactions between themselves and others. Ultimately, this can help us determine which ego state is most heavily influencing our behavior and the behavior of other people with whom we interact.

Two types of transactions may be useful for managers to know: *open* (complementary) and *blocked* (crossed).[32] There are many combinations of open transactions; however, the basic principle to remember is that the ego state that is addressed is the one that responds. Therefore, the response to the stimulus is the expected or predictable one. When this occurs, communication can continue. (This in no way suggests effective communication or indicates any openness between individuals, for, in fact, the content of the communication may be a distortion of true data.) Open transactions are Adult to Adult, Child to Child, Parent to Child, and Parent to Parent. Not all open transactions are beneficial. What we want to strive for in our relationships are OK open transactions—Happy Child to Happy Child. Nurturing Parent to Happy Child, Adult to Adult, and Nurturing Parent to Nurturing Parent. Not OK open transactions involve any of the less healthy ego states—for example, Critical Parent, Rebellious Child, or Compliant Child (when complying does not make sense to the person's Adult ego state.) Examples of both OK and not OK open transactions are shown in Figure 3-7.

As illustrated in Transaction 1, if a manager says to one of her staff members from her Nurturing Parent, "I want you to be more careful in

FIGURE 3-7 Two types of open transactions

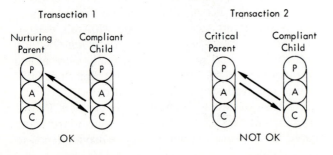

writing your reports because I found a number of typographical and grammatical errors in this report," and her staff member responds from this Compliant Child, "OK, Mrs. Jones, I didn't notice all those mistakes," then we have a completed communication in which information has been easily shared and everyone still feels OK about themselves. If, however, as illustrated in Transaction 2, this manager was coming from her Critical Parent and said something like, "How can you be so stupid? The last report you gave me had all kinds of typographical and grammatical errors. I don't see how you can possibly do your job if you don't know how to write a decent report," and her staff member responded from Compliant Child back to his manager's Critical Parent by meekly saying, "I'm sorry, I'll try not to make those mistakes next time," we have a completed communication in which information is shared with a minimum effort. But the staff member feels put down by his boss and does not feel OK.

A blocked transaction is one that results in the closing, at least temporarily, of communications. Unlike open transactions, the response is either inappropriate or unexpected, as well as being out of context with what the sender of the stimulus had originally intended. This occurs when a person responds with an ego state different from the one the other person was addressing. In other words, it occurs when the stimulus from one ego state to another ego state is responded to as if the source were some other ego state, such that the sender feels misunderstood, confused, or even threatened. When this occurs, sharing and listening stop, at least temporarily. For example, if Alan asks a co-worker a question from his Adult ego state "What time is it, John?" he would expect John to respond from his Adult ego state and share information with him; that is, tell him what time it is. If, however, John responds from his Critical Parent and answers, "Don't ask so many questions," then a blocked transaction has taken place, as illustrated in Figure 3-8.

The example in Figure 3-8 illustrates that in a blocked transaction the lines of communication get crossed and stop effective communication (although talking may continue).

Blocked transactions can either be helpful or destructive to the devel-

FIGURE 3-8   A blocked transaction

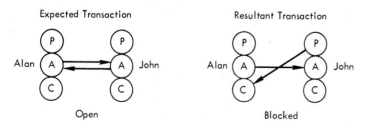

opment of people. The preceding example was a destructive transaction because the Critical Parent response to Alan's Adult question leaves Alan with not OK feelings. Destructive blocked transactions occur between people when either responds to the other from the Critical Parent or the Rebellious or Compliant Destructive Child.

When people argue or fight, a destructive blocked transaction is usually involved. For example, if a manager makes a statement in a Critical Parent manner ("I don't think you should hire that person for your staff assistant. There will be nothing but trouble.") directed toward the staff member's Compliant (happy) Child and the staff member responds from the Rebellious (destructive) Child ("You have no right to tell me who I can hire for my staff assistant.") to the boss's Child, the lines of communication get blocked and the manager and the subordinate stop listening (although talking or yelling may continue). Now the interaction becomes a win-lose power struggle. Manager and staff member seem to be talking past each other, matching "oughts and shoulds" with the other's "oughts and shoulds." If, in this example, the boss wins—and bosses usually do—the win has a cost. It forces the staff member to become Destructive (compliant) Child and teaches the staff member either go "underground" with feelings in the future, plot how to get out from under the command of the boss, or become compliant and do what others say because "I'm not OK."

In some situations, we may find blocked transactions useful in helping people to switch out of the less healthy Rebellious Child, Compliant Child, and Critical Parent ego states into their Adult, Nurturing Parent, or Happy Child. This will become clear as we integrate concepts from TA with other theories in later chapters.

By analyzing open and blocked transactions, it is possible to determine the various strengths of the three ego states. This in turn provides an indication of which life position the individual has selected. We can thus gather data on individuals in a way that will help to predict future patterns of behavior.

Ulterior transactions, like blocked transactions, are generally not desired. "An ulterior transaction happens when someone appears to be sending one kind of message but is secretly sending another. Thus, the real message is disguised.[33] An example of an ulterior transaction is when Alice says to her boss, "I'd be happy to add up all those figures, Mr. Johnson. It looks like it would be a real challenge."

In this example of an ulterior transaction (see Figure 3-9), Alice is not talking straight about her needs but is sending her message in a disguised way. She appears to be giving Mr. Johnson factual information in an Adult to Adult transaction. Actually, she is probably annoyed about all of the routine, boring tasks that she's continually asked to do. Perhaps she would like to ask Mr. Johnson directly if there's a way that she could expand her responsibilities and take on more exciting tasks. "It should be challenging to

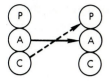

Alice   Mr. Johnson   **FIGURE 3-9** **Ulterior transaction**

add up all those figures" may be a plea for more challenging work from Alice's Child to Mr. Johnson's Parent.

Strokes

It is important to recognize one more thing about transactions. "Strokes" are being exchanged *whenever* two people are transacting. According to Jongeward and Seyer,[34] in TA language:

> The term "stroke" refers to giving some kind of recognition to a person. This may or may *not* involve physical touching. As we grow from infancy into child and adulthood, we do not entirely lose our need for stroking. Part of our original need for physical stroking seems to be satisfied with symbolic stroking. We no longer need constant cuddling, but we need attention. When we receive a stroke, we choose to feel either good or bad. If we chose to feel good, we think of the stroke as a "warm fuzzy" or "positive" stroke. On the flip side, if we choose to feel bad, we can think of it as a "cold prickly" or "negative" stroke.

If it is true that people have a basic need for strokes, they will work hard to get them. For example, ignored people will engage in all sorts of creative activities to get strokes. Often, such people quickly learn at work that they can get strokes from their boss by

- fighting with co-workers.
- doing sloppy work.
- injuring themselves.

A person who carries out one of these actions is likely to get a cold prickly (negative) stroke. But given a choice between no strokes or negative strokes, most people will opt for negative strokes. To such a person, any kind of stroke is better than no stroke at all; a cold prickly is better than nothing. The same is true for children who live in a stroke-deprived home.

Psychological Game Analysis

When people don't get enough strokes at work, they will try a variety of things, some harmful, to make up their "stroke deficit." To do that, they may play *psychological games.*[35] A psychological game is a set of trans-actions with the following characteristics:

- Transactions tend to be repeated.
- They make sense on a superficial or social level.
- One or more of the transactions is ulterior.
- A set of transactions ends with a predictable payoff—a negative feeling. Payoffs usually reinforce the decision made in childhood about oneself or about others. They reflect feelings of not okayness, as we shall see.

Let's look at an example of a psychological game called *Yes, But:*

Doug: "I need your help again, Ken. I just don't seem to be very excited about my job. I really can't remember a job that really 'turned me on.' "
Ken: "Why don't you go to a career-planning center and take some of those tests to find out what you might really be interested in?"
Doug: "Yes, I've thought of doing that, but they cost quite a bit of money and our budget is a little tight right now."
Ken: "Why don't you talk to your boss and see if there's any opportunity to enlarge or expand your job?"
Doug: "Yes, that's possible, but he's awfully busy and is hard to get to see."
Ken: "I know! Why don't you try to get a teaching job? You could go over and see . . . ?"
Doug: "Yes, but teaching jobs are really hard to find these days."
Ken: (Silent)

Let's examine how each of the characteristics of a psychological game is present in this example:[36]

- *Repeated transactions:* Doug and Ken have played this game before. Note Doug's opening line, "I need your help *again*, Ken."
- *Transactions make sense:* Outwardly, it seems Doug is honestly asking Ken for help. Ken's suggestions are reasonable and Doug's replies also seem to make sense.
- *Ulterior transactions:* Notice that Doug consistently rejects all of Ken's advice. At one level, Doug seems to be giving reasons why Ken's advice won't work. But he is also simultaneously sending an ulterior message that says, "Nobody's going to tell me what to do." Doug may still be rebelling against the advice his parent figures gave him when he was young. He operates from a belief that authority figures are not OK.
- *Predictable payoff:* According to TA theory,
  The game of *Yes, But* is often played by people whose parents either domi-nated them or didn't give them reasonable answers. So they tend to take a stand against parental figures. They play *Yes, But* to prove to themselves that nobody can tell them anything they don't already know. The feeling of power they get becomes a payoff for playing the game, which they seek over and over again. They prove once more that "Parents can't tell me anything."[37]

SCRIPT ANALYSIS

As we have pointed out, the life positions (I'm OK, you're OK, etc.) that people act out tend to vary according to the situation. The life position that people take and the games that they learn to play are part of what TA calls a "script":

> In everyday language, a script is the text of a play, motion picture, or radio or TV program. In TA, a person's life is compared to a play and the script is the text of that play. A person's psychological script is a life plan—a drama he or she writes and then feels compelled to live out. These plans may be positive, negative, or circular—endless repetition headed nowhere.[38]

All people have a script. People develop their scripts based on their experiences as a child. The most important influence on how one's script develops is through interactions with parents or other authority figures. These interactions in turn lead us to make certain decisions, formulate our life positions, play psychological games, and start the drama of our script.

Jongeward and Seyer[39] cite an excellent example of script development and its impact on later life:

> As Edwin was growing up, he was frequently put down and compared to his older brother, Sid. He constantly heard things like:

> - "Well, Edwin, you only got 60% on this test, but gee, that's pretty good for you, considering your ability."
> - "Edwin! You spilled the soda all over my new chair. What's wrong with you? Why are you always doing such dumb things? Don't you have a brain in your head?"
> - "Edwin is not as bright as Sid, you know, so don't expect much from him"
> - "What a stupid thing to do, Edwin. Sid would never have done a thing like that."

> Given this background, what psychological position do you think Edwin usually took as a child? Edwin most likely took an I'm not OK position on many occasions as a child. He often felt not OK about himself because of all the negative things he heard from his parents. He probably felt his parents (and others) were not OK because of the cruel way they spoke to him.
> Assuming that Edwin believed what he heard about himself, imagine him as a high school student. Do you think he likes school? Do you think he was a good student? Given his predominant psychological position, Edwin would probably dislike school and be a poor student. (Occasionally, however, a person like Edwin takes an "I'll show you" stance and knocks himself out trying to be perfect at everything, yet rarely satisfied with how he's doing.)
> Now imagine Edwin on the job later in life. He is talking to one of his co-workers about a report he is working on. Which one of these things would he be most likely to say? (a) "I feel concerned about the progress I've made on

this project" or (b) "I'm just a bungling idiot, I misplaced that report again! I'll never learn, will I?" Undoubtedly, he would have taken (b).

Do you think it is clear that Edwin was born with inferior mental capacity? Edwin might have a good brain and the potential to become a brilliant executive. But he has come to believe that he *is* stupid. Consequently, Edwin may have unconsciously (and compulsively) arranged things to strengthen this script.

We must remember that all of us have scripts. And, like Edwin, without being aware of it, we often arrange our environment so that our script prevails. Sometimes managers have to deal with the scripts that people bring with them to the world of work. In later chapters we will be discussing some concepts that may be useful to managers in helping people write new scripts.

SUMMARY AND CONCLUSION

We have tried through the material presented to examine what is known today about understanding and motivating employees. The attempt has been to review theoretical literature, empirical research, and case examples with the intention of integrating these sources into frameworks that may be useful to managers for analyzing and understanding behavior. In reflecting upon the theories we have discussed, we can easily isolate two polar positions. At one extreme (and most people still think it is the most common extreme) are organizations that are dominated by Theory X assumptions about human nature, bureaucratic/pyramidal values, and Pattern A behavior. As a result, these organizations tend to be managed by Critical Parent managers with I'm OK, you're not OK life positions, who think people are only motivated by physiological and safety needs and satisfied hygiene factors. The subordinates in these organizations tend to be passive, dependent, and childlike, with "I'm not OK, you're not OK" or "I'm not OK, you're OK" feelings.

At the other extreme are the "ideal" organizations with their Theory Y assumptions about human nature, humanistic/democratic values, and pattern B behavior. As a result, these organizations tend to be managed by people with a good balance of Parent-Adult-Child (P.A.C.), "I'm OK, you're OK" feelings and a sense that people are also motivated by affiliation, esteem, and self-actualization needs as job-related "motivators." The style(s) of these managers fosters similar feelings among subordinates and evokes Adult problem-solving behavior. Although the differences between these two extremes and the suggested movement are obvious, as Argyris argues, the journey from XA to YB is not an "easy road to haul." To prepare for this journey, analyzing and understanding are necessary, but real skills are also needed in directing, changing, and controlling behavior. Beginning with Chapter 4, a framework for applying leader behavior may help get us "on the road."

NOTES

1. For detailed descriptions of this research, see F. J. Roethlisberger and W. J. Dickson, *Management and the Worker* (Cambridge: Harvard University Press, 1939); T. N. Whitehead, *The Industrial Worker*, 2 vols. (Cambridge: Harvard University Press, 1938); Elton Mayo, *The Human Problems of an Industrial Civilization* (New York: Macmillan, 1933); Elton Mayo, *The Human Problems of an Industrial Civilization* (Salem, N.H.: Ayer Company, 1977). See also R. E. Dutton, "On Alix Carev's Radical Criticism of the Hawthorne Studies: Comment," *Academy of Management Journal*, 14 (September 1971), pp. 394–396; Randolph M. Hale, "Managing Human Resources: Challenge for the Future," *Enterprise*, June 1985, pp. 6–9.

2. Douglas McGregor, *The Human Side of Enterprise* (New York: McGraw-Hill, 1960). See also McGregor, *Leadership and Motivation* (Boston: MIT Press, 1966); Craig C. Pinder, *Work Motivation: Theory, Issues, and Applications* (Glenview, Ill.: Scott, Foresman, 1984).

3. Chris Argyris, *Management and Organizational Development: The Path from XA to YB* (New York: McGraw-Hill, 1971); Walter E. Natemeyer, ed., *Classics of Organizational Behavior* (Oak Park, Ill.: Moore Publishers, 1978); David R. Hampton, *Organizational Behavior and the Practice of Management* (Glenview, Ill.: Scott, Foresman, 1986).

4. *Ibid.*, p. 12.

5. George C. Homans, *The Human Group* (New York: Harcourt, Brace & World, 1950).

6. Anthony G. Athos and Robert E. Coffey, *Behavior in Organization: A Multidimensional View* (Englewood Cliffs, N.J.: Prentice-Hall, 1968), p. 101.

7. S. E. Asch, "Effects of Group Pressure upon the Modification and Distortion of Judgments," in *Groups, Leadership and Men*, ed. Harold Guetzkow (New York: Russell and Russell, 1963), pp. 177–90. Also in Dorwin Cartwright and Alvin Zander, *Group Dynamics.*, 2nd ed. (Evanston, Ill.: Row, Peterson, 1960), pp. 189–200.

8. *Ibid.*

9. Chris Argyris, *Interpersonal Competence and Organizational Effectiveness* (Homewood, Ill.: Irwin, Dorsey Press, 1962).

10. This table was taken with minor changes from Warren G. Bennis, *Organizational Development in Nature, Origins, Prospects* (Reading, Mass.: Addison-Wesley, 1969), p. 13.

11. *Ibid.*

12. *Ibid.*

13. Chris Argyris, *Personality and Organization* (New York: Harper & Row, 1957); *Interpersonal Competence and Organizational Effectiveness* (Homewood, Ill: Irwin, Dorsey Press, 1962); and *Integrating the Individual and the Organization* (New York: Wiley, 1964).

14. N. Breman, *The Making of a Moron* (New York: Sheed & Ward, 1953).

15. For other examples of successful interventions, see Argyris, *Intervention Theory and Method: A Behavioral Science View* (Reading, Mass.: Addison-Wesley, 1970); Robert W. Nay, *Behavioral Intervention: Contemporary Strategies* (New York: Gardner Press, 1976).

16. Frederick Herzberg, Bernard Mausner, and Barbara Snyderman, *The Motivation to Work* (New York: WIley, 1959); and Herzberg, *Work and the Nature of Man* (New York: World Publishing, 1966). See also R. M. Steers and L. W. Porter *Motivation and Work Behavior*, 2nd ed. (New York: McGraw-Hill, 1979); A. J. Stewart (ed.), *Motivation and Society* (San Francisco: Jossey-Bass, 1982); Terence R. Mitchell, "Motivation: New Directions for Theory, Research and Practice," *Academy of Management Review*, January 1982, pp. 80–88.

17. Herzberg, Mausner and Snyderman, *The Motivation to Work*, p. ix.

18. Scott M. Meyers, "Who Are Your Motivated Workers?" in David R. Hampton, *Behavioral Concepts in Management* (Belmont, Calif.: Dickenson Publishing, 1968). p. 64. Originally published in *Harvard Business Review*, January-February 1964, pp. 73–88.

19. David C. McClelland, J. W. Atkinson, R. A. Clark, and E. L. Lowell, *The Achievement Motive* (New York: Appleton-Century-Crofts, 1953); and *The Achieving Society* (Princeton, N.J.: D. Van Nostrand, 1961).

20. A. J. Marrow, D. G. Bowers, and S. E. Seashore, eds., *Strategies of Organizational Change* (New York: Harper & Row, 1967).

21. Eric Berne, *Games People Play* (New York: Grove Press, 1964).

22. Thomas Harris, *I'm OK—You're OK: A Practical Guide in Transactional Analysis* (New York: Harper & Row, 1969).

23. Muriel James and Dorothy Jongeward, *Born to Win* (Reading, Mass.: Addison-Wesley, 1971).

24. Abe Wagner, *The Transactional Manager: How to Solve Your People Problems with T.A.* (Englewood Cliffs, N.J.: Prentice-Hall, 1981). See also Muriel James and Louis Savary, *A New Self: Self Therapy with Transactional Analysis* (Reading, Mass.: Addison-Wesley, 1977).

25. Dorothy Jongeward, *Everybody Wins: Transactional Analysis Applied to Organizations* (Reading, Mass.: Addison-Wesley, 1973). See also Dorothy Jongeward and Muriel James, *Born to Win* (NAL, 1978); Dorothy Jongeward and Muriel James, *Born to Win: Transactional Analysis with Gestalt Experiments* (Reading, Mass.: Addison-Wesley, 1971); Dorothy Jongeward and Dru Scott, *Women as Winners: Transactional Analysis for Personal Growth* (Reading, Mass.: Addison-Wesley; *Transactional Analysis Bulletin: Selected Articles from Volume 1–9*, (San Francisco: TA Press, 1976).

26. Wagner, *The Transactional Manager*.

27. Sigmund Freud, *The Ego and the Id* (London: Hogarth Press, 1927).

28. Eric Berne, *Principles of Group Treatment* (New York: Oxford University Press, 1964), p. 281.

29. The most popular classification of child ego states in Natural Child, Adaptive Child, and Little Professor.

30. Abe Wagner was very helpful in the writing of this particular section.

31. Harris, *I'm OK—You're OK*.

32. The work of Dorothy Jongeward and Abe Wagner was very helpful in this section. See Dorothy Jongeward and Phillip C. Seyer, *Choosing Success: Transactional Analysis on the Job* (New York: Wiley, 1978), and Wagner, *The Transactional Manager*.

33. Jongeward and Seyer, *Choosing Success*, p. 21.

34. *Ibid.*, p. 26.

35. *Ibid.*, pp. 28–29.

36. This information was adapted from Jongeward and Seyer, *Choosing Success*, p. 28.

37. *Ibid.*

38. *Ibid.*, p. 34.

39. *Ibid.*, pp. 35–36.

CHAPTER 4

LEADERSHIP:
Trait and Attitudinal Approaches

The successful organization has one major attribute that sets it apart from unsuccessful organizations: dynamic and effective leadership. Peter F. Drucker points out that managers (business leaders) are the basic and scarcest resource of any business enterprise.[1] Statistics from recent years make this point more evident: "Of every one hundred new business establishments started, approximately fifty, or one half, go out of business within two years. By the end of five years, only one-third of the original one hundred will still be in business."[2] Most of the failures can be attributed to ineffective leadership.

On all sides there is a continual search for persons who have the necessary ability to lead effectively. This shortage of effective leadership is not confined to business but is evident in the lack of able administrators in government, education, foundations, churches, and every other form of organization. Thus, when we decry the scarcity of leadership talent in our society, we are not talking about a lack of people to fill administrative bodies. What we are agonizing over is a scarcity of people who are willing to assume significant leadership roles in our society and who can get the job done effectively.

LEADERSHIP DEFINED

According to George R. Terry, "Leadership is the activity of influencing people to strive willingly for group objectives."[3] Robert Tannenbaum, Irving R. Weschler, and Fred Massarik define leadership as "interpersonal influence exercised in a situation and directed, through the communication process, toward the attainment of a specialized goal or goals."[4] Harold Koontz and Cyril O'Donnell state that "leadership is *influencing* people to follow in the achievement of a common goal."[5]

A review of other writers reveals that most management writers agree that leadership is *the process of influencing the activities of an individual or a group in efforts toward goal achievement in a given situation*. From this definition of leadership, it follows that the leadership process is a function of the *leader*, the *follower*, and other *situational* variables— $L = f(l,f,s)$.

It is important to note that this definition makes no mention of any particular type of organization. In any situation in which someone is trying to influence the behavior of another individual or group, leadership is occurring. Thus, everyone attempts leadership at one time or another, whether activities are centered on a business, educational institution, hospital, political organization, or family.

It should also be remembered that when this definition mentions leader and follower, one should not assume that we are talking only about a hierarchical relationship such as suggested by superior (boss)/subordinate. Any time an individual is attempting to influence the behavior of someone else, that individual is the *potential leader* and the person subject to the influence attempt is the *potential follower*, no matter whether that person is the boss, a colleague (associate), a subordinate, a friend, a relative, or a group.

SCHOOLS OF ORGANIZATIONAL THEORY

We have defined leadership as the process of influencing the activities of an individual or a group in efforts toward goal achievement in a given situation. In essence, leadership involves accomplishing goals with and through people. Therefore, a leader must be concerned about tasks and human relationships. Although using different terminology, Chester I. Barnard identified these same leadership concerns in his classic work *The Functions of the Executive*, in the late 1930s.[6] These leadership concerns seem to be a reflection of two of the earliest schools of thought in organizational theory—scientific management and human relations.

Scientific Management Movement

Frederick Winslow Taylor

In the early 1900s one of the most widely read theorists on administration was Frederick Winslow Taylor. The basis for his *scientific management* was technological in nature. It was felt that the best way to increase output was to improve the techniques, or methods, used by workers. Consequently, he has been interpreted as considering people as instruments or machines to be manipulated by their leaders. Accepting this assumption, other theorists of the scientific management movement proposed that an organization as rationally planned and executed as possible be developed to create more efficiency in administration and consequently increase production. Management was to be divorced from human affairs and emotions. The result was that the workers had to adjust to the management and not the management to the workers.

To accomplish this plan, Taylor initiated time and motion studies to analyze work tasks to improve performance in every aspect of the organization. Once jobs had been reorganized with efficiency in mind, the economic self-interest of the workers could be satisfied through various incentive work plans (piece rates and such).

The function of the leader under scientific management or classical theory was obviously to set up and enforce performance criteria to meet organizational goals. The main focus of a leader was on the needs of the organization and not on the needs of the individual.[7]

Human Relations Movement

Elton Mayo

In the 1920s and early 1930s the trend started by Taylor was to be replaced at center stage by the *human relations* movement, initiated by Elton Mayo and his associates. These theorists argued that in addition to finding the best technological methods to improve output, it was beneficial to management to look into human affairs. It was claimed that the real power centers within an organization were the interpersonal relations that developed within the working unit. The study of these human relations was the most important consideration for management and the analysis of organization. The organization was to be developed around the workers and had to take into consideration human feelings and attitudes.[8]

The function of the leader under human relations theory was to facilitate cooperative goal attainment among followers while providing opportunities for their personal growth and development. The main focus, contrary to scientific management theory, was on individual needs and not on the needs of the organization.

In essence, then, the scientific management movement emphasized a concern for task (output), while the human relations movement stressed a concern for relationships (people). The recognition of these two concerns has characterized the writings on leadership ever since the conflict between the scientific management and the human relations schools of thought became apparent.

Looking specifically at leadership, we find that basic approaches to leadership have moved through three rather dominant phases: trait, attitudinal, and situational.

TRAIT APPROACH TO LEADERSHIP

Prior to 1945, the most common approach to the study of leadership concentrated on leadership traits per se, suggesting that there were certain characteristics, such as physical energy or friendliness, that were essential for effective leadership. These inherent personal qualities, like intelligence, were felt to be transferable from one situation to another. Since all individuals did not have these qualities, only those who had them would be considered potential leaders. Consequently, this approach seemed to question the value of training individuals to assume leadership positions. It implied that if we could discover how to identify and measure these leadership qualities (which are inborn in the individual), we should be able to screen leaders from nonleaders. Leadership training would then be helpful only to those with inherent leadership traits.

A review of the research literature using this trait approach to leadership has revealed few significant or consistent findings.[9] As Eugene E. Jennings concluded, "Fifty years of study have failed to produce one personality trait or set of qualities that can be used to discriminate leaders and nonleaders."[10]

This is not to say that certain traits may hinder or facilitate leadership; the key is that no set of traits has been identified that clearly predicts success or failure. As Yukl has observed, "The old assumption that 'leaders are born' has been discredited completely, and the premise that certain leader traits are absolutely necessary for effective leadership has never been substantiated in several decades of trait research. Today there is a more balanced viewpoint about traits. It is now recognized that certain traits increase the likelihood that a leader will be effective, but they do not guarantee effectiveness, and the relative importance of different traits is dependent upon the nature of the leadership situation."[11]

What are some traits and skills found to be most characteristic of successful leaders? Yukl has offered the following in Table 4-1.

Trait research is still continuing. Warren Bennis recently completed a five-year study of ninety outstanding leaders and their subordinates. On

TABLE 4-1   Traits and Skills Found Most Frequently to Be Characteristic of Successful Leaders[12]

Traits	Skills
Adaptable to situations	Clever (intelligent)
Alert to social environment	Conceptually skilled
Ambitious and achievement-oriented	Creative
Assertive	Diplomatic and tactful
Cooperative	Fluent in speaking
Decisive	Knowledgeable about group task
Dependable	Origanized (administrative ability)
Dominant (desire to influence others)	Persuasive
Energetic (high activity level)	Socially skilled
Persistent	
Self-confident	
Tolerant of stress	
Willing to assume responsibility	

Source: Gary A. Yukl, *Leadership in Organizations*, © 1981, p. 70. Reprinted with permission of Prentice-Hall, Inc., Englewood Cliffs, New Jersey.

the basis of this research, he identified four common traits or areas of competence shared by all ninety leaders.[13]

1. *Management of attention*—The ability to communicate a sense of outcome, goal, or direction that attracts followers.
2. *Management of meaning*—The ability to create and communicate meaning with clarity and understanding.
3. *Management of trust*—The ability to be reliable and consistent so people can count on them.
4. *Management of self*—The ability to know one's self and to use one's skills within limits of strengths and weaknesses.

Bennis suggests leaders empower their organizations to create an environment where people feel significant, learning and competence matter, people are part of the community or team, and work is exciting. It is also an environment where quality matters and dedication to work energizes effort.[14]

As Yukl indicated, there may be negative traits that hinder a person from reaching leadership potential. In one such study, Geier[15] found three traits that kept group members from competing for a leadership role. These three traits were, in order of importance, the perception of being uninformed, of being nonparticipants, or of being extremely rigid. Why were these traits so critical? Because the other group members believed members who were uninformed, disinterested, or overly rigid would hinder the group's accomplishment of its goals. As an aside, isn't our general educational system designed to make students more informed, more motivated, and less rigid? We think so.

McCall and Lombardo have examined differences between executives who went all the way to the top and those who were expected to go to the top but were "derailed" just before reaching their goal. Both winners and losers were a patchwork of strengths and weaknesses, but those who fell short seemed to have one or more of what McCall and Lombardo call "fatal flaws." These included:

1. Insensitive to others: abrasive, intimidating, bullying style.
2. Cold, aloof, arrogant.
3. Betrayal of trust.
4. Overly ambitious: thinking of next job, playing politics.
5. Specific performance problems with the business.
6. Overmanaging—unable to delegate or build a team.
7. Unable to staff effectively.
8. Unable to think strategically.
9. Unable to adapt to boss with different style.
10. Overdependent on advocate or mentor.[16]

While the most frequent cause for derailment was insensitivity to others, the one "unforgivable sin" was betrayal of trust—not following through on promises or double-dealing.[17]

In summary, empirical research studies[18] suggest that leadership is a dynamic process, varying from situation to situation with changes in the leader, the followers, and the situation. Because of this, while there may be helping or hindering traits in a given situation, there is no universal set of traits that will ensure leadership success. The lack of validation of trait approaches led to other investigations of leadership. Among the most prominent areas were the attitudinal approaches.

ATTITUDINAL APPROACHES

The main period of the attitudinal approaches to leadership occurred between 1945, with the Ohio State and Michigan studies, and the mid-1960s, with the development of the Managerial Grid.[19]

By attitudinal approaches, we mean approaches that use paper and pencil instruments such as questionnaires to measure attitudes or predispositions toward leader behavior. For example, the dimensions of the Managerial Grid, Concern for Production, and Concern for People are *attitudinal*. Concern may be defined as a predisposition or feeling toward or against production and people. In contrast, Situational Leadership uses the *observed* behavior dimensions of task behavior and relationship behavior. Situational Leadership thus describes how people are actually behaving. In this section, we will look specifically at three attitudinal approaches to leadership: the Ohio State Studies; the Michigan Studies, including Rensis Likert's work; and the Managerial Grid.

Ohio State Leadership Studies

The leadership studies initiated in 1945 by the Bureau of Business Research at Ohio State University attempted to identify various dimensions of leader behavior.[20] The staff, defining leadership as the behavior of an individual when directing the activities of a group toward a goal attainment, eventually narrowed the description of leader behavior to two dimensions: *Initiating Structure* and *Consideration*. Initiating Structure refers to "the leader's behavior in delineating the relationship between himself and members of the work group and in endeavoring to establish well-defined patterns of organization, channels of communication, and methods of procedure." On the other hand, Consideration refers to "behavior indicative of friendship, mutual trust, respect, and warmth in the relationship between the leader and the members of his staff."[21]

To gather data about the behavior of leaders, the Ohio State staff developed the Leader Behavior Description Questionnaire (LBDQ), an instrument designed to describe *how* leaders carry out their activities.[22] The LBDQ contains fifteen items pertaining to Consideration and an equal number for Initiating Structure. Respondents judge the frequency with which their leader engages in each form of behavior by checking one of five descriptions—always, often, occasionally, seldom, or never—as it relates to each particular item of the LBDQ. Thus, Consideration and Initiating Structure are dimensions of observed behavior as perceived by others. Examples of items used in the LBDQ for both these dimensions follow in Table 4-2.

Although the major emphasis in the Ohio State Leadership Studies was on *observed behavior*, the staff did develop the Leader Opinion Questionnaire (LOQ) to gather data about the self-perceptions that leaders have about their own leadership style. The LBDQ was completed by leaders'

TABLE 4-2 Examples of LBDQ Items

Consideration	Initiating Structure
The leader finds time to listen to group members.	The leader assigns group members to particular tasks.
The leader is willing to make changes.	
The leader is friendly and approachable.	The leader asks the group members to follow standard rules and regulations.
	The leader lets group members know what is expected of them

subordinate(s), superior(s), or associates (peers), but the LOQ was scored by the leaders themselves.

In studying leader behavior, the Ohio State staff found that Initiating Structure and Consideration were separate and distinct dimensions. A high score on one dimension does not necessitate a low score on the other. The behavior of a leader could be described as any mix of both dimensions. Thus, it was during these studies that leader behavior was first plotted on two separate axes rather than on a single continuum. Four quadrants were developed to show various combinations of Initiating Structure (task behavior) and Consideration (relationship behavior), as illustrated in Figure 4-1.

Michigan Leadership Studies

In the early studies of the Survey Research Center at the University of Michigan, there was an attempt to approach the study of leadership by locating clusters of characteristics that seemed to be related to each other and various indicators of effectiveness. The studies identified two concepts, which they called *employee orientation* and *production orientation*.

Leaders who are described as employee oriented stress the relationships aspect of their job. They feel that every employee is important and take interest in everyone, accepting their individuality and personal needs. Production orientation emphasizes production and the technical aspects of the job; employees are seen as tools to accomplish the goals of the organization. These two orientations parallel the authoritarian (task) and democratic (relationship) concepts of the leader behavior continuum.

Figure 4-1   The Ohio State leadership quadrants

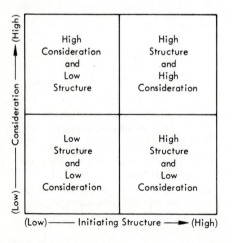

Group Dynamics Studies

Dorwin Cartwright and Alvin Zander, summarizing the findings of numerous studies at the Research Center for Group Dynamics, claim that group objectives fall into one of two categories: (1) the achievement of some specific group goal or (2) the maintenance or strengthening of the group itself.[22]

According to Cartwright and Zander, the type of behavior involved in goal achievement is illustrated by these examples: the manager "initiates action . . . keeps members' attention on the goal . . . clarifies the issue and develops a procedural plan."[23]

On the other hand, characteristic behaviors for group maintenance are the manager "keeps interpersonal relations pleasant . . . arbitrates disputes . . . provides encouragement . . . gives the minority a chance to be heard . . . stimulates self-direction . . . and increases the interdependence among members."[24]

Goal achievement seems to coincide with the task concepts discussed earlier (authoritarian and production orientation), while group maintenance parallels the relationship concepts (democratic and employee orientation).

Research findings in recent years indicate that leadership styles vary considerably from leader to leader. Some leaders emphasize the task and can be described as authoritarian leaders; others stress interpersonal relationships and may be viewed as democratic leaders. Still others seem to be both task oriented and relationship oriented. There are even some individuals in leadership positions who are not concerned about either. No dominant style appears. Instead, various combinations are evident. Thus, task and relationship are not either/or leadership styles, as the preceding continuum suggests. They are separate and distinct dimensions that can be plotted on two separate axes rather than on a single continuum.

Rensis Likert's Management Systems

Using the earlier Michigan studies as a starting place, Rensis Likert did some extensive research to discover the general pattern of management used by high-producing managers in contrast to that used by the other managers. He found that "supervisors with the best records of performance focus their primary attention on the human aspects of their subordinates' problems and on endeavoring to build effective work groups with high performance goals."[25] These supervisors were called "employee-centered." Other supervisors who kept constant pressure on production were called "job-centered" and were found more often to have low-producing sections. Figure 4-2 presents the findings from one study.

Likert also discovered that high-producing supervisors "make clear to their subordinates what the objectives are and what needs to be accom-

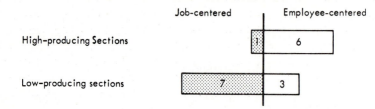

NUMBER OF FIRST-LINE SUPERVISORS WHO ARE

Figure 4-2 Employee-centered supervisors are higher producers than job-centered supervisors[26]

plished and then give them freedom to do the job."[27] Thus, he found that general rather than close supervision tended to be associated with high productivity. This relationship, found in a study of clerical workers, is illustrated in Figure 4-3.

His continuing research together with his colleagues at the Institute for Social Research at the University of Michigan emphasized the need to consider both human resources and capital resources as assets requiring proper management attention. He found that most managers when asked what they would do if they suddenly lost half of their plant, equipment, or capital resources were quick to answer that they would depend upon insurance or borrowed money to keep them in business. Yet when these same managers are asked what they would do if they suddenly lost half of their human resources—managers, supervisors, and hourly employees—they are at a loss for words. There is no insurance against outflows of human resources. Recruiting, training, and developing large numbers of new personnel into a working team takes years. In a competitive environment, this is almost an impossible task. Organizations are only beginning to realize that their most important assets are human resources and that the managing of these resources is one of their most crucial tasks.

As a result of behavioral research studies of numerous organizations,

Figure 4-3 Low-production section heads are more closely supervised than high-production heads[28]

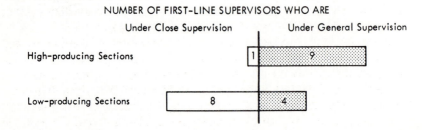

NUMBER OF FIRST-LINE SUPERVISORS WHO ARE

Likert implemented organizational change programs in various industrial settings. These programs were intended to help organizations move from Theory X to Theory Y assumptions, from fostering immature behavior to encouraging and developing mature behavior, from emphasizing only hygiene factors to recognizing and helping workers to satisfy the motivators.

Likert in his studies found that the prevailing management styles of organizations can be depicted on a continuum from System 1 through System 4. These systems might be described as follows:[29]

System 1—Management is seen as having no confidence or trust in subordinates since they are seldom involved in any aspect of the decision-making process. The bulk of the decisions and the goal setting of the organization are made at the top and issued down the chain of command. Subordinates are forced to work with fear, threats, punishment, and occasional rewards and need satisfaction at the physiological and safety levels. The limited superior–subordinate interaction that does take place is usually with fear and mistrust. Although the control process is highly concentrated in top management, an informal organization generally develops in opposition to the goals of the formal organization.

System 2—Management is seen as having condescending confidence and trust in subordinates, such as a master has toward the servants. The bulk of the decisions and goal setting of the organization are made at the top, but many decisions are made within a prescribed framework at lower levels. Rewards and some actual or potential punishment are used to motivate workers. Any superior–subordinate interaction takes place with some condescension by superiors and fear and caution by subordinates. Although the control process is still concentrated in top management, some is delegated to middle and lower levels. An informal organization usually develops, but it does not always resist formal organizational goals.

System 3—Management is seen as having substantial but not complete confidence and trust in subordinates. Broad policy and general decisions are kept at the top, but subordinates are permitted to make more specific decisions at lower levels. Communication flows both up and down the hierarchy. Rewards, occasional punishment, and some involvement are used to motivate workers. There is a moderate amount of superior–subordinate interaction, often with a fair amount of confidence and trust. Significant aspects of the control process are delegated downward, with a feeling of responsibility at both higher and lower levels. An informal organization may develop, but it may either support or partially resist goals of the organization.

System 4—Management is seen as having complete confidence and trust in subordinates. Decision making is widely dispersed throughout the organization, although well integrated. Communication flows not only up and down the hierarchy but among peers. Workers are motivated by participation and involvement in developing economic rewards, setting goals, improving methods, and appraising progress toward goals. There is extensive friendly superior–subordinate interaction, with a high degree of confidence and trust. There is widespread responsibility for the control process, with the lower units fully involved. The informal and formal organizations are often one and the same. Thus, all social forces support efforts to achieve stated organizational goals.

In summary, System 1 is a task-oriented, highly structured authoritarian management style; System 4 is a relationships-oriented management style based on teamwork, mutual trust, and confidence. Systems 2 and 3 are intermediate stages between two extremes, which approximate closely Theory X and Theory Y assumptions.

To expedite the analysis of a company's present behavior, Likert's group developed an instrument that enables members to rate their organization in terms of its management system. This instrument is designed to gather data about a number of operating characteristics of an organization. These characteristics include leadership, motivation, communication, decision making, interaction and influence, goal setting, and the control process used by the organization. Sample items from this instrument are presented in Table 4-3. The complete instrument includes more than twenty such items. Various forms of this instrument have been adapted to be situation specific. For example, a version for school systems is now available with forms for the school board, superintendent, central staff, principals, teachers, parents, and students.

In testing this instrument, Likert asked hundreds of managers from many different organizations to indicate where the *most* productive department, division, or organization they have known would fall between System 1 and System 4. Then these same managers were asked to repeat this process and indicate the position of the *least* productive department, division, or organization they have known. While the ratings of the most and the least productive departments varied among managers, almost without exception each manager rated the high-producing unit closer to System 4 than the low-producing department. In summary, Likert has found that the closer the management style of an organization approaches System 4, the more likely it is to have a continuous record of high productivity. Similarly, the closer this style reflects System 1, the more likely it is to have a sustained record of low productivity.

Likert has also used this instrument not only to measure what individuals believe are the present characteristics of their organization but also to find out what they would like these characteristics to be. Data generated from this use of the instrument with managers of well-known companies have indicated a large discrepancy between the management system they feel their company is now using and the management system they feel would be most appropriate. System 4 is seen as being most appropriate, but few see their companies presently utilizing this approach. These implications have led to attempts by some organizations to adapt their management sys-

TABLE 4-3 Examples of Items from Likert's Table of Organizational and Performance Characteristics of Different Management Systems[30]

Organizational Variable	System 1	System 2	System 3	System 4
Leadership processes used				
Extent to which superiors have confidence and trust in subordinates	Have no confidence and trust in subordinates	Have condescending confidence and trust, such as master has to servant	Substantial but not complete confidence and trust; still wishes to keep control of decisions	Complete confidence and trust in all matters
Character of motivational forces				
Manner in which motives are used	Fear, threats, punishment, and occasional rewards	Rewards and some actual or potential punishment	Rewards, occasional punishment, and some involvement	Economic rewards based on compensation system developed through participation; group participation and involvement in setting goals, improving methods, appraising progress toward goals, etc.
Character of interaction-influence process				
Amount and character of interaction	Little interaction and always with fear and distrust	Little interaction and usually with some condenscension by superiors; fear and caution by subordinates	Moderate interaction, often with fair amount of confidence and trust	Extensive, friendly interaction with high degree of confidence and trust

tem to approximate more closely System 4. Changes of this kind are not easy. They involve a massive reeducation of all concerned, from the top management to the hourly workers.

Theory into Practice

One instance of a successful change in the management style of an organization occurred with a leading firm in the pajama industry.[31] After being unprofitable for several years, this company was purchased by another corporation. At the time of the transaction, the purchased company was using a management style falling between System 1 and System 2. Some major changes were soon implemented by the new owners. The changes that were put into effect included extensive modifications in how the work was organized, improved maintenance of machinery, and a training program involving managers and workers at every level. Managers and supervisors were exposed in depth to the philosophy and understanding of management approaching System 4. All of these changes were supported by the top management of the purchasing company.

Although productivity dropped in the first several months after the initiation of the change program, productivity increased by almost 30 percent within two years. Although it is not possible to calculate exactly how much of the increased productivity resulted from the change in management system, it was obvious to the researchers that the impact was considerable. In addition to increases in productivity, manufacturing costs decreased 20 percent, turnover was cut almost in half, and morale rose considerably (reflecting a more friendly attitude of workers toward the organization). The company's image in the community was enhanced, and for the first time in years the company began to show a profit.

The implication throughout Likert's writings is that the ideal and most productive leader behavior for industry is employee-centered or democratic. Yet, his own findings raise questions as to whether there can be an ideal or single normatively good style of leader behavior that can apply in all leadership situations. As the preceding figures revealed, one of the eight job-centered supervisors and one of the nine supervisors using close supervision had high-producing sections; also, three of the nine employee-centered supervisors and four of the thirteen supervisors who used general supervision had low-producing sections. In other words, in almost 35 percent of the low-producing sections, the suggested ideal type of leader behavior produced undesirable results and almost 15 percent of the high-producing sections were supervised by the suggested "undesirable" style.

Similar findings and interpretations were made by Halpin and Winer in a study of the relationship between aircraft commanders' leadership patterns and the proficiency rating of their crews.[32] Using the LBDQ, they found that eight of ten commanders with high-proficiency ratings were described as using above average Consideration and Initiating Structure and that six of seven commanders with low ratings were seen as below average in Consideration and Initiating Structure. As Likert did, Halpin and Winer reported only that the leaders above average in both Consideration and Initiating Structure are likely to be effective and did not discuss the two high proficiency, low Consideration, low Initiating Structure commanders and the one low producing, high Initiating Structure, high Consideration commander.

Evidence suggesting that a single ideal or normative style of leader behavior is unrealistic was provided when a study was done in an industrial setting in Nigeria.[33] The results were almost the exact opposite of Likert's findings. In that country the tendency was for job-centered supervisors who provide close supervision to have high-producing sections and for employee-centered supervisors who provide general supervision to have low-producing sections. Thus, a single normative leadership style does not take into consideration cultural differences, particularly customs and traditions as well as the level of education, the standard of living, or industrial experience. These are examples of cultural differences in the followers and the situations that are important in determining the appropriate leadership style to be used. Therefore, based on the definition of leadership process as a function of the leader, the followers, and other situational variables, *a single ideal type of leader behavior seems unrealistic.*

Managerial Grid

Robert R. Blake and Jane S. Mouton

In discussing the Ohio State, Michigan, and Likert leadership studies, we concentrated on two theoretical concepts—one emphasizing *task* accomplishment and the other stressing the development of personal *relationships*. Robert R. Blake and Jane S. Mouton have popularized these concepts in their Managerial Grid and have used them extensively in organization and management development programs.[34]

In the Managerial Grid, five different types of leadership based on concern for production (task) and concern for people (relationship) are located in four quadrants (see Figure 4-4) similar to those identified by the Ohio State studies.

Concern for production is illustrated on the horizontal axis. Production becomes more important to the leader as the rating advances on the horizontal scale. A leader with a rating of nine on the horizontal axis has a maximum concern for production.

Concern for people is illustrated on the vertical axis. People become more important to leaders as their ratings progress up the vertical axis. A leader with a rating of nine on the vertical axis has maximum concern for people.

The five leadership styles are described as follows:

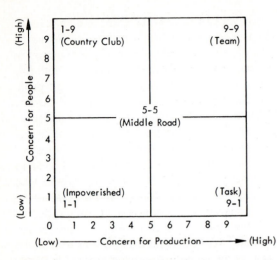

Figure 4-4 The Managerial Grid leadership styles[35]

Impoverished. Exertion of minimum effort to get required work done is appropriate to sustain organization membership.

Country Club. Thoughtful attention to needs of people for satisfying relationships leads to a comfortable, friendly organization atmosphere and work tempo.

Task. Efficiency in operations results from arranging conditions of work in such a way that human elements interfere to a minimum degree.

Middle-of-the-Road. Adequate organization performance is possible through balancing the necessity to get out work while maintaining morale of people at a satisfactory level.

Team. Work accomplishment is from committed people; interdependence through a "common stake" in organization purpose leads to relationships of trust and respect.[36]

In essence, we feel the Managerial Grid has given popular terminology to five points within the four quadrants of the Ohio State studies. However, we want to point out one significant difference between the two frameworks. "Concern for" is a predisposition about something, or an attitudinal dimension. Therefore, the Managerial Grid tends to be an attitudinal model that measures the values and feelings of a manager, while the Ohio State framework attempts to include behavioral concepts (items) as well as attitudinal items. A diagram combining the two frameworks could be illustrated, as shown in Figure 4-5.

IS THERE A BEST STYLE OF LEADERSHIP?

While some researchers such as Blake, Mouton, and McGregor have argued that there is "one best" style of leadership—a style that maximizes produc-

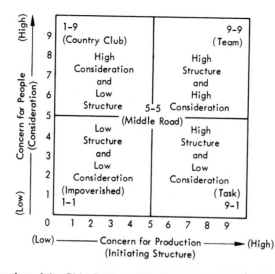

Figure 4-5 Merging of the Ohio State and the Managerial Grid theories of leadership

tivity and satisfaction, and growth and development in all situations, further research in the last several decades has clearly supported the contention that there is no one best leadership style.[37] Successful and effective leaders are able to adapt their style to fit the requirements of the situation. To amplify this idea, it is necessary to place the current state of leadership theory and Situational Leadership, in particular, into perspective.

First, *all* leadership theories, like the vast majority of behavioral science theories (one is attempted to say *all*), have not been conclusively validated by scientific research. As Robbins has observed, " . . . simple and universal principles [of organizational behavior] are avoided because there exist no simple and universal truths or principles that consistently explain organizational behavior."[38] But just because research does not conclusively validate a behavioral science theory does not necessarily make it invalid. If this were not true, there probably wouldn't be any organizational behavior theories (or books such as this one based on the behavioral sciences). For example, as Miner and Robbins suggested in their appraisal of Maslow's Hierarchy of Needs," . . . remember that there is a difference between finding 'insufficient evidence' for a theory and labeling it 'invalid.' It is clear that the available research does not support the Maslow theory to any significant degree. *This does not imply that the theory is wrong, merely that it has not been supported*" (emphasis added).[39]

The lack of solid scientific evidence supporting *all* leadership theories may be because leadership "theories" are, at this point, sets of empirical generalizations and have not developed into scientifically testable theories. This does not make them "wrong," merely that they have not been supported.[40]

Perhaps the problem is that we have been expecting too much from so-called leadership "theories." They really are not "theories" at all but, as we have suggested, descriptions of concepts, procedures, actions, and outcomes that exist. This is why we refer to Situational Leadership as a model.

The primary reason why there is no "one best way" of leadership is that leadership is basically situational, or contingent. All of the leadership theories of House, Fiedler, Kerr, Reddin, Vroom-Yetten, Yukl—to name a few—are situational and represent, together with Situational Leadership, the mainstream of leadership thought. As Robbins has stated, " . . . OB concepts are founded on situational conditions; that is, if X, then Y, but only under conditions specified in Z (the contingency variables). . . . [41] In other words, the effectiveness of a particular leadership style is contingent upon the situation in which it is utilized. As several researchers have noted, one of the most important contributions of Situational Leadership is its attention to the situational nature of leadership.[42]

It is also important to know that effective managers not only have the diagnostic ability to determine the most appropriate leadership style, but they also have the ability to correctly apply that style. As Owens has observed:

> These managers expressed a virtual consensus that, based on their actual experience, each situation they handled demanded a different leadership style. No single style could suffice under the day-to-day, even minute-by-minute, varying conditions of different personalities and moods among their employees, routine process vs. changing or sudden deadlines, new and ever-changing government regulations and paperwork, ambiguous roles of workers, wide ranges in job complexity from simple to innovation-demanding, changes in organizational structure and markets and task technologies and so on. Contingency theory has come to mean, therefore, that the effective manager has, and knows how to use, many leadership styles as each is appropriate to a particular situation.[43]

We believe that Owens has correctly described the situational nature of leadership and that no "one best way" approach can adequately describe what leaders must do to cope with the challenges facing them. Perhaps Ralph Stogdill, author of the *Handbook of Leadership* and a distinguishd leadership researcher for more than forty years, has said it best: "The most effective leaders appear to exhibit a degree of versatility and flexibility that enables them to adapt their behavior to the changing and contradictory demands made on them."[44]

What are some of these "changing and contradictory demands"? How do they influence leadership? How does a potential leader diagnose the situation to determine the high probability leadership style to use? These and many other important issues will be the subjects for Chapter 5 and the following chapters.

NOTES

1. Peter F. Drucker, *The Practice of Management* (New York: Harper & Row, 1954). See also Allen L. Appell, *A Practical Approach to Human Behavior in Business* (Columbus: Merrill,1984).

2. George R. Terry, *Principles of Management*, 3rd ed. (Homewood, Ill.: Irwin, 1960). p. 5.

3. Terry, *Principles of Management*, p. 493.

4. Robert Tannenbaum, Irwin R. Weschler, and Fred Massarik, *Leadership and Organization: A Behavioral Science Approach* (New York: McGraw-Hill, 1959).

5. Harold Koontz and Cyril O'Donnell, *Principles of Management*, 2nd ed. (New York: McGraw-Hill, 1959), p. 435.

6. Chester I. Barnard, *The Functions of the Executive* (Cambridge, Mass.: Harvard University Press, 1938).

7. Frederick W. Taylor, *The Principles of Scientific Management* (New York: Harper & Brothers, 1911).

8. Elton Mayo, *The Social Problems of an Industrial Civilization* (Boston: Harvard Business School, 1945), p. 23.

9. Cecil A. Gibb, "Leadership," in *Handbook of Social Psychology*, Gardner Lindzey, ed. (Cambridge, Mass.: Addison-Wesley, 1954). See also Roger M. Stogdill, "Personal Factors Associated with Leadership: A Survey of Literature," *Journal of Psychology*, 25 (1948), pp. 35–71.

10. Eugene E. Jennings, "The Anatomy of Leadership," *Mangement of Personnel Quarterly*, 1, No. 1 (Autumn 1961). See also A. G. Jago, "Leadership: Perspectives in Theory and Research," *Management Science*, March 1982, pp. 315–336.

11. Gary A. Yukl, *Leadership in Organizations* (Englewood Cliffs, N. J.: Prentice-Hall, 1981), p. 70.

12. *Ibid.*, p. 12.

13. Warren Bennis, "The 4 Competencies of Leadership," *Training and Development Journal*, August 1984, pp. 15–19. See also Warren Bennis and Bert Nanus, *Leaders: The Strategies for Taking Charge* (New York: Harper & Row, 1986).

14. *Ibid.*

15. John G. Geier, "A Trait Approach to the Study of Leadership in Small Groups," *Journal of Communications*, December 1967.

16. Morgan W. McCall, Jr. and Michael M. Lombardo, "What Makes a Top Executive?" *Psychology Today*, February 1983, pp. 26–31.

17. *Ibid.*

18. See cited research by Bennis, McCall, Owens, Yukl, and others.

19. Robert R. Blake and Jane S. Mouton, *The Managerial Grid III*, 3rd ed. (Houston, Tex.: Gulf Publishing, 1984). See also Robert R. Blake and Jane S. Mouton, "The Managerial Grid III," *Personnel Psychology*, 39 (Spring 1986), pp. 238–240.

20. Ralph M. Stogdill and Alvin Coons, eds., *Leader Behavior: Its Description and Measurement*, Research Monograph No. 88 (Columbus: Bureau of Business Research, Ohio State University, 1957). See also Fred E. Fiedler and M. M. Chemers, "Improving Leadership Effectiveness," *Personnel Psychology*, 38 (Spring 1985), pp. 220–222.

21. Andrew W. Halpin, *The Leadership Behavior of School Superintendents* (Chicago: Midwest Administration Center, University of Chicago, 1959), p. 4.

22. Dorwin Cartwright and Alvin Zander, eds., *Group Dynamics: Research and Theory*, 2nd ed. (Evanston, Ill.: Row, Peterson, 1960). See also Patrick R. Penland, *Group Dynamics and Individual Development* (New York: Dekker, 1974); R. H. Guest, *Work Teams and Team Building* (New York: Pergamon, 1986).

23. *Ibid.*, p. 496. See also *Group Plannings and Problems—Solving Methods in Engineering Management*, ed. by Shirley A. Olsen (New York: Wiley, 1982).

24. *Ibid.*

25. Rensis Likert, *New Patterns of Management* (New York: McGraw-Hill, 1961), p. 7.

26. *Ibid.*

27. *Ibid.*, p. 9.

28. *Ibid.*

29. Adapted from Table 2-1, Table of Organizational and Performance Characteristics of Different Management Systems, in Rensis Likert, *The Human Organization* (New York: McGraw-Hill, 1967), pp. 3–10.

30. *Ibid*, pp. 197–211.

31. L. Coch and J. R. P. French, Jr., "Overcoming Resistance to Change," *Human Relations*, 1, No. 4 (1948), pp. 512–532.

32. Andrew W. Halpin and Ben J. Winer, *The Leadership Behavior of Airplane Commanders* (Columbus: Ohio State Research Foundation, 1952).

33. Paul Hersey, an unpublished research project, 1965.

34. Robert R. Blake and Jane S. Mouton, *The Managerial Grid* (Houston, Tex.: Gulf Publishing, 1964). See also R. R. Blake and J. S. Mouton, "The Managerial Grid III," *Personnel Psychology*; R. R. Blake and J. S. Mouton, *The Versatile Manager: A Grid Profile* (Homewood, Ill.: Irwin, 1982); R. R. Blake and J. S. Mouton, *The Secretary Grid: A Program for Increasing Office Synergy* (New York: AMACOM, 1983); Robert Blake et al., *The Academic Administration Grid: A Guide to Developing Effective Management Teams* (San Francisco: Jossey-Bass, 1981).

35. *Ibid*.

36. Robert Blake et al., "Breakthrough in Organizational Development," *Harvard Business Review*, November–December 1964, p. 136.

37. See research by Bennis, Kerr, Yukl, House, Robbins, Tannenbaum and Schmidt, Fiedler, Reddin, Bass, Vroom.

38. Stephen P. Robbins, *Organizational Behavior: Concepts Controversies, and Applications*, 2nd ed. (Englewood Cliffs, N. J.: Prentice-Hall, 1983), pp. 11–12.

39. *Ibid*, p. 136.

40. John B. Miner, *Theories of Organizational Behavior* (Hinsdale, Ill.: Dryden Press, 1980).

41. Robbins, *Organizational Behavior*, p. 12.

42. Yukl, *Leadership in Organizations*, p. 144.

43. James Owens, "A Reappraisal of Leadership Theory and Training," *Personnel Administrator*, 26 (November 1981), p. 81.

44. Ralph M. Stogdill, "Historical Trends in Leadership Theory and Research," *Journal of Contemporary Business*, Autumn 1974, p. 7.

CHAPTER 5

LEADERSHIP:
Situational Approaches

The focus in situational approaches to leadership is on observed behavior, not on any hypothetical inborn or acquired ability or potential for leadership. The emphasis is on the behavior of leaders and their group members (followers) and various situations. With this emphasis on behavior and environment, more encouragement is given to the possibility of training individuals in adapting styles of leader behavior to varying situations. Therefore, it is believed that most people can increase their effectiveness in leadership roles through education, training, and development. From observations of the frequency (or infrequency) of certain leader behavior in numerous types of situations, models can be developed to help leaders make some predictions about the most appropriate leader behavior for their present situation. For these reasons, in this chapter we will talk in terms of leader behavior rather than leadership traits, thus emphasizing the situational approach to leadership.

SITUATIONAL APPROACHES TO LEADERSHIP

As we noted in the last chapter, current organizational behavior theory views leadership as well as other organizational behavior concepts and theories as situational, or contingent in nature. While we cited Robbins, his views are not unique. Schriesheim, Tolliver, and Behling have noted," . . . the literature supports the basic notion that a situational view is necessary to portray accurately the complexities of the leadership process."[1] Vroom concurs, "I do not see any form of leadership as optimal for all situations. The contribution of a leader's actions to the effectiveness of his organization cannot be determined without considering the nature of the situation in which that behavior is displayed."[2]

Earlier we identified the three main components of the leadership process as the leader, the follower, and the situation. Situational approaches to leadership examine the interplay among these variables in order to find causal relationships that will lead to predictability of behavior. You will find a common thread among the situational approaches that we will elaborate upon in this and in subsequent chapters. This common thread is that all situational approaches require the leader to behave in a flexible manner, to be able to diagnose the leadership style appropriate to the situation, and to be able to apply the appropriate style.

While there are many situational models and theories, we will focus on five that have received wide attention in leadership research: the Tannenbaum and Schmidt Continuum of Leader Behavior, Fiedler's Contingency Model, the House–Mitchell Path–Goal Theory, Vroom–Yetten Contingency Model, and the Hersey–Blanchard Tri-Dimensional Leader Effectiveness Model.[3]

TANNENBAUM–SCHMIDT CONTINUUM OF LEADER BEHAVIOR

Robert Tannenbaum and Warren H. Schmidt's 1957 *Harvard Business Review* article "How to Choose a Leadership Pattern" was one of the initial and certainly one of the most significant situational approaches to leadership.[4] The leader selects one of seven possible leader behaviors depending upon the forces among the leader, follower, and situation. As Figure 5-1 indicates, the range or continuum of choices is between democratic or relationship-oriented behaviors and authoritarian or task-oriented behaviors. You will remember that these are dimensions from the Michigan and Ohio State studies, respectively.

Past writers have felt that concern for task tends to be represented by authoritarian leader behavior, while a concern for relationships is represented by democratic leader behavior. This feeling was popular because it was generally agreed that leaders influence their followers in either of two ways: (1) they can tell their follows what to do and how to do it or (2) they can share their leadership responsibilities with their followers by involving

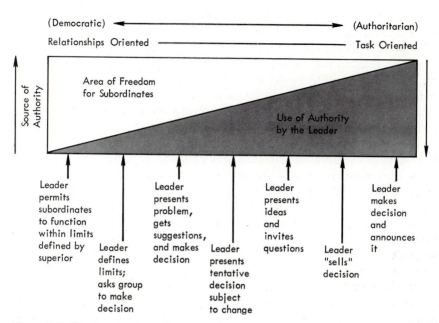

(Democratic) ←————————————————————→ (Authoritarian)

Relationships Oriented ————————————————— Task Oriented

Source of Authority

Area of Freedom for Subordinates

Use of Authority by the Leader

Leader permits subordinates to function within limits defined by superior

Leader defines limits; asks group to make decision

Leader presents problem, gets suggestions, and makes decision

Leader presents tentative decision subject to change

Leader presents ideas and invites questions

Leader "sells" decision

Leader makes decision and announces it

Figure 5-1   Continuum of leader behavior[6]

them in the planning and execution of the task. The former is the traditional authoritarian style, which emphasizes task concerns. The latter is the more nondirective democratic style, which stresses the concern for human relationships.

The differences in the two styles of leader behavior are based on the assumptions leaders make about the source of their power or authority and human nature. The authoritarian style of leader behavior is often based on the assumption that the power of leaders is derived from the position they occupy and that people are innately lazy and unreliable (Theory X). The democratic style assumes that the power of leaders is granted by the group they are to lead and that people can be basically self-directed and creative at work if properly motivated (Theory Y). As a result, in the authoritarian style, all policies are determined by the leader; in the democratic style, policies are open for group discussion and decision.

There are, of course, a wide variety of styles of leader behavior between these two extremes. Robert Tannenbaum and Warren H. Schmidt depicted a broad range of styles as a continuum moving from authoritarian, or boss-centered, leader behavior at one end to democratic, or subordinate-centered, leader behavior at the other end,[5] as illustrated in Figure 5-1. Tannenbaum and Schmidt now refer to these two extremes as manager power and influence and nonmanager power and influence.

Leaders whose behavior is observed to be at the authoritarian end of the continuum tend to be task oriented and use their power to influence their followers; leaders whose behavior appears to be at the democratic end tend to be group-oriented and thus give their followers considerable freedom in their work. Often this continuum is extended beyond democratic leader behavior to include a *laissez-faire* style.[7] This style of behavior permits the members of the group to do whatever they want to do. No policies or procedures are established. Everyone is left alone. No one attempts to influence anyone else. As is evident, this is not included in the continuum of leader behavior illustrated in Figure 5-1. This was done because it was felt that in reality, a *laissez-faire* atmosphere represents an absence of formal leadership. The formal leadership role has been abdicated and, therefore, any leadership that is being exhibited is informal and emergent.

It is interesting to note that in the 1973 reprint of their article in the *Harvard Business Review*, Tannenbaum and Schmidt commented that the interrelationships among leader, follower, and situation were becoming increasingly complex.[8] With this complexity it becomes more difficult to identify causes and effects, particularly when more forces outside the traditional situation are exerting influences. As the world becomes more international, as more stakeholders come into play, and as more traditional customs, practices and authorities are eroded, the leadership process becomes more difficult. Warren Bennis's "Where Have All the Leaders Gone?" is one astute commentary on this phenomenon.[9]

FIEDLER'S LEADERSHIP CONTINGENCY MODEL

Widely respected as the Father of the Contingency Theory of Leadership, Fred Fiedler has developed the Leadership Contingency Model. He suggests that three major situational variables seem to determine whether a given situation is favorable to leaders: (1) their personal relations with the members of their group (leader–member relations), (2) the degree of structure in the task that their group has been assigned to perform (task structure), and (3) the power and authority that their position provides (position power).[10] Leader–member relations seem to parallel the relationship concepts discussed earlier, while task structure and position power, which measure very closely related aspects of a situation, seem to be associated with task concepts. Fiedler defines the *favorableness of a situation* as "the degree to which the situation enables the leader to exert his influence over his group."[11]

In this model, eight possible combinations of these three situational variables can occur. As a leadership situation varies from high to low on these variables, it will fall into one of the eight combinations (situations). The most favorable situation for leaders to influence their group is one in which they are well liked by the members (good leader–member relations),

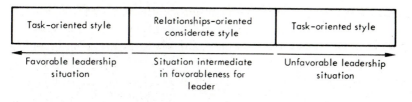

Task-oriented style	Relationships-oriented considerate style	Task-oriented style

Favorable leadership situation ←——— Situation intermediate in favorableness for leader ———→ Unfavorable leadership situation

Figure 5-2   Leadership styles appropriate for various group situations[12]

have a powerful position (high position power), and are directing a well-defined job (high task structure); for example, a well-liked general making inspection in an army camp. On the other hand, the most unfavorable situation for leaders is one in which they are disliked, have little position power, and face an unstructured task—such as an unpopular head of a voluntary hospital fund-raising committee.

Having developed this model for classifying group situations, Fiedler has attempted to determine what the most effective leadership style—task oriented or relationship oriented—seems to be for each of the eight situations. In a reexamination of old leadership studies and an analysis of new studies, Fiedler has concluded that:

1. *Task-oriented* leaders tend to perform best in group situations that are either very favorable or very unfavorable to the leader.
2. *Relationship-oriented* leaders tend to perform best in situations that are intermediate in favorableness.

Although Fiedler's model is useful to a leader, he seems to be reverting to a single continuum of leader behavior, suggesting that there are only two basic leader behavior styles, task-oriented and relationship-oriented. Most evidence indicates that leader behavior must be plotted on two separate axes rather than on a single continuum. Thus, a leader who is high on task behavior is not necessarily high or low on relationship behavior. Any combination of the two dimensions may occur.

HOUSE-MITCHELL PATH-GOAL THEORY

The Path−Goal model builds upon two concepts that we have looked at earlier—the Ohio State leadership studies and the expectancy model of motivation.[13] You will recall that the expectancy model focused on the effort−performance and the performance−goal satisfaction (reward) linkages.[14]

You will also remember that the key dimensions of the Ohio State model are initiating structure and consideration and that the model suggested that the most effective leaders would score high on both the initiating structure and the consideration dimensions.

Robert House did much of his leadership research at Ohio State University and was interested in explaining the contradictions in the Ohio State model; for example, the situations where initiating structure, consideration, or certain combinations of the two variables were not the most effective. In other words, he was interested in those situations where initiating structure was most appropriate and those situations where consideration was most appropriate. Furthermore, he was interested in explaining *why* a certain style of leadership was effective. Before we go further, it is important to state why this theory is called the path−goal theory. House and Mitchell explain it in this manner:

> According to this theory, leaders are effective because of their impact on subordinates' motivation, ability to perform effectively and satisfactions. The theory is called Path−Goal because its major concern is how the leader influences the subordinates' perceptions of their work goals, personal goals and paths to goal attainment. The theory suggests that a leader's behavior is motivating or satisfying to the degree that the behavior increases subordinate goal attainment and clarifies the paths to these goals.[15]

How does the Path−Goal Theory relate to the expectancy model and the Ohio State Leadership Model? The expectancy model tells us that " . . . people are satisfied with their job if they think it leads to things that are highly valued, and they work hard if they believe that effort leads to things that are highly valued."[16] Leadership is related to this because " . . . subordinates are motivated by leader behavior to the extent that this behavior influences expectancies . . . ."[17] Leaders do this best according to Path−Goal Theory when they supply what is missing from the situation. For example, in an unstructured task situation, leaders may increase job satisfaction by supplying leader directiveness. This can be seen in Figure 5-3.

In this figure, task structure is the contingency variable. Job satisfaction is highest in a situation that is *unstructured*—for example, a basic research lab, when leader directiveness is high; job satisfaction would be low if leader directiveness is low. In a *structured* task situation—for example, an assembly line, job satisfaction would be highest when leader directiveness is low and job satisfaction would be lowest when leader directiveness is high. Why is this so? House and Mitchell propose that if followers are performing highly structured tasks, the most effective leader behavior style is one that is high on supportive (relationship) behavior and low on instrumental (task) behavior. This proposition is based on the assumption that highly structured tasks are inherently less satisfying and a source of frustration and stress for followers. Leader relationship behavior should help reduce the frustration and mitigate the dissatisfying nature of highly structured tasks. Further, it is assumed that if followers' tasks are highly structured, the required activities are clear to followers and leader task behavior (providing direction and instruction) is less important.

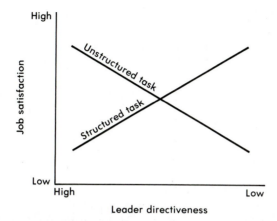

Figure 5-3 **Hypothetical relationship between directive leadership and subordinate satisfaction with task structure as a contingency factor.**[18]

If followers are performing relatively unstructured tasks, the Path−Goal Theory proposes that a leadership style high on task behavior and low on relationship behavior will be most effective. It is assumed that required activities and performance expectations are unclear and leader task behavior is needed to provide direction and role structuring. Unstructured tasks, however, are assumed to be more challenging, more intrinsically satisfying, and less frustrating and stressful. Under these conditions, leader relationship behavior is less important.[19]

Research by John E. Stinson and Thomas W. Johnson[20] has suggested that the relationship between leader behavior and task structure is somewhat more complex than was proposed by House. Stinson and Johnson found that although leader relationship behavior is more important if followers are performing highly structured tasks, the amount of task behavior the leader should use depends on the nature of the followers as well as the type of task the followers are performing.

Specifically, they propose that high leader task behavior is most effective if:

1. Followers' tasks are highly structured *and* followers have strong needs for achievement and independence and a high level of education and/or experience (that is, followers are overqualified for the job).
2. Followers' tasks are unstructured *and* followers have weak needs for achievement and independence and a low level of task relevant education and/or experience (that is, followers are underqualified for the job).

Low task behavior by the leader is most effective if:

1. Followers' tasks are highly structured *and* followers share weak needs for achievement and independence but an adequate level of task relevant education and/or experience.
2. Followers' tasks are unstructured *and* followers have strong needs for achievement and independence and a high level of education and/or experience.

Figure 5-4 shows the high probability leader behavior style for different combinations of task structure and follower capacity. Follower capacity refers to the degree of achievement motivation, need for independence, and task-relevant education and experience.

As Figure 5-4 suggests, a high task/low relationship tends to be an effective leadership style if a manager is supervising an unstructured task being performed by followers with low capacity; high task/high relationship style seems to be appropriate for high-capacity followers performing a structured task; high relationship/low task behavior tends to be effective with low-capacity followers performing a highly structured task; and finally, low relationship/low task behavior seems appropriate for high capacity followers performing an unstructured task.

VROOM–YETTEN CONTINGENCY MODEL

The Contingency Model developed by Victor Vroom and Phillip Yetten is based on a model commonly used by researchers who take a contingency approach to leadership. This model, shown in Figure 5-5,[21] is based on the assumption that situational variables interacting with personal attributes or characteristics of the leader result in leader behavior that can affect organizational effectiveness. This change in the organization—because the organi-

Figure 5-4 The relationship between leadership style and different combinations of task structure and follower capacity

		TASK STRUCTURE	
		Low	High
Follower Capacity	High	Low Relationship Low Task	High Task High Relationship
	Low	High Task Low Relationship	High Relationship Low Task

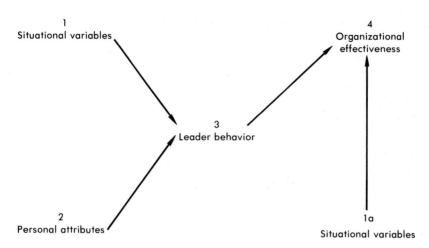

Figure 5-5 Schematic representation of variables used in leadership research

zation is part of the situation—can, in turn, affect the next leadership intervention.

Because Figure 5-5 blends several of the ideas we have and will be considering in our discussion of leadership, it is important that we pause to look at it in some detail. Figure 5-5 assumes that situational variables [1] such as followers, time, and job demands interacting with personal attributes [2] of the leader such as experience and/or communication skills result in leader behavior [3] such as a directive style of leadership to influence organizational effectiveness [4] which is also influenced by other situational variables [1a] outside the control of the leader; for example, world economic conditions, actions of competitors, government legislation. We will look in greater detail at situational variables in a subsequent chapter. Before we leave Figure 5-5, you will note that it draws upon not only the situational approach to leadership, but also upon some of the aspects of the trait approach that we considered earlier.

How does the Vroom-Yetten Contingency Model Work? Assume that you have decided to let your group participate in making a decision. You can use Figure 5-6, Decision Model, as a guide, by asking questions A through F in sequence. Table 5-1, Types of Managerial Decisions, describes the five different types of decision styles possible in this model. Let's try an example.

As we suggested in discussing Figure 5-5, the manager should first diagnose the situational variable. Table 5-2, Problem Attributes Used in the Model, is very useful for this purpose and has been found to have a high success rate in improving decision quality. After asking these seven questions, the manager should refer to Figure 5-6 and work through this decision

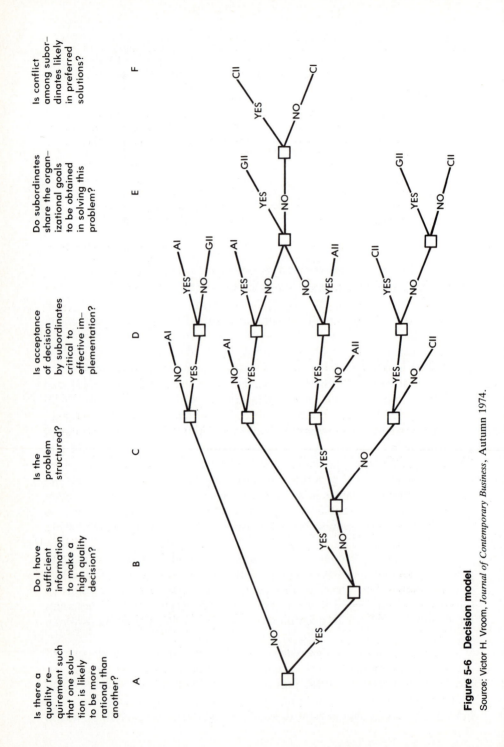

Figure 5-6 Decision model

Source: Victor H. Vroom, *Journal of Contemporary Business*, Autumn 1974.

TABLE 5-1   Types of Managerial Decision Styles

AI   You solve the problem or make the decision yourself, using information available to you at the time.

AII   You obtain the necessary information from your subordinate(s), then decide on the solution to the problem yourself. You may or may not tell your subordinates what the problem is in getting the information from them. The role played by your subordinates in making the decision is clearly one of providing the necessary information to you, rather than generating or evaluating alternative solutions.

CI   You share the problem with relevant subordinates individually, getting their ideas and suggestions without bringing them together as a group. Then *you* make the decision that may or may not reflect your subordinates' influence.

CII   You share the problem with your subordinates as a group, collectively obtaining their ideas and suggestions. Then *you* make the decision that may or may not reflect your subordinates' influence.

GII   You share a problem with your subordinates as a group. Together you generate and evaluate alternatives and attempt to reach agreement (consensus) on a solution. Your role is much like that of chairman. You do not try to influence the group to adopt "your" solution and you are willing to accept and implement any solution that has the support of the entire group.

Source: Victor H. Vroom, *Journal of Contemporary Business,* Autumn 1974

TABLE 5-2   Problem Attributes Used in the Model

Problem Attributes	*Diagnostic Questions*
A. The importance of the quality of the decision.	Is there a quality requirement such that one solution is likely to be more rational than another?
B. The extent to which the leader possesses sufficient information/expertise to make a high-quality decision.	Do I have sufficient information to make a high-quality decision?
C. The extent to which the problem is structured.	Is the problem structured?
D. The extent to which acceptance or commitment on the part of subordinates is critical to the effective implementation of the decision.	Is acceptance of the decision by subordinates critical to effective implementation?
E. The prior probability that the leader's autocratic decision will receive acceptance by subordinates.	If I were to make the decision by myself, is it reasonably certain that it would be accepted by my subordinates?
F. The extent to which subordinates are motivated to attain the organizational goals as represented in the objectives explicit in the statement of the problem.	Do subordinates share the organizational goals to be obtained in solving the problem?
G. The extent to which subordinates are likely to be in conflict over preferred solutions.	Is conflict among subordinates likely in preferred solutions?

Source: Victor H. Vroom, *Journal of Contemporary Business,* Autumn 1974

tree from left to right asking the questions. When the response indicates a type of decision, for example AI, then the manager should turn to Table 5-1 for a description of the appropriate decision style.

This model is a contingency model because the leader's possible behaviors are contingent upon the interaction between the questions and the leader's assessment of the situation in developing a response to the questions. Perhaps you recognized that the questions used the quality and acceptance aspects of decision making popularized by Norman R. R. Maier. The first three questions concern the quality or technical accuracy of the decision, and the last four concern the acceptance of the decision by the group members. The questions are designed to eliminate alternatives that would jeopardize the quality or the acceptance of the decision, as appropriate.

The Vroom—Yetten approach is important for several reasons. One is that it is widely respected among researchers in leadership behavior. Another reason is that the authors believe that leaders have the ability to vary their styles to fit the situation. This point is critical to acceptance of situational approaches to leadership. A third reason is that they believe that people can be developed into more effective leaders.

HERSEY-BLANCHARD TRI-DIMENSIONAL LEADER EFFECTIVENESS MODEL

In the leadership models developed by Paul Hersey and Kenneth H. Blanchard in their research efforts, the terms *task behavior* and *relationship behavior* are used to describe concepts similar to Consideration and Initiating Structure of the Ohio State studies. The four basic leader behavior quadrants are labeled: high task and low relationship; high task and high relationship; high relationship and low task; and low relationship and low task (see Figure 5-7).

These four basic styles depict essentially different leadership styles. The *leadership style* of an individual is the behavior pattern that person exhibits when attempting to influence the activities of others as perceived by those others. This may be very different from the leader's perception of leadership behavior, which we shall define as *self-perception* rather than style. A person's leadership style involves some combination of task behavior and relationship behavior. The two types of behavior—task and relationship— which are central to the concept of leadership style, are defined as follows:

> *Task behavior*—The extent to which leaders are likely to organize and define the roles of the members of their group (followers); to explain what activities each is to do and when, where, and how tasks are to be accomplished; characterized by endeavoring to establish well-defined patterns of organization, channels of communication, and ways of getting jobs accomplished.

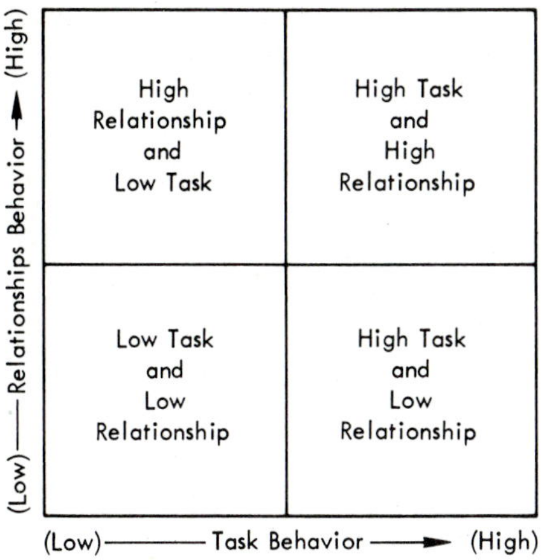

High Relationship and Low Task	High Task and High Relationship
Low Task and Low Relationship	High Task and Low Relationship

(Low) ———— Task Behavior ——➤ (High)

(High) ↑ Relationships Behavior ———— (Low)

Figure 5-7   Basic leader behavior styles

Relationship behavior—The extent to which leaders are likely to maintain personal relationships between themselves and members of their group (followers) by opening up channels of communication, providing socioemotional support, "psychological strokes," and facilitating behaviors.[24]

Effectiveness Dimension

Recognizing that the effectiveness of leaders depends on how their leadership style interrelates with the situation in which they operate, an effectiveness dimension should be added to the two-dimensional model. This is illustrated in Figure 5-8.

In his 3-D Management Style Theory, William J. Reddin was the first to add an effectiveness dimension to the task concern and relationship concern dimensions of earlier attitudinal models such as the Managerial Grid.[23] Reddin, whose pioneer work influenced us greatly in the development of our Tri-Dimensional Leader Effectiveness Model presented in this book, felt that a useful theoretical model "must allow that a variety of styles may be effective or ineffective depending on the situation."[24]

By adding an effectiveness dimension to the task behavior and relationship behavior dimensions of the earlier Ohio State leadership model, we are attempting in the Tri-Dimensional Leader Effectiveness Model to integrate the concepts of leader style with situational demands of a specific environment. When the style of a leader is appropriate to a given situation, it is termed *effective*; when the style is inappropriate to a given situation, it is termed *ineffective*.

If the effectiveness of a leader behavior style depends on the situation in which it is used, it follows that any of the basic styles may be effective or ineffective, depending on the situation. The difference between the effective and ineffective styles is often not the actual behavior of the leader but the

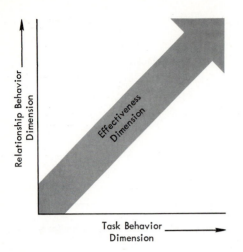

Figure 5-8   Adding an effectiveness dimension

appropriateness of this behavior to the environment in which it is used. In reality, the third dimension is the environment. It is the interaction of the basic style with the environment that results in a degree of effectiveness or ineffectiveness. We call the third dimension *effectiveness* because in most organizational settings various performance criteria are used to measure the degree of effectiveness or ineffectiveness of a manager or leader. But the authors feel it is important to keep in mind that the third dimension is the environment in which the leader is operating. One might think of the leader's basic style as a particular stimulus, and it is the response to this stimulus that can be considered effective or ineffective. This is an important point because theorists and practitioners who argue that there is one best style of leadership are making value judgments about the stimulus, while those taking a situational approach to leadership are evaluating the response or the results rather than the stimulus. This concept is illustrated in the diagram of the Tri-Dimensional Leader Effectiveness Model presented in Figure 5-9.

Although effectiveness appears to be an either/or situation in this model, in reality it should be represented as a continuum. Any given style in a particular situation could fall somewhere on this continuum, from extremely effective to extremely ineffective. Effectiveness, therefore, is a matter of degree, and there could be an infinite number of faces on the effectiveness dimension rather than only three. To illustrate this fact, the effectiveness dimension has been divided into quartiles, ranging on the effective side from +1 to +4 and on the ineffective side from -1 to -4.

The four effective and the four ineffective styles are, in essence, how appropriate a leader's basic style is to a given situation as seen by the leader's followers, superiors, or associates. Table 5-1 describes briefly one of

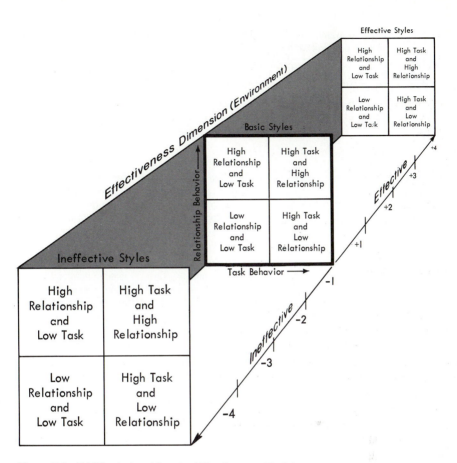

Figure 5-9 Tri-Dimensional Leader Effectiveness Model

many different ways each style might be perceived as effective or ineffective by others.[25]

A model such as the Tri-Dimensional Leader Effectiveness Model is distinctive because it does not depict a single ideal leader behavior style that is suggested as being appropriate in all situations. For example, the high task and high relationship style is appropriate only in certain situations. In basically crisis-oriented organizations such as the military or the fire department, there is considerable evidence that the most appropriate style would be high task and low relationship, since under combat, fire, or emergency conditions success often depends on immediate response to orders. Time demands do not permit talking things over or explaining decisions. But once the crisis is over, other styles might become appropriate. For example, although the fire chief may have to initiate a high level of structure at the

TABLE 5-1 How the basic leader behavior styles may be seen by others when they are effective or ineffective

Basis Styles	Effective	Ineffective
High Task and Low Relationship Behavior	Seen as having well-defined methods for accomplishing goals that are helpful to the followers.	Seen as imposing methods on others; sometimes seen as unpleasant and interested only in short-run output.
High Task and High Relationship Behavior	Seen as satisfying the needs of the group for setting goals and organizing work, but also providing high levels of socioemotional support.	Seen as initiating more structure than is needed by the group and often appears not to be genuine in interpersonal relationships.
High Relationship and Low Task Behavior	Seen as having implicit trust in people and as being primarily concerned with facilitating their goal accomplishment.	Seen as primarily interested in harmony; sometimes seen as unwilling to accomplish a task if it risks disrupting a relationship or losing "good person" image.
Low Relationship and Low Task Behavior	Seen as appropriately delegating to subordinates decisions about how the work should be done and providing little socioemotional support where little is needed by the group.	Seen as providing little structure or socioemotional support when needed by members of the group.

scene of a fire, upon returning to the firehouse it may be appropriate for the chief to engage in other styles while his staff is participating in ancillary functions such as maintaining the equipment or studying new firefighting techniques.

Instrumentation

To gather data about the behavior of leaders, the Leader Effectiveness and Adapatability Description (LEAD)[26] instruments were developed for use in training settings. The LEAD-Self contains twelve leadership situations in which respondents are asked to select from four alternative actions—a high task/low relationship behavior, a high task/high relationship behavior, a high relationship/low task behavior, and a low relationship/low task behavior—the style they felt would most closely describe their own behavior in that type of situation. An example of a situation–action combination used in the LEAD-Self follows:

The LEAD-Self was designed to measure self-perception of three as-

TABLE 5-2 Sample Item from Lead-Self Instrument[27]

Situation	Alternative Actions
Your subordinates, usually able to take responsibility, are not responding to your recent redefinition of standards.	A. Allow group involvement in redefining standards, but don't push. B. Redefine standards and supervise carefully. C. Avoid confrontation by not applying pressure. D. Incorporate group recommendations, but see that new standards are met.

pects of leader behavior: (1) style, (2) style range, and (3) style adaptability. Style and style range are determined by four style scores, and the style adaptability (effectiveness score) is determined by one normative score. The LEAD-Self was originally designed as a training instrument and should be properly used only in training situations and not, as some researchers have done, as a research instrument. The length of the scale (twelve items) and time requirement (ten minutes) clearly reflect the intended function.

We have also developed the LEAD-Other to gather leadership-style information in training situations. The LEAD-Self is scored by leaders themselves, but the LEAD-Other is completed by leaders' subordinate(s), superior(s), or associates (peers). We will discuss both these instruments in more detail in Chapter 12.

WHAT ABOUT CONSISTENCY?

What is consistent leadership behavior? Consistent leadership is not using the same leadership style all of the time but using the style appropriate for the followers' level of readiness in such a way so the followers understand *why* they are getting a certain behavior, a certain style from the leader. Inconsistent is using the *same* style in *every* situation. Therefore, if a manager uses a supportive high relationship/low task style with a staff member when that person is performing well and also when that staff member is performing poorly, that manager would be inconsistent, not consistent. Managers are consistent if they direct their subordinates and even sometimes discipline them when they are performing poorly but support and reward them when they are performing well. Managers are inconsistent if they smile and respond supportively when their subordinates are not doing their job as well as when they are.

To be *really* consistent (in our terms) managers must behave the same way in similar situations for all parties concerned. Thus, a consistent manager would not discipline one subordinate when the person makes a costly mistake but not another staff member, and vice versa. It is also important for managers to treat their subordinates the *same way* in *similar circumstances* even when it is *inconvenient*—when they don't have time or when they don't feel like it.

Some managers are consistent only when it is convenient. They may praise and support their people when they feel like it and redirect and supervise their activities when they have time. This leads to problems. Parents are probably the worst in this regard. For example, suppose Wendy and Walt get upset when their children argue with each other and are willing to clamp down on them when it happens. However, there are exceptions to their consistency in this area. If they are rushing off to a dinner party, they will generally not deal with the children's fighting. Or if they are in the supermarket with the kids, they will frequently permit behavior they would normally not allow because they are uncomfortable disciplining the children in public. Since children are continually testing the boundaries or limits of their behavior (they want to know what they can do and cannot do), Walt and Wendy's kids soon learn that they should not fight with each other except when "Mom and Dad are in a hurry to go out or when we're in a store." Thus, unless parents and managers are willing to be consistent even when it is inconvenient, they may actually be encouraging misbehavior.

Another thing that frequently happens is instead of using appropriate leader behavior matched with follower readiness, performance, and demonstrated ability, privileges are based upon chronological age or gender. For example, it is OK for an irresponsible 17-year-old to stay out until 2:00 A.M. but it is not OK for a very responsible 15-year-old daughter to stay out until 12:00 P.M..

ATTITUDE VERSUS BEHAVIOR

One of the ideas behind the old definition of consistency was the belief that your behavior as a manager *must* be consistent with your attitudes. This was a problem with some people who were heavily involved with the human relations or sensitivity-training movement. They believed that if you care about people and have positive assumptions about them, you should also treat them in high relationship ways and seldom in directive or controlling ways.

We feel that much of this problem stemmed from the failure of some theorists and practitioners to distinguish between an attitudinal model and a behavioral model. For example, in examining the dimensions of the Managerial Grid (concern for production and concern for people) and Reddin's 3-D Management Style Theory (task orientation and relationship orientation), one can see that these appear to be *attitudinal* dimensions. Concern or orientation is a feeling or an emotion toward something. The same can be said about McGregor's Theory X and Theory Y assumptions about human nature. Theory X describes negative feelings about the nature of people, and Theory Y describes positive feelings. These are all models that describe attitudes and feelings.

On the other hand, the dimensions of the Tri-Dimensional Leader Effectiveness model (task behavior and relationship behavior) are dimensions of *observed* behavior. Thus, the Leader Effectiveness model describes *how* people behave, while the Managerial Grid, the 3-D Management Style Theory, and Theory X−Theory Y describe *attitudes* or *predispositions* toward production and people.[28]

Although attitudinal models and the Leader Effectiveness model examine different aspects of leadership, they are not incompatible. A conflict develops only when behavioral assumptions are drawn from analysis of the attitudinal dimension of models such as the Managerial Grid and theories such as Theory X−Theory Y. First of all, it is very difficult to predict behavior from attitudes and values. In fact, it has been found that you can actually do better the other way around. You can do a much better job of predicting values or attitudes from behavior. If you want to know what's in a person's heart, look at what that person does. Look at the person's behavior.

For example, assume that a person has a very high concern for conditions in the ghetto—for poverty. Does that tell you what that person's going to do about it? No. You may have one person who has a high concern for conditions in the ghetto and poverty who engages in the following behavior: "Don't even talk to me about it. I don't want to go on that side of town." In other words, the person engages in avoidance or withdrawal behavior (low relationship behavior and low task behavior). You may have another person who has a very high concern for conditions in the ghetto and poverty, who goes down into the ghetto and begins to tell people what to do, how to do it, when to do it, and where to do it (high task behavior and low relationship behavior). You may have another person who has high concern for conditions in the ghetto and poverty who would go down to the ghetto areas saying, "Gee, I'm sorry you have problems. Do you want to talk to me about it? Let's discuss it. Gosh, I'm sympathetic" (high relationship behavior and low task behavior). Finally, you might get someone else who has a high concern for conditions in the ghetto and poverty who would try to provide high amounts of both task behavior and relationship behavior.

What we're suggesting is that the same value set can evoke a variety of behaviors. You cannot easily predict behaviors from values. A look at one of the simplest models in the behavior sciences may help to emphasize our point of view. The model is the S−O−R (a stimulus directed toward an organism produces some response). The trap that many of the humanistic trainers fall into is to suggest that we assess the effectiveness of management by looking at the stimulus, or the leadership style. In other words, they say there are good styles and bad styles. What we are saying is that if you are going to assess performance, you don't evaluate the stimulus, you assess the results—the response. It's here that we need to make assessments in terms of performance. This is exactly what we suggest. There is no best leadership style, or stimulus. Any leadership style can be effective or ineffective depending on the response that style gets in a particular situation. We also have to look at the impact the leaders have on the human resources. It's not enough to have a tremendous amount of productivity for the next six months and then have your people get upset and leave and join your competitors in other organizations. You've also got to be concerned about what impact you are having on the human resources, on developing their competency and their commitment. So when we talk about response, or results, we're talking about output and impact on the human resources.

There is another reason to be careful about making behavioral assumptions from attitudinal measures. Although high *concern* for both production and people (9-9 attitude) and positive Theory Y assumptions about human nature are basic ingredients for effective managers, it may be appropriate for managers to engage in a variety of behaviors as they face different problems in their environment. Therefore, the high task/high relationship style often associated with the Managerial Grid 9-9 Team style or the participative high relationship/low task behavior that is often argued as consistent with Theory Y may not always be appropriate. For example, if a manager's subordinates are emotionally mature and can take responsibility for themselves, the appropriate style of leadership for working with them may be low task and low relationship. In this case, the manager delegates to those subordinates the responsibility of planning, organizing, and controlling their own operation. The manager plays a background role, providing socioemotional support only when necessary. In using this style appropriately, the manager would not be "impoverished" (low concern for both people and production), or Theory X. In fact, delegating to competent and confident people is the best way a manager can demonstrate a 9-9 attitude and Theory Y assumptions about human nature. The same is true for using a directive high task/low relationship style. Sometimes the best way you can show your concern for people and production (9-9) is to direct, control and closely supervise their behavior when they are insecure and don't have the skills yet to perform their job.

In summary, empirical studies tend to show that there is no normative (best) style of leadership.[29] Effective leaders adapt their leader behavior to meet the needs of their followers and the particular environment. If their followers are different, they must be treated differently. Therefore, effectiveness depends on the *leader*, the *follower*(s), and other *situational* variables: $E=f(l, f, s)$. Anyone who is interested in success as a leader must give serious thought to these behavioral and environmental considerations.

We have now discussed a number of approaches to the study of leader behavior, concluding with the Tri-Dimensional Leader Effectiveness model. In Chapter 6 we will discuss the effectiveness dimension in this model.

NOTES

1. Chester A. Schriesheim, James M. Tolliver, and Orlando C. Behling, "Leadership Theory: Some Implications for Managers," *MSU Business Topics*, 22:2 (Summer 1978), pp. 34–40, in William E. Rosenbach and Robert L. Taylor, eds., *Contemporary Issues in Leadership* (Boulder, Colo. Westview Press, 1984), p. 128.

2. Victor Vroom, "Can Leaders Learn to Lead?" *Organizational Dynamics*, 4 (Winter 1976). See also R. Tannenbaum and W. H. Schmidt, "How to Choose a Leadership Pattern," *Harvard Business Review*, July–August 1986, p. 129.

3. These models and theories are frequently cited in management and organizational behavior texts.

4. Robert Tannenbaum and Warren H. Schmidt, "How to Choose a Leadership Pattern," *Harvard Business Review*, May–June 1973. This is an update of their original 1957 article, one of the landmarks in leadership research.

5. *Ibid.*

6. *Ibid.*

7. K. Lewin, R. Lippitt and R. White identified *laissez-faire* as a third form of leadership style. See Lewin, Lippitt, and White, "Leader Behavior and Member Reaction in Three 'Social Climates,'" in *Group Dynamics: Research and Theory*, 2nd ed., Dorwin Cartwright and Alvin Zander, eds. (Evanston, Ill.: Row, Peterson, 1960).

8. Tannenbaum and Schmidt, "How to Choose a Leadership Pattern," *Harvard Business Review*, May–June 1973.

9. Warren G. Bennis, "Where Have All The Leaders Gone?" *Technology Review*, 758:9 (March–April 1977), pp. 3–12.

10. Fred E. Fiedler, *A Theory of Leadership Effectiveness* (New York: McGraw-Hill, 1967). See also Fred E. Fiedler and P. M. Bons, "Changes in Organizational Leadership and the Behavior of Relationship- and Task-motivated Leaders," *Administrative Science Quarterly*, 21 (September 1976), pp. 453–473; Fred E. Fiedler and M. M. Chemers, "Improving Leadership Effectiveness," *Personnel Psychology*, 38 (Spring 1985), pp. 220–222; Fred E. Fiedler and M. M. Chemers, *Improving Leadership Effectiveness: The Leader Match Concept* (New York: Wiley, 1984).

11. *Ibid.*, p. 13.

12. Adapted from Fiedler, *A Theory of Leadership Effectiveness*, p. 14. See also N. H. Snyder, "Leadership: The Essential Quality for Transforming United States Business," *Advanced Management Journal*, 51 (Spring 1986), pp. 15–18.

13. See Chapter 3.

14. See Chapter 3.

15. R. J. House and T. R. Mitchell, "Path-Goal Theory of Leadership," *Journal of Contemporary Business*, Autumn 1974, p. 81. See also Mark J. Knoll and Charles D. Pringle, "Path-Goal Theory and the Task Design Literature: A Tenuous Linkage," *Akron Business and Economic Review*, 17, No. 4 (Winter 1986), pp. 75–83.

16. *Ibid.*

17. *Ibid.*

18. *Ibid*, p. 86.

19. Robert J. House, "A Path-Goal Theory of Leader Effectiveness," *Administrative Science Quarterly*, 16 (1971), pp. 321–338. See also House and G. Dressler, "The Path-Goal Theory of Leadership: Some Post Hoc and a Priori Tests," in J. G. Hunt and L. L. Larson, eds., *Contingency Approaches to Leadship* (Carbondale, Ill.: Southern Illinois University Press, 1974), pp. 29–55.

20. John E. Stinson and Thomas W. Johnson, "The Path-Goal Theory of Leadership: A Partial Test and Suggested Refinement," *Academy of Management Journal*, 18, No. 2 (June 1975), pp. 242–252.

21. Victor H. Vroom and Philip W. Yetton, *Leadership and Decision-Making* (Pittsburgh: University of Pittsburgh Press, 1973), p. 198.

22. Since our model is an outgrowth of the Ohio State Leadership Studies, these definitions have been adapted from their definitions of "Initiating Structure" (task) and "Consideration" (relationship): R. M. Stogdill and Alvin E. Coons, eds. , *Leader Behavior: Its Description and Measurement*, Research monograph no. 88 (Columbus: Bureau of Business Research, Ohio State University, 1957), pp. 42–43.

23. William J. Reddin, "The 3-D Management Style Theory," *Training and Development Journal*, April 1967, pp. 8–17; see also *Managerial Effectiveness* (New York: McGraw-Hill, 1970).

24. Reddin, "The 3-D Management Style Theory," p. 13.

25. Parts of this table were adapted from the managerial style descriptions of William J. Reddin, *The 3-D Management Style Theory*, Theory Paper #2—Managerial Styles (Fredericton, N. B., Canada: Social Science Systems, 1967), pp. 5–6.

26. The first publication on the LEAD (formerly known as the Leader Adaptabilty and Style Inventory [LASI]) appeared as Paul Hersey and Kenneth H. Blanchard, "So You Want to Know Your Leadership Style?" *Training and Development Journal*, February 1974. LEAD instruments are distributed through Center for Leadership Studies, Escondido, Calif.

27. Instrument is available from Center for Leadership Studies, Escondido, Calif.

28. Fiedler in his Contingency Model of Leadership Effectiveness (Fiedler, *A Theory of Leadership Effectiveness*) also tends to make behavioral assumptions from data gathered from an attitudinal measure of leadership style. A leader is asked to evaluate his least preferred co-worker (LPC) on a series of semantic differential type scales. Leaders are classified as high or low LPC depending on the favorableness with which they rate their LPC.

29. See cited research by Owens, House, Bennis, Kerr, and others.

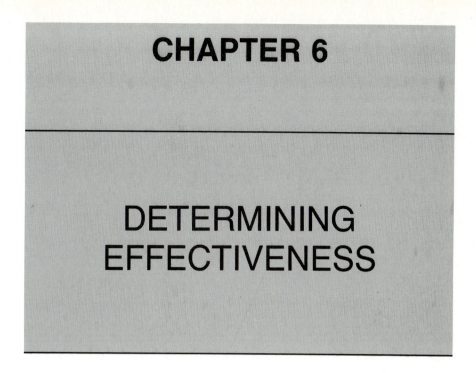

CHAPTER 6

DETERMINING EFFECTIVENESS

One of the most important issues facing the applied behavioral sciences is that of human productivity—the quality and quantity of work. Productivity concerns both effectiveness (the attainment of goals) and efficiency (resource costs, including those human resource costs affecting the quality of life). Our focus in this chapter will be primarily on effectiveness because, as the *Wall Street Journal* has noted, "The first job of the manager is to make the organization perform."[1]

MANAGEMENT EFFECTIVENESS VERSUS LEADERSHIP EFFECTIVENESS

The most important aspect of the Tri-Dimensional Leader Effectiveness Model is that it adds *effectiveness* to the task and relationship dimensions of earlier leadership models. For this reason, it seems appropriate to examine closely the concept of effectiveness.

In discussing effectiveness, it is important once again to distinguish between *management* and *leadership*. As we discussed in Chapter 1, leadership is a broader concept than management. Management is thought of as a special kind of leadership in which the accomplishment of organizational goals is paramount. Leadership is simply an attempt to influence, for whatever reason. Influence and leadership may be used interchangeably. It should be noted that not all of your leadership behavior is directed toward accomplishing organizational goals. In fact, many times when you are trying to influence someone else you are not even part of an organization. For example, when you are trying to get some friends to go someplace with you, you are not engaging in management, but you certainly are attempting leadership. If they agree to go, you are an effective leader but not an effective manager. Even within an organizational setting, managers may attempt to engage in leadership rather than management since they are trying to accomplish personal goals, not organizational ones. For example, a vice-president may have a strong personal goal to become the company president. In attempting to achieve this goal, this executive may not be concerned with organizational goals at all but only with undermining the plans of the president and other executives who may be contenders for the job. The vice-president may accomplish this personal goal and, in that sense, be a successful leader. However, this individual cannot be considered an effective manager because these actions were probably disruptive to the effective operation of the firm. *Parkinson's Law*[2] suggests a clear example of a person's personal goals being placed before organizational goals. His law states that in bureaucracies managers often tend to try to build up their own departments by adding unnecessary personnel, more equipment, or expanded facilities. Although this tendency may increase the prestige and importance of these managers, it often leads to "an organizational environment which not only is inefficient but stifling and frustrating to the individuals who must cope with [it]."[3] Thus, in discussing effectiveness we must recognize the differences between *individual goals, organizational goals, leadership,* and *management.*

SUCCESSFUL LEADERSHIP VERSUS EFFECTIVE LEADERSHIP

If an individual attempts to have some effect on the behavior of another, we call this stimulus *attempted* leadership. The response to this leadership attempt can be successful or unsuccessful. Since a basic responsibility of managers in any type of organization is to get work done with and through people, their success is measured by the output or productivity of the group they lead. With this thought in mind, Bernard M. Bass suggests a clear distinction between *successful* and *effective* leadership or management.[4]

Suppose manager A attempts to influence individual B to do a certain job. A's attempt will be considered successful or unsuccessful depending on the extent to which B accomplishes the job. It is not really an either/or situation. A's success could be depicted on a continuum (Figure 6-1) ranging

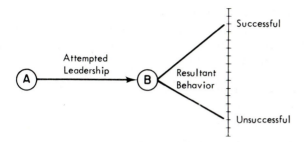

FIGURE 6-1 Successful and unsuccessful leadership continuum

from very successful to very unsuccessful, with gray areas in between that would be difficult to ascertain as either.

Let us assume that A's leadership is successful. In other words, B's response to A's leadership stimulus falls on the successful side of the continuum. This still does not tell the whole story of effectiveness.

If A's leader style is not compatible with the expectations of B, and if B is antagonized and does the job only because of A's position power, then we can say that A has been successful but not effective. B has responded as A intended because A has control of rewards and punishment, and not because B's needs are being accomplished by satisfying the goals of the manager or the organization.

On the other hand, if A's attempted leadership leads to a successful response, and B does the job because it's personally rewarding, then we consider A as having not only position power but also personal power. B respects A and is willing to cooperate, realizing that A's request is consistent with some personal goals. In fact, B sees these personal goals as being accomplished by this activity. This is what is meant by effective leadership, keeping in mind that effectiveness also appears as a continuum that can range from very effective to very ineffective, as illustrated in Figure 6-2.

Success has to do with how the individual or the group behaves. On the other hand, effectiveness describes the internal state, or predisposition of an individual or a group, and thus is attitudinal in nature. If individuals are interested only in success, they tend to emphasize their position power and use close supervision. However, if they are effective, they will also depend on personal power and be characterized by more general supervision. Position power tends to be delegated down through the organization, while personal power is generated upward from below through follower acceptance.

In the management of organizations, the difference between successful and effective often explains why many supervisors can get a satisfactory level of output only when they are right there looking over the worker's

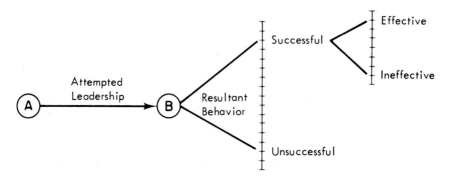

FIGURE 6-2 Successful and effective leadership continuums[5]

shoulder. But as soon as they leave, output declines and often such things as horseplay and scrap loss increase. We have seen this phenomenon occur in schools with some teachers who, if they left the room during an exam, upon returning would find the kids exchanging papers and answers without any regard for rules. Other teachers could leave the room and the kids would behave no differently from the way they would if the teacher were there. In fact, if someone started to cheat, a student might even stop the violator and say, "We don't do that *in this class!*

The phenomenon described applies not only to educational and business organizations but also to less formal organizations such as the family. If parents are successful and effective, have both position and personal power, their children accept family goals as their own. Consequently, if the husband and wife leave for the weekend, the children behave no differently than if their parents were there. If, however, the parents continually use close supervision and the children view their own goals as being stifled by their parents' goals, the parents have only position power. They maintain order because of the rewards and the punishments they control. If these parents went away on a trip leaving the children behind, upon returning they might be greeted by havoc and chaos.

In summary, managers could be successful but ineffective, having only a short-lived influence over the behavior of others. On the other hand, if managers are both successful and effective, their influence tends to lead to long-run productivity and organizational development.

It should be pointed out that this *successful versus effective framework is a way of evaluating the response to a specific behavioral event and not of evaluating performance over time.* Long-term evaluation is not a result of a single leadership event but a summation of many different leadership events. The evaluation of a leader or an organization over time will be discussed in the following section.

WHAT DETERMINES ORGANIZATIONAL EFFECTIVENESS

In discussing effectiveness we have concentrated on evaluating the results of individual leaders or managers. These results are significant, but perhaps the most important aspect of effectiveness is its relationship to an entire organization. Here we are concerned not only with the outcome of a given leadership attempt but with the effectiveness of the organizational unit over a period of time. Rensis Likert identifies three variables—causal, intervening, and end result—which are useful in discussing effectiveness over time.[6]

Causal Variables

Causal variables are those factors that influence the course of developments within an organization and its results or accomplishments. These independent variables can be altered by the organization and its management; they are not beyond the control of the organization, such as general business conditions. Leadership strategies, skills, and behavior; management's decisions; and the policies and structure of the organization are examples of causal variables.

Intervening Variables

Leadership strategies, skills, and behavior, and other causal variables affect the human resources or intervening variables in an organization. According to Likert,[7] intervening variables represent the current condition of the internal state of the organization. They are reflected in the commitment to objectives, motivation, and morale of members and their skills in leadership, communications, conflict resolution, decision making, and problem solving.

Output or End-Result Variables

Output or end-result variables are the dependent variables that reflect the achievements of the organization. In evaluating effectiveness, perhaps more than 90 percent of managers in organizations look at measures of output alone. Thus, the effectiveness of business managers is often determined by net profits; the effectiveness of college professors may be determined by the number of articles and books they have published; and the effectiveness of basketball coaches may be determined by their won—lost record.

Many researchers talk about effectiveness by emphasizing similar output variables. Fred E. Fiedler, for example, in his studies evaluated "leader effectiveness in terms of group performance on the group's primary assigned task."[8] William J. Reddin, in discussing management styles, thinks in similar terms about effectiveness. He argues that the effectiveness of a manager should be measured "objectively by his profit center performance"— maximum output, market share, or other similar criteria.[9]

We might visualize the relationship between the three classes of variables as stimuli (causal variables) acting upon the organism (intervening variables) and creating certain responses (output variables), as illustrated in Figure 6-3.[10]

The level or condition of the intervening variables is produced largely by the causal variables and in turn has influence upon the end-result variables. Attempts by members of the organization to improve the intervening variables by endeavoring to alter these variables directly will be much less successful usually than efforts directed toward modifying them through altering the causal variables. Similarly, efforts to improve the end-result variables by attempting to modify the intervening variables usually will be less effective than changing the causal variables.

Long-Term Goals versus Short-Term Goals

Intervening variables are concerned with building and developing the organization, and they tend to be long-term goals. This is the part of effectiveness that many managers overlook because it emphasizes long-term potential as well as short-term performance. This oversight is understandable because most managers tend to be promoted on the basis of short-term output variables, such as increased production and earnings, without concern for the long-run potential and organizational development. This creates a dilemma.

Organizational Dilemma

One of the major problems in industry today is that there is a shortage of effective managers. Therefore, it is not uncommon for managers to be pro-

FIGURE 6-3 Relationship between causal, intervening, and output variables[11]

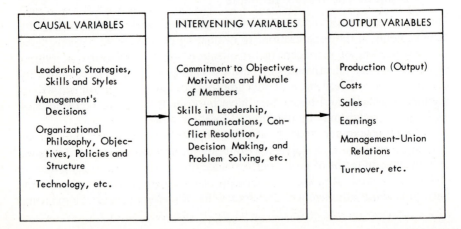

CAUSAL VARIABLES	INTERVENING VARIABLES	OUTPUT VARIABLES
Leadership Strategies, Skills and Styles Management's Decisions Organizational Philosophy, Objectives, Policies and Structure Technology, etc.	Commitment to Objectives, Motivation and Morale of Members Skills in Leadership, Communications, Conflict Resolution, Decision Making, and Problem Solving, etc.	Production (Output) Costs Sales Earnings Management–Union Relations Turnover, etc.

moted in six months or a year if they are "producers." Since the basis on which top management promotes is often short-run output, managers attempt to achieve high levels of productivity and often overemphasize tasks, placing extreme pressure on everyone, even when it is inappropriate.

We probably all have had some experience with coming into an office or a home and raising the roof with people. The immediate or short-run effect is probably increased activity. We also know that if this style is inappropriate for those concerned and if it continues over a long period of time, the morale and climate of the organization will deteriorate. Some indications of deterioration of these intervening variables at work may be turnover, absenteeism, increased accidents, scrap loss, and numerous grievances. Not only the number of grievances but the nature of grievances is important. Are grievances really significant problems or do they reflect pent-up emotions due to anxieties and frustration? Are they settled at the complaint stage between the employee and the supervisor or are they pushed up the hierarchy to be settled at higher levels or by arbitration? The organizational dilemma is that in many instances a manager who places pressure on everyone and produces in the short run is promoted out of this situation before the disruptive aspects of the intervening variables catch up.

There tends to be a time lag between declining intervening variables and significant restriction of output by employees under such a management climate. Employees tend to feel things will get better. Thus, when high-pressure managers are promoted rapidly, they often stay "one step ahead of the wolf."

The real problem is faced by the next manager. Although productivity records are high, this manager has inherited many problems. Merely the introduction of a new manager may be enough to collapse the slowly deteriorating intervening variables. A tremendous drop in morale and motivation leading almost immediately to a significant decrease in output can occur. Change by its very nature is frightening; to a group whose intervening variables are declining, it can be devastating. Regardless of this new manager's style, the present expectations of the followers may be so distorted that much time and patience will be needed to close the now apparent "credibility gap" between the goals of the organization and the personal goals of the group. No matter how effective this manager may be in the long run, superiors in reviewing a productivity drop may give the manager only a few months to improve performance. But as Likert's studies indicate, rebuilding a group's intervening variables in a small organization may take one to three years, and in a large organization it may extend to seven years.

This dilemma is not restricted to business organizations. It is very common in school systems where superintendents and other top administrators can get promoted to better, higher paying jobs in other systems if they are innovative and implement a number of new programs in their systems. One such superintendent brought a small town national prominence by putting every new and innovative idea being discussed in education into a school. In this process, there was almost no involvement or participation by the teachers or building administrator(s) in the decision making that went into these programs. After two years, the superintendent, because of his innovative reputation, was promoted to a larger system with a $15,000-a-year raise. A new superintendent was appointed in the "old" system, but almost before the new superintendent unpacked turmoil hit the system with tremendous teacher turnover, a faculty union, and a defeated bond issue. As things became unglued, people were heard saying that they wished the old superintendent were back. And yet, in reality, it was the old superintendent's very style that deteriorated the intervening variables and set up the trouble that followed the entrance of the new superintendent. Examples in other types of organizations are also available.

Most people tend to evaluate coaches on won-and-lost records. Let's look at an example. Charlie, a high school coach, has had several good seasons. He knows if he has one more such season he will have a job offer with a better salary at a more prestigious school. Under these conditions, he may decide to concentrate on the short-run potential of the team. He may play only his seniors and he may have an impressive record at the end of the season. Short-run output goals have been maximized, but the intervening variables of the team have not been properly used. If Charlie leaves this school and accepts another job, a new coach will find himself with a tremendous rebuilding job. But because developing the freshman and sophomores and rebuilding a good team take time and much work, the team could have a few poor seasons in the interim. When the alumni and fans see the team losing, they soon forget that old adage "It's not whether you win or lose, it's how you play the game." They immediately consider the new coach a bum. After all, "We had some great seasons with good old Charlie." They don't realize that the previous coach concentrated only on short-run winning at the expense of building for the future. The problem is that the effectiveness of a new coach is judged immediately on the same games-won basis as the predecessor. The new coach may be doing an excellent job of rebuilding and may have a winning season in two or three years, but the probability of that coach's being given the opportunity to build a future winner is low. Problems don't occur just when leaders concentrate on output without taking into consideration the condition of the human resources. For example, in the classic World War II movie about the Air Force *Twelve O'Clock High*, Frank Savage (played by Gregory Peck) is asked suddenly to take over a bomber group from a commanding officer whom everyone loves and respects but whose overidentification with his men and concern about his human resources have resulted in an outfit that is not producing and is hurting the war effort.[12]

Thus, it should be clear that we do not think this is an either/or process. It is often a matter of determining how much to concentrate on each—output and intervening variables. In our basketball example, suppose a women's team has good potential, with a large number of experienced senior players, but as the season progresses it does not look as if it is going to be an extremely good year. There comes a point in this season when the coach must make a basic decision. Will she continue to play her experienced seniors and hope to win a majority of her final games, or should she forget about concentrating on winning the last games and play her sophomores and juniors to give them experience, in hopes of developing and building a winning team for future years? The choice is between short- and long-term goals. If the accepted goal is building the team for the future, then the coach should be evaluated on these terms and not entirely on her present won –lost record.

Although intervening variables do not appear on won–lost records, balance sheets, sales reports, or accounting ledgers, we feel that these long-term considerations are just as important to an organization as short-term output variables. Therefore, although difficult to measure, intervening variables should not be overlooked in determining organizational effectiveness. One of the instruments used by Likert to measure these variables was discussed in Chapter 4.

In summary, we feel that effectiveness is actually determined by whatever the manager and the organization decide are their goals and objectives, but they should remember that *effectiveness is a function of*:

1. Output variables (productivity/performance).
2. Intervening variables (the condition of the human resources).
3. Short-range goals.
4. Long-range goals.

FORCE FIELD ANALYSIS

Kurt Lewin

Force field analysis, a technique developed by Kurt Lewin for diagnosing situations, may be useful in looking at the variables involved in determining effectiveness.[13]

Lewin assumes that in any situation there are both driving and restraining forces that influence any change that may occur. *Driving forces* are those forces affecting a situation that are pushing in a particular direction; they tend to initiate a change and keep it going. In terms of improving productivity in a work group, pressure from a supervisor, incentive earnings, and competition may be examples of driving forces. *Restraining forces* are forces acting to restrain or decrease the driving forces. Apathy, hostility, and poor maintenance of equipment may be examples of restraining forces against increased production. Equilibrium is reached when the sum of the driving forces equals the sum of the restraining forces. In our example, equilibrium represents the present level of productivity, as shown in Figure 6-4.

This equilibrium, or present level of productivity, can be raised or lowered by changes in the relationship between the driving and the restraining forces. For illustration, let us look again at the dilemma of the new manager who takes over a work group in which productivity is high but whose predecessor drained the human resources (intervening variables). The former manager had upset the equilibrium by increasing the driving forces (that is, being autocratic and keeping continual pressure on subordinates) and thus achieving increases in output in the short run. By doing this, however, new restraining forces developed, such as increased hostility and antagonism; and at the time of the former manager's departure the restraining forces were beginning to increase and the results manifested themselves in turnover, absenteeism, and other restraining forces, which lowered productivity shortly after the new manager arrived. Now a new equilibrium at a significantly lower productivity is faced by the new manager.

Now just assume that our new manager decides not to increase the driving forces but to reduce the restraining forces. The manager may do this by taking time away from the usual production operation and engaging in problem solving and training and development. In the short run, output will tend to be lowered still further. However, if commitment to objectives and technical know-how of the group are increased in the long run, they may become new driving forces, and that, along with the elimination of the hostility and the apathy that were restraining forces, will now tend to move the balance to a higher level of output.

Managers are often in a position in which they must consider not only

FIGURE 6-4   Driving and restraining forces in equilibrium[14]

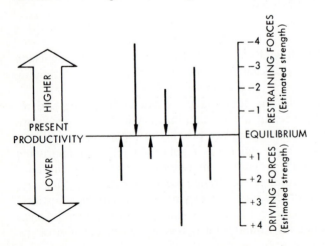

output but also intervening variables and not only short-term but also long-term goals. A framework that is useful in diagnosing these interrelationships is available through force field analysis.

INTEGRATION OF GOALS AND EFFECTIVENESS

The extent that individuals and groups perceive their own goals as being satisfied by the accomplishment of organizational goals is the degree of integration of goals. When organizational goals are shared by all, this is what McGregor calls a true "integration of goals."[15]

To illustrate this concept, we can divide an organization into two groups, management and subordinates. The respective goals of these two groups and the resultant attainment of the goals of the organization to which they belong are illustrated in Figure 6-5.[16]

In this instance, the goals of management are somewhat compatible with the goals of the organization but are not exactly the same. On the other hand, the goals of the subordinates are almost at odds with those of the organization. The result of the interaction between the goals of management and the goals of subordinates is a compromise, and actual performance is a combination of both. It is at this approximate point that the degree of attainment of the goals of the organization can be pictured. This situation can be much worse when there is little accomplishment of organizational goals, as illustrated in Figure 6-6.

In this situation, there seems to be a general disregard for the welfare of the organization. Both managers and workers see their own goals con-

FIGURE 6-5 Directions of goals of management, subordinates, and the organization—*moderate* organizational accomplishment

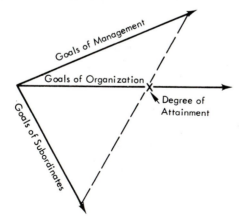

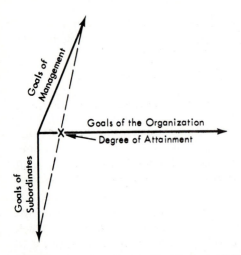

FIGURE 6-6   Little organizational accomplishment

flicting with those of the organization. Consequently, both morale and performance will tend to be low and organizational accomplishment will be negligible. In some cases, the organizational goals can be so opposed that no positive progress is obtained.

The result often is substantial losses, or draining off of assets (see Figure 6-7). In fact, organizations are going out of business every day for these very reasons.

The hope in an organization is to create a climate in which one of two things occurs. The individuals in the organization (both managers and subordinates) either perceive their goals as being the same as the goals of the organization or, although different, see their own goals being satisfied as a direct result of working for the goals of the organization. Consequently, the

FIGURE 6-7   No positive organizational accomplishment

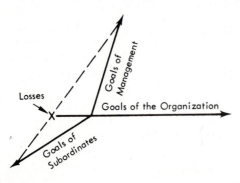

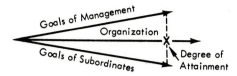

FIGURE 6-8 An integration of the goals of management, subordinates, and the organization—*high* organizational accomplishment

closer we can get the individual's goals and objectives to the organization's goals, the greater will be the organizational performance, as illustrated in Figure 6-8.

One of the ways in which effective leaders bridge the gap between the individual's and the organization's goals is by creating a loyalty to themselves among their followers. They do this by being an influential spokesperson for followers with higher management.[17] These leaders have no difficulty in communicating organizational goals to followers, and these people do not find it difficult to associate the acceptance of these goals with accomplishment of their own need satisfaction.

PARTICIPATION AND EFFECTIVENESS

In an organizational setting, it is urged that the criteria for an individual's or a group's performance should be mutually decided in advance. In making these decisions, managers and their subordinates should consider output and intervening variables, short- and long-range goals. This process has two advantages. First, it will permit subordinates to participate in determining the basis on which their efforts will be judged. Second, involving subordinates in the planning process will increase their commitment to the goals and objectives established. Research evidence seems to support this contention.

One of the classic studies in this area was done by Coch and French in an American factory.[18] They found that when managers and employees discussed proposed technological changes, productivity increased and resistance to change decreased when these procedures were initiated. Other studies have shown similar results.[19] These studies suggest that involving employees in decision making tends to be effective in our society. Once again, we must remember that the success of using participative management depends on the situation. Although this approach tends to be effective in some industrial settings in America, it may not be appropriate in other countries.

This argument was illustrated clearly when French, Israel, and Ås attempted to replicate the original Coch and French experiment in a Norwegian factory.[20] In this setting, they found no significant difference in productivity between work groups in which participative management was used and those in which it was *not* used. In other words, increased participation in decision making did not have the same positive influence on factory workers in Norway as it did in America. Similar to Hersey's replication of one of Likert's studies in Nigeria, this Norwegian study suggests that cultural differences in the followers and the situation may be important in determining the appropriate leadership style.

Management by Objectives

We realize that it is not an easy task to integrate the goals and objectives of all individuals with the goals of the organization. Yet it is not an impossible task. A participative approach to this problem, which has been used successfully in some organizations in our culture, is a process called *Management by Objectives* (MBO). The concepts behind MBO were introduced by Peter Drucker[21] in the early 1950s and have become popularized throughout the world, particularly through the efforts of George Odiorne[22] and John Humble.[23] Through their work and the efforts of others,[24] managers in all kinds of organizational settings, whether they be industrial, educational, governmental, or military, are attempting to run their organizations with the MBO process as a basic underlying management concept.

Management by objectives is basically:

> A process whereby the superior and the subordinate managers of an enterprise jointly identify its common goals, define each individual's major areas of responsibility in terms of the results expected of him, and use these measures as guides for operating the unit and assessing the contribution of each of its members.[25]

This process in some cases has been successfully carried beyond the managerial level to include hourly employees. The concept rests on a philosophy of management that emphasizes an integration between external control (by managers) and self-control (by subordinates). It can apply to any manager or individual no matter what level or function, and to any organization, regardless of size.

The smooth functioning of this system is an agreement between a manager and a subordinate about that subordinate's own or group performance goals during a stated time period. These goals can emphasize either output variables or intervening variables or some combination of both. The important thing is that goals are jointly established and agreed upon in advance. This is then followed by a review of the subordinate's peformance in relation to accepted goals at the end of the time period. Both superior and subordinate participate in this review and in any other evaluation that takes place. It has been found that objectives that are formulated with each person participating seem to gain more acceptance than those imposed by an authority figure in the organization. Consultation and participation in this area tend to establish personal risk for the attainment of the formulated objective by those who actually perform the task.

Prior to setting individual objectives, the common goals of the entire organization should be clarified, and, at this time, any appropriate changes in the organizational structure should be made: changes in titles, duties, relationships, authority, responsibility, span of control, and so forth.

Throughout the time period, what is to be accomplished by the entire organization should be compared with what is being accomplished; necessary adjustments should be made and inappropriate goals discarded. At the end of the time period, a final mutual review of objectives and performance takes place. If there is a discrepancy between the two, efforts are initiated to determine what steps can be taken to overcome these problems. This sets the stage for the determination of objectives for the next time period.

The entire cycle of management by objectives is represented graphically in Figure 6-9.[26]

FIGURE 6-9   The cycle of management by objectives

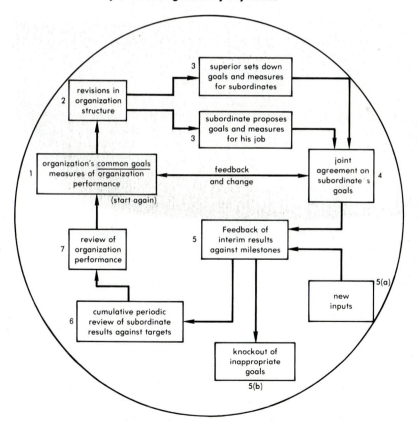

Management by objectives may become a powerful tool in gaining mutual commitment and high productivity for an organization in which management realizes this type of involvement of subordinates is appropriate in its situation.

STYLE AND EFFECTIVENESS

Examples of research that support the argument that all the basic leader behavior styles may be effective or ineffective depending on the situation are readily available.

A. K. Korman gathered some of the most convincing evidence that dispels the idea of a single best style of leader behavior.[27] Korman attempted to review all studies that examined the relationships between the Ohio State behavior dimensions of Initiating Structure (task) and Consideration (relationship) and various measures of effectiveness, including group productivity, salary, performance under stress, administrative reputation, work group grievances, absenteeism, and turnover. In all, more than twenty-five studies were reviewed. In every case the two dimensions were measured by either the Leadership Opinion Questionnaire or the Leader Behavior Description Questionnaire. The former is used to assess how leaders think they should behave in a given situation; the latter measures follower perceptions of leader behavior. Korman concluded that:

> Despite the fact that "Consideration" and "Initiating Structure" have become almost bywords in American industrial psychology, it seems apparent that very little is now known as to how these variables may predict work group performance and the conditions which affect such predictions. At the current time, we cannot even say whether they have any predictive significance at all.[28]

Thus, Korman found that Consideration and Initiating Structure had no significant predictive value in terms of effectiveness. This suggests that since situations differ, so must leader style.

Fred Fiedler, in testing his contingency model of leadership in more than fifty studies covering a span of sixteen years (1951−67), concluded that both directive, task-oriented leaders and nondirective, human relations-oriented leaders are successful under some conditions. As Fiedler argues:

> While one can never say that something is impossible, and while someone may well discover the all-purpose leadership style or behavior at some future time, our own data and those which have come out of sound research by other investigators do not promise such miraculous cures.[29]

A number of other investigators besides Korman and Fiedler have also shown that *different leadership situations require different leader styles*.[30] In summary, the evidence is clear that there is no single all-purpose leader behavior style that is effective in all situations.

While our basic conclusion in this chapter is that the type of leader behavior needed depends on the situation, this conclusion leaves many questions unanswered for a specific individual in a leadership role. Such individuals may be personally interested in how leadership depends on the situation and how they can find some practical value in theory. To accommodate this type of concern, in Chapter 7 we will discuss the environmental variables that may help a leader or a manager to make effective decisions in problematic leadership situations.

NOTES

1. *Wall Street Journal*, January 9, 1978, p. 12.
2. C. Northcote Parkinson, *Parkinson's Law* (Boston: Houghton Mifflin, 1957).
3. Fred J. Carvell, *Human Relations in Business* (Toronto: Macmillan, 1970), p. 182.
4. Suggested by Bernard M. Bass in *Leadership, Psychology, and Organizational Behavior* (New York: Harper & Brothers, 1960).
5. *Ibid.*
6. Rensis Likert, *The Human Organization* (New York: McGraw-Hill, 1967), pp. 26-29.
7. Rensis Likert, *New Patterns of Management* (New York: McGraw-Hill, 1961), p. 2.
8. Fred E. Fiedler, *A Theory of Leadership Effectiveness* (New York: McGraw-Hill, 1967), p. 9.
9. William J. Reddin, "The 3-D Management Style Theory," *Training and Development Journal*, April 1967. This is one of the critical differences between Reddin's 3-D Management Style Theory and the Tri-Dimensional Leader Effectiveness Model. Reddin in his model seems to consider only output variables in determining effectiveness, while in the Tri-Dimensional Leader Effectiveness Model both intervening variables and output variables are considered.
10. Adapted from Likert, *The Human Organization*, pp. 47–77.
11. *Ibid.*
12. This classic film is an excellent illustration of the concepts of motivation, Situational Leadership, and improving organizational performance.
13. Kurt Lewin, "Frontiers in Group Dynamics: Concept, Method, and Reality in Social Science; Social Equilibria and Social Change," *Human Relations*, 1, No. 1 (June 1947), pp. 5–41.
14. *Ibid.*
15. Douglas McGregor, *The Human Side of Enterprise* (New York: McGraw-Hill, 1960). See also McGregor, *Leadership and Motivation* (Boston: MIT Press, 1966).
16. In reality, the schematics presented in the following pages are simplifications of vector analyses and therefore would be more accurately portrayed as parallelograms.
17. Saul W. Gellerman, *Motivation and Productivity* (New York: American Management Association, 1963), p. 265. See also Gelleman, *Management by Motivation* (New York: American Management Association, 1968).
18. L.Coch and J. R. P. French, "Overcoming Resistance to Change," in Dorwin Cartwright and Alvin Zander, eds., *Group Dynamics: Research and Theory*, 2nd ed. (Evanston, Ill.: Row, Peterson, 1960).
19. See Kurt Lewin, "Group Decision and Social Change," In G. Swanson, T. Newcomb, and E. Hartley, eds., *Readings in Social Psychology* (New York: Henry Holt, 1952), pp. 459–73; K. Lewin, R. Lippitt, and R. White, "Leader Behavior and Member Reaction in Three 'Social Climates,' " in Cartwright and Zander, *Group Dynamics: Research and Theory*; and N. Morse and E. Reimer, "The Experimental Change of a Major Organizational Variable," *Journal of Abnormal Social Psychology*, 52(1956), pp. 120–29.

20. John R. P. French, Jr., Joachim Israel, and Dagfinn Ās, "An Experiment on Participation in a Norwegian Factory," *Human Relations*, 13 (1960), pp. 3−19.

21. Peter F. Drucker, *The Practice of Management* (New York: Harper and Row, 1964).

22. George S. Odiorne, *Management by Objectives: A System of Managerial Leadership* (New York: Pitman Publishing, 1965); Odiorne, *The Human Side of Management* (San Diego, Calif.: University Associates, 1987); Odiorne et al., *Executive Skills: A Management Objectives Approach* (Dubuque, Iowa: Brown, 1980); Odiorne, *MBO II: A System of Managerial Leadership for the 80's* (Belmont, Calif.: Pitman, Learning, 1979); Odiorne, "The Managerial Bait-and-Switch Game," *Personnel*, 63, No. 3 (March 1986), pp. 32−37.

23. John W. Humble, *Management by Objectives* (London: Industrial Education and Research Foundation, 1967); Humble, *Management Objectives in Action* (New York: McGraw-Hill, 1970).

24. See also J. D. Batten, *Beyond Management by Objectives (New York: American Management Association, 1966);* Ernest C. Miller, *Objectives and Standards Approach to Planning and Control*, AMA Research Study '74 (New York: American Management Association, 1966); and William J. Reddin, *Effective Management by Objectives: The 3-D Method of MBO* (New York: McGraw-Hill, 1971).

25. Odiorne, *Management by Objectives, pp. 55−56.*

26. *Ibid.*, p. 78.

27. A. K. Korman, " 'Consideration, Initiating Structure,' and Organizational Criteria—A Review," *Personnel Psychology: A Journal of Applied Research*, 19, No. 4 (Winter 1966), pp. 349−61.

28. *Ibid.*, p. 360.

29. Fiedler, *A Theory of Leadership Effectiveness*, p. 247.

30. See C. A. Gibb, "Leadership," in *Handbook of Social Psychology*, Gardner Lindzey, ed. (Cambridge, Mass.:L Addison-Wesley, 1964); A. P. Hare, *Handbook of Small Group Research* (New York: Wiley, 1965); and D. C. Pelz, "Leadership within a Hierarchial Organization," *Journal of Social Issues*, 7 (1961), pp. 49−55. See also J. R. Nicholls, "Congruent Leadership," *Leadership and Organization Review Journal*, 7, No. 1 (1986), pp. 27−31; John H. Zenger, "Leadership: Management's Better Half," *Training*, 22, No. 12 (December 1985), pp. 44ff. See also previously cited research by Bennis, Schriesheim, Yukl, Kerr, and many others.

CHAPTER 7

DIAGNOSING THE ENVIRONMENT

The situational approach to leadership is built on the concept that effectiveness results from a leader's using a behavioral style that is appropriate to the demands of the environment. The key for managers or leaders is learning to diagnose their environment, the first of the three important leadership competencies.

ENVIRONMENTAL VARIABLES

The environment in an organization consists of the leader, that leader's follower(s), superior(s), associates, organization, and job demands.[1] This list is not all-inclusive, but it contains some of the interacting components that tend to be important to a leader.[2] As illustrated in Figure 7-1, the environment a leader faces may have some other situational variables that are unique to it, as well as an external environment that has an impact on it.

Except for job demands, each of these environmental variables can be viewed as having two major components—style and expectations. Thus, our list of variables is expanded to include the following:

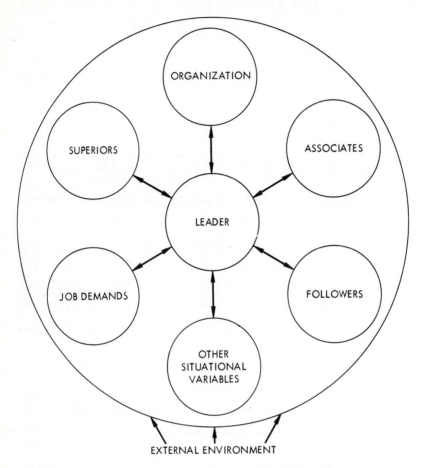

FIGURE 7-1   Interacting components of an organizational setting

Leader's style	Leader's expectations
Followers' styles	Followers' expectations
Superiors' styles	Superiors' expectations
Associates' styles	Associates' expectations
Organization's style	Organization's expectations

Job demands

Style Defined

As discussed in Chapter 5, the style of leaders is the consistent behavior patterns that they use when they are working with and through other people, as perceived by those people. These patterns emerge in people as they begin to respond in the same fashion under similar conditions; they develop habits of action that become somewhat predictable to those who work with them.

Some writers, including the authors of this text, have used style and personality interchangeably. In Chapter 10 we will distinguish between these two terms.

Expectations Defined

Expectations are the perceptions of appropriate behavior for one's own role or position or one's perception of the roles of others within the organization. In other words, the expectations of individuals define for them what they should do under various circumstances in their particular job and how they think others—their superiors, peers, and subordinates—should behave in relation to their positions. To say that a person has *shared expectations* with another person means that each of the individuals involved perceives accurately and accepts a personal role and the role of the other. If expectations are to be compatible, it is important to share common goals and objectives. While two individuals may have differing personalities because their roles require different styles of behavior, it is imperative for an organization's effectiveness that they perceive and accept the institution's goals and objectives as their own.

The task of diagnosing a leader environment is very complex when we realize that the leader is the pivotal point around which all of the other environmental variables interact, as shown in Figure 7-1. In a sense, all these variables are communicating role expectations to the leader.

STYLE AND EXPECTATIONS

The behavior of managers in an organization, as Jacob W. Getzels suggests, results from the interaction of style and expectations.[3] Some managerial positions or roles are structured greatly by expectations; that is, they allow people occupying that position very little room to express their individual style. The behavior of an army sergeant, for example, may be said to conform almost completely to role expectations. Little innovative behavior is tolerated. In supervising highly structured, routine jobs based on Theory X assumptions about human nature, the behavior required by a manager is almost predetermined, that is, close supervision, firm but fair, and so on.

On the other hand, some managerial positions have fewer formal expectations, allowing for more individual latitude in expressing one's style of operating. The behavior of a research and development manager, for example, is derived extensively from that person's style, as innovation and creativity are encouraged. It seems that as a manager moves from supervising a

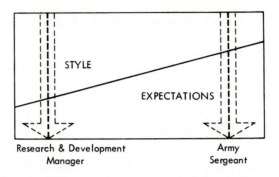

Research & Development
Manager

Army
Sergeant

FIGURE 7-2 Style and expectations as related to two different positions or roles

structured job to working with people on a more structured job, style tends to play a more important role than expectations.

The difference between these two positions in terms of style and expectations is illustrated in Figure 7-2.[4]

While the mix varies from job to job, behavior in an organization remains a function of both style and expectations and involves some combination of task and relationship orientation.

Leader's Style and Expectations

One of the most important elements of a leadership situation is the style of the leader(s). Leaders develop their style over a period of time from experience, education, and training. Tannenbaum and Schmidt suggest there are at least four internal forces that influence a manager's leadership style: the manager's value system, confidence in subordinates, leadership inclinations, and feelings of security in an uncertain situation.[5]

A manager's value system consists of the answers to such questions as how strongly does a manager feel that individuals should have a share in making the decisions that affect them or how convinced is the manager that the person who is paid to assume responsibility should personally carry the burden of decision making? The strength of a manager's convictions on questions such as these will tend to affect that manager's leadership style, particularly in terms of the amount of direction or support that manager is willing to provide for staff members.

Confidence in subordinates is often influenced by the manager's Theory X or Theory Y assumptions about human nature. In other words, the amount of control or freedom a manager gives to staff members depends on whether that manager believes that people are basically lazy, unreliable, or irresponsible or that people can be creative and self-motivated in an environment if properly motivated. In addition, a manager's confidence in subordinates also depends on feelings about the knowledge and competence of staff members in a particular area of responsibility.

A manager's own inclinations have an impact on leadership style; thus, some managers are much more comfortable being directive (controlling and supervising). Other managers operate more comfortably in a team management situation in which they are providing some direction and/or facilitating the interactions of subordinates. Still other managers are at ease in delegating and letting staff members run with the ball on specific problems and issues.

Feelings of security in an uncertain situation have a definite impact on the manager's willingness to release control over decision making to other people in an uncertain environment. What might be involved here is the manager's tolerance for ambiguity. Another factor that might be influenced is the leader's life position in terms of personal feelings of OKness, as well as OKness about others in the environment.

While it important to recognize that managers have different leadership styles, it is important to remember that style is not how leaders *think* they behave in a situation but how others (most importantly, their followers) perceive their behavior. This is often a difficult concept for leaders to understand. For example, if Jane's followers think that she is a hard-nosed, task-oriented leader, this is very valuable information for her to know. In fact, it makes little difference whether *she* thinks she is a relationship-oriented, democratic leader because her followers will behave according to how *they* perceive her behavior. In this case, the followers will treat the leader as if she were a hard-nosed, task-oriented leader. Thus, leaders have to learn how they are coming across to others. Yet this kind of information is difficult to obtain. People are often reluctant to be honest with one another on this subject, especially in a superior—subordinate relationship.

One method that has been developed to help individuals learn how others perceive their behavior is sensitivity, or T-group, training. This method was developed at Bethel, Maine, in 1947 by Leland P. Bradford, Kenneth D. Benne, and others.[6] It is based on the assumption that a number of individuals meeting in an unstructured situation in an open climate will develop working relations with each other and will learn a great deal about themselves, as perceived by the other group members.

> The training process relies primarily and almost exclusively on the behavior experienced by the participants; i.e., the *group itself* becomes the focus of inquiry. . . . In short, the participants learn to analyze and become more sensitive to the processes of human interaction and acquire concepts to order and control these phenomena.[7]

An example follows of one of Chris Argyris's experiences with a T-group in which the president and nine vice-presidents of a large industrial organization went to a retreat for a week to discuss their problems.

At the outset, after defining the objectives of this educational experience, the seminar leader said, in effect, "Okay. Let's go." There was a very loud silence and someone said, "What do you want us to do?"

(Silence.)

"Where's the agenda?"

(Silence.)

"Look, here, what's going on? Aren't you going to lead this?"

(Silence.)

"I didn't come up here to feel my stomach move. What's up?"

(Silence.)

"Fellows, if he doesn't speak in five minutes, I'm getting out of here."

"Gentlemen," said the treasurer, "We've paid for the day, so let's remain at least till five."

"You know, there's something funny going on here."

"What's funny about it?"

"Well, up until a few minutes ago we trusted this man enough that all of us were willing to leave the company for a week. Now we dislike him. Why? He hasn't done anything."

"That's right. And it's his job to do something. He's the leader and he ought to lead."

"But I'm learning something already about how we react under these conditions. I honestly feel uncomfortable and somewhat fearful. Does anybody else?"

"That's interesting that you mention fear, because I think that we run the company by fear."

The president turned slightly red and became annoyed: "I don't think that we run this company by fear and I don't think you should have said that."

A loud silence followed. The vice-president thought for a moment, took a breath, looked the president straight in the eye and said, "I still think we run this company by fear and I agree with you. I should not have said it."

The group laughed and the tension was broken.

"I'm sorry," the president said, "I wanted all you fellows with me here so that we can try to develop a higher sense of openness and trust. The first one that really levels with us, I let him have it. I'm sorry—but it isn't easy to hear about management by fear. . . ."

"And it's not easy to tell you."

"Why not? Haven't I told you that my door is open?"

And the group plunged into the issue of how they judge the openness of a person—by the way he speaks or by the way he behaves?[8]

Argyris reported that:

The group explored their views about each other—the way each individual tended unintentionally to inhibit the other (the vice-presidents learned that they inhibited each other as much as the president did but for years had felt it was his fault); their levels of aspiration, their goals in their company life and in their total life; their ways of getting around each other, ranging from not being honest with one another to creating organizational fires which had to be put out by someone else; their skill at polarizing issues when deep disagreements occurred so that the decisions could be bucked right up to the president, who would have to take the responsibility and the blame; their techniques in the game of one-upmanship. . . .[9]

The result was highly satisfying. Once these top executives returned home, they found that they could reduce the number of meetings, the time spent at meetings, the defensive politicking, and the windmilling at the lower levels. In time they also found that they could truly delegate more responsibility, get more valid information up from the ranks, and make decisions more freely.

Although the main objective of T-group training was originally personal growth or self-insight, the process has been used extensively to implement organizational improvement or change.[10] It has some critics as well as advocates among organizations that have experimented with these techniques.

A central problem according to some is that sensitivity training is designed to change individuals, not necessarily to change the environment in which they work. When individuals attempt to use what they have learned, they often find their co-workers unwilling to accept it or, even worse, what they have learned may not be appropriate for their back-home situation. In an article from the *Wall Street Journal* entitled "The Truth Hurts," an example was cited in which this very thing happened:

> A division manager at one big company was described by a source familiar with his case as "a ferocious guy—brilliant but a thoroughgoing autocrat—who everyone agreed was just what the division needed, because it was a tough, competitive business." Deciding to smooth over his rough edges, the company sent him to sensitivity training, where he found out exactly what people thought of him. "So he stopped being a beast," says the source, "and his effectiveness fell apart." The reason he'd been so good was that he didn't realize what a beast he was. Eventually, they put in a new manager.

All leaders have expectations about the way they should behave in a certain situation. How they actually behave often depends on these expectations. The resulting behavior, however, is sometimes modified by the impact of how they interpret the expectations of other persons in their environment, such as their boss or subordinates.

Followers' Styles and Expectations

The styles of followers (subordinates) are an important consideration for leaders in appraising their situation. In fact, as Fillmore Sanford has indicated, there is some justification for regarding the followers "as the most crucial factor in any leadership event."[11] Followers in any situation are vital, not only because individually they accept or reject the leader but because as a group they actually determine whatever personal power that leader will have. If the follower decides not to follow, it really doesn't matter what the other elements in the situation are.

This is important at all levels of management. Victor H. Vroom has uncovered evidence that the effectiveness of a leader is dependent to a great extent on the style of the individual workers.[12]

> Place a group with strong independence drives under a supervisor who needs to keep his men under his thumb, and the result is very likely to be trouble. Similarly, if you take docile men who are accustomed to obedience and respect for their supervisors and place them under a supervisor who tries to make them manage their own work, they are likely to wonder uneasily whether he really knows what he is doing.[13]

It has been argued that a manager can permit subordinates greater freedom if the following essential conditions exist:[14]

> If the subordinates have relatively high needs for independence.
> If the subordinates have a readiness to assume responsibility for decision making.
> If they have a relatively high tolerance for ambiguity.
> If they are interested in the problem and feel it is important.
> If they understand and identify with the goals of the organization.
> If they have the necessary knowledge and experience to deal with the problem.
> If they have learned to expect to share in decision making.

Therefore, even though managers would prefer to change their followers' styles, they may find that they must adapt, at least temporarily, to the followers' present behavior. For example, a supervisor who wants subordinates to take more responsibility and to operate under general rather than close supervision cannot expect this kind of change to take place overnight. The supervisor's current behavior, at least to some extent, must be compatible with the present expectations of the group, with planned change taking place over a long-term period. We have seen numerous examples of the need for this kind of diagnosis in schools where humanistic teachers have tried to turn over significant responsibility to students without recognizing that many of these students expect teachers to tell them what to do. This rapid change in style often produces irresponsibility rather than more student initiative.

Leaders should know the expectations that followers have about the way they should behave in certain situations. This is especially important if leaders are new in their position. Their predecessor's leader behavior style is then a powerful influence. If this style is different from the one they plan to use, this may create an immediate problem.[15] Leaders must either change their style to coincide with followers' expectations or change follower expectations. Since the style of leaders often has been developed over a long period of time, it can be difficult for them to make any drastic changes in the short run. It may, therefore, be more effective if leaders concentrate on changing the expectations of their followers. In other words, in some cases they may be able to convince their followers that their style, although not what they as followers would normally expect, if accepted, will be adequate.

Superiors' Styles and Expectations

Another element of the environment is the leadership style of one's boss. By "boss" we mean the leader's leader. Just about everyone has a boss of one kind or another. Most managers give considerable attention to supervising subordinates, but some do not pay enough attention to being a subordinate themselves. Yet meeting the superior's expectations is often an important factor affecting one's style, particularly if one's boss is located in close proximity. If a boss is very task oriented, for example, the boss might expect subordinate(s) to operate in the same manner. Relationship-oriented behavior might be evaluated as inappropriate, without even considering results. This has become evident when first-line supervisors are sent to training programs to improve their human relations skills. Upon returning to the company, they try to implement some of these new ideas in working with their people. Yet, because the superior has not accepted these concepts, the superior becomes impatient with the first-line supervisor's newfound concern for people: "Joe, cut out all that talking with the men and get the work done." With such reactions, it would not take this supervisor long to revert to the previous style, and in the future, it will be much more difficult to implement any behavioral change.

It is important for managers to know their boss's expectations, particularly if they want to advance in the organization. If they are predisposed toward promotion, they may tend to adhere to the customs and mores (styles and expectations) of the group to which they aspire to join rather than those of their peer group.[16] Consequently, their superiors' expectations may become more important to them than those of the other groups with which they interact—their followers or associates.

The importance of the expectations of one's boss and the effect it can have on leadership style was vividly illustrated by Robert H. Guest in a case analysis of organizational change.[17] He examined a large assembly plant of an automobile company, Plant Y, and contrasted the situation under two different leaders.

Under Stewart, the plant manager, working relationships at Plant Y were dominated by hostility and mistrust. His high task style was characterized by continual attempts to increase the driving forces pushing for productivity. As a result, the prevailing atmosphere was that of one emergency following on the heels of another, and the governing motivation for employee activity was fear—fear of being chewed out right on the assembly line, fear of being held responsible for happenings in which one had no clear authority, fear of losing one's job. Consequently, of the six plants in this division of the corporation, Plant Y had the poorest performance record, and it was getting worse.

Stewart was replaced by Cooley, who seemed like an extremely effective leader. Over the next three years dramatic changes took place. In various cost and performance measures used to rate the six plants, Plant Y was now truly the leader; and the atmosphere of interpersonal cooperation and personal satisfaction had improved impressively over the situation under Stewart. These changes, moreover, were efffected through an insignificant number of dismissals and reassignments. Using a much higher relationship style, Cooley succeeded in turning Plant Y around.

On the surface, the big difference was style of leadership. Cooley was a good leader. Stewart was not. But Guest points out clearly in his analysis that leadership style was only one of two important factors. The other was that while Stewart received daily orders from division headquarters to correct specific situations, Cooley was left alone. Cooley was allowed to lead; Stewart was told how to lead.[18] In other words, when productivity in Plant Y began to decline during changeover from wartime to peacetime operations, Stewart's superiors expected him to get productivity back on the upswing by taking control of the reins, and they put tremendous pressure on him to do just that. Guest suggests that these expectations forced Stewart to operate in a very crisis-oriented, autocratic way. However, when Cooley was given charge as plant manager, a hands-off policy was initiated by his superiors. The fact that the expectations of top management had changed enough to put a moratorium on random troublesome outside stimuli from headquarters gave Cooley an opportunity to operate in a completely different style.

Associates' Styles and Expectations

A leader's associates, or peers, are those individuals who have similar positions within the organization. For example, the associates of a vice-president for production are the other vice-presidents in the company; the associates of a teacher would be other teachers. Yet not all associates are significant for leaders; only those they interact with regularly are going to have impact on their style and effectiveness.

The styles and expectations of one's associates are important when a leader has frequent interactions with them, for example, a situation that involves trading and bargaining for resources such as budget money.[19]

In discussing superiors, we mentioned the manager who has a strong drive to advance in an organization. Some people, however, are satisfied with their present positions. For these people, the expectations of their associates may be more important in influencing their behavior than those of their superiors. College professors tend to be good examples. Often they are more concerned about their peer group, other professors, or colleagues in their area of expertise than they are in being promoted to administrative positions. As a result, college presidents and deans often have little position power with professors.

Organization's Style and Expectations

The style and expectations of an organization are determined by the history and tradition of the organization, as well as by the organizational goals and objectives that reflect the style and expectations of present top management.

Over a period of time, an organization, much like an individual, becomes characterized by certain modes of behavior that are perceived as its style. The development of an organizational style, or corporate image, has been referred to as the process of institutionalization.[20] In this process, the organization is infused with a system of values that reflects its history and the people who have played vital roles in its formation and growth. Thus, it is difficult to understand Ford Motor Company without knowing the impact that Henry Ford had on its formation. Some organizations, for example, hold to the notion that the desirable executive is one who is dynamic, imaginative, decisive, and persuasive. Other organizations put more emphasis on the importance of the executive's ability to work effectively with people—human relations skills.[21]

Members of the organization soon become conscious of the value system operating within the institution and guide their actions from many expectations derived from these values. The organization's expectations are most often expressed in forms of policy, operating procedures, and controls, as well as in informal customs and mores developed over time.

Organizational goals. The goals of an organization usually consist of some combination of output and intervening variables. As we discussed earlier, output variables are those short-run goals that can easily be measured, such as net profits, annual earnings, and won−lost records. On the other hand, intervening variables consist of those long-run goals reflecting the internal condition of the organization that *cannot* easily be measured, such as its capacity for effective interaction, communication, and decision making. These organizational goals can be expressed in terms of task and relationship, as illustrated in Figure 7-3.

OTHER SITUATIONAL VARIABLES

Job Demands

Another important element of a leadership situation is the demands of the job that the leader's group has been assigned to perform. Fiedler[22] called this situation variable *task structure*—the degree of structure in the task that the group has been asked to do. He found that a task that has specific instructions on what leaders and their followers should do requires a different leadership style than an unstructured task with no prescribed operating procedure.[23] Research findings indicate that highly structured jobs that

155

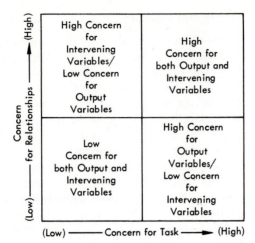

FIGURE 7-3 Organizational goals as expressed in terms of task and relationship

need directions seem to require high task behavior, while unstructured jobs that do not need directions seem to favor relationship-oriented behavior.[24]

The *amount of interaction* the job requires of subordinates is an important consideration for managers in analyzing their work environment. Victor H. Vroom and Floyd C. Mann studied this aspect of a job in a large trucking company.[25] They investigated two groups of workers. One group was involved in the package and handling operation and the other consisted of truck drivers and their dispatchers. The nature of the work in the package and handling operation required that the men work closely together in small groups. Cooperation and teamwork were required not only among the workers but also between the workers and their superiors. In this situation, the workers preferred and worked better under employee-centered supervisors. The truck drivers, on the other hand, usually worked alone, having little contact with other people. These men did not depend on others for accomplishing their task, except for the dispatchers from whom they needed accurate information. Since the truck drivers generally worked alone, they were not concerned about harmony but were concerned about the structure of the job in terms of where and when they were to deliver or pick up. In this situation, they preferred task-oriented supervisors.

Another important aspect of job demands that managers should consider is the type of control system being used. In our work, we have identified three types of control systems, as shown in Figure 7-4.

As illustrated, Type I shows the simplest and most structured of the control systems. The boss controls the activities of three separate functions and the horizontal arrows show the work moving in an assembly-line fashion to completion.

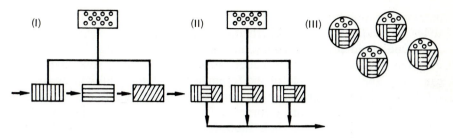

FIGURE 7-4 Three fundamental types of control systems

Type II depicts an organization in which work has been "enlarged." The boss still controls the activities of three people but now all three functions are combined in each job and the three employees see end-product results (vertical arrows).

Type III is the least structured organization model ("enriched"), with each employee having the advantage of Type II plus decision-making responsibility, reserved only for the boss in Types I and II.

In an example of producing booklets, under a Type I control system employee A is responsible for typing, B for mimeographing, and C for proofreading. The boss is responsible for coordination, end results, and customer relations.

In Type II, job enlargement takes place, and the boss is now responsible for directing the activities of three people who type, mimeograph, and proofread their own work. Here, some motivational or job satisfaction considerations come into play. The boss gets satisfaction by relating directly to the customer (or persons needing booklets). The employees' satisfaction comes closer to being served in Type II since they can now see a new dimension of their work, and psychologically they come closer to understanding the customer.

In Type III, all four members of the group act as separate decision-making and functional units, having the advantages reserved for only the manager in Types I and II: contact with the customer and control of work.

Time

Another important element in the environment of a leader is the *time available for decision making*. If a manager's office burst into flames, he could not seek opinions and suggestions from his followers or use other methods of involvement to determine the best way to leave the building. The leader must make an immediate decision and point the way. Therefore, short-time demands, such as in an emergency, tend to require task-oriented behavior. On the other hand, if time is not a major factor in the situation, there is more opportunity for the leader to select from a broader range of leadership styles, depending on the other situational variables.

One could probably enumerate many more variables. For example, even the physical stature of a leader can affect the kind of style that leader can use. Take the example of the foreman in the steel mill who is six feet six inches tall and weighs over two hundred fifty pounds. He may be able to use a different style than a foreman five feet four inches tall weighing ninety-eight pounds, since their subordinates' expectations about their behavior will probably be influenced by their physical appearance. Sex may be similar. For example, some men may respond and interact very differently with a female boss, associate, or subordinate than a male, and vice versa. This undoubtedly is influenced by the amount of past experience one has had in working with members of the opposite sex. But it certainly may be a situational variable worth examining in a leadership environment.

The kinds of environmental variables we have been discussing tend to be important whether one is concerned about an educational, an informal, or a business organization. But specific organizations may have additional variables unique to themselves that must be evaluated before determining effectiveness.

External Environment

Years ago, managers didn't worry much about the external environment because it didn't seem to affect them or their decisions. Today, this is no longer true. Organizations are continually influenced by external variables. Reality dictates that organizations do not exist in a vacuum but are continually affected in numerous ways by changes in the society.

In the last several decades we have been bombarded by numerous movements that have challenged many of our society's core beliefs and practices. Consider the implications for organizations of such social developments as the youth revolution and its distrust and contempt for the "establishment"; the civil rights movement and the opening of wider opportunities in organizations for all minority groups; the ecology and consumer movements and their demands on organizations from the outside; and the increasing widespread concern for the quality of working life and its relationship to worker productivity, participation, and satisfaction.[26]

> These and other societal changes make effective leadership in the future a more challenging task, requiring even greater sensitivity and flexibility than was ever needed before. Today's manager is more likely to deal with employees who resent being treated as subordinates, who may be highly critical of any organizational system, who expect to be consulted and to exert influence, and who often stand on the edge of alienation from the institution that needs their loyalty and commitment. In addition, he is frequently confronted by a highly turbulent, unpredictable environment.[27]

DEVELOPING STRATEGIES

Changing Style

One of the most difficult changes to make is a complete change in the style of a person, and yet industry invests many millions of dollars annually for training and development programs that concentrate on changing the style of its leaders. As Fiedler suggests:

> A person's leadership style reflects the individual's basic motivational and need structure. At best it takes one, two, or three years of intensive psychotherapy to effect lasting changes in personality structure. It is difficult to see how we can change in more than a few cases an equally important set of core values in a few hours of lectures and role playing or even in the course of a more intensive training program of one or two weeks.[28]

Fiedler's point is well taken. It is indeed difficult to effect changes in the styles of managers overnight. While not completely hopeless, it is a slow and expensive process that requires creative planning and patience. In fact, Likert found that it takes from three to seven years, depending on the size and complexity of the organization, to implement a new management theory effectively.

> Haste is self-defeating because of the anxieties and stresses it creates. There is no substitute for ample time to enable the members of an organization to reach the level of skillful and easy, habitual use of the new leadership.[29]

What generally happens in present training and development programs is that managers are encouraged to adopt certain normative behavior styles. In our culture, these styles are usually high relationship/low task or high task/high relationship styles. Although we agree that there is a growing tendency for these two styles to be more effective than the high task/low relationship or low relationship/low task styles, we recognize that this is not universally the case even in our own culture. In fact, it is often not the case even within a single work group. Most people might respond favorably to the high relationship styles, but a few might react in a negative manner, taking advantage of what they consider a soft touch. As a result, certain individuals will have to be handled in a different way. Perhaps they will respond only to the proverbial kick in the pants or close supervision (a high task/low relationship style). Thus, it is unrealistic to think that any of these styles can be successfully applied everywhere. In addition to considering application, it is questionable whether every leader can adapt to one normative style.

Most training and development programs do not recognize these two considerations. Consequently, a foreman who has been operating as a task-oriented, authoritarian leader for many years is encouraged to change style—get in step with the times. Upon returning from the training program, the foreman will probably try to utilize some of the new relationship-oriented techniques. The problem is that the style the foreman has used for a long time is not compatible with the new concepts. As long as things are running smoothly, there is no difficulty in using them. However, the minute an important issue or a crisis develops, the foreman tends to revert to the old basic style and becomes inconsistent, vacillating between the new relationship-oriented style and the old task-oriented style, which has the force of habit behind it.

This idea was supported in a study that the General Electric Company conducted at one of its turbine and generator plants.[30] In this study the leadership styles of about ninety foremen were analyzed and rated as "democratic," "authoritarian," or "mixed." In discussing the findings, Saul W. Gellerman reported that:

> The lowest morale in the plant was found among those men whose foremen were rated *between* the democratic and authoritarian extremes. The GE research team felt that these foremen may have varied inconsistently in their tactics, permissive at one moment and hardfisted the next, in a way that left their men frustrated and unable to anticipate how they could be treated. The naturally autocratic supervisor who is exposed to human relations training may behave in exactly such a manner . . . a pattern which will probably make him even harder to work for than he was before being "enlightened."[31]

In summary, changing the style of managers is a difficult process and one that takes considerable time. Expecting miracles overnight will only lead to frustration and uneasiness for both managers and their subordinates. Consequently, we recommend that change in overall management style in an organization should be planned and implemented on a long-term basis so that expectations can be realistic for all involved.

Changes in Expectations versus Changes in Style

Using the feedback model discussed in Chapter 2, we can begin to explain why it is so difficult to make changes in leader style in a short period of time.

As discussed earlier, when a person behaves in a motivating situation, that behavior becomes a new input to the individual's inventory of past experience. The earlier in life that this input occurs, the greater its potential effect on future behavior. At that time, this behavior represents a larger portion of the individual's total past experience than the same behavior input will later in life. In addition, the longer a behavior is reinforced, the more patterned it becomes and the more difficult it is to change. That is why it is easier to make personality changes early in life. As a person gets older, more time and new experiences are necessary to effect a change in behavior.

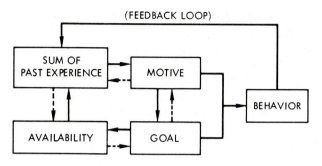

FIGURE 7-5 Feedback model

As discussed in Chapter 1, changes in behavior are much more difficult and time-consuming than changes in knowledge and attitudes if force is not a factor. Since changes in expectations, in reality, are changes in knowledge and attitudes, these can be implemented more rapidly than changes in style. In fact, changes in expectations may be accomplished merely by having leaders sit down and clarify what their behavior will be with the individuals involved. Once they understand their leader's style, followers can more easily adjust their expectations to it. This is easier than attempting the tedious task of changing the basic style of leader.

Team Building: Selection of Key Subordinates

It is important to point out that it is not always necessary for superiors and subordinates within an organization to have similar styles. People do not have to have the same personalities to be compatible. What is necessary is that they share perceptions of each other's roles and have common goals and objectives. It is often more appropriate for a manager to recruit key subordinates who can compensate for areas in which they have shortcomings than to surround themselves with aides who are all alike. And yet there are large companies today that have created problems for themselves by a testing and selection process that eliminates personalities not congruent with the norm. The usual process is to measure the values and styles of the top management and then select new people who are compatible with those patterns. The assumption is that if those people got to the top, their values and styles must be what are needed to be successful in the organization. When these norms become part of the screening process, what the organization is saying is that there is a best style, at least for this organization.

One of the reasons that hiring "likes" became popular is that it led to a more harmonious organization. For example, if we have the same set of values and behave in similar ways, will we tend to get along? Yes, because we will tend to be compatible. There will probably not be much conflict or confrontation. On the surface, this kind of screening appears to be very positive. Yet we have found that this approach can lead to organizational or management inbreeding, which tends to stifle creativity and innovation. To be effective in the long run, we feel that organizations need an open dialogue in which there is a certain amount of conflict, confrontation, and differing points of view to encourage new ideas and patterns of behavior so that the organization will not lose its ability to adjust to external competition. Organizations that have had these problems almost have been forced to break their prior policy of promoting only from within and have had to hire some key people from the outside who can encourage open dialogue.

What is often needed in organizations is more emphasis on team building in which people are hired who complement rather than replicate a manager's style. For example, Henry Ford, who was considered a paternalistic leader, placed in key positions in the organization men who supplemented him rather than duplicated his style. Henry Bennett, for one, acted as a hatchet man, clearing deadwood from the organization (high task). Another subordinate acted as a confidant to Henry (high relationship). While these styles differed considerably, Ford's success during that time was based on compatibility of expectations; each understood the other's role and was committed to common goals and objectives.

Other examples could be cited. This kind of team building is common in sports such as football. Assistant coaches not only may have differential task roles; that is, line coach, backfield coach, and so forth, but may have different behavioral roles with the players; the same with principals and vice-principals, and so on.

Changing Situational Variables

Recognizing some of the limitations of training and development programs that concentrate only on changing leadership styles, Fiedler has suggested that "it would seem more promising at this time to teach the individual to recognize the conditions under which he can perform best and to modify the situation to suit his leadership style."[32] This philosophy, which he calls "organizational engineering," is based on the following assumption: "It is almost always easier to change a man's work environment than it is to change his personality or his style of relating to others."[33] Although we basically agree with Fiedler's assumption, we want to make it clear that we feel changes in both are difficult but possible. In many cases, the best strategy might be to attempt to make some changes in both the style of leaders and the expectations of the other variables of their situation, rather than concentrating on one or the other.

Fiedler is helpful, however, in suggesting ways in which a leadership situation can be modified to fit the leader's style. These suggestions are based on his Leadership Contingency Model, which we discussed in Chapter 5. As you will recall, Fiedler feels there are three major situational variables that seem to determine whether a given situation is favorable or unfavorable to leaders: (1) *leader−member relations*—their personal relations with the members of their group, (2) *position power*—the power and authority that their position provides, and (3) *task structure*—the degree of structure (routine versus challenging) in the task that the group has been assigned to perform. The changes in each of these variables that Fiedler recommends can be expressed in task or relationship terms; each change tends to favor either a task-oriented or a relationships-oriented leader, as illustrated in Table 7-1.

With changes such as these, Fiedler suggests that the situational variables confronting leaders can be modified to fit their style. He recognized, however, as we have been arguing, that the success of organizational engineering depends on training individuals to be able to diagnose their own leadership style and the other situational variables. Only when they have

TABLE 7-1 Changes in the leadership situation expressed in terms of task and relationship[34]

Variable Being Changed	Change Made	
	Style Favors	
	Task	*Relationship*
Leader—Member Relations	Leaders could be given: 1. Followers who are quite different from them in a number of ways. 2. Followers who are notorious for their conflict.	Leaders could be given: 1. Followers who are very similar to them in attitude, opinion, technical background, race, etc. 2. Followers who generally get along well with their superiors.
Position Power of the Leader	Leaders could be given: 1. High rank and corresponding recognition, i.e., a vice-presidency. 2. Followers who are two or three ranks below them. 3. Followers who are dependent upon their leader for guidance and instruction. 4. Final authority in making all the decisions for the group. 5. All information about organizational plans, thus making them expert in their group.	Leaders could be given: 1. Little rank (office) or official recognition. 2. Followers who are equal to them in rank. 3. Followers who are experts in their field and are independent of their leader. 4. No authority in making decisions for the group. 5. No more information about organizational plans than their followers get, placing the followers on an equal "footing" with the leaders.
Task Structure	Leaders could be given: 1. A structured production task that has specific instructions on what they and their followers should do.	Leaders could be given: 1. An unstructured policy-making task that has no prescribed operating procedures.

accurately interpreted these variables can they determine whether any changes are necessary. If changes are needed, leaders do not necessarily have to initiate any in their own particular situation. They might prefer to transfer to a situation that better fits their style. In this new environment, no immediate changes may be necessary.

DIAGNOSING THE ENVIRONMENT—A CASE

Any of the situational elements we have discussed may be analyzed in terms of task and relationship. Let us take the case of Steve, a general foreman who has been offered a promotion to superintendent in another plant. In his present position, which he has held for fifteen years, Steve has been extremely effective as a task-oriented manager responsible for the operation of several assembly-line processes.

Steve's first impulse is to accept this promotion in status and salary and move his family to the new location. But, instead, he feels it is important first to visit the plant and to talk with some of the people with whom he will be working. In talking with these people, Steve may gain some insight into some of the important dimensions of this new position. An analysis of all these variables in terms of task and relationship could be summarized together, as illustrated in Figure 7-6.[35]

If Steve, using diagnostic skills, makes this type of analysis, he has gone a long way toward gathering the necessary information he needs for effectively determining his appropriate actions.

The circle designated for the leader represents Steve's leadership style, which has been reinforced over the past fifteen years. The other circles represent the expectations of all the other environmental variables in terms of what is considered appropriate behavior for a foreman. In this plant, all of

FIGURE 7-6 An example of all the environmental variables being analyzed together in terms of task and relationship

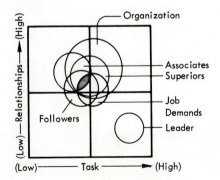

the situational variables seem to demand a high task/high relationship or high relationship/low task superintendent. Unfortunately, Steve's style does not seem appropriate for any of the situational variables, for he tends to be a high task/low relationship manager. Thus, if he accepts the job and makes no changes, there is a high probability that Steve will be ineffective. At this point, he has to make a decision. Several alternatives are available to him.

1. He can attempt to change his style of behavior, thus permitting him to work effectively with the various situational variables in the new environment.
2. He can attempt to change some or all of the situational elements. For example, he can attempt to change the behavior and the expectations of his followers through training and development programs and/or coaching and counseling.
3. He can attempt to make *some* changes in both his own range of behavior and some or all of the situational elements, thus attempting in the long run to have the two move toward each other rather than concentrating only on changing one or the other.
4. He can reject the job and seek another superintendent's position in an environment in which his range of behavior is more compatible with the demands of the other situational elements.
5. He can remain in his present position, where he knows he has been effective and will probably continue to be.

Reddin,[36] in doing a similar analysis, would attempt to find an area where the expectations of the organization, superiors, associates, followers, and job demands intersected. It is within this area that he would suggest that a leader would probably have to behave to maximize effectiveness. While that averaging process perhaps could be used for a case such as Steve's in which the expectations of all the other situational variables are grouped closely together, it would not be useful in other situations.

When the expectations of various key variables do not intersect, it is not possible to use a generalized style but will require that leaders use different styles with each of the important situational variables in their environment. Thus, Dorothy, a sales manager, may have to treat her boss differently from the way she treats any of her subordinates or associates. Even among the salespeople who report to her, she will probably have to treat some differently from others.

Although these examples have been written from the point of view of an individual, this type of analysis is just as important from an organization's point of view. It is vital that the people placed in key positions throughout the organization have the prerequisites for carrying out the organizational goals effectively. Management must realize that it does not follow that a person will be effective in one position merely because the person has been effective in another situation. Laurence J. Peter writes about such assumptions. The Peter Principle is stated as follows: "In a hierarchy every employee tends to rise to his level of incompetence."[37]

Anti-Peter Principle Vaccine

The dilemma expressed by Peter is not necessarily a self-fulfilling prophecy or principle. There are several ways an organization can develop an immunity to the problem. One method is appropriate training and development before upward mobility takes place. This training may often include, prior to movement, the delegation of some responsibility, so that the person has had an opportunity for some real experience that approximates the new position. Another part of the solution is careful selection of those whose personality and expectations are appropriate for the new job, instead of having upward mobility depend only on good performance at the preceding level.

HOW CAN MANAGERS LEARN TO DEAL WITH ALL THESE ENVIRONMENTAL VARIABLES?

It is our feeling that it would be an impossible task for managers to attempt to look at all the interacting influence variables discussed in this chapter every time they had to make a leadership decision. As a result, in the next chapter we are going to zero in on what we think is the key—the relationship between the leader and the follower.

Why do we say that the relationship between the leader and the follower is the key for diagnosing a situation? The main reason is that our work confirms Sanford's[38] work. We have found that if the follower decides not to follow, it really doesn't matter what the boss thinks, what the nature of the work is, how much time is involved, or what the other situational variables are.

NOTES

1. These environmental variables have been adapted from a list of situational elements discussed by William J. Reddin in *The 3-D Management Style Theory*, Theory Paper #5—Diagnostic Skill (Fredericton, N.B., Canada: Social Science Systems, 1967), p. 2.

2. Robert Tannenbaum and Warren H. Schmidt indicate that the appropriate leadership style that should be used in a given situation is the function of factors in the leader, the follower, and the situation. What constitutes the situation can vary in different environmental settings. See Tannenbaum and Schmidt, "How to Choose a Leadership Pattern," *Harvard Business Review*, March–April, 1957.

3. The introductory section here was adapted from a model that discusses the interaction of personality and expectations. See Jacob W. Getzels and Egon G. Guba, "Social Behavior and the Administrative Process," *The School Review*, 65, No. 4 (Winter 1957), pp. 423–441. See also Getzels "Administration as a Social Process," in Andrew W. Halpin, ed., *Administrative Theory in Education* (Chicago: Midwest Administration Center, University of Chicago, 1958).

4. Adapted from Getzels, p. 158

5. Tannenbaum and Schmidt, "How to Choose a Leadership Pattern."

6. Leland P. Bradford, Jack R. Gibb, and Kenneth D. Benne, *T-Group Theory and Laboratory Method* (New York: Wiley, 1964).

7. Warren G. Bennis, *Changing Organizations* (New York: McGraw-Hill, 1966), p. 120; Warren G. Bennis, *The Planning of Change* (New York: Harper & Row, 1985); D. G. Bowers, "Organizational Development: Promises, Performances, Possibilities," *Organizational Dynamics*, Spring 1976, pp. 50–62.

8. Chris Argyris, "We Must Make Work Worthwhile," *Life*, May 5, 1968, pp. 67–68. See also Chris Argyris, "Beyond Freedom and Dignity by B. F. Skinner, "A Review Essay," *Harvard Educational Review*, 41 (1971), pp. 550–567.

9. *Ibid.*

10. See Chris Argyris, "T-Groups for Organization Effectiveness," *Harvard Business Review*, 42 (1964), pp. 60–74; Edgar H. Schein and Warren G. Bennis, *Personal and Organizational Change through Group Methods* (New York: Wiley 1965); Robert R. Blake et al., "Breakthrough in Organization Developement," *Harvard Business Review*, November–December 1964; and Chris Argyris, *Interpersonal Competence and Organizational Effectiveness* (Homewood, Ill.: Dorsey Press, 1962). See also E. H. Schein, *Organizational Psychology*, 2nd ed. (Englewood Cliffs, N. J.: Prentice-Hall, 1977); Robert R. Blake and Jane S. Mouton, *Consultation: A Comprehensive Approach to Individual and Organization Development* (Reading, Mass.: Addison-Wesley, 1983).

11. Fillmore H. Sanford, *Authoritarianism and Leadership* (Philadelphia: Institute for Research in Human Relations, 1950).

12. Victor H. Vroom, *Some Personality Determinants of the Effects of Participation* (Englewood Cliffs, N.J.: Prentice-Hall, 1960).

13. Saul W. Gellerman, *Motivation and Productivity* (New York: American Management Association, 1963).

14. Tannenbaum and Schmidt, "How to Choose a Leadership Pattern."

15. Reddin, *The 3-D Management Style Theory*, Theory Paper #5—Diagnostic Skill, p. 4.

16. William E. Henry, "The Business Executive: The Psychodynamics of a Social Role," *The American Journal of Sociology*, 54, No. 4 (January 1949), pp. 286–291.

17. Robert H. Guest, *Organizational Change: The Effect of Successful Leadership* (Homewood, Ill.: Irwin, Dorsey Press, 1964). See also Robert Guest, Paul Hersey, and Kenneth Blanchard, *Organizational Change through Effective Leadership*, 2nd ed. (Englewood Cliffs, N. J.: Prentice-Hall 1986).

18. *Ibid.*

19. Reddin, *The 3-D Management Style Theory*, Theory Paper #5—Diagnositc Skill, p. 4.

20. Waino W. Suojanen, *The Dynamics of Management* (New York: Holt, Rinehart & Winston, 1966).

21. Tannenbaum and Schmidt, "How to Choose a Leadership Pattern."

22. Fred E. Fiedler, *A Theory of Leadership Effectiveness* (New York: McGraw-Hill, 1967).

23. *Ibid.*

24. Edwin P. Hollander, *Leadership Dynamics: A Practical Guide to Effective Relationships* (New York: Free Press, 1978).

25. Victor H. Vroom and Floyd C. Mann, "Leader Authoritarianism and Employee Attitudes," *Personnel Psychology*, 13, No. 2 (1960).

26. Robert Tannenbaum and Warren H. Schmidt, "How to Choose a Leadership Pattern," *Harvard Business Review*, May–June 1973.

27. *Ibid.*

28. Fiedler, *A Theory of Leadership Effectiveness*, p. 248.

29. Rensis Likert, *New Patterns of Management* (New York: McGraw-Hill, 1961), p. 248.

30. *Leadership Style and Employee Morale* (New York: General Electric Company, Public and Employee Relations Services, 1959).

31. Gellerman, *Motivation and Productivity*, p. 43.

32. Fiedler, *A Theory of Leadership Effectiveness*, p. 255.

33. *Ibid.*

34. This table was adapted from Fiedler's discussion in *A Theory of Leadership Effectiveness*, pp. 255–256.

35. Adapted from Reddin, Theory Paper #6—Style Flex, p. 6

36. Reddin, Theory Paper #6—Style Flex.

37. Laurence J. Peter and Raymond Hull, *The Peter Principle: Why Things Go Wrong* (New York: Morrow, 1969).

38. Fillmore H. Sanford, *Authoritarianism and Leadership* (Philadelphia: Institute for Research in Human Relations, 1950).

CHAPTER 8

SITUATIONAL LEADERSHIP

The importance of a leader's *diagnostic ability* cannot be overemphasized. Edgar H. Schein expresses it well when he contends that *the successful manager must be a good diagnostician and must value a spirit of inquiry. If the abilities and motives of the people under him are so variable, he must have the sensitivity and diagnostic ability to be able to sense and appreciate the differences.*[1] In other words, managers must be able to identify clues in an environment. Yet even with good diagnoistic skills, leaders may still not be effective unless they can *adapt* their leadership style to meet the demands of their environment. This is the second of the three important leadership competencies. "He must have the personal flexibility and range of skills necessary to vary his own behavior. If the needs and motives of his subordinates are different, they must be treated differently."[2]

It is easier said than done to tell practicing managers that they should use behavioral science theory and research to develop the necessary diagnostic skills to maximize effectiveness. First, much of the research currently published in the field of applied behavioral sciences is not even understood by practitioners, and often appears in final form to be more an attempt to impress other researchers than to help managers to be more effective. Second, even if practitioners could understand the research, many would argue that it is impractical to consider every situational variable in every decision, as advised by the management theorists and behavioral scientists.

As a result, one of the major focuses of our work has been the development of a practical model that can be used by managers, salespeople, teachers, or parents to make the moment-by-moment decisions necessary to effectively influence other people. The result: Situational Leadership.[3]

This approach uses as its basic data the perceptions and observations made by managers—parents in the home or supervisors on the job—on a day-to-day basis in their own environments, rather than data gathered only by professional researchers and consultants through instrumentation, systematic observation, and interviews.

SITUATIONAL LEADERSHIP

Paul Hersey and Kenneth H. Blanchard

Situational Leadership is based on an interplay among (1) the amount of guidance and direction (task behavior) a leader gives, (2) the amount of socioemotional support (relationship behavior) a leader provides, and (3) the readiness level that followers exhibit in performing a specific task, function or objective. This concept was developed to help people attempting leadership, regardless of their role, to be more effective in their daily interactions with others. It provides leaders with some understanding of the relationship between an effective style of leadership and the level of readiness of their followers.[4]

Thus, while all the situational variables (leader, follower(s), superior(s), associates, organization, job demands, and time) are important, the emphasis in Situational Leadership will be on the behavior of a leader in relation to followers. As Fillmore H. Sanford has indicated, there is some justification for regarding the followers "as the most crucial factor in any leadership event."[5] Followers in any situation are vital, not only because individually they accept or reject the leader, but because as a group they actually determine whatever personal power the leader may have.

It may be appropriate at this point to note the difference between a model and a theory. A theory attempts to explain *why* things happen as they do. As such, it is not designed to recreate events. A model, on the other hand, is a pattern of already existing events that can be learned and therefore repeated. For example, in trying to imagine why Henry Ford was motivated to mass-produce automobiles, you would be dealing with a theory. However, if you recorded the procedures and sequences necessary for mass-production, you would have a model of the process.

Situational Leadership is a model, *not* a theory. Concepts, procedures, actions, and outcomes are based upon tested methodologies that are practical and easy to apply.

It was emphasized in Chapter 4 that when discussing leader/follower relationships, we are not necessarily talking about a hierarchical relationship, that is, superior/subordinate. The same caution will hold during our discussion of Situational Leadership. *Thus, any reference to leader(s) or follower(s) in this model should imply potential leader and potential follower.* As a result, although our examples may suggest a hierarchical relationship, the concepts presented in Situational Leadership should have application no matter whether you are attempting to influence the behavior of a subordinate, your boss, an associate, a friend, a relative, or a group.

Basic Concept of Situational Leadership

According to Situational Leadership, there is no one best way to influence people. Which leadership style a person should use with individuals or groups depends on the readiness level of the people the leader is attempting to influence, as illustrated in Figure 8-1.

Figure 8-1   Situational Leadership[7]

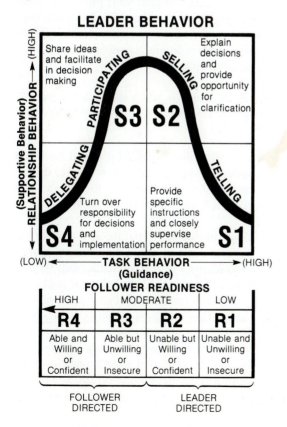

Before we look at the application of the Situational Leadership model, it is important that we understand leadership styles as they are used in the model and the idea of follower readiness.

Our earlier discussion of different leadership theories in Chapters 4 and 5 introduced us to our definition of leadership style—behavior by the leader as perceived by the follower(s). We also saw the ways that classifying leader behaviors developed, including the identification of task and relationship behavior.[6]

> *Task behavior* is defined as the extent to which the leader engages in spelling out the duties and responsibilities of an individual or group. These behaviors include telling people what to do, how to do it, when to do it, where to do it, and who is to do it.

An example of high amounts of task behavior might be the last time you asked someone for directions. The person was probably very precise and clear about telling you what streets to take and what turns to make. You were told where to start and where to finish. It is important to notice that being directive does not mean being nasty or short-tempered. The person helping you might have been very plesant toward you, but the actions and statements were aimed at completing the task—that of helping you find your way. Task behavior is characterized by one-way communication from the leader to the follower. The person was not so much concerned with your feelings but with how to help you achieve your goal.

> *Relationship behavior* is defined as the extent to which the leader engages in two-way or multi-way communication. The behaviors include listening, facilitating, and supportive behaviors.[8]

An example of high amounts of relationship behavior might be when you reach an impasse with an assignment. You basically know how to do the assignment but need some encouragement to get you over the hump. The listening, encouraging, and facilitating a leader does in this example is an illustration of relationship behavior.

Task behavior and relationship behavior are separate and distinct dimensions. They can be placed on separate axis of a two-dimensional graph, and the four quadrants can be used to identify four basic leadership styles.[9] Figure 8-1 illustrates these styles. You will note that task behavior is plotted from low to high on the horizontal axis while relationship behavior is plotted from low to high on the vertical axis. This makes it possible to describe leader behavior in four ways or styles.

By using the four quadrants as the basis for assessing managerial success in different work settings, it became clear that it wasn't just one style that was effective. Each style was appropriate, depending on the situation.

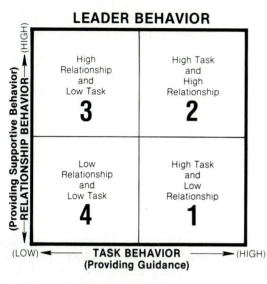

LEADER BEHAVIOR

(High)

(Providing Supportive Behavior) → (HIGH)
RELATIONSHIP BEHAVIOR

| High Relationship and Low Task **3** | High Task and High Relationship **2** |
| Low Relationship and Low Task **4** | High Task and Low Relationship **1** |

(LOW) ← **TASK BEHAVIOR** → (HIGH)
(Providing Guidance)

Figure 8-2 Leadership styles[10]

The following descriptions apply to the four styles:

- Style 1: This leadership style is characterized by above-average amounts of task behavior and below-average amounts of relationship behavior.
- Style 2: This leadership style is characterized by above-average amounts of both task and relationship behavior.
- Style 3: This style is characterized by above-average amounts of relationship behavior and below-average amounts of task behavior.
- Style 4: This style is characterized by below-average amounts of both task behavior and relationship behavior.

The important information presented by this model is in the operational *definitions* of task behavior and relationship behavior presented earlier. In leadership situations involving the family, schools, or other settings, different words may be more appropriate than *task* and *relationship*—for example, *guidance* and *supportive* behavior or *directive* behavior and *facilitiating* behavior—but the underlying definitions remain the same.

Readiness of the Followers or Group

In Chapter 7 we looked at the situation—the complex pattern of conditions that exist within a given environment. We have noted that there is no one best style of leadership; it depends upon the situation within which the attempt to influence takes place. The more that leaders can adapt their behaviors to the situation, the more effective their attempts to influence become. The situation, in turn, is influenced, as we have noted, by the various conditions that are present.

Some of the primary factors in the situation that influence leader effectiveness include the:

- Leader
- Followers
- Boss
- Key associates
- Organization
- Job demands
- Decision time

These variables do not operate in isolation. They are interactive. For example, style 1 is often referred to as "crisis leadership" because it is appropriate in times of crisis. The important thing to remember is that we should use it to *respond* to crises, not to create them. *If we treat an organization as if it is in crisis, that's what we get . . . crisis. If we treat people like children, they will often begin to behave like children.* This is one of the most important concepts in the field of applied behavioral sciences—the concept of the *self-fulfilling prophecy.* In working with others and helping them grow, leaders should have positive assumptions about followers' potential. Effective leaders believe that people have the potential to grow and, given an opportunity, can and will respond.[11]

We need to remind ourselves that the relationship between leaders and followers is the crucial variable in the leadership situation. If the followers decide not to follow, it doesn't matter what the boss or key associates think or what the job demands may be. *There is no leadership without someone following.*

In order to maximize the leader–follower relationship, the leader must first determine the task-specific outcomes the followers are to accomplish— on an individual and group basis. Without creating clarity on outcomes, objectives, subtasks, milestones, and so on, the leader has no basis for determining follower readiness or the specific behavioral style to use for that level of readiness.

Readiness Defined

Readiness in Situational Leadership is defined as the extent to which a follower has the ability and willingness to accomplish a specific task. People tend to be at different levels of readiness depending on the *task* they are being asked to do. Readiness is *not* a personal characteristic; it is not an evaluation of a person's traits, values, age, and so on. *Readiness is how ready a person is to perform a particular task*. This is to say, an individual or a group is ready or *not* ready in any *total* sense. All persons tend to be more or less ready in relation to a specific task, function, or objective that a leader is attempting to accomplish through their efforts. Thus, a salesperson may be very responsible in securing new sales but very casual about completing the paper work necessary to close on a sale. As a result, it is appropriate for the manager to leave the salesperson alone in terms of closing on sales but to supervise closely in terms of paper work until the salesperson can start to do well in that area too.

In addition to assessing the level of readiness of individuals within a group, a leader may have to assess the readiness level of the group as a group, particularly if the group interacts frequently together in the same work area, as happens with students in the classroom. Thus, a teacher may find that a class as a group may be at one level of readiness in a particular area, but a student within that group may be at a different level. When the teacher is one-to-one with that student, the teacher may have to behave very differently than when working with the class as a group. In reality, the teacher may find a number of students at various readiness levels. For example, the teacher may have one student who is not doing the assigned work regularly; when the work is turned in, it is poorly organized and not very academic. With that student, the teacher may have to initiate some structure and supervise closely. Another student, however, may be doing good work but is insecure and shy. With that student, the teacher may not have to engage in much task behavior in terms of schoolwork but may need to be supportive, to engage in two-way communication, and to help facilitate the student's interaction with others in the class. Still another student may be competent and confident in the schoolwork and thus can be left alone. So leaders have to understand that they may have to behave differently one-on-one with members of their group from the way they do with the group as a whole.

The two major components of readiness are *ability* and *willingness*.[12]

Ability is the knowledge, experience, and skill that an individual or group brings to a particular task or activity.

When considering the ability level of others, it is very important to be *task specific*. A person who has a Ph.D. in music and twenty years of professional experience playing the piano may be of little help in the design of a new jet engine. It is essential to focus on the specific outcome desired and to consider the ability of the followers in light of that outcome.

Willingness is the extent to which an individual or group has the confidence, commitment, and motivation to accomplish a specific task.

Willingness is only one word that describes the issue. Sometimes, it isn't so much that people are really unwilling, it's just that they've never done a specific task before. Perhaps they don't have any experience with it, so they're insecure or afraid. Generally, *if it is an issue of never having done something, the problem is insecurity.* The term "unwilling" might be most appropriate when, for one reason or another, the individuals have slipped, or lost some of their commitment and motivation. It might imply that they are regressing.

Even though the concepts of ability and willingness are different, it is important to remember that they are an *interacting influence system.* This means that *a significant change in one will affect the whole.* The extent to which followers bring willingness into a specific situation affects the use of their present ability. And it affects the extent to which they will grow and develop competence and ability. Similarly, the amount of knowledge, experience, and skill brought to a specific task will often affect competence, commitment, and motivation.

Readiness levels are the different combinations of ability and willingness that people bring to each task. (See Figure 8-3.)

The continuum of follower readiness can be divided into four levels. Each represents a different combination of follower ability and willingness or confidence:[14]

- Readiness Level One (R1)
  Unable and unwilling
  The follower is unable and lacks commitment and motivation.
  Unable and insecure
  The follower is unable and lacks confidence.
- Readiness Level Two (R2)
  Unable but willing
  The follower lacks ability but is motivated and making an effort.
  Unable but confident
  The follower lacks ability but is confident as long as the leader is there to provide guidance.

Figure 8-3   Follower readiness[13]

HIGH	MODERATE		LOW
R4	R3	R2	R1
Able and Willing or Confident	Able but Unwilling or Insecure	Unable but Willing or Confident	Unable and Unwilling or Insecure

■ Readiness Level Three (R3)
Able but unwilling
The follower has the ability to perform the task but is not willing to use that ability.
Able but insecure
The follower has the ability to perform the task but is insecure or apprehensive about doing it alone.
■ Readiness Level Four (R4)
Able and willing
The follower has the ability to perform and is committed.
Able and confident
The follower has the ability to perform and is confident about doing it.

Note: Some people have difficulty understanding the development of followers from R1 to R2 to R3. How can one go from being insecure to confident and then become insecure again? The important thing to remember is that at the lower levels of readiness, the leader is providing the direction—the what, where, when, and how. Therefore, the decisions are *leader directed*. At the higher levels of readiness, *followers* become responsible for task direction, and the decisions are *follower-directed. This transition from leader-directed to self-directed may result in apprehension or insecurity*.

As followers move from low levels of readiness to higher levels, the combinations of task and relationship behavior appropriate to the situation begin to change.

The curved line through the four leadership styles shown in Figure 8-1 represents the high probability combination of task behavior and relationship behavior. These combinations correspond to the readiness levels directly below. To use the model, identify a point on the readiness continuum that represents follower readiness to perform a specific task. Then construct a perpendicular line from that point to a point where it intersects with the curved line representing leader behavior. This point indicates the most appropriate amount of task behavior and relationship behavior for that specific situation.

In selecting the high probability combination of task behavior and relationship behavior, it isn't necessary to be exact. As you move away from the optimal combination, the probability of success gradually falls off, slowly at first and then more rapidly the farther away you move. Because of this, you don't need a direct hit—a close approximation keeps the probability of success high.

Selecting Appropriate Styles

Readiness Level 1: Style 1 Match—Telling

For a follower or group that is at Readiness Level 1 for a specific task, it is appropriate to provide high amounts of guidance but little supportive behavior. A word that describes this specific leadership style is *telling*—telling the followers what to do, where to do it, and how to do it. This style is appropriate when an individual or group is low in ability and willingness and needs direction. Other one-word descriptors for this leadership style include *guiding*, *directing*, or *structuring*.

Readiness Level 2: Style 2 Match—Selling

The next range of readiness is Readiness Level 2. This is an individual or group that is still unable, but they're trying. They're willing or confident. The high probability styles are combinations of high amounts of both task and relationship behavior. The task behavior is appropriate because people are still unable. But since they're trying, it is important to be supportive of their motivation and commitment.

This style is *selling*. It is different from *telling* in that the leader is not only providing the guidance but is also providing the opportunity for dialogue and for clarification, in order to help the person "buy in" psychologically to what the leader wants. If a leader simply says "go stand by the door and keep people from coming through," that is *telling*. On the other hand, if the leader suggests "I'd sure appreciate it if you would be willing to stand by the door to guide people around the classroom because people coming through have been disruptive," this would be an example of *selling*. The follower can ask questions and get clarification, even though the leader has provided the guidance.

The definition of task behavior includes providing the *what*, *how*, *when*, *where*, and *who*. The reason that *why* isn't included is that efforts to explain *why* bridge both task and relationship behaviors. One of the differences between *telling* and *selling* is the explanation of *why*. Other words for this leadership style include *explaining*, *persuading*, or *clarifying*.

Readiness Level 3: Style 3 Match—Participating

Readiness Level 3 would be a person or group that's able but they've just developed this ability and haven't had an opportunity to gain confidence in doing it on their own. An example is the fledgling salesperson who goes out on a sales call for the first time without the sales manager.

Readiness Level 3 could also be a person or group that was able and willing but for one reason or another is slipping in terms of motivation. Perhaps they're upset, mad at the boss, or just tired of performing this behavior and, therefore, are becoming *unwilling*.

In either case, the appropriate behavior would be high amounts of two-way communication and supportive behavior but low amounts of guidance. Since they have already shown that they are able to perform the task, it isn't necessary to provide high amounts of what to do, where to do it, or how to do it. Discussion and supportive and facilitating behaviors would tend to be more appropriate for solving the problem or soothing the apprehension.

In *participating*, the leader's major role becomes encouraging and communicating. Other descriptors for this style of leadership include *collaborating*, *facilitating*, or *committing*. Each of these implies high relationship, low task behaviors.

Readiness Level 4: Style 4 Match—Delegating

Readiness Level 4 is where the individual or group is both ready and willing, or ready and confident. They've had enough opportunity to practice, and they feel comfortable without the leader providing direction.

It is unnecessary to provide direction about where, what, when, or how because the followers already have the ability. Similarly, above-average amounts of encouraging and supportive behaviors aren't necessary because they are confident, committed, and motivated. The appropriate style involves giving them the ball and letting them run with it.

This style is call *delegating*. Other words for this leadership style include *observing* or *monitoring*. Remember—some relationship behavior is still needed, but it tends to be less than average. It is still appropriate to monitor the pulse of what's going on, but it is important to give these followers an opportunity to take responsibility and implement on their own.

One point to remember is that when an individual or group is developing, the issue is usually one of insecurity; when they are regressing, the issue is usually one of unwillingness. We will go into these ideas in greater detail in subsequent chapters.

It should be clear that the appropriate leadership style for all four of the readiness designations—low (R1), low to moderate (R2), moderate to high (R3), and high (R4)—correspond to the following leadership style designations: *telling* (S1), *selling* (S2), *participating* (S3), and *delegating* (S4). That is, low readiness needs a *telling* style, low to moderate readiness needs a *selling* style, and so on. These combinations are shown in Table 8-1.

Situational Leadership not only suggests the high-probability leadership style for various readiness levels, but it also indicates the probability of success of the other style configurations if a leader is unable to use the desired style. The probability of success of each style for the four readiness levels, depending on how far the style is from the high-probability style along the prescriptive curve in the style of leader portion of the model, is as follows:

R1	S1 high, S2 2nd, S3 3rd, S4 low probability
R2	S2 high, S1 2nd, S3 2nd, S4 low probability
R3	S3 high, S2 2nd, S4 2nd, S1 low probability
R4	S4 high, S3 2nd, S2 3rd, S1 low probability

TABLE 8-1 Leadership styles appropriate for various readiness levels

Readiness Level	Appropriate Style
R1 *Low Readiness* Unable and unwilling or insecure	**S1** *Telling* High task Low relationship behavior
R2 *Low to Moderate Readiness* Unable but willing or confident	**S2** *Selling* High task High relationship behavior
R3 *Moderate to High Readiness* Able but unwilling or insecure	**S3** *Participating* High relationship Low task behavior
R4 *High Readiness* Able/competent and willing/confident	**S4** *Delegating* Low relationship Low task behavior

In Situational Leadership, who has the problem? The *follower*. The follower can get any behavior desired depending upon the *follower's* behavior. The follower's behavior determines the leader's behavior. What a marvelous thing we now have available to use at home, at the office, in any kind of interpersonal situation. For example, how much easier parenting would be if children were to realize that it is not Mom and Dad who determine and control the children's behavior; it is *they* who control their own behavior.

Another important consideration: Why is it that a leadership style that may not be our "natural" style is frequently our most *effective* style? This is because we have worked at these styles, we have practiced and practiced those behaviors, and we have worked at them with some expert help. We have also paid attention to the details of applying these learned styles. Those styles that we are most comfortable with we use as we are presently using them. Why? Because they are OK. We do not put the same amount of skill practice into them as we do our learned styles. As a consequence, they are not as effective.

One last thought: Situational Leadership is not a prescription with hard and fast rules. In the behavioral sciences, there are no rules. Situational Leadership as a major contribution to the behavioral sciences is attempting to improve the odds. In so doing, managers will be able to achieve the productivity of human resources they have been seeking.

APPLICATION OF SITUATIONAL LEADERSHIP

In using Situational Leadership, it is useful to keep in mind that there is no "one best way" to influence others. Rather, any leader behavior may be more or less effective depending on the readiness level of the person you are attempting to influence. Shown in Figure 8-4 is a more comprehensive version of the Situational Leadership Model that brings together our discussion of the past several pages. It will provide you with a quick reference to assist in (1) diagnosing the level of readiness, (2) adapting by selecting high probability leadership styles, and (3) communicating these styles effectively to influence behavior. Implicit in Situational Leadership is the idea that a leader should help followers grow in readiness as far as they are able and willing to go. This development of followers should be done by adjusting leadership behavior through the four styles along the prescriptive curve in Figure 8-4.

Situational Leadership contends that strong direction (task behavior) with followers with low readiness is appropriate if they are to become productive. Similarly, it suggests that an increase in readiness on the part of people who are somewhat unready should be rewarded by increased positive reinforcement and socioemotional support (relationship behavior). Finally, as followers reach high levels of readiness, the leader should respond by not only continuing to decrease control over their activities but also by continuing to decrease relationship behavior as well. With people with high readiness the need for socioemotional support is no longer as important as the need for autonomy. At this stage, one of the ways leaders can prove their confidence and trust in these people is to leave them more and more on their own. It is not that there is less mutual trust and friendship between leader and follower; in fact, there is more, but it takes less supportive behavior on the leader's part to prove this to them.

Regardless of the level of readiness of an individual or group, change may occur. Whenever a follower's performance begins to slip—for whatever reason—and ability or motivation decreases, the leader should reassess the readiness level of this follower and move backward through the prescriptive curve, providing appropriate socioemotional support and direction.

These developmental and regressive processes will be discussed in depth in Chapters 10 and 11. At this point, though, it is important to emphasize that Situational Leadership focuses on the appropriateness or effectiveness of leadership styles according to the task-relevant readiness of the followers.

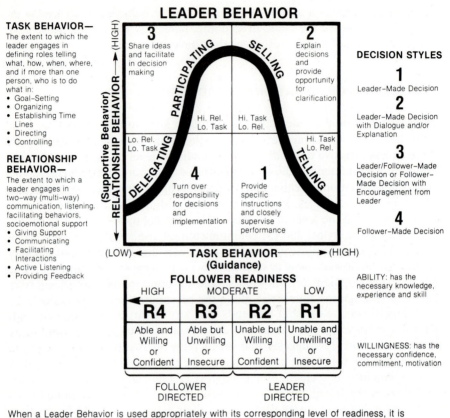

TASK BEHAVIOR—
The extent to which the leader engages in defining roles telling what, how, when, where, and if more than one person, who is to do what in:
• Goal–Setting
• Organizing
• Establishing Time Lines
• Directing
• Controlling

RELATIONSHIP BEHAVIOR—
The extent to which a leader engages in two–way (multi–way) communication, listening, facilitating behaviors, socioemotional support
• Giving Support
• Communicating
• Facilitating Interactions
• Active Listening
• Providing Feedback

LEADER BEHAVIOR

(Supportive Behavior)
RELATIONSHIP BEHAVIOR
(HIGH)

3
Share ideas and facilitate in decision making
PARTICIPATING
Hi. Rel.
Lo. Task

2
SELLING
Explain decisions and provide opportunity for clarification
Hi. Task
Lo. Rel.

Lo. Rel.
Lo. Task
DELEGATING

Hi. Task
Lo. Rel.
TELLING

4
Turn over responsibility for decisions and implementation

1
Provide specific instructions and closely supervise performance

(LOW) ◄———— **TASK BEHAVIOR** ————► (HIGH)
(Guidance)

DECISION STYLES

1
Leader–Made Decision

2
Leader–Made Decision with Dialogue and/or Explanation

3
Leader/Follower–Made Decision or Follower–Made Decision with Encouragement from Leader

4
Follower–Made Decision

FOLLOWER READINESS

HIGH	MODERATE		LOW
R4	**R3**	**R2**	**R1**
Able and Willing or Confident	Able but Unwilling or Insecure	Unable but Willing or Confident	Unable and Unwilling or Insecure

FOLLOWER DIRECTED

LEADER DIRECTED

ABILITY: has the necessary knowledge, experience and skill

WILLINGNESS: has the necessary confidence, commitment, motivation

When a Leader Behavior is used appropriately with its corresponding level of readiness, it is termed a High Probability Match. The following are descriptors that can be useful when using Situational Leadership for specific applications:

S1	**S2**	**S3**	**S4**
Telling	Selling	Participating	Delegating
Guiding	Explaining	Encouraging	Observing
Directing	Clarifying	Collaborating	Monitoring
Establishing	Persuading	Committing	Fulfilling

Figure 8-4 Expanded Situational Leadership Model[15]

Determining Appropriate Style

To determine what leadership style you should use with a person in a given situation, you must do several things.

First, you must decide what areas of an individual's or a group's activities you would like to influence. In the world of work, those areas would vary according to a person's responsibilities. For example, a salesperson might have responsibility in sales, administration (paper work), service, and team development. Therefore, before managers can begin to determine the appropriate leadership style to use with an individual, they must decide what aspect of that person's job they want to influence.

Once this decision has been made, the second step is to determine the ability and motivation (readiness level) of the individual or group in each of the selected areas.

The third and final step is deciding which of the four leadership styles (see Table 8-1) would be appropriate with this individual in each of these areas. Let us look at an example. Suppose a manager has determined that a subordinate's readiness level, in terms of administrative paper work, is low (R1); that is, the staff member is unable and unwilling to take reponsibility in this area. Using Table 8-1, the manager would know that when working with this subordinate, a directive *telling* (S1) style (high task/low relationship behavior) should be used.

In this example, low relationship behavior does not mean that the manager is unfriendly to the subordinate. We merely suggest that the manager, in supervising the subordinate's handling of administrative paper work, should spend more time directing the person in what to do and how, when, and where to do it than providing socioemotional support and reinforcement. Increased relationship behavior should occur only when the subordinate begins to demonstrate the ability to handle necessary administrative paper work. At this point, a movement from *telling* to *selling* would be appropriate.

Components of Readiness

It has been argued that the key to effective leadership is to identify the *readiness level* of the individual or group you are attempting to influence and then bring to bear the appropriate leadership style. If that is true, how can managers get a better handle on what readiness actually means?

In examining the components of readiness, several comments should be made. First, according to David C. McClelland's research,[16] achievement-motivated people have certain characteristics in common, including the capacity to set high but obtainable goals, the concern for personal achievement rather than the rewards of success, and the desire for task-relevant feedback (how well am I doing?) rather than for attitudinal feedback (how well do you like me?). Of these characteristics we are most interested, in terms of task-relevant readiness, in the capacity to set high but attainable goals.

Second, in terms of education and/or experience, we are contending that there is no conceptual difference between the two. One can gain task-relevant readiness through education or experience or some combination of both. The only difference between the two is that when we are talking about education, we are referring to formal classroom experiences, and experience involves what is learned on one's own or on the job.

Third, in our recent work, we have argued that education and/or experience affects ability and that achievement motivation affects willingness. As a result, in discussing readiness in terms of ability and willingness, we are suggesting that the concept of ability consists of two dimensions: ability and willingness.

Ability (job readiness) is related to the ability to do something. It has to do with knowledge and skill. Individuals who have high job readiness in a particular area have the knowledge, ability, and experience to perform certain tasks without direction from others. A person high in job readiness might say: "My talent really lies in that aspect of my job. I can work on my own in that area without much help from my boss."

Willingness (psychological readiness) is related to the willingness, or motivation, to do something. It has to do with confidence and commitment. Individuals who have high psychological readiness in a particular area or responsibility think that responsibility is important and have self-confidence and good feelings about themselves in that aspect of their job. They do not need extensive encouragement to get them to do things in that area. A comment from a person high in psychological readiness might be: "I really enjoy that aspect of my job. My boss doesn't have to get after me or provide any encouragement for me to do work in that area."

It should be remembered that although readiness is a useful concept for making diagnostic judgments, other situational variables—the boss's style (if close by), a crisis or time bind, the nature of the work—can be of equal or greater importance. Yet, the readiness concept is a solid bench mark for choosing the appropriate style with an individual or group at a particular time.

Instruments to Measure Readiness

To help managers and their followers make valid judgments about follower readiness, Hambleton, Blanchard, and Hersey have developed two different maturity instruments: the *Manager's Rating Form* and the *Self-Rating Form*.[17]

Both readiness instruments measure *ability* and *willingness* by using five rating scales. Examples of these rating scales from the *Manager's Rating Form* are given in Figure 8-5.

The five ability scales and five willingness scales were selected after pilot research from a pool of about thirty potential indicators of both dimensions. As is clear from Figure 8-5, corresponding to each scale, "behavioral indicators" of the end points were produced. Also, eight-point rating scales are used in the instrument. Low to high designations correspond to the four readiness levels (R1 to R4) associated with Situational Leadership.

ABILITY SCALES

This person |................................. in performing this objective

	High				Moderate			Low
	R4			R3		R2		R1
Scales	8	7	6	5	4	3	2	1
1. Past Job Experience	Has experience relevant to job	7	6	5	4	Does not have relevant experience	2	1
	8					3		
2. Job Knowledge	Possesses necessary job knowledge	7	6	5	4	Does not have necessary job knowledge	2	1
	8					3		
3. Understanding of Job Requirements	Thoroughly understands what needs to be done	7	6	5	Has little understanding of what needs to be done	3	2	1
	8				4			

WILLINGNESS SCALES

This person |................................. in performing this objective

	High				Moderate			Low
	R4			R3		R2		R1
Scales	8	7	6	5	4	3	2	1
1. Willingness to Take Responsibility	Is very eager	7	6	5	4	Is very reluctant	2	1
	8					3		
2. Achievement Motivation	Has a high desire to achieve	7	6	5	Has little desire to achieve	3	2	1
	8				4			
3. Commitment	Is very dedicated	7	6	5	4	3	Is uncaring	1
	8						2	

Figure 8-5 A portion of the Manager's Rating Form of readiness

185

In more recent work, Hersey, Blanchard, and Keilty developed a Readiness Style Match rating form that measures readiness using only one scale for each dimension—one measuring *ability* and the other measuring *willingness*.[18] In this instrument, a person's ability (knowledge and skill) is thought of as a matter of degree. That is, an individual's ability does not change drastically from one moment to the next. At any given moment, an individual has a little, some, quite a bit, or a great deal of ability.

Willingness (confidence and motivation), however, is different. A person's motivation can, and often does, fluctuate from one moment to another. Therefore, a person is seldom, on occasion, often, or usually willing to take responsibility in a particular area.

The availability of both a *Manager's Rating Form* and a *Staff Member Form* of the *Readiness Style Match* is necessary to initiate a program combining *Situational Leadership* with *Contracting for Leadership Style*.[19] We will discuss that process in some detail in Chapter 12.

Components of Leadership Style

Once managers have identified the readiness level of the individual or group they are attempting to influence, the key to effective leadership then is to bring to bear the *appropriate leadership style*. If that is true, how can managers get a better handle on the behaviors that comprise each of the four leadership styles?

Instruments to measure leader behavior. To help managers and their staff members make better judgments about leadership style, Hersey, Blanchard, and Hambleton have developed two different leadership scales: the *Manager's Rating Form* and the *Staff Member Form*.[20] Both leadership instruments measure task and relationship behavior on five behavioral dimensions. The five task behavior dimensions and five relationship behavior dimensions are listed in Table 8-2.

After the five dimensions were established for both leader behaviors, behavioral indicators of the extreme of each of these dimensions were identified to help managers and their staff members differentiate between high and low amounts of each leader behavior. For example, with the task–behavior dimension "organizing" on the Staff Member Form, the end points of a rating scale were chosen to be "organizes the work situation for me" and "lets me organize the work situation." For the relationship–behavior dimension "providing feedback," the end points of the rating scale were chosen to be "frequently provides feedback on my accomplishments" and "leaves it up to me to evaluate accomplishments."

In the Readiness Style Match instrument discussed earlier, each of the four basic leadership styles are described, rather than the separate behavioral dimensions that make up each style. The descriptions of the four leader behaviors follow:

TABLE 8-2 Task behavior and relationship behavior dimensions and their behavior indicators

Task—Behavior Dimensions	Behavioral Indicator
	The extent to which a leader . . .
Goal setting	Specifies the goals people are to accomplish.
Organizing	Organizes the work situation for people.
Setting time lines	Sets time lines for people.
Directing	Provides specific directions.
Controlling	Specifies and requires regular reporting on progress.

Relationship—Behavior Dimensions	Behavioral Indicator
	The extent to which a leader . . .
Giving support	Provides support and encouragement.
Communicating	Involves people in give-and-take discussions about work activities.
Facilitating interactions	Facilitates people's interactions with others.
Active listening	Seeks out and listens to people's opinions and concerns.
Providing feedback	Provides feedback on people's accomplishments.

- Telling (S1) Provide specific instructions and closely supervise performance
- Selling (S2) Explain decisions and provide opportunity for clarification
- Participating (S3) Share ideas and facilitate in making decisions
- Delegating (S4) Turn over responsibility for decisions and implementation

The advantage of using the readiness *Style Match* is that it permits managers and their staff members to rate leadership style and readiness on the same instrument. Figure 8-6 shows that integration. This figure provides a good summary of the key components involved in Situational Leadership.

SITUATIONAL LEADERSHIP AND VARIOUS ORGANIZATIONAL SETTINGS

We have found that Situational Leadership has application in every kind of organizational setting, whether it be business and industry, education, government, military, or even the family. The concepts apply in any situation in which people are trying to influence the behavior of other people.

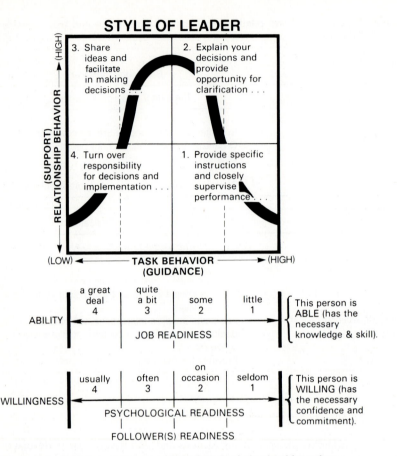

STYLE OF LEADER

3. Share ideas and facilitate in making decisions . . .	2. Explain your decisions and provide opportunity for clarification . . .
4. Turn over responsibility for decisions and implementation . . .	1. Provide specific instructions and closely supervise performance . . .

RELATIONSHIP BEHAVIOR (SUPPORT) — (HIGH)

(LOW) ◄—— **TASK BEHAVIOR** ——► (HIGH)
(GUIDANCE)

	a great deal 4	quite a bit 3	some 2	little 1	This person is ABLE (has the necessary knowledge & skill).
ABILITY					
		JOB READINESS			

	usually 4	often 3	on occasion 2	seldom 1	This person is WILLING (has the necessary confidence and commitment).
WILLINGNESS					
		PSYCHOLOGICAL READINESS			

FOLLOWER(S) READINESS

Figure 8-6   Defining readiness and the four basic leadership styles

The only problem we have found in working in various organizational settings is that some of the language has to be adapted to fit specific vocabularies. For example, we found that in training nonworking spouses, when we talked about task and relationship behavior, that did not ring any bells for them. We soon realized that in working in such family settings, it was much easier for parents and children to identify with "directive" behavior than with task behavior and to identify with "supportive" behavior than with relationship behavior.

On the other hand, when working with trainers and facilitators who have had a lot of personal growth experience and, therefore, are high on human relation quotients, even directive behavior will often tend to be a negative stimulus. Therefore, in working with these people we have found the word *guidance* is a good substitute for *directive behavior*. We want to emphasize that in utilizing various labels for the two basic leader behaviors—task behavior and relationship behavior—we are not changing the definitions at all. Task behavior is essentially the extent to which a leader engages in one-way communication by explaining what each staff member is to do as well as when, where, and how tasks are to be accomplished. Relationship behavior, even when we call it supportive behavior, is still the extent to which a leader engages in two-way communication by providing socioemotional support, "psychological strokes," and facilitating behaviors.

The reason it is important to modify the use of various words is that a key concept in all behavioral sciences is communication. If you're going to help people grow and develop, you have to learn to put frameworks, concepts, and research results into terminology that is acceptable to the groups you are attempting to influence. This has to be done if you want to have the highest probability of gaining acceptance and, therefore, affecting their growth.

Parent–Child Relationships

We have found tremendous application of Situational Leadership to the family and the parent–child relationship. The book *A Situational Approach to Parenting* is devoted completely to applying Situational Leadership to the family setting.

We suggest that when working with children (while they will need "different strokes even for the same folks"), there is a general pattern and movement in leadership style over their developmental years. Thus, when working with children who are low in maturity on a particular task, a directive parent style has the highest probability of success. This is especially true during the first few years of children's lives when they are unable to control much of their own environment. This whole developmental process will be discussed in more depth in Chapter 10.

Ineffective Parent Styles

One of the useful aspects of Situational Leadership is that one can begin to predict not only the leadership styles with the highest probability of effectiveness but also which styles tend to be ineffective in what circumstances. For instance, we can take four examples of parents who tend to use a single leadership style during the child's entire developmental period (see Figure 8-7).

First, let us look at the parent who uses a high directive/low supportive style (S1) with their children throughout the developmental years, that is, "As long as you're living in this house, you'll be home at ten o'clock and abide by the rules I've set." Two predictions might be made. The first one is that the children might pack their bags and leave home at the earliest oppor-

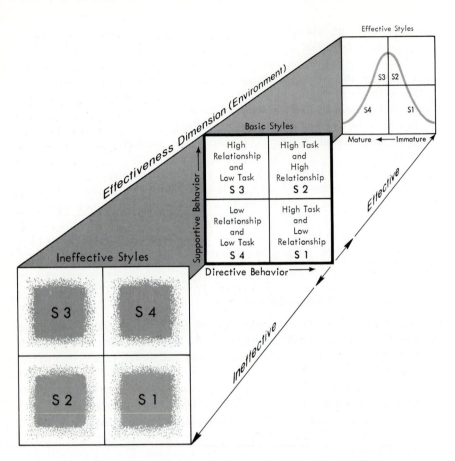

Figure 8-7 Consequences of using a *single* parent–child style over time

tunity. If this does not occur, they may succumb to their parents' authority and become very passive, dependent individuals throughout their lives, always needing someone to tell them what to do and when to do it.

A high probability result of a parent using exclusively a style of high directive/high supportive behavior (S2) might be called the "Mama's boy" or "Daddy's little girl" syndrome. Even when the children get older, they may chronologically be adults but they are still psychologically dependent on their parent(s) to make decisions for them. Since most of the direction for their behavior and socioemotional support has been provided by their parents(s), these young people are unable to provide it for themselves.

What happens when parents are unfailingly supportive and never structure or direct any of their children's activities? The response to this high supportive/low directive style (S3) may be called a "spoiled brat" syndrome, for the children develop into individuals who have little regard for rules and little consideration for the rights of others.

A low directive/low supportive behavior style (S4) seems to be characteristic of two of the socioeconomic classifications described by Lloyd Warner, the *upper-upper* level and the *lower-lower* level.[22] In both cases, the children may become products of their environment rather than products of the parents' style. In the upper-upper level, this responsibility may be delegated to a private school; in the lower-lower level, children are often left on their own and learn appropriately or inappropriately from their peers how to cope with the day-to-day contingencies of their environment.

As we mentioned in Chapter 5, some people might question why it is inappropriate to use the same leadership style all the time—"after all, we've been told that consistency is good." This advice might have been given in the past, but, as we argue, according to Situational Leadership, consistency is *not* using the same style all the time. Instead, consistency is using the same style for all similar situations but varying the style appropriately as the situation changes. Parents are consistent if they tend to discipline their children when they are behaving inappropriately and reward them when they are behaving appropriately. Parents are inconsistent if they smile and engage in other supportive behavior when their children are bad as well as when they are good.

This discussion of consistency urges parents to remember that children are often at different levels of readiness in various aspects of their lives. Thus, parental style must vary as children's activities change.

Management of Research and Development Personnel

In working with highly trained and emotionally stable people, an effective leader behavior style in many cases is low relationship/low task behavior.[23] This was dramatically demonstrated in a military setting. Normally, in basically crisis-oriented organizations such as the military or the fire department, the most appropriate style tends to be high task (S1), since under combat or fire conditions success often depends on immediate response to orders. Time demands do not permit talking things over or explaining decisions. For success, behavior must be almost automatic. Although a high task style may be effective for a combat officer, it is often ineffective in working with research and development personnel within the military. This was pointed out when line officers trained at West Point were sent to command outposts in the DEW line, part of the American advanced-warning system. The scientific and technical personnel involved, living in close quarters in an Arctic region, did not respond favorably to the high levels of task behavior of the combat-trained officers. The levels of education, research experience, and readiness of these people were such that they did not need their commanding officer to initiate a great deal of structure in their work. In fact, they tended to resent it. Other experiences with scientific and research-oriented personnel indicate that many of these people also desire or need a limited amount of socioemotional support.

Educational Setting

Educational settings provide us with numerous examples of Situational Leadership in operation.[24]

Teacher–student relationship. In an educational setting, Situational Leadership is being used in studying the teacher–student relationship.

For example, Paul Hersey and two colleagues in Brazil, Arrigo L. Angelini and Sofia Caracushansky,[25] conducted a study applying Situational Leadership to teaching. In the study, an attempt was made to compare the learning effectiveness scores between (1) students who attended a course in which a conventional teacher–students relationship prevailed (control subgroups) and (2) students who attended a course in which Situational Leadership was applied by the same teacher (experimental subgroups). In the control group classes, lectures prevailed, but group discussions, audiovisual aids, and other participative resources were also used. In the experimental classes, the readiness level of students (willingness and ability to direct their own learning and provide their own reinforcement) was developed over time by a systematic shift in teaching style. The teacher's style started at S1 (high task/low relationship—teacher in front of the class lecturing), then moved to S2 (high task/high relationship behavior—group discussions in a circular design with the teacher directing the conversation), then to S3 (high relationship/low task—group discussions with the teacher participating as a supportive but nondirective group member), and finally to S4 (low relationship/low task—the group continuing to discuss with the teacher involved only when asked by the class). The development of student readiness was a slow process at first, with gradual decreases in teacher direction and increases in teacher encouragement. As the students demonstrated their ability not only to assume more and more responsibility for directing their own learning but also to provide their own reinforcement (self-gratification), decreases in teacher socioemotional support accompanied continual decreases in teacher direction.

In two experiments with this design, the experimental classes showed not only higher performance on content exams but were also observed to have a higher level of enthusiasm, morale, and motivation, as well as less tardiness and absenteeism.

Administrator–governing board relationship. An important area for the top administrator (college president or superintendent) in an educational institution is the relationship this person maintains with the governing board. Since these boards have the ultimate power to remove college presidents or superintendents when they lose confidence in their leadership, these administrators often tend to use a high relationship style (S3), providing only a limited amount of structure for these decision-making groups.[26] In fact, they sometimes seem to shy away from directing the activities of their board for fear of arousing their criticism. Situational Leadership questions this behavior.

Although the members of the governing board are often responsible, well-educated individuals, they tend to have little work experience in an educational setting. For example, in a survey of college trustees in New York State, it was found that less than 10 percent of the trustees serving on these boards had any teaching or administrative experience in an educational institution.[27] In fact, the large majority of the 1,269 trustees sampled were employed primarily in industry, insurance and banking, merchandising and transportation, and medicine and law. Virtually half acted as corporation officials with the rank of treasurer, director, or above. In addition to their involvement in other than educational institutions, these trustees tended to be overcommitted and were probably unable to give the time to university problems they would have liked to give. In fact, the most frequent dissatisfaction expressed by trustees was the lack of time to devote to the board.

The relative inexperience of the trustees and the heavy commitment elsewhere suggest that it may be appropriate for college presidents to combine with their high relationship behavior an increase of task behavior in working with their trustees. In fact, the responsibility for defining the role of trustees and organizing their work should fall on the college president. Henry Wriston, former president of Brown University, has said it well:

> It may seem strange, at first thought, that this should be a president's duty. A moment's reflection makes it clear that it can evolve on no other person. Trustees are unpaid; they have no method of analyzing talents and making assignments. The president is in a position to do so.[28]

Administrator–faculty relationship. In working with experienced faculty, the low relationship/low task style (S4) characterized by a decentralized organization structure and delegation of responsibility to individuals may be appropriate. The level of education and experience of these people is often such that they do not need their principal or department chairperson to initiate much structure. Sometimes they tend to resent it. In addition, some teachers desire or need only a limited amount of socioemotional support (relationship behavior).

Often an effective leader style in working with faculty tends to be low relationship/low task, but certain deviations may be necessary. For example, during the early stages of a school year or a curriculum change, a certain amount of structure as to the specific areas to be taught, by whom, when, and where must be established. Once these requirements and limitations are understood by the faculty, the administrator may move rapidly back to low relationship/low task style appropriate for working with experienced, responsible, self-motivated personnel.

Other deviations may be necessary. For example, a new, inexperienced teacher might need more direction and socioemotional support until gaining experience in the classroom.

UNDERSTANDING EARLIER RESEARCH

One of the major contributions of Situational Leadership is that it provides a way of understanding much of the research findings that prior to a situational approach seemed to be incompatible with each other.

For example, at first glance, the extensive research that Likert[29] did in industrial sections of the United States in the 1950s and a similar study that Hersey[30] conducted in western Africa in the 1960s seem to be in conflict. Likert found in his studies that the tendency is for employee-centered supervisors who provide general supervision to have high-producing sections, while the low-producing sections tend to have job-centered supervisors who provide close supervision. Hersey's findings were almost the exact opposite of the results generated by Likert. In emerging industrial settings in western Africa, he found the more effective style to be job-centered close supervision. However, by examining these different results using Situational Leadership, one may gain some insights into why these differing results are predictable.

As indicated, the population for Likert's research was drawn from industrial sections of the United States. This is particularly relevant when one considers what we have come to call "cultural readiness" or "work force." We have found that three phenomena—level of education, standard of living, and industrial experience—can have a pronounced effect on the task-relevant readiness level of the work force from which an organization is attempting to draw its employees.

In terms of Likert's research, the level of readiness of the work force of his sample upon examination appears to be quite advanced. The level of education, standard of living, and industrial experiences of people in industrial sections of the United States in the 1950s were probably moderate to high. This is not surprising when one examines the research in terms of Situational Leadership. Likert found that moderate to low task behavior and relatively high relationship behavior (S3) tended to be the most effective leadership styles—that is, they had the highest probability of being effective given the cultural readiness involved. At the same time, it is not surprising to see the results Hersey found. In the middle 1960s, emerging countries in Africa seemed to have labor forces characterized for many by very little formal education, a subsistence standard of living, and little or no industrial experience. Considering this low level of work force readiness at that time, one could predict from Situational Leadership that the highly structured, close supervision style that Hersey found would have the highest probability of being effective in that environment.

The same kind of analysis can be made in comparing the results of the classical participation study done by Coch and French[31] in an American factory in the Northeast and a replication of their study by French, Israel and Ās[32] in a Norwegian factory. In the industrial setting in the United States, it was found that involving employees in decision making tends to be effective, but in Norway there was not significant difference in productivity between work groups in which participative management was used and those in which it was *not* used. Once again, these two studies support Situational Leadership and suggest that readiness levels and/or cultural work force differences in the followers and the situation are important in determining the appropriate leadership style.

Determining the Effectiveness of Participation

An analysis of studies in participation[33] in terms of Situational Leadership also suggests some interesting things about the appropriate use of participation. Situational Leadership suggests that the higher the level of task-relevant readiness of an individual or group, the higher the probability that participation will be an effective management technology. The less task-relevant readiness, the lower the probability that participation will be a useful management practice.

Involvement and participation in decision making with people at extremely low levels of readiness might be characterized by a pooling of ignorance, or the blind leading the blind, and, therefore, directive leadership might have a higher probability of success. At the other end of the readiness continuum (extremely high levels of task-relevant readiness), some of these people tend to resist engaging in "group think." Thy would prefer the individual with the highest level of expertise in an area to make the decisions there. "Bill, how do you think we should go on this? It's your area.".Thus, according to Situational Leadership, participation as a management technique has a higher probability of success as one moves from low to moderate levels of readiness, and then begins to plateau in potential effectiveness as one's followers become high in task-relevant readiness, as illustrated in Figure 8-8.

One further point about participation. Although participation tends to satisfy affiliation and esteem needs by giving people a chance to feel in on things and be recognized as important in the decision-making process, it

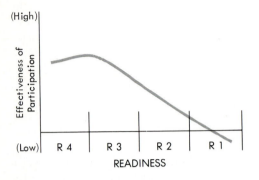

Figure 8-8 Participation as an effective management technique

should be remembered that self-actualization may not result from participation. The high-level need satisfaction most often occurs in a work environment where people are given a job that allows them an opportunity for achievement, growth and development, and challenge.

The Influence of Cultural Change[34]

The scientific and technical advancements in United States society since the turn of the century almost stagger the imagination. As a result, we have become a dynamic, industrial society with a higher level of education and standard of living then ever thought possible. This phenomenon is beginning to have a pronounced effect on much of the work force utilized by organizations.

Today, many employees enjoy a higher standard of living and tend to be better educated and more sophisticated than ever before. As a result, these workers have increased potential for self-direction and self-control. Consistent with these changes in readiness, a large majority of our population, in Maslow's terms, now have their basic physiological and safety-security needs fairly well satisfied. Management can no longer depend on the satisfaction of these needs—through pay, incentive plans, hospitalization, and so on—as primary motivating factors that influence industrial employees. In our society today, there is almost a built-in expectation in people that physiological and safety needs will be fulfilled. In fact, most people do not generally have to worry about where their next meal will come from or whether they will be protected from the elements of physical danger. They are now more susceptible to motivation from other needs: people want to belong, to be recognized as "somebody," and to have a chance to develop to their fullest potential. As William H. Haney has said:

SELF-CONTROL

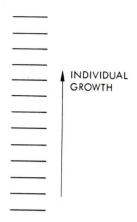

INDIVIDUAL
GROWTH

EXTERNAL CONTROL

Figure 8-9   External control versus self-control

The managerial practice, therefore, should be geared to the subordinate's *current level of maturity with the overall goal of helping him to develop, to require progressively less external control, and to gain more and more self-control.* And why would a man want this? Because under these conditions he achieves satisfaction on the job at the levels, primarily the ego and self-fulfillment levels, at which he is the most motivatable.[35]

This concept is illustrated in Figure 8-9.

This shift in the readiness level and need disposition of our general population helps us to understand why the findings of many studies of the relationship between leadership styles and productivity, such as those conducted by Likert and Halpin, seem to cluster around styles 2 and 3 but not at the extremes (1 and 4).

DOES SITUATIONAL LEADERSHIP WORK?

The widespread acceptance of Situational Leadership for more than two decades as a concept with face validity is well documented.[36] Practicing managers, parents, teachers, and administrators throughout the world say it has given them a practical, easy-to-use approach for determining what they should do in challenging situations. It has been a major factor in training and development programs for more than 400 of the Fortune 500 companies, such as Bank of America, Caterpillar, IBM, Mobil Oil, Union 76, and Xerox. It has been widely accepted in all of the military services and numerous fast-growing entrepreneurial companies. More than one million leaders received Situational Leadership development in 1987. While research studies have attempted to validate Situational Leadership from various directions, the real question that managers, teachers, parents, and administrators ask is: Does Situational Leadership work? We would like to present just two of the many studies that attempt to answer this question.

In 1974 the Information Systems Group (ISG) of Xerox, responsible for copier/duplicator products, made a major commitment to Situational Leadership as a training concept. Situational Leadership now is a cornerstone of ISG's building-block training strategy and is taught to middle-level as well as new first-level managers. As Gumpert and Hambleton indicate:

> Despite the model's intuitive appeal and quick acceptance by our managers, because of the training resources required, ISG management development had to answer a critical question: Are managers who use the model correctly in their interactions with employees more effective than those who do not? After all, if they are no more effective, there would be no point to training in situational leadership.[37]

Sixty-five managers in sales, service, administration, and staff functions participated in the study. These managers completed three types of forms.[38]

- A *manager questionnaire*, which was constructed to provide demographic data, such as age, sex, years of service, and so on. The questionnaire also asked for perceptions of the managers' job performance and use of Situational Leadership.
- A *professional maturity scale*, which was used to determine a subordinate's level of maturity for a set of major job objectives. Each manager assessed one to four employees.
- A *manager rating form*, which allowed the managers to assess their own leadership styles and their subordinates' job performance for each major job objective. The following job performance rating scale, identical to Xerox's appraisal scale, was used:

Rating	Performance Description
5	Exceptional
4	Consistently exceeds expected level
3	Expected level
2	Meets minimal requirements
1	Unsatisfactory

To test the validity of Situational Leadership, data were collected for two predictions:

- Highly effective managers will indicate more knowledge and use of Situational Leadership than less effective managers.
- Employee job performance will be higher when managers apply Situational Leadership correctly than when they apply it incorrectly.[39]

The study led to these conclusions:

- Highly effective managers indicate greater knowledge and use of Situational Leadership than less effective ones.
- All managers in the study reported using Situational Leadership at least some of the time. This finding demonstrates that training in this area has had substantial on-the-job impact.
- On the average, managers who apply the model correctly rate their subordinates' job performance higher than managers who do not. The data in this area are highly supportive of the Hersey–Blanchard model of leadership effectiveness.[40]

Gumpert and Hambleton conclude:

Stated simply, highly effective managers knew more about Situational Leadership and used it more than less effective managers. Data supporting this came from the managers themselves. Also, there is strong evidence suggesting that when Situational Leadership was applied correctly, subordinate job performance was judged higher, and the gains in job performance were practically and statistically significant.[41]

Research was conducted on the impact of the video interactive Situational Leadership program on managers of a large firm that was undergoing major changes and internal restructuring. The sample of 161 managers who had received the training nine to eighteen months prior to the research completed a questionnaire booklet that included four sections: (1) an appraisal of training course content, (2) a test of skill/knowledge retention, (3) a report of a critical incident involving use of the training, and (4) an open-ended opportunity to provide feedback.

The results indicated that Situational Leadership was highly effective. Managers offered favorable appraisals of the course; they demonstrated an impressive level of mastery (retention) of course skills; and they reported successful outcomes as a consequence of using the skills on the job. The findings lend support to the claim that managerial training can improve managerial performance, even under conditions of change in the work place.[42]

CHANGING LEADERSHIP STYLE APPROPRIATELY

If managers are currently using a style that is appropriate for the level of readiness of their group, as Fred Finch of the University of Massachusetts suggested to the authors,[43] one of the indicators that they can use in determining when and to what degree they should shift their style is performance, or results. How well is their group performing in their present activities? If performance is increasing, it would be appropriate for managers to shift their style to the left along the curvilinear function of the Situational Leadership model. This would indicate that task-relevant readiness is increasing. If performance results are on the decline, it gives managers a clue that they may need to shift their leader behavior to the right along the curvilinear function. In the next chapter, we will discuss specifically the implications and implementation of these processes.

NOTES

1. Edgar H. Schein, *Organizational Psychology* (Englewood Cliffs, N. J.: Prentice-Hall, 1965), p. 61.
2. *Ibid.*
3. Situational Leadership was developed by Paul Hersey and Kenneth H. Blanchard at the Center for Leadership Studies. It was first published by those authors as "Life Cycle Theory of Leadership" in *Training and Development Journal*, May 1969. The concept has continually been refined until its present form presented in this book.

Since the fourth edition of *Management of Organizational Behavior*, Ken Blanchard and his colleagues at Blanchard Training and Development (BTD), Escondido, California, have modified the original Situational Leadership model as it appeared in the fourth edition of *Mangement of Organizational Behavior*. Their current approach to Situational Leadership, called SLII, is described in *Leadership and The One Minute Manager* by Kenneth Blanchard, Patricia Zigarmi, and Rhea Zigarmi (New York: William Morrow and Company, 1985). BTD has developed diagnostic instruments and training materials to support SLII in training seminars and presentations.
4. We now use readiness in place of maturity because it is a more descriptive term of a person's ability and willingness to perform a specific task.
5. Fillmore H. Sanford, *Authoritarianism and Leadership* (Philadelphia: Institute for Research in Human Relations, 1950).
6. The following section has been adopted from Paul Hersey, *Situational Selling* (Escondido, Calif.: Center for Leadership Studies, 1985), p. 19 and following.
7. *Ibid.*, p. 19.
8. *Ibid.*
9. *Ibid.*
10. *Ibid.*, p. 20.
11. *Ibid.*, p. 22.
12. *Ibid.*, pp. 25–26.
13. *Ibid.*, p. 27.
14. *Ibid.*, pp. 28–31.
15. *Ibid.*, p. 32.
16. David C. McClelland, J. W. Atkinson, R. A. Clark and E. L. Lowell, *The Achievement Motive* (New York: Appleton-Century-Crofts, 1953); and *The Achieving Society* (Princeton, N. J.: D. Van Nostrand, 1961).
17. These two instruments were developed by Ronald K. Hambleton, Kenneth H. Blanchard, and Paul Hersey through a grant from Xerox Corporation. We are grateful to Xerox Corporation not only for providing financial support for the instrument development project but also for allowing us to involve many of their managers and employees in our development and validation work. In particular, we would like to acknowledge Audian Dunham, Warren Rothman, and Ray Gumpert for their assistance, encouragement, and constructive criticism of our work. The instruments are available through the Center for Leadership Studies, Escondido, Calif.

18. The Maturity Style Match instruments were developed by Paul Hersey, Kenneth H. Blanchard, and Joseph Keilty. Information on these instruments is available through Center for Leadership Studies, Escondido, Calif.

19 The *Integration of Situational Leadership with Contracting for Leadership Styles* was first published as Paul Hersey, Kenneth H. Blanchard, and Ronald K. Hambleton, "Contracting for Leadership Style: A Process and Instrumentation for Building Effective Work Relationships" in *The Proceedings of OD'78*, San Francisco, Calif., sponsored by University Associates/LRC. This presentation is available through the Center for Leadership Studies, Escondido, Calif.

20. These leadership scales were developed by Paul Hersey, Kenneth H. Blanchard, and Ronald K. Hambleton. Information on these instruments is available through the Center for Leadership Studies, Escondido, Calif.

21. Paul Hersey and Kenneth H. Blanchard, *The Family Game* (Escondido, Calif.: Center for Leadership Studies, 1979).

22. W. Lloyd Warner, *Social Class in America* (New York: Harper & Row, 1960).

23. See Paul Hersey and Kenneth H. Blanchard, "Managing Research and Development Personnel: An Application of Leadership Theory," *Research Management*, September 1969.

24. See Kenneth H. Blanchard and Paul Hersey, "A Leadership Theory for Educational Administrators," *Education*, Spring 1970.

25. Arrigo L. Angelini, Paul Hersey and Sofia Caracushansky, "The Situational Leadership Theory Applied to Teaching: A Research on Learning Effectiveness," São Paulo, Brazil.

26. Kenneth H. Blanchard, "College Boards of Trustees: A Need for Directive Leadership," *Academy of Management Journal*, December 1967.

27. F. H. Stutz, R. G. Morrow, and K. H. Blanchard, "Report of a Survey," in *College and University Trustees and Trusteeship: Recommendations and Report of a Survey* (Ithaca: New York State Regents Advisory Committee on Educational Leadership, 1966).

28. Henry M. Wriston, *Academic Procession* (New York: Columbia University Press, 1959), p. 78.

29. Rensis Likert, *New Patterns of Management* (New York: McGraw-Hill, 1961).

30. Paul Hersey, an unpublished research project, 1965.

31. L. Coch and J. R. P. French, "Overcoming Resistance to Change," in Dorwin Cartwright and Alvin Zander, eds., *Group Dynamics: Research and Theory*, 2nd ed. (Evanston, Ill.: Row, Peterson, 1960).

32. John R. P. French, Jr., Joachim Israel, and Dagfinn Ås, "An Experiment on Participation in a Norwegian Factory," *Human Relations*, 13 (1960), 3–19.

33. A classic study in the area of participation is Victor H. Vroom, *Some Personality Determinants of the Effects of Participation* (Englewood Cliffs, N. J.: Prentice-Hall, 1960).

34. See Paul Hersey and Kenneth H. Blanchard, "Cultural Changes: Their Influence on Organizational Structure and Management Behavior," *Training and Development Journal*, October 1970.

35. William H. Haney, *Communication and Organizational Behavior: Text and Cases*, rev. ed. (Homewood, Ill.: Irwin, 1967), p. 20.

36. Research summaries available from the Center for Leadership Studies.

37. Raymond A. Gumpert and Ronald K. Hambleton, "Situational Leadership: How Xerox Managers Fine-Tune Managerial Styles to Employee Maturity and Task Needs," *Management Review*, December 1979, p. 9.

38. *Ibid.*, p. 11.

39. *Ibid.*

40. *Ibid.*, p. 12.

41. *Ibid.*

42. Research summary available from Center for Leadership Studies, Escondido, Calif.

43. Suggestion made at the Faculty Club, University of Massachusetts, Fall 1974.

CHAPTER 9

SITUATIONAL LEADERSHIP, PERCEPTION, AND THE IMPACT OF POWER

The concepts of leadership and power have generated lively interest, debate, and occasionally confusion throughout the evolution of management thought. The concept of power is closely related to the concept of leadership, for power is one of the means by which a leader influences the behavior of followers.[1] Given this integral relationship between leadership and power, leaders must not only assess their leader behavior in order to understand how they actually influence other people, but they must also examine their possession and use of power.[2]

POWER DEFINED

We earlier defined leadership as an attempt to influence another individual or group and concluded that leadership is an influence process. How do you influence? Through power. Power is influence potential—the resource that enables a leader to gain compliance or commitment from others. Despite its critical importance, power is a subject that is often avoided. This is because power can have its seamy side, and many people want to wish it away and pretend it is not there. But power is a real-world issue. Leaders who understand and know how to use power are more effective than those who do not or will not use power. It is important to understand that to successfully influence the behavior of others, the leader should understand the impact of power on the various leadership styles. In today's world, many sources of power within organizations have been legislated, negotiated, or policied away. Since leaders now have less power to draw from, it is more important to be effective in the use of what is available. Since power bases drive your leadership styles, using them appropriately can enhance your effectiveness as a leader.[3]

In spite of the widespread usage of the term "power" in the management literature, there is considerable confusion over its definition. Power and other concepts, such as influence and authority, are often definitionally indistinct among scholars.[4] Russell[5] defined power as "the production of intended effects." Bierstedt[6] defined power as "the ability to employ force." Wrong[7] limited power to the intended, successful control of others. French[8] defined the power that person A has over person B as "equal to the maximum force which A can induce on B minus the maximum force which B can mobilize in the opposing direction." For Dahl,[9] "A has power over B to the extent that A can get B to do something that B would otherwise not do."

Rogers[10] attempted to clear up the terminological confusion by defining power as "the potential for influence." Thus, power is a resource which may or may not be used. The use of power resulting in a change in the probability that a person or group will adopt the desired behavioral change is defined as "influence." Accepting Rogers's definition, we make this distinction between leadership and power. As was suggested in Chapter 4, leadership is defined as the process of influencing the activities of an individual or a group in efforts toward goal accomplishment in a given situation. Therefore, leadership is simply any attempt to influence, while power is well described as a leader's *influence potential*. It is the resource that enables a leader to induce compliance from or influence others.

POWER: AN ERODING CONCEPT

If power is defined as influence potential, how does one describe authority? Authority is a particular type of power that has its origin in the position that a leader occupies. Thus, authority is the power that is legitimatized by virtue of an individual's formal role in a social organization.

Hundreds of years ago the kings and queens had all the power; the serfs had none. After all, their positions gave them ultimate authority. For years it was almost a similar case with managers. They could make all the decisions. If they didn't like the way you looked or the way you combed your hair, they could fire you, and workers could do very little to stop such arbitrary action. Today, that is no longer the case. What does that mean in terms of a leader's influence potential?

First of all, managers must realize that power is finite. There is only so much power around. If someone else has it, you don't. If your power is legislated or negotiated away, it is no longer there. The amount of power available does not expand in different situations. As James A. Lee argues, "Leader power is what is left after subtracting all subordinate power (i.e., collective, legal, economic independence, and expertise), power removed from their grasp by the nature of the task (i.e., a machine-paced assembly line, lack of proximity, and physical barriers), and that removed by power sources outside their organizational unit (organizational policies, intrusions from their boss, and public sentiment).[11] Thus, today's manager only has a limited amount of power.

Second, if managers have only a portion of the total power available, they must learn ways to use the power they have in realistic and meaningful ways. In addition, where managers used to rely on the power of their position, they now have to look for other bases, or sources, of power.

POSITION POWER AND PERSONAL POWER

One of the characteristics of leadership is that leaders exercise power. Amitai Etzioni discusses the difference between *position power* and *personal power*. His distinction springs from his concept of power as the ability to induce or influence behavior. He claims that power is derived from an organizational office, personal influence, or both. Individuals who are able to induce other individuals to do a certain job because of their position in the organization are considered to have position power; individuals who derive their power from their followers are considered to have personal power. Some individuals can have both position power and personal power.[12]

Where do managers get the position power that is available to them? Although Etzioni would argue that it comes from the organizational office of a manager, we feel it comes from above and, therefore, is not inherent in the office. Managers occupying positions in an organization may have more or less position power than their predecessor or someone else in a similar position in the same organization. It is not a matter of the office having power, but rather the extent to which those people to whom managers report are willing to delegate authority and responsibility down to them. So position power tends to flow down in an organization. This is not to say that leaders do not have any impact on how much position power they accrue. They certainly do. The confidence and trust they develop with the people above them will often determine the willingness of superior(s) to delegate down to them. And remember, it is not just a downward delegation; their boss can take it back. We have all seen this occur on occasions when managers still have the same responsibilities but all of a sudden their authority (reward system and sanctions) to get the job done in the way they once did is taken away.

Personal power is the extent to which followers respect, feel good about, and are committed to their leader, and see their goals as being satisfied by the goals of their leader. In other words, personal power is the extent to which people are willing to follow a leader. As a result, personal power in an organizational setting comes from below—the followers. Thus, we must be careful when we say that some leaders are charismatic or have personal power that flows from them. If that were true, we would have to be able to say that managers with personal power could take over any department and have the same commitment and rapport they had in their last department. We know that is not true. Although managers certainly can influence the amount of personal power they have by the way they treat their people, it is a volatile kind of power. It can be taken away rapidly by followers. Make a few dramatic mistakes and see how many people are willing to follow. Personal power is a day-to-day phenomenon—it can be earned and it can be taken away.

Etzioni suggested that the best situation for leaders is when they have both personal power and position power. But in some cases it is not possible to build a relationship on both. Then the question becomes whether it is more important to have personal power or position power. Happiness and human relations have been culturally reinforced over the past several decades. With this emphasis, most people would pick personal power as being the most important. But there may be another side of the coin.

In his sixteenth-century treatise *The Prince*, Machiavelli presents an interesting viewpoint when he raises the question of whether it is better to have a relationship based on love (personal power) or fear (position power).[13] Machiavelli, as does Etzioni, contends that it is best to be both loved and feared. If, however, one cannot have both, he suggests that a relationship based on love alone tends to be volatile, short-lived, and easily terminated when there is no fear of retaliation. On the other hand, Machiavelli contends that a relationship based on fear tends to be longer lasting, in that the individual must be willing to incur the sanction (pay the price) before terminating the relationship. This is a difficult concept for many people to accept, and yet one of the most difficult roles for leaders—whether they be a boss, teacher, or parent—is disciplining someone about whom they care. Yet to be effective, leaders sometimes have to sacrifice short-term friendship for long-term respect if they are interested in the growth and development of the people with whom they are working. Machiavelli warns, however, that one should be careful that fear does not lead to hatred. For hatred often evokes overt behavior in terms of retaliation, undermining, and attempts to overthrow.

In summary, *position power* is the extent to which the leader has rewards, punishments and sanctions to bring to bear in reference to follow-ers.[14] It tends to come from above in the organization. Position power can be thought of as the authority to use the rewards and sanctions that are dele-gated down. But one must be careful. Just because you have position power today does not mean that you will have it tomorrow. People above you can delegate it, but they can also take it back. It doesn't mean you don't have any impact on how much you receive. That is the result of the trust and confidence you build with your people.

Personal power is defined as the extent to which leaders gain the confi-dence and trust of those people that they're attempting to influence. It's the cohesiveness, commitment, and rapport between leaders and followers. It is also impacted by the extent to which followers see their own goals as being the same, similar to, or at least dependent upon the accomplishment of the leader's goals.

While position power comes from above in the organization, personal power flows from the followers. Personal power is not inherent in the leader. It has to be earned from the followers on a day-to-day basis. Just because you've got it today doesn't mean you've got it tomorrow. This coun-try re-elected Richard Nixon with a landslide victory in 1972 and just a few months later took back its commitment. Personal power is not within the leader but comes from the people the leader is attempting to influence.

Although personal and position power are unique and distinct, they are an interacting influence system: one directly affects the other. Often followers are affected by their perception of the leader's ability to provide rewards, punishments and sanctions, and influence up the organization. Also, the extent to which people above you in the organization are willing to delegate position power is often dependent on their perception of the fol-lowers' commitment to you. *So it is not sufficient just to have either position or personal power alone—you need to work at gaining both.*

Selling Within Your Own Organization[15]

It is important to keep in mind that no matter where you are within your organization, you are trying to influence people. If you are managing, you can use both position power and personal power to influence the people who report directly to you. However, when attempting to influence your boss, senior executives, and associates, you must depend almost exclusively on personal power. Therefore, you are selling. When you have little or no position power, you must learn to develop rapport through personal power, because it is through this trust and confidence that an effective relationship can be built. Figure 9-1 illustrates this important idea. Keep in mind that power is a real-world issue. People who understand and know how to use power are more effective than those who do not or will not. Recognition of the fact that all managers are in the business of selling is an important aspect of this understanding.

Boss/Associates

SELLING

Leadership = Influence

MANAGING

Staff members/Followers   **Figure 9-1   Selling up/Managing down**[16]

ADDITIONAL BASES OF POWER

While position power and personal power are important and useful in examining power, they are limited because you are always forced to divide "the pie" into just two pieces.

Natemeyer cites a number of other attempts to classify bases of power.[17] Peabody[18] classified the statements of respondents in a police department, a welfare office, and an elementary school into four categories. These were power of legitimacy (laws, rules, policies), of position, of competence (professional and technical expertise), and of person.

A study by Filley and Grimes[19] identified eleven reasons why an individual would seek a decision from another on various work-related matters in a professional organization. These reasons, from most frequently to least frequently mentioned, were responsibility and function (the person is responsible for the particular matter); formal authority (the person is in a position to make decisions generally); control of resources (the person controls money, information, and so on); collegial (a group of peers has the right to be consulted); manipulation (the person can get the decision made in the manner desired); default or avoidance (the person is available and will deal with the problem); bureaucratic rules (the rules specify the person to consult); traditional rules (custom, tradition, or seniority specify the person to consult); equity (the person is a fair decision maker); friendship (the person is personally liked); and expertise (the person has superior knowledge of the subject).

Many other power base classification systems have been developed,[20] but the framework devised by French and Raven[21] appears to be the most widely accepted. They propose that there are five different bases of power: coercive power, expert power, legitimate power, referent power, and reward power.

Later, Raven collaborating with Kruglanski,[22] identified a sixth power base—information power. Then, in 1979,[23] Hersey and Goldsmith proposed

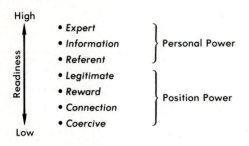

Figure 9-2 Power bases important at various levels of readiness[24]

a seventh basis of power—connection power. These seven bases of power, identified as potential means of successfully influencing the behavior of others, are shown in Figure 9-2 and discussed following.

Readiness, Styles, and Power Bases[25]

The relationship between readiness, the appropriate style, and the power base that drives that style will be explained from the aspects of managing and leading.

Coercive power—the perceived ability to provide sanctions.

Followers at readiness level R1 need guidance. It is important to remember that too much supportive behavior with people who are not performing may be perceived as permissive or as rewarding the lack of performance. Without some coercive power to drive the *telling* style, attempts to influence may be like water off a duck's back. Followers need to know that if they do not respond, there may be some costs, sanctions, or other consequences. These may take the form of a reprimand, cut in pay, transfer, demotion, or even dismissal.

Managers often erode their coercive power by not following through. They may have the ability to impose sanctions but for one reason or another are unwilling to do so. This can result in a loss of power.

Another way to erode coercive power is by not differentiating in the use of sanctions based upon performance. If people feel they will be punished regardless of performance, coercive power has little impact.

It is even possible to "talk" coercive power away. A manager begins a performance appraisal interview with a low performer by saying, "Now, look, both of us know that you've been here over twenty years and I can't get rid of you . . . ." In just a few words, the manager has stripped away any coercive power the follower might have perceived.

> *Connection power—the perceived association with
> influential persons or organizations.*

Connection power is an important driver for *telling* and *selling* leadership styles. Usually followers at R1 and R2 want to avoid the sanction or gain the favor they associate with powerful connections. The important issue is not whether there is a real connection but whether there is a perception of a real connection.

For example, a first-level supervisor may be regarded as having limited power. But, if that supervisor is married to a relative of the company president, the perceived connection may provide added influence with others in the organization.

> *Reward power—the perceived ability to provide things
> that people would like to have.*

Reward power is enhanced if managers are seen as having the ability to give appropriate rewards. Followers who are unable but willing are more likely to try on new behaviors if they feel increases in performance will be rewarded. Rewards may include raises, bonuses, promotions, or transfers to more desirable positions. They may also include intangibles such as a pat on the back or feedback on accomplishment.

A significant amount of reward power has been legislated, negotiated, and policied away. Yet managers themselves often erode the power that remains by making promises they don't keep. For example:

Salesperson: "I did it! I made the fifteen percent over quota with room to spare. When am I going to get that ten percent bonus?"

Sales Mgr: "I'm sorry, but economic conditions are such that we'll have to postpone it for a while. But don't worry, if you keep up the good work, I promise I'll make it up to you."

Other managers erode their reward power by hoping for *A* but rewarding *B*. An example might be an organization that gives all salespeople a 10 percent cost-of-living adjustment and yet the difference between reward for *average* sales and *outstanding* sales is only 1 or 2 percent. In this case, "hanging around" for another year is significantly rewarded. This often results in high performers losing their motivation and commitment or looking outside the company for opportunities.

> *Legitimate power—the perception that it is appropriate
> for the leader to make decisions due to title or position
> in the organization.*

Legitimate power can be a useful driver for the *selling* and *participating* styles. Followers who are both unable and unwilling could care less about whether someone's title is "manager," "regional manager" or "vice-president." By the same token, followers high in readiness are far less impressed with title or position than they are with expertise or information that the leader has to offer. But followers in the moderate ranges of readiness can often be influenced if they feel it is appropriate for a person in *that* position or with *that* title to make *that* decision. For example, a salesperson commenting to a peer about the department's recent reorganization: ". . . Pat should be making those kinds of decisions . . . that's what the Sales Manager gets paid to do."

Referent power—the perceived attractiveness of inter-acting with another person.

In attempting to influence people who have the ability but are insecure or unwilling, high relationship behavior is necessary. If people have a confidence problem, the manager needs to *encourage*. If they have a motivation problem, the manager needs to *discuss* and *problem solve*. In either case, if the manager has not taken time to build rapport, attempts to participate may be perceived as adversarial rather than helpful. Confidence, trust, and rapport are important in influencing people. If a follower feels that the manager will provide encouragement and help when it is needed, it can make an important difference in the success of the influence attempt.

Referent power is based on the manager's personal traits. A manager high in referent power is generally liked and admired by others because of personality. It is this liking for, admiration for, and identification with the manager that influences others.

Information power—the perceived access to—or possession of—useful information.

The styles that tend to effectively influence followers at above average readiness levels, R3 and R4, are *participating and delegating*. Information Power is helpful in driving these styles.

This power source has grown in importance during the high tech explosion, with the emphasis on data storage and data retrieval.

Information power is based on perceived access to data. This is different from expert power, which is the *understanding* of or ability to *use* data. For example, in a recent study, it was found that secretaries in a major corporate office had a significant amount of information power but little expert power in some technical areas. They were able to help gain or prevent access to information, but in a few technical areas had little expertise themselves.

Expert power—the perception that the leader has relevant education, experience, and expertise.

Followers who are competent and confident require little direction or supportive behavior. They are able and willing to perform on their own. The driver for influencing these followers is expert power. With followers who are able and willing, leaders are more effective if they possess the expertise, skill, and knowledge that followers respect and regard as important.

IS THERE A BEST TYPE OF POWER?

Even though the French and Raven initial classification system was not derived from research, it motivated a number of scholars to try to answer the following question: Given the wide variety of power bases available to the leader, which type of power should be emphasized in order to maximize effectiveness? In any attempt to answer this question, it is important to remember the definition of effectiveness. As stated in Chapter 6, organizational effectiveness, as well as leader effectiveness, is a function of both performance (output variables) and satisfaction (intervening variables). Natemeyer[26] reviewed the various studies that attempted to investigate the relationship between work group effectiveness and the degree to which a leader utilizes various power bases.

Student[27] studied forty production groups in two plants of a company that manufactured home appliances. Employees rated the extent to which they complied with their foremen due to each of the five French and Raven power bases. Legitimate power was found to be the strongest reason for compliance, followed by expert power, reward power, referent power, and last, coercive power.

Student also related the foreman's power base utilization (as perceived by the workers) to a number of measures of performance. He found that legitimate power, while most important among the reasons for compliance, was not related to the performance of the work groups. Reward and coercive power were positively related to some performance measures (suggestions submitted, supply cost performance) but negatively related to others (average earnings, maintenance cost performance). Expert and referent power were significantly and positively related to four and five measures of performance, and thus emerged as the most effective base of supervisory power. Student explains these results by suggesting that expert and referent power are qualitatively different from legitimate, reward, and coercive power. Expert and referent power are considered idiosyncratic in character and dependent on an individual's unique role behavior, while legitimate, reward, and coercive power are organizationally determined and designed to be equal for supervisors at the same hierarchical level. Implicit in Student's conclusions is the contention that subordinates are more responsive to and satisfied with a leader whose influence attempts are not based entirely on position-based power (that is, legitimate, reward, and coercive).

Similar results were obtained in a study by Bachman, Smith, and Slesinger.[28] Data were obtained from thirty-six branch offices of a national sales organization. Each office was managed by a single office supervisor. Employees were asked to rank each of the five power bases according to the extent to which it was a reason for compliance. These results were then correlated with satisfaction and performance measures. Legitimate and expert power again emerged as numbers 1 and 2 in importance, followed by referent, reward, and coercive power.

In those offices in which referent and expert power predominated, performance and satisfaction were high. In those offices in which reward power was high, performance tended to be poor and there was marked dissatisfaction. Coercive and legitimate bases of power were associated with dissatisfaction, but they were unrelated to performance.

The findings of Student and Bachman and others were included in a comparative study of five organizations by Bachman, Bowers, and Marcus.[29] In addition to the appliance firm and the sales organization, other organizations examined were twelve liberal arts colleges, forty agencies of a life insurance company, and twenty-one work groups of a large Midwestern utility company. A ranking procedure was used to ascertain the strength of the supervisors' power bases in the colleges and the utility company, while an independent rating procedure for each power base was used with the life insurance agencies.

Expert and legitimate power were again the most important reasons for complying with superiors in all three organizations. Expert power was most important and legitimate, second, in the colleges and insurance agencies, while the order was reversed in the utility company. Referent power was third in importance in the colleges, fourth in the insurance agencies, and fifth in the utility companies. Reward power was third in importance in the utility company and the agencies, and fourth in the colleges. Finally, coercive power was least important in the colleges and the insurance agencies, and fourth in the utility company.

Expert and referent power were again strongly and positively related to satisfaction in these three additional organizations, while reward and legitimate power were not strongly related to the satisfaction measures. Coervive power was consistently related to dissatisfaction. Performance data were obtained from the insurance agencies but not from the colleges or utility company. Expert and reward power were positively related to insurance agency performance measures, while coercive, legitimate, and referent power yielded insignificant correlations.

Ivancevich and Donnelly[30] studied salesmen's perceptions of their managers' power bases in thirty-one branches of a large firm that produces food products. The employees were asked to rank the power bases in order of importance for compliance. Expert power was most important, followed by legitimate, reward, referent, and coercive power. Referent and expert power were positively related to performance, while reward, legitimate, and coercive power showed no relationship.

Burke and Wilcox[31] conducted a study of leader power bases and subordinate satisfaction in six offices of a large public utility company. Using a 1 to 5 ranking method, expert power emerged as most important, followed by legitimate, coercive, referent, and reward power. Referent and expert power were associated with greatest satisfaction; legimate and reward power were intermediate; and coercive power was associated with least satisfaction.

Jamieson and Thomas[32] conducted a study of power in the classroom. Data were collected from high school, undergraduate, and graduate students on their teachers' bases of power, and results were correlated with several measures of student satisfaction. For the high school students, legitimate power was most important, followed by coercive, expert, referent, and reward power. The undergraduate students viewed coercive power as most important, followed by legitimate, expert, reward, and referent power. The graduate students perceived expert power as the strongest, followed by legitimate, reward, coercive, and referent power. Coercive power was strongly and negatively associated with satisfaction among all three groups, while the other four power bases yielded insignificant results.

In summarizing his review of the most important research that has been done relating supervisory power bases to subordinate satisfaction and performance, Natemeyer[33] made the following general conclusion. While expert and legitimate power bases appear to be the most important reason for compliance, and expert and referent power bases tend to be often strongly and consistently related to subordinate performance and satisfaction measures, the results are not clear enough to generalize about a *best* power base. In fact, the results suggest that the appropriate power base is largely affected by situational variables. In other words, leaders may need various power bases, depending on the situation.[34]

Power Bases and Readiness Level

Hersey, Blanchard, and Natemeyer[35] suggest that there appears to be a direct relationship between the level of readiness of individuals and groups and the kind of power bases that have a high probability of gaining compliance from those people. Situational Leadership views readiness as the ability and willingness of individuals or groups to take responsibility for directing their own behavior in a particular situation. Thus, it must be reemphasized that readiness is a task-specific concept and depends on what the leader is attempting to accomplish.

As people move from lower to higher levels of readiness, their compe-

High readiness

↑

expert
information
referent
legitimate
reward
connection
coercive

Low readiness

**Figure 9-3   The impact of power bases
at various levels of readiness**

tence and confidence to do things increase. The seven power bases appear to have significant impact on the behavior of people at various levels of readiness, as seen in Figure 9-3.

INTEGRATING POWER BASES, READINESS LEVEL, AND LEADERSHIP STYLE THROUGH SITUATIONAL LEADERSHIP

Situational Leadership can provide the basis for understanding the potential impact of each power base. It is our contention that the readiness of the follower not only dictates which style of leadershp will have the highest probability of success, but that the readiness of the follower also determines the power base that the leader should use in order to induce compliance or influence behavior.

The Situational Use of Power

Even if the leader is using the appropriate leadership style for a given readiness level, that style may not be maximizing the leader's probability of success if it does not reflect the appropriate power base. Therefore, just as an effective leader should vary leadership style according to the readiness level of the follower, it may be appropriate to vary the use of power in a similar manner. The power bases that may influence people's behavior at various levels of readiness are pictured in Figure 9-4.

Figure 9-4 shows a relationship only between power bases and readiness level. There also appears to be a direct relationship between the kind of power bases a person has and the corresponding leadership style that will be effective for that person in influencing the behavior of others at various readiness levels.

Coercive power.   A follower low in readiness generally needs strong directive behavior in order to become productive. To engage effectively in

214

Figure 9-4   Power bases necessary to influence people's behavior at various levels of readiness

this *"telling"* style, coercive power is often necessary. The behavior of people at low levels of readiness seems to be influenced by the awareness that costs will be incurred if they do not learn and follow the rules of the game. Thus, if people are *unable and unwilling*, sanctions—the perceived power to fire, transfer, demote, and so on—may be an important way that a leader can induce compliance from them. The leader's coercive power may motivate the followers to avoid the punishment or "cost" by doing what the leader tells them to do.

Connection power.   As a follower begins to move from *readiness level* R1 to R2, directive behavior is still needed, but increases in supportive behavior are also important. The *"telling"* and *"selling"* leadership styles appropriate for these levels of readiness may become more effective if the leader has connection power. The possession of this power base may induce compliance because a follower at these readiness levels tends to aim at avoiding punishments or gaining rewards available through the powerful connection.

Reward power.   A follower at a low to moderate level of readiness often needs high amounts of supportive behavior and directive behavior. This *"selling"* style is often enhanced by reward power. Since individuals at this readiness level are *willing* to "try on" new behavior, the leader needs to be perceived as having access to rewards in order to gain compliance and reinforce growth in the desired direction.

Legitimate power.   The leadership styles that tend to influence effectively those at both *moderate levels of readiness* (R2 and R3) are *"selling"* and *"participating."* To engage effectively in these styles, legitimate power seems to be helpful. By the time a follower reaches these moderate levels of readiness, the power of the leader has become legitimized. That is, the leader is able to induce compliance or influence behavior by virtue of the leader's position in the organizational hierarchy.

Referent power. A follower at a moderate to high level of readiness tends to need little direction but still requires a high level of communication and support from the leader. This *participating* style may be effectively utilized if the leader has referent power. This source of power is based on good personal relations with the follower. With people who are *able but unwilling or insecure*, this power base tends to be an important means of instilling confidence and providing encouragement, recognition, and other supportive behavior. When that occurs, followers will generally respond in a positive way, permitting the leader to influence them because they like, admire, or identify with the leader.

Information power. The leadership styles that tend to motivate followers effectively at *above-average readiness levels* (R3 and R4) are *participating* and *delegating.* Information power seems to be helpful in using these two styles. People at these levels of readiness look to the leader for information to maintain or improve performance. The transition from moderate to high readiness may be facilitated if the follower knows that the leader is available to clarify or explain issues and provide access to pertinent data, reports, and correspondence when needed. Through this information power the leader is able to influence those people who are both willing and able.

Expert power. A follower who develops to a high level of readiness often requires little direction or support. This follower is *able and willing* to perform the tasks required and tends to respond most readily to a *delegating* leadership style and expert power. Thus, a leader may gain respect from and influence most readily a person who has both competence and confidence by possessing expertise, skill, and knowledge that this follower recognizes as important.

An easy way to think about sources of power in terms of making diagnostic judgments is to draw a triangle, as shown in Figure 9-5, around the

Figure 9-5   Power bases necessary to influence people at various readiness levels

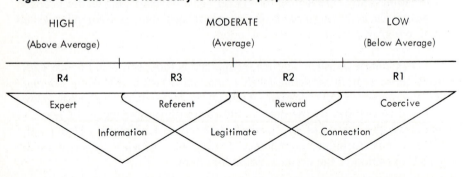

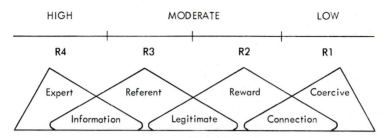

Figure 9-6   Power bases necessary to influence people's behavior at *specific* levels of readiness

three power bases necessary to influence below-average, moderate, and above-average levels of readiness. It is important to stress here that with people of below-average readiness, the emphasis is on compliance; with people of average readiness, it is on compliance and influence; and with people with above-average readiness, it is on influence.

A way to examine the high-probability power base for a specific readiness level is to draw inverted triangles, as shown in Figure 9-6. Note that R1 and R4, the extreme readiness levels, include only two power bases instead of three.

Developing Sources of Power

Although these seven power bases are potentially available to any leader as a means of inducing compliance or influencing the behavior of others, it is important to note that there is significant variance in the powers that leaders may actually possess. Some leaders have a great deal of power while others have very little. Part of the variance in actual power is due to the organization and the leader's position in the organization (position power), and part is due to individual differences among the leaders themselves (personal power), as shown in Figure 9-7.

The power bases that are most relevant at the below-average levels of readiness tend to be those that the organization or others can bestow upon the leader. The power bases that influence people who are above average in readiness must, to a large degree, be earned from the people the leader is attempting to influence. Therefore, we suggest that position power, the word *compliance*, and the phrase *power over* are most descriptive with coercive, connection, reward, and legitimate power bases; and we suggest that personal power, the word *influence*, and the phrase *power with* more accurately describe the effect on behavior from referent, information, and expert power.

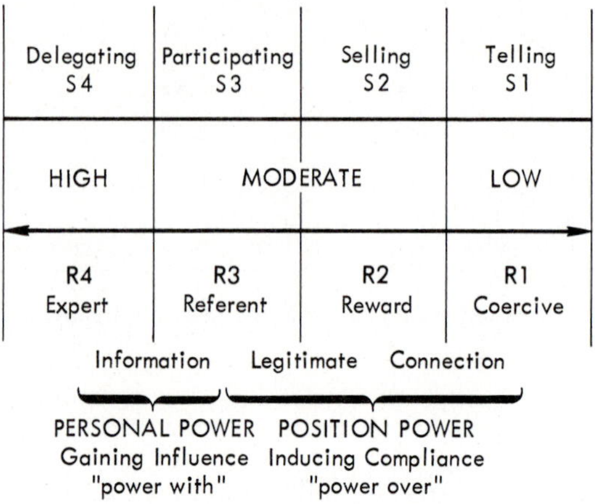

Delegating S4	Participating S3	Selling S2	Telling S1
HIGH	MODERATE		LOW
R4 Expert	R3 Referent	R2 Reward	R1 Coercive

Information   Legitimate   Connection

PERSONAL POWER   POSITION POWER
Gaining Influence   Inducing Compliance
"power with"   "power over"

Figure 9-7   Summary of relationships between power bases, readiness level, and leadership style

Sources of Power

Just as some leaders start off with little power in the beginning and gradually build and develop various power sources, other leaders gradually let their power bases erode and lose them. Why does this happen? Before we answer this question, managers need to understand where position and personal power sources come from.

As we discussed earlier, position power can be thought of simply as the authority that is delegated down in an organization. It is important to remember that just because a manager has position power today, it doesn't mean that the manager will have it tomorrow. Not only can the people above delegate the authority to provide rewards and sanctions, they can also take that authority away. So managers must remember that position power is volatile.

This is not to suggest that managers do not have some impact on how much coercive, connection, reward, and legitimate power they get. Of course they do. The extent to which they develop rapport, confidence, and trust between themselves and their superiors will determine how willing those above will be to delegate power. But position power is something that a manager has to earn on a day-to-day basis.

The same can be said about personal power, except the reward, information, and expert power that managers possess depend on the confidence and trust these managers generate from the people they are attempting to influence. For example, people might think that some leaders have charisma and other leaders don't. Leaders don't have charisma; followers *give* leaders charisma. We have all seen that phenomenon with elected officials. They are often carried into office because of their charisma, but when their actions do not gain general approval, they may lose their charisma overnight. Again, this is not to say that managers do not have some impact on how much personal power they get, but it's something that they have to earn on a day-to-day basis.

It should be remembered that position power and personal power bases together constitute an interaction-influence system. That is, power does not develop in a vacuum. Each power base tends to affect each of the other power bases. Thus, it has been found that the extent to which people are willing to grant personal power to a manager depends a great deal on their perception of a leader's ability to provide rewards, punishment, or sanctions (position power). At the same time, the willingness of managers above a leader to delegate position power is often determined by the extent to which they perceive that leader as being liked and respected and having information and expertise (personal power) with their people. Keep in mind that we did not say how much personal power or position power affects whether leaders will be delegated authority or treated with respect. It's the *perception* that others have of those power bases that is crucial. So, the key word, perhaps, in the whole area of the behavioral sciences is *perception*.

The Perception of Power[36]

The key issue in the concept of power is that it is not based on the reality of how much power the manager has but rather on the followers' perception of that power. *Truth and reality evoke no behavior. All behavior is based on people's perception and interpretation of truth and reality.* For example, when a couple has a fight, it does not matter whether the cause was real or imagined—it was just as much of a fight. It is the perception others hold about power that gives people the ability to influence.

We operate using psychological maps. The caution that one must make is that no matter how hard we work or how detailed our psychological maps, the map is not the territory. But the closer and closer we match our psychological map to the territory, the higher the probability that we will effectively be able to operate within that territory. We have to remember, however, that the map is not the territory—no matter how much information and specificity we have in terms of our psychological map.

Get the Data Out[37]

With power, people must not only perceive you as having it, they must see you as able and willing to use it. Because power is a matter of perception, it is important that you get out the data. It's not enough to have access to power. You have to let people know you're willing to use it. You can't hide your light under a bushel. Information has no value in a data bank. It has value only when you get it out to the end user in a fashion that can be understood and accepted. It means simply that, if you don't blow your own horn, somebody else will use it as a spitoon! Some leaders *have* plenty of power but are unwilling to *use* it.

Consider a father examining his son's report card and suffering mild cardiac tremors as he sees a solid column of *D* grades. Outraged that a product of his genes could so disgrace the family, he confronts his son and says, "Dave, this just won't do. I can't tolerate these grades, and if you don't show me an immediate turn-around, you're going to be grounded!"

Six weeks later, Dave brings home another report card. This time the *D* grades are written in red ink with exclamation points. The father says, "David, get in here! I'm really upset, and now you have no choice at all. Hit those books hard or you're definitely going to be grounded!

Next time it's the same except that the teacher has added some pointed remarks about Dave's inattentive behavior in class. Dave's father turns crimson, crumples his beer can, and shouts, "David Ralph, this is it . . . last chance city . . . you're in real trouble with the old man now!"

What has Dave learned? That his father, who has the ability to ground him, won't use the power! Because of his Dad's reluctance to follow through with his threatened punishments, Dave knows that all he has to do is take heat for six minutes and he's off the hook for six weeks!

Power is a matter of perception—use it or lose it!

Eroding Sources of Power

Since leaders have only a limited amount of power available to them, one would hope for their sake that they would hold on to whatever power bases they have. And, yet, some leaders who often start off with significant power gradually lose their power bases and let them erode. The key to avoiding such erosion is using your power bases (in the eyes of others). For example, a leader could have a significant amount of coercive power but gradually lose it by threatening. If a leader continually threatens followers with some kind of punishment but never delivers the punishment, the people will start to think that the leader really does not have any coercive power. Similarly, leaders can lose their reward power if everyone gets the same reward whether they perform or not, or just because they have seniority in industry, or are older in the family. Some parents establish age requirements when kids can get to do things. "When you're thirteen, you'll be able to stay out past ten o'clock. When you're sixteen, you'll be able to stay home alone." The problem with using age as a factor in determining when people can do things is that all they have to do is get older. When that is done, reward power as a parent or a leader is lost. What is happening is that people are getting rewards for being older, not for being more mature.

Connection power can be eroded when people begin to see that the sponsor or connection does not make any disciplinary interventions or provide any favors or sanctions. In other words, to be maintained, connection power needs occasional interventions from the sponsor.

Managers can lose their legitimate power by not making decisions that people think they ought to make, given their position. Erosion of this power base can also occur if a manager continually makes decisions that are not fruitful. After a while, their staff members will no longer look to them to make decisions even if they have the title of Senior Research Scientist or Department Chairman.

This process also works with referent power. When you give "strokes" to those who are performing and the same strokes to those who are not performing, you begin to erode your referent power. If people do not have to earn strokes, then you no longer have referent power.

Leaders also have to be careful about eroding their information and expert power. This is particularly a concern if you give away expertise and information to people whose goals are not organizational goals. If you give away too much information and knowledge, eventually they will not need you. The only way you can get around this is to continually develop new information and new expertise so that they have to come back to the source.

If leaders let their power bases erode, they will also reduce the effectiveness of their leadership attempts. For example, an effective "telling" (S1) leadership style depends on having some coercive power. If leaders are not seen as being able to deliver punishments and sanctions, their use of that style is limited.

The same can be said about a *"selling"* (S2) style. Without some control over rewards, leaders are seen as not able to reinforce or reward increased performance as people grow and develop their skills.

A *"participating"* (S3) style won't work if people don't like and respect a manager. If a manager has let reward power erode because the manager hasn't been good to people, then a participative/high relationship style is going to be seen not as a reward but as a punishment. It's like a manager who has ignored and left a staff member alone for a along time, then, suddenly, when that person's family life begins to deteriorate, the manager tries to "fill the void." Since the manager has eroded available referent power, these supportive leadership attempts are not seen as rewards but as sanctions and punishments. Time with the boss is not seen as a positive situation.

If a manager is supervising highly competent and motivated people, that manager needs to have some expert power to make any kind of significant intervention with these people. If the manager has eroded any information and expert power that the manager had, the possibility of influencing these people in any significant way will be very limited.

Willingness to Take a Power Role

As we just noted, a person desiring a leadership role must also be willing to assume the responsibilities of that role. This means gaining and exercising power. Managing, supervising, and leading are all influencing behaviors. If a person is unwilling or unable to exercise power, any attempt to manage, supervise, or lead is doomed to failure.

Katherine Benzinger has provided some special insights into the process of gaining and using power.[38] While her views are primarily directed toward women, her observations also have direct relevance to men. We will spend the next few paragraphs summarizing her important contributions.

Benzinger defines power as "the ability to get your way."[39] She notes that there are important differences between personal and organizational power. In the former, a person has freedom of choice as far as who to influence and the size of the group(s) is much smaller. In the later, a person is not free to chose co-workers and bosses and there are many more people in the group. These differences are very significant, particularly in the way men and women approach these differences.

Men, Benzinger observes, have been trained since childhood—particularly in athletic groups—to develop trust and respect among fellow group members, even those they may personally dislike. Women, on the other hand, have been socialized to use personal power. When confronted with an unpleasant situation, they may choose to either avoid the threatening person or accommodate.

We have equated leadership with influence, but as Benzinger has correctly concluded, accommodation does not influence. Therefore, "The first difference between personal and organizational power is: in seeking organizational power, you must consciously try to build the trust and respect of your co-workers.[40]

As was just noted, women have a tendency when faced with a difficult situation to rely on past experience; that is, to seek a family-sized group such as their own staff or peer group as a power base. If they had control of their own staff, women believe, they would be perceived as competent and doing an effective job. But this neglects contextual power—power external to one's immediate staff. Men assume that they have control of their immediate staff and place their primary focus of power on persons *external* to their unit or department. This brings up the second difference between personal and organizational power. "The second difference is the need to develop influence with a large number of people."[41]

Do You Want Power?

Benzinger suggest that "If . . . you want to climb a career ladder or influence your organization significantly, you must not only understand power, you must seek it actively and skillfully . . . . To protect yourself from frustration and burn-out, you must therefore decide consciously whether you want power and are willingly to do what it takes to acquire it."[42] She suggests three guidelines:

1. Earning power requires a very substantial time commitment. If you are not willing to invest the time, perhaps gaining power is not right for you.
2. Gaining power in organizations requires confrontation. If you are not willing to play "King of the Mountain" to get on top and stay on top, then you may not wish to seek power.
3. You may want to check to see if research on hemispheric accessing patterns of the brain and personal styles can give you some insights into whether or not you will be comfortable with power. This research suggests that if organizational demands are congruent with areas of hemispheric dominance, then the person will function with a greater degree of comfort.[43]

Once you have decided to acquire power, you may wish to consider the following 12-step strategy:

1. Learn and use your organization's language and symbols.
2. Learn and use your organization's priorities.
3. Learn the power lines.
4. Determine who has power and get to know these people.
5. Develop your professional knowledge.
6. Develop your power skills.
7. Be proactive.
8. Assume authority.
9. Take risks.
10. Beat your own drum.
11. Meet the boss's needs.
12. Take care of yourself.[44]

Benzinger concludes this list with a worthwhile personal note, " . . . you may discover that being powerful is not as exhausting as some people might have you believe. What's more you might discover having power is fun—it gets things you want done."[45]

THE POWER PERCEPTION PROFILE

To provide leaders with feedback on their power bases so that they can determine which power bases they already have and which they need to develop, Hersey and Natemeyer developed the Power Perception Profile.[46] There are two versions of this instrument: one measures self-perception of power and the other determines an individual's perception of another's power.

Development of the Power Perception Profile

The Power Perception Profile contains twenty-one forced-choice pairs of reasons often given by people when asked why they do things that a leader suggests or wants them to do. Each statement reflects one of the seven sources of power just discussed. In the following pair of statements, referent power is represented by the first statement and coercive power is depicted by the second statement.

> I like this person and want to do things that will please.
>
> This person can administer sanctions and punishments to those who do not cooperate.

Respondents are asked to allocate three points between each set of two alternative choices. They are asked to base their judgments on the relative importance of each alternative, judging either their perception of why people comply with their wishes (self-perception) or why they comply with a particular leader's wishes (other perception).

Respondents are asked to allocate the points between the first item and the second item based on perceived importance in any of the following fashions:

3	2	1	0
0	1	2	3

After completing the Power Perception Profile, respondents are able to obtain a score of the relative strength of each of the seven bases of power. This score represents the perception of influence for themselves or some other leader.

One of the shortcomings of most forced-choice instruments is that they provide comparisons only between items or categories but they do not offer any perspective on the overall scope of the concepts. In other words, a leader might score high or low on a certain power base when compared with each of the other power bases but no indication is given of how that power base score compares with the score another leader might receive. For example, even if a leader's score on coercive power is low in relation to the other six power bases, the leader may be relatively high in coercive power when compared with other leaders the respondent has known. To correct this deficiency, the Power Perception Profile goes one step farther than most forced-choice questionnaires and asks respondents to compare the leader with other leaders they have known, in reference to each of the seven power bases.

Uses of the Power Perception Profile

The Power Perception Profile can be used to gather data in actual organizational settings or any learning environment—for example, student or training groups.

In learning groups, the instrument is particularly helpful in groups that have developed some history—that is, they have spent a considerable amount of time interacting with each other analyzing or solving cases, participating in simulations or other training exercises, and so on. In this kind of situation, it is recommended that the group fill out one instrument together, using a particular member as the subject and arriving at a consensus on each of the items on the instrument. During each discussion, the person whose power bases are being examined should play a nonparticipant role. That person should not ask any questions or attempt to clarify, justify, or explain actions. An appropriate response might be, "Could you tell me more about that?" or "I'd like to hear more on that point." Then, at the end of the group's assessment, the person whose power bases were being examined is given an opportunity to respond to the group's discussion. This process is repeated until every participant has had a turn to get feedback from the group.

If the Power Perception Profile is being used to gather data in an organization, each organizational member from whom perceptions are desired should fill out a separate instrument. In this case, it is strongly suggested that the leaders not collect the data themselves. Instead, a third party who has the trust and confidence of all involved—such as a representative from personnel or human resource management—should administer the questionnaire. It is also important to assure respondents that only generalized data will be shared with the leader, not the scores from any particular instrument. These suggestions are important because if leaders collect their own data, even if the instruments are anonymous, there is a tendency for some respondents to answer according to what they feel the leaders do or do not want to hear. Thus, to help establish a valid data base, leaders may want to have their data gathered by a third party.

Another value of understanding power bases is important to mention. If you understand which power bases tend to influence a group of people, you have some insight into who should be given a particular project assignment or responsibility. The person you assign to a particular task should have the power bases and be comfortable in using the appropriate leadership styles that are required in a particular setting. If someone really wants an assignment and doesn't have the appropriate power bases, it's a problem of self-development. You can work out a program to build that power base or appropiate style. What all this means is that we can increase the probability of success of a particular manager if we understand the territory—if we know what power bases and corresponding leadership styles are needed to influence the people involved in the new situation effectively. That's the whole concept of team building. We will be talking about this in much greater depth in later chapters.

CONCLUSIONS

As has been emphasized throughout this chapter, whether or not a leader is maximizing effectiveness is not a question of style alone. It is also a question of what power bases are available to that leader and whether or not these power bases are consistent with the readiness levels of the individual or group that the leader is trying to influence. As managers consider these relationships, it appears that dynamic and growing organizations gradually move away from reliance on power bases that emphasize compliance and move toward the utilization of power bases that aim at gaining influence with people. It is important to keep in mind that many times this change, by necessity, will be evolutionary rather than revolutionary.

In the next chapter, we will show how leaders can develop their people from lower levels of readiness to higher levels. After all, the growth and development of people is the key to the long-term effectiveness of an organization.

NOTES

1. R. M. Stogdill, *Handbook of Leadership* (New York: Free Press, 1974).
2. Many of the concepts in this chapter were first published in Paul Hersey, Kenneth H. Blanchard, and Walter E. Natemeyer, "Situational Leadership, Perception, and the Impact of Power," *Group and Organizational Studies*, 4, No. 4 (December 1979), pp. 418–428.
3. Adapted from Paul Hersey, *The Situational Leader* (Escondido, Calif.: Center For Leadership Studies, 1985), p. 27.
4. This section on defining power and other concepts originated with Walter E. Natemeyer, *An Empirical Investigation of the Relationships Between Leader Behavior, Leader Power Bases, and Subordinate Performance and Satisfaction*, an unpublished dissertation, University of Houston, August 1975. See also J. J. Gibson, J. M. Ivancevich, and J. H. Donnelly, *Organizations* (Dallas: Business Publications, 1973). See also K. D. Mackenzie, "Virtual Position and Power," *Managerial Science*, 32 (May 1986), pp. 622–624.
5. B. Russell, *Power* (London: Allen and Unwin, 1938). See also Geoffrey Kemp, *Projection of Power: Perceptives, Perceptions, and Problems* (Hamden, Conn.: Archon Books, 1982).
6. R. Beirstedt, "An Analysis of Social Power," *American Sociological Review*, 15 (1950), pp. 730–736.
7. D. H. Wrong, "Some Problems in Defining Social Power," *American Journal of Sociology*, 73 (1968), pp. 673–681.
8. J. R. P. French, "A Formal Theory of Social Power," *Psychology Review*, 63

(1956), pp. 181–194. See also P. P. Poole, "Coalitions: The Web of Power," in D. J. Vreden-burgh and R. S. Schuler (eds.), *Effective Management: Research and Application, Proceedings of the 20th Annual Eastern Academy of Management*, Pittsburgh, May 1983, pp. 79–82.

9. R. A. Dahl, "The Concept of Power," *Behavioral Science*, 2 (1957), pp. 201–215.

10. M. F. Rogers, "Instrumental and Infra-Resources: The Bases of Power," *American Journal of Sociology*, 79, 6 (1973), 1418–1433. See also Rosabeth M. Kanter, "Power Failure in Management Circuits," *Harvard Business Review*, July–August 1979.

11. James A. Lee, "Leader Power and Managing Change," an unpublished paper writ-ten at the College of Business Administration, Ohio University, Athens, Ohio. See. also J. Pfeffer, *Power In and Around Organizations* (Englewood Cliffs, N. J.: Prentice-Hall, 1983).

12. Amitai Etzioni, *A Comparative Analysis of Complex Organizations* (New York: Free Press, 1961).

13. Niccolo Machiavelli, "Of Cruelty and Clemency, Whether It Is Better to Be Loved or Feared," *The Prince and the Discourses* (New York: Random House, 1950), Chap. 17.

14. This summary section adapted from Paul Hersey, *Situational Selling* (Escondido, Calif.: Center For Leadership Studies, 1985), pp. 14–15.

15. *Ibid.*

16. *Ibid.*, p. 15.

17. See note 4.

18. R. L. Peabody, "Perceptions of Organizational Authority: A Comparative Analy-sis," *Administrative Quarterly*, 6 (1962), pp. 463–482.

19. A. C. Filley and A. J. Grimes, "The Bases of Power in Decision Processes" (Indus-trial Relations Research Institute, University of Wisconsin, Reprint Series 104, 1967).

20. K. D. Beene, *A Conception of Authority* (New York: Teachers College, Columbia University, 1943); H. C. Kelman, "Compliance, Identification, and Internalization: Three Pro-cesses of Attitude Change," *Journal of Conflict Resolution*, 158, 2, pp. 51–60; and G. Gilman, "An Inquiry into the Nature and Use of Authority," in M. Haire, *Organization Theory in Industrial Practice* (New York: Wiley, 1962).

21. J. R. P. French and B. Raven, "The Bases of Social Power," in D. Cartwright, *Studies in Social Power* (Ann Arbor: University of Michigan, Institute for Social Research, 1959).

22. B. H. Raven and W. Kruglanski, "Conflict and Power," in P. G. Swingle, ed., *The Structure of Conflict* (New York: Academic Press, 1975), pp. 177–219.

23. Five of these descriptions of power bases (coercive, expert, legitimate, referent, and reward) have been adapted from the work of French and Raven, "The Bases of Social Power." One power base (information) was introduced by Raven and Kruglanski, "Conflict and Power." In addition to modifying some of these definitions, Paul Hersey and Marshall Gold-smith added a seventh power base: connection power.

24. Hersey, *Situational Selling*, p. 114.

25. This section adapted from Hersey, *Situational Selling*, pp. 114–120.

26. Natemeyer, *An Empirical Investigation of the Relationships Between Leader Behavior*.

27. K. R. Student, "Supervisory Influence and Work-Group Performance, *Journal of Applied Psychology, 52, 3 (1968), pp. 188–194.*

28. J. G. Bachman, C. G. Smith, and J. A. Slesinger, "Control, Performance, and Satis-faction: An Analysis of Structural and Individual Effects," *Journal of Personality and Social Psychology*, 4, 2 (1966), pp. 127–136.

29. J. G. Bachman, D. G. Bowers and P. M. Marcus, "Bases of Supervisory Power: A Comparative Study in Five Organizational Settings," in Arnold S. Tannenbaum, *Control in Organizations* (New York: McGraw-Hill, 1968).

30. J. M. Ivancevich and J. H. Donnelly, "Leader Influence and Performance," *Person-nel Psychology*, 23, 4 (1970), 539–549.

31. R. J. Burke and D. S. Wilcox, "Bases of Supervisory Power and Subordinate Job Satisfactions," *Canadian Journal of Behavioral Science* (1971).

32. D. W. Jamieson and K. W. Thomas, "Power and Conflict in the Student-Teacher Relationship," *Journal of Applied Behavioral Science*, 10, 3 (1974).

33. Natemeyer, *An Empirical Investigation of the Relationships Between Leader Behavior*.

34. Adapted from D. Kipnis, *The Powerholders* (Chicago: University of Chicago Press, 1976). See also J. Ivancevich, "An Analysis of Control, Bases of Control, and Satisfactional Setting," *Academy of Management Journal*, December 1970, pp. 427−436.

35. Hersey, Blanchard, and Natemeyer, "Situational Leadership, Perception, and the Impact of Power."

36. This section adapted from Hersey, *The Situational Leader*, pp. 82−83.

37. *Ibid.*, pp. 222−223.

38. Katherine Benziger, "The Powerful Woman," *Hospital Forum* May−June 1982, pp. 15−20.

39. *Ibid.*, p. 15.

40. *Ibid.*, pp. 15−16.

41. *Ibid.*, p. 16.

42. *Ibid.*, pp. 16−17.

43. *Ibid.*

44. *Ibid.*, pp. 18−20.

45. *Ibid.*, p. 20. For a related discussion, see Jane Covey Brown and Rosabeth Moss Kanter, "Empowerment: Key To Effectiveness," *Hospital Forum*, May−June, 1982, pp. 6−12.

46. This instrument was developed by Paul Hersey and Walter E. Natemeyer. Published by the Center for Leadership Studies, Escondido, Calif.

CHAPTER 10

DEVELOPING HUMAN RESOURCES

In Chapter 4 we stated that in evaluating performance, a manager ought to consider both output (productivity) and intervening variables (the condition of the human resources). We urged that both these factors should be examined in light of short- and long-term organizational goals. If the importance of intervening variables is accepted, then one must assume that one of the responsibilities of managers, regardless of whether they are parents in the home or managers in a business setting, is developing the human resources for which they are responsible. Managers need to devote time to nurture the leadership potential, motivation, morale, climate, commitment to objectives, and the decision-making, communication, and problem-solving skills of their people. Thus, an important role for managers is the development of the task-relevant readiness of their followers.

We think it is vital to emphasize this developmental aspect of Situational Leadership. Without emphasizing that aspect, there is a danger that managers could use Situational Leadership to justify the use of any behavior they wanted. Since the concept contends that there is no "best" leadership style, the use of any style could be supported merely by saying "the individual or group was at such-and-such readiness level." Thus, while close supervision and direction might be necessary initally when working with individuals who have had little experience in directing their own behavior, it should be recognized that this style is only a first step. In fact, managers should be rewarded for helping their people develop and be able to assume more and more responsibility on their own. For example, in some progressive companies in which we have worked we have been able to introduce a new policy, which essentially states: No managers will be promoted in this organization unless they do at least two things. First, they have to do a good job in what they are being asked to do; that is, good "bottom line" results (output variables). Second, they have to have a ready replacement who can take over their job tomorrow (intervening variables).

This means that if managers are using a leadership style with a high probability of success for working with a given level of readiness (as discussed in the last chapter), this perhaps is not really enough. These managers may be getting a reasonable amount of output but their responsibilities may not stop there. Besides maintaining an adequate level of output, managers may want to develop the ability and effectiveness of their human resources (their followers).

INCREASING EFFECTIVENESS

Likert found that employee-centered supervisors who use general supervision *tend* to have higher producing sections than job-centered supervisors who use close supervision.[1] We emphasize the word *tend* because this seems to be increasingly the case in our society; yet we must also realize that there are exceptions to this tendency, which are even evident in Likert's data. What Likert found was that subordinates generally respond well to their superior's high expectations and genuine confidence in them and try to justify their boss's expectations of them. Their resulting high performance will reinforce their superior's high trust for them; it is easy to trust and respect people who meet or exceed your expectations.

J. Sterling Livingston,[2] in discussing this phenomenon, refers to the words of Eliza Doolittle from George Bernard Shaw's play *Pygmalion* (the basis of the musical hit *My Fair Lady*):

> You see, really and truly, apart from the things anyone can pick up (the dressing and the proper way of speaking, and so on), the difference between a lady and a flower girl is not how she behaves but how she's treated. I shall always be a flower girl to Professor Higgins, because he always treats me as a flower girl, and always will; but I know I can be a lady to you, because you always treat me as a lady, and always will.

Livingston has found from his experience and research that:

FIGURE 10-1   Effective cycle

Some managers always treat their subordinates in a way that leads to superior performance. But most managers, like Professor Higgins, unintentionally treat their subordinates in a way that leads to lower performance than they are capable of achieving. The way managers treat their subordinates is subtly influenced by what they expect of them. If a manager's expectations are high, productivity is likely to be excellent. If his expectations are low, productivity is likely to be poor. It is as though there were a law that caused a subordinate's performance to rise or fall to meet his manager's expectations. . . .

Cases and other evidence available from scientific research now reveal:

What a manager expects of his subordinates and the way he treats them largely determine their performance and career progress.

A unique characteristic of superior managers is their ability to create high performance expectations that subordinates fulfill.

Less effective managers fail to develop similar expectations, and, as a consequence, the productivity of their subordinates suffers.

Subordinates, more often than not, appear to do what they believe they are expected to do.

When people respond to the high expectations of their managers with high performance, we call that the "effective cycle," as illustrated in Figure 10-1.

Yet, as we have pointed out earlier, the concentration on output variables as a means of evaluating effectiveness tends to lead to short-run task-oriented leader behavior. This style, in some cases, does not allow much room for a trusting relationship with employees. Instead, subordinates are told what to do and how to do it, with little consideration expressed for their ideas or feelings. After a while, the subordinates respond with minimal effort and resentment; low performance results in these instances. Reinforced by low expectations, it becomes a vicious cycle. Many other examples could be given that result in this all-too-common problem in organizations, as shown in Figure 10-2.

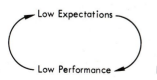

FIGURE 10-2   Ineffective cycle

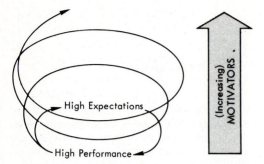

FIGURE 10-3   Spiraling effect of effective cycle

These cycles are depicted as static, but in reality 'they are very dynamic. The situation tends to get better or worse. For example, high expectations result in high performance, which reinforces the high expectations and produces even higher productivity. It almost becomes a spiral effect, as illustrated in Figure 10-3.

In many cases, this spiraling effect is caused by an increase in leverage created through the use of the motivators. As people perform they are given more responsibility and opportunities for achievement and growth and development.

This spiraling effect can also occur in a downward direction. Low expectations result in low performance, which reinforces the low expectations and produces even lower productivity. It becomes a spiral effect like a whirlpool, as shown in Figure 10-4.

FIGURE 10-4   Spiraling effect of ineffective cycle

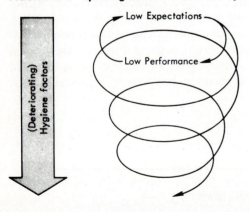

If this downward spiraling continues long enough, the cycle may reach a point where it cannot be turned around in a short period of time because of the large reservoir of negative past experience that has built up in the organization. Much of the focus and energy is directed toward perceived problems in the environment such as interpersonal relations and respect for supervision rather than toward the work itself. Reaction to deteriorating hygiene factors takes such forms as hostility, undermining, and slowdown in work performance. When this happens, even if a manager actually changes behavior, the credibility gap based on long-term experience is such that the response is still distrust and skepticism rather than change.

One alternative that is sometimes necessary at this juncture is to bring in a new manager from the outside. The reason this has a higher probability of success is that the sum of the past experience of the people involved with the new manager is likened to a "clean slate" and thus different behaviors are on a much more believable basis. This was evident in the case of Plant Y described by Guest, which was discussed in Chapter 7. The ineffective cycle had been in a downward spiral far past the point where Stewart would have had an opportunity to make significant changes. But, with the introduction of a new manager, Cooley, significant changes were now possible.

Breaking the Ineffective Cycle

Although new managers may be in a better position to initiate change in a situation that has been spiraling downward, they still do not have an easy task. Essentially, they have to break the ineffective cycle. There are at least two alternatives available to managers in this situation. They can either fire the low-performing personnel and hire people whom they expect to perform well or they can respond to low performance with high expectations and trust.

The first choice is not always possible because competent replacements are not readily available or the people involved have some form of job security (civil service or union tenure), which means they cannot be fired without considerable cost in time, energy, and hassle.

The latter choice for managers is difficult. In effect, the attempt is to change the expectations or behavior of their subordinates. It is especially difficult for managers to have high expectations about people who have shown no indication that they deserve to be trusted. The key, then, is to change appropriately.

From our work with Situational Leadership, we have identified two different cycles that managers can use for changing or maximizing the task-relevant readiness of their followers—the developmental cycle and the regressive cycle.

In this chapter we will discuss the developmental cycle. In Chapter 11 we will present the regressive cycle.

DEVELOPMENTAL CYCLE

The role managers play in developing the readiness level of their people is extremely important. Too often managers do not take responsibility for the performance of their people, especially if they are not doing well. If they're having problems, often managers will say, "I have an example of a Peter Principle," and not take responsibility for the poor performance. It has been our experience that when managers have to fire someone or find a place to hide them (this is what Peter called a "lateral arabesque"), or when they are downright worried about someone's performance, these managers should look in the mirror. In most cases, the biggest cause of the performance problem is looking back at them. Managers are responsible for making their people "winners," and this is what the developmental cycle is all about. Managers are involved in the developmental cycle any time they attempt to increase the present readiness level of an individual or group in some aspect of their work. In other words, the developmental cycle is a growth cycle.

What's in It for the Manager?[3]

When followers are at low levels of readiness, the manager must take the responsibility for the "traditional" management functions such as planning, organizing, motivating, and controlling. The manager's role is that of supervisor of the group. However, when managers develop their people and have followers at high levels of readiness, the followers can take over much of the responsibility for these day-to-day traditional management functions. The manager's role can then change from supervisor to the group's representative in the next level of the organization.

Through the development of people, managers can invest their time in the "high payoff" management functions. These "linking pin" activities enhance the group's performance. When followers can take responsibility for their own tasks on a day-to-day basis, the manager can focus on these activities. These functions include acquiring resources necessary for maximizing the group's productivity, communicating both horizontally and vertically, and coordinating their group's efforts with that of other departments to improve overall productivity. The manager, instead of getting trapped in tunnel vision, has time for long-range strategic planning and creativity.

Initially, close supervision and direction are helpful when working with individuals who have little experience in directing their own behavior. The manager recognizes that this style is only a first step. In order to maximize their potential in the high-payoff functions, managers must change their style and take an *active* role in helping others grow. The development of followers depends not only on the manager's behavior, but also on values and expectations.

What Do We Want to Influence?

As we suggested in Chapter 8, the first question managers have to ask themselves when they are thinking about the development of their people is: What area of my subordinate's job do I want to influence? In other words, what are their responsibilities or goals and objectives? A foreman, for example, might want to influence subordinates' productivity, quality, waste, absenteeism, accident rate, and so on. A university department chairman might want to affect the faculty's writing and research and teaching and service.

Once the objectives or responsibilities are identified and understood, managers must clearly specify what constitutes good performance in each area, so that both they and their subordinates know when their performance is approaching the desired level. What does a good sales record mean? Does it mean a number of sales made or volume of sales? What is meant by developing your people or being a good adminstrator? Managers have to specify what good performance *looks like*. Just telling a person, "I want you to make widgets" is not as helpful as saying, "I want you to make widgets at the rate of two hundred a day." For managers and staff members to know how well someone is doing, good performance has to be clearly specified. Managers cannot change and develop their subordinate's behavior in areas that are unclear.

How Is the Person Doing Now?

Before beginning the developmental cycle with an individual in a work situation, the manager must decide how well that person is doing right now. In other words, what is the person's readiness level right now in a specific aspect of the job? How able is the person to take responsibility for specific behavior? How willing or motivated is the person? As was discussed earlier, readiness is not a global concept. That is, people do not have a degree of readiness in any total sense. How can we know what a person's readiness level is in a given situation?

Determining Readiness

In assessing the readiness level of an individual, we will have to make judgments about that person's ability and motivation. Where do we get the information to make these judgments? We can either *ask the person* or *observe* the person's behavior. We could ask a person such questions as, "How well do you think you are doing at such and such?" or "How do you feel about doing that?" or "Are you or are you not enthusiastic and excited about it?" Obviously, with some people, asking for their own assessment of their readiness won't be productive. However, it has been surprising how even young children are able to share that kind of information. Phil and Jane learned that when they used to ask their two-year-old daughter, Lee, to do something. Often Lee would reply, "I can't want to!" When translated, what Lee was really saying (in our terms) is, "I'm both unable and unwilling to do what you want me to do." If Lee's parents still wanted her to do it, they soon learned that they had to direct and closely supervise her behavior in this area (S1—"telling"). As children get older, they can play an even more significant role in determining their own readiness level. That process will be discussed in much more detail in Chapter 12.

You might be wondering whether people will always tell their managers the truth or just tell what is necessary to keep the manager off their backs. If managers doubt what their people tell them about their ability or willingness to do something, those managers can check out their opinion by observing staff members' behavior. Ability can be determined by examining past performance. Has the person done well in this area before or has performance been poor or nonexistent? Does the staff member have the necessary knowledge to perform well in the area or does that person not know how to do what needs to be done?

Willingness can be determined by watching a person's behavior in a particular case. What is the person's interest level? Does the person seem enthusiastic or interested? What is the person's commitment to this area? Does the person appear to enjoy doing things in this area or merely anxious to get them over with? Is the person's self-confidence secure in this area or does the person lack confidence and feel insecure? Remember that people can be at any of four levels of readiness in each of their various areas of responsibility. A person's readiness level gives us a good clue to how to begin any further development of that individual. If a manager wants to influence a staff member in an area in which the person is both unable and unwilling (low readiness level), the manager must begin the developmental cycle by directing, controlling, and closely supervising ("telling") the staff member's behavior. If, however, the person is willing (motivated) to do something but not able to do it (low to moderate readiness), the manager must begin the cycle by both directing and supporting ("selling") the desired behavior. If the person is able to do something without direction but is unwilling to do it or is insecure (moderate to high readiness), the manager is faced with a motivational problem. Individuals reluctant to do what they are able to do are often insecure or lacking confidence. In this case, the manager should begin the developmental cycle by using a supportive style ("participating") to help the individual become secure enough to do what the individual already knows how to do. Finally, if staff members are both able and willing to direct their own behavior (high readiness), we can merely delegate responsibility to them and know that they will perform well. When that occurs, there is no need for beginning the development cycle. The person already has a high degree of readiness in that area.

Increasing Readiness

Managers are engaged in the developmental cycle any time they attempt to increase the task-relevant readiness of an individual or group beyond the level that individual or group has previously reached. In other words, the developmental cycle is a growth cycle.

To explain fully how the developmental cycle works, let us look at an example. Suppose a manager has been able to diagnose the environment and finds that the task-relevant readiness of a staff member is low (R1) in the area of developing a departmental budget. If the manager wants the staff member to perform well in this area without supervision, the manager must determine the appropriate leadership style for starting the develop-mental cycle. As can be seen in Figure 10-5, once this manager has diagnosed the readiness level of the follower as low, the appropriate style can be determined by constructing a right angle from a point on the readiness continuum to where it meets the curved line in the style-of-leader portion of the model. In this case, it would be appropriate to start the developmental cycle by using a directive "telling" style (S1). What would a "telling" style look like in this situation?

It would involve several things for the manager. First, the manager would have to tell the staff member exactly what was involved in developing

FIGURE 10-5   Determining an appropriate leadership style

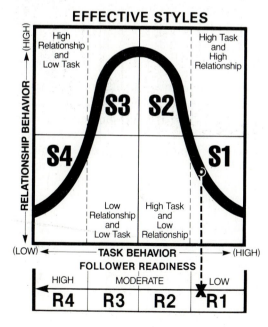

a departmental budget—taking inventory, processing manpower and material requests, comparing present costs with last year's budget, and so on. Second, the manager would begin to show the staff member how to do each of the tasks involved. Thus, "telling" in a teaching situation involves "show and tell"; the staff member must be told what to do and then shown how to do it. Although this "telling" style is high on direction and low on support, this does not mean that the manager is not being friendly to the staff member. Low supportive behavior in this situation merely means that the manager is not patting the staff member on the back before the member has earned it. Till then, the manager emphasizes explaining the what, when, where, and how of the job.

If the manager uses an S1 "telling" style in this situation, the departmental budget will probably be done fairly well, since the manager is working closely with the staff member. But if this same manager or leader assumes a responsibility to increase the task-relevant readiness of the follower(s), then the manager has to be willing to *take a risk* and begin to *delegate some responsibility* to the followers. This is particularly true when supervising an individual or group that has not assumed much responsibility in the past; and yet, if one is going to develop people—children in the home, employees on the job—one has to take that risk. While taking a risk is a reality in the developmental cycle, managers have to keep the degree of risk reasonable; it should not be too high. For example, suppose a mother wants to teach her eight-year old daughter how to wash the dishes. The risk is a few broken dishes. It would be wise, then, to start the daughter off on old dishes, or even plastic dishes, rather than Grandma's priceless bone china. It's not a question of whether to take a risk or not; it's a matter of taking a calculated risk.

Successive Approximations

If a manager asks a staff member to do something the member has never been taught to do and expects good performance the first time, and doesn't offer any help to the staff member, the manager has set the person up for failure and punishment. This begins the widely used "tell, leave alone, and then 'zap'" approach to managing people. The manager tells the staff member what to do (without bothering to find out if the person knows how to do it), leaves the staff member alone (expecting immediate results), and then yells at and "zaps" the staff member when the desired behavior does not follow.

If the manager in our budget example used that approach, the events might look something like this. The manager might assume that anyone could prepare the departmental budget. So the manager tells the staff member to prepare the budget and have it within ten days. Not bothering to analyze whether the staff member is able or willing to prepare the budget alone, the manager gives the order and then goes about his own responsibilities. When the staff member produces the budget ten days later, the manager finds all kind of mistakes and problems with it and screams and yells at the staff member about the poor quality of the work.

Managers should remember that no one (including themselves!) learns how to do anything all at once. We learn a little bit at a time. As a result, if a manager wants someone to do something completely new, the manager should reward the slightest progress the person makes in the desired direction.

Many parents use this process without really being aware of it. For example, how do you think we teach a child to walk? Imagine if we stood Eric up and said, "Walk," and then when he fell down we spanked him for not walking. Sound ridiculuous? Of course. But it's not really any different from the manager's anger with the staff member about the poorly prepared budget. A child spanked for falling down will not try to walk because the child knows this leads to punishment. At this point Eric is not even sure what his legs are for. Therefore, parents usually first teach children how to stand up. If the child stays up even for a second or two, his parents get excited and hug and kiss him, call his grandmother, and the like. Next, when the child can stand and hold onto a table, his parents again hug and kiss him. The same happens when he takes his first step, even if he falls down. Whether or not his parents know it, they are postively rewarding the child for small accomplishments as he moves closer and closer to the desired behavior—walking.

Thus, in attempting to help an individual or group develop—to get them to take more and more responsibility for performing a specific task—a leader must first tell and show the follower(s) what to do; second, delegate *some* responsibility (not too much or failure might result); and, third, reward soon as possible any behavior in the desired direction. This process should continue as the individual's behavior comes closer and closer to the leader's expectations of good performance. What would relationship behavior look like in this situation?

Relationship behavior would involve providing "positive strokes" and reinforcement. Positive reinforcement strokes are anything that is desired or needed by an individual whose behavior is being reinforced. While task behavior precedes the desired behavior, relationship behavior or positive reinforcement follows the desired behavior and increases the likelihood of its recurring. It is important to remember that reinforcement must immediately follow any behavior in the desired direction. Reinforcement at a later time will be of less help in getting the individual or group to do something they've never done before on their own.

This three-step process of (1) initiating structure or providing direction (task behavior), (2) reducing the amount of direction and supervision, and (3) after adequate performance follows, increasing socioemotional support (relationship behavior) is known as *positively reinforcing successive approxi-*

mations. This concept is associated with behavior modification and reinforcement theory,[4] and more recently, in industrial circles it has been called performance management.[4] This field will be discussed in more depth later in this chapter and in Chapter 11. Let us look at an example to illustrate this concept. Suppose a manager wanted to change leadership style with an individual from Point A to Point C along the curved line or curviliner function of Situational Leadership, as illustrated in Figure 10-6. The first step of the process would be to provide some structure and direction for the individual at Point A. The next step would be to delegate some responsibility by decreasing task behavior to Point B. This is a risky step since the manager is turning over the direction and the supervision of some of the tasks to the follower. If the follower responds well to the increased responsibility, then it is appropriate to engage in Step 3—positively reinforcing this behavior by increasing socioemotional support (relationship behavior) to the higher level Point C, as shown in Figure 10-6.

It is important to remember that a leader must be careful not to delegate too much responsibility too rapidly. This is a common error that many managers make. If this is done before the follower can handle it, the leader may be setting the follower up for failure and frustration that could prevent that person from wanting to take additional responsibility in the future. The process is often started off by good intentions. The manager provides direction and structure but then moves too quickly to a "leave-alone" leadership style. This abrupt movement from "telling" to "delegating" often sets the person up for failure and punishment, since it assumes that telling is learning. The manager is likely to return to Style 1 rapidly in a punitive way if the job is not getting done.

FIGURE 10-6 Three-step process of the developmental cycle

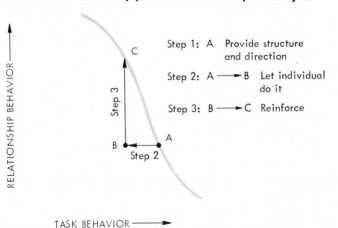

In addition, a manager should be warned not to increase socioemotional support (relationship behavior) without first getting the desired performance. In postively reinforcing nonperformance, this manager may be viewed as a soft touch. That is why the manager in our example does not immediately move from Point A to Point C along the curved line in Figure 10-6. If the manager moved from Point A to Point C without some evidence that the individual could assume responsibility at Point B, it would be like giving the reward before the person has earned it. It would be like paying a person twenty dollars an hour right now who at present is worth only five dollars an hour. For many people, if you gave them twenty dollars an hour up front, there would be very little incentive to improve their performance. Thus, the leader should develop the readiness of followers slowly on each task that they must perform, using less task behavior and more relationship behavior as they become more willing and able to take responsibility. When an individual's performance is low on a specific task, one must not expect drastic changes overnight.

If the manager (in our example) finds that the follower is unable to handle that much added responsibility when task behavior is decreased to Point B, the manager might have to return to a moderate level of direction (where the follower is able to take responsibility) somewhere between Point A and Point B. This new level of task behavior is indicated by Point B^1 in Figure 10-7. If the subordinate is now able to be effective at that level, then the manager can appropriately increase socioemotional support (relationship

FIGURE 10-7   Adjustment when growth expectation is too high

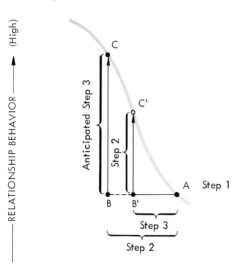

behavior) to Point C^1. Although this level of socioemotional support is less than depicted at Point C, it is appropriate to the amount of task behavior that the follower, at that time, is able to assume.

As shown in Figure 10-8, this three-step process—telling and showing, cutting back structure and then increasing socioemotional support if the follower can respond to the additional responsibility—tends to continue in small increments until the individual is assuming moderate levels of readiness. This continual decreasing of task behavior does not mean the individual will have less structure, but that rather than being externally imposed by the leader, the structure can now be internally provided by the follower.

An interesting phenomenon occurs in the developmental cycle when the high point of the curvilinear function in the leadership style portion of the model is reached. This is where the function crosses the mean, or average, of task behavior. Past this point, a leader who is appropriately using leadership style 3 or style 4 is supervising people at moderate to high levels of readiness (R3 and R4). At that time, the process changes and becomes one whereby the leader not only reduces structure (task behavior), but, when the followers can handle their responsibility, reduces socioemotional support as well. This continuation of the successive approximation process is illustrated by the downward steps in Figure 10-8.

Sometimes the following question is raised: Doesn't the reduction of

FIGURE 10-8   Development cycle as people mature over time

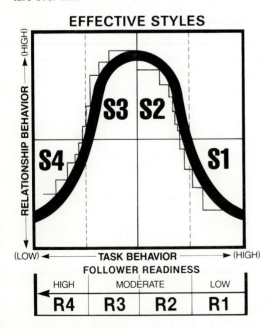

socioemotional support mean that there is a lack of confidence and trust between manager and follower(s)? In reality, when a manager reduces the amount of socioemotional support and structure appropriately, this indicates that there is more mutual trust and confidence between the leader and the follower(s). This suggests that as people change, their motives and needs hierarchy often change too. For example, people who have low levels of readiness tend to view increased socioemotional support and facilitating behavior as positive reinforcement. In fact, if the leader left them too much on their own, this behavior would create insecurities and help reinforce fear and anxiety on the part of the follower(s). As a result, this low relationship behavior could be perceived as punishment rather than reward.

On the other hand, as people move to high levels of readiness, they do not require as much encouragement or psychological "stroking." As people become high on task-relevant readiness, one way the leader can demonstrate confidence and trust in the follower(s) is to leave them more and more on their own. Just as socioemotional support from the leader tends to be positive reinforcement for persons with low levels of readiness, too much socioemotional support or relationship behavior for people at high levels of readiness is not seen as a reward. In fact, this supportive behavior is often seen as dysfunctional and can be interpreted by these high-readiness people as a lack of confidence and trust on the part of the leader.

Time and the Developmental Cycle

There is no set blueprint in terms of the amount of time necessary to develop an individual or group. A manager may be doing very well to move a group from readiness level 1 to level 2 over a period of eighteen months to two years. On the other hand, within that group there may be an individual or several individuals who will develop much more rapidly than the group as a whole. Thus, time is a function of the complexity of the job being performed and the performance potential of the individual or group. For example, one might take someone on a specific task through the total cycle— from low to high levels of readiness—in a matter of minutes. And yet, in other tasks with that same individual, the readiness development process may take a much greater amount of time. In fact, it could take weeks, months, or even years to move through the complete cycle in terms of appropriate leadership style from telling (S1) to delegating (S4). To illustrate a short development process, an example of teaching a child to tie her shoes may be helpful.

If the child has not made any attempt to learn to tie shoes, this fact may, in a sense, become a problem to the parent. In that case, the parent needs to provide some high task behavior for the child. Since the child has low readiness on this task, the parent should explain what to do, how to do it, and where to do it. In essence, the parent must move into the early stages of coaching and counseling by providing the child with a "hands-on experience." As the child begins to show the ability to do some of those functions, the parent reduces the amount of telling behavior and increases, to some extent, supportive behavior. "That's fine! Good! You're getting it!" And perhaps in a matter of minutes, the behavior of the parent may change from a "hands-on" highly structured style to just being in close proximity, where this adult can provide a moderate amount of structure but also high levels of both verbal and nonverbal supportive and facilitative behavior. In another few minutes, the parent may leave the child to practice alone while staying close enough to make an intervention if there should be some regression. Thus, in a matter of ten to fifteen minutes, the parent has taken the child in that specific task of shoe tying from style 1 through styles 2 and 3 to almost a complete delegation of that function to the child in a manner characteristic of style 4. This does not mean that the parent's style with that child should now always be style 4. It just means that in that specific task (shoe tying), the most appropriate style to use with that child is style 4.

CHANGING READINESS THROUGH BEHAVIOR MODIFICATION

In our discussion of the developmental cycle, we made reference to behavior modification and, in particular, the concept of positively reinforcing successive approximations. This section will elaborate on some other concepts from this behavioral science field and attempt to show how these concepts provide guidelines for changing one's leadership style with shifts in readiness.[6]

Behavior modification is a useful tool for managers and leaders because it can be applied in almost all environments. Although it may involve a reassessment of customary methods for obtaining compliance and cooperation, it has relevance for persons interested in accomplishing objectives through other people. This may not be the case with some methods of psychotherapy.

For example, one form of psychotherapy is based on the assumption that to change behavior one must start with the feelings and attitudes within an individual. Although the introduction of transactional analysis (TA) has helped, the problem with psychotherapy from a practitioner's viewpoint is that it tends to be too expensive and is appropriate for use only by professionals. One way of illustrating the main difference between these two approaches is to go back to a portion of the basic motivating situation model as illustrated in Figure 10-9.

Figure 10-9 shows that both psychotherapy and behavior modification are interested in affecting behavior. The emphasis in psychotherapy is on analyzing the reasons underlying behaviors that are often the result of early

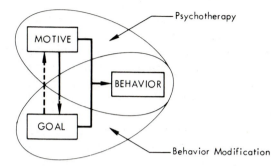

FIGURE 10-9 **Comparison of psychotherapy and behavior modification**

experiences in life. Behavior modification concentrates on observed behavior and uses goals or rewards outside the individual to modify and shape behavior toward the desired performance.

Behavior modification theory is based on observed behavior and not on internal unobserved emotions, attitudes, or feelings. Its basic premise is that *behavior is controlled by its immediate consequences*. Behavior can be increased, suppressed, or decreased by what happens immediately after it occurs. Because probabilities are difficult to work with, we use observations of the future frequency of the behavior as a measure of the effectiveness of a consequence. Five of the major concepts of reinforcement that help one to make behavioral changes are positive reinforcement, punishment, negative reinforcement, extinction, and schedule of reinforcement. In our discussions in this chapter we have and will continue to emphasize positive reinforcement and schedule of reinforcement. In the next chapter, "Constructive Discipline," we will examine punishment, negative reinforcement, and extinction.

Positive Reinforcement

Positive reinforcement, as mentioned earlier, can be anything that is desired or needed by the individual whose behavior is being reinforced. A positive reinforcer tends to strengthen the response it follows and make that response more likely to recur.

To increase the probability that desirable behavior will occur, reinforcement should *immediately* follow the response. Reinforcement at a later time may be of less help in making the desired behavioral change.

Individualizing Reinforcement

When thinking about this concept of positive reinforcement, managers should remember that reinforcement depends on the individual. What is reinforcing to one person may not be reinforcing to another. Money may motivate some people to work harder. But to others, money may not be a positive reinforcer; the challenge of the job might be the most rewarding aspect of the situation. In addition, the same individual at different times will be motivated by different things, depending on present need satisfaction. Thus, at one time an individual might respond to praise as a reinforcer, but at another time that same individual might not respond to praise but be eager for more responsibility. Managers must recognize the dangers of over-generalizing and not only look for unique differences in their people but also be aware of the various fluctuations in need satisfaction within a person.

For a desirable behavior to be obtained, the slightest appropriate behavior exhibited by the individual in that direction must be rewarded as soon as possible. This is the basic premise for the concept of *reinforcing positively successive approximations* of a certain response. For example, when an individual's performance is low, one cannot expect drastic changes overnight, regardless of changes in expectations for the individual or the type of reinforcers (rewards) used.

A child learning some new behavior is not expected to give a polished performance at the outset. So, as parent, teacher, or supervisor, we use positive reinforcement as the behavior approaches the desired level of performance. Managers must be aware of any progress of their subordinates so as to be in a position to reinforce this change appropriately.

This strategy is compatible with the concept of setting short-term goals rather than final performance criteria and then reinforcing appropriate progress toward the final goals as they are met. In setting goals it is important that they be programmed to be difficult but obtainable so that the individual proceeds along a path of gradual and systematic development. Eventually this individual will reach the point of a polished performance.

The type of consequence individuals experience as a result of their behavior will determine the speed with which they approach the final performance. Behavior consequences can be either positive (money, praise, award, promotion), negative (scolding, fines, layoffs, embarrassment), or neutral. The difference between positive and negative consequences is important to reiterate. Postive consequences tend to result in an increase in the rewarded behavior in the future. Negative consequences, as you will discover in the discussion of punishment, merely disrupt and suppress on-going behavior. Negative consequences tend to have neither a lasting nor a sure effect on future behavior.

Schedule of Reinforcement

Once a manager has someone engaging in a new behavior, it is important that the new behavior is not extinguished over time. To ensure that this does not happen, reinforcement must be scheduled in an effective way. Most experts agree that there are two main reinforcement schedules: continuous and intermittent.[7] Continuous reinforcement means that the individuals being changed are reinforced each time they engage in the desired new pattern. With intermittent reinforcement, on the other hand, not every desired response is reinforced. Reinforcement either can be completely random or can be scheduled according to a prescribed number of responses occurring or a particular interval of time elapsing before reinforcement is given. With continuous reinforcement, the individual learns the new behavior faster; but if the environment for that individual changes to one of nonreinforcement, extinction can be expected to take place relatively soon. With intermittent reinforcement, extinction is much slower because the individual has been conditioned to go for periods of time without any reinforcement. Thus, for fast learning, a continuous reinforcement schedule should be used. But once the individual has learned the new pattern, a switch to intermittent reinforcement should insure a long-lasting change.

How does the concept of reinforcement relate to Situational Leadership? In the early stages of a developmental cycle, whenever a manager delegates some responsibility to a person at a low level of readiness and that person responds well, the manager should provide reinforcement. That is, every time the manager cuts back on task behavior and the staff member responds well, the manager should immediately increase relationship behavior appropriately. This kind of reinforcement should continue until the manager's style is between "selling" and "participating" and the readiness of the person shifts toward higher levels (R3 and R4). At that time, the manager should begin periodically to reinforce, so that the manager's decreased support and direction will not be seen by the staff member as punishment. When the style of a manager moves toward the "delegating" style, the person's behavior is self-reinforcing, and external "strokes" from the manager are significantly reduced. In sum, the developmental cycle moves from continual reinforcement to periodic reinforcement to self-reinforcement.

Consistency in Reinforcement

In Chapter 5 consistency was defined as behaving the same way in similar circumstances. This is very important when it comes to reinforcement. Many managers are reinforcing or supportive of their people only when they feel like it. While that's probably more convenient for managers, it is not helpful if they want to have an impact on *other* people's behavior. Managers should know when they are being supportive and should be careful not to be supportive when their people are performing poorly. Be consistent! Only good behavior or improvement—not just any behavior—should be rewarded.

Isn't All This Reinforcement a Form of Bribery?

The ultimate goal of the developmental process discussed in this chapter is to shift people toward self-management so that they can eventually assume responsibility for motivating their own behavior. This ultimate goal is mentioned to reassure people who have some real doubts about the use of reinforcement. Some readers may say, "People should be motivated by a desire to succeed or the desire to please people around them, not by a hoped-for reward," or "This sounds like bribery to me," or "If I use positive reinforcement with people, won't they always expect rewards for every little thing they do?"

Although we have shared similar concerns in the past, our experience in observing people in organizations has been reassuring. It has been found that people who are reinforced when they are first learning new behaviors and performance areas and then gradually allowed to be more and more on their own turn out to be happy, eager to help, self-motivated people who can be left alone without productivity dropping significantly.

In this chapter we have discussed how managers increase the readiness level of their followers in a developmental process that emphasizes the use of positive reinforcement. In the next chapter we will discuss the regressive cycle and will consider what has to be done when followers begin, for whatever reason, to decrease in their task-relevant readiness.

NOTES

1. Rensis Likert, *New Patterns of Management* (New York: McGraw-Hill, 1961), p.7.

2. J. Sterling Livingston, "Pygmalion in Management," *Harvard Business Review*, July–August 1969, pp. 81–82.

3. Adapted from Paul Hersey, *The Situational Leader* (Escondido, Calif.: Center for Leadership Studies, 1985), pp. 92–94.

4. The most classic discussions of behavior modification, reinforcement theory, or operant conditioning have been done by B. F. Skinner. See Skinner, *Science and Human Behavior* (New York: Macmillan, 1953). See also A. Bandura, *Principles of Behavior Modification* (New York: Holt, Rinehart & Winston, 1969) and C. M. Franks, *Behavior Therapy: Appraisal and Status* (New York: McGraw-Hill, 1969). B.F. Skinner, *Contingencies of Reinforcement: A Theoretical Analysis* (Englewood Cliffs, N.J.: Prentice-Hall, 1969); B. F. Skinner, *About Behaviorism* (New York: Knopf, 1974).

5. One of the first applications of behavior modification and reinforcement theory to organizations was done by Fred Luthans and Robert Kreitner. See Luthans and Kreitner, *Organizational Behavior Modification* (Glenview, Ill.: Scott, Foresman, 1975). See also Thomas K. Connelian, *How to Improve Human Performance: Behaviorism in Business and in Industry* (New York: Harper & Row, 1978); Lawrence M. Miller, *Behavior Management: The New Science of Managing People at Work* (New York: Wiley, 1978); and Fred Luthans, *Introduction to Management: Organizational Behavior* (New York: McGraw-Hill, 1981).

6. Helpful resources in developing this section in addition to those mentioned above were provided by Glenna Holsinger, *Motivating the Reluctant Learner* (Lexington, Mass: Motivity, Inc., 1970); Madeline Hunter, *Reinforcement Theory for Teachers* (El Segundo, Calif., TIP Publications, 1967); and Lawrence M. Miller, *Behavior Management: New Skills for Business and Industry* (Atlanta: Behavioral Systems, Inc., 1976). Discussions with friend and colleague Bob Lorber, President of Performance Systems, International (PSI), a division of Continuing Education Corp. in Tustin, Calif., were also extremely helpful.

7. *Skinner for the Classroom: Selected Papers* (Champaign, Ill.: Research Press, 1982).

CHAPTER 11

CONSTRUCTIVE DISCIPLINE

In the last chapter we discussed how to develop readiness and independence in people through the use of positive reinforcement and changing leadership styles. However, you should be aware that for one reason or another, people's performance may begin to slip. And one of the most difficult challenges managers face is working with performance problems. That's because discipline is often viewed as a negative intervention. However, the origin of the word *discipline* is "disciple." A disciple is a learner.

Unfortunately in our culture many people interpret discipline as punishment. It is the problem-solving nature of *constructive discipline* that differentiates it from punitive discipline. As such, constructive discipline is designed to be a learning process that provides an opportunity for positive growth. Effective managers use constructive discipline when people slip in readiness.[1] In this chapter we will attempt to help managers determine what needs to be done when this happens.

THE REGRESSIVE CYCLE

Managers may need to make a regressive intervention when their followers begin to behave less willingly than they have in the past. Thus, in a developmental cycle, managers are attempting to increase the task-relevant readiness of an individual or group beyond where it has been in the past. The regressive cycle involves an intervention that leaders need to make when an individual or a group is becoming less effective. Thus, in a regressive cycle, managers must use a leadership style appropriate to the present level of readiness rather than the style that might have been effective when the individual or group was at a higher level of readiness.

Decreases in readiness are often the result of what might be called "high strength competing responses" in the environment. Other things are competing with the goals of the leader or the organization and, therefore, have become higher strength needs to the followers in terms of their behavior.

Decreases in readiness occur for a variety of reasons. Followers can have problems with the boss, problems with co-workers, suffer burnout, boredom, and have other problems on or off the job. These are just a few of the things that can have a negative impact on people's performance. Let's take an example of a performance problem.[2]

While consulting with a large research and development laboratory, one of the authors worked with a manager who was responsible for supervising John, one of the most motivated scientists on the staff. John was so committed to his job that even if the manager went into the laboratory at eight o'clock in the evening, it was not unusual to see a light under his laboratory door. Even on weekends, John was often found working in the laboratory. He probably had more patents and made more contributions to the overall program than any other person in the laboratory.

From the author's observations, this manager was behaving appropriately in using a low relationship/low task style (S4) for the high readiness level (R4) of this scientist. Thus, rather than operating as John's supervisor, the manager was behaving more as John's representative to higher levels in the organization. John's manager was attempting to maximize John's potential by engaging in such "linking pin" activities as acquiring necessary resources and coordinating his activities with the activities of other staff members.

Although John was at a high level of readiness in this organizational setting, we learned that John's behavior was seen in a different light in his interactions with another organization—his family. In that organizational setting, his wife saw his behavior of long hours and weekends at work as an indication that he no longer cared about her and their young daughter. So in his wife's eyes, John was behaving at a low readiness level. As a result, John went home one evening and found a note from his wife in which she told him that she had packed her bags and taken their daughter away to start a new life. John was shocked by his wife's action since he had perceived his own behavior quite differently from the way she did. He felt that he was attempting to provide for his wife and child all those things he was not able to have as a youngster.

What happened on the job was that now, with these family problems on his mind, John's effectiveness began to decrease. It has been said many times that you should leave your family problems at home and your job problems at work, but in reality we tend to carry problems both ways. Problems at home affect our behavior in the work environment and problems at work affect our home environment. This was certainly true in John's case. As his concerns for his family began to take effect, his performance and corresponding level as a scientist began to shift from readiness level 4 into level 3, as shown in Figure 11-1. Although his work emphasized technical competency, his declining psychological readiness was now affecting his performance. John did not seem to be able to cope with these problems at home. This meant that to maximize performance, John's manager had to shift behavior from style 4 to style 3 to deal with this lowering readiness level of a follower (Figure 11-1). As a result, a moderate increase in direction and structure as well as significant increases in socioemotional support, two-way communication, and the willingness to listen actively and be supportive (relationship behavior) were necessary. At this point, the situation was still more of a problem to the follower than the leader. However, the high relationship intervention by the manager seemed to help the situation.

Once John was able to cope with his problem and put it in perspective,

FIGURE 11-1 An example of a regressive cycle intervention

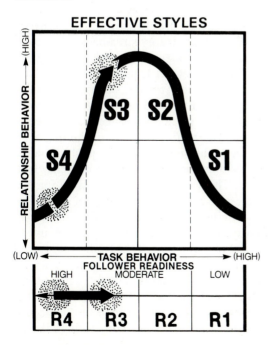

it was possible for his manager to move directly back to style 4. This illustrates one of the basic differences between a developmental cycle and a regressive cycle. In a regressive cycle, once an appropriate intervention has been made, the leader may often move back to the former leadership style without going through the process of positively reinforcing successive approximations. This is because the follower has previously demonstrated an ability to function at this level.

However, it should be pointed out in this example that if John's performance had continued to decline, the situation clearly would have become a problem to both leader and follower and would have demanded an eventual shift by the manager to a high task/high relationship style (S2).

In another example, Henry, a construction engineer, was operating as a project consultant; that is, he had a special expertise that was useful for a variety of projects. As a result, rather than being assigned to a specific project, he worked with a half-dozen projects at different construction sites. Since his readiness level was extremely high, his boss was also treating him appropriately in a style 4 manner. His supervisor was acting more as a linking pin with the rest of the organization than as his supervisor.

This style was effective until Henry began to take an active interest in golf. As a result of this new high strength competing response, no longer was anybody able to get in touch with Henry after two o'clock in the afternoon. It took several months for his boss to make this discovery, since his co-workers just assumed that he was at one of the other construction sites. The supervisor finally became aware of Henry's behavior and discovered that his activity on the golf course was causing problems with the construction progress at some of the sites. As a result, Henry's readiness level as a project consultant in terms of the accomplishment of organizational goals had moved from readiness level 4 to readiness level 1, particularly from 2 to 5 in the afternoon. Thus, it became appropriate for the supervisor to shift his leadership style from S4 to S1 to deal with this drastic change in readiness. What might be called a disciplinary intervention was necessary to redefine roles and expectations for Henry. Once this was done, if the manager was able to unfreeze this new pattern of the subordinate, he might be able to shift his style back to S4. This is possible, once again, because Henry had been at a high readiness level before. Thus, it may not be necessary for the manager to positively reinforce successive approximations before he moves back to the previously appropriate style used with Henry. This is much like the story about the mule and the two-by-four. Often in a disciplinary intervention, all managers have to do is get the attention of their followers to get them moving back in the right direction.

The regressive cycle should be taken one step at a time. Thus, if we are letting individuals operate on their own ("delegating") and performance declines, we should move to "participating" and support their problem solving. If we are being supportive but not directive with individuals (S3) and performance declines, we should move to "selling" and continue to engage in two-way communication, but we should also be more directive. If we are providing both task and relationship behavior (S2) and performance declines, we should move to "telling" and reduce some of our supportive behavior and increase direction and supervision. In both the regressive and developmental cycles, we should be careful not to jump from "delegating" (S4) to "selling" (S2) or "telling" (S1) or from "telling" to "participating" or "delegating." Making a drastic shift backward in leadership styles is one of the common mistakes managers make with their people. It sets up the "leave alone and 'zap'" (punish) style of management—an approach that is not only disruptive to the relationship a manager has with a staff member but is also disruptive to that person's growth and development.

Relationship between Ability and Willingness in the Developmental and Regressive Cycles

Sometimes we are asked, "How can a person go from 'unable but willing or confident' (R2) to 'able but unwilling or insecure' (R3)?" Figure 11-2 answers this question. As people grow in their task-specific readiness, the behaviors they need from the leader also change. Followers who are performing at readiness levels 1 and 2 need structure and guidance in order to

FIGURE 11-2   Relationship between ability and willingness in the developmental and regressive cycles

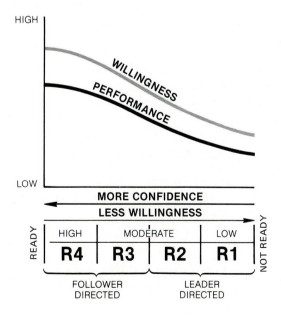

perform well and grow. They also need increased supportive behavior as they move from R1 to R2 as reward and reinforcement for their efforts.

Often managers will observe followers moving from being unable and insecure, R1, to unable but confident, R2. They perform well as long as the leader is there providing direction. But as people grow and are given responsibility to accomplish tasks on their own, there is usually some apprehension with taking charge the first few times. Insecurity increases as the follower moves from R2 to R3. This is a new realm of *follower-directed* behavior versus *leader-directed* behavior.

Think about the first time you had to make a presentation in front of a group. Even though you practiced in front of a mirror and on a tape recorder, you probably had some "butterflies" and insecurity right before the moment of truth. But after you had a few wins under your belt, you became both able and confident about performing on your own. Your insecurity came about, in part, because the leader was not right there to bail you out when you got in trouble.

Figure 11-2 further clarifies the ability and willingness issues. Performance slippage in the short run is usually a willingness problem. It is not that an individual's or a group's ability has deteriorated significantly, but it is the *use* of ability that is causing the performance slippage. It is a motivation problem, not an ability problem. So if performance starts to slip, the person may be giving verbal and nonverbal clues about being upset with the boss, with a peer, or with the organization about not getting an expected raise or promotion or whatever it happens to be. The person's mental attitude is now focused on personal troubles rather than work requirements. If there are problems at home, you may have the same things occurring.

Figure 11-2 further clarifies these ability and willingness issues. First comes the decline in willingness, as shown by the top gray line, followed by a decline in performance, shown by the bottom solid line. There is a lead–lag relationship. There is another related point. During the developmental cycle, issues of confidence or insecurity predominate psychological readiness; during the regressive cycle, it is issues of willingness and commitment.

Some Things to Remember When Disciplining an Individual

If a disciplinary intervention is called for, how can it be carried out effectively? Here are a few helpful guidelines.[3]

Timeliness

Problem solving needs to be done in a timely manner. The sooner the intervention, the better the chance of stopping the performance slippage. The longer a manager waits, the more directive the intervention will have to be. Therefore, a manager may risk a follower's becoming anxious, frustrated, or resentful. Even if the directive intervention is appropriate, this may lead to attempts to get out from under the manager or get the manager out.

For example, Peter's parents expect him to keep his room clean. Over the past few months the child has done a good job at keeping it in good shape. Lately, however, when the parents walk by his room, it's a mess. They begin to complain about Peter's lack of performance to themselves but still haven't talked with him. Finally one day they have had it. The room is a disaster and they can't wait for him to get home so that they can really let him have it. Peter may then feel "zapped," be bitter toward his parents, and not focus on the importance of keeping his room clean.

If the parents had intervened earlier, a participative style would probably have been enough to turn the problem around. But now, the highly structured style is necessary and creates resentment in the child. This is a trap that managers fall into when making disciplinary interventions. First they engage in "ostrich" leadership by sticking their heads in the sand and hoping the problem will go away. And then when it doesn't, they get angry and "zap" the follower.

By timing interventions appropriately and treating people where they are currently performing, managers can begin to take a proactive approach to problem solving, as opposed to just reacting to each new crisis.

Unless discipline occurs as close to the misbehavior or the poor performance as possible, it won't be helpful in influencing future behavior. Some managers are gunnysack discipliners. That is, they store up observations of poor behavior and then one day when the bag is full, they charge in and "dump everything on the table." Often, managers wait until the yearly performance review. That is why some people call an annual performance review program an "NIHYYSOB"—"Now I have you, you S.O.B." Managers using the "NIHYYSOB" performance review tell their people all the bad things they have done over the last months or year. Manager and employee usually end up arguing about the "facts," and the employee doesn't really hear what is wrong. This is a version of the "leave alone and 'zap'" form of discipline. If managers would only intervene early, they could calmly deal with one behavior at a time, and the person could "hear" the feedback.

Varying the Emotional Level

The emotional level of the intervention is different for constructive discipline than it is for developing people. When developing people, you are attempting to expand the present ability of the follower. Therefore, it helps to keep the emotional content of a development intervention at a low level. People often misinterpret Situational Leadership because they think a "telling" style is raising your voice, hollering, or blowing your cool. Actually, a style 1 can be a very soft and caring approach by providing the needed demonstration of how to do things with some hands-on guidance. It would be inappropriate to shout at or raise the emotional level with people who are developing. It could tend to make them insecure about taking risks and continuing to learn in the future.

However, when followers choose not to use their present ability and constructive discipline is appropriate, you can raise the emotional content to a *moderate* level. This helps to get people's attention and lets them know that you are aware of the performance problem and that you care. It also helps to unfreeze the inappropriate behavior so that change can take place.

Focus on Performance

The next thing to consider in working with constructive discipline is *don't attack personality—focus on performance.*

If you attack personality and the person becomes angry, the probability of being able to successfully work with the person is much lower. So often a manager starts off a disciplinary intervention with, "I just told you that a week ago. Can't you remember to do anything, you dumb son of a gun? . . ." All this does is raise the emotional level of other people. It doesn't get them to focus on the problem. If the focus is on performance, not personality, both leader and follower can talk about it and problem solve.

Be Specific . . . Do Your Homework

Being specific about performance problems is important. When using constructive discipline, be careful of *glittering generalities*. So often managers on the job do all the other aspects of constructive discipline well; they treat people where they are, have good timing, keep a moderate emotional profile, and focus on performance. However, their intervention sounds like this, "Look, you're just not doing the kind of performance that we both know you're capable of; now let's get back on track." Then the manager is bewildered or gets angry when followers don't understand.

These kinds of glittering generalities don't get the job done. You have to do your homework before the intervention and gather specific details that may be useful in problem solving. With specific information the interventions might sound like, "Productivity is down fourteen and a half percent," "Scrap loss is up six and a half percent," or "Project Z is five days late and we've got three other departments depending on us for that component." This provides specificity so that the manager and followers together can work on developing a solution.

Keep It Private

The last thing to remember is to keep disciplinary interventions private. As a guideline, it's a good idea to praise people in public and problem solve in private. If you address followers about problems when others are around, you run the risk of having them more concerned about being seen "catching hell" than on solving the problem. Discussing problems in private tends to make it easier to get your points across and keep the other person focused on the problem-solving process.

The goal of constructive discipline is to make problem solving a positive growth-oriented opportunity instead of a punitive experience. It is important to:

- Treat people where they are presently performing
- Make the intervention timely
- Use an appropriate emotional level
- Focus on performance, not personality
- Be specific . . . do your homework
- Keep the intervention private

Managers find that by keeping these factors in mind when making disciplinary interventions, discipline is not seen as a destructive intervention but as a helping relationship.

Punishment and Negative Reinforcement

Punishment, as we discussed earlier, is a negative consequence. A negative consequence tends to weaken the response it immediately follows; that is, it prevents the recurrence of that behavior. It is a stimulus that an individual "will reject, if given a choice between the punishment and no stimulus at all."[4] As punishment suppresses the behavior that brought it (the punishment) on, *negative reinforcement* strengthens the response(s) that eliminates the punishment.

An example of both punishment and negative reinforcement may be helpful. Suppose whenever a manager brings the work group together to share some new information with them, Bill, one of the subordinates, usually pays little attention and often talks to people around him. As a result he is uninformed and his manager is irritated. The manager decides to punish Bill's whispering behavior by stopping in the middle of a sentence and looking at Bill whenever she sees him talk. The unexpected silence (a negative consequence) causes the whole work group to focus on what stopped the manager's sharing of information (Bill's talking). The silence from the manager and all eyes on him are uncomfortable to Bill (punishment). He stops talking and starts listening to his manager resume sharing information. His manager's use of a negative consequence or punishment (silence and look) has weakened and suppressed his whispering behavior. At the same time it has operated as negative reinforcement in strengthening his listening, the behavior that took the punishment away (his manager stops looking at him and starts talking).

It is important to remember that a manager has to be careful in using punishment because one does not always know what a person will do when punished. For example, suppose a manager reprimands Al, a subordinate, for sloppy work. If Al settles down, figures out what he has done wrong, and begins working carefully (negative reinforcement), the punishment has been helpful. After having this good experience in "shaping up," the manager might try the same technique with Mary, another employee who is doing sloppy work. But rather than the punishment (reprimand) getting Mary to behave more carefully, her work becomes worse, and she begins to become disruptive in other areas. Thus, while Al shaped up with a reprimand, Mary became more troublesome after the same intervention from the manager.

Another important point to keep in mind when using punishment is that punishment shows one what *not* to do but does not show one what *to* do. This was vividly pointed out by John Huberman in a case study[5] about a Douglas fir plywood mill in which the management had continually used punitive measures to deal with sloppy workmanship and discipline problems. Although punishment seemed to stop the inappropriate behavior for the moment, it had little long-term effect. When top management finally analyzed the system during the preparation for the doubling of its capacity, they were amazed that:

> . . . *not a single desirable result* could be detected.
> The people who had been disciplined were generally still among the poorest workers; their attitude was sulky, if not openly hostile. And they seemed to be spreading this feeling among the rest of the crew.[6]

This reality and the findings that "85 percent of all those who entered the local prison returned there within three years of their release . . ."[7] made management seriously question their system. Eventually they worked out a new and highly effective system, which Huberman called "discipline *without* punishment." One of the main ingredients of the new method was that rather than a punitive approach to unsatisfactory work or a discipline problem, a six-step process was initiated that clearly spelled out appropriate behavior and placed "on the employee the onus" of deciding whether the employee wished (or was able) "to conform to the requirements of a particular work situation."[8]

As this illustrates, it is essential when making a disciplinary intervention that task behavior follows immediately. That is, once an intervention has been made, the manager must identify the new behavior that is to replace the undesired behavior. Only when that occurs can positive reinforcement be used to increase the likelihood of the new behavior recurring.

Extinction

When reinforcement is withheld after a behavior occurs, the behavior is said to be on extinction. Punishment tends only to suppress behavior; extinction tends to make it disappear. To extinguish a response, nothing must happen as a result of behavior. For example, suppose a child finds that stomping up and down and crying gets the attention of the parents and usually receives something wanted, say a cookie. Now, if the parents don't want that kind of behavior, they could extinguish it by not responding to the child (either in a positive or negative way). After a while, when the child sees that stomping and crying do not get anything, this behavior will tend to decrease. People seldom continue to do things that do not provide positive reinforcement.

Although extinction can help to eliminate undesirable behavior, one should be careful not to use it when it is not intended. Let's look at our example of Al again.

Imagine that Al has adjusted pretty well to his setting. He works carefully and neatly because that is what pays off. But, suddenly, the boss stops rewarding Al for neat work. Al goes for perhaps a week or two weeks working neatly with no reward. He may not be able to tell us what is different but gradually his behavior gives us a clue. He soon begins to try other behaviors. He becomes less careful and neat. If the former negative consequences (punishment) are also withheld, we see that within days he has reverted to his earlier behavior pattern. In essence, neatness and carefulness have been extinguished. As stated earlier, people seldom continue to do things that do not provide positive reinforcement, either through external reward or internal satisfaction. In Al's case, he does not yet find working carefully or neatly as rewarding in itself. The intervention by his manager helped his task readiness, but Al is not psychologically ready enough in this job (and he may never become so if it is a boring and unsatisfying job) to be left alone and not periodically reinforced for his neatness and carefulness.

In addition to its effect on the continuation of a particular behavior, extinction also can sometimes have an emotional impact on that behavior. We could predict, for example, with an excellent chance of being correct, that Al will likely become surly, may complain more than before, or may have problems getting along with his co-workers. Emotional behavior usually accompanies extinction in performance when expected reinforcement or former punishment is withheld.

Parents often have problems with extinction when they do not realize what they are doing and tend to pay attention to their children only when they are behaving poorly. When the children are behaving appropriately, they may pay little or no attention to them, which in a sense puts that behavior on extinction. If a child wants attention from the parents (it is rewarding to him), the child may be willing to endure what the parents think is punishment for that attention. So, in the long run, the parents might be reinforcing the very behavior they do not want and extinguishing more appropriate behavior.

Leaders in all kinds of settings must be careful of the possibility of positively reinforcing inappropriate behavior, and yet it happens all the time. Have you ever given a crying child a piece of candy? *"Don't cry, John. Here's some candy."* It works. The child eats the candy and stops crying. But does it really work? Behavior Modification Theory suggests that the next time the child wants a piece of candy (or your attention), he knows exactly how to get it—by crying. You have made the mistake of positively reinforcing inappropriate behavior.[9]

This phenomenon does not just happen at home but is very common in the world of work. For example, a manager's work group had responded well to a high task/low relationship behavior of always spelling out tasks specifically and dealing firmly with anyone who did not demonstrate appropriate behavior. Now suddenly this behavior is not achieving results, and followers are being disruptive and making unreasonable demands. What should the manager do? The first impulse of most managers is to think "maybe I've been too hard on them" and begin to give in to their demands. Although perhaps the manager should have increased relationship behavior earlier and moved to a high task/high relationship leadership style, if the manager does it now it may be perceived as positively reinforcing inappropriate behavior—every time the work group wants something, they will become disruptive. Positively reinforcing inappropriate behavior generally results in more unwanted behavior.

When to Use Punishment or Extinction

In essence, what we are saying is that leaders must think before they behave because they never know what they may or may not be reinforcing. This is particularly true when it comes to using punishment and extinction. And yet, these can be useful concepts that managers can learn to use effectively for unfreezing inappropriate behavior so that they can begin to reinforce positively more desirable behavior. It should be remembered, however, in using punishment or extinction that it is important to know what behavior you want to change and communicate that in some way to the person(s) with whom you are working. To determine when to use punishment and when to ignore (extinguish by withholding reinforcement), managers need to estimate how long the undesirable behavior has been occurring. If the behavior is new, ignoring it (extinction) may get results and cause a person to abandon an inappropriate behavior. But if the behavior has been occurring for some time, it may be necessary to suppress this behavior through some form of punishment until some desirable behavior has a chance to become strong enough as a result of positive reinforcement to replace the undesirable behavior. As we discussed in Chapter 2, the larger the reservoir of past experience that a person has in a particular behavior, the tendency is that the more difficult the behavior will be to change, and, thus, the harder the initial intervention may have to be before positive reinforcement can be used effectively to strengthen a new behavior.

An Example of Using Behavior Modification

Consider the behavior of Tony, a new employee right out of high school, who can be described as a very aggressive and competitive individual. During his first day on the job he argues over tools with another young employee. To make certain that a manager would not be unsure about what to do with Tony's behavior and to summarize our discussion of Behavior Modification, some steps that managers can use in attempting to change employee behavior are presented here.[10]

> *Step 1:* Identify (for yourself and then with Tony) the behavior to be changed and the new behavior that is to replace the old and discover what Tony would consider to be positive reinforcement and punishment. Devise a strategy to get the new behavior and determine the way you will positively reinforce it.
>
> *Step 2:* Attempt to find out whether the old behavior (arguing over tools) is such a strong behavior that you need to suppress it through punishment or whether it is a new enough behavior that a lack of any kind of reinforcement will extinguish it. If you decide to use punishment, determine what it will be. Remember, this punishment could operate as negative reinforcement and thus strengthen the behavior that removes the punishment. So be careful!
>
> *Step 3:* Develop a strategy to get Tony to practice the new behavior and positively reinforce it on a regular schedule. As soon as Tony has practiced the new behavior so that it is more likely to occur than the old behavior, change to an intermittent schedule of reinforcing the new behavior (make the intervals between reinforcement increasingly long) so that new behavior will resist extinction.

In examining these steps, one could get the impression that the manager is dominating the process with little if any involvement from Tony. According to Situational Leadership this may be appropriate in working with people at low levels of readiness, such as a new and inexperienced employee like Tony. But, as the readiness level of the people that a manager supervises begins to increase, this process of change becomes much more of a collaborative process. As we will discuss in Chapter 12, the extent of involvement of subordinates in the change process will vary from situation to situation.

PROBLEMS AND THEIR OWNERSHIP—WHO'S GOT THE MONKEY?

As we have been suggesting in this chapter, effective managers are not only able to develop the readiness and independence of their people, they are also able to spot "slippage" in readiness and intervene early enough to turn the situation around. How can managers know when to intervene? What should they look for?

As a simple guideline, whenever managers receive feedback, either verbal (one of their people tells them) or nonverbal (they observe the performance of one of their people), indicating that that person is having a problem in some area, it's time to think about stepping in. A *problem* exists when there is a difference between what someone is doing and what that person's manager and (or) that individual believes what is really happening. Thus, detecting problems is all-important in determining what areas of a person's job require attention.

Thomas Gordon, in his book *P.E.T., Parent Effectiveness Training,*[11] contends that one of the most important steps in becoming more effective in rearing responsible self-motivated children is determining whether their behavior is acceptable or unacceptable to their parents as well as to themselves. Once the acceptance question has been answered, then "who owns the problem" in terms of a child's behavior can be identified. Although the work of Gordon originated from observations of parents and teachers, the concepts behind the ownership of problems seem to apply to any organizational setting in which a leader is trying to influence the behavior of others.

Combining this concept of "who owns the monkey?" with William Onchen's helpful "monkey-on-the-back" analogy,[12] we arrive at four potential "monkey business' (problem) situations.

1. *The leader has a "monkey."* The follower's behavior is a problem to the leader but not to the follower. Thus, the "monkey" is on the leader's back.
2. *Both leader and follower have a "monkey."* The follower's behavior is a problem to both the leader and the follower. Thus, both have a "monkey."
3. *The follower has a "monkey."* The follower's behavior is a problem to the follower but not to the leader. Thus, the "monkey" is on the follower's back.
4. *Neither leader nor follower has a "monkey."* The follower's behavior is a problem to neither leader nor follower. There is no problem; the "monkey" is gone.

If managers can identify who has the monkey, then they are in a position to determine which leadership style has the best chance of success and thus when and how to intervene with followers in each of the four problem situations:

If the behavior of a follower is acceptable to a leader, it represents moderate to high levels of readiness (R3 and R4), and thus a leader can use a "participating" (S3) or "delegating" (S4) style. However, if the behavior of a follower is unacceptable to a leader, it represents low to moderate levels of readiness (R1 and R2), and thus a "telling" (S1) or "selling" (S2) leadership style is appropriate.

To differentiate further between "telling" and "selling" or "participating" and "delegating," leaders need to determine who has the monkey. Imagine that a leader is confronted with a problem that the leader does not know how to handle. As the leader looks at who has the monkey, the leader can begin to determine whether to take action and, if so, what leadership style would be appropriate with each of the four problem situations:

1. If the leader owns the problem and the follower sees no issue, the appropriate leadership style for the leader would be high task/low relationship (S1), similar to what Gordon would refer to as "you or I messages"; that is, statements of role definition and clarification. In this situation, since the follower sees no problem, the leader must initiate some structure to make any change in the follower's behavior.

2. If both leader and follower own the problem, the appropriate leadership style for the leader would be high on both task and relationship behavior, (S2), since the follower needs some direction. Yet because the follower also sees the behavior as a problem, some relationship behavior in terms of two-way communication and facilitating behavior is also necessary.

3. If the follower owns the problem but the leader sees no problem in the follower's behavior, the leader needs to make an intervention that is high on relationship behavior and low on task behavior (S3), similar to what Gordon would refer to as "active listening." Thus, the leader needs to provide the follower with supportive behavior to facilitate two-way communication. The tragedy is that managers often treat this problem situation as if it were a problem to neither. If a supportive intervention is not made here, there is a high probability that the situation will become a problem to both.

4. If neither the leader nor the follower owns the problem, the most appropriate leadership style for the leader is low relationship/low task behavior (S4), since no intervention is necessary.

Let's look at some examples of how this concept might be used as a diagnostic tool. Mary, a junior in high school, is avoiding the use of drugs. Since she is not using drugs, her behavior is not a problem to her parents. However, her behavior may be a problem to the girl herself, since all her friends are involved with drugs and are putting pressure on her. If her parents treat this situation as if it were a problem to neither and leave their daughter alone, this situation can quickly become a problem to both. Because of the competing pressures at school, no socioemotional support or active listening at home could lean the girl toward the drugs and acceptance by her peers. Thus, by not making a high relationship intervention at the appropriate time, the parents have helped to create a problem for all involved.

If the situation is one in which the behavior of the child is a problem to the parent but not to the child, the parent does not have to provide socioemotional support or facilitating behaviors. The parent merely needs to provide the child with an understanding of where the limits are (an S1 intervention). The child wants to know what are the barriers, what are the parent's expectations. Since the situation is not a problem to the child, the child does not want to spend fifteen or twenty minutes discussing it. The child just wants to know what the rules are. For example, a teacher who is making an assignment for the next day may ask the class to read fifteen, twenty, or twenty-five pages. That doesn't really matter to the students; any of those reading assignments are okay. All the students want to know is the expectations of the teacher; they don't want to sit around and talk about it. But if the teacher says the assignment is one hundred pages, the situation might quickly become a problem to both the students and the teacher. Now that the situation is also a problem to the students, the teacher has to engage in "selling" behavior rather than "telling." The teacher has to open up channels of communication and discussion, and engage in facilitating behaviors. The teacher has to get the students to understand the why of the large assignment and have them "buy in" psychologically to the decision. The teacher might say, "There is a top lecturer coming this week and, for that reason, a heavy assignment is being made for tomorrow; but later in the week we'll have no reading assignment." In other words, the teacher attempts to make some trades to facilitate interaction but is still trying to get the students to buy into the decision.

As the discussion and examples suggest, it is felt that this integration of Situational Leadership with problem ownership (Gordon) and monkey business (Oncken) can be helpful in determining the appropriate leadership style in various situations. Remember, even if the follower's behavior is acceptable to the leader, the leader may still have to take action if the follower needs support and encouragement to keep up the good work. If the follower's behavior is unacceptable to the leader, a more directive intervention is needed to turn the situation around. How direct the intervention must be ("telling" or just "selling") depends on whether the follower also sees this behavior as a problem and "owns the monkey" too.

As is being suggested, one of the key factors in determining readiness is problem solving—or the care and feeding of monkeys. If leaders are going to help their people grow and develop into mature, self-motivated individuals, they must gradually let them think for themselves and solve their own problems. Many managers have trouble dealing with people when they have a problem.

Inappropriate Responses to People with a Monkey

In transactional analysis (TA), a concept known as the Karpman triangle [13] is helpful in recognizing some dysfunctional reactions when a follower or staff member has a problem. As Figure 11-3 indicates, there are three basic roles in the triangle: victim, persecutor, and rescuer.

If we adapt Karpman's concept to problem solving in an organization, we see that the victim would be a person with a monkey. A manager could respond to a monkey on a staff member's back from either the persecutor or the rescuer role. If a manager responds from the persecutor role, the manager puts the person down for having a problem. For example, a staff member, Carlos, might tell his boss that he has not been getting along lately with a co-worker. Ted and his boss might respond by saying, "That's ridiculous. You and Ted have worked together for years. You've never fought before and I can't believe you are having trouble getting along now." The manager doesn't even want to recognize that a problem exists for his staff member.

If a manager responds from the rescuer role, the manager tries to solve the problem for the person. In our example with Carlos and Ted, the manager may respond by saying, "That's too bad, Carlos. Why don't you contact Ted and ask him to come over here this afternoon and maybe the three of us could talk this out. I was always able to iron things out with my co-workers and I would be happy to talk with you and Ted." In TA and Situational Leadership terms, the persecutor and rescuer tend to both be coming from a Critical Parent ego state, with the Critical Parent using an ineffective supportive leadership style. Both roles are considered Critical Parent roles because in both instances messages are sent to the victim that the person is not OK. The persecutor denies that a monkey exists and tells the person to forget it; the rescuer takes the monkey back and tends to let the victim (the staff member with the monkey) "off the hook." Neither of these responses teaches people to solve their own problems.

FIGURE 11-3   The Karpman triangle

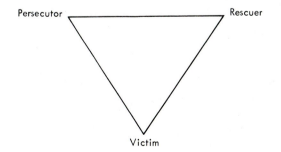

Persecutor

Rescuer

Victim

The triangle gets really interesting when a drama develops and people start to change roles. In our example of Carlos and Ted, if the manager responds to Carlos' problem with Ted from the persecutor role and puts Carlos down for having a problem and if Carlos does a good job as the victim (mumbles to himself about Ted, looks downcast and thoroughly victimized), his boss may begin to feel guilty and realize that maybe Carlos really has a monkey. When this happens, the manager usually moves from the persecutor role to the rescuer role and attempts to rescue the victim (Carlos, in this case) and take the monkey on his back. "I'm sorry, Carlos, for yelling at you. I didn't realize how serious your disagreements with Ted were to you. Maybe I can help out."

At this point, the plot can thicken (as it often does) if Carlos moves quickly from victim to persecutor and attacks his boss (now the rescuer) for not being more understanding earlier. "You never listen to me when I try to tell you something. All I want from you is support, but you always jump to your own conclusions and start yelling." Now the persecutor turned rescuer (Carlos' boss) is the new victim.

The drama can also start when the manager initially tries to rescue the victim—the person with a monkey. What we often find is that most victims don't really want to be rescued. Either they want support or they only want to complain. So when the rescuing manager starts to make suggestions, the victimized staff member "yes buts" every suggestion. "Sounds like a good idea having a talk with Ted this afternoon, *but* he has another appointment." Then when the rescuing manager runs out of good suggestions (that the staff member didn't want to use anyway), the person moves quickly from victim to persecutor and "pounds" his or her manager for not being more helpful. "I thought you said you were good at working things out with co-workers. Not one of your solutions will work for Ted and me." So, once again, the manager ends up as the victim.

The drama gets even more exciting when there are three actors instead of just two. The drama usually unfolds when one manager responds to the person with the monkey from either the persecutor or rescuer role and another manager plays the unfulfilled role. Suppose that when Carlos' manager is persecuting him for having a problem with Ted, his boss's assistant jumps in to rescue Carlos. "Don't be so hard on Carlos. His relationship with Ted is very important to him." The rescue attempt makes Carlos' manager so angry that he stops persecuting Carlos and attacks the assistant as if she were the victim. "Why don't you stay out of this? It's between Carlos and me." When that happens, the victim escapes unharmed and the two managers battle it out.

The drama does not always start with the staff member, follower, or child (in the family) as the victim. Sometimes the triangle starts off with the manager or parent being persecuted. Jongeward and Seyer give a beautiful family example of this kind of situation.[14]

    Son: (as persecutor, yells angrily at mother)   You know I hate blue. Here you went and bought me another blue shirt!

Mother: (as victim)   I never do anything right as far as you're concerned.

Father: (rescues mother, persecutes son)   Don't you dare yell at your mother like that, young man. Go to your room and no dinner!

    Son: (now as victim sulking in his room)   They tell me to be honest, and when I tell them what I don't like, they put me down. How can you satisfy people like that?

Mother: (now rescuer, sneaks him a tray of food)   Now don't tell your father! We shouldn't get so upset over a shirt.

Mother: (returning to father as persecutor)   John, you're so tough with our son. I'll bet he's sitting in his room right now hating you.

Father: (as victim)   Gee, honey, I was only trying to help you, and you kick me where it hurts the most.

    Son: (calling out as rescuer)   Hey, Mom, lay off, will ya? Dad's just tired.

How can managers stop games like this and the drama of the triangle? As discussed in Chapter 3, managers are best able to use theories and concepts when they have their Adult ego state in the executive position; that is, when they are able to think before they act.

The way to avoid the role of persecutor is to listen to your people before you begin to evalute what they are saying. Active listening helps managers gather information so that their intervention will be effective, and it helps their staff members begin to identify and solve their own problems. How about the rescuer? How do managers avoid playing that role?

Keep the Monkey Where It Belongs

William Oncken, Jr., who developed the monkey-on-the-back analogy, warns us not to take on other people's monkeys.[15] In terms of the TA triangle, rescuing is letting a monkey jump from another person's back onto our own back. For example, suppose a son comes home and says to his parents that he has made the club's junior tennis team but practices are on Tuesdays and Thursdays at three-thirty and he doesn't know how he will get there. Most parents would immediately say, "I think I can drive you." If, however, they normally have something planned on Tuesday and Thursday afternoons and cannot make an immediate commitment, they might tell their son, "We'll try to work something out."

Now let's analyze what has just happened. Before the son entered the house, on whose back was the monkey (how he was going to get to tennis practice)? The child's. After he and his parents talked about it, on whose back was the monkey? The parents'. Now who is in the superior position? The child. And in case the parents forget who's in charge, the child periodically checks in to see how the parents are doing in terms of rearranging their Tuesday and Thursday afternoons. In essence, the parents are working for the child.

That's what often happens in organizations. Managers are exhausted from trying to solve all their subordinates' problems. This all occurs as if managers did not have their own responsibilities to handle. Subordinate-imposed time begins the moment a monkey successfully executes a leap from the back of the subordinate to the back of the subordinate's manager and does not end until the monkey is returned to its proper owner for care and feeding.[16]

What a leader needs to do is get rid of a follower's monkey as the follower begins to mature. The first step, as suggested earlier, is for the leader to determine who owns the monkey. Let's look again at the four problem situations:

1. If a follower's behavior is unacceptable but is only a problem to the leader, then the leader owns the monkey and should do the initial care and feeding. But once the leader and follower know the monkey exists, the follower should take over its care and feeding. Staying with a "telling" (S1) style will guarantee only that the monkey will stay on the leader's back.

2. If a follower's behavior is unacceptable and a problem to both the leader and the follower, then the monkey is astride both backs. The follower needs some direction on how to feed this monkey. The leader should be careful not to use a "selling" style too long, but as soon as possible get the developmental cycle going and move to a "participating" style in which the monkey and its care and feeding are now on the follower's back. A "selling" style (S2) can be a rescuing style, which sometimes is acceptable in the short run, but it could lead to full-time caring and feeding if it becomes a status quo.

3. If a follower's behavior is acceptable to the leader but is a problem to the follower, the leader should only be supportive of the follower's efforts to solve the follower's problem. The leader must be careful in this process that the monkey does not leap on the follower's back. The leader should be supportive but should not rescue the follower and take over the care and feeling of the follower's monkey.

4. If the follower's behavior is acceptable and neither the leader nor the follower owns a problem, then no leadership intervention is needed (use of a "delegating" style), since there is no monkey in need of care and feeding. Some leaders get nervous, however, when everything is going well with their people and start "hunting down monkeys and feeding them on a catch-as-catch-can basis."[17] This is a useless activity that may grow large monkeys where none really existed before.

The purpose of this chapter has been to help leaders develop strategies for turning around a decrease in readiness. The hope was to make leaders realize why it is important to work their way out of their traditional job of directing, controlling, and supervising their followers so that these people can learn to stand on their own feet and be effective in a world that is full of monkeys (problems).

NOTES

1. Adapted from Paul Hersey, *The Situational Leader* (Escondido, Calif.: Center for Leadership Studies, 1985), p. 114.

2. *Ibid.*

3. Adapted from Paul Hersey, *Situational Selling* (Escondido, Calif.: Center for Leadership Studies, 1985), pp. 115–120.

4. R. L. Solomon, "Punishment," *American Psychologist*, 19 (1964), p. 239.

5. John Huberman, "Discipline Wtihout Punishment," *Harvard Business Review,* May 1967, pp. 62–68.

6. *Ibid.*, pp. 64–65.

7. *Ibid.*, p. 65.

8. *Ibid.*

9. Taken from an enjoyable popular article on this subject by Alice Lake, "How to Teach Your Child Good Habits," *Redbook Magazine*, June 1971, pp. 74, 186, 188, 190.

10. These steps were adapted from seven steps identified by Madeline Hunter, *Reinforcement Theory for Teachers* (El Segundo, Calif., TIP Publications, 1967), pp. 47–48.

11. Thomas Gordon, *P.E.T., Parent Effectiveness Training* (New York: Peter H. Wyden, 1970). See also Muriel James and Louis Savary, *A New Self: Self Therapy with Transactional Analysis* (Reading, Mass.: Addison-Wesley, 1977); Abe Wagner, *The Transactional Manager: How to Solve Problems with Transactional Analysis* (Englewood Cliffs, N.J.: Prentice-Hall, 1981).

12. William Oncken, Jr., and Donald L. Wass, "Management Time: Who's Got the Monkey?" *Harvard Business Review*, November–December 1974, pp. 75–80.

13. Stephen B. Karpman, *"Fairy Tales and Script Drama Analysis," Transactional Analysis Bulletin* VII, No. 26 (April 1968), pp. 39–43.

14. Dorothy Jongeward and Philip C. Seyer, *Choosing Success: Transactional Analysis on the Job* (New York: Wiley, 1978).

15. Oncken and Wass, "Management Time."

16. *Ibid.*, p. 76.

17. *Ibid.*, p. 80.

CHAPTER 12

BUILDING EFFECTIVE RELATIONSHIPS

In the last two chapters the emphasis was on helping leaders to develop people to their fullest potential. This involves shifting their leadership style forward and backward (according to Situational Leadership), thus utilizing various degrees of direction and support as followers increase or decrease in readiness or development levels. This continual shifting of leadership styles seems to require leaders to be flexible; that is, to be able to use a variety of leadership styles depending on the situation. That raises two questions: (1) Are most leaders able to be that flexible or do they tend to be limited only to one or two leadership styles? (2) If leaders continually change their leadership styles, how will that affect their followers' perception of their intentions?

The first question is something that has been examined at the Center for Leadership Studies for more than a decade through the use of Leader Effectiveness and Adaptability Description (LEAD) instruments.[1] Answering the second question was an important impetus in the development of the Contracting for Leadership Style[2] process developed by Hersey and Blanchard to increase the effectiveness of management by objectives (MBO), a widely used formal superior–subordinate negotiation system.[3]

LEAD INSTRUMENTATION

The LEAD instrument developed by Hersey and Blanchard was designed to measure three aspects of leader behavior: (1) style, (2) style range, and (3) style adaptability.

The *leadership style* of an individual is the behavior pattern that person exhibits when attempting to influence the activities of others—as perceived by those others. This may be very different from the leader's perception, which we will define as *self-perception* rather than style. Comparing one's self-perception of leadership style with the perceptions of others can be very useful, particularly since one's self-perception may or may not reflect actual leadership style, depending on how close a person's perceptions are to the perceptions of others. For this reason, two LEAD instruments were developed: LEAD-Self and LEAD-Other. The LEAD-Self measures self-perception of how an individual behaves as a leader; the LEAD-Other reflects the perceptions of a leader's subordinates, superiors, and peers or associates.[4]

Leadership Style

Our extensive research over many years has revealed that most leaders have a *primary* leadership style and a *secondary* leadership style. A leader's primary style is defined as the behavior pattern used most often when attempting to influence the activities of others. In other words, most leaders tend to have a favorite leadership style.

A leader's supporting style(s) is a leadership style that person tends to use on occasion. It is important to note that all leaders have a primary leadership style; that is, they tend to use one of the four basic leadership styles described in Situational Leadership more often than not in leadership situations. However, they may *not* have any secondary leadership style. Therefore, a leader could have no secondary styles or up to three secondary styles, but a leader would always have at least one primary style.

Style Range or Flexibility

Leaders' *style range* is the extent to which leaders are able to vary their leadership style. Leaders differ in their ability to vary their style in different situations. Some leaders seem to be limited to one basic style: these rigid people tend to be effective only in situations in which their styles are compatible with the environment. Other leaders are able to modify their behavior to fit any of the four basic styles; still others can utilize two or three styles. Flexible leaders have the *potential* to be effective in a number of situations.

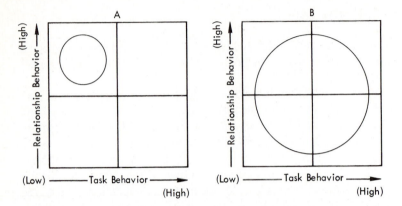

FIGURE 12-1 Style range in terms of task behavior and relationship behavior

The style range of a leader can be illustrated in terms of task and relationship behavior, as shown in Figure 12-1. The area of the circle indicates the range of style. If the area is small, as in A, then the range of behavior of the leader is limited; if the area is large, as in B, the leader has a wide range of behavior.

Leadership situations vary in the extent to which they make demands on flexibility. Reddin has cited some of the conditions that demand, in his terms, low and high flexibility. These conditions are listed in Table 12-1.[5]

TABLE 12-1 Low and high flexibility demands

Low Flexibility Demands	High Flexibility Demands
Low level managerial jobs	High level managerial jobs
Simple managerial jobs	Complex managerial jobs
Established goals	Emerging goals
Tight procedures	Fluid procedures
Established tasks	Unstructured tasks
Routine, automated decision making	Nonroutine decision making
Little environmental change	Rapid environmental change
Manager has complete power	Manager does not have complete power
Following plans essential	Using initiative essential
Manager accepted or rejected by subordinates	Subordinates neutral to manager
Few interconnecting jobs	Many interconnecting jobs

Style Adaptability

Style range indicates the extent to which leaders are able to vary their style; style *adaptability* is the degree to which they are able to vary their style appropriately to the demands of a given situation, according to Situational Leadership. People who have a narrow style range can be effective over a long period of time if they remain in situations in which their style has a high probability of success. Conversely, people who have a wide range of styles may be ineffective if these behaviors are not consistent with the demands of the situation.

Thus, style range is not as relevant to effectiveness as style adaptability; a wide style range will not guarantee effectiveness. For example, in A in Figure 12-1, the leader has a dominant relationship style with no flexibility; in B, the leader has a wide range of leadership styles because the leader is able to use all four leadership styles on various occasions. In this example, A may be effective in situations that demand a relationship-oriented style, such as in coaching or counseling situations. In B, however, the potential exists to be effective in a wide variety of instances. It should be remembered, however, that the B style range will not guarantee effectiveness. The B style will be effective only if the leader makes style changes appropriate to the situation.

Flexibility: A Question of Willingness

The importance of a leader's *diagnostic ability* cannot be overemphasized. It is the key to adaptability. However, most leaders are more concerned about flexibility than when to use which leadership style. That gets us back to one of the questions raised at the beginning of the chapter: Are most leaders able to be that flexible or do they tend to be limited only to one or two leadership styles?

It has been our experience based on our research that there are few, if any, leaders who cannot learn to use all four basic leadership styles. In fact, people use those behaviors almost every day. At least once a day you probably tell somebody what to do and watch them closely (style S1), explain what you want somebody to do and permit them to ask clarifying questions (style S2), share ideas with people and support their efforts (style S3), and turn over responsibility to someone to "run with the ball" (style S4).

Learning to use the four basic styles is not the issue; the question is one of willingness. Anyone has the ability, but if the person does not want to learn, then there is not much that you can do. It is like the old saying, "You can lead a horse to water but you can't make him drink."

When people are willing to learn to use all the leadership styles, we have found an interesting phenomenon. When people learn to use the leadership style that previously was not even considered a secondary style, the compensating styles often become their most effective styles. While these styles may never become comfortable, they can become the most effective, in many cases, because they've been learned. Therefore, such leaders know a lot more about these styles because they have practiced them consciously. People often use their comfortable or primary leadership styles by the "seat of their pants." This is true not only in terms of leadership styles but also in many other areas of their lives.

For example, suppose you are a golfer who enjoys and excels at hitting a drive; yet you realize that the "drive is for show but the putt is for the dough," so you decide to take lessons in putting. If you consciously make an effort and take lessons and practice to become a good putter, very often it is this part of the game that becomes your most effective weapon. That does not mean that you would not still be more comfortable hitting the ball off the tee, but since you have studied putting in considerable detail, you now know much more about that particular part of the game.

The same goes for leaders. Your primary style is often one that you do not have to think about using. But once you learn other styles through conscientious study, these compensating styles can be your most effective. Thus, we find willingness—not ability—is the main issue in terms of style flexibility.

Is There Only One Appropriate Style?

The concept of adaptability implies that the effective leader is able to use the right style at the right time. What if a leader makes a good diagnosis and then is unwilling or is unable to use the "best" style? Is that leader doomed to failure? Situational Leadership not only suggests the high probability leadership styles for various readiness levels but also indicates the probability of success of the other styles if the leader is unwilling or unable to use the "desired" style. The probability of success of each style for the four readiness levels is shown in Table 12-2.

As Table 12-2 indicates, the "desired" style always has a second "best" style choice; that is, a style that would probably be effective if the highest probability style could not be used. In attempting to influence people at the low to moderate (R2) and moderate to high (R3) readiness levels, you will notice that there are two second "best" style choices: which one should be used depends on whether the readiness of the individual is getting better, indicating that the leaders should be involved in a developmental cycle (Chapter 10), or getting worse, revealing that a regressive cycle is occurring (Chapter 11). If the situation is improving, "participating" and "delegating" would be the "best" second choices, but if things are deteriorating, "telling" and "selling" would be the most appropriate backup choices.

Table 11-2 also suggests that "telling" and "delegating" are the risky

Readiness	"Best" Style	Second "Best" Style	Third "Best" Style	L. Effe.. Style
R1 Low	S1 Telling	S2 Selling	S3 Participating	S4 Delegating
R2 Low to Moderate	S12 Selling	S1 Telling or S3 Participating		S4 Delegating
R3 Moderate to High	S3 Participating	S2 Selling or S4 Delegating		S1 Telling
R4 High	S4 Delegating	S3 Participating	S2 Selling	S1 Telling

styles because one of them is always the lowest probability style. However, even though this appears to be true, later in this chapter we will discuss why it is so important for leaders to learn to use these styles effectively.

Use of LEAD Instrumentation

When staff members at the Center for Leadership Studies diagnose an organization, part of that diagnosis often involves use of the LEAD instruments. The process consists of having managers throughout the organization complete the LEAD-Self Instrument (how they perceive their own leadership style). At the same time each of these managers' subordinates, superior, and several associates or peers fill out the LEAD-Other instrument. All the instruments are sent directly to the Center for Leadership Studies for analysis. Once the data have been analyzed, a LEAD-Profile is prepared for each individual manager. On that profile the managers are given an opportunity to see if there is any significant difference between how they perceive their own leadership style and how others in the environment perceive their style.

The purpose of distributing and analyzing the LEAD-Self and LEAD-Other data is to determine if there is any discrepancy between self-perception and the perception of others. In analyzing that data and feeding it back to participating managers, a useful framework developed by Joseph Luft and Harry Ingham[6] is used.

JOHARI WINDOW

The framework developed by Luft and Ingham is called the *Johari window* (taken from the first names of its authors). The Johari window is used in our consulting to depict leadership personality, not overall personality, as it is sometimes used. The difference between leadership personality and leadership style in this context is that leadership personality includes self-perception and the perception of others; leadership style consists only of an individual's leader behavior as perceived by others, that is, superior, subordinate(s), associates, and so on. Thus, leadership personality equals self-perception plus other perception (style).

According to this framework, there are some attitudes or behaviors engaged in by leaders that they themselves know about. This *known-to-self* area includes their knowledge of the way they are coming across—the impact they are having with the people they are trying to influence. At the same time, part of the leader's personality is *unknown to self*; that is, in some areas leaders are unaware of how they are coming across to others. It may be that their followers have not given them feedback or it may be that a leader has not been alert enough to pick up some of the verbal or nonverbal feedback that actually exists within the environment.

We can also look at leadership personality that includes behaviors and attitudes *known to others* in a leader's organizational setting, as well as areas *unknown to others*. In terms of what is known and unknown to self and known and unknown to others, we can create four areas that comprise the total window, as depicted in Figure 12-2.

The arena that is known to self and also known to others in any specific organizational setting is called the *public* arena—it is known to all (the leader and others; that is, superior, subordinate(s), and peers) within that organizational setting.

The arena that is unknown to self (the leader) but is known to others is

FIGURE 12-2   The Johari window

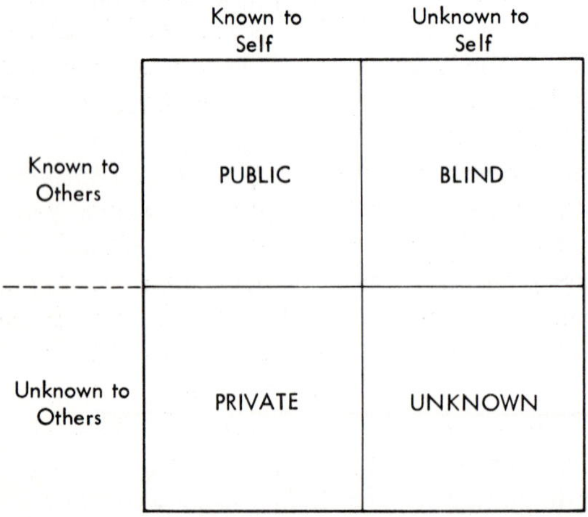

	Known to Self	Unknown to Self
Known to Others	PUBLIC	BLIND
Unknown to Others	PRIVATE	UNKNOWN

referred to as the *blind* arena. It is unknown to the leader either because followers have been unwilling to share feedback with or communicate ("level") to that leader, or it may be that the data are there in terms of verbal and nonverbal behavior but the leader is not able or does not care to "see" them.

The arena that is known to self but unknown to others is referred to as the *private* arena since it is only known to the leader. Again, it may be private because the leader has been unwilling to share or disclose this to others in the organizational setting, or it may be private because the others in the system are not picking up the nonverbal and verbal responses that are available from the leader in the system.

The last arena, unknown to self and unknown to others, is called the *unknown*. In Freudian psychology this would be referred to as the subconscious or unconscious.[7] As you will recall from Chapter 2, Freud describes personality much like an iceberg. There is a certain portion of a leader's personality that is above the surface—that is, it is very graphic. Anyone who looks in that direction can hardly help but see the basic size, consistency, makeup, and configuration. But much of this iceberg exists beneath the surface, and unless we make conscious efforts to probe and understand, we will really never have any insight into its consistency. And yet much of that part of a leader's personality referred to as unknown may be having a relevent impact in terms of the kinds of behaviors in which a leader engages when trying to influence the behavior of others.

Feedback

There are two processes that affect the shape of the Johari window (the configuration of the four arenas). The first, which operates in the direction illustrated in Figure 12-3, is called *feedback*. This is the extent to which others in the organizational setting are wlling to share with the leader. It is the willingness of others to be open and level and to give relevant feedback to the leader. But again, you have to look at it from both perspectives. It is also the extent to which the leader is attempting to perceive the verbal and nonverbal feedback that exists in the system.

Many managers cut off and eventually stifle feedback from their people by arguing with them about their feelings and perceptions. The late Haim Ginott, author of the well-known book *Between Parent and Child*,[8] and his wife, Alice Ginott,[9] who has been carrying on some of his work, believe that people should be allowed to have any feelings they want. Feelings are to be heard and accepted; it's only behavior that should be limited. In other words, people are experts on their own feelings and perceptions. Managers should never say to their people, "You don't really feel that way" or "That's not true" because, obviously, these people do know how they feel about things.

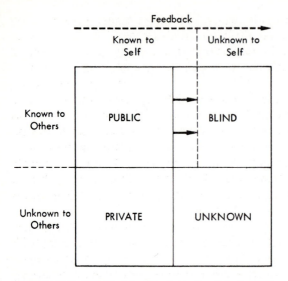

FIGURE 12-3   Effect of feedback on the Johari window

To illustrate this point, let's look at an example. A mother is walking through a department store with her young son when the child notices a beautiful bicycle. He says, "Boy, would I like to have a bike like that!" His mother, rather than hearing his feelings, replies harshly, "You're such an ungrateful child. We just got you a new bike for Christmas and already you want a new one. I've had enough of your spoiled attitude. See if you get anything new again for a long time." Now, what exactly has this child learned from this experience? He has learned that he should never tell his mother how he feels about anything; he will only get punished. If this scene is repeated often enough, the mother may soon lose any chance of ever receiving feedback from her son again—which is certainly a high price to pay!

What should the mother do in this situation? Alice Ginott suggests that she should recognize her son's wish and rephrase it in simple words; for example, "I bet you wish you could get a new bike any time you wanted." The child undoubtedly would agree. Then the mother should follow up with a statement or question such as, "Why don't you think you can get that new bike?" The boy knows and will probably say, "Because I just got a new one for Christmas." After agreeing, the mother could conclude the conversation on a supportive note: "When you've gotten good use out of your bike and it starts to get too small for you, then you probably can get a new one." With this kind of interaction, the child won't be afraid to share his feelings with his mother again.

This same situation occurs day after day in every organization. For example, a staff member tells the boss, "Those staff meetings we have on Thursday run too long and I think generally are a waste of time." The boss, rather than listening to feelings and trying to find out why the staff member feels that way responds quickly and harshly: "What do you mean those meetings are a waste of time? I'm sick and tired of your attitude around here. I think those meetings are the most productive sessions that we've had around here for a long time. And I'm sick and tired of this kind of ridiculous comment." Will this manager get much more feedback from the staff member? Probably not. The staff member has learned that with the boss "feelings are not allowed" unless they are "company line." That is unfortunate because in many ways "feedback is the breakfast of champions." Without feedback from their people, managers will develop significant blind areas that will eventually damage their effectiveness.

Another suggestion can give managers an additional clue to how they can encourage their people to share their feelings and perceptions with them. Why treat your people differently from the way you would treat a stranger, acquaintance, or friend? For example, Henry, a guest at a party in your home, forgets his hat and you discover it just after he has headed out to his car. Would you run out the door waving the hat and yelling, "How stupid can you be to leave your hat behind? How many times have I had to run after you with something you left? If your head wasn't glued on your shoulders, you'd probably forget that, too!" Of course you wouldn't. You would probably just say, "I'm glad I caught you. You left your hat!" And that's how staff members and family members deserve to be treated as well.

Treating staff members with respect will lead to a relationship in which they feel free to share and talk. As can be seen in Figure 12-3, the more relative feedback that takes place within an organization, the more the public arena of a leader begins to extend into and displace the blind arena and thus the smaller the blind arena that leader has.

Disclosure

The other process that affects the shape of the Johari window is *disclosure*. This is the extent to which leaders are willing to share with others in their organizational setting data about themselves.

The way we use the term disclosure is different from the way others in the field often use it. First, the most relevant disclosure is not what people say about themselves but rather their behavior. It is not words that mean, it is people that mean. And if you want to understand people better you really have to look at the behavior those people engage in to gain relevant insights into their values and what this behavior represents.

Second, we think disclosure is appropriate in organizations only when such disclosure is organizationally relevant. This is a different way of viewing disclosure than is urged by some people in the sensitivity training and personal growth field, who feel all disclosure is appropriate. In fact, some contend that it is appropriate for a leader or manager in an organizational setting to be open and disclose as much as possible and that the organization should process that data. Our experience from numerous organizational development interventions suggests that two of the scarcest resources in any organizational setting are time and energy. Therefore, if people disclosed almost everything about themselves within the organizational setting and others took time to process these various agendas, there would not be much time left to accomplish other organizational goals and objectives. We feel disclosure is important and helpful in organizations as long as it is relevant to the operation of the organization. For example, suppose a manager is having an affair with a neighbor down the street and it does not affect the manager's work environment. It might be inappropriate to disclose and process that situation in that work setting. But it might be very appropriate to discuss it with a marriage counselor if the situation is causing problems in that environment. Therefore, what may be organizationally relevant in one setting might be inappropriate in another.

In the process of disclosure, the more and more organizationally relevant the information that leaders disclose about the way they think or behave, the more the public arena opens into the private arena and the smaller and smaller that arena becomes, as shown in Figure 12-4. An interesting phenomenon occurs in settings where there is simultaneous feedback and disclosure between leaders and the people with whom they work. Not only does the public arena of these leaders begin to extend itself into the blind

FIGURE 12-4   Effect of feedback and disclosure on the Johari window

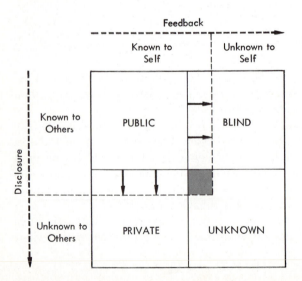

and the private arenas, but there is also a high probability that some of what was previously unknown (not known to either the leaders or other people in the organization) will begin to surface into the public arena.

A psychiatrist working with a patient in psychotherapy hopes to create an environment in which this process of simultaneous feedback and disclosure occurs. If that happens, the doctor can begin to release and understand some of the phenomena that have been evoking behavior in the patient that was unknown to the patient as well as to the psychiatrist. This is also the same process that Carl Rogers[10] refers to in his work on coaching and counseling.

Self-perception versus Style

When we do an organizational diagnosis, the data from the LEAD-Self, as we explained, denote self-perception. In terms of the Johari window, the self-perception of leaders would represent what is known to them about their leadership style and would include both their public and private arenas. This self-perception of leadership style can be measured using the LEAD-Self. On the other hand, an individual's leadership style would represent what is known to others and would include on the Johari window both that person's public and blind arenas. Leadership style can be measured using the LEAD-Other. The relationship between self-perception, leadership style, and the Johari window is presented in Figure 12-5.

FIGURE 12-5   Self-perception and other perception (style)

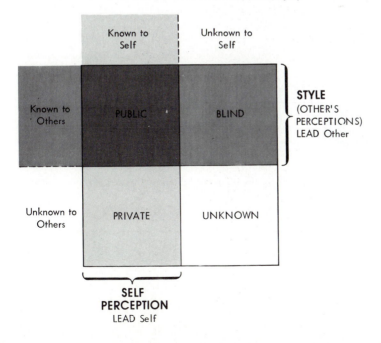

One of the interesting phenomena that we have discovered at the Center for Leadership Studies is that we can predict the shape of the public arena within the Johari framework. For instance, if there is a great discrepancy between self-perception and the way others perceive a manager (style), the public arena in that manager's Johari window would tend to be very small. as illustrated in Figure 12-6.

But if there is no significant difference between self-perception and the perception of others within a leader's organizational setting, the public arena in that person's leadership Johari window would be large, as illustrated in Figure 12-7. LEAD data can actually measure the shape of the arenas in a person's leadership Johari window in each of the organizational settings in which that person operates.

For example, a manager responsible for three departments may find that in Department A, where there is good feedback and disclosure, the public window is very open. In Department B, where there is very little contact, and thus infrequent feedback and disclosure, the public window might be small. And finally, in Department C, where there is average interaction, the public arena might be moderate in size.

Another interesting result of the work at the Center for Leadership Studies is a realization that there tends to be a high correlation between the openness of a leader's public arena and that person's effectiveness within that specific organizational setting. Since people often have different config-

FIGURE 12-6 Public arena when there is a large discrepancy

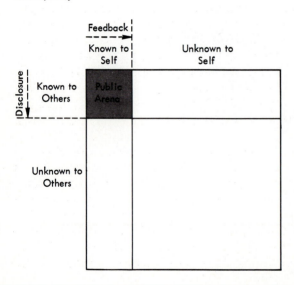

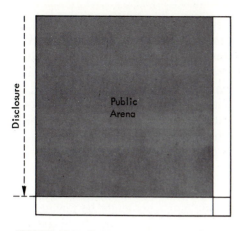

FIGURE 12-7 Public arena when there is a small discrepancy

urations for their leadership Johari window depending on the organizational setting in which they are operating, these people could vary in their effectiveness in these various settings. This is why some managers who have a very open public arena on the job and are very effective there are not as effective at home. It is often the case of managers coming home, picking up the paper, and having a drink. They are tired and don't want to be bothered by children or any problems of the home. Therefore, in their home environment there tends to exist far less feedback and disclosure. We could predict that these managers would not be as effective in their interactions at home as at work. And yet they have trouble understanding why they are not having an effective impact on the development of their children because they see themselves as effective leaders in terms of the feedback they get on the job. On the other hand, there are individuals who are quite effective in the home and wonder why they are not effective on the job. We have to recognize that each organizational setting in which we are involved is unique, and if we want to have an impact on that setting, we have to be willing to engage in relevant feedback and disclosure.

Another thing managers must recognize is that within a given organizational setting they need to be effective on both individual and group levels, and both levels involve separate Johari windows. Thus, we have found it helpful in a family, for example, for the parents to get together with each of their children individually, as well as with all the children as a family. One might begin with something like taking each child out to dinner once a month, giving the child a chance to choose where and what to eat. The important thing is to create a situation in which the focus is on the child and the child's problems. You would be surprised how willing the child will be to open up and engage in feedback and disclosure when alone with the parent(s) than when brothers and sisters are there to create many competing responses in that environment. This process over time will help to develop an open public arena between children individually with their parents, as well as developing feedback and disclosure within the family as a total group. We need to build into our domestic environment, as well as our work setting, opportunities to work with groups as a whole, at the same time developing openness with individuals within that system.

Is It Too Late?

In reading about communication problems, managers might be feeling discouraged or even guilty. Maybe they have a problem employee or a child or two and are thinking they really have done a poor job as a manager or parent. Yet, as Wayne Dyer so aptly argues in his book *Your Erroneous Zones*,[11] guilt is a useless feeling.

> It is by far the greatest waste of emotional energy. Why? Because, by definition, you are feeling immobilized in the present over something that has already taken place, and no amount of guilt can ever change history.[12]

Managers can never do what they should have done at an earlier time. Maybe you have made some mistakes. But that was yesterday; what are you going to do today? Today is the beginning of the rest of your life as a leader, manager, or parent. It is never too late to turn a situation around, as long as there is enough time. We mention time because it is a key factor. Why? Let us try to explain from a child-rearing point of view.

The earlier in a child's life a parent attempts to have an impact the greater will be that parent's potential influence on the child's future behavior. During the early years, an intervention by a parent represents a substantial portion of the child's sum experience in that area of the child's life; the same intervention later can never carry the same weight. In addition, the longer the behavior is reinforced, the more patterned it becomes, and the more difficult it is to change. That's why as a child gets older, it takes more time and more new experiences to bring about a change in behavior. Think of it this way: one drop of red food coloring in a half-pint bottle of clear liquid may be enough to change drastically the appearance of the total contents. But the same drop in a gallon jug may make little, if any, noticeable difference.

If our children are now teenagers—young adults—it is still possible, though difficult, to bring about some change in their behavior. Now it becomes a matter of economics: how much time are we willing to invest in implementing such a change.

Let's take an extreme case. Suppose a teenage son is discovered by his parents to be into drugs and in trouble with the law. What can his parents do now? One choice is to feel guilty and try to make up for past mistakes by putting all kinds of time in with the son now. But the son might resent all this attention from his parents after having been left on his own for so long. If the son doesn't resent the sudden attention from his parents, then it becomes an economic question: our children have unlimited needs, but we have limited time. Where can we put in the most effective time with the biggest payoff?

If the parents have plenty of time and decide to attempt to change their son's behavior (even though it's an old pattern), the concepts presented in this book should provide some helpful hints as to where and how to begin. Probably they will have to do some "telling" (S1) and "selling" (S2), both of which are time-consuming styles. But with some concentrated effort, the parents can probably have an impact on this boy's behavior.

Before parents throw themselves into a change effort with one of their kids, it's a wise idea to consider what impact this attention will have on the other children in the family. By devoting all their time and energy to one problem, the parents may unwittingly create other problems. If all the parents' time is spent on this teenage son, the other children still at home may get the impression that the only way to get time with mom and dad is by getting into trouble (in effect, the parents have put all their good behavior on "extinction"). And soon one problem child has mushroomed into other problem children. Therefore, it's important always to look at the big picture and allot time accordingly.

The lesson to be learned in this example as a manager is to "get your shots in early" with your people. As we stated in Chapter 11, loosening up is much easier than tightening up. Rescue and salvage work is tough and time-consuming and often comes too late to do much good.

LEAD PROFILES

As was indicated earlier, LEAD data are gathered in organizations to give managers feedback on how they perceive their own leadership style as compared with how others see their style. Once a manager has learned that subordinates perceive that one style or another is used most of the time with them, what does it all mean?

Sample

In this section we will examine and interpret some of the common profiles that we have found from analysis of LEAD-Self and LEAD-Other data accumulated at the Center for Leadership Studies.[13] The information was generated from a LEAD sample of over twenty thousand leadership events from fourteen different cultures. A "leadership event" occurs when we have data not only in terms of self-perception (LEAD-Self) but also the perception of others (LEAD-Other) in that leadership environment. Of these respondents, we have interviewed some two thousand middle managers from industry and education; of that number, we have conducted more than five hundred in-depth interviews. The interviews have not only included the leaders in terms of self-perception but also a sample of the leaders' followers and their perceptions of the leaders' style.

What Is a Two-Style Profile?

In our in-depth interviews the emphasis has been on what we call "two-style profiles." A two-style profile includes either (1) a basic style that encompasses two of the four posssible configuration styles or (2) a basic style and a supporting style.

It is suggested that as feedback is given on the specific two-style profiles you keep in mind what you know about your own leadership style. If you think you have a one-style profile (you tend to use only one primary leadership style with little flexibility), then you need to remember that your profile represents only a portion of the two-style profile. If you think you have a three- or four-style profile (you have more than one supporting style in addition to your primary style), you may have to integrate the feedback that will be given to you into several of the two-style profiles. It must be pointed out that unless you have gathered specific data on how your leadership style is perceived by others, your perception of your own leadership style is only that—your perception.

Wide Flexibility

We have found that in working with people who have a wide range of styles, even though their effectivness score may be low, a shorter period of time is needed to increase their effectivness than is needed with people who have a smaller range of behavior. If people are engaging in a wide range of behavior, all you have to do to make a significant change in their effectiveness is to change their knowledge and attitude structure—in other words, teach them diagnostic skills. On the other hand, for people who have had no experience in using a variety of styles, much more time is necessary for them to become comfortable in using different styles.

Reference to Situational Leadership

Since we will be referring to Situational Leadership throughout the discussion of the two-style profiles, the basic framework is reproduced for your use in Figure 12-8.

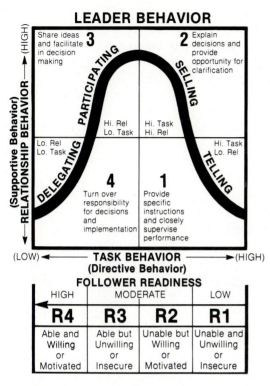

FIGURE 12-8   Situational Leadership model

Style Profile 1−3

People who are perceived as using predominately styles 1 and 3 fall into what is called the Theory X−Theory Y profile. What we have found is that people who have a style profile 1−3, with little flexibility to styles 2 and 4, generally view their subordinates with either Theory X or Theory Y assumptions about human nature. They see some people as lazy, unreliable, and irresponsible. The only way to get anything out of these people is to coerce, reward and punish, and closely supervise them. Other people they see very positively as creative and self-motivated; the only thing they have to do with these people is to provide socioemotional support. In fact, in interviewing managers with this profile, it has been found that they talk about individuals they supervise as "good people" or "bad people," "with me" or "against me." Their subordinates, when interviewed, tend to agree. They see their managers as labeling people, and thus being very supportive (S3) with people they see in their "camp," but closely supervising, controlling (S1), and even punishing people whom they perceive as against them.

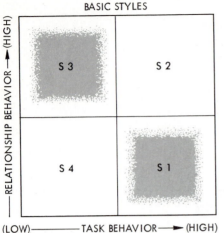

BASIC STYLES

RELATIONSHIP BEHAVIOR ———➤(HIGH)

S 3   S 2

S 4   S 1

(LOW)————— TASK BEHAVIOR ——➤ (HIGH)   **FIGURE 12-9   Style profile 1—3**

One of the interesting things that occurs with this style profile is that it often becomes a self-fulfilling prophecy. A manager with this style takes people who are at moderate readiness levels (R2) and either moves them up to moderate to high (R3) or moves them down to low levels of readiness (R1). Thus, this manager tends to be effective working with low levels of readiness or moderate to high levels of readiness.

A problem with this style is that the leaders who adopt it often are doing little to develop the potential of the people they don't like; they keep them locked into low levels of readiness by always relying on S1 (high task/ low relationship behavior) with them. They lack the interim behaviors between style 1 and style 3 to operate effectively in the developmental cycle. At the same time, their style 3 (high relationship/low task behavior) with people of moderate levels of readiness might keep these people psychologically dependent on them too long. These kinds of leaders do not seem to allow people to develop fully through delegation.

It is also interesting that people who work for leaders with this style profile claim that if there is any change in their leader's style with them, it usually occurs in a movement from style 3 to style 1. In other words, it is very difficult if you are being treated in a style 1 fashion by these leaders ever to receive style 3 types of behavior from them. But it is not too difficult to move from receiving style 3 behaviors to receiving style 1 behaviors. All you have to do is make some mistakes and these leaders tend to respond with highly structured behavior.

Style Profile 1—4

People who are perceived as using mainly styles S1 and S4 have some similarity to the Theory X—Theory Y profile of style 1—3 leaders. But rather

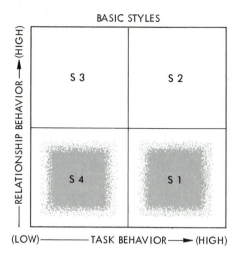

BASIC STYLES

RELATIONSHIP BEHAVIOR ⟶ (HIGH)

S 3   S 2

S 4   S 1

(LOW) ——————— TASK BEHAVIOR ⟶ (HIGH)

FIGURE 12-10   Style profile 1−4

than assessing people on whether they are good or bad in terms of personal attachment to them, the sorting mechanism for this kind of leader often becomes competency. When interviewed, these managers suggest that if you are competent you will be left alone; but if you are incompetent, they will "ride you" and closely supervise your activities. Their style is either "telling" or "delegating." A leader with this style is effective at crisis interventions. This is the kind of style we might look for to make an intervention into an organization with severe problems where there are short-time restrictions to solve them. This kind of leader is quite capable of making disciplinary interventions, going in and turning around a situation, and hopefully moving people back to a higher level of readiness. But again, much like the style 1−4 profile, this type of leader lacks the developmental skills to take people from low levels of readiness and develop them into higher levels of readiness.

An interesting thing occurs when leaders with this type of profile are introduced into a group with a normal distribution of readiness. What tends to happen is that the leader treats people in such a way that they either progress in their readiness or they regress, so that now, rather than a normal distribution of readiness levels, followers are clustered at the high end (R4) or low end (R1) of the readiness continuum. Once again, this becomes a self-fulfilling prophecy.

Style Profile 2−3

People who are perceived as using predominantly styles S2 and S3 tend to do well working with people of average levels of readiness but find it difficult handling discipline problems and work groups at low levels of readiness

(R1), as well as "delegating" with competent people to maximize their development. This style tends to be the most frequently identified style in the United States and other countries that have a high level of education and extensive industrial experience. Managers in some of the emerging cultures tend to have a more structured style profile (S1 and S2).

This style leader tends to be effective more often than not, because most people in work settings usually fall in readiness levels R2 and R3. We find far fewer people on the whole at readiness levels R1 and R4.

If styles S2 and S3 are considered "safe styles," then we would have to say that styles S1 and S4 are the "risky styles." We say "risky" because if they are used inappropriately, they can result in a great deal of crisis. For instance, if someone is supervising a very low level of readiness and uses style S4, leaving people on their own, there is a high probability that the environment is going to deteriorate and serious problems will result. On the other hand, if you have an extremely high level of readiness among your followers and you are attempting to use style S1 interventions, you are likely to generate much resentment, anxiety, and resistance, which may lead to what Machiavelli refers to as attempts to undermine, overthrow, or get out from under the leader; that is, hatred rather than fear. Although style S1 and S4 are risky styles, if you are going to maximize your role as leader, you have to be willing to take the risk and use these styles when the situation is appropriate. One caution is that if you feel style 1 or style 4 is needed in a situation, you should be more careful in your diagnostic judgments before you make these kinds of interventions.

You need to learn to make style S1 interventions for the following reasons. First, they are effective interventions when beginning the process of developing the task-relevant readiness of people with low readiness levels.

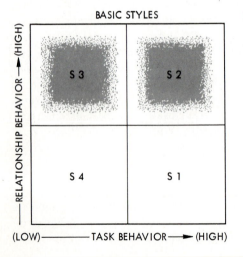

FIGURE 12-11   Style profile 2–3

Second, this style is often necessary in making disciplinary interventions. On the other hand, S4 is often necessary if you are going to allow people to reach self-actualization by satisfying their need for achievement and desire to maximize their potential.

Learning to use style S4 is also important to leaders themselves. In any of the organizations for which we work, there are at least two prerequisites for promotion. The first is that managers have to do an outstanding job in their present position. In other words, their output in terms of that organization has to be high. The second prerequisite is that they have to have a ready replacement—someone who is ready and able to take over their responsibilities. To have this kind of ready replacement, managers must have at least one of several key subordinates with whom they are able to use style S4 and delegate significant responsibilities. If this is not so, the probability of these managers having a ready replacement is very low. In summary, the style profile S2–S3 is an excellent style for working with individuals at moderate levels of readiness, but if leaders with this profile are going to maximize their potential as leaders, they need to learn to use styles S1 and S4 when necessary.

Style Profile 1–2

People who are perceived as using predominantly styles S1 and S2 tend to be able to raise and lower their socioemotional support or relationship behavior, but they often feel uncomfortable unless they are "calling the shots"; that is, when they are providing the structure and direction. In our sample, we found that this style profile tends to be characteristic of engineers who have become supervisors of other engineers but tend to be reluc-

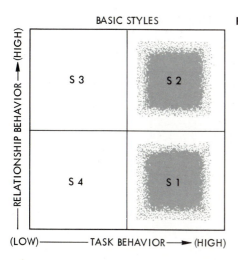

BASIC STYLES

FIGURE 12-12   Style profile 1–2

RELATIONSHIP BEHAVIOR ⟶ (HIGH)

S 3

S 2

S 4

S 1

(LOW) ——— TASK BEHAVIOR ⟶ (HIGH)

.ant to give up their engineering; salespersons who have become sales managers yet still love to sell; and teachers who have become administrators but still want to be directing the activities of children. These leaders often project in interviews that "no one can do things as well as I can," and this often becomes a self-fulfilling prophecy.

The style profile S1—S2 tends to be effective with low to moderate levels of readiness. It is often an extremely effective style for people engaged in manufacturing and production where managers have real pressures to produce, as well as with leaders in crisis situations where time is an extremely scarce resource. But when the crisis or time pressure is over, leaders with this style often are not able to develop people to their fullest potential. And this remains true until they learn to use styles S3 and S4 appropriately.

Style Profile 2—4

People who are perceived as using mainly styles S2 and S4 usually have a primary style of S2 and a secondary style of S4. This style seems to be characteristic of managers who do not feel secure unless they are providing much of the direction, as well as developing a personal relationship with people in an environment characterized by two-way communication and socioemotional support (high relationship behavior). Only occasionally do these people find a person to whom they feel comfortable delegating. And when they do delegate, their choice may not be able to handle the project. Thus, such a person may not be able to complete the task or may come to the manager for help because the person is used to the leader's providing direction and socioemotional support. The reason that style profile S2—S4 leaders tend not to be successful in delegating is that they generally move

FIGURE 12-13 Style profile 2—4

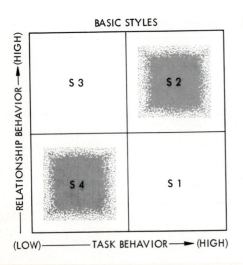

BASIC STYLES

RELATIONSHIP BEHAVIOR ——► (HIGH)

S 3

S 2

S 4

S 1

(LOW)———— TASK BEHAVIOR ——► (HIGH)

from style S2 to style S4 without moving through style S3. Let's look at an example.

Suppose Mac, a supervisor, usually directs and closely supervises (high task behavior) your activities, but you also have a good rapport with this supervisor and open communication and you receive socioemotional support from these interactions (high relationship behavior). One day Mac puts a couple of projects on your desk and tells you that they must be completed in a couple of weeks. You don't see Mac during that time. You would probably respond to that behavior from Mac as if it were a punishment rather than a reward. You might respond by saying, "What's Mac giving me all this work for?" and "Mac must not care about me much anymore because I never see him now!" So rather than suddenly shifting from style S2 to S4, managers with this style—if they are going to be effective in delegating—have to learn to move from "selling" (S2) through "participating" (S3) and then to "delegating" (S4).

In the previous example, if this strategy were followed by your supervisor, he should provide you with some socioemotional support, telling you that you have been doing a good job, that he has confidence in you, and that he feels that you will be able to take on some additional responsibility. Then he might give you a choice of several projects so that you could then participate in choosing which of the projects you would be interested in taking over. So your supervisor would be moving from style S2 into style S3 (participation and supportive behavior). Then he might say, "Look, I think you can run with this project on your own. If you get into some problems, give me a call." Now, because your supervisor has moved from style S2 through the supportive relationship behaviors (S3) to delegation (S4), you would tend to see this behavior as a reward rather than a punishment.

Style Profile 3–4

People who are perceived as using predominantly styles 3 and 4 tend to be able to raise and lower their socioemotional support or relationship, but they often feel uncomfortable if they have to initiate structure or provide direction for people. Thus, while this style profile is appropriate for working with moderate to high levels of readiness, it tends to create problems with people who are decreasing in readiness and need a regressive intervention or with inexperienced people who require more direction during the early phases of the developmental cycle.

We have found style profile S3–S4 to be characteristic of certain types of individuals or groups. It tends to be representative of very effective top managers in organizational settings where they have an experienced, competent staff that needs little direction from the top. It has also been found to be characteristic of managers who have been very deeply involved in sensitivity training, personal growth groups, or laboratory training. These manag-

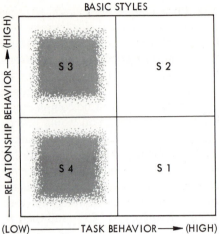

BASIC STYLES

RELATIONSHIP BEHAVIOR ⟶ (HIGH)

S 3   S 2

S 4   S 1

(LOW) ⟶ TASK BEHAVIOR ⟶ (HIGH)   **FIGURE 12-14** Style profile 3−4

ers sometimes become more interested in how people feel and the process of interpersonal relationships than what people do in terms of organizational goals. We also have found this profile among people who have studied or are practicing in the area of humanistic education. For example, teachers with this kind of profile tend to be comfortable in "student-centered" environments where the norm is not for teachers to direct, control, and closely supervise the learning activities of children. However, because many youngstes are not yet ready to assume direction of their own learning, this style universally applied can lead to problems. In fact, some parents complain today that although youngsters seem to be much more willing to level, share, and be open about their feelings with adults—teachers in school and parents in the home—they often seem to lack the solid technical skills of reading, writing, and arithmetic, which tend to require for development in the initial stage more directive teacher behavior, with an emphasis on the technical as well as the human skills.

Another group we have found, in several dozen cases, to have style profile 3−4 is women who have recently been promoted into significant middle-management positions. In interviewing these women, it has been noted that prior to their promotion, top management had not given them opportunities to engage in much "telling" (S1) or "selling" (S2) leader behavior; that is, they had little practice in initiating structure within the organizational setting. As a result, the only way they had an impact in the past was by raising or lowering socioemotional support. In terms of training experience, we found that with very little training these women respond quickly to trying on some of the other styles. It is just a matter of exposing them to concepts such as Situational Leadership to get them to feel comfortable trying these new behaviors. The tragedy is that women and other minorities restricted from management positions often have not received this training prior to promotion. And yet, they may find that they are dealing with people who need direction and supervision. When they initially use a high relationship (S3) style, it is much more difficult to use other styles later, even though they now understand that they are appropriate.

Implications for Growth and Development

If we look at an organizational hierarchy from very low levels of supervision to what we might call top management, we find that effective managers at each level require different profiles, as shown in Figure 12-15.

We have found that effective managers at the lower levels tend to have style profile S1–S2. The reason is that at these lower levels of management (in industry, the general foremen and first- and second-line supervisors), there is an emphasis on productivity—getting the work out. At the other end of the management hierarchy, however, effective top managers tend to engage in more "participating" and "delegating." The reason seems to be that as you move up in an organizational hierarchy, the greater and greater the probability that the subordinates who report directly to you will have a high level of task-relevant readiness. So you can see that as you progress through an organization, you learn to engage in styles 3 and 4, as well as those styles that might be effective at lower ends of the hierarchy (styles S1 and S2). Thus, we have found in working with manufacturing organizations that while it may be appropriate for first-line supervisors to have a basic style of S1 and a supporting style of S2, when those people get promoted, it would be more appropriate if they had a basic style of S2 with supporting

FIGURE 12-15 Style needs for different level of management

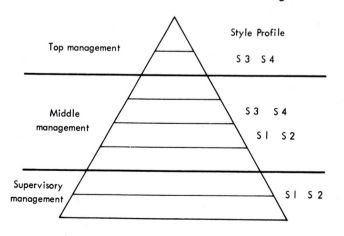

styles in S1 and S3. At this new supervisory level, they are no longer managers of hourly employees but have now become managers of managers.

Another interesting observation in terms of the management hierarchy is that it is the middle managers who really have to wear "both hats"—they need the most flexibility. They have to be able to provide the structured style S1 and style S2 interventions when appropriate but they also must be able to use "participating" and "delegating" styles when necessary. It is interesting to think of this phenomenon in terms of the Peter Principle.

As you will recall, the Peter Principle states: "In a hierarchy every employee tends to rise to his level of incompetence.[14] What we find in our work at the Center for Leadership Studies is that this is *not* a principle. In other words, it does not hold as a universal truth. In fact, as we suggested in Chapter 7, one might think of the Anti-Peter Principle vaccine as being the appropriate training and development or experience prior to moving up to the next level of the hierarchy. Better than training and development *after* being appointed to the new position is having worked for a boss who is willing to delegate responsibilities and provide on-the-job experience for future higher level positions. Another interesting observation is that although the Peter Principle is not really a principle, it occurs often enough to merit some attention. There certainly is a tendency for people to reach their level of incompetency. So often when we interview people who are in a position they are having trouble handling, it turns out that they have the technical skills and conceptual skills required. In most cases, their incompetence is a result of not having the human skills. Many times they are not able to adapt their leadership style to the new environment.

Although this lack of flexibility does occur, we have found in working with managers in a variety of settings and cultures that given some training in Situational Leadership, they seem willing and able, almost without exception, to expand their adaptability. They are able to take on new leadership styles effectively. The most important criterion here is motivation—people have to want to do this. But if they want to, we feel strongly that most people have the capacity to increase their style range and adaptability provided they think through the appropriate leadership style needed and then seriously try to use a new style if it is appropriate for a particular situation. This assumption is an important difference between our approach and the thinking of some other people in the field, such as Fiedler,[15] who contend that if a leader's style is not appropriate to a given situation, what really needs to be done is either change the leader or change the job demands to fit the style of the leader. We feel that approach implies Theory X assumptions about human nature; and yet our work suggests strongly that the potential of people to operate under Theory Y assumptions is there to be tapped. Although this lack of flexibility does occur, as we indicated earlier, we found that managers in a variety of settings and cultures, once exposed to training in Situational Leadership, seem willing and able almost without exception to expand their adaptability.

Team Building

If managers have a narrow range of behavior, one way that they can expand their flexibility (without changing their own behavior) is by carefully choosing the people they gather around them. If leaders are careful to bring into the organization key subordinates who complement their leadership style rather than replicate it, the organization may develop a wider range of potential styles that can be brought to bear on the contingencies they face. As we cautioned in Chapter 7, to avoid personality conflict and to increase the likelihood of building on the strength of others, it is important to select subordinates who understand each others' roles and have the same goals and objectives, even though their styles might be somewhat different.

Who Determines the Leadership Style of a Manager?

In the beginning of the chapter we raised the following question: If leaders continually change their leadership styles, how will that affect their followers' perception of their intentions?

From our experience, the sooner managers begin to share Situational Leadership with their key subordinates and clarify what is expected of them, this question no longer becomes an issue. When that occurs, managers no longer are the sole determiners of the style they use with their people. Their key staff now play a vital role. If their managers are not practicing situational leaders, they start to realize that it is *their behavior* (not their managers) that determines the leadership style to be used with them. Thus, if everyone in a management team knows Situational Leadership, the key staff realize how they can keep their boss off their backs. All they have to do is perform in responsible ways—ways that everyone has agreed are appropriate—and their manager will be supportive (S3) or leave them alone (S4). But if they do not produce and perform in responsible ways, they know their boss will be on them. They know why they are getting that kind of treatment from their manager and they know how they can get their boss to treat them in a more supportive way again—by getting back on track. It must be remembered though that this is effective only if managers are consistent (that is, that they treat their people the same way in similar circumstances) even when it is inconvenient and/or unpopular with their people.

Thus, Situational Leadership is a vehicle to help managers and their staff understand and share expectations in their organizational setting. If people know what is expected of them, they can gradually learn to supervise their own behavior and become responsible, self-motivated individuals.

CONTRACTING FOR LEADERSHIP STYLE[16]

The process that was developed at the Center for Leadership Studies for sharing Situational Leadership with key staff and helping to open everyone's public window (in Johari window terms) is called "Contracting for Leadership Style." This process is a helpful addition to management by objectives (MBO) program.

Of all the management concepts and techniques developed over the past several decades, few have received such widespread attention as management by objectives. Theoretically, MBO, discussed in Chapter 6, offers tremendous potential as a participatory management approach, but problems have developed in implementation. Consequently, although many attempts have been made to utilize MBO, ineffective implementations have occurred. As a result, success stories do not occur as often as anticipated by theorists who have written about MBO or practitioners who have applied it. One reason is that often the role of the leader in helping subordinates accomplish objectives is not clearly defined in MBO.

What often happens in the MBO process is that once a superior and subordinate have negotiated and agreed upon goals and objectives for the subordinate, the superior may or may not engage in the appropriate leader behavior that will facilitate goal accomplishment for the subordinate. For example, if the superior leaves the subordinate completely alone, the superior will be unaware until the next interim check period that this low relationship/low task leadership style is appropriate for accomplishing objectives in areas where the subordinate has had significant experience but inappropriate when the subordinate lacks sufficient technical skill and know-how in a particular area. Conversely, if, after negotiating goals and objectives, a leader continually hovers over and directs the activities of the subordinates, this high task/low relationship style might alienate subordinates working in areas where they are competent and capable of working alone. Problems may occur when a superior uses too much of any one style.

Adding the Contracting Process

In terms of Situational Leadership, once a superior and subordinate have agreed upon and contracted certain goals and objectives for the subordinate, the next logical step would be a negotiation and agreement about the appropriate leadership style that the superior should use in helping the subordinate accomplish each one of the objectives. For example, an individual and the boss may agree on five objectives for the year. After this agreement, the next step would be the negotiation of leadership style. In areas where the person is experienced and has been successful in accomplishing similar objectives over a period of time, the negotiated leadership contract might be for the boss to leave the subordinate alone. In this case, rather than directing and closely supervising behavior, the role of the boss would be to make sure that the resources necessary for goal accomplishment are available and to coordinate the results of this project with other projects being supervised. With another goal, the subordinate might be working on a new project with little prior experience, while the boss does have some expertise in this area. In this case, the subordinate and superior might negotiate significant structure, direction, and supervision from the boss until the subordinate is familiar with the task. To accomplish all the goals, a variety of leadership styles may be appropriate at any given time, depending on the subordinate's readiness in relation to the specific task(s) involved.

Two things should be emphasized in discussing the negotiation of leadership style. First, it should be an open contract. Once style has been negotiated for accomplishing a particular goal, it can be opened for renegotiation by either party. For example, an individual may find on a particular task that working without supervision is not realistic. At this point, the subordinate may contact the boss and set up a meeting to negotiate for more direction from the boss. The superior, at the time, may gather some data that suggest the style being used with an individual on a particular task is not producing results. The boss in this case can ask for a renegotiation of style.

Second, when a boss–subordinate negotiation over leadership style occurs, it implies a shared responsibility if goals are not met. For example, if a subordinate has not accomplished the agreed-upon goals and the leader or boss has not provided the contracted leadership style or support, the data then become part of the evaluation of both people. This means that if a boss has contracted for close supervision, help cannot be withheld from a subordinate (even though the boss may be busy on another project) without the boss sharing some of the responsibility for lack of accomplishment of that goal.

MAKING THE PROCESS WORK

Initially, as people were exposed to Situational Leadership concepts and began to apply them in daily superior and subordinate interactions, they sought some general ways to judge similarities and differences between leadership styles and subordinate expectations.

An Example—Contracting for Leadership Styles in a School

Some interesting results of the Contracting for Leadership Style process occurred in an elementary school in eastern Massachusetts. In many school systems, the principal of a school is required by school policy to visit each classroom a certain number of times each year. This visitation policy is dysfunctional for principals who recognize that their teachers vary in their experience and competence and therefore have varying needs for supervision from the principal. If a principal decides to schedule visitations according to a perception of the competence of the teachers, problems often occur with teachers at either end of the extreme. As we discussed earlier, left alone, a highly experienced teacher may be confused by the lack of contact with the principal and may even interpret it as a lack of interest. At the same time, an inexperienced teacher may interpret the frequent visits of the principal as a sign of lack of trust and confidence. In both cases, what the principal does may be interpreted as negative by the teachers.

These problems were eliminated in this elementary school when the principal shared Situational Leadership with the staff and then attempted to negotiate what the principal's leadership style should be with each of the teachers. It was found that when low relationship/low task leadership style was negotiated between the principal and teachers because both agreed that these teachers were capable of working on their own, infrequent visits from the principal were perceived by the teachers as a reward rather than a punishment.

The same thing held true at the other end of the continuum. It was found that when negotiation for leadership style took place with inexperienced teachers (who realized that the system was designed to help teachers learn to work on their own) these teachers were less reluctant to share anxieties about certain aspects of their teaching. If the negotiation led to initial close supervision and direction, the teachers were able to view this interaction as positive not punitive, because it was a temporary style and demonstrated the principal's interest in helping them to operate on their own.

Using the Readiness Style Match

Since those early days, a useful instrument has been developed by Hersey, Blanchard, and Keilty at the Center for Leadership Studies. The instrument formalizes the process of implementing Contracting for Leadership Style between superior and subordinate. It's called the Readiness Style Match.[17] As discussed in Chapter 8, the Readiness Style Match measures readiness using two dimensions: (1) *ability*, or job readiness, and (2) *willingness*, or psychological readiness. The rating form also describes precisely the four basic leadership styles. The description of those styles and the two readiness scales are depicted in Figure 12-16.

As indicated in Figure 12-16, a person's ability (knowledge and skill) is thought of as a matter of degree. That is, an individual's ability does not change drastically from one moment to the next. At any given moment, an individual has a little, some, quite a bit, or a great deal of ability. Willingness (competence and motivation), however, is different. A person's psychological readiness can, and often does, fluctuate from one moment to an-

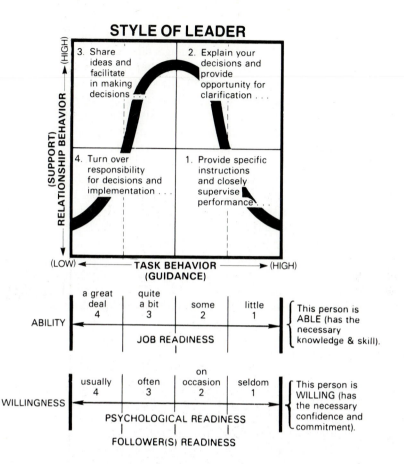

STYLE OF LEADER

RELATIONSHIP BEHAVIOR (SUPPORT) — (HIGH)

3. Share ideas and facilitate in making decisions . . .

2. Explain your decisions and provide opportunity for clarification . . .

4. Turn over responsibility for decisions and implementation . . .

1. Provide specific instructions and closely supervise performance . . .

(LOW) ◄——— TASK BEHAVIOR ———► (HIGH)
(GUIDANCE)

ABILITY	a great deal 4	quite a bit 3	some 2	little 1	This person is ABLE (has the necessary knowledge & skill).

JOB READINESS

WILLINGNESS	usually 4	often 3	on occasion 2	seldom 1	This person is WILLING (has the necessary confidence and commitment).

PSYCHOLOGICAL READINESS

FOLLOWER(S) READINESS

FIGURE 12-16   Defining readiness and the four basic leadership styles

other. Therefore, a person is seldom, on occasion, often, or usually willing to take responsibility in a particular area.

Combining establishing objectives and reaching consensus on performance criteria in a traditional MBO program with a similar process for negotiating the appropriate leadership style that a manager should use to facilitate goal accomplishment in a specific task area can be accomplished through the following steps. (1) Manager and staff member independently establish objectives and performance criteria for the staff member. (2) Manager and staff member come together to reach agreement on objectives and performance criteria. (3) Both manager and staff member are introduced to Situational Leadership, if they have not already been exposed to the concept (which can be accomplished by reading Chapter 8 of this book). (4) Manager and staff member independently complete a Readiness Style Match rating form. The staff member records what is believed the primary and secondary leadership styles are that the manager has been using on each of the agreed upon goals and objectives. The manager does the same, indicating what leadership style has been used with the staff member on each of the agreed upon goals and objectives. If the staff member has never had a particular objective area before, no past leadership style can be diagnosed. After analyzing leadership style, both the staff member and manager make judgments on the ability and the willingness of the staff member to accomplish each of the goals and objectives established at the desired performance level without any supervision. In other words, the staff member participating in this process would analyze the leadership style that the boss has been using, as well as self-assessment judgments of the readiness level. At the same time, the manager would be analyzing the readiness level of the staff member as well as making leadership style self-assessment judgments. (5) Manager and staff member meet together and share the data from their Readiness Style Match rating forms. It is recommended that they consider one objective or responsibility at a time. The purpose of sharing data is to agree upon the readiness level and appropriate leadership style that can be utilized with the staff member to maximize performance. During this process both manager and staff member should bring their calendars. Once they have determined the appropriate leadership style to make this commitment and turn it into behavior, they will require scheduled meetings. For example, in a particular objective area, any one of the four leadership styles may. have been agreed upon as appropriate. If the staff member is inexperienced and insecure about performing in a particular area, a "telling" (S1) style would be appropriate for the manager to use. If this is the case, they should schedule frequent meetings so that the manager can work closely with the staff member.

If the staff member is willing but inexperienced in a particular area, the manager should utilize a "selling" (S2) style. This would involve scheduling meetings to work with the staff member, but not as frequently as under S1 supervision.

If the staff member is able in a particular area but is a little insecure about working completely alone, a participating (S3) leadership style would be appropriate. That may involve meeting periodically over lunch so that the staff member can show the manager what has been accomplished and the proper support and encouragement can be given.

If the staff member is able and willing to perform at the desired level in a particular objective area, no meetings are necessary unless called by the staff member. In this case, performance review can occur on an infrequent basis.

If the Contracting for Leadership Style process is utilized, the frequency of performance review will change depending on the ability and the motivation of the staff member to perform at the desired level without supervision. As stated earlier, if this process is used, the negotiation of leadership style should be an open contract and imply shared responsibility if goals are not met. In particular, if a staff member is improving in a particular area, there should be a renegotiation of leadership style to a less directive leadership style. At the same time, if a staff member's performance is not being maximized utilizing a particular leadership style, that will signal the need to move back to a more directive style. A give and take process should occur between superior and subordinate.

The Readiness Style Match Matrix, part of the Readiness Style Match, is useful in providing insight into whether or not your manager is using "overleadership"—you have high levels of readiness but your manager is using "telling" and "selling" styles to a greater degree than necessary. "Underleadership" is where you have low levels of readiness but your manager is using "participating" and "delegating" styles more than is appropriate. A high probability style match would be when the style(s) of your manager tends to correspond with the readiness level(s) you exhibit.

One warning should be given in using the Contracting for Leadership style process and the Readiness Style Match rating forms. When managers go through that process, their public arena in the Johari window becomes wide open. Very little about what these managers think and feel about the staff member is unknown to that staff member, and vice versa. Feedback and disclosure become an ongoing process. If managers do not want their people to know what they think and feel about them, then they should be careful about using the described process. With some people they might want to remain tight-lipped and aloof. When managers make that choice, they must remember that with those people the blind and private arenas in their Johari window will be large. In some cases, that may very well be appropriate.

In summary, combining the establishment of goals and objectives and criteria performance with appropriate leadership style may help to make MBO more of a developmental process, which can be effective in working with all levels of readiness. Establishing such a program may be a significant change for an organization and its managers. In Chapter 15 we will discuss how to implement change in an effective way.

NOTES

1. The development of LEAD (formerly known as the Leader Adaptability and Style Inventory (LASI) is based on Situational Leadership discussed earlier. The first publication on this LEAD instrument appeared as Paul Hersey and Kenneth H. Blanchard, "So You Want to Know Your Leadership Style?" *Training and Development Journal*, February 1974. Copies of the LEAD-Self and LEAD-Others can be ordered from the Center for Leadership Studies, Escondido, CA 92025.

2. This contracting process first appeared as Paul Hersey and Kenneth H. Blanchard, "What's Missing in MBO?" *Management Review*, October 1974. Much of the discussion that follows was taken from that article.

3. G. S. Odiorne, *The Human Side of Management* (San Diego, Calif.: University Associates, 1987).

4. The LEAD-Other is the same instrument as the LEAD-Self but written so a subordinate, superior, or peer could fill it out on a leader. Instruments are available from the Center for Leadership Studies, Escondido, CA 92025.

5. William J. Reddin, *The 3-D Management Style Theory*, Theory Paper #6—Style Flex (Fredericton, N.B., Canada: Social Science Systems, 1967), p. 6.

6. Joseph Luft and Harry Ingham, "The Johari Window, A Graphic Model of Interpersonal Awareness," *Proceedings of the Western Training Laboratory in Group Development* (Los Angeles: UCLA, Extension Office, 1955). A more up-to-date version of the framework is presented in Joseph Luft, *Group Process: An Introduction to Group Dynamics,* 2nd ed. (Palo Alto, Calif.: National Press Book, 1970).

7. Sigmund Freud, *The Ego and the Id* (London: Hogarth Press, 1927).

8. Haim Ginott, *Between Parent and Child: New Solution to Old Problems* (New York: Avon Books, 1965).

9. Kenneth Blanchard was a faculty resource with Alice Ginnott at the February 1977 YPO (Young Presidents' Organization) University of Honolulu, Hawaii. The discussions of what she said at a session entitled "Between Parent and Child" are taken from Blanchard's notes and do not represent her exact words.

10. Carl R. Rogers, *Client-centered Therapy* (Boston: Houghton Mifflin, 1951); see also *Freedom to Learn* (Columbus, Ohio: Merrill, 1969).

11. Wayne W. Dyer, *Your Erroneous Zones* (New York: Funk & Wagnalls, 1976).

12. This sentence is adapted from a quotation by Dorothy Canfield Fisher that Wayne Dyer referred to in *Your Erroneous Zones*, p. 195.

13. The analysis of LEAD data was first published in Paul Hersey, *Situational Leadership: Some Aspects of Its Influence on Organizational Development*, an unpublished dissertation, University of Massachusetts, 1975.

14. Laurence J. Peter and Raymond Hull, *The Peter Principle: Why Things Always Go Wrong* (New York: Morrow, 1969). See also Laurence J. Peter, *The Peter Plan: A Proposal for Survival* (New York: Morrow, 1976); Laurence J. Peter, *Peter's Quotations: Ideas for Our Time* (New York: Morrow, 1977).

15. Fred E. Fiedler, "Engineer the Job to Fit the Manager," *Harvard Business Review*, 51 (1965), pp. 115–122. See also Fred E. Fiedler, *Leader Attitudes and Group Effectiveness* (Westport, Conn.: Greenwood, 1981); Fred E. Fiedler and Martin M. Chemers, *Improving Leadership Effectiveness: The Leader Match Concept* (New York: Wiley, 1984).

16. This contracting process first appeared as Paul Hersey and Kenneth H. Blanchard, "What's Missing in MBO?" *Management Review*, October 1974. Much of the discussion that follows was taken from that article.

17. Readiness Style Match instruments were developed by Paul Hersey, Kenneth H. Blanchard, and Joseph Keilty. Information on these instruments is available through the Center for Leadership Studies, Escondido, CA 92025.

CHAPTER 13

COMMUNICATING WITH RAPPORT

Very early in this book we defined leadership as an attempt to influence, for whatever reason. We also noted that leadership and influence may be used interchangeably. You will also recall that we discussed the three basic competencies in influencing as (1) diagnosing—being able to understand the situation you are attempting to influence, (2) adapting—being able to adapt your behavior . . . and the other things that you have control over . . . to the contingencies of the situation, and (3) communicating—being able to put the message in a way that people can easily understand and accept. This chapter is about the third competency—communicating with rapport.[1]

HOW IMPORTANT IS EFFECTIVE COMMUNICATION?

All of the evidence clearly shows that written and oral communication skills are critical not only in obtaining a job but also in performing effectively on the job. For example, in a study reported in *Personnel*, a survey questionnaire was sent to the personnel managers of 175 of the largest companies in a western state.[2] One of the key questions in this study concerned the factors and skills most important in helping graduating business students obtain employment. The personnel managers' responses to this question are shown

TABLE 13-1   Factors or skills considered most important by personnel managers in helping business graduates obtain employment

Rank/Score	Factor/Skill	Score
1	Oral communication skills	6.294
2	Written communication skills	6.176
3	Work experience	5.706
4	Energy level (enthusiasm)	5.706
5	Technical competence	5.647
6	Persistence/determination	5.529
7	Dress/grooming	5.235
8	Personality	5.118
9	Resumé	5.118
10	Appearance	5.000
11	Poise	4.882
12	Specific degree held (finance, marketing, accounting, and so forth)	4.867
13	Grade point average	4.235
14	Letters of recommendation	4.059
15	Interview skills	4.059
16	Accreditation of the school/college	3.941
17	Social graces	3.824
18	Physical characteristics	3.647
19	School attended	2.941
20	Age	2.529
21	Marital status	2.000
22	Race	1.588
23	Sex	1.471
24	Religion	1.000

in Table 13-1.[3] Written and oral communication skills were the two most important factors or skills in obtaining employment. But what about effective performance on the job?

Most Chief Operating Officers (COOs) rate employee communication skills as vital, using such phrases as "extremely important," "very important," or "tops".[4] Other COOs say that "There is a direct correlation between employee communication and profitability" and "I find that making good profits really goes hand in hand with having good communication." Perhaps the importance of good communication is best summarized by a senior executive who noted:

> The best business plan is meaningless unless everyone is aware of it and pulling together to achieve its objectives. Good communications are the lifeblood of

any enterprise, large or small. Communications are essential to keep our entire organization functioning at maximum levels and to make the most of our greatest management resource—our people.[5]

But how can we, as leaders and potential leaders, improve our communication competency? One way is to understand and use the process of communicating with rapport.

The Communication Process

When communicating with other people, the message passes through perceptual "filters," as shown in Figure 13-1, The Communications Process, which follows. And because of these filters, there is the potential for a communication breakdown at any point in the process. It is as if "I know you think you understood what I said, but I'm not sure that what you heard is what I meant."

The following descriptions relate to the three areas of Figure 13-1.

Leader

Leaders spend more time communicating than doing any other single activity; yet studies summarized in Table 13-2, Communication Skills Training, show that many need to develop their ability to communicate more effectively. This may result from the complexity of the interaction between leader and follower, as well as the nature of the training that the average person receives.

Research also shows that people spend about 45 percent of their communication time listening. Despite this, the average listener understands and retains about half of what is said immediately after a presentation . . . and within 48 hours, this level drops off to 22 percent.

FIGURE 13-1 The communication process

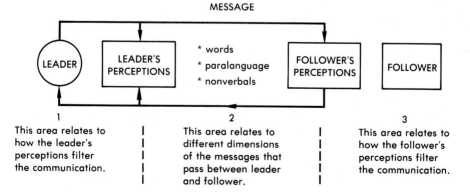

MESSAGE

1	2	3
This area relates to how the leader's perceptions filter the communication.	This area relates to different dimensions of the messages that pass between leader and follower.	This area relates to how the follower's perceptions filter the communication.

TABLE 13-2 Communication skills training (average person)

Skills	Years of Training	Extent Used in Adult Life
Writing	14	Little
Reading	8	Some
Speaking	1	Quite a bit
Listening	0	A great deal

This data would suggest that listening is one of the most critical skills in the communication process.[6] It helps leaders to determine followers' needs, problems, moods, or levels of interest.

In order to become effective communicators, leaders need to tune in not only to words—and the way those words are expressed—but to nonverbal cues. Effective communication requires responses that demonstrate interest, understanding, and concern for the follower, as well as for the follower's needs and problems.

Message

Communication effectiveness is also dependent upon the following message forms:

Words—the phrases that we select to express the thought that we intend to communicate, including
- Vocabulary
- Language
- Phrases
- Sentence structure
- Sentence clarity

Words can insult, injure, or exalt. They can lead to costly errors, false hopes, or disillusionment. They can evoke pride, loyalty, action, or silence and are critical to the influence process. However, they are not the sole basis for how people represent and interpret reality.

Paralanguage—the characteristics of the voice, such as
- Rate of speech (speed)
- Diction
- Tone
- Rhythm
- Volume

Your voice is a highly versatile instrument. Through it you can convey enthusiasm, confidence, anxiety, urgency, serenity, and other states of mind and intent. The ability of the voice to affect how something is said is known as paralanguage. Timing when you speak, increasing or decreasing voice intensity, pausing, varying pitch, and other aspects of speech patterns can increase your ability to influence. By closely attending to the follower's paralanguage, you can pick up clues about your progress in influencing your followers.

Nonverbal behavior—anything that can be "seen" by the other person, such as
- Gestures
- Facial expressions
- Eye contact
- Body language
- Positioning

How you enter an office, how you support your message through gestures and facial expressions, how you imply interest and vitality through eye contact and other nonverbal behaviors affect other people's reaction to you. In turn, the nonverbal cues of followers serve as windows to their emotions, desires, and attitudes.

Changes in a follower's body postures and gestures often signal a change in readiness. Movement toward the front of a chair may indicate interest. Relaxation of the body may reflect acceptance. Mirroring of your nods, smiles, and gestures could indicate acceptance.

As a leader, it is also important to understand how followers view space and its relationship to you. It is important to monitor how you position yourself in relation to followers. People have levels of comfort when it comes to how close they want you to be. The general rule is, if you are making them uncomfortable, then change. This may involve moving closer or farther away.

When you first encounter a prospective follower, before you say your first word you have already made a statement about yourself. Part of this statement involves body language in terms of how confidently you carry yourself, how you walk, and your general manner. Part of it involves the clothing you wear and your accessories. Grooming, neatness, hairstyle, and other personal features also enter into the equation.

Many of these nonverbals are under your direct control. You can make them what you want them to be. To the extent possible, your attire and general appearance should reflect a sense of personal dignity and self-worth. They should be appropriate to your followers' environment and should reflect your personal and your organization's values.[7]

Follower

In interpersonal communications, 7 percent of your meaning is from followers' interpretation or perception of your words—that is, *what* you say; 38 percent is conveyed by their perception of your voice—that is, *how* you say the words; and approximately 55 percent comes from their interpretation of your nonverbal signals.[8] As a leader, you need to monitor both the message you are sending—words, voice, and nonverbals—and follower feedback. It is also important to keep in mind that it is not the followers' perceptions that evoke behavior. It is their perceptions of the messages they receive from you that cause them to act.

Pacing, Then Leading

Leaders, as we have seen, influence from both personal power and position power. You can begin building personal power by establishing rapport. Part of establishing rapport is the ability to communicate effectively in a way that is comfortable with people you are attempting to influence. For people to feel comfortable, you have to get in step with them—pace with them.

In order to understand how to establish rapport, it is important to keep some key concepts in mind:

- *Rapport*—being in sync with other people verbally or nonverbally so that they are comfortable and have trust and confidence in you.
- *Pacing*—establishing rapport by reflecting what others do, know, or assume to be true (matching some part of their ongoing experience).
- *Leading*—getting other people to pace with *you* (attempting to influence them to consider other possibilities).
- *Behavioral adaptability*—having enough range in your own behavior to pace with the person or persons that you are interacting with.

The secret of establishing rapport with people is pacing. To pace with other people you need to adapt to match their behavior . . . to get in sync with them so that they feel comfortable with you. This means getting in alignment with their words, their voice characteristics, and their nonverbals.[9]

When you have established rapport with people, they are more apt to follow when you lead. The general pattern can be thought of in this way:

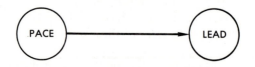

When you're interacting with other people, you're either pacing—doing something similar—or leading—having them pace with you. If your primary objective is to gain acceptance, then pacing may be enough. But if your objective is to influence them to consider other alternatives, then you must also lead.

Managers or parents can sometimes lead first and then pace to get results, since they often have access to position power.[10]

How to Test for Rapport

Sometimes, it is useful to test the level of rapport you have established. In the following example, the salesperson attempts to lead the customer to a buying decision after *pacing* with the customer through the early part of the sales process:

Salesperson attempts to lead customer:	(leaning forward and showing interest) Tom, we've agreed that increasing sales is important. Our program has demonstrated a significant impact on that objective. You viewed turnover as the major problem your marketing group is presently facing. Our training program, through its emphasis on professionalism, can impact that directly.
Customer accepts lead:	(leaning forward, partially mirroring the salesperson's posture) Yes, if we could cut down our turnover, this would be a positive step in cost containment.
Salesperson continues leading:	(sensing that they now have rapport and are in agreement and alignment at both the verbal and nonverbal levels) You might consider conducting some pilot programs. Although our minimum order is two hundred units, training one hundred new hires with the five-day design and one hundred experienced representatives with a combination of the other designs would give you a chance to evaluate actual results.

If the customer continues to pace, then the salesperson can keep leading.

In the following example, the customer does not respond on a verbal or nonverbal basis, as the salesperson would like. The key here is to return to pacing to reestablish comfort and rapport.

Salesperson attempts to lead customer:	(leaning forward and showing interest) Are we in agreement that turnover is the major problem your marketing group is presently facing?
Customer resists lead:	(remaining in the same posture) I'm not so sure. The real issue might be our advertising program.
Salesperson returns to pacing:	(mirroring customer's posture) I can understand how advertising can impact your sales . . .

In summary, the general rules of pacing, as shown in Figure 13-2 are (1) if your boss, associates, or followers go with your lead, continue to lead

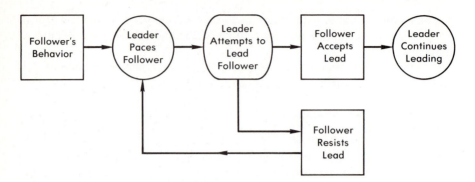

FIGURE 13-2   Influencing from Personal Power: The Pace-Lead Process

and (2) if your boss, associates, or followers resist your lead, go back to pacing—and look for new opportunities to lead.

PREFERRED REPRESENTATIONAL SYSTEMS

People do not behave based on truth and reality. Their behavior is evoked from their *perception* and *interpretation* of truth and reality.

These perceptions and interpretations are the product of data taken in through the senses: sight, hearing, smell, taste, and touch. So much data come in that people cannot attend to it all. Through selective awareness, psychological maps are formed from only part of the data. Behavior is based upon these maps. And the maps affect what people perceive. Communication effectiveness is enhanced if you understand the way people map their psychological worlds.

People use their psychological maps to make decisions, to get around in life. However, the map is not the territory. It is based upon perceptions of that territory. And these perceptions differ from person to person.[11]

"Rep" Systems and Communication

People tend to perceive their worlds through the sensing systems they most prefer—the ones they're most comfortable with. It's like speaking five languages. You probably don't speak all of them with the same fluency. You prefer one over the other as your primary language. And that's the primary one you use to represent your psychological world.

These preferred sensory representational—or "Rep"—systems are important to you as a leader. You will have a higher probability of influencing people if you know how they map their psychological worlds through what they see, what they feel, or what they hear. They do not map exclusively in one of these modes but tend to be more comfortable with the one they prefer.

- Some people are picture people, or "visuals." They are comfortable mapping their psychological worlds in *pictures*.
- Others are feelings people, or "kinesthetics." They are most comfortable mapping their psychological worlds from internal and external *feelings*.
- Some people are sounds people, or "auditories." Also referred to as "tonals," they tend to map their psychological worlds from *sounds*.
- Word people, or "digitals," are a hybrid of the other three. They have to make a transition from raw data-sensing into a specific language—through *words* or numbers or computer symbols—before they can map their psychological worlds.

When attempting to communicate, you are in a better position if you know that person's primary Rep system. You may then be able to transmit your message in a way that that person can better encode and decode . . . understand . . . and, therefore, accept.[12]

For example, auditories don't always "look people in the eye" because they're "tuning an ear." During a conversation or presentation, they may look elsewhere because they are listening and trying to take in data. Their intention is not to be rude or inattentive; they are trying to understand.

Children who are auditories often get in trouble with their parents because they look down when Mom or Dad talks to them. Parents make the mistake of telling the child, "You look at me when I talk to you!" because they feel the child isn't listening. The child looks up and has more difficulty understanding the data. The result often leads to further misunderstandings, anger, and frustration.

Picture people tend to like space. If you visit them in the office, they want you to sit across from them at the desk—back far enough to keep comfortably within their visual range. Feelings people prefer you to be closer. They often set up their office suites so that you can move closer and interact in a more personal way.

Digitals like written information presented to them in a logical fashion. Terms should be defined, and all spelling, punctuation, grammar, margins, and layout should be correct. Auditories, on the other hand, like short paragraphs, headings, italics, and indented areas. To get their attention, just underline or circle any parts of a message they shouldn't miss.

During group presentations, visuals tend to cluster to the rear of the room to keep all the data out in front of them, in their field of vision. The kinesthetics tend to cluster up front, close to the speaker; they want to feel they are part of the presentation. The auditories cluster to the side and, depending on their best ear (which ear they favor), sit to the left or right side of the room. For digitals, it's hard to predict where they will place themselves. Much of it depends on where they think they should be to filter data to the level of abstraction they are comfortable with. Because of these preferences, the message should be put in a variety of ways to increase the probability of communicating with all of those involved. This means when making a presentation, try to pace with the:

- Visuals by using diagrams, flow charts and other graphics, particularly when presenting complex information.
- Digitals by defining terms and providing order and sequence to the information.
- Auditories by providing pizzazz—moving around, energizing, varying voice speed and delivery.
- Kinesthetics by sitting down occasionally—talking to them from a relaxed, nonthreatening position. Whenever possible, try to get your eye level lower than the group's to help the kinesthetics feel more comfortable.[13]

Matching Predicates to Rep Systems

People will often provide you with direct cues to their preferred Rep system. One of the more frequent cues they provide are *words* or "predicates" that reflect their Rep systems. Visuals use picture words: "I can see that" or "Looks good to me." Auditories use words such as "Sounds good to me" or "I hear you." Kinesthetics use feelings words: "I sense that you're uncomfortable" or "How do you feel about that?" Digitals use expressions such as "That seems to be a reasonable approach" or "Have you verified the results?" Table 13-3 gives examples of preferred representational system predicates.

To build rapport, it is important to use predicates that are comfortable for the person you are attempting to influence.[14] If you do not match predicates, it is harder to communicate.

Sales manager: (visual)	It appears problems are developing with our delivery service. Let's take a look at what's happening. Visualize a customer who has been waiting for our shipment that hasn't shown up.
Salesperson: (auditory)	I hear you, but I'm not tuning in.
Sales manager:	Imagine a concerned customer, loosening his tie, tapping his fingers, glancing up at the clock. Do you get the picture?
Salesperson:	OK, OK, so what are you trying to tell me?
Sales manager:	I'm trying to provide you with a picture of a good client examining other alternatives because they have a negative view of us.
Salesperson:	Before you sound the alarm, you ought to tune in to the other problems that are crying for attention.

TABLE 13-3   Preferred representational system predicates

Pictures (Visual)	Sounds (Auditory)	Feelings (Kinesthetic)	Words (Digital)
clear	tune	touch	logical
focus	note	handle	data
perspective	accent	block	facts
see	ring	finger	information
outlook	shout	shock	results
spectacle	tone	stir	compute
preview	sing	strike	articulate
shortsighted	hear	impress	reasonable
illustrate	alarm	move	statistical
show	scream	hit	rational
reveal	click	grasp	conclude
hazy	static	impact	propose
glimpse	rattle	stroke	analyze
clarify	chord	tap	sequence
graphic	amplify	rub	verify
cloud	harmonize	sense	relevant
expose	key	tense	specific
bright	muffle	pressure	predict
flash	voice	irritate	objective
picture	sound	feel	word

> *Sales manager:* What other problems? I don't see what that has to do with following up on late orders.
>
> *Salesperson:* You haven't heard a word I've said. You're obviously not listening. I've got nothing more to say.

In the previous example, the predicates did not match and there was less opportunity for a positive consequence.

In the following example, predicates do match—and the probability of rapport, comfort, and positive action increases:

> *Sales manager:* *(visual)* It appears problems are developing with our delivery service. Let's take a look at what's happening. Visualize a customer who has been waiting weeks for our shipment that hasn't shown up.
>
> *Salesperson:* *(visual)* Yes, I see what you mean.
>
> *Sales manager:* Imagine a concerned customer, loosening his tie, tapping his fingers, glancing up at the clock. Do you get the picture?
>
> *Salesperson:* Mmmm! Clearly a potential problem. We can't afford to have

> our customers looking elsewhere for service. As I see it, clarifying our shipment policies with the transportation people might help. It is apparent that we need to develop a control system to ensure timely delivery. By keeping an eye on shipping dates, we can spot delays before they become a problem.

Sales manager: Good idea. When you have something to show me, I'd like to look at it.

Pacing predicates is important. There are times when someone's preferred representational system may not be clear to you. That person may even switch among predicates during a discussion. The best thing to do in this circumstance is to pace the predicates you hear.

Matching predicates is crucial, particularly when summarizing, advocating, and asking for assistance. It is also important when you are managing the interface between your company and customers, suppliers, and other outside groups. Matching predicates with people in your own organization can also help in following through on special requirements and resolving problems.

You need to practice and learn to become proficient in all of the representational systems. This kind of behavioral adaptability will help you to improve your communication ability, increase your effectiveness, and build ongoing relationships. Irving S. Shapiro thinks this is important as he has noted:

> One important day-to-day task for the CEO (Chief Executive Officer) is communication—digesting information and shaping ideas, yes, but even more centrally, the business of listening and explaining. Decisions and policies have no effect nor any real existence unless they are recognized and understood by those who must put them into effect. . . . It sounds banal to say that a CEO is first and foremost in the human relations and communication business—what else could the job be?—but the point is too important to leave to inference. No other item on the chief executive's duty list has more leverage on the organization's prospects.[15]

NOTES

1. This chapter has been generally adapted from Paul Hersey, *Situational Selling* (Escondido, Calif.: Center for Leadership Studies, 1985), pp. 123–138.
2. Gary L. Benson, "On the Campus: How Well do Business Schools Prepare Graduates for the Business World?" *Personnel*, July–August 1983, pp. 63–65.
3. *Ibid.*
4. Louis C. Williams, Jr., "What 50 Presidents and Chief Executive Officers Think About Employee Communication," *Public Relations Quarterly*, Winter 1978, p. 7. See also "Information Mapping—The Fast Track to Better Business Communication," *Administrative Management*, 47 (May 1986), p. 6.
5. "Listening Your Way to the Top," *Graduating Engineer*, Winter 1980.
6. Anthony J. Allessandra, Phillip S. Wexler, and Jerry D. Deem, *Non-Manipulative Selling* (Reston, Virginia: Reston Publishing, 1979), pp. 81–118.

7. George Walter, "Communicating Clearly," *Profitable Telemarketing Audiocassette Program*, Tape No. 2 (Chicago: Nightengale-Conant Corporation, 1984).

8. Genie Z. LaBorde, *Influencing with Integrity*, (Palo Alto: Science and Behavior Books, 1983), pp. 27–74.

9. Jerry Richardson and Joel Margulis, *The Magic of Rapport* (San Francisco: Harbor Publishing, 1981), pp. 19–59.

10. John Grinder and Richard Bandler, *The Structure of Magic II* (Palto Alto: Science and Behavior Books, 1976), pp. 4–6.

11. Byron A. Lewis and R. Frank Pucelik, *Magic De-Mystified* (Lake Oswego: Metamorphous Press, 1982), pp. 11–49.

12. Hersey, *Situational Selling*, p. 135.

13. For a technical introduction to verbal and nonverbal predicate matching, see Robert Dilts, John Grinder, Richard Bandler, Leslie C. Bandler, and Judith DeLozier, *Neuro-Linguistic Programming: Volume I—The Study of the Structure of Subjective Experience* (Cupertino: Meta Publications, 1980), pp. 69–179.

14. Hersey, *Situational Selling*, p. 138.

15. Irving S. Shapiro, "Executive Forum: Managerial Communication: The View from Inside," *California Management Review*, Fall 1984, p. 157.

CHAPTER 14

GROUP DYNAMICS: *Helping and Hindering Roles in Groups*

One of the realities of organizational behavior is that we must work in and with problem-solving groups to accomplish our aspirations. No matter how much we value and protect our individuality, almost everything we value can only be achieved as a group member. Although the following description of this reality was presented by Krech, Crutchfield, and Ballachey more than two decades ago, it is probably even more true today.

> The paradox of modern man is that only as the individual joins with his fellows in groups and organizations can he hope to control the political, economic, and social forces which threaten his individual freedom. This is especially true now that massive social groupings—in nations and combinations of nations—are the order of the day. Only as the individual in society struggles to preserve his individuality in common cause with his fellows can he hope to remain an individual.[1]

It is, therefore, important to be able to apply behavioral science principles and concepts to make problem-solving groups more effective. In this chapter we will describe how Situational Leadership through an understanding of helping and hindering roles can accomplish this goal.

Is group effectiveness an operational problem? The answer is a resounding yes! For example, despite the rush to implement Quality Circles, studies have shown very low success rates.[2] Other researchers, such as Hartenstein and Huddleston, have noted that the results, at best, are mixed.[3]

Why is this so? One reason is that labor and management lack shared values.[4] Another is because the structure and function of problem-solving groups was not established according to behavioral science concepts and techniques. Too often Quality Circles and other problem-solving groups are overly focused on participation as a single problem-solving mode, thus neglecting the potential richness of other possible modes. Where problem-solving groups have been effective—much as in the groups cited in the Plant Y Study by Guest, Hersey, and Blanchard[5]—it is because values were shared and the groups were structured to take advantage of all of the group problem-solving modes. Only then can groups reach their full potential payoff both in terms of goal achievement and in quality of life—the true components of productivity.[6]

Before we look at specific techniques, it is important that we review some fundamental group definitions and concepts.

INDIVIDUALS AND GROUPS

While much of the previous discussion has focused on one-on-one leadership, it is important to remember that the Situational Leadership model is equally applicable—whether you are working with a group or organization or with an individual. Certainly there are some complicating factors when you are working with groups, but you still have to apply the three basic competencies in influencing—diagnosing, adapting, and communicating. It is also important to remember that you may have to deal with individual group members differently when you are in a one-on-one situation than when you are working with the entire group as a group. This is because individual group members may be at different levels of readiness from the entire group.

Just as individuals may be at different levels of readiness, so may groups. For example, most graduate classes are at a high level of readiness. Class members are there because they want to be, and they bring considerable academic and work experience to the class. There might be some insecurity due to some of the material being new or especially difficult, but on balance, most graduate classes are at an R3−R4 level.

A group consisting of managers attending a training program might be at a lower readiness level. They have made a considerable investment in time, transportation costs, and tuition to attend the class, and are probably very willing. However, since they are attending the training program to learn new knowledge and skills, they are probably somewhat unable. It is also true that individuals in groups may be higher or lower than the entire group in readiness.

IMPORTANT DEFINITIONS

Before we continue, it is important that we define three key terms—group, organization, and collection.

There are, perhaps, as many definitions of groups as there are definitions of leadership. This lack of common definition creates problems in terms of communicating, diagnosing, and being able to think through strategies for change. To help reduce this confusion, we suggest this working definition of a group:

> *Group*—Two or more people interacting in which the existence of all (the existence of the group as a group) is necessary for the needs of the individual group members to be satisfied.

The group gives individual members a way to meet needs and to grow. Since groups can be fulfilling and rewarding, energies can be expanded to achieve goals.[7]

An important point to keep in mind is that individual needs satisfaction may be quite different for each member of the group. This is the ingredient that is missing from most definitions of groups. One of the principal problems with most definitions is that they assume that group members have common goals and purposes. There are many examples of groups devoid of common goals or purposes. For example, you may have three people in a group who have very different needs. One person may have joined the group because of a need for power; another because of the need for interaction with other people, a social need; while a third may have joined because of a need for status, for esteem. While the individual group members do not necessarily have to have common needs, goals, or purposes, the key is that the satisfaction, at least in part, of these individual needs is dependent upon the accomplishment of group goals. The degree to which individual need satisfaction is achieved differentiates effective from ineffective groups. When the needs are harmonious, the group is probably effective. When they are not, the group is probably ineffective. Common goals or purposes are, therefore, not criteria of groups but of *effective* groups.[8]

A group without clear-cut objectives lack guidelines for the behavior of its members.[9] For the group to be productive, it must have goals that are understood by all participants.[10] Progress toward these goals is the best way to measure effectiveness. Research has consistently shown that group productivity is highest in those groups in which techniques are used that simultaneously further the attainment of group goals and bring fulfillment of the needs of individual group members.

What is the difference between groups and organizations? Again, it is not commonality of goals or purposes. Do owners, managers, first-line supervisors, and line workers have the same goals? Not in very many organizations. Our definition of an organization is one in which a group has stated and formal goals. Organizations exist for various reasons and have different organizational goals. Organizational goals are targets toward which input, process, and output are directed;[11] for example, make a 10 percent return on investment, help mankind conquer hunger, increase sales 20 percent during the current fiscal year. Which of the three entities has the best chance of having common goals? Not a group or an organization but a collection. Twenty-seven people standing on a corner waiting for a bus have a common goal—everyone is waiting there for the bus. Interdependence of all of them is not necessary. Twenty-six people waiting for a bus would still be a collection, just like two hundred and fifty people waiting in line to see a movie.

Suppose you wanted to swim across San Francisco Bay from Oakland to San Francisco, a very difficult swim because of the severe tides and currents. You dive in and about halfway across you are in trouble. You feel a cramp coming on and you are beginning to get tired. Just then you see another swimmer coming alongside. What are the two of you now? A group? No, a collection because you only have a common goal—to get to San Francisco. There is no interdependence. If, however, you start to interact, give encouragement, support each other so that the existence of both is necessary for the satisfaction of individual member needs, then you have a group.[12] Once you both get to the other side, you decide to meet three times a week to swim to San Francisco to get in shape. Now you are an organization because you have stated or formal goals. Does it mean that you both necessarily share the same goal? No, but you both agree on the formal, stated goals.

GROUP PROBLEM-SOLVING MODES

Groups develop personalities—mores, customs, traditions—that tend to differentiate them from other groups and are characteristic of that group. It is the collective behavior of people within that group that makes it have its special personality, its individuality as a group. Just as leaders have styles—patterns of behavior as perceived by the follower—so do groups have modes, or patterns of behavior as perceived by others. We can take a look at group modes in the same way that we can look at leadership styles. The different modes of group behavior, as shown in Figure 14-1, are helpful because we can use these different modes to help us recognize and organize patterns of group behavior.[13]

As in the Situational Leadership model, we place Task Behavior on the horizontal, or X, axis and Relationship Behavior on the vertical, or Y, axis. When a group faces a situation that requires significant amounts of task behavior—lots of what, when, where, and how but not a lot of time for dialogue and discussion—they may be heavily into high task behavior and low relationship behavior. When used appropriately for problem solving, this is

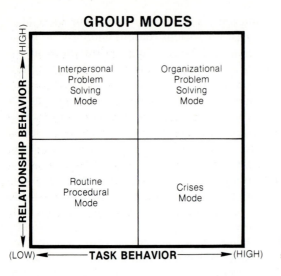

GROUP MODES

RELATIONSHIP BEHAVIOR → (HIGH)

Interpersonal
Problem
Solving
Mode

Organizational
Problem
Solving
Mode

Routine
Procedural
Mode

Crises
Mode

(LOW) ◄── TASK BEHAVIOR ──► (HIGH)

FIGURE 14-1 Group problem-solving modes

the Crises Mode. The very nature of many crisis situations makes this the best approach for problem solving. The danger is that many organizations use this mode inappropriately and treat *every* situation as a crisis, just as individuals treat every situation as a "telling" situation whether or not it is.

The Organizational Problem-Solving Mode when used appropriately requires high amounts of both task and relationship behavior. In this type of situation, considerable emphasis must be placed on structuring group activities, as well as motivating group members.

For example, eight teachers met with the principal and the superintendent of a school district. The job at hand was to revise the general curriculum. The curriculum had been neglected in the past because energies had been directed toward student disciplinary problems. The superintendent and principal both spelled out what needed to be done at the present meeting. The principal then elicited ideas from each group member and encouraged dialogue among the group members. By giving the group both content, structure, and a motivating process, the principal assured a productive group meeting.

In the Interpersonal Problem-Solving Mode, a high relationship. low task approach is appropriate. For example, if after a group is given a problem, cliques develop that serve to disrupt the group, relationship behaviors need to be used to increase interaction of all group members.

When appropriately used, the Routine Procedural Mode requires low task and low relationship behaviors. For example, a group of managers finds that they need to reassemble an important report before an early meeting the next day. The clerical staff has gone home. They quickly decide who is going to do what task and play what role. The emphasis is on getting the job done through performing the assigned roles with a minimum of structuring activities and socioemotional support.

In all of these modes, the focus must be on producing quality decisions in a timely manner. Quality decisions have no value if they are not timely. You may be highly skilled at picking the winners of Saturday's football games on Monday morning, but by then it's too late to do you any good.

A characteristic of effective groups is that they can move rapidly and easily from one mode to another without getting hung up on a normative mode. We enrich the ability of the group to respond to different situations and face different problems and contingencies if we build into them the ability and fluidity to move from one mode to another. Adaptability is very important. It is a product of growth and development. Mental receptiveness to the concept of change is the essence of adaptability. This is a positive virtue needed by persons in a group.[14]

HELPING AND HINDERING ROLES

Individuals within groups play roles—the individual behavior each member exhibits. It is not that a particular role by itself is helping or hindering to group performance, but it is that a high-performing group member plays a role that in a given situation contributes to maximizing the productivity of the group. This is the same principle that underlies leadership styles. A particular style is not intrinsically good or bad. The key is whether or not it is appropriate to the situation.

For some time the literature has given us lists of helping roles and lists of hindering roles. When these roles are researched, we find that the same roles are helping in some situations and hindering in others. So it is not that any combination of behavior by itself is a helping or hindering role, but it is the particular role in a particular contingency that makes the determination.

If we are to be effective in groups, all of us need to be able to adapt our roles to the needs of the group. We need to get rid of the idea that there are certain behaviors that are always good and certain behaviors that are always bad. There are behaviors that tend to be functional in some situations and dysfunctional in others.

In our extensive work with organizations in helping them improve their Quality Circles and other productivity programs, we have found that the material in Figure 14-2 has been particularly useful in giving people insights into roles they are and should be exhibiting in group settings. You will note that it is organized in much the same way as the Situational Leadership model, with the dimensions of Task Behavior and Relationship Behavior. It is a taxonomy of influence. Each style, S1–S4, represents a *behavioral competency*. Within each *competency* there are two *categories* of behavior—one helping and one hindering. These *categories* are further divided into *indica-*

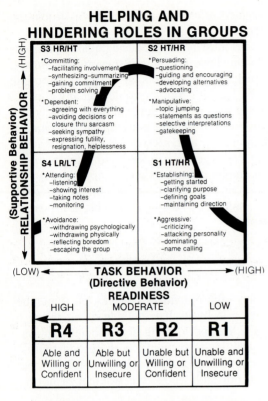

HELPING AND HINDERING ROLES IN GROUPS

S3 HR/HT

*Committing:
  –facilitating involvement
  –synthesizing–summarizing
  –gaining commitment
  –problem solving

*Dependent:
  –agreeing with everything
  –avoiding decisions or
   closure thru sarcasm
  –seeking sympathy
  –expressing futility,
   resignation, helplessness

S2 HT/HR

*Persuading:
  –questioning
  –guiding and encouraging
  –developing alternatives
  –advocating

*Manipulative:
  –topic jumping
  –statements as questions
  –selective interpretations
  –gatekeeping

S4 LR/LT

*Attending:
  –listening
  –showing interest
  –taking notes
  –monitoring

*Avoidance:
  –withdrawing psychologically
  –withdrawing physically
  –reflecting boredom
  –escaping the group

S1 HT/HR

*Establishing:
  –getting started
  –clarifying purpose
  –defining goals
  –maintaining direction

*Aggressive:
  –criticizing
  –attacking personality
  –dominating
  –name calling

(Supportive Behavior)
RELATIONSHIP BEHAVIOR → (HIGH)

(LOW) ◄─── **TASK BEHAVIOR** ───► (HIGH)
(Directive Behavior)

READINESS

HIGH	MODERATE		LOW
R4	**R3**	**R2**	**R1**
Able and Willing or Confident	Able but Unwilling or Insecure	Unable but Willing or Confident	Unable and Unwilling or Insecure

FIGURE 14-2   Helping and hindering roles in groups

tors of the types of behavior an individual could engage in under each *category*.

Some people seem to be fairly predictable in the roles that they play. They frequently enter into a series of transactions when interfacing with the group. In Transactional Analysis, this repetitive series of transactions is called a "psychological game." Because of their importance, we will include brief illustrations of some of the psychological games associated with hindering roles.

S1 (HT/LR) COMPETENCY

Helping Role Category

Establishing.   Helps start the group along new paths. Proposes tasks and goals, defines problems, helps set rules, and contributes ideas. May suggest a plan of attack to handle a problem. Interprets issues and helps

324

clear up ambiguous ideas or suggestions. Focuses attention on the alternatives and issues before the group.

Establishing Indicators

Getting started.   Initiating action. Suggesting roles, structure, or procedures for the group to use. For example, "I suggest we go once around the table. Each of us will have an opportunity to give input."

Clarifying purpose.   Stating why the group has been called together. Ensuring commonality of the intended result. "We are not here to play games. We have a responsibility to develop a workable strategic plan for our company."

Defining goals.   Specifying what is needed to fulfill the group's purpose; the steps necessary for purpose attainment. For example, "To meet budget guidelines, we must submit our plan by December first and within the target of two and a half million. The first step is to agree on the line items."

Maintaining direction.   Keeping the group on track; focusing on the stated goals and purpose. For example, "I think we're missing the point. We are not here to redefine the company's mission, we are here to agree on funding for each of the line items."

Hindering Role Category

Aggressive.   Asserts personal dominance and attempts to get own way regardless of others. May react with hostility toward aspects of the problem of individuals who appear to be blocking progress. Criticism may be offered, either directly or through sarcasm and innuendo. May refuse to cooperate by rejecting all ideas or by interrupting, monopolizing the conversation, or by acting as an authority. May also engage in other aggressive behaviors such as bullying, discounting ideas, and boasting.

Aggressive Indicators

Criticizing.   Downgrading, putting down, or otherwise finding fault with the suggestions or input or others. For example, "You keep coming up with these bright sayings. Why don't you try to sell them to the *Readers' Digest.*"

Attacking personality.   Focusing on someone's personal attributes instead of the performance issue or problem the group is facing. For example, "That's one of the dumbest things I've heard. Why do you keep coming up with such stupid comments?"

Dominating.   Taking "air time" and blocking other group members' opportunity to make suggestions. For example, "Just be quiet a minute. I've got something to say."

Name calling.   Stereotyping. Using labels that generalize about a person or group in a demeaning manner. For example, "You staff types really don't know what is going on in this company."

Games Played by People in This Role

Uproar.   Beginning with some form of critical statement that triggers an attack/defense series of transactions. The game ends with group members arguing in loud voices with any (or all) aggressive role category behaviors represented.

See What You Made Me Do? and/or If It Weren't For You.   Using *blaming* games. The purpose is to transpose ownership or accountability for an error to another person, usually in a forceful, attacking manner. The message is: "My lack of influence, or the group's ineptness, is *your* fault."

S2 (HT/HR) COMPETENCY

Helping Role Category

Persuading.   Requests the facts and relevant information on the problem. Seeks out expressions of feelings and values. Asks for suggestions, estimates, and ideas. Responds openly and freely to others. Encourages and accepts contributions of others, whether expressed orally or nonverbally.

Persuading Indicators

Questioning.   Asking questions for the sake of clarity and shared understanding of a point. Productive questioning enhances group process and quality of content. For example, "Of your training objectives, which one do you consider to be the most important?"

Encouraging and guiding responses.   It isn't sufficient to ask good questions. It is also people's willingness to respond that helps surface information and insights into their feelings and values. For example, "That is an excellent idea. Please tell us more about it."

Developing alternatives.   Creating options. Coming up with various interpretations or multiple conclusions or strategies for consideration. For example, "Perhaps we should look at the financial plan from a 'best case'/'worst case' set of scenarios."

Advocating. Suggesting that the group pursue one suggestion or alternative over another. For example, "Since we seem to be stuck for a next step, I'd like to suggest that we talk about the Johnson Tool acquisition next."

Hindering Role Category

Manipulative. Responds to a problem rigidly and persists in using stereotypical responses. Makes repeated attempts to use solutions that are ineffective in achieving group goals. Selectively interprets data so as to validate personal opinions and censure nonsupportive input. Responds to personal motives, desires, and aspirations to the exclusion of the public agenda. Attempts to lure others into joining the position. Evaluates communication context. Judges remarks before they are understood and cross-examines the input of others.

Topic jumping. Getting off course, such as talking about X and suddenly discussing Y. Or, hairsplitting—overly focusing on and debating one detail so much that it is taken out of context and becomes a topic of its own. For example, "I agree that a business plan is important, but I think it is time that we rethink our company's mission statement."

Masking statements as questions. Saying something in question form or a one-liner that is actually a statement of justification or criticism. For example, "Don't you think it's time you got this meeting going again? We're not getting anything accomplished here."

Selective interpretation. Twisting what was said to discredit someone's point or taking a point out of context. For example, "That may be true, but we have never been successful in introducing a product without television advertising."

Gatekeeping. Hearing what you want to hear. Attempting to control the input to match one's own assessment of significance and responding accordingly. For example, "Thank you for your suggestion." (writes it down) "That is interesting." (does not write it down) "Worthwhile idea." (writes it down)

Games Played by People in This Role

Blemish. Becoming the group's nit-picker. Sifting through positive contributions looking for the chink in the armor and focusing on existing weak points.

Corner. Manuevering other people through a series of seemingly plausible questions into a situation in which, no matter what they do, they never come out right.

"Now I've Got You. Listening carefully to what is said, even questioning to get information, then once the ammunition is gathered, unloading on whoever makes the mistake or steps into the trap.

S3 (HR/LT) COMPETENCY

Helping Role Category

Committing. Helps to ensure that all members are part of the decision-making process. Shows relationships between ideas. May restate suggestions to pull them together. Summarizes and offers potential decisions for the group to accept or reject. Asks to see if the group is nearing a decision. Attempts to reconcile disagreements and facilitate the participation of everyone in the decision. Helps keep communication channels open by reducing tension and getting people to explore differences.

Committing Indicators

Facilitating involvement. Making sure that people are getting enough air time to provide input. Making efforts to tap into the resources that are available in the group. For example, "Come on, fella, you're doing a fine job. Nobody wants to cut into what you have to say."

Synthesizing/summarizing. Taking a variety of inputs and putting them into a new idea. Integrating what people say into a holistic framework. Summarizing existing ideas. For example, "If we take Joe's idea for a redesigned package and Mary's suggestion for in-store promotion, we may be able to launch the product introduction two months ahead of schedule."

Gaining commitment. Tapping into the group to ensure members are on board and buying into the group's progress or results. Securing a shared sense of ownership. For example, "How many of you are willing to sign on to our commitment to ship fifty thousand units by November first?"

Problem solving. Dealing with problems affecting group commitment near the point of implementation. If there is skepticism, offer proof; if there is misunderstanding, clarify; a drawback, be creative; procrastination, create a sense of urgency; a solution not within the group's scope of authority, identify who is in authority, ask for support, and make suggestions. For example, "We have not been making very good progress. If we are going to wind this up today, we have to reach agreement before lunch on this personnel evaluation system."

Hindering Role Category

Dependent. Reacts to people as authority figures. May acquiesce to anyone who is seen as an overt leader. Abdicates problem solving to others and expects someone else to lead to the solution. Unwilling to use leadership resources available within self or others. Attempts to escape tension through diversions or the inappropriate use of humor. Easily embarrassed and vulnerable to criticism. Often apologizes for given input. Requires constant encouragement to participate. Seeks sympathy.

Dependent Indicators

Agreeing with everything. Deferring to others. Suppressing one's feelings. Appears to be on board with all members on all issues. For example, "No, I guess you're right. I'm out of ideas."

Avoiding decisions or closure through sarcasm. Making an inappropriate attempt at humor that keeps issues open when the group could be making a decision. For example, "Did you hear the story about the. . . . "

Seeking sympathy. Attempting to gain attention or concessions from other group members through sulking, looking dejected, or similar behaviors. Using such behaviors as manipulative ploys to gain influence. For example, "You always make my department take more than our share of the cuts. Why do we always have to give in? Why do we have to be punished?"

Expressing futility, resignation, or helplessness. Blowing smoke rings, drawing, playing paper-and-pencil games and doing things that distract group members and demonstrate noninvolvement. Announcing all the reasons why something is wrong or will not work. The aim is to convince others that the group is powerless and lacks control. For example, "Management is never going to listen to our ideas anyway. It is just another waste of time."

Games Played by People in This Role

"Ain't It Awful?" Presenting superficial concern and commitment to the group's efforts when really attempting to thwart those efforts through statements such as: "It will take too much work" or "There'll be no support" or "No one ever listens to us."

Wooden leg.   Trying to avoid accomplishment, accountability, work, or to gain sympathy. Using some contrived or exaggerated handicap as an excuse for not being able to fulfill their good intentions.

"Poor Me."   Behaving in a way that reinforces some form of self-pity and self-negation. The game is played to seek sympathy. Griping continues, but the person makes no real effort to change or improve the situation.

S4 (LR/LT) COMPETENCY

Helping Role Category

Attending.   Listens as well as speaks. Easy to talk to. Encourages input from group members and tries to understand as well as be understood. Records input for use later. Demonstrates a willingness to become involved with other people. Takes time to listen and avoids interrupting.

Attending Indicators

Listening.   Remaining silent, maintaining eye contact, and paying attention to what is being said with the purpose of *understanding*; not agreeing. For example, "I've been listening very carefully and it seems Tom has some very good points."

Showing interest.   Communicating in a way that shows one is involved in the group's process and concerned with its workings. The communication is usually nonverbal and is a type of emotionally neutral reinforcement. For example, leaning forward, visibly concentrating on discussions.

Taking notes (for oneself) *or recording* (for the group).   Keeping some form of registered evidence of the group's inputs, activities, and decisions that will make them accessible at a later point. For example, "I've made some notes and I'd like to say something. . . . "

Monitoring or observing.   Auditing or examining the group. Paying special attention to the impact things have on the group's process or performance. For example, showing alertness during discussions.

Hindering Role Category

Avoidance.   Retreats emotionally in thought and/or physically. Daydreams, avoids the topics, or remains indifferent. Engages in individualistic activity that has little or nothing to do with group activity. May withdraw from the group. Scoffs at group effort, rolls eyes in disgust, or demonstrates aloofness nonverbally. Will occasionally preplan a means to leave the group early.

Avoidance Indicators

Withdrawing Psychologically. Being unresponsive, withdrawn, seemingly checked out from the group's activities—preoccupied with thoughts other than the issues before the group. For example, trying not to be involved in the group's activities—looking intently at pictures and so on.

Withdrawing physically. Stationing oneself away from the group. Creating a physical distance between oneself and the group's activities. For example, getting up from the group discussion area and walking over to the windows, a few feet away.

Reflecting boredom. Pouting, physically conveying the message "I'd rather not be here." Being an active competing response for the group. For example, slouching in the chair and appearing disinterested.

Escaping the group. Physically leaving the environment, planning to be late, intentionally absenting oneself from the group. For example, phone rings as secretary makes prearranged call. "Sorry, folks, got to leave to take care of some important business."

Games Played by People in This Role

Harried. Appearing too overworked or busy to meet deadlines and commitments. To sustain the game and maintain this image the player will take on and even solicit added responsibilities to an already overfilled plate. This provides the basis for permission to be late, to leave meetings before the group comes to closure, and to turn over unfinished work with incomplete instructions to other group members—guilt-free and with justification.

Kick me. Making a mistake, that is, coming to work late or unprepared and hoping that someone in the group will provide the desired kick—criticism, questions, and so on. This kick provides the payoff the player seeks. An eventual result of this is that the person may withhold contributions or withdraw psychologically or physically from the group.

Withdrawing psychologically or physically from the group can be an outcome of any of these games. Although this may give the hinderer some short-term satisfaction, it undermines the group process.

These are some of the behavioral indicators reflecting helping and hindering roles in each of the four competencies. They are illustrations of the types of activities that contribute to or detract from functional and constructive group problem solving. We want to emphasize again that these roles are not by themselves helping or hindering—there are no generic helping or hindering roles. A role may be helping or hindering depending upon the situation. Your awareness of these roles will make a very real contribution toward increasing your effectiveness in groups.

NOTES

1. David Krech, Richard S. Crutchfield, and Egerton L. Ballachey, *Individual in Society* (New York: McGraw-Hill, 1962), p. 529.

2. Sandy J. Wayne, Ricky W. Griffin, and Thomas S. Bateman, "Improving the Effectiveness of Quality Circles," *Personnel Administrator*, March 1986, pp. 79–88. See also Merle O'Donnel and Robert J. O'Donnel, "Quality Circles: Latest Fad or Real Winner?" *Business Horizons*, May–June 1984, pp. 48–52; Edward E. Lawler III and Susan A. Mohrman, "Quality Circles After the Fad," *Harvard Business Review*, January–February 1985, pp. 64–71.

3. Annette Hartenstein and Kenneth F. Huddleston, "Values: The Cornerstone of QWL," *Training and Development Journal*, October 1984, pp. 65–66. See also Shoichi Suzawa, "How The Japanese Achieve Excellence," *Training and Development Journal*, May 1985, pp. 110–117.

4. *Ibid.*

5. Robert H. Guest, Paul Hersey, and Kenneth H. Blanchard, *Organizational Change through Effective Leadership*, 2nd ed. (Englewood Cliffs, N.J.: Prentice-Hall, 1986).

6. *Ibid.*

7. Kenneth H. Blanchard and Spencer Johnson, *The One Minute Manager* (New York: Morrow, 1982).

8. Kenneth Blanchard and Robert Lorber, *Putting the One Minute Manager to Work* (New York: Morrow, 1984).

9. *Ibid.*

10. *Ibid.*

11. Sam Certo, *Principles of Modern Management: Functions and Systems* (Dubuque, Iowa: Brown, 1983).

12. Guest, Hersey, and Blanchard, *Organizational Change through Effective Leadership*.

13. The definition of leadership style in individuals we used in earlier chapters can also be applied to group behavior.

14. Guest, Hersey, and Blanchard, *Organizational Change through Effective Leadership*.

CHAPTER 15

PLANNING AND IMPLEMENTING CHANGE

In the dynamic society surrounding today's organizations, the question of whether change will occur is no longer relevant. Instead, the issue is, How do managers and leaders cope with the inevitable barrage of changes that confront them daily in attempting to keep their organizations viable and current? Although change is a fact of life, if managers are to be effective, they can no longer be content to let change occur as it will. They must be able to develop strategies to plan, direct, and control change.

To be effective managers of change, leaders must have more than good *diagnostic skills*. Once they have analyzed the demands of their environment, they must be able to *adapt* their leadership style to fit these demands and develop the means to *change* some or all of the other situational variables. Recognizing that sometimes the only avenue to effectiveness is through change, in this chapter we will concentrate on the processes and strategies for planning and implementing change.

GENERAL FRAMEWORK
FOR UNDERSTANDING CHANGE

Managers who are interested in implementing some change in their group or organization should have (or be able to obtain people with) skills, knowledge, and training in at least two areas:

1. *Diagnosis.* The first, and in some ways the most important, stage of any change effort is diagnosis. Broadly defined, the skills of diagnosis involve techniques for asking the right questions, sensing the environment of the organization, establishing effective patterns of observation and data collection, and developing ways to process and interpret data. In diagnosing for change, managers should attempt to find out: (1) what is *actually* happening now in a particular situation, (b) what is *likely* to be happening in the future if no change effort is made, (c) what would people *ideally* like to be happening in this situation, and (d) what are the *blocks*, or restraints, stopping movement from the actual to the ideal.

2. *Implementation.* This stage of the change process is the translation of diagnostic data into change goals and plans, strategies and procedures.Questions such as the following must be asked: How can change be effected in a work group or organization and how will it be received? What is adaptive and what is resistant to change within the environment?

Diagnosis

There are at least three steps in the diagnostic process: point of view, identification of problem(s), and analysis.

Point of View

Before beginning to diagnose in an organization, you should be clear through whose eyes you will be observing the situation—your own, those of your boss, your associates, your subordinates, an outside consultant, or others.

Ideally, to get the full picture you should look at the situation from the points of view of as many as possible of the people who will be affected by any changes. Reality, however, sometimes restricts such a broad perspective. At any rate, you should be clear about your frame of reference from the start.

Identification of Problem(s)

Any change effort begins with the identification of the problem(s). A problem in a situation exists when there is a discrepany between what is actually happening (the *real*) and what you or someone who hired you (point of view) would like to be happening (the *ideal*). For example, in a given situation, there might be tremendous conflict occurring among individuals in a work group. If this kind of conflict is not detrimental, there may be no problem. Until you can explain precisely what you would like to be occurring and unless that set of conditions is different from the present situation, no problem exists. On the other hand, if you would ideally like this work group to be harmonious and cooperative, then you have a problem—there is a discrepancy between the real and the ideal. *Change efforts involve attempting to reduce discrepancies between the real (actual) and the ideal.* It should be pointed out that change efforts may not always involve attempting to move the real closer to the ideal. Sometimes after diagnosis you might realize that your ideal is unrealistic and should be brought more in line with what is actually happening.

It is in problem identification that the concepts and theoretical frameworks presented in this book begin to come into play. For example, two important potential areas for discrepancy are, in Likert's terms, output/end-result variables and intervening variables.

In examining *end-result variables*, the question becomes: Is the organization, work group, or individual doing an effective job in what it was asked to do; that is, production, sales, teach the 3 Rs, and so on? Are short-term goals being accomplished? How does the long-term picture look? If performance is not what it should be, there is an obvious discrepancy.

If performance is a problem, you might want to look for discrepancies in the *intervening variables* or condition of the human resources. For example, is there much turnover, absenteeism, or tardiness? How about grievances, accident rate, and such? The theories and framework of people that you have been reading can generate all kinds of diagnostic questions for the change situation you are examining, such as:

- What leadership, decision-making, and problem-solving skills are available? What is the motivation, communication, commitment to objectives, and climate (morale)? (Likert)
- What is the readiness level of the people involved? Are they willing and able to take significant responsibility for their own performance? (Hersey and Blanchard)
- What need level seems to be most important for people right now? (Maslow)
- How are the hygiene factors and motivators? Are people getting paid enough? How are the working conditions? Is job security an issue? How are interpersonal relations? Do people complain about the manager? Are people able to get recognition for their accomplishments? Is there much challenge in the work? Are there opportunities for growth and development? Are people given much responsibility? (Herzberg)

Good theory is just organized common sense. So use the theories and questions presented here to help you sort out what is happening in your situation and what might need to be changed.

Analysis—An Outgrowth of Problem Identification

Problem identification flows almost immediately into analysis. Once a discrepancy (problem) has been identified, the goal of analysis is to determine why the problem exists. The separation between problem identification and analysis is not always that clear, however, because identifying areas of discrepancy is often a part of analysis.

Once a discrepancy has been identified in the end-result variables or intervening variables, the most natural strategy is to begin to examine what Likert calls "causal variables"—the independent variables that can be altered or changed by the organization and its management, such as leadership or management style, organizational structure, organizational objectives. In other words, can you identify what in the environment might have caused the discrepancy? Again, different theorists come to mind and stimulate various questions.

- What is the dominant leadership style being used? How does it fit with the readiness level of the people involved? (Hersey and Blanchard)
- What are the prevailing assumptions about human nature adhered to by management? How well do those assumptions match the capabilities and potential of the people involved? (McGregor)
- Are people able to satisfy a variety of needs in this environment? How do the opportunities for need satisfaction compare with the high strength needs of the people involved? (Maslow)
- How do the expectations of the various situational variables compare with the leadership style being used by management? (Hersey and Blanchard)

Again, these theories and questions are presented to suggest how the concepts studied can help you to analyze problems that exist in your environment and provide guidelines for developing strategies for implementing change.

Implementation

The implementation process involves the following: identifying alternative solutions and appropriate implementation strategies to use in attempting to reduce the discrepancy between what is actually happening and what you would like to be happening; anticipating the probable consequences of using each of the alternative strategies; and choosing a specific strategy and implementing it.

Once your analysis is completed, the next step is to determine alternative solutions to the problem(s). Hand in hand with developing alternative solutions is determining appropriate implementation strategies. Three theories seem helpful in designing change strategies.

Force Field Analysis

In Chapter 6 force field analysis was examined as a useful technique in looking at the variables involved in determining effectiveness. This technique for diagnosing situations, which was developed by Kurt Lewin,[1] also may be useful in analyzing the various change strategies that can be used in a particular situation.

Once you have determined that there is a discrepancy between what is actually happening and what you would like to be happening in a situation—

and have done some analysis on why that discrepancy exists—then force field analysis becomes a helpful tool. Before embarking on any change strategy, it seems appropriate to determine what you have going for you in this change effort (driving forces) and what you have going against you (restraining forces). We have found from our experience that if managers start implementing a change strategy without doing that kind of analysis, they can get blown out of the water and not know why. An example might help.

In August, an enthusiastic superintendent of schools and his assistant took over a suburban school district outside a large urban area in the Midwest. Both men were committed to "humanizing" the schools. In particular, they wanted to change the predominant teaching approach used in the system from a teacher-centered approach in which the teachers always tell the students what to do, how to do it, when to do it, and where to do it (high task/low relationship style) to a child-centered approach in which students play a significant role in determining what they are to do (high relationship/low task or low relationship/low task style).

To implement the changes they wanted, the two administrators hired a business manager to handle the office and the paper work. They themselves essentially had no office. They put telephones in their cars and spent most of their time out in the schools with teachers and students. They spent fifteen to eighteen hours a day working with and supporting teachers and administrators who wanted to engage in new behavior. Then, suddenly, in January, only six months after they had been hired, the school board called a special meeting and fired the superintendent by a seven to two vote.

The administrators could not believe what had happened. They immediately started a court suit against the school board for due process. They charged that the board had served as both judge and jury. In addition to the court actions, the administrators became educational martyrs and began to hit the lecture tour to talk about the evils of schools. During one of their trips, the assistant superintendent was asked by one of the authors of this book to come to his graduate seminar on the management of change. The class at that time was discussing the usefulness of force field analysis. The administrator, who did not know Lewin's theory, was asked to think about the driving and restraining forces that had been present in the change situation. In thinking about the driving forces that were pushing for the change they wanted, the administrator was quick to name the enthusiasm and commitment of the top administrators, some teachers, and some students, but really could not think of any other driving forces. When asked about the number of teachers and students involved, the administrator suggested that they were a small but growing group.

In thinking about restraining forces, the assistant superintendent began to mention one thing after another. The assistant or administrator said that they had never really had a good relationship with the mayor, chief of police, or editor of the town paper. These people felt that the two administrators were encouraging permissiveness in the schools. In fact, the town paper printed several editorials against their efforts. In addition, the teachers' association had expressed concern that the programs being pushed were asking the teachers to assume responsibilities outside their contract. Even the Parent—Teachers Association (PTA) had held several meetings because of parent concerns about discipline in the schools. The administrator also reported the fact that the superintendent had been hired by a five to four vote of the board and that some of his supporters had been defeated in the November election. In general, he implied that the town had been traditionally very conservative in educational matters, and on and on.

Figure 15-1 suggests the relationship between driving and restraining forces in this change situation. As can be seen, even with adding some board members as driving forces and not mentioning some teachers and students as restraining forces, the restraining forces for changing this school system from a teacher-centered approach to a child-centered approach not only outnumbered but easily outweighed the driving forces. As a result, the restraining forces eventually overpowered the driving forces and pushed the equilibrium even more in the direction of a teacher-centered approach.

In utilizing force field analysis for developing a change strategy, there are a few guidelines that can be used:

1. If the driving forces far outweigh the restraining forces in power and frequency in a change situation, managers interested in driving for change can often push on and overpower the restraining forces.

FIGURE 15−1 Driving and restraining forces in an educational change example

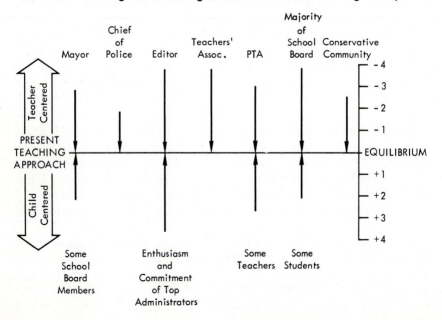

2. If the reverse is true and the restraining forces are much stronger than the driving forces, managers interested in driving for change have several choices. First, they can give up the change effort, realizing that it will be too difficult to implement. Second, they can pursue the change effort but concentrate on maintaining the driving forces in the situation while attempting, one by one, either to change each of the restraining forces into driving forces or somehow immobilize each of the restraining forces so that they are no longer factors in the situation. The second choice is possible but very time consuming.
3. If the driving forces and restraining forces are fairly equal in a change situation, managers probably will have to begin pushing the driving forces, while at the same time attempting to convert or immobilize some or all of the restraining forces.

In this school example, the situation obviously represented an imbalance in favor of restraining forces, yet the administrators acted as if the driving forces were clearly on their side. If they had used force field analysis to diagnose their situation, they would have seen that their change strategy was doomed until they took some time to try to work on the restraining forces.

Once force field analysis has been completed and managers have decided whether to increase the driving forces, work on the restraining forces, or both, some understanding of the levels of change and the change cycles available might be useful.

Change Cycles

Levels of change. In Chapter 1 four levels of change were discussed: knowledge changes, attitudinal changes, individual behavior changes, and group or organizational performance changes.

Changes in knowledge tend to be the easiest to make; they can occur as a result of reading a book or an article or hearing something new from a respected person. Attitude structures differ from knowledge structures in that they are emotionally charged in a positive or negative way. The addition of emotion often makes attitudes more difficult to change than knowledge.

Changes in individual behavior seem to be significantly more difficult and time consuming than either of the two previous levels. For example, managers may have knowledge about the advantages of increased follower involvement and participation in decision making and may even feel that such participation would improve their performance, and, yet, they may be unable to delegate or share decision-making responsibilities significantly with subordinates. This discrepancy between knowledge, attitude, and behavior may be a result of their own authoritarian management–subordinate upbringing. This past experience has led to a habit pattern that feels comfortable.

While individual behavior is difficult enough to change, it becomes even more complicated when you try to implement change within groups or organizations. The leadership styles of one or two managers might be effectively altered, but drastically changing the level of follower participation throughout an entire organization might be a very time-consuming process. At this level you are trying to alter customers, mores, and traditions that have developed over many years.

Levels of change become very significant when you examine two different change cycles—the participative change cycle and the directive change cycle.[2]

Participative change. A participative change cycle is implemented when new knowledge is made available to the individual or group. It is hoped that the group will accept the data and will develop a positive attitude and commitment in the direction of the desired change. At this level an effective strategy may be to involve the individual or group directly in helping to select or formalize the new methods for obtaining the desired goals. This is group participation in problem solving.

The next step will be to attempt to translate this commitment into actual behavior. This step is significantly more difficult to achieve. For example, it is one thing to be concerned about increased follower participation in decision making (attitude) but another thing to be willing actually to get involved in doing something (behavior) about the issue. An effective strategy may be to identify the informal and formal leaders among the work group(s) and concentrate on gaining their behavioral support for the desired change. Once this is accomplished, organizational change may be effected by getting other people to begin to pattern their behavior after those persons whom they respect and perceive in leadership roles. This participative change cycle is illustrated in Figure 15−2.

FIGURE 15−2 Participative change cycle

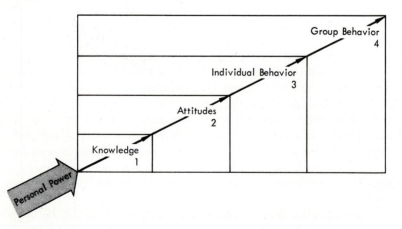

Directive change. We have all probably been faced with a situation similar to the one in which there is an announcement on Monday morning that "as of today all members of this organization will begin to operate in accordance with Form 10125." This is an example of a directive change cycle. It is through this change cycle that many managers in the past have attempted to implement such innovative ideas as management by objectives, job enrichment, and the like.

This change cycle begins by change being imposed on the total organization by some external force, such as higher management, the community, new laws. This will tend to affect the interaction network system at the individual level. The new contacts and modes of behavior create new knowledge, which tends to develop predispositions toward or against the change. The directive change cycle is illustrated in Figure 15−3.

In some cases where change is forced, the new behavior engaged in creates the kind of knowledge that develops commitment to the change, and, therefore, begins to approximate a participative change as it reinforces the individual and group behavior. The hope is that "if people will only have a chance to see how the new system works, they will support it."

Is there a "best" strategy for change? Given a choice between the polarities of directive and participative change, most people would tend to prefer the participative change cycle. But just as we have argued that there is no "best" leadership style, there also is no best strategy for implementing change. Effective change agents are identified as those who can adapt their strategies to the demands of their unique environment. Thus, the participative change cycle is not a better change strategy than the directive change

FIGURE 15−3 Directive change cycle

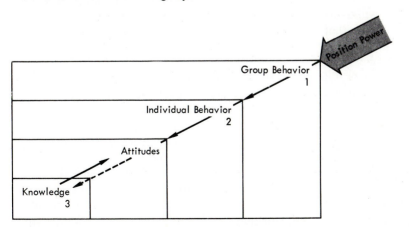

cycle, and vice versa. The appropriate strategy depends on the situation, and there are advantages and disadvantages to each.

Advantages/disadvantages of change cycles. The participative change cycle tends to be more appropriate for working with individuals and groups who are achievement motivated, seek responsibility, and have a degree of knowledge and experience that may be useful in developing new ways of operating—in other words, people with task-relevant readiness. Once the change starts, these people are much more capable of assuming responsibilities for implementation of the desired change. Although these people may welcome change and the need to improve, they may become very rigid and opposed to change if it is implemented in a directive (high task/low relationship) manner. A directive change style is inconsistent with their perceptions of themselves as responsible self-motivated people who should be consulted throughout the change process. When they are not consulted and change is implemented in an authoritarian manner, conflict often results. Examples of this occur frequently in organizations in which a manager recruits or inherits a competent, creative staff that is willing to work hard to implement new programs and then proceeds to bypass the staff completely in the change process. This style results in resistance and is inappropriate to the situation.

A coercive, directive change style might be very appropriate and more productive with individuals and groups who are less ambitious, are often dependent, and who are not willing to take on new responsibilities unless forced to do so. In fact these people *might prefer* direction and structure from their leader to being faced with decisions they are not willing or experienced enough to make. Once again, diagnosis is all-important. It is just as inappropriate for a manager to attempt to implement change in a participative manner with a staff that has never been given the opportunity to take responsibility and has become dependent on its manager for direction as it is to implement change in a coercive manner with a staff that is ready to change and willing to take responsibility for implementing it.

There are other significant differences between these two change cycles. The participative change cycle tends to be effective when induced by leaders who have personal power; that is, they have referent, information, and expert power. On the other hand, the directive cycle necessitates that a leader have significant position power; that is, coercive, connection, reward, and legitimate power.

If managers decide to implement change in an authoritarian, coercive manner, they would be wise to have the support of their superiors and other sources of power or they may be effectively blocked by their staff.

With the participative change cycle, a significant advantage is that once the change is accepted it tends to be long lasting. Since everyone has been involved in the development of the change, each person tends to be more highly committed to its implementation. The disadvantage of participative change is that it tends to be slow and evolutionary—it may take years to implement a significant change. An advantage of directive change, on the other hand, is speed. Using position power, leaders can often impose change immediately. A disadvantage of this change strategy is that it tends to be volatile. It can be maintained only as long as the leader has position power to make it stick. It often results in animosity, hostility, and, in some cases, overt and covert behavior to undermine and overthrow.

In terms of force field analysis, discussed earlier, the directive change cycle could be utilized if the power of the driving forces pushing for change far outweighed the restraining forces resisting change. On the other hand, a directive change cycle would be doomed to failure if the power of the restraining forces working against the change was more frequent and powerful than the power of the driving forces pushing for the change.

A participative change cycle that depends on personal power could be appropriate in either of the cases just described. With frequent and powerful driving forces pushing for change in a situation, a leader might not have to use a high task, directive change cycle since the driving forces are ready to run with the change already and do not have to be forced to engage in the new desired behavior. At the same time, when the restraining forces could easily overpower the driving forces, managers would be advised to begin with participative change techniques designed gradually to turn some of the restraining forces into driving forces or at least immobilize their influence in the situation. In other words, when things are stacked against you, it would seem to be more effective to try to reeducate the forces against the change than to try to force change in a situation when little power is on the side of the change effort.

These two change cycles have been described as if they were either/or positions. The use of only one of these change cycles exclusively, however, could lead to problems. For example, if managers introduce change only in a directive, high task/low relationship manner without any movement toward participative change, members of their staff—if they decide to remain—may react in one of two ways. Some may fight the managers tooth and nail and organize efforts to undermine them. Others may buckle under to their authority and become very passive, dependent staff members, always needing the manager to tell them what to do and when to do it before doing anything. These kinds of people say yes to anything the manager wants and then moan and groan and drag their feet later. Neither of these responses makes for a very healthy organization. At the other extreme, managers who will not make a move without checking with their staff and getting full approval also can immobilize themselves. They may establish such a complicated network of "participative" committees that significant change becomes almost impossible.

Thus, in reality, it is more a question of the proper blend of the directive and participative change cycles, depending on the situation, than a forced choice between one or the other.

Patterns of Communication

One of the most important considerations in determining whether to use a participative or directive change strategy or some combination of both is how communication patterns are structured within a group or organization prior to implementing a change.[3] Two of the most widely used ways of structuring communications, illustrated in Figure 15–4, are the star and the circle.

The arrowed lines represent two-way communication channels. In the circle each person can send messages in either direction to two colleagues on either side, and, thus, the group is free to communicate all around the circle. In other words, nothing in the structure of the communication pattern favors one group member over another as leader. In essence, this depicts an open, democratic organization in which there is participation in decision making by all members. In the star communication pattern, however, one individual (C) is definitely in a leadership position; C can communicate with the other four members of the group and they can communicate with C but not with each other. This group represents an autocratic structure, with C acting as the boss. Either of these groups might be analogous to groups of department heads, each having a department but all reporting eventually to the same manager. In both patterns, A, B, D, and E are department heads and C is the manager.

Is there a "best" pattern of communication? Once these two patterns of communication have been identified, the usual question arises about which is the "best" pattern. Some classic experiments conducted by Alex Bavelas[4] attempted to answer that question. In particular, Bavelas was interested in determining how each of these communication patterns affected the efficiency of a group's performance as well as the group's morale.

FIGURE 15–4 **Two ways of structuring communications**

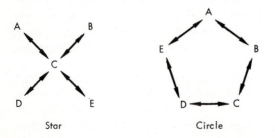

Star   Circle

In one experiment, the two groups were put to work in the star and circle patterns. Sets of five marbles were given to each of the five group members. The marbles of each set had different colors but one color was common to all sets. Both groups were to discover the common color. When that had been accomplished, the task was completed. In essence, it was the star, or autocratic, pattern against the circle, or democratic, pattern.

The autocratic star pattern was much faster. Its four subordinate members simply had to describe their marbles to the leader. After noting the common color, the designated leader sent correct information back. In trial after trial, the star group arrived at correct answers in an average of about thirty to forty seconds. The circle group took sixty to ninety seconds. The star group was not only faster but used fewer messages and developed more efficient ways of solving problems. In addition, group members respected their communication pattern.

The star pattern, although fast, tended to have a negative effect on morale. While group members had a high opinion of their communication pattern or organization, they had a low opinion of themselves except for the leader (C). With each ensuing trial they felt less important and more dissatisfied. In fact, on one occasion the leader received a message, "Enough of this game; let's play tic-tack-toe." On other occasions, messages were torn up or written in French and Spanish; yet, on the whole, the group still was faster and more productive than the circle group.

The circle could be described as "slow, inaccurate, but happy." It developed no system for working on problems and no one leader seemed to emerge. While members were openly critical of the organization's productivity, they seemed to enjoy the tasks. No one attempted to sabotage.

In terms of performance, everything seemed to be in favor of the autocratic groups, until Bavelas created a so-called emergency. He changed the marbles. Instead of simple solid colors, each group was given odd-colored marbles that were difficult to describe. The task, as before, was to find out which marble all members of the group had in common. The new marbles required close observation to tell one from another. In fact, two group members could be looking at identical marbles and describe them quite differently.

Since morale and the condition of the human resources were good in the circle group, members pulled together in the "emergency" and were able to solve the problem by utilizing all the available resources. On the other hand, the star pattern was a leader-dominated system; so group members looked to the leader in the emergency to solve the problem with little commitment from them.

The new task confused both groups. Errors mounted, and it took ten minutes or more to solve the problem. Yet, eventually, the circle seemed to adapt to the crisis, and after a number of trials had restored its efficiency completely. On the other hand, the star could not seem to cope with it, taking twice as much time and committing three to four times as many errors.

Why was the star communication pattern faster? Essentially, because it was a one-way communication system dominated by a single leader. With this communication pattern, an orderliness was imposed on the group that eliminated extra messages. In the circle, no such clear organization existed. Group members could communicate with two people. Since they had this kind of mobility, they seemed to get around more and thus spend more time. However, since the members of a circle group sent more messages, they could take advantage of more checkpoints and, thus, could locate and correct more of their errors.

Members of the circle group had more chance to participate and take responsibility. They were less dependent on one person since they could check with another member. Thus, they were more satisfied and happy. The leader (C) in the star also felt quite happy and satisfied, probably for the same reasons as the members of the circle pattern—C was given responsibility and had several sources of information and checkpoints. In essence, C was independent and powerful.

In summary, these experiments suggest that the mere structure of communication patterns can influence how people feel and act in terms of independence, security, and responsibility. This same structure also can influence the total operational efficiency of a group in terms of speed, accuracy, and adaptability. In essence, the structure seems to influence the way people feel in one direction and their speed and accuracy in another. Although the two communication patterns discussed have been described as if they were either/or structures, in reality, the design for an effective organization may need to incorporate both. For example, with the professional teaching staff, a school principal might find it most appropriate to structure the communication pattern in a democratic, free-wheeling manner, as in the circle. However, with the nonprofessional service personnel, the principal might find it appropriate to operate in a more autocratic manner, as in the star pattern. These groups may be at different levels of commitment, motivation, and ability to take responsibility, and therefore different kinds of communication patterns are needed.

Relationship between communication patterns and change strategies. The structure of communication patterns seems to have two significant relationships with the participative and directive change strategies discussed earlier. First, in implementing a change strategy, managers or leaders have to incorporate into the strategy the development of an appropriate communication pattern. In that sense, the unstructured democratic wheel pattern seems very compatible with the participative change cycle, while the structured, autocratic star pattern seems appropriate for the directive change cycle. In fact, the results of Bavelas's experiments with the circle and star patterns of communication seem to support the suggested advantages and disadvantages of the participative and directive change cycles; that is, the participative change cycle is slow but tends to develop involvement and commitment; the directive change cycle is fast but can create resentment and hostility.

Second, before implementing a change strategy in an organization or group, it is important for the change agent to know the present communication structure in operation. For example, if an organization has been run in a democratic manner in which the communication pattern did not favor the manager as a leader over any of the subordinates, a new manager should probably think twice before implementing a directive, coercive change. The structure of communication required of a directive change strategy would be alien to the already established communication pattern. The same warning applies to a manager attempting to implement change in a participative manner in an organization that for years has been organized with the manager in a strong leadership position. In such a situation, supervisors and staff members often learn to be more dependent and less responsible because the manager always seems to assume leadership. As a result, they may not be ready for a more open, democratic system at this time.

In conclusion, there is no one "best" strategy for implementing change in organizations. The strategy used—whether participative, directive, or some combination of both—depends on the situation. One variable that seems important to analyze in developing an appropriate change strategy is the present structure of communication patterns within the target group or organization.

Change Process

In examining change, Lewin identified three phases of the change process—unfreezing, changing, and refreezing.[t]

Unfreezing

The aim of unfreezing is to motivate and make the individual or the group ready to change. It is a thawing out process in which the forces acting on individuals are rearranged so that now they see the need for change. According to Edgar H. Schein, when drastic unfreezing is necessary, the following common elements seem to be present: (1) the physical removal of the individuals being changed from the accustomed routines, sources of information, and social relationships; (2) the undermining and destruction of all social supports; (3) demeaning and humiliating experience to help individuals being changed to see their old attitudes or behavior as unworthy and thus to be motivated to change; (4) the consistent linking of reward with willingness to change and of punishment with unwillingness to change.[6]

In brief, unfreezing is the breaking down of the mores, customs, and traditions of individuals—the old ways of doing things—so that they are ready to accept new alternatives. In terms of force field analysis, unfreezing may occur when either the driving forces are increased or the restraining forces that are resisting change are reduced.

Changing

Once individuals have become motivated to change, they are ready to be provided with new patterns of behavior. This process is most likely to occur by one of two mechanisms: identification and internalization.[7] *Identification* occurs when one or more models are provided in the environment—models from whom individuals can learn new behavior patterns by identifying with them and trying to become like them. *Internalization* occurs when individuals are placed in a situation in which new behaviors are demanded of them if they are to operate successfully in that situation. They learn these new behavior patterns not only because they are necessary to survive but because of new high strength needs induced by coping behavior.

> Internalization is a more common outcome in those influence settings where the direction of change is left more to the individual. The influence that occurs in programs such as Alcoholics Anonymous, in psychotherapy or counseling for hospitalized or incarcerated populations, in religious retreats, in human relations training of the kind pursued by the National Training Laboratories (1953), and in certain kinds of progressive education programs is more likely to occur through internalization or, at least, to lead ultimately to more internalization.[8]

Identification and internalization are not either/or courses of action, but effective change is often the result of combining the two into a strategy for change.

Force or compliance is sometimes discussed as another mechanism for inducing change.[9] It occurs when an individual is forced to change by the direct manipulation of rewards and punishment by someone in a power position. In this case, behavior appears to have changed when the change agent is present, but it is often dropped when supervision is removed. Thus, rather than discussing force as a mechanism of changing, we should think of it as a tool for unfreezing.

Refreezing

The process by which the newly acquired behavior comes to be integrated as patterned behavior into the individual's personality and/or ongoing significant emotional relationships is referred to as *refreezing*. As Schein contends, if the new behavior has been internalized while being learned, "this has automatically facilitated refreezing because it has been fitted naturally into the individual's personality. If it has been learned through identification, it will persist only so long as the target's relationship with the original influence model persists unless new surrogate models are found or social support and reinforcement is obtained for expressions of the new attitudes."[10]

This highlights how important it is for an individual engaged in a change process to be in an environment that is continually reinforcing the desired change. The effect of many training programs has been short-lived when the person returns to an environment that does not reinforce the new patterns or, even worse, is hostile toward them.

What we are concerned about in refreezing is that the new behavior does not get extinguished over time. To keep this from happening, reinforcement must be scheduled in an effective way. There seem to be two main reinforcement schedules: continuous and intermittent.[11] As we discussed in Chapter 10, with continuous reinforcement, the individuals learn the new behavior quickly, but if their environment changes to one of nonreinforcement, extinction can be expected to take place relatively soon. With intermittent reinforcement, extinction is much slower because the individuals have been conditioned to go for periods of time without any reinforcement. Thus, for fast learning, a continuous reinforcement schedule should be used. But once the individual has learned the new pattern, a switch to intermittent reinforcement should ensure a long-lasting change.

Change Process—Some Examples

To see the change process in operation, several examples can be cited.

A college basketball coach recruited Bob Anderson, a six-foot four-inch center, from a small town in a rural area where six feet four inches was a good height for a center. This fact, combined with his deadly turnaround jump shot, made Anderson the rage of his league and enabled him to average close to thirty points a game.

Recognizing that six feet four inches is small for a college center, the coach hoped that he could make Anderson a forward, moving him inside only when they were playing a double pivot. One of the things the coach was concerned about, however, was how Anderson, when used in the pivot, could get his jump shot off when he came up against other players ranging in height from six feet eight inches to seven feet. He felt that Anderson would have to learn to shoot a hook shot, which is much harder to block, if he were going to have scoring potential aginst this kind of competition. The approach that many coaches would use to solve this problem would probably be as follows: On the first day of practice the coach would welcome Anderson and then explain the problem to him as he had analyzed it. As a solution, he would probably ask Anderson to start to work with the varsity center, Steve Cram, who was six feet ten inches tall and had an excellent hook. "Steve can help you start working on that new shot, Bob," the coach would say. Anderson's reaction to this interchange might be one of resentment, and he would go over and work with Cram only because of the coach's position power. After all, he might think to himself, "Who does he think he is? I've been averaging close to thirty points a game for three years now and the first day I show up here the coach wants me to learn a new shot." So he may start to work with Cram reluctantly, concentrating on the hook shot only when the coach is looking but taking his favorite jump shot when not being observed. Anderson is by no means unfrozen, or ready to learn to shoot another way.

Let us look at another approach the coach might use to solve this problem. Suppose that on the first day of practice he sets up a scrimmage between the varsity and the freshmen. Before he starts the scrimmage he takes big Steve Cram, the varsity center, aside and tells him, "Steve, we have this new freshman named Anderson who has real potential to be a fine ball player. What I'd like you to do today, though, is not to worry about scoring or rebounding—just make sure every time Anderson goes up for a shot you make him eat it. I want him to see that he will have to learn to shoot some other shots if he is to survive against guys like you." So when the scrimmage starts, the first time Anderson gets the ball and turns around to shoot, Cram leaps up and stuffs the ball right down his throat. Time after time this occurs. Soon Anderson starts to engage in some coping behavior, trying to fall away from the basket, shooting from the side of his head rather than from the front in an attempt to get his shot off. After the scrimmage, Anderson comes off the court dejected. The coach says, "What's wrong, Bob?" Bob replies, "I don't know, coach, I just can't seem to get my shot off against a man as big as Cram. What do you think I should do, Coach?" he asks. "Well, Bob, why don't you go over and start working with Steve on a hook shot. I think you'll find it much harder to block. And with your shooting eye I don't think it will take long for you to learn." How do you think Anderson would feel about working with Cram now? He'd probably be enthusiastic and ready to learn. Being placed in a situation in which he learns for himself that he has a problem will go a long way in unfreezing Anderson from his past patterns of behavior and preparing him for making the attempt at identification. Now he'll be ready for identification. He has had an opportunity to internalize his problem and is ready to work with Steve Cram.

So often the leader who has knowledge of an existing problem forgets that until the people involved recognize the problem as their own, it is going to be much more difficult to produce a change in their behavior. Internalization and identification are not either/or alternatives, but they can be parts of developing specific change strategies appropriate to the situation.

Another example of the change processes in operation can be seen in the military, particularly in the induction phase. There are probably few organizations that have people entering who are less motivated and committed to the organization than the recruits the military gets. And yet in a few short months they are able to mold these recruits into a relatively effective combat team. This is not an accident. Let us look at some of the processes that help accomplish this.

The most dramatic and harsh aspect of the training is the unfreezing phase. All four of the elements that Schein claims drastic unfreezing situations have in common are present. Let us look at some specific examples of these elements in operation.

1. The recruits are *physically removed from their accustomed routines, sources of information, and social relationships* in the isolation of Parris Island (Marine training base in South Carolina).

   During the first week of training at Parris Island, the recruit is . . . hermetically sealed in a hostile environment, required to rise at 4:55 A.M., do exhausting exercises, attend classes on strange subjects, drill for hours in the hot sun, eat meals in silence and stand at rigid attention the rest of the time; he has no television, no radio, no candy, no Coke, no beer, no telephone—and can write letters only during one hour of free time a day.[12]

2. *The undermining and destruction of social supports* is one of the DI's (drill instructor's) tasks. "Using their voices and the threat of extra PT (physical training), the DI . . . must shock the recruit out of the emotional stability of home, pool hall, street corner, girl friend, or school."[13]

3. *Demeaning and humiliating experiences* are commonplace during the first two weeks of the training as the DIs help the recruits *see themselves as unworthy and thus motivated to change* into what they want a marine to be. "it's a total shock. . . . Carrying full seabags, 80 terrified privates are herded into their "barn," a barracks floor with 40 doubledecker bunks. Sixteen hours a day, for two weeks, they will do nothing right.[14]

4. Throughout the training there is *consistent linking of reward with willingness to change and of punishment with unwillingness to change.*

   Rebels or laggards are sent to the Motivation Platoon to get "squared away." A day at Motivation combines constant harassment and PT (physical training), ending the day with the infiltration course. This hot 225-yard ordeal of crawling, jumping, and screaming through ditches and obstacles is climaxed by the recruit dragging two 30-pound ammo boxes 60 yards in mud and water. If he falters, he starts again. At the end, the privates are lined up and asked if they are ready to go back to their home platoons . . . almost all go back for good.[15]

While the recruits go through a severe unfreezing process, they quickly move to the changing phase, first identifying with the DI and then emulating informal leaders as they develop. "Toward the end of the third week a break occurs. What one DI calls 'that five percent—the slow, fat, dumb, or difficult' have been dropped. The remaining recruits have emerged from their first week vacuum with one passionate desire—to stay with their platoon at all costs."[16]

Internalization takes place when the recruits through their forced interactions develop different high strength needs. "Fear of the DI gives way to respect, and survival evolves into achievement toward the end of training. 'I learned I had more guts than I imagined' is a typical comment."[17]

Since the group tends to stay together throughout the entire program, it serves as a positive reinforcer, which can help to refreeze the new behavior.

The three theories discussed—force field analysis, change cycles, and change process—should help a person interested in change determine some alternative solutions to the identified problem(s) and suggest appropriate implementation strategies. For example, let us reexamine the case of our enthusiastic school administrators who wanted to humanize the schools in their system and change the predominant teaching approach from teacher-centered to child-centered. As we suggested, if they had done a force field analysis, they would have realized that the restraining forces working against this change far outweighed the driving forces in power and frequency. The analysis would have suggested that a directive, coercive change strategy would have been ineffective for implementing change since significant unfreezing had to occur before the restraining forces against the change could have been immobilized or turned into driving forces. Thus, a participative change effort probably would have been appropriately aimed at reeducating the restraining forces by exposing them in a nonthreatening way (through two-way communication patterns) to new knowledge directed at changing their attitudes and eventually their behavior.

While this participative reeducative approach might be appropriate, it also must be recognized that it will be time consuming (four to seven years). The superintendent and his assistant just might not be willing to devote that kind of time and effort to this change project. If they are not, then they could decide not to enter that school system or charge on in a coercive, directive manner and be ready for the consequences. Or they could choose their action from a number of other alternatives that may have been generated at this time.

Change Process—Recommended Action

After suggesting various alternative solutions and appropriate implementation strategies, a leader/manager interested in change should anticipate the probable consequences (both positive and negative) of taking each of the alternative actions. *Remember* (1) Unless there is a high probability that a desired consequence will occur and that consequence will be the same as the conditions that would exist if the problem were not present, then you have not solved the problem or changed the situation. (2) The ultimate solution to a problem (the change effort) may not be possible overnight, and, therefore, interim goals must be set along the path to the final goal (the solving of the problem).

The end result of analysis (which includes determining alternative solutions) should be some recommended action that hopefully will decrease the discrepancy between the actual and the ideal. Although action is the end result, you must remember that action based on superficial analysis may be worse than taking no action at all. Too frequently, people want to hurry on to the action phase of a problem before they have adequately analyzed the situation. The importance of the analysis part cannot be given too much emphasis—a good analysis frequently makes the action obvious.

MANAGING INTERGROUP CONFLICT

One of the problems that often occurs during a change effort is intergroup conflict. A total organization is really a composite of its various working units or groups. The important thing for organizational accomplishment— whether these groups be formal or informal—is that these groups either perceive their goals as being the same as the goals of the organization or, although different, see their own goals being satisfied as a direct result of working for the goals of the organization.

On occasion, groups or parts of an organization come into conflict. The atmosphere *between* groups can affect the total productivity of the organization. According to Schein,

> this problem exists because as groups become more commited to their own goals and norms, they are likely to become competitive with one another and seek to undermine their rivals' activities, thereby becoming a liability to the organization as a whole. The overall problem, then, is how to establish high-productive, *collaborative* intergroup relations.[18]

Consequences of Group Competition

Sherif was the first to study systematically the consequences of intergroup conflict.[19] His original studies and more recent replications have found the effects of competition on individuals consistent to the extent that they can readily be described.[20] As Schein reports, some interesting phenomena occur both *within* and *between* each competing group.[21]

During competition, each group becomes more cohesive; internal differences are forgotten for the moment as increased loyalty takes over. The group atmosphere becomes more task oriented as group accomplishment becomes paramount. The leadership shifts more toward an autocratic style as the group becomes more tolerant of someone's taking the lead. The group becomes more organized and highly structured, and with this demands more loyalty and conformity from its members in order to present a "solid front."

At the same time that these phenomena are occurring *within* the group, the relationship *between* the groups has some common characteristic.

Each group starts to see the other as the enemy and distorts perceptions of reality—recognizing only their own strengths and the weaknesses of the other group. Hostility toward the other group increases, while communication decreases. This makes it easier to maintain negative feelings and more difficult to correct false perceptions. If the groups are forced to interact, as at a bargaining table, neither one really listens to the other but only listens for cues that support its arguments.

Schein stresses that while competition and the responses it generates may be very useful to a group in making it more effective and achievement motivated, "the same factors which improve intragroup effectiveness may have negative consequences for intergroup effectiveness."[22] Labor–management disputes are cases in point because the more these parties perceive themselves as competitors, the more difficult they find it to resolve their differences.

When win–lose confrontations occur between two groups or teams, even though there eventually is a winner, the loser (if it is not a clear-cut win) is not convinced that it lost, and intergroup tension is higher than before the competition began. If the win is clear-cut, the winner often loses its edge, becomes complacent, and is less interested in goal accomplishment. The loser in this case often develops internal conflict while trying to discover the cause of the loss or someone to blame. If reevaluation takes place, however, the group may reorganize and become more cohesive and effective.[23]

When the negative consequences of intergroup conflict outweigh the gains, management seeks ways to reduce this intergroup tension. As Schein suggests, "the basic strategy of reducing conflict, therefore, is to find goals upon which groups can agree and to reestablish valid communication between the group."[24] He contends that this strategy can be implemented by any combination of the following: *locating a common enemy, inventing a negotiation strategy which brings subgroups of the competing groups into interaction with each other,* and *locating a superordinate goal.*

Preventing Intergroup Conflict

Since it is difficult to reduce intergroup conflict once it has developed, it is desirable to prevent its occurrence in the first place. This might be done in several ways. First of all, management should emphasize the contributions to total goals rather than the accomplishment of subgroup goals. Second, an attempt should be made to increase the frequency of communication and interaction between groups and develop a reward system for groups who help each other. Third, whenever possible individuals should be given experiences in a wide range of departments to broaden their base for empathy and understanding of intergroup problems.[25]

Collaborative organizations often appear to have an abundance of task-relevant conflict, which improves overall effectiveness. This may occur because under these conditions individuals trust each other and are frank and open in sharing information and ideas. In competitive situations characterized by win—lose confrontations, observations may suggest lower levels of open conflict, since total interaction is significantly less and each group is committed to withholding its resources and information from the other groups, thus lowering the potential for overall organizational effectiveness.

Blake, Shepard, and Mouton Model

According to Blake, Shepard, and Mouton,[26] there are three attitudinal sets or basic assumptions that people can have toward intergroup conflict: (1) conflict is inevitable, agreement is impossible; (2) conflict is not inevitable, yet agreement is impossible; and (3) although there is conflict, agreement is possible. These attitudinal sets will lead to predictable behavior depending on the way the people involved see the "stakes"; that is, the extent to which they see the conflict as important or having value.

As illustrated in Figure 15—5, if people think that conflict is inevitable and agreement is impossible, their behavior will range from being passive to very active. When the stakes are low, they will tend to be passive and willing to let fate (like a flip of a coin) decide the conflict. When the stakes are moderate, they will permit a third-party judgment to decide the conflict. And, finally, when the stakes are high, they will actively engage in a win—lose confrontation or power struggle.

If people think that conflict is not inevitable, yet if it occurs then agreement is impossible, they will be passive and indifferent if the stakes are low. When the stakes are moderate, they will isolate themselves from such a con-

FIGURE 15—5 Three basic attitudes toward conflict and the behavior each evokes as involvement (stakes) increase and decrease[27]

	Conflict Inevitable, Agreement Impossible	Conflict Not Inevitable, Yet Agreement Not Possible	Although There Is Conflict, Agreement Is Possible	
ACTIVE	Win—Lose Power Struggle	Withdrawal	Problem-Solving	HIGH STAKES
	Third-Party Intervention	Isolation	Splitting the Difference (Compromise, Bargaining, etc.) Mediation	MODERATE STAKES
PASSIVE	Fate	Indifference or Ignorance	Peaceful Coexistence ("Smoothing Over")	LOW STAKES

flict situation. And when the stakes are high and they find themselves actively involved, they will eventually withdraw.

If people think that although there is conflict, agreement is possible, they will be passive and attempt to smooth over the situation when the stakes are low. When the stakes are moderate, they will engage in bargaining or some form of negotiation. And if the stakes are high, they will actively engage in problem solving.

In using this model in consulting, we contend that if you have some knowledge of the attitudes people have about a potential conflict and what the stakes are for them, you can predict their behavior, and vice versa. If you observe the behavior of people during a conflict, you can usually predict their assumptions about conflict in this situation. For example, if you see people actively engaging in a win−lose power struggle, you can predict that the stakes in this conflict are high and that they think agreement is impossible. At the same time, if you learn that people think that a certain conflict is inevitable but agreement is impossible and the stakes are high in this situation, you can predict that if the conflict occurs the situation will deteriorate to a win−lose power struggle. If such a win−lose power struggle occurs, one possible intervention might be to attempt initially to lower the stakes so that the conflicting parties will at least permit a third-party intervention. When that intervention is made, efforts can be directed toward changing the assumptions of the people involved to "although there is conflict, agreement is possible." When that is done, an attempt to increase commitment again will tend to move them into an active problem-solving mode.

ORGANIZATIONAL GROWTH

Our discussions in this chapter have focused on changing or working on problems in organizations that are already established. How different are the issues in new or emerging organizations? A developmental theory developed by Larry E. Greiner[28] is helpful in examining growing organizations.

Greiner argues that growing organizations move through five relatively calm periods of *evolution*, each of which ends with a period of crisis and revolution. According to Greiner, "each evolutionary period is characterized by the dominant *management* style used to achieve growth, while each revolutionary period is characterized by the dominant *management* problem that must be solved before growth will continue."[29]

As illustrated in Figure 15−6, the first stage of organizational growth is called *creativity*. This stage is dominated by the founders of the organization, and the emphasis is on creating both a product and a market. These "founders are usually technically or entrepreneurially oriented, and they dis-

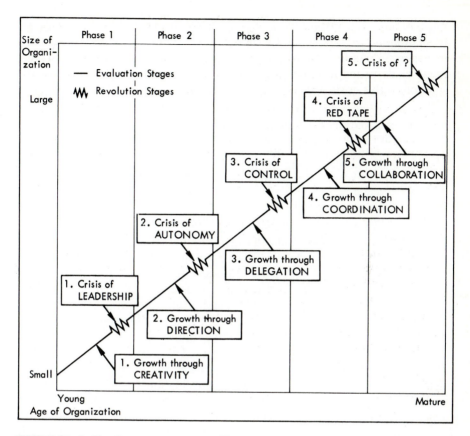

FIGURE 15–6 The five stages of growth[30]

dain management activities; their physical and mental energies are absorbed entirely in making and selling a new product."[31] But as the organization grows, management problems occur that cannot be handled through informal communication and dedication. "Thus the founders find themselves burdened with unwanted management responsibilities . . . and conflicts between the harried leaders grow more intense."[32]

It is at this point that the *crisis of leadership* occurs and the first revolutionary period begins. "Who is going to lead the organization out of confusion and solve the management problems confronting the organization?" The solution is to locate and install a strong manager "who is acceptable to the founders and who can pull the organization together."[33] This leads to the next evolutionary period—growth through *direction*.

During this phase the new manager and key staff "take most of the responsibility for instituting direction, while lower level supervisors are treated more as functional specialists than autonomous decision-making managers."[34] As lower level managers demand more autonomy, this eventually leads to the next revolutionary period—the *crisis of autonomy*. The solution to this crisis is usually greater delegation.

> Yet it is difficult for top managers who were previously successful at being directive to give up responsibility. Moreover, lower level managers are not accustomed to making decisions for themselves. As a result numerous [organizations] flounder during this revolutionary period, adhering to centralized methods, while lower level employees grow more disenchanted and leave the organization.[35]

When an organization gets to the growth stage of *delegation*, it usually begins to develop a decentralized organizational structure, which heightens motivation at the lower levels. Yet, eventually, the next crisis begins to evolve as the top managers "sense that they are losing control over a highly diversified field operation . . . freedom breeds a parochial attitude."[36]

The *crisis of control* often results in a return to centralization, which is now inappropriate and creates resentment and hostility among those who had been given freedom. A more effective solution tends to initiate the next evolutionary period—the *coordination* stage. This period is characterized by the use of formal systems for achieving greater coordination with top management as the "watchdog." Yet most coordination systems eventually get carried away and result in the next revolutionary period—the *crisis of red tape*. This crisis most often occurs when "the organization has become too large and complex to be managed through formal programs and rigid systems."[37]

If the crisis of red tape is to be overcome, the organization must move to the next evolutionary period—the phase of *collaboration*. While the coordination phase was managed through formal systems and procedures, the collaboration phase "emphasizes greater spontaneity in management action through teams and the skillful confrontation of interpersonal differences. Social control and self-discipline take over from formal control."[38]

Greiner is not certain what the next revolution will be, but he anticipates that it will "center around the 'psychological saturation' of employees who grow emotionally and physically exhausted by the intensity of teamwork and the heavy pressure for innovative solutions."[39]

It is felt that to overcome and even avoid the various crises, managers could attempt to move through the evolutionary periods more consistently with the sequencing that Situational Leadership would suggest—direction to coordination to collaboration to delegation—rather than the ordering depicted by Greiner.

ORGANIZATIONAL DEVELOPMENT

Throughout this chapter we have been discussing various frameworks that managers may find useful in helping them initiate change in their organizations. The need for managers to be able to plan and implement change in the future is a given, particularly as people begin to demand more and more that organizations be more than just a place to "pick up a pay check." As Richard Beckhard views it,[40] the challenge of change facing managers is

> How can we optimally mobilize human resources and energy to achieve the organization's mission and, at the same time, maintain a viable, growing organization of people whose personal needs for self-worth, growth and satisfaction are significatly met at work?

An attempted response to this dilemma and the corresponding need for changes in the way organizations operate has been the growing field of organizational development (O.D.).

Organizational Effectiveness and O.D.

In defining O.D. from our perspective, it is important to remember, as we discussed in Chapter 6, that the effectiveness of a particular organization depends on its goals and objectives. Thus, we do not accept a set of normative goals that are right for all organizations, as many O.D. theorists and practitioners seem to do.[41] As Bennis suggests, the philosophy and values of O.D. change agents provide the "guidelines and directions for *what* will be undertaken in an organization development effort and *how* the program will evolve and be sustained."[42] With the humanistic values that are communicated by O.D. practitioners and theorists, it is not hard to understand why the goals of organizational development are generally reported as aiming toward an open, trusting type of organization and O.D. interventions seem to stress the use of collaborative or interpersonal strategies for change. As Bennis argues:[43]

> I have yet to see an organization development program that uses an intervention strategy other than an interpersonal one, and this is serious when one considers that the most pivotal strategies of change in our society are political, legal and technological.

A Problem with Organizatinal Development

If it is true that most O.D. consultants and practitioners use collaborative or interpersonal strategies of change and thus almost always concentrate on the "people variable" in helping organizations, it becomes clear why there are more O.D. intervention failures than successes. First, as we have suggested throughout this chapter, using the same strategy for change all the time will lead to effective change in some situations but in many others might be ineffective. Thus, there is no one best strategy of change. Effective O.D. interventions depend on diagnosing the situation and determining the highest probability success approach for the particular environment.

Second, if one analyzes the interpersonal change strategy so often used in O.D. interventions, one can see that it tends to be related to high relationship/low task(S3). According to Situational Leadership, this interpersonal change strategy would be most appropriate in organizations in which members tend to have moderate to high levels of readiness; that is, they are able to take responsibility for implementing the desired change but just need someone to help facilitate it. Such an organization, as we discussed in Chapter 3, would probably be classified by Argyris as a YB organization. And yet as Argyris[44] contends, most organizations are not operating in YB patterns but are more typically XA organizations. These organizations, in terms of Situational Leadership, would be at low levels of readiness since they are not only unable to direct their own change but are often even unwilling. Thus, one of the greatest challenges facing the field of organizational development is developing strategies to move organizations from XA to YB and from low levels of readiness (in terms of implementing their own change) to higher levels. As a result, O.D. practitioners and change agents need to develop their skills in structural, directive change strategies, as well as to maintain their skills in interpersonal, participative change strategies so that the movement toward "self-renewing" organizations can begin with some hope of success.

IMPACT OF CHANGE ON THE TOTAL SYSTEM

In Chapter 1 the importance of combining the social and the technical into a unified social systems concept was stressed. As Robert H. Guest argues:

> On his part the social scientist often makes the error of concentrating on human motivation and group behavior without fully accounting for the technical environment which circumscribes, even determines, the role which the actors play. Motivation, group structure, interaction processes, authority—none of these abstractions of behavior takes place in a technological vacuum.[45]

A dramatic example of the consequences of introducing technical change and ignoring its consequences on the social system is the case of the introduction of the steel axe to a group of Australian aborigines.[46]

This tribe remained considerably isolated, both geographically and socially, from the influence of Western cultures. In fact, their only contact was an Anglican mission established in the adjacent territory. The polished stone axe was traditionally a basic part of the tribe's technology. Used by men, women, and children, the stone axe was vital to the subsistence economy. But more than that, it was actually a key to the smooth running of the social system; it defined interpersonal relationships and was a symbol of masculinity and male superiority. "Only an adult male could make and own a stone axe; a woman or a child had to ask his permission to obtain one."[47]

The Anglican mission, in an effort to help improve the situation of the aborigines, introduced the steel axe, a product of European technology. It was given indiscriminately to men, women, and children. Because the tool was more efficient than the stone axe, it was readily accepted; but it produced severe repercussions unforeseen by the missionaries or the tribe. As Stephen R. Cain reports:

> The adult male was unable to make the steel axe and no longer had to make the stone axe. Consequently, his exclusive axe-making ability was no longer a necessary or desirable skill, and his status as sole possessor and dispenser of a vital element of technology was lost. The most drastic overall result was that traditional values, beliefs, and attitudes were unintentionally undermined.[48]

The focus in this book has been on the management of human resources, and as a result we have spent little time on how technical change can have an impact on the total system. Our attempt in this example was to reiterate that an organization is an "open social system"; that is, all aspects of an organization are interrelated; a change in any part of an organization may have an impact on other parts or on the organization itself. Thus, a proposed change in any part of an organization must be carefully assessed in terms of its likely impact on the rest of the organization.

NOTES

1. Kurt Lewin, *Field Theory in Social Science*, D. Cartwright, ed. (New York: Harper & Brothers, 1951).

2. Paul Hersey and Kenneth H. Blanchard, "Change and the Use of Power," *Training and Development Journal*, January 1972. See also Chris Argyris, *Strategy, Change and Defensive Routines* (Cambridge: Ballenger Publishing, 1985).

3. Kenneth H. Blanchard and Paul Hersey, "The Importance of Communication Patterns in Implementing Change Strategies," *Journal of Research and Development in Education*, 6, No. 4 (Summer 1973), pp. 66–75.

4. Alex Bavelas, "Communication Patterns in Task-Oriented Groups" in Dowin Cartwright and Alvin Zander, eds., *Group Dynamics: Research and Theory* (Evanston, Ill.: Row, Peterson, 1953).

5. Kurt Lewin, "Frontiers in Group Dynamics: Concept, Method, and Reality in Social Science; Social Equilibria and Social Change," *Human Relations*, I, No. 1 (June 1974), pp. 5–41. See also Kenneth D. Beene et al., eds. *Laboratory Method of Changing and Learning Theory and Application* (Palo Alto, Calif.: Science and Behavior Books, 1975); Amitai Etzioni

and Richard Remp, *Technological Shortcuts to Social Change* (New York: Russell Sage Foundation, 1973).

6. Edgar H. Schein, "Management Development as a Process of Influence," in David R. Hampton, *Behavioral Concepts in Management* (Belmont, Calif.: Dickinson Publishing, 1968), p. 110. Reprinted from *Industrial Management Review*, II, No. 2 (May 1961) pp. 59–77.

7. The mechanisms are taken from H. C. Kelman, "Compliance, Identification and Internalization: Three Processes of Attitude Change," *Conflict Resolution*, (1958), pp. 51–60.

8. Schein, "Management Development," p. 112.

9. Kelman discussed compliance as a third mechanism for attitude change.

10. Schein, "Management Development," p. 112.

11. See C. B. Ferster and B. F. Skinner, *Schedules of Reinforcement* (New York: Appleton-Century-Crofts, 1957).

12. "Marine Machine," *Look Magazine*, August 12, 1969.

13. *Ibid.*

14. *Ibid.*

15. *Ibid.*

16. *Ibid.*

17. *Ibid.*

18. Edgar H. Schein, *Organizational Psychology* (Englewood Cliffs, N.J.: Prentice-Hall, 1965), p. 80.

19. M. Sherif, O.J. Harvey, B. J. White, W. R. Hood, and Carolyn Sherif, *Intergroup Conflict and Cooperation: The Robbers Cave Experiement* (Norman, Okla.: Book Exchange, 1961).

20. Robert R. Blake and Jane S. Mouton, "Reactions to Intergroup Competition under Win-Lose Conditions," *Management Science*, 7(1961), pp. 420–35.

21. Schein, *Organizational Psychology*, p. 81.

22. *Ibid.*

23. *Ibid.*, p. 82.

24. *Ibid.*, p. 83.

25. *Ibid.*, p. 85.

26. Robert R. Blake, Herbert Shepard, and Jane S. Mouton, *Managing Intergroup Conflict in Industry* (Houston: Gulf Publishing, 1964). See also Robert R. Blake and Jane S. Mouton, *Solving Costly Organizational Conflicts: Achieving Intergroups Trust, Cooperation, and Teamwork* (San Francisco: Jossey-Bass, 1984); Alan C. Filley, *Interpersonal Conflict Resolution* (Glenview, Ill.: Scott, Foresman, 1975); Rensis Likert and Jane G. Likert, *New Ways of Managing Conflict* (New York: McGraw-Hill, 1976).

27. *Ibid.*, p. 13. Minor changes made in the figure but major change in the figure title so it is more consistent with the way we use the model in consulting.

28.Larry E. Greiner, "Evolution and Revolution as Organizations Grow," *Harvard Business Review*, July–August 1972, pp. 37–46. See also Larry E. Greiner and Robert O. Metzger, *Consulting to Management* (Englewood Cliffs, N.J.: Prentice-Hall, 1983); Jack R. Gibb, *A New View of Personal and Organizational Development* (La Jolla, Calif.: Omicron Press, 1978).

29. *Ibid.*, p. 40.

30. *Ibid.*, p. 41.

31. *Ibid.*, p. 42.

32. *Ibid.*

33. *Ibid.*

34. *Ibid.*

35. *Ibid.*, p. 43.

36. *Ibid.*

37. *Ibid.*

38. *Ibid.*

39. *Ibid.*, p. 44

40. Richard Beckhard, *Organization Development: Strategies and Models* (Reading, Mass.: Addison-Wesley, 1969), p. 3.

41. Warren G. Bennis, *Organization Development: Its Nature, Origins, and Prospects* (Reading, Mass.: Addison-Wesley, 1969) p. 13. See also Warren G. Bennis, *The Planning of*

Change (New York: Harper & Row, 1985); Warren G. Bennis, *Beyond Bureaucracy: Essays on the Develoment and Evolution of Human Organization* (New York: McGraw-Hill, 1973).

42. *Ibid.*

43. Bennis, "Editorial," *Journal of Applied Behavioral Science*, 4, No. 2 (1968), p. 228.

44. Chris Argyris, *Management and Organization Development: The Path From XA to YB* (New York: McGraw-Hill, 1971).

45. Robert H. Guest, *Organizational Change: The Effect of Successful Leadership* (Homewood, Ill.: Irwin, Dorsey Press, 1964), p. 4. See also Robert H. Guest, Paul Hersey, and Kenneth Blanchard, *Organizational Change through Effective Leadership*, 2nd ed. (Englewood Cliffs, N.J.: Prentice-Hall, 1986); Stanley E. Seashore, ed., *Assessing Organizational Change: A Guide to Methods, Measures, and Practices* (New York: Wiley, 1983).

46. Lauriston Sharp, "Steel Axes for Stone Age Australians," in *Human Problems in Technology Changes*, ed. Edward H. Spicer (New York: Russell Sage Foundation, 1952), pp. 69–94.

47. Stephen R. Cain, "Anthropology and Change," taken from *Growth and Change*, University of Kentucky, I, No. 3 (July 1970).

48. *Ibid.*

CHAPTER 16

IMPLEMENTING SITUATIONAL LEADERSHIP:
Managing People to Perform

This is the first in a series of four chapters that builds upon or uses significant aspects of Situational Leadership together with One Minute Management in bottom-line approaches to managing people to perform. We emphasize bottom-line because regardless of how a leadership or management concept might appear to be initially, the most fundamental issue is *does it contribute to organizational productivity*. This is what we mean by effective management.

Our approach in these four chapters is to draw upon some of the most significant contributions to effective management in recent years, using as the key points of focus Situational Leadership and One Minute Management. In this chapter, we will begin with a strategic model, the Satellite Model of Organizational Performance, and then follow up with several tactical or operational approaches to management. The first, the ACHIEVE model, will be presented in this chapter. The next two chapters, 17 and 18, will use the powerful insights of One Minute Management. The last of the four chapters, Chapter 19, will focus on important contributions to decision-making and building commitments. While the approaches in these four chapters may differ in terminology and in specific areas of emphasis, they all are related to Situational Leadership and the achievement of organizational productivity through effective leadership and management.

ORGANIZATIONAL PERFORMANCE

We need to remind ourselves again through a strategic model that organizational performance is the product of many factors, as shown in Figure 16−1, Satellite Model of Organizational Performance.[1] This model identifies several of the most important factors, including organizational structure, knowledge, nonhuman resources, strategic positioning, and human process. A strategy is a broad integrated plan of action to accomplish organizational goals; in our frame of reference, the goal of improving human productivity. Because a strategy is an integrated plan, you will note that all of the factors or variables are interrelated. You should also note that all of the factors contribute to performance, which is defined in the model as achieving or surpassing business and social objectives and responsibilities from the perspective of the judging party. But integration is not only essential to meeting current business and social needs but as Figure 16−2[2] suggests, it is essential to the change process necessary to meet future business and social needs of the organization.

While all of these factors are important and are certainly worthy of study, our primary emphasis in this book is on human resources. This em-

FIGURE 16−1 Satellite model of organizational performance

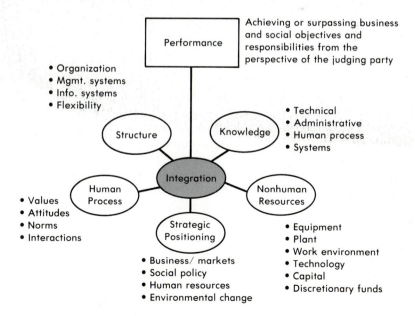

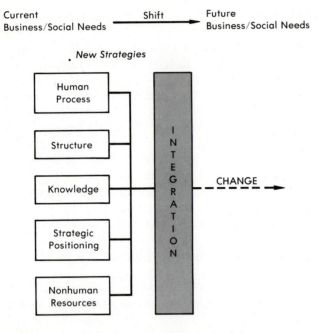

FIGURE 16—2 Positioning for future performance

Reprinted, by permission of the publisher, from "Strategies and Actions for Improving Organizational Performance," Alan A. Yelsey, *Management Review*, June 1984, pp. 45, 46. © 1984 American Management Association, New York. All rights reserved.

phasis is justified because increasing attention is being directed toward human resources, not only in their traditional roles but also in their influence on the other key performance factors.[3] For example, MacMillan and Schuler suggest that "focusing on a firm's human resources could provide a significant opportunity to secure a sustained edge over competitors."[4] Let's take a brief look at this interesting idea. Using superior human resources as a competitive weapon in improving organizational performance is certainly a new dimension in the management of organizational behavior. But how can organizations use human resources as strategic weapons?

MacMillan and Schuler have found that companies have gained an edge by either capturing or developing greater shares of critically needed human resource skills or by leveraging existing human resources to gain a competitive advantage. This cannot be done in isolation. There must be very close coordination between human resources planning and the other performance factors.

Increasingly, human resources managers will come under pressure to anticipate the major gaps in key skills needed for the firm. . . . The role of human resources management (HRM) in developing strategy will become critical. Clearly these managers are best equipped to identify the key skills that can be applied to create the competitive edge, and clearly they can play a major role in managing any transfer of skills to the strategic target, as well as assure the quality and quantity and continuity of the existing in-house skills. So it becomes vital for the HRM staff to become involved in the strategic process—not only in the traditional sense as a support function that assures the availability of human resources to support the strategic effort, but also as an aggressive participant that helps identify significant strategic advantages based on the corporation's existing human resources or to identify areas in which emerging skill needs can be preempted ahead of competitors.[5]

Questions MacMillan and Schuler recommend be asked include:

1. Which human resources in the company are unequivocally excellent?
2. How must HRM practices be applied to motivate the employees who possess the key skills?
3. What strategic targets could be pursued?
4. What strategic thrusts will be critical in the industry chain in the future?[6]

Their main argument that "Companies can gain a competitive advantage through their human resources by making sure that employees both have the appropriate skills and are suitably motivated"[7] is the same argument that we have been using for more than twenty-five years. Managing people to perform can make a very significant difference. We hope that the ACHIEVE model that follows and the other tactical approaches discussed in the subsequent chapters will give you useful ideas in your own human resources management.

Background of the ACHIEVE Model[8]

A common problem that occurs in the management process is that many managers tend to be effective in letting followers know *what* performance problems exist but they are not as effective in helping followers determine *why* these problems exist. In other words, many managers are strong in problem identification but are much weaker in problem analysis or diagnosis.

In order to be most effective in evaluating and solving performance problems, managers need to determine why problems have occurred. The ACHIEVE model was designed by Hersey and Goldsmith to help managers determine why performance problems may have occurred and then to develop change strategies aimed at solving these problems.[9]

In developing a model for analyzing human-performance problems Hersey and Goldsmith had two primary goals in mind: to determine the key factors that can influence staff members' performance and to present these factors in a way that can be used and remembered by practicing managers.

The first step in the development of the ACHIEVE model was to isolate the key factors that influence performance management. Earlier work by Atkinson[10] indicated that performance is a function of motivation and ability. Put in simple terms, the follower has to have a certain degree of willingness to do the job and the necessary skills for task completion. Porter and Lawler[11] expanded this idea by including role perception or job understanding, noting that followers can have all the willingness and skills needed to do the job but will not be effective unless there is a clear understanding of what to do and how to do it.

Lorsch and Lawrence[12] approached the topic from a different perspective and concluded that performance was not merely a function of attributes possessed by the individual but also depends on the organization and the environment. Individuals can be highly motivated and have all the skills to do the job but will not be effective unless they get needed organizational support and direction and unless their work fits the needs of their organizational environment.

The ACHIEVE model uses two more factors in the performance management equation. The first factor is feedback, which means that the followers need to know not just what to do but also how well they are doing it on an ongoing basis. Feedback includes day-to-day coaching and formal performance evaluation. The other performance management factor is validity. In today's environment managers need to be able to document and justify decisions that affect people's careers. Valid personnel practices have become a legal necessity in the United States. In analyzing performance, managers need to continually check for validity in all personnel practices, such as job analyses, recruitment, appraisal, training, promotion, and dismissal.

Hersey and Goldsmith have isolated seven variables related to effective performance management: (1) motivation, (2) ability, (3) understanding, (4) organizational support, (5) environmental fit, (6) feedback, and (7) validity. Their next step was to put these factors together in a manner that managers could easily remember and use. One technique for making items on a list easy to remember is to make their first letter form a common word, an acronym. A seven-letter word that is synonymous with "to perform" is *achieve*. By substituting *incentive* for the motivation factor; *clarity* for understanding; *help* for organizational support; and *evaluation* for performance feedback, the ACHIEVE model was developed. The seven factors in the model are listed as follows:

A— Ability
C— Clarity
H— Help
I — Incentive
E— Evaluation
V— Validity
E— Environment

Using the Achieve Model

In using the ACHIEVE model the manager evaluates how each factor will affect the present or potential performance of followers for a given task. Then the manager should take the steps that "fit" the unique cause(s) of the performance problem. The seven factors in the ACHIEVE model, along with typical problem-solving alternatives are

A—Ability (knowledge and skills). In the ACHIEVE model the term *ability* refers to the follower's knowledge and skills—the ability to complete the specific task successfully. It is important to remember that individuals are not universally competent. Key components of ability include task-relevant education (formal and informal training that facilitates the successful completion of the specific task); task-relevant experience (prior work experience that contributes to the successful completion of the task); and task-relevant aptitudes (potential or traits that enhance the successful completion of the task). In analyzing follower performance, the manager should ask, Does this follower have the knowledge and skills to complete this task successfully?

If the person has an ability problem, solutions may include specific training, coaching, formal educational courses, or reassignment of specific duties or responsibilities. These alternatives should be considered from the viewpoint of cost effectiveness.

C—Clarity (understanding or role perception). Clarity refers to an understanding and acceptance of what to do, when to do it, and how to do it. To have a thorough understanding of the job, the follower needs to be clear on the major goals and objectives, how these goals and objectives should be accomplished, and the priority of goals and objectives (which objectives are most important at what times).

If the follower has a problem in clarity or understanding, there may well be a problem in the performance-planning phase. In many cases, oral agreement on objectives is insufficient. The manager should assure that all objectives are formally recorded. The follower should be encouraged to ask questions for further clarification.

H—Help (organizational support). The term *help* refers to the organizational help, or support, that the follower needs for effective task completion. Some organizational support factors might include adequate budget, equipment and facilities that are suitable for task completion, necessary support from other departments, product availability and quality, and an adequate supply of human resources.

If there is a lack of help or organizational support, managers should clearly identify where the problem exists. If the problem is lack of money, human resources, equipment, or facilities, the manager should see whether the necessary resources can be acquired in a cost-effective manner. If the resources cannot be acquired, the manager may have to revise objectives to avoid holding followers responsible for circumstances beyond their control.

I—Incentive (motivation or willingness). The term *incentive* refers to the follower's task-relevant incentive—the motivation to complete the specific task under analysis in a successful manner. In evaluating incentive it is important to remember that most people are not equally motivated to complete all tasks. Followers tend to be more motivated toward the successful completion of tasks that will bring them either intrinsic or extrinsic rewards.

If the follower has an incentive problem, the first step is to check the use of rewards and punishments. The follower should clearly understand that performance on this task is related to pay, promotion, recognition, and job security. Research indicates that managers sometimes hope followers will engage in certain behaviors without rewarding these behaviors.[13] People have a natural tendency to pursue tasks that are rewarded and to avoid tasks that are not. Rewards can be tangible or intangible; feedback on performance, such as recognition or a pat on the back, can be an important part of the overall incentive system.

E—Evaluation (coaching and performance feedback). Evaluation refers to informal day-to-day performance feedback as well as formal periodic reviews. An effective feedback process lets followers know how well they are doing the job on a regular basis. It is unrealistic to expect followers to improve performance if they are unaware that performance problems exist. People should know how they are being evaluated on a regular basis before their formal periodic evaluation occurs. Many performance problems can be caused by a lack of necessary coaching and performance feedback.

If there is an evaluation problem, it may be caused by the lack of day-to-day feedback on both effective and ineffective performance. Many managers tend to focus on the bad news and forget to recognize when things are going well. Recognition for a job well done can be a vital part of the ongoing evaluation process. It can increase motivation and cost the organization very little.

One method that helps to highlight extremes in performance is the "significant incident" process, which includes formally documenting highly positive or negative performance. This ensures that the follower receives feedback that is part of the formal record.

V—Validity (valid and legal personnel practices). The term *validity* refers to the appropriateness and legality of human resources decisions made by the manager. Managers need to make sure that decisions about people are appropriate in light of laws, court decisions, and company policies. The manager should make sure that personnel practices do not discriminate against any specific group or individual and should be aware that organizations need valid and legal performance evaluations, training and promotion criteria selection techniques, and so on.

If there is a validity problem, the manager should know that the trend of the law in management is clear: personnel decisions need to be documented and justified on the basis of performance-oriented criteria. Managers uncertain about validity issues should discuss them with the personnel department or the organization's legal office.

E—Environment (environmental fit). The term *environment* refers to the external factors that can influence performance even if the individual has all the ability, clarity, help, and incentive needed to do the job. Key elements of the environmental factors include competition, changing market conditions, government regulations, suppliers, and so on.

If there is an environmental problem beyond their control, followers should not be rewarded or reprimanded for performance. In short, followers should be expected to perform at a level consistent with the limitations of their environment.

As stated earlier, performance management integrates the widely used Situational Leadership concept and the ACHIEVE model. In explaining how to implement performance management, the major steps required in performance planning will be outlined, including the coaching process that can be used to reinforce performance plans and develop followers. Finally, guidelines on conducting the formal performance review, which completes the performance management cycle, will be provided.

THE THREE FUNCTIONS OF PERFORMANCE MANAGEMENT

Performance management includes three major functions:

1. *Performance planning*—setting objectives and directions for followers at the beginning of a planning period and developing plans for achieving these objectives.
2. *Coaching*—day-to-day feedback and development activities aimed at the enhancement of performance plans.
3. *Performance review*—overall evaluation of performance for the specific planning period.

The situational approach to performance management enables managers to individualize performance planning, coaching, and review by choosing managerial techniques that fit the unique situation faced by each of their followers.

Performance Planning

Many traditional MBO approaches indicate that managers and followers should always develop objectives in a joint decision-making process. Situational Leadership suggests that degrees of joint decision making may be appropriate for followers at moderate readiness levels (R2 or R3) but not as appropriate with followers who have very high or very low readiness levels (R1 or R4).

In cases where followers have low readiness levels for setting certain goals, managers may be better off setting the goals and communicating them to the low-readiness level follower. In cases where follower readiness is extremely high, followers may take the key role in the goal-setting process due to their readiness regarding a particular task. If the follower is at a very high readiness level it may be acceptable (and even desirable) for the follower to take the major leadership responsibility in setting more specific objectives. In summary, Situational Leadership suggests that managers should involve followers in the performance-planning process at a level consistent with the follower's readiness concerning the task under discussion.

Another use of Situational Leadership in the performance-planning process involves the idea of contracting for leadership style.[14] In setting objectives it is not enough for the manager and follower to determine what objectives should be achieved; it is also useful for them to agree upon their respective roles in the achievement of objectives. Managers and followers should agree up front on the degree of managerial involvement expected for each specific task. Managers should let followers know where structure and direction can be expected and where delegation may be appropriate. By clarifying their roles in the performance-planning process, both managers and followers can help avoid unnecessary stress and surprises in the implementation phase.

One weakness of many MBO-type systems is that the manager and follower negotiate only for what the follower is going to contribute. The ACHIEVE system suggests that the manager and follower also need to get a clear idea of what needed support the organization is going to contribute. Using the ACHIEVE model in performance planning, the manager can deal with questions such as, Does the follower have the ability to do the job? Does the follower clearly understand what to do and how to do it? What degree of support is needed from the organization? Is there a process for ongoing coaching and feedback?

The ACHIEVE model gives the manager a clear analysis of performance potential. If any problems appear to exist, the manager should address these problems before the individual is assigned specific objectives. For example, if the manager feels the follower lacks ability, necessary training should occur before the follower starts unsuccessfully trying to achieve the objective.

An analysis of each performance factor in the ACHIEVE model before the follower starts to work increases the probability of setting challenging, realistic objectives. Special attention should be paid to the validity factor. If performance objectives have been set in a way that may unfairly discriminate against any individual or group, the company personnel staff may be contacted and the objectives changed.

Coaching

Managers can develop a situational approach to coaching by actually using the leadership styles contracted for during the performance-planning process.

In coaching, Situational Leadership helps managers make clear connections between their leadership styles, the objectives set in the performance-planning process, and the follower's readiness level for achieving each specific objective.

One serious problem mangers have in coaching is the lack of sufficient analysis before making a coaching intervention.[15] Managers can use the ACHIEVE model to analyze performance problems quickly before deciding what remedial actions to take.

Performance problems need to be faced as early as possible—before they turn into disasters. Managers observing a problem in its early stages often refrain from taking action because they hope the problems will go away. Very seldom does this happen. With the ACHIEVE model, the manager has a quick mental checklist for day-to-day problem solving that can be used without formal meetings, documents, or office appointments. After using the ACHIEVE model to diagnose a unique problem, the manager can dramatically increase the probability of making a problem-solving intervention that fits the situation faced by the follower.

In the final performance appraisal meeting between manager and follower there should be no surprises. If the manager has done a thorough job of performance planning and day-to-day coaching, both parties should see this meeting as a review of what happened during the planning period. The manager can use Situational Leadership to determine the degree of follower involvement in the formal review process.

Managers may want followers at high readiness levels to complete self-evaluations, which can be discussed before final managerial ratings. Followers at moderate readiness levels may require a joint decision-making process, with the degree of follower direction depending on readiness level for each specific goal. Followers at low readiness levels may require a directive review, with most of the information going from the manager to the follower. Managers can use a situational approach to avoid the issue of determining what levels of follower participation in reviews are "good" or "bad."

The Situational Leadership framework allows followers to engage in the degree of participation that works for their particular review.

In the final performance review mangers can use the ACHIEVE model to analyze why performance results did or did not meet the standards set in the performance-planning process. After the causes of performance problems have been determined by the manager and follower, developmental strategies can be designed to fit the specific performance problems that have occurred. The ACHIEVE model can help the manager attain specific performance-related data that can be used in future training, transfer, and personnel decisions. The ACHIEVE model also helps managers decide whether failure to meet performance standards was due to a lack of follower performance or managerial, organizational, or environmental problems.

Performance management builds upon the basic philosophy of Situational Leadership. There is no one best way to solve human resource problems. The manager should use the problem-solving strategy tht best fits the needs of followers in their unique situations. Performance management provides managers with easy-to-use guidelines for analyzing work situations, determining why performance problems may exist, and choosing solution strategies to fit the problems faced by their followers.

Also, a significant benefit of the situational approach to performance management is that it provides an effective framework that trainers can use for developing managers in performance planning, coaching, and review.

The next two chapters will present one of the most important concepts in the behavioral sciences in recent years, One Minute Management. Chapter 17 will introduce One Minute Management, while Chapter 18 will discuss the concepts of putting One Minute Management to work, including the interrelation of Situational Leadership and One Minute Management.

NOTES

1. Alan A. Yelsey, "Strategies and Actions for Improving Organizational Performance," *Academy of Management Review*, June 1984, p. 25.

2. *Ibid*, p. 26.

3. See, for example, the increasing importance of human resources in "Human Resources Managers Aren't Corporate Nobodies Anymore," *Business Week*, December 2, 1987, pp. 58–59. See also William A. Medlin, "Managing People to Perform," *The Bureaucrat*, Spring 1985, pp. 52–55; Jac Fritz Enz, "Human Resource: Formulas for Success," *Personnel Journal*, 64, No. 10 (October 1985), pp. 52–60; Philip H. Mirvis, "Formulating and Implementating Human Resource Strategy," *Human Resource Management*, 24, No. 4 (Winter 1985), pp. 385–412.

4. Ian C. MacMillan and Randall S. Schuler, "Gaining a Competitive Edge through Human Resources," *Personnel*, April 1985, p. 24. See also Dave Ulrich, "Human Resource Planning as a Competitive Edge," *Human Resource Planning*, 9, No. 2 (1986), pp. 41–49.

5. *Ibid*., p. 27.

6. *Ibid*., p. 28.

7. *Ibid*., p. 28–29.

8. This section on the ACHIEVE model is adapted from Paul Hersey and Marshall Goldsmith, "A Situational Approach to Performance Planning," *Training and Development*, 34 (November 1980), pp. 38–40.

9. This has been a primary research objective at the Center for Leadership Studies.

10. J. W. Atkinson, *An Introduction to Motivation* (New York: Van Nostrand, 1958).

11. Lyman Porter and Edward Lawler, *Managerial Attitudes and Performance* (Homewood, Ill.: Irwin, 1968. See also G. Miller, "Management Guidelines: The Right Perspective," *Supervisory Management*, 26 (March 1981), pp. 22–28; Charles R. Gowen, "Managing Work Group Performance by Individual Goals and Group Goals for an Interdependent Group Task," *Journal of Organizational Behavior*, 7, No. 3 (Winter 1986), pp. 5–27.

12. Jay Lorsch and Paul Lawrence, "The Diagnosis of Organizational Problems" in Newton Margulies and Anthony P. Raia, *Organizational Development: Values, Processes, and Technology* (New York: McGraw-Hill, 1972).

13. Steven Kerr, "On the Folly of Hoping for A While Rewarding B," *Academy of Management Journal*, 4 (1975), pp. 76–79. See also Thomas Kemper, "Motivation and Behavior, A Personal View," *Journal of General Management*, 9, No. 3 (Fall 1983), pp. 51–57; Martin Gevans, "Organizational Behavior: The Central Role of Motivation," *Journal of Management*, 12, No. 2 (Summer 1986), pp. 203–222.

14. See discussion in Chapter 12.

15. Ferdinand Fournies, *Coaching for Improved Work Performance* (New York: Van Nostrand, 1978).

CHAPTER 17

IMPLEMENTING SITUATIONAL LEADERSHIP:
One Minute Management

The previous chapters have introduced and elaborated upon the Situational Leadership model, including a discussion of the behavioral science foundations of modern leadership theory. These chapters, and the ones that follow, illustrate adaptations and extensions of Situational Leadership that have been developed by the Center for Leadership Studies and other internationally recognized management development organizations with extensive experience in working with managers, administrators, teachers, parents, and other leaders concerned with improving human performance.

Several of the concepts presented in this chapter were more academically discussed in previous chapters, especially Chapter 10, "Developing Human Resources," and Chapter 11, "Constructive Discipline." In this chapter, however, the concepts are presented with more of an eye toward implementation. For example, a previous discussion of behavior modification and reinforcement theory focused on its importance in shaping human performance. While the concepts associated with those two theories are powerful, they have not been used widely in organizations per se for two reasons. First, the terminology—*reinforcement, extinction, successive approximations* and the like—is not palatable to most managers. The terms are too academic. Second, the concepts have been associated with animal research and have a connotation of controlled manipulation; that is, getting people to do what *you* want them to do, not necessarily what *they* want to do. In this chapter managers are shown how the theories discussed earlier in this book can be applied to day-to-day management situations. For example, we translate the theory of behavior modification into the more memorable technique of "catching people doing things right."

Spencer Johnson and Blanchard attempted to overcome some of the objections to the academic nature of behavior modification in their best-selling book, *The One Minute Manager*.[1] The book focused on three powerful concepts derived from behavior modification principles: One Minute Goal Setting, One Minute Praisings, and One Minute Reprimands. The notion of a "One Minute Manager" was developed to encourage managers to take an extra minute to make sure they are focusing on those things that have the most impact in obtaining desired performance from workers. Managers need to concentrate on setting clear goals with their people, praising good performance, and reprimanding or redirecting poor performance when necessary.

This chapter is primarily based on the work of Blanchard and his colleagues at Blanchard Training & Development Inc., a human resources organization based in Escondido, California. Since 1981, associates at BTD have been implementing and refining the One Minute Management concepts with their version of Situational Leadership[2] into the management systems of organizations throughout the United States and abroad.

ONE MINUTE GOAL SETTING

The first key to being a One Minute Manager is One Minute Goal Setting. All good performance starts with clear goals. This involves making sure that all employees are clear about two things: what they are being asked to do (their areas of accountability) and what good performance looks like (performance standards by which they will be evaluated). While these two stipulations may seem simple, they are often lacking in organizations.

Areas of Accountability

To obtain desired performance from its employees, an organization must first have a well-defined accountability system. For example, when employees are asked what they do and their managers are asked what their people do, widely divergent answers typically are given. This is particularly so if each group is asked to prioritize their list of responsibilities. As a consequence, individuals in organizations often get punished for not doing what they didn't know they were supposed to do in the first place.

One of the biggest obstacles to productivity improvement stems from this problem of unclear organizational expectations and accountability. At times those individuals whom management deems most responsible for a specific activity may be unaware of their role altogether. For example, a group of restaurant managers concerned about sales were asked: "Who is responsible for generating sales in your organization?" The almost unanimous reply was: "The waiters and waitresses." But when the waiters and waitresses were asked what the primary responsibilities of their jobs were, their reply was consistently: "Serving food and taking orders." No reference was made to selling. So although it may seem very basic, managers need to make sure their people know what is expected of them.

Performance Standards

Employees must also know what good performance looks like. This is accomplished through *performance standards*. Performance standards help managers and employees more easily monitor performance and serve as a basis for evaluation. To determine whether an organization has clear performance standards, employees can be asked: "Are you doing a good job?" Most people will respond to this question by saying: "Yes, I think so." A revealing follow-up question would then be: "How do you know?" The typical response: "I haven't been criticized by my manager lately." Such an answer implies that employees receive very little encouragement concerning mistakes or delays. This is a sad state of affairs. A habitual practice by managers leads to the most commonly used management style in America: the "leave alone/zap," S4–S1 style of management, discussed in Chapter 11, "Constructive Discipline." This style of managing can also be called "seagull management." A seagull manager flies in, makes a lot of noise, dumps on everyone, and flies out. Since this is the predominant style of management in most organizations, it is no wonder that the motivation of people is a major organizational behavior problem today.

Scott Meyers,[3] a long-time consultant in the field of motivation, makes the same point with a novel analogy. Meyers was struck by the contrast between workers when they worked and the same individuals when they were involved in a social or recreational activity, such as bowling. While bowling, it was common to see someone get excited after throwing a strike—perhaps the person would jump up and down or yell. The same individual would seldom if ever get as excited at work. Meyers wondered why they didn't. He posed the questions: "Why aren't people jumping up and down and yelling in most organizations?" and "What can be done to make work a more exciting environment and workers more highly motivated?"

Goals Need to Be Clear

The reasons people are not yelling in organizations, Meyers contends, is in part because it is not clear what is expected of them. To continue his bowling analogy, when they approach the alley, they notice there are no pins at the other end; that is, they don't know what their goals are. How long would you want to bowl without any pins? Yet every day in the world of work, people are bowling without any pins, and as a result cannot tell how well they are doing.

Reaching Goals Requires Feedback

A second obstacle to obtaining good performance involves feedback to employees on how they are doing. It's as if when an employee goes to bowl, a sheet is covering the pins. When the ball is rolled down the alley, it goes through the sheet and a crack is heard. When asked, "How did you do?" an employee might reply: "I don't know, but I thought it was OK." To move toward goals, employees need feedback on their performance.

This feedback can serve to motivate employees. There seems to be adequate evidence that the number one motivator of people is feedback on results. Another way of emphasizing this is with the slogan: "Feedback is the Breakfast of Champions."[4] Can you image training for the Olympics with no one telling you how fast you had run or how high you had jumped? The idea seems ludicrous, yet many employees operate in a vacuum, without knowing essential information to do their jobs well—if at all.

Money is only a motivator of people if it's feedback on results. Have you ever gotten a raise that you were pleased with only to find out that somebody else who you don't think works as hard as you got the same or even a better raise? Not only is that increase in money *not motivating*, it became *demotivating* once you know it had nothing to do with results. Suddently, it didn't seem to matter how hard you worked at all.

Once managers are convinced that the number one motivator of people is feedback on results, they usually start giving feedback—but not always the right type. Back to our analogy: When employees go to the line to roll the ball, they notice that the boss is standing on the other side of the sheet. When the ball is rolled down the alley, it goes through the sheet, they hear a crack, and then the boss holds up two fingers and says, "You knocked down two." In fact, most bosses would not phrase the feedback so positively but would say, "You missed eight." Thus we come to a central point that will be elaborated upon later in this chapter as well as in the next chapter: Positive feedback is more effective at shaping desired performance than negative feedback.

Performance Review Can Undermine Performance

Why don't managers lift the sheet so everyone can see the pins? Because there is a strong tradition in organizations known as the performance review. We called it NIHYYSOB, and it stands for "Now I have you, you S.O.B." Sadly, many managers use the performance review as a once-a-year opportunity to get even with an employee.

The performance review process is also used to spread people over a distribution curve, thus categorizing employees and distorting their performance. In most organizations, if you have six or seven people reporting to you, the practice of rating them all high—even if they all deserve it—is discouraged. For example, it doesn't take managers very long to realize that if they rate all of their people high, then they subsequently will get rated low by *their* managers. The only way they can get rated high is if they rate some of their people low. This practice is often encouraged by having a set budget or percentage for a group's salary increases.

One of the toughest jobs a manager can have is to decide who gets the low ratings. Most Americans grew up with this win-lose mentality in which some people in every group must lose. It pervades our educational system. For example, a fifth grade teacher giving a test on state capitals to her class would never consider making atlases available during the test to allow the class to get up and look up the answers. Why not? Because all the children would get 100. Can you imagine what would happen to American education if kids who had to take vocabulary tests were allowed dictionaries on their desks? There would be an uproar!

As we discussed in the last chapter, "Managing People to Perform," Hersey and Goldsmith have identified three parts of a performance review: (1) performance planning, in which you set the goals and objectives (2) day-to-day coaching, in which you work with your people to help them reach their goals; and (3) performance evaluation, in which you evaluate progress toward goals. Of these three steps, most organizations tend to start with performance evaluation. The personnel department comes up with some form to be filled out once a year on every employee. Then somebody might say that some goals ought to be set. Notebooks are filled with goals and job descriptions—many of which are never looked at until someone decides a year or more later that they should be revised. The only part of the performance-review process that is seldom done on a systematic basis is the most important of the three steps: day-to-day coaching. The primary value of Situational Leadership is obtained in working daily with people at different levels of readiness to help them win.

Limit the Number of Goals

All the research on high performance shows that three to five goals are the ideal number of goals peak performers concentrate on. Remember Pareto's 80/20 rule: 80 percent of the results you want to obtain from people comes from 20 percent of their activites. Therefore, you want to limit the number of goals employees have and attempt to identify the few key activities that will have the highest impact and yield the greatest results. Once these goals are established, they should be written down so they can be frequently used to compare actual behavior against targeted behavior.

Often goal setting is considered a paperwork activity—a necessary evil of organizational life but one that seemingly has little value in getting the job done. When this is the case, goals are filed and people go off and do whatever they want until a performance review draws near. In One Minute Goal Setting the philosophy is that you should keep your goals close at hand. Goals should be able to be read in a minute and be written in no more than 250 words.

Although most managers we've worked with agree with the importance of setting goals, many do not take the time to clearly develop their own goals and to write them down. They tend to get caught in the "activity trap," in which they become busy doing things but not necessarily the right things—that is, those activities they would deem most important. To help out with this problem, Kelsey Tyson and Drea Zigarmi have developed two instruments[5] managers can use to set goals for both themselves and those with whom they work. These instruments systematically guide the user through nine steps for establishing goals in a way that increases the probability for their successful achievement. We will briefly discuss each of these steps.

Step 1: Setting Goals "What is the person's job?" Specifically list the most important activities you want a person to accomplish in the next three to six months.

Step 2: Setting Priorities "Which goals are most important?" Rank the priority of achieving the goals, with a specific deadline for each goal.

Step 3: Measurable Indicators "How will you know if the person is doing the job well?" This should include two or three specific variables within the person's control that need to be tracked for changes and improvements.

Step 4: Standards of Performance "What does outstanding performance look like?" There should be minimal, acceptable, and outstanding levels of performance determined for each goal. For example, different amounts of time or different degrees of quality, quantity and cost.

Step 5: Incentives and Benefits "What will the person gain by doing a good job?" These can include such items as increased autonomy, flextime, increased responsibilities, or additional money.

Step 6: Obstacles to Goal Accomplishment "What could get in the way of accomplishing the person's goals?" Consider both factors within the person's control and likely factors beyond personal control.

Step 7: Action Steps "What steps will the person take to accomplish the goals?" Determine what is the most feasible plan for success, including the help and support that will be needed from others. Most goals can be successfully accomplished in a variety of ways.

Step 8: Praising and Rewards "What happens if the goal is accomplished?" Recognition should be planned for both final completion and progress toward final completion. Don't overlook one of the simplest yet important and powerful forms of recognition: sincere appreciation.

Step 9: Reprimands and Redirection "What happens if the goal is not accomplished?" If the person has the necessary skills to complete a task but doesn't, the person should be reprimanded. If the person lacks the necessary skills, redirection is more appropriate. When redirecting, goals and action steps are redetermined and the person tries again.

Diagnosing Blocks to Goal-setting

If the goal-setting process is unsuccessful, check the goals you have set for clarity, feasibility, and unanticipated problems, using the following questions, also taken from Tyson and Zigarmi's instruments:[6]

> Are the time lines you have established realistic? Will other competing demands cause delay? Will the person be able to overcome those demands to accomplish the goals you have agreed on, on time?
>
> How central to the long-range goals of your department are the goals that you have established?
>
> Will the goals you have established have the impact you want for the effort needed to achieve them?
>
> How will these goals help move the company ahead? Are the goals in keeping with the prevailing thrust of the organization?
>
> How will these goals help the person develop new skills? How will these goals help him or her to build confidence? What is the likely reaction if the employee fails to achieve the predetermined goals? Will the person be able to accept a reprimand if necessary or redirection to get back on track?

Good Goals Are SMART Goals

SMART is an acronym for the most important factors in setting quality goals.

S—Specific. You just don't say to somebody, "I want you to improve." The area and method of improving must be specifically defined.

M—Measurable. An important thing to remember is, "If you can't measure it, you can't manage it." Therefore, the goals have to be observable and measurable. If somebody says, "That leaves my job out—you can't measure my job" offer to eliminate it to see if it will be missed.

A—Attainable. You need to be able to reach your goals and stretch yourself in the process. This relates back to the research conducted by David McClelland on achievement motivation, presented in Chapter 2, "Motivation and Behavior." He found that high achievers like to set moderately difficult but obtainable goals; that is, goals that stretch the individual.

R—Relevant. You want to set goals in areas that are important to the job.

T—Trackable. You need to set interim goals so that people's progress can be praised along the way. If a goal consists of completing a report due June 1, the chances of receiving an acceptable report will increase if interim reports are required. Remember, good performance is a journey, not a destination. The goal is the destination. What managers have to do is manage the journey. This is best done through One Minute Praisings.

THE ONE MINUTE PRAISING

Once your people are clear on what you are asking them to do and what good behavior looks like, you are ready for the second key to obtaining desired performance: One Minute Praisings. Praising is the most powerful activity a manager can do. In fact, it is the key to training people and making winners of everyone working for you. The One Minute Praising focuses on reinforcing behavior that is moving an employee closer to the goals. While all the keys of the One Minute Manager—Goal Setting, Praising, Reprimanding—are important, One Minute Praising is the most important. Look around your organization and see if you can "catch people doing something right." When you do, give them a One Minute Praising that is immediate and specific, and share your feelings.

Be Immediate and Specific

In order for praising to be effective, it must be *immediate and specific.* Tell people exactly what they did right as soon as possible. For example, "You submitted your report on time Friday and it was well written; in fact, I used it in a meeting today and that report made you and me and our whole department look good." Use examples such as, "I see productivity in your department is up ten percent" or "Your report helped us win the contract with the Jones Company." If comments are too general, such as "Appreciate your efforts," "Thank you very much," "I don't know what I'd do without you," or "Keep up the good work," they are less likely to seem sincere and thus are not likely to be effective. Instead of praising people at random, first find out what they have done right. A manager should schedule time to observe employees' behavior and specifically praise improvements that are noticed.

State Your Feelings

After you praise employees, tell them how you *feel* about what they did. Don't intellectualize. State your gut feelings: "Let me tell you how I feel. I was so proud after hearing your financial report presentation at the Board of Director's meeting that I want you to know I really feel good about your being on our team. Thanks a lot." Although praisings do not take very long, they can have lasting effects. To help managers master the important skill of praising, Tyson and Zigarmi developed The One Minute Manager Praising Planning Guide.[7] This instrument systematically takes the user through the steps for a quality praising on a specific person who works for or with the manager. It lists sample items, questions for consideration in planning specific praisings, and a means for evaluating the effectiveness of praisings after they are delivered. Following are some sample questions from the instrument.

Pre-Planning Analysis

Are you considering a praising because you feel good today or because you feel the person deserves the praise?

Is the praising related to performance demonstrated in accomplishing a new task assignment or to the improved performance of previously performed tasks/assignments?

Have you praised this person before for the same behavior?

Is there a chance that the person will feel manipulated by the praising?

Were any other people involved whom you should praise?

Post-Planning Analysis

Did the praising result in increased commitment and motivation for you and the person being praised?

Did you deliver any "bad news" or assign additional work as part of the praising? If so, why?

Did you add a "but" and give some critical feedback?

Praisings drive all effective human interaction. These same concepts apply to any relationship, not only making people better managers but also better parents, spouses, friends, and customers. Consider marriage, for example. A recent study reported that second marriages are breaking up at a higher rate than first marriages. This is grimly amusing because some people argue that success in marriage is merely a matter of selection—that if you could only get a second chance, you could do much better. What this study confirmed was that, "if you are a jerk in one relationship, you'll probably be a jerk in your next relationship as well"—*unless* you learn the basics of human interaction.

Just trace the demise of a love relationship. When people fall in love, they seldom see the faults or limitations of the loved one. Have you ever seen a couple in love in a restaurant? When one is talking, the other is very attentive—listening, smiling, and supporting. They don't seem to care if their meal ever comes.

In contrast, have you ever seen a couple in a restaurant who are not really happy together? They may look as if they have nothing to say to each other. They may not say four sentences to each other in two-and-a-half hours. Perhaps the man finally says, "How is your meal?" And the woman counters with, "Fine! How's yours?" That is the extent of their conversation. Their marriage is dead, but nobody has buried it!

How do two people go from being excited over each other's words to having nothing to say? It's really quite simple. Good relationships are all about the frequency with which you catch each other doing something right!

When you first fall in love, everything is right. Then when you decide to get married or commit to some permanency in your relationship, you often start to see things wrong with each other. You begin to say things such as, "I didn't know that!" or "That's strange you should do something like that!" After awhile you might become critical, and your emphasis is on what's wrong with the other person, rather than what's right. In fact, the final demise of a loving relationship is when you do something right and you get yelled at because you didn't do it *exactly* right—"You had to ask" or "You should have done it earlier."

Being Close Counts

This brings up one of the most important points to remember about praising. Don't wait for exactly the right behavior before praising; catch people doing things *approximately* right. What we expect from each other is exactly right behavior. And yet, if you wait for exactly right behavior before you recognize it, you'll probably never get it. What we have to remember is that *exactly right* behavior is made up of a whole series of *approximately right* behaviors.

Bob Davis, president of Chevron Chemical, has as one of his favorite mottos: "Praise progress—it's at least a moving target." What a powerful statement! What we need to do in all of our interactions at work and at home is to reward or praise people for performing.

Another example is childrearing. Teenagers are a problem for many parents. Why? Before kids become teenagers, their parents think they are "cute," and when "cute" kids do something wrong they are usually forgiven. Cute kids are caught doing things approximately right. But the minute teenagers walk in the house, they get yelled at. "Where have you been?" or "Why didn't you do this?" or "That sure was a stupid mistake." It doesn't take teenagers long to figure out that they don't like hanging around at home. Parents lose influence with their children because they catch them doing things wrong more frequently than they catch them doing things right.

Think about this in relation to your children. Parents tell us they can't understand why their children are so different. For example, "Mary is a model child. She does well in school, helps around the house, is polite and friendly to adults. But Harry and Alice—my other children—are nothing but trouble." In every case we find that Mary is caught doing things right, while Harry and Alice are caught doing things wrong.

If you are having difficulty with a spouse, a child, an employee, your boss, or friends, ask yourself, "Do I want this relationship to work?" When you are looking for an answer, go to your gut feelings. If deep down you don't want to make the relationship work, you won't. Why? Because you have control of the qualifier—the "yes, but." If you want to make the relationship work, you will catch the other person doing things right. But if you don't want to make it work, for whatever reason, you can easily undermine another person's best efforts to please you. No matter what that person does right, you will say, "Yes, but . . . you didn't do this or that right."

Make Time for Praisings

You should set aside at least two hours a week for "praisings." Write it on your calendar just like your appointments. Then use the Hewlett-Packard philosophy of MBWA—Management by Wandering Around—made famous by Peters and Waterman in their book *In Search of Excellence.*[8] Wander around your operation and catch people doing things right—and tell them about it. Do the same with your spouse, children, friends. At home you may not need two hours per week—but ten minutes surely wouldn't hurt. Are you doing that much?

Try it. You'll like catching people doing things right. It will put a spring in your step and a sparkle in your eye. And just imagine what it will do for the people you catch!

THE ONE MINUTE REPRIMAND

People often comment about One Minute Management, as they do of other research-based behavioral science approaches, "It just isn't tough enough." They say, "In the real world you have to be tough. The third key to One Minute Management focuses on reprimanding others.

There are four keys to remember about a reprimand. First, as with One Minute Praising, reprimand as *soon as possible* after an incident. Do not save up your feelings. If you "gunnysack" and store up your feelings, when you finally let go of them, they are apt to be out of proportion to the event that triggered your emotional release. This will make the mistake—and the situation—seem much worse than it really is. Such is often the case with personality attacks. The longer you wait to give someone negative feedback, the more emotional it becomes. So give negative feedback as soon as possible—it causes fewer problems.

Second, *be specific*. Tell people specifically what they did wrong. For example, "John, you didn't get your report in on time on Friday" or "I notice your sales were down twenty percent this quarter" or whatever. Be specific with people.

Third, *share your feelings* about what was done. "Let me tell you how I feel about the late report, John. I'm angry because everyone else got their report in on time and not having your report delayed my analysis of our market position. It really frustrated me!" Don't intellectualize about what the person did wrong—it is more important to just focus on how you feel. Describe your feelings sincerely and honestly.

Fourth—and this is probably the most important of the steps—*reaffirm* the person. In the late report example, you might say: "Let me tell you one other thing. You're good. You're one of my best people. That's why I was angry about your late report. It's so unlike you. I count on you to set an example for others. That's why I'm not going to let you get away with that late report behavior. You're better than that."

To help managers integrate these steps into their own behavior, Tyson and Zigarmi developed The One Minute Manager Reprimand Planning Guide,[9] which—like the Praising Planning Guide—can be used to focus on actual people and situations with which a manager works. Following are some of the questions from the instrument.

Pre-Reprimand Analysis

Is this person a learner or has he or she previously demonstrated expertise in the area of responsibility?

What are the specific behaviors that you want discontinued? What behavior/performance do you want increased?

Are you convinced that this poor performance is within the control of the person you are about to reprimand?

Why do you feel you should reprimand rather than redirect?

What are the possible positive and negative outcomes of this reprimand?

Post-Reprimand Analysis

Was the reprimand given as soon after the behavior as possible?

Did you affirm their past performance in this area?

Did you threaten or attack the person personally?

Did you pause in order to let the reprimand sink in and to let go of your feelings?

Reprimand Behavior, Not the Person

Many people can't understand why you would praise someone just after you have reprimanded them. You do it for two very important reasons. First, you want to separate people's behavior from them as individuals. That is, you want to keep the people but get rid of their poor behavior. By reaffirming people after you have reprimanded them, you focus on their behavior without attacking them personally.

Second, when you walk away after reprimanding, you want people thinking about what they did wrong, not about how you treated them. If no reaffirmation is done, people who are reprimanded tend to direct their energy back to you, the reprimander. Why? Because of the way they are treated. For example, many reprimands not only don't end with a praising but with a comment such as, "And let me tell you one other thing . . ." and then the individual is given one last shot—". . . if you think you're going to get that promotion, you have another thing coming."

Then when you walk away, the person who has been reprimanded often turns to a co-worker and instead of discussing the poor performance, talks about the incident and the manager's poor performance. That person is psychologically off the hook with the poor behavior, and the manager becomes the villain.

If, however, you end a reprimand with a praising, the person you reprimand is less likely to turn to a co-worker and complain about you after you walk away because you just told that individual how good the person was. Now that person has to think about what was wrong, not about your leadership style.

Many problems in life stem not from making mistakes but from not *learning from* our mistakes. Whenever we do not learn from our mistakes, it is often because we are attacked personally for those mistakes. We are called names such as idiot or stupid and generally downgraded by other people who discover our mistakes.

When our self-concept is under attack, we feel the need to defend ourselves and our actions, even to the extent of distorting the facts. When people become defensive, they never hear the feedback they are getting. As a result, little learning takes place. The effective use of the One Minute Reprimand with someone who makes a mistake will hopefully eliminate this defensive behavior.

Remember, people are OK. It is just their behavior that is sometimes a problem. The proper use of the One Minute Reprimand will help to communicate important information necessary to get poor performance back on track. How the One Minute Management skills are used together to achieve better performance is discussed in greater detail in *The One Minute Manager* and graphically presented in The One Minute Manager Gameplan.[10]

THE ONE MINUTE APOLOGY

Since everyone makes mistakes, the ability to apologize is a valuable addition to the three original One Minute Management skills. The One Minute Apology has the same first three steps as the One Minute Praising and the One Minute Reprimand. In apologizing to someone, it is important to do it as soon as possible. The longer you wait, the harder it is to say you are sorry. When you apologize, you also need to be specific with people; otherwise, you are like the little boy who hears his dad yell for him and enters the room saying "I'm sorry, I'm sorry, I'm sorry," trying to cover the possibility that he might have done something wrong. You also need to tell the other person how you feel about what you did wrong; that is, embarrassment, disappointment, remorse, or whatever.

The fourth step of the One Minute Apology is, however, slightly different from the final step of the One Minute Reprimand. Instead of reaffirming the other person by saying how the person is better than that, in the One Minute Apology you reaffirm *yourself* and say, for example, how the behavior you are apologizing for is unlike you or, "That isn't my typical behavior, and if I had thought about it more first I wouldn't have done it." So often when people do something wrong, not only do they not apologize, but they also may feel guilty for something they have done. By apologizing and reaffirming yourself, you can release the guilt for the inappropriate behavior and move forward with a stronger, more productive relationship.

Managers may be hesitant to use One Minute Apologies because (1) it might appear as a weakness and (2) there is a fear that others might use the apology against them. Both concerns are unfounded. Apologies need to be thought of as a legitimate behavioral alternative in organizations, so that managers and employees can stop expending so much energy trying to "be right" and instead more quickly pinpoint and correct problems as they arise.

Contrary to the popular phrase from Erich Segal's book *Love Story*, "Love means never having to say you're sorry,"[11] we believe that in organizations and families alike, "Love is being able to say you're sorry." One Minute Apology can help to make saying you are sorry easier and more productive.

INTEGRATION WITH SITUATIONAL LEADERSHIP

The keys of the One Minute Manager integrate well into Situational Leadership and enhance several very important aspects of that model. For example, One Minute Goal Setting starts the Contracting for the Leadership Style process, as discussed earlier in Chapter 12, "Building Effective Relationships," and elsewhere in this book. Without clear goals, people don't know where they are going. If you don't know where you are going, any road will get you there or get you lost! Once goals are clear between a manager and the employees, they will be prepared to contract for a leadership style according to their level of readiness for each of the goals. Goal setting thus fits closely with an analysis of employee readiness.

The One Minute Praising plays a key role in the *developmental cycle* of the Situational Leadership model used with employees, as discussed in

Chapter 10, "Developing Human Resources," when you are trying to increase an employee's level of readiness. When you attempt to develop somebody, remember the three key steps are to (1) provide direction, (2) let them try, and (3) reinforce good behavior. Praising comes into play when you observe performance and catch employees doing the right things. Praising is thus crucial in the reinforcement process. Praising is one of the driving forces moving a manager from the more directive leadership styles to the participating and delegating styles. Praising is thus a very important part of the developmental process.

The One Minute Reprimand comes into play in the *regressive cycle* of the Situational Leadership model when an employee declines in level of readiness. For example, when you have delegated to someone and something goes wrong so that task is not completed properly, you should return to a participating style to find out what went wrong. After you know what went wrong, you can decide whether the performance failure was due to a lack of ability or a lack of motivation. If there is an ability problem, then you move back to an S2 style and redirect, using both direction and support. If there is a motivation problem, the reprimand can be effective. Reprimanding is also a selling style, in that you are directing the person—being honest about what the person has done wrong—but also providing supportive behavior with the use of the reaffirmation.

In summary, three of the secrets of The One Minute Manager—One Minute Goal Setting, Praisings, and Reprimands—describe three management behaviors that are key to making Situational Leadership come alive for managers. Goal setting is a key part of Contracting for Leadership Style—it permits a manager to analyze task-specific aspects of an employee's level of readiness. One Minute Praising is an important part of the developmental process, and the One Minute Reprimand is a potentially useful strategy for dealing with regressions when and if they occur.

In Chapter 18, "Implementing Situational Leadership: Effective Follow-up," we discuss other methods for successfully implementing the behavioral science concepts discussed earlier in this book.

NOTES

1. Kenneth Blanchard and Spencer Johnson, *The One Minute Manager* (New York: Morrow, 1982).
2. The version of the Situational Leadership Model advocated by Blanchard Training and Development consists of the four styles of Directing (S1), Coaching (S2), Supporting (S3), and Delegating (S4). The first publication of this version appeared in a series of three articles by Kenneth Blanchard in *Executive Excellence* during January–March 1985: "A Situational Approach to Managing People," "Situational Leadership II: A Dynamic Model for Managers and Subordinates," and "Contracting for Leadership Style: The Key to Effective Communications."
3. Scott Meyers, *Every Employee a Manager* (New York: McGraw-Hill, 1970).

4. The slogan "Feedback is the Breakfast of Champions" was coined by Rick Tate, a BTD associate, when he was conducting leadership training for the U.S. Coast Guard.

5. These instruments, Goal Setting-Self and Goal Setting-Other, are available from Blanchard Training and Development, Escondido, CA 92025.

6. *Ibid.*

7. Available from Blanchard Training and Development, Escondido, CA 92025.

8. Thomas J. Peters and Robert H. Waterman, Jr., *In Search of Excellence* (New York: Harper & Row, 1982).

9. Available from Blanchard Training and Development, Escondido, CA 92025.

10. *Ibid.*

11. Erich Segal, *Love Story* (New York: Harper & Row, 1970), p. 131.

CHAPTER 18

IMPLEMENTING SITUATIONAL LEADERSHIP:
Effective Follow-Up

We have repeatedly emphasized the difficulty organizations face in implementing applied behavioral science concepts and techniques. Research has shown that implementation is both problem laden and time consuming. This chapter addresses one of the primary reasons why most companies fail to implement their plans *most* of the time: the lack of follow-up. The problem of little or no follow-up was summarized in Kenneth Blanchard and Robert Lorber's *Putting the One Minute Manager to Work*[1] when they noted, "Most companies spend all their time looking for another management concept and very little time following up the one they have just taught their managers." It seems to be human nature to always look for the next quick fix rather than to use the knowledge and skills that already exist.

Why is this so? We believe it is because top management views training as a fringe benefit—a nice frill that can be given employees as the budget permits. Management often doesn't seem to really believe that what their people learn can make a significant and lasting difference in individual and organizational performance. It is important to overcome this false belief about training and instead become committed to making a difference with training. The veteran manager in the parable presented in *Putting the One Minute Manager to Work* said it well:

I'm enthusiastic right now and so are they, but that has happened before when a new management system has been introduced. My question is, how do you put One Minute Management to work in a way that makes a difference where it really counts—in performance?

Suppose a manager was really committed to effectively implementing One Mintute Management? What would that manager have to do? Two practical approaches, which we will discuss in depth in this chapter, are the ABC's of Management and the PRICE system.

THE ABC's OF MANAGEMENT

In *Putting the One Minute Manager to Work*, Lorber and Blanchard discussed the "ABC's of Management," which stand for A*ctivators*, *B*ehavior, and *C*onsequences.

Activators are things you have to do before you can expect good performance. The ACHIEVE model presented in Chapter 16 is a good checklist of what managers should be doing ahead of time to ensure that desired performance is obtained. Activators are essential to good performance planning.

Goal setting clearly is an activator. Before a person can be expected to perform well, you need to know what you are being asked to do and what good behavior looks like. These principles were discussed in greater depth in the last chapter. If done after performance, goal setting usually comes across to people as punitive and unfair. For example, if you ask, "Why didn't you turn in a report on the Johnson situation?" and that is the first the employee heard of the need or desire for a report, the employee might rightfully wonder: "What report?"

Behavior is the performance you want. In most of their activities, managers try to influence the performance behavior of others. This can be done primarily with activators, as was just discussed, or with consequences; that is, anything that happens after behavior.

Consequences are what follow behavior. While goal setting can set the stage for good performance, it does little to ensure the desired performance will continue. That's where managing consequences comes into play. As we discussed in Chapter 10, "Developing Human Resources," there are three main consequences that can follow someone's performance: something positive, something negative, or nothing at all. If you do something and that performance is followed by a *positive consequence*, you will want to repeat that performance. Positive consequences tend to increase the frequency of a particular behavior. If you do something and that behavior is followed by a *negative consequence*, you will probably not want to do it again. Negative consequences tend to decrease the frequency of a particular behavior.

What happens when you work hard on a project but no one seems to notice or say anything about it? You might work harder the next time to see if you get any attention. But after a while, when your hard work gets no response, motivation and subsequent performance drop. Thus, *no consequence* at all also tends to decrease the frequency of a particular behavior.

The only consequence that tends to increase the frequency of behavior is a positive consequence. And yet, the two most frequent responses people consistently get to their performance are negative responses and no responses. This leads to the "leave along/zap" style of management, mentioned in Chapter 17, that has come to be the predominant management style in most organizations.

Once managers know their ABC's, they usually want to know what impacts behavior more—activators or consequences. Most managers tend to think that activators like goal setting have more of an impact than consequences on obtaining desired behavior. We have found the reverse to be true. While activators are important, only about 20 percent of what influences people's performance come from these factors—the other 80 percent

FIGURE 18-1   The ABC's of Management
Source: Blanchard and Lorber, *Putting the One Minute Manager to Work* (New York: Morrow, 1984).

The term:

A	**B**	**C**
ACTIVATOR	BEHAVIOR	CONSEQUENCE

What it means:

What a manager does before performance	Performance: What someone says or does	What a manager does after performance

Examples:

One Minute Goal Setting • Areas of accountability • Perfomance standards • Instructions	• Writes report • Sells product • Comes to work on time • Misses deadline • Types letter • Makes mistake • Fills order	*One Minute Praising* • Immediate, specific • Shares feelings *One Minute Reprimand* • Immediate, specific • Shares feelings • Supports individual *No Response*

come from consequences. As we have said before, behavior is primarily controlled by its consequences.

The power of the ABC model for managers is that whenever somebody is not performing at the level you want, you can attribute the behavior to either an activator problem or a consequence problem. An *activator problem* could stem from a number of factors. An employee could lack training or clarity as to what to do. Also, the person may not have known what help and support was available to complete an assigned task. As mentioned, the ACHIEVE model, presented in Chapter 16, is a good activator checklist of things that should be done beforehand to obtain the desired performance.

The most common *consequence problem* occurs when employees do something and nobody says anything. The only time many employees are approached is when they do something wrong. As a result, people's performance deteriorates because they spend all of their time trying to avoid being punished or, rather, trying to avoid the punisher. It can be helpful then for managers to ask: "Why is this person not performing? Did I not provide adequate activators or am I not adequately managing consequences?" Sometimes managers do not do either, and obtaining desired performance becomes almost a random activity. The following is an example of the use of the ABC model to manage employee behavior.

Bob Lorber and his staff were working on a productivity improvement project one time in a manufacturing plant where there was a very high noise density. People working in the plant were expected to wear hearing protection during working hours to conform to legal requirements and to avoid hearing loss. While everyone was issued hearing protection, few people wore the apparatus in the plant with any consistency. When Bob's staff was asked to see if they could improve the frequency and use of hearing protection in the plant, they immediately wondered whether this contrary behavior was a result of poor goal setting and training (activators) or inappropriate responses to performance (consequences).

They found that hearing protection was discussed and demonstrated in orientation meetings for new employees, so Lorber's staff eliminated the possibility that the low use was an activator problem. They turned their attention to an examination of consequences; that is, what happened when employees wore or did not wear their hearing protection.

They found that most new employees started wearing their hearing protection because of what they learned at their orientation session; however, they soon stopped wearing the protection once on the job. Why was this?

When supervisors noticed a new employee wearing hearing protection, they reported "feeling pleased," yet they seldom communicated any of their thoughts to the new employee. As a result, new employees who conformed to the safety guidelines received no positive supervisory response as a consequence of their behavior. This highlights a point all managers (and parents and spouses, for that matter) should remember: unless good feelings and kind thoughts are expressed, they mean nothing.

So new employees received no positive feedback from their supervisors. But they did get a clear message from other co-workers: they got kidded and called names for being so soft and willing to "butter up to the boss." In other words, a negative consequence. New employees quickly found themselves in a dilemma. If they wore the hearing protection, they got zapped by co-workers; if they did not wear the hearing protection, they got zapped by supervisors. They spent all their time putting the headphones on and off and dodging supervisors to avoid reprimands! It was a wonder they were able to do their jobs at all!

The only way out of this lose-lose dilemma was for supervisors to start to provide a positive consequence. The moment a new employee was seen wearing hearing protection, the supervisor needed to praise the employee: "I see you're wearing your hearing protection. I really appreciate that—it's important. I appreciate your cooperation and feel good about having you on my team." Now the new employee has a positive consequence to match up against a negative one received from co-workers. The positive consequence will tend to influence behavior more strongly over time.

When self-assessment instruments are given to managers, they usually evaluate themselves as supportive, caring people. And yet often when these same managers are evaluated on the same instrument by the people who work for them, they are not seen as supportive, caring people. The reality is that unless you express your good feelings, people often do not know they exist. People are not mind readers.

This point is humorously illustrated by a story of a Swedish couple, Olaf and Anna, who had been married for more than thirty years. Anna said, "Olaf, you never say you love me." Olaf was quick to reply, "Anna, I told you I loved you the day we got married. If I change my mind, you'll be the first to know."

Communication once every thirty years is not enough. Nor is once-a-year feedback delivered during a performance review adequate. Most people need to know how they are performing on a daily basis. You can do this by making use of the ABC's of Management, another simple yet powerful management technique. Putting this concept into practice can make your job as a manager easier and more fulfilling.

THE PRICE SYSTEM

Although learning the ABC's of management and recognizing that any performance problem is either an activator problem or a consequence problem is important, applied behavioral science concepts also come alive when they are integrated into the PRICE system. The PRICE system is a five-step productivity improvement system developed by Robert Lorber and his associates. Lorber's consulting firm, RL Lorber and Associates, and Blanchard Training and Development have been using the PRICE system to improve companies' performance for almost a decade. Both firms have a long list of clients, mentioned in greater detail at the end of this chapter, who have achieved significant bottom-line results using the principles discussed here. The PRICE acronym stands for Pinpoint, Record, Involve, Coach, and Evaluate. We will discuss each of these factors in turn along with general advice for establishing and implementing a performance-improvement plan.

P—Pinpoint

Pinpoint refers to identifying one or more key performance areas that a manager wants to improve. Remember the 80/20 rule. Most of the performance you want from people—80 percent—comes from 20 percent of their activities. You want to pinpoint performance-improvement areas that will focus on the 20 percent that have the biggest impact. Pinpointing involves a tentative analysis of the problem which will be refined and changed as the PRICE process unfolds.

The areas for improvement may vary quite a bit, depending on you, your unit, and your company. During pinpointing ask yourself, Where is current performance not meeting expectations? Where is the biggest discrepancy between the *real* and the *ideal* level of performance as I see it? Some areas that companies have focused on include:

- Enhanced customer satisfaction
- Improved employee productivity
- Improved return on equipment
- Improved return on capital investment
- Creation of better inventory procedures
- More timely receipt of accounts receivable
- Stimulated innovation
- Expanded managerial training and development
- Increased organizational accountability

If You Can't Measure It, You Can't Manage It

It is important to remember in pinpointing a performance-improvement area that you must be able to measure progress in that area. In other words, you have to be able to observe and quantify performance. There is very little room for vagueness in a successful performance-improvement plan. You must be able to specifically describe the current and desired level of performance and how you will measure improvement as it is made. The five key measurement areas used in many companies are quantity (how many), quality (how good), cost (amount of money), timeliness (on or off schedule), and amount of change (the difference between past and present performance).

You must also establish what you think might be reasonable levels of improvement. Ask how much, how often, by when, and what is an outstanding level of improvement? What is acceptable or minimal? For example, the closure of half of the sales presentations made by a sales staff would most likely be considered outstanding, a closure rate of 10 percent might be considered minimal.

Measurement Formats

Measurements can be made through observations, surveys, interviews, or analyses of reports and records. Which format you use depends on a number of factors, including available time and staff, ease of data collection, and the method that gives you the information you most need. There are several other points to keep in mind regarding measurements:

1. Select measurements that are simple and easy to understand by those who will be held accountable for the measures.
2. Select measurements that are reliable. A measure is reliable if it measures what you say it measures. For example, the number of cold calls made may not measure an increase in the number of division-wide sales. Cold calls are related to the number of division-wide sales but are not a reliable predictor of increased sales. You could have an increase in cold calls but not a corresponding increase in division sales.
3. Use measures that are fair and unbiased. Measurements become unfair or biased when those collecting the information have a vested interest in the outcome or when the measure involves a great deal of subjectivity. If the outcomes are observable and verifiable by anyone who cares to examine the results, the measurements are fair and unbiased. In the sales example, the measurements would most likely be unbiased if the accounting office confirms or verifies the sales and forwards the figures to you.
4. Organize measurements so that they can reflect the performance of the smallest work unit. In the sales example, the division may be divided into four regions. You might want to measure and compare region-wide sales figures for each region. These figures would allow you to place greater focus on those regions that require more of your time and expertise to improve performance.
5. Choose measurements that are stable and not subject to too many outside influences and contingencies. In the sales example, if the price for the product changes randomly due to the availability of raw materials, this product might not be an effective outcome area on which to focus—too many variables are outside of one's control.

Although it may not initially seem so, almost anything can be measured. For example, we were asked to increase the "friendliness" of the tellers in a bank that we were working with. When we asked the top manager what was meant by "friendliness," the manager was stumped and finally said: "If you're so smart, why don't you find out for me?" So we set out to find out what a friendly teller was. We asked customers since they were in the best position to evaluate teller friendliness.

We found there were three ways that people determined whether or not a teller was friendly, and these three ways apply in any situation where people are dealing with customers.

The first thing that was mentioned about a friendly teller was that the teller was good at *name−face recognition*. It is very important to people that they be recognized for who they are. If you don't know their name at first, it is desirable to use it as soon as you do learn it. Customers reported very little name and face recognition on the part of tellers in this bank. In fact, the typical teller used the customer's name only once or less per interaction.

The second thing that people talked about when they talked about a friendly teller was that the teller had a *friendly face*. How would you measure a friendly face? Again, we asked customers to show us a friendly face versus a very businesslike face. They identified distinctions that we were able to describe to a cartoonist who consequently was able to sketch five faces, from very businesslike to very friendly. After the drawings were prepared, we were able to show them to customers in the bank and ask people to rate the face of each of the tellers on a scale of 1 (very unfriendly) to 5 (very friendly). We found that the average teller's face in this bank was rated 1.5. If any of these tellers were in a good mood, they sure weren't letting their faces know about it!

The third factor that determined friendliness was whether tellers *discussed nonbusiness topics*. A business-related topic would be, "Would you please sign here?" or "Would you like it all in twenties?" A friendly topic would be, "Isn't the weather lovely today?"

Once we knew about the difference between friendly and unfriendly conversation, we were able to specifically observe tellers' interaction and track the instances of "friendly" and "unfriendly" conversation. Every time the teller changed the topic, it would be indicated whether the teller had gone from a business to business topic, or business to friendly, or friendly to friendly, and the like. We found out that the tellers were engaging in less than 10 percent nonbusiness-related conversation. All in all, the tellers communicated professionalism but not all that much warmth and friendliness toward customers. Since friendliness was an important factor to customers, this was a worthwhile area in which to improve the bank's performance and perceptions.

Prioritize Areas for Improvement

When pinpointing, you will probably identify more than one or two areas to improve. You might want to list several areas to be worked on. Then separate those areas into two groups: those that demand your immediate attention (top priority) and those that aren't quite as pressing (lower priority). Your criteria for separation might be cost, impact on the company's human resources, degree of difficulty for change, centrality to the company mission, or the time the change will take. Initially, with a first or second productivity effort, you might want to choose an area in which you can have a significant impact and where the chances of success are high. Do not try to impact more than three or four areas at once.

To summarize, benefits of the pinpoint step include:

1. Enables managers to see and understand where unit performance improvement is most needed.
2. Helps managers to determine effective measurements for evaluating improvement.
3. Assists managers in selecting priorities for performance improvement.

R—Record

Once you have identified a performance area that you want to improve, the next step is to record present performance in that area. You want to do this for several reasons. First, you don't want to "fix what isn't broken." So many managers tend to generalize from a population of one. To illustrate, we once worked with a manager who owned more than twenty restaurants. When we asked him in what areas he would like to improve performance, he said, "One of the things that really bugs me is that a machine will break down in a restaurant and employees will take their 'own sweet time' to report the broken machine to the central office so we can get it fixed." We asked him, "How many times has that occurred in the last three months?" He said, "What do you mean?" We answered, "Just what we said. How many times has it occurred in the last three months?" The manager said, "I don't know, but yesterday I saw a broken machine that had not been reported." Based on a single incident he was ready to launch an organization-wide performance improvement program!

Start with a Base Line of Data

Make sure you have base-line data before implementing strategies to improve performance. Base-line data are developed by tracking and recording performance or behavior in the area you want to improve so that it can be compared with future data. If you have no base line, it is difficult to assess improvements or changes. Make sure your base line is based on the most recent information.

Record Systematically on an Ongoing Basis

Once data have been collected for problem diagnosis and strategies have been decided upon, tracking data must continue through to the point where you evaluate and decide to de-emphasize this particular productivity improvement effort. Recording data also allows you to identify trends that will give you greater problem definition and clarity and possibly will help to suggest ideas for solutions. There needs to be enough information to show a trend. Trends are influenced by many factors, such as client needs or even in some instances the weather. Data gathered over several months or even years might be appropriate. For example, if you were tracking sales by region and it was found that one sales region out of four had abnormally good performance, you might begin to examine what this region is doing that the other regions are not. The recording is done on an ongoing basis to track progress against performance goals.

In order to increase your effectiveness and collect data most consistently, keep the following points in mind as measurements are recorded:

1. Collect your data regularly and at short intervals. Don't allow lengthy amounts of time to go between data collection points. Opportunities for on-line corrections may be lost, or your people may be waiting for the positive feedback that comes with productivity improvement. It may also be hard to retrieve the data if they are not collected at short, regular intervals.

2. Collect data in a consistent fashion. If the same person collects data at the same time of the week or month in the same way, the incidence or error in the data will be minimized. Otherwise, collection errors can be misleading and frustrating to those trying to improve.

3. Collect data that cover all relevant aspects of the productivity improvement effort. In the sales example, the number of division-wide sales of a product may be the only outcome measure that will effectively evaluate the program's value.

4. Make sure your data are accurate. Continuously be on the lookout for inaccuracies in your data. Check your figures with data recorded in the past. Use some measures to validate other measures.

Prominently Display Progress

Another crucial factor we have found in tracking progress involves data display procedures. Data that are tracked should be graphically depicted in a prominent place for those individuals who can most impact and benefit from the productivity improvement effort. This becomes an automatic feedback mechanism that can help motivate employees. When progress is being made, the graph can be a source of pride to workers and managers.

To return to our teller example, performance could be tracked on a graph. The horizontal axis represents time—when and how often performance will be observed. The vertical axis is used to track performance improvement. So if you are going to measure friendliness once a week for ten weeks, each of the weeks (one through ten) would be indicated at the bottom of the graph. If the person was initially identified as engaging in 8-percent friendly conversation and the goal was to get that teller up to 35

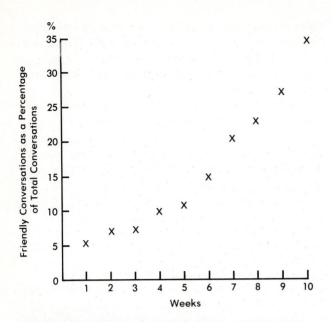

FIGURE 18-2   Percentage of a teller's total conversations
measured as friendly

percent, that measure would appear on the vertical axis. The same with sales, profits, or any other area you have decided to track.

To summarize, benfits derived from the record state include:

1. Prevents managers from "fixing what is not broken."
2. Gives managers a clear starting point for improvement.
3. Sets up opportunities for managers to praise future progress.
4. Enables managers to track performance and to make decisions about how to improve performance.
5. Allows managers to check on the validity and reliability of outcome measures.
6. Results in a clear graphic representation of past and ongoing performance.
7. Provides managers with an opportunity to reevaluate the pinpoint stage and refine their perceptions of the problem.

I—Involve

Once you have recorded in order to present performance in a pinpointed area you are now ready to involve others. A manager can personally do the pinpoint and record stage, but to effectively implement a performance-improvement project, the people who can most influence that area must be involved.

This stage requires you to work in two different ways with your people. First, you need to work with the *group* as a group or team to build consensus around goals, standards, and strategies. Then you need to work with *individuals* in the group to set personal performance goals that correspond with the group goals. Individual involvement provides an opportunity to identify the people who can influence the problem and get them squarely behind the effort to improve unit performance.

You need to engage your people in dialogue that may refine or redefine the area of improvement, based on the perceptions and contributions of the group members. Involving is a mutual process of setting standards to which your people can be committed, as well as brainstorming strategies and incentives for reaching the desired performance outcomes. The most important thing to realize is that for any productivity improvement program to succeed this step must be a group effort. The involve stage consists of four steps: (1) inform, (2) agree on standards and strategy formulation, (3) set goals with individuals that correspond with unit goals, and (4) establish rewards and incentives.

Inform the Group

In this step you share the information gathered in the record stage. In presenting the results of your investigation, you focus on the performance of the unit as a whole, rather than evaluating the problem on an individual performance basis. To be effective, informing should allow for an exchange of data wherein you can ask your group's opinion of the accuracy of the problem and the feasibility and appropriateness of different solutions. Remember that your view of the problem may change, depending on the data and the perceptions of others.

Agree on Standards and Strategies

After you have passed on the data, your group must focus on setting performance standards. Share with your group the tentative performance standards you established in the pinpoint stage. Even though you have developed your own ideas, the group should agree on the standards, since they will be required to maintain them. That's why it is important to develop reasonable standards with the group. Standards should be determined for three levels of performance: minimal, acceptable, and outstanding. To gain perspective and help determine reasonable ranges for each of these three levels, look to past performance, industry averages, and the capabilities of those involved.

The group must then develop strategies for achieving the levels of expected improvement in the targeted areas. The group must reach some agreement as to how the improvement will occur. The means of doing this may depend upon such factors as cost, manpower, time, and customer/client reaction. How the group goes about arriving at suitable strategies will depend on the group's history and patterns of working together and the manager's management style. The manager should facilitate an open exploration of all alternatives. Strategies that you come up with as a group may lead to further data collection or to the establishment of strategy measures to be collected during the productivity improvement effort. At the end of this step, a group action plan should be in place that will facilitate a group effort toward the intended change. It should no longer be your plan but the group's plan—one they have generated and one to which they can be committed.

Set Individual Goals

Much has already been said about goal setting, and the point that is to be emphasized here is that individual goals need to mesh well with those of the overall group. Because different employees perform different functions in the organization, the goals will vary quite a bit. A person in sales uses different skills from one in training or advertising, yet each will contribute to the overall effort of improvement. The variation in function becomes more diverse as the unit involved in the project increases in size or the goal itself becomes more complex.

Determine Rewards and Feedback

If productivity is to be sustained, it will be necessary to set up a system of feedback for performance at each level and for each phase of the performance-improvement project. As mentioned in the record step, managers should use the ongoing posting of information in graphs as an opportunity to celebrate the progress being made. People take pride in their own performance and like to see and be recognized for a job well done. As the members of the group reinforce each other's performance, group pride develops. Managers can have an enormous impact on shaping the work atmosphere. It is useful to explore specific ways to create a climate of appreciation. For instance, incentives can help increase the chances of performance improvement. At the very least, healthy amounts of praise and encouragement are important, and sincere appreciation for work well done is a must!

To summarize, the benefits of the involve step include:

1. Allows for employee commitment as to how the performance is improved.
2. Allows for employee input into the standards and levels of performance. How much can be done by when is as important to the employee as it is to you.
3. Allows for employee understanding as to how their individual goals fit into the overall unit goal.
4. Emphasizes informal and formal incentives to reinforce outstanding performance.

C—Coach

In many ways the pinpoint, record, and involve steps are all activators. They are all things that need to be done *before* you can expect performance improvement. It is in the fourth step—coaching—that managers begin to deal with consequences. Coaching involves the management of consequences by praising progress, reprimanding poor performance, and redirecting the errors of inexperienced people. As such, this step is closely associated with some of the principles discussed in the last chapter involving One Minute Management. People need to be praised for good performance. When performance is not measuring up, you may need to restate what you want and how it is to be done. When good performance drops off, a reprimand may be necessary. In Situational Leadership, coaching occurs when you deliver and use the agreed-upon leadership style.

Coaching Requires Constant Communication

Sometimes managers monitor the performance of individuals but fail to give them feedback on their efforts until they make a mistake. Even worse, some managers do not even monitor the job being done until a problem arises. In addition, many managers do not think of showing sincere appreciation for a job well done when the goal is accomplished. Nor do they think about reinforcing "successive approximations" of goal accomplishment when the task is new or difficult. Too often performance is regarded as "what we pay them for."

Consequences Must Be Clear

As described earlier in this chapter in the ABC's of Management, it can't be emphasized enough that good performance is managed by its consequences. You must notice your people's efforts and apply consequences to their behavior. When you ignore performance, your people may initially try harder so as to receive some kind of recognition. But if that recognition does not come, they usually stop trying as hard because from what they've seen where they work, good performance makes no difference. As a manager, you must use consequences to separate good performers from poor performers. If you do not treat the two differently, there is little motivation to be a good performer (except for self-pride), and you will demotivate your good performers or lose them to another company.

Poor performers also need to know of the consequences, the available assistance, and the feedback that you will provide them in order to help them to succeed. When working with a new person or a new task, the employee is in a training mode. Training takes time, and the learner needs to know that you will be there to support and encourage and to apply consequences as learning and performance occur.

Types of Consequences

There are four types of consequences that make a difference when working with people: praise, redirection, renegotiation of goals and/or standards, and reprimands.

Praise. Praise is showing sincere appreciation for a job well done. It should follow the accomplishment of a goal or the successful completion of interim steps toward a goal.

Redirection. Redirection is the restatement of what is to be accomplished and how. Simply stated, redirection involves returning to the beginning and restating with greater clarity the goals and a revised plan for reaching those goals.

Renegotiation. In this case, you change a person's goals, strategies, or standards because existing ones are inappropriate for some reason. The standard might be too low or too high, strategies no longer suitable, or the goal no longer relevant or feasible.

Reprimand. A reprimand is stating your displeasure with performance. It should follow instances of poor performance or when a person who has demonstrated ability should be doing better. Reprimands should not be used with learners or until all the facts concerning performance have been gathered.

To summarize, the benefits of the coaching step include:

1. Employees get immediate feedback on performance.
2. Feedback is specific and concerned with behavior.
3. Employees feel appreciated and recognized for their efforts.
4. Learners are not punished while they learn.
5. Renegotiation is built in as the situation changes.

E—Evaluate

Since data is constantly being collected and you are continually coaching, it could be asked why evaluation is a separate step in the PRICE system. Evaluation allows a formal way to recognize progress and evaluate future strategies and directions. It sets a date in the future with enough time allowed for trends to develop. Month by month coaching and evaluation of individual performance may not allow for total project evaluation, so the evaluation stage is of value for its overall analysis for the group.

At predetermined, periodic intervals, managers and their people need to sit down and evaluate performance. At this time, there should be no surprises. Interaction between the manager and employees will be reviewed and progress toward goals assessed. In this step, you might also find that you obtained the results you wanted and are ready to put your efforts elsewhere. If the project shows positive impact, you should celebrate the improvement.

Or you might determine that strategies are not working and that you must create some alternatives. If the data reveal little or no progress, then you must return to the involve stage and get your people to generate different strategies, assuming the incentives and standards were initially valid. Go back and restrategize, set standards, and apply consequences to individual goals with the knowledge gained from this overall evaluation of the project. If you choose to discontinue the effort, leave the tracking mechanisms in place to review the data at a future date.

In the event there is little or no progress, avoid punishing the group. When you evaluate, try to focus on results and reasons why they weren't realized, as well as new strategies that can be generated to obtain the desired results. There can be many reasons for lack of progress since performance can break down at every stage of the PRICE system. You might have pinpointed an irrelevant area, or you could have been recording data ineffectively. In the involve stage, your people might have agreed to too high or too low a goal. Your feedback may have been erratic or your consequences not sufficiently motivating.

In many ways, responsibility for the success of the project rests on the manager's shoulders, who must take significant responsibility for ensuring that employees perform well. If proper results are not obtained, try to learn why and attack the problem again, this time armed with new knowledge and experience. The evaluation stage also includes an examination of a manager's own leadership behavior. Did you continually emphasize and reinforce the change you requested? Did you use consequences effectively? Did you allow enough time for the desired improvement to occur? Were there unexpected internal or external conditions that might have influenced the data?

To summarize, the benefits of the evaluation step include:

1. Formalizes the examination of project results and the group effort.
2. Allows for further group strategy generation and problem solving.
3. Requires alternative actions if little or no progress has resulted.

Many of the principles of the PRICE system that we have elaborated on here are taken from the Blanchard Trucking and Distribution Case, by Zigarmi, Blanchard, and Lorber.[2]

The principles of the PRICE system and the ABC's of Management are both discussed in *Putting the One Minute Manager to Work*. They are graphically illustrated and explained in the Putting the One Minute Manager to Work Gameplan.[3]

PRINCIPLES IN PRACTICE

We have presented some very powerful principles in this chapter. To demonstrate the impact they can have, we'd like to share the experiences we've had with three companies that incorporated these principles into their organizations. We believe that the results obtained by these organizations are both realistic and typical of any organization that makes a firm commitment to install and maintain a system in which the principles of Situational Leadership and One Minute Management are practiced. Following are the results of application at Transco, Canadian Pacific, and Fairweather.

Transco Energizes

Transco Energy Company became committed to learning and applying the principles discussed in this chapter and, working with Blanchard Training and Development, implemented a three-phrase approach that involved:

- *Phase Ia*—Five one-day training sessions given over a two-month period for the top one hundred managers, which focused on developing the three skills of the One Minute Manager.
- *Phase Ib*—The training of eight in-house trainers on the One Minute Manager skills. These trainers later provided workshops for the lower level management down through the supervisory management level over an eight-month period (this overlapped with the training in Phase Ia).
- *Phase II*—Five two-day sessions focused on Leadership and Group Development for the top one hundred managers of Transco over a two-month period.
- *Phase III*—The development of Productivity Improvement Projects and Teams focused on increasing productivity by improving operations and cutting costs. BTD's goals were the creation of eight to fifteen projects within six months.

As a result of this effort, the company closely tracked its costs and savings that could be directly attributed to the extensive training and were able to document savings of more than $2 million in a nine-month period. Based on a $159,000 training investment, that's a ten-to-one return. Some twenty-four performance improvement projects were initiated within six months that involved sixty-four core team members.

Says George Slocum, President of Transco:

We project $18 million in savings over the next two and one-half to three years. In addition, there has been a noticeable movement toward collaborative and participative management styles at Transco as a result of our managers learning the secrets of One Minute Management, developing the flexibility of a Situational Leader, functioning more effectively in teams, and mastering the PRICE Model for productivity improvement. . . . I couldn't be more positive about the ability of these principles to make a difference in the companies in which they are applied.

Canadian Pacific Keeps Trucking

The scenario was repeated at Canadian Pacific Trucking, where fuel costs were reduced by 10 percent in four months; claims by 50 percent in eight months; and accounts receivable dropped from an average collection period of forty-nine days to forty-one days in a nine-month period.

Training at Canadian Pacific also involved a three-stage approach: unfreezing/initial training, skill training and ongoing consultation, and refreezing/evaluation. Prior to the start of any training, an "implemention team" was established to help monitor the project, several days of confidential interviews were conducted with selected top- and mid-level managers, and an extensive survey of all employees was taken that covered the topics of leadership, communication patterns, decision-making patterns, meeting effectiveness, performance appraisal practice, training opportunities, role clarity and standards, role conflict and overload, feedback and rewards on performance, and equal employment opportunity practice.

Phase I: Unfreezing/initial training. After the initial data collection and planning, a two-and-one-half day Situational Leadership/One Minute Management seminar was conducted for the company's senior management staff. During the workshop, each senior manager planned how the manager intended to implement Situational Leadership back on the job. Each manager was also encouraged to begin a performance/productivity improvement project. Five one-day videotape workshops were conducted on the same material for mid-level managers at various company sites.

Phase II: Skill training and ongoing consultation. More specific skill training was then conducted with senior management staff during two two-day workshops given a month apart. In these sessions, management was taught to determine the development level, needs for direction, and support needs of each of their subordinates. Managers were taught how to be more flexible with their management styles as the situation warranted. The skills of effective performance planning, performance monitoring, and performance evaluation were also taught. Individual coaching and counseling were provided to managers as they implemented these skills and their performance/productivity improvement plans.

Phase III: Refreezing/evaluation. At this stage specific work was done with the company's performance review system, including new performance planning, monitoring, and evaluation polices and procedures, and record-keeping forms, based on Situational Leadership and One Minute Management. New positions were designed as needed to maintain ongoing progress of the initial work that had been done. Once the new system was developed, consultants worked with the implementation team and in-house trainers to assure that managers were adequately trained on how to use the system. Additional follow-up training using a variety of diagnostic instruments focused on management styles during crisis situations.

The final impact of the training and development efforts was made and provided to top management and the implementation team. the president of that company, Karl Wahl, claims:

> The PRICE Model has been a major tool in improving results in the key accountability areas of safety and cargo claims prevention, and has resulted in significant savings to our company.

A Fairweather Forecast

What happened at the Fairweather stores—a moderately priced women's fashion chain with one hundred and fifty stores in Canada—also serves as a good example. As part of our training sessions, we had initially explained to managers at Fairweather how most businesses are organized like a pyramid, with hourly employees at the bottom and the chairman at the top. There is nothing wrong with pyramid organizations unless people *think* in terms of the pyramid. When that happens, they work for the person above them. When this occurs, managers think they are responsible, and the people who report to them must be responsive to them. People think they are at the mercy of their boss's whims.

At our suggestion, they turned the pyramid upside down, so that the customers were placed at the top of the organization and given greater service. With the inverted triangle philosophy, managers work for their people and are thus responsive to their people's needs.

In the summer of 1985 we heard seven Fairweather store managers and Rick Colbear, the company's director of training, share with top management of the division how they had implemented the PRICE system and the inverted triangle philosophy. By implementing the PRICE model throughout key stores in the Toronto area and adopting the "inverted triangle" philosophy, Fairweather made tremendous gains in performance. The difference between 1984−85 earnings and those of 1983−84 was almost a million dollars in terms of productivity improvement.

One of the more exciting aspects about the implementation of One Minute Management concepts at Fairweather is that they did it by themselves. For a long time, we knew that organizations didn't need consultants if they were really committed to implementing and using concepts they had learned. Managers at Fairweather proved this was true by showing the initiative and follow-through necessary to stick with implementing management techniques they believed in.

In the final analysis, the most important thing about any management concept is whether or not it works on a day-to-day basis. The proof is in the application. And at the three sample companies discussed in this chapter—Transco, Canadian Pacific, and Fairweather—the application became proof.

Applications of the principles discussed in this chapter are further discussed in Chapter 19, "Implementing Situational Leadership: Making Decisions That Stick." As is the case in learning about leadership concepts and techniques and *not* applying them, that chapter will show how making decisions and not following up on them leads to an ineffective decision-making process.

NOTES

1. This chapter is adapted from Kenneth Blanchard and Robert Lorber, *Putting the One Minute Manager to Work* (New York: Morrow, 1984).
2. *Ibid.* p. 21. See also Ray E. Keefe, "How Good Are You as an Executive?" *Today's Executive*, Winter/Spring 1987, pp. 3–9.
3. *Ibid*, p. 17.
4. This case study with worksheets and exercises for classroom or individual use is available from Blanchard Training and Development, Escondido, CA 92025.
5. Available from Blanchard Training and Development, Escondido, Calif.

CHAPTER 19

IMPLEMENTING SITUATIONAL LEADERSHIP: *Making Decisions That Stick*

Making decisions that stick and building commitments are two of the most important activities a manager can perform. Both are essential to managerial success. In this chapter we will first look at an application of Situational Leadership to making good decisions, an indispensable skill at every level of management. We will then examine a major contribution of the management consulting firm of Keilty, Goldsmith, and Boone[1]—building commitments, which uses Situational Leadership as an important aspect of their approach.

MAKING EFFECTIVE DECISIONS

Managers spend much of their time reviewing and acting on the proposals of associates, upper management, and nonmanagement personnel. As such, it is common to hear some managers spoken of as "decisive" or as "having good business sense." Unfortunately, it is also common to hear other managers spoken of as "wishy-washy" or as "lacking prudent judgment." That's why your chances for present success and future career advancement are helped if you can (1) make the right decisions in areas you control and (2) submit sound recommendations when requested by your boss.[2]

Viewed in a vacuum, decision making seems like a fairly straightforward process. There appear to be simple steps for collecting and analyzing data, weighing alternatives, testing possible solutions, and arriving at a course of action.

But the world rarely rotates so conveniently. Real-life decisions are usually called for in a pressure-packed environment of inadequate input, conflicting information, budget restraints, time squeezes, scarce resources, and many other elements that cloud the issues and threaten the quality of decisions. Despite all this, poor decision making is not likely to be excused because of the complexities of the manager's workload. The manager needs a simple and logical framework for making decisions that stick.

Situational Leadership can serve as that framework. Just as your diagnosis of follower readiness can determine the high-probability leadership style, it can also indicate which style of decision making is most apt to succeed in a given situation.

Figure 19−1, Problem-solving and decision-making styles, not only describes four problem-solving situations but also suggests four basic decision-making styles—authoritative, consultative, facilitative, and delegative. Each

Figure 19−1 Problem-solving and decision-making styles

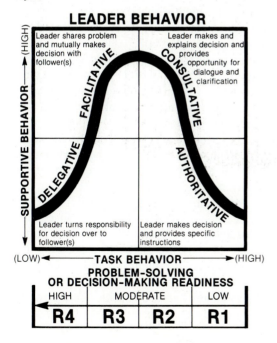

decision-making style has a high probability of getting results depending on the readiness of the followers and the situation.

Decision Styles

Authoritative decision making applies in situations where the manager has the necessary experience and information to reach a conclusion and followers do not possess the ability, willingness, or confidence to help. In this case the manager should make the decision without seeking assistance.[3]

The authoritative style requires directive leader behavior. Followers are usually not actively involved in determining the course of action. Therefore, they hear little about the decision until the manager announces it. Authoritative decisions are commonly communicated with phrases such as "I've decided that . . . " and "Here's what we're going to do . . . ."

What kinds of circumstances require leader-made authoritative decisions? Suppose that your background in product development is all that is needed to set the budget for next year's research program. You've managed your department for four years. You know the goals set for your work group. You are aware of all budgeting policies governing staff, supplies, travel, and so on. Further, your followers know little about budgeting and are new to your department (R1 for most tasks). They are still learning the basics and just are not ready to assist you in making this decision. Therefore, you need to make this decision yourself. Your experience in this area assures you that (1) your conclusion has a high probability of being correct and (2) your proposed budget has a high probability of being accepted by your boss.

Authoritative decisions are also required in cases where you are the *only* source of information or expertise. If a co-worker suddenly begins choking—even though your knowledge of first aid is limited—you may be the *only* available resource. While your experience may not provide all the answers you need, there are no other alternatives.

Consultative decision making is a valuable strategy when the manager recognizes that the followers also possess *some* experience or knowledge of the subject and are willing but not yet able to help. In this case the best strategy is to obtain their input before making the decision.

When using the consultative approach, the manager selects those followers who can help to reach a decision and asks their assistance with phrases such as "What do you know about . . . " and "I'd like some information on . . . ." The manager may or may not share all aspects of the problem. After hearing from the followers, *the manager makes the final decision*.

Suppose you are a marketing manager and are considering a new ad campaign for one of your company's products. Two members of your staff have some experience in this area, so you ask their assistance in determining the product market strategy.

Your consultative strategy has two immediate benefits. First, by enlisting the cooperation of your somewhat knowledgeable resources, you increase the likelihood that your decision will be correct. Second, by giving your followers a chance to contribute, you reinforce their motivation and help them identify more closely with the goals of your department.

A word of caution: Whenever you bring others into the decision-making process, you must make the ground rules very clear. Followers low to moderate in readiness, (R2), can be included in the process but are not ready to run with the ball on their own. A consultative decision is still leader-made. To avoid misunderstandings you should let your people know you'll weigh their input carefully but may not follow their advice in reaching a final conclusion.[4]

Facilitative decision making is a cooperative effort in which manager and follower(s) work together to reach a shared decision. In situations where followers are moderate to high in readiness, (R3), the manager can enlist their help with phrases such as "Let's pool our thoughts and decide on . . . " or "We've got a problem and I'd like your opinion . . . ." The implication is that these followers are capable of sharing the authority to decide what should be done.

For example, let us assume that both you and your assistant have been through project management situations before. You know how the scheduling and work assignments should be handled. Your assistant can administer "process" items such as communication, record keeping, reporting procedures, and so forth. Your best approach is to work together in deciding how the new project should be set up. In this case you are effectively committing yourself to a shared decision-making process—a perfectly good leadership style when dealing with an able but not yet confident follower.[5]

Finally, *delegative* decision making is used with followers high in readiness, (R4), who have the experience and information needed to make the proper decision or recommendation.

In situations where delegation is appropriate, the manager can look forward to a high level of performance simply by saying, "you know this subject . . . work on it and let me know what you come up with."

For example, your plant supervisors are old pros who know how to schedule their swing shifts so that all your requirements are met. Although you could accomplish this task yourself, you recognize that your people are self-motivated and capable of self-direction in this specific situation. Therefore, your high-probability strategy is to delegate this task to them and await their decision.[6]

As a general rule, you can select the appropriate decision-making style by using Situational Leadership to determine "who owns the decision."

- If none of your followers have experience or information in the specific area, they cannot own any part of the decision. You should make the *authoritative* decision by yourself and tell them what to do.
- If your followers have some knowledge of the subject, they may be capable of contributing to (but not making) the final decision. You should seek their help in a *consultative* manner and make your decision after considering their input.
- If your followers have quite a bit of experience, they can take some of the responsibility for making the decision. You should use a *facilitative* strategy to share the decision-making process with them.
- If your followers have a thorough understanding of the subject and a willingness to deal with it, you should use a *delegative* style. Give them the ball and let them run with it.

It is important to remember that although you may choose to give others a degree of authority in making decisions, the ultimate responsibility is yours alone. However, that's usually no problem for the manager who uses a logical approach to guide the decision maker's process. Followers are usually more likely to approve, follow, and support the decisions of someone who knows not only where to go but also the best way to get there!

DECISION MAKING AND LEADER LATITUDE

The LaJolla-based management consulting firm of Keilty, Goldsmith, and Boone have adapted the Situational Leadership model to an approach to decision making that combines the leader's decision-making latitude with follower readiness.[7] As illustrated in Figure 19–2, Selecting your decision-making style, the basic decision-making styles of directing (high task/low relationship), guiding (high task/high relationship), supporting (high relationship/ low task) and delegating (low task/low relationship) are combined with four degrees of decision-making latitude. These are L1 (little or no latitude), L2 (low to moderate latitude), L3 (moderate to high latitude), and L4 (high latitude). And, as in Figure 19–1, follower readiness is a key variable.

Keilty, Goldsmith, and Boone illustrate the relationships in Table 19–1, Decision-Making Characteristics. This table integrates your decision-making style, characteristics of the decision, your decision-making latitude, followers' decision-making readiness, and the characteristics of effective decision makers. Working through this table in much the same way as a decision-logic table will help you improve your decision-making skills.

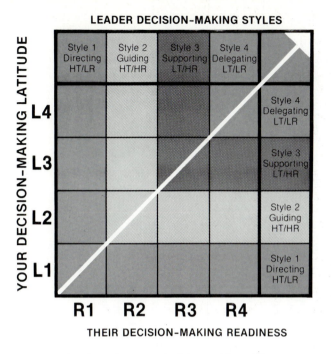

LEADER DECISION-MAKING STYLES

YOUR DECISION-MAKING LATITUDE

| | Style 1 Directing HT/LR | Style 2 Guiding HT/HR | Style 3 Supporting LT/HR | Style 4 Delegating LT/LR | |

L4 — Style 4 Delegating LT/LR

L3 — Style 3 Supporting LT/HR

L2 — Style 2 Guiding HT/HR

L1 — Style 1 Directing HT/LR

R1   R2   R3   R4

THEIR DECISION-MAKING READINESS

Figure 19–2   **Selecting your decision-making style**

BUILDING COMMITMENTS

Keilty, Goldsmith, and Boone have performed extensive research in identifying and defining the qualities that make managers successful and helping their clients apply these qualities within their own corporation or organization. As frequently happens, some individuals are admired and respected for the way that they manage others, but the reasons for their success are not always apparent. Building on the work of McKinsey and Company, the internationally respected management consulting firm, and through their experience with many excellent companies and managers, they have developed valuable insights and a very useful model concerning managerial excellence, The Five Key Commitments model, shown in Figure 19–3.[8]

The essential qualities and relationships necessary to successful management can be explained and understood. Managerial excellence stems from *commitment*, a characteristic common to all individuals recognized for successful management.

Managers carry out their tasks in an interpersonal world. Other people continually view the manager's manner, bearing, and conduct. From their

TABLE 19-1 Decision-Making Characteristics

Your Decision-Making Style	Characteristics of the Decision	Your Decision-Making Latitude	Their Decision-Making Readiness	Characteristics of Effective Decision-Makers
Style 1 Directing		L1	R1	
High Task and Low Relationship HT/LR	The decision is made by you or from top down with little input from them	Little or no latitude Decision is already made Decision is nonnegotiable Examples: rules, regulations, clearly defined procedures	They lack the motivation, ability, or understanding to make the decision	Makes the rules clearly understood Levels with people on what is not negotiable Gives specific direction when it is needed Maintains tight controls when necessary
Style 2 Guiding		L2	R2	
High Task and High Relationship HT/HR	The decision is primarily made by you or with high input from them	Low to moderate latitude Decision can be changed but will be made top down Examples: decisions on strategy implementation	They want to be involved, but lack the ability and understanding to make the decision	Gives orientation to people in new assignments Build's people's understanding and ability Takes time to answer questions and explain decisions Provides coaching and guidance when needed

TABLE 19-1 (*continued*)

Your Decision-Making Style	Characteristics of the Decision	Your Decision-Making Latitude	Their Decision-Making Readiness	Characteristics of Effective Decision-Makers
Style 3 Supporting		L3	R3	
Low Task and High Relationship LT/HR	The decision is primarily their responsibility with high input from you	Moderate to high latitude Decision must involve you but need not be controlled by you Examples: decisions requiring your feedback to higher management	They have the ability and understanding to make the decision with high input from you	Colloborates appropriately in setting objectives Encourages participation in decision making when appropriate Provides support when needed Builds and maintains people's confidence
Style 4 Delegating		L4	R4	
Low Task and Low Relationship LT/LR	The decision is their responsibility with little input from you	High latitude Decision can legitimately be made by them Examples: their defined job responsibilities	They are willing and have the ability to make the decision with little input from you	Delegates when possible Lets others make decisions when appropriate Encourages others to take as much responsibility as they can handle Gives people the freedom to do their job well

observations, they form impressions of the manager's values, beliefs, and attitudes. Excellent managers make a powerful and positive impression on others because they blend a set of positive beliefs with an equally appropriate set of positive behaviors. These beliefs and actions form "commitments." The most effective managers share a fundamentally similar set of five commitments. These are

- Commitment to the customer
- Commitment to the organization
- Commitment to self
- Commitment to people
- Commitment to task

Separately, each commitment is extremely important to effective management. Together, these commitments form the essential framework for long-term achievement of managerial excellence. True excellence seems to result from genuine dedication and positive service in all five areas of commitment. Figure 19−3 shows the five key commitments and their interrelationships.

Commitment to the Customer

The first and probably most important management commitment focuses on the customer. Excellent managers strive to provide useful service to custom-

Figure 19−3   The Five Key Commitments model

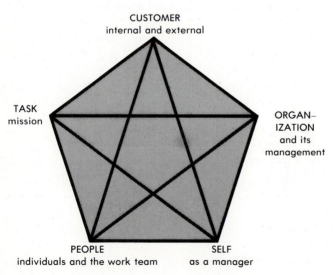

ers. A customer is defined as anyone who rightly should benefit from the work of a manager's unit. For some managers, their work directly affects the external customer. For other managers, the essential customer is internal. Employees in one unit often serve members of another unit in the same organization. Whether the customer is primarily external or internal, the key to this commitment is service. The two primary ways in which an excellent manager demonstrates strong commitment to the customer are serving the customer and building customer importance.

Serving the customer boils down to consistent, conscientious dedication to customer needs. This requires responsiveness to customers through continually encouraging and listening to input from the people who use the manager's services or products. Clear, current identification of customer needs is necessary to genuinely serve the customer. In addition to knowing the customer and the needs of the customer, the excellent manager acts to solve customer problems in a timely manner.[10]

Building customer importance means presenting the customer in a positive manner to those who actually provide service to the customer. The customer is not always appreciated by others within an organization. In fact, some employees view the customer as a necessary evil. To these employees, the customer is the source of most problems and often is viewed as someone to be tolerated. Excellent managers build customer importance by (1) clearly communicating the importance of the customer to employees, (2) treating the customer as a top priority, and (3) prohibiting destructive comments about the people who use their work group's products or services.

Commitment to the Organization

The second management commitment focuses on the organization. Effective managers personally project pride in their organizations. They also instill the same pride in others. A manager positively demonstrates this commitment in three ways: building the organization, supporting higher management, and operating by the basic organizational values.

Building the organization is achieved by constantly presenting the organization in a positive way. Most people lose their motivation if they are ashamed of where they work or embarrassed by what they do. They want to be part of something positive. The excellent manager builds support for what the organization does and effectively prevents destructive comments.

Supporting higher management is essential to the loyalty any organization needs in order to function. Excellent managers add value to the organization by showing and inspiring this necessary loyalty. These managers view their position in the organization as involving a dual responsibility. (See Figure 19–4.) The first responsibility is to actively challenge and lead "up" in the organization. The excellent manager takes decisions from above in the organization, makes them work, and expects others to do likewise. This

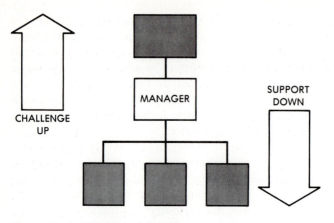

Figure 19-4   The roles of the manager

manager does not blame higher management or pass the buck. The excellent manager's behavior strengthens the organization's ability to implement decisions and achieve objectives.

Operating by the basic organizational values clearly communicates the importance of what the organization stands for. A difficult aspect of managerial excellence is living the values of the organization, especially when those values are challenged during trying times. If an organization has a clearly defined and communicated set of basic beliefs, it is the manager's responsibility to function in a manner consistent with those fundamental beliefs. Managers are the clearest models of what the organization stands for. The excellent manager lives up to this challenge and this commitment.[11]

Commitment to Self[12]

The third management commitment focuses on the manager personally. Excellent managers present a strong, positive image to others. They act as a positive force in all situations. This is not to be mistaken as self-serving or selfish. Excellent managers are seen as individuals who combine strength with a sense of humility. Commitment to self is evidenced in three specific activities: demonstrating autonomy, building self as a manager, and accepting constructive criticism.

Demonstrating autonomy is an important dimension for an effective manager. Within their own organizational units, excellent managers act as though they are running their own businesses. They take responsibility and ownership for decisions. They stand up for personal beliefs. When taking risks, they are reasonable and more concerned with achieving excellence than "playing it safe."

Building self as a manager deals with the self-image a manager projects to others. Excellent managers appear confident and self-assured. They act on the basis of total integrity. They do not belittle or overplay their own accomplishments. It becomes obvious to others that these managers belong in their jobs. Excellent managers live up to the faith others place in them. They act on the basis of honesty and expressly behave with exceptional integrity.

Accepting constructive criticism forms a balance with the first two aspects of a positive commitment to self. Many people act autonomously and deserving of their positions. It is the truly excellent manager who remains receptive to criticism or comment in order to become even better. Excellent managers demonstrate long-term ability to admit mistakes, encourage and accept constructive criticism, and avoid recrimination or adverse reaction. In other words, after receiving personal feedback, excellent managers do not "shoot the messenger" or discount the message. It is not easy to graciously accept criticism. However, the ability to listen and act positively to improve oneself is essential to sustain personal excellence over time.

Commitment to People

The fourth management commitment focuses on the work team and individual group members. Excellent managers display a dedication to the people who work for them. This denotes the manager's use of the proper style of leadership to help individuals succeed in their tasks. Figure 19−5 reinforces the developmental process of matching leadership style to the ability and motivation of subordinates. Positive commitment to people is demonstrated daily by a manager's willingness to spend the necessary time and energy working with subordinates. Specifically, three vital activities comprise this commitment: showing positive concern and recognition, giving developmental feedback, and encouraging innovative ideas.

Showing positive concern and recognition focuses on the positive aspects of making people feel and act like winners. This is accomplished through rewarding and reinforcing others' performance. It also involves the creation of an environment in which people treat each other with courtesy and respect. For example, destructive comments concerning other people are not acceptable.

Giving developmental feedback is a realistic method of dealing with individual performance failure or setback. People sometimes fail to live up to positive expectations. The excellent manager is willing to intervene when performance does not meet established standards. Using honest feedback, the excellent manager works with the individual to reestablish realistic performance goals. Also, the manager is willing to take the time to guide and coach the individual to improve performance.

Encouraging innovative ideas demonstrates interest in others and stimulates individual and group progress. This positive action is often the differ-

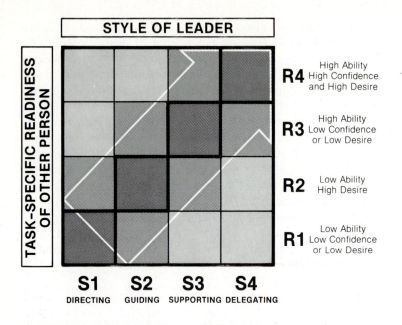

Figure 19—5 Using the leadership style that fits

ence between successful work teams and those that stagnate or disintegrate. The excellent manager taps into the full capacity of subordinates through such common-sense actions as listening to others' ideas, providing opportunities to test ideas, and directing the credit for a successful idea to its originator. These actions tend to create a desirable atmosphere of confidence, accomplishment, and trust.

Commitment to the Task

The fifth management commitment concentrates on the tasks that need to be done. Successful managers give meaning and relevance to the tasks people perform. They provide focus and direction for subordinates, assuring successful completion of tasks. The durability of a manager's excellence is demonstrated through the sustained high performance of the organizational unit managed. This commitment is effected by keeping the right focus, keeping it simple, being action oriented, and building task importance.

Keeping the right focus refers to maintaining the proper perspective on tasks. The excellent manager concentrates everyone's atention on what is most important. This is determined through knowledge and support of the organization's overall mission. The manager consistently ties individual objectives into larger organizational goals.

Keeping it simple entails breaking work down into achievable components while avoiding unnecessary complications and procedures. The excellent manager fully considers objectives, tasks, and human capabilities, thus restraining the natural tendency to try to accomplish too much. Focus is clearly centered on major objectives within organizational priorities.

Being action oriented is simply described as accomplishing. Excellent managers get things done. They execute. They maintain positive momentum. Realistic deadlines are set and met. People are encouraged to take action, and a sense of positive direction and accomplishment results.

Building task importance is the element that completes the fabric of managerial excellence. People generate excitement and action about what they feel is important. The excellent manager plays up the importance of the work. Excellence in task achievement is an expected result. Continuous excellence becomes the hallmark of the manager and the group.

Consistently applied, the five commitments are the keys to effective management. The manager is the critical link among each of the commitments. The excellent manager takes a personal perspective with regard to the five commitments. (See Figure 19−6.)

The excellent manager is central to the process of developing and sustaining commitments. By taking personal responsibility and acting as a positive force, the manager can strongly influence the organization and its people, tasks, and customers. The active involvement and personal integrity of excellent managers flow to others. Excellent companies have long realized that "they are their people." What separates the excellent companies from

Figure 19−6 The central perspective of the manager

TABLE 19-2   What Does the Excellent Manager Do

COMMITMENT TO THE CUSTOMER
internal and external
THE EXCELLENT MANAGER:
Serves the Customer
Knows who the customers are.

Is dedicated to meeting the needs of people who use the organization's services or products.

Encourages and listens to input from the people who use the organization's services or products.

Acts to solve customers' problems in a timely manner.

Builds Customer Importance
Consistently treats the users of the organization's products or services as a top priority.

Clearly communicates the importance of the people who use the organization's products or services.

Does not allow destructive comments about the people who use the organization's products or services.

Is more committed to customers' long-term satisfication than the organization's short-term gain.

COMMITMENT TO THE ORGANIZATION
and its management
THE EXCELLENT MANAGER:
Builds the Organization
Knows and supports the mission of the overall organization.

Discourages destructive comments about the organization.

Is honest and positive in describing organizational benefits.

Inspires pride in the organization.

Supports Higher Management
Describes higher level managers in a positive way.

Avoids destructive comments about higher level managers.

Personally supports higher level management decisions.

Does not pass the buck or blame higher level management.

Operates by the Basic Values
Understands the basic values of the organization.

Manages using the basic values of the organization.

Encourages others to operate using the basic values of the organization.

Takes corrective action when basic organizational values are compromised.

COMMITMENT TO SELF
as a manager
THE EXCELLENT MANAGER:
Demonstrates Autonomy
Stands up for personal beliefs.

Takes responsibility and ownership for decisions.

Takes reasonable risks in trying out new ideas.

Is more concerned with achieving excellence than playing it safe.

Builds Self as a Manager
Shows a high degree of personal integrity in dealing with others.

Presents self in a positive manner.

Demonstrates confidence as a manager.

Avoids destructive self-criticism.

Accepts Constructive Criticism

Is willing to admit mistakes.

Encourages and accepts constructive criticism.

Acts on constructive advice in a timely manner.

Does not discourage people from giving constructive criticism.

COMMITMENT TO PEOPLE
individuals and the work team

THE EXCELLENT MANAGER:

Shows Positive Concern and Recognition

Consistently shows respect and concern for people as individuals.

Gives positive recognition for achievement without discomfort to either party.

Adequately rewards and reinforces top performance.

Makes people feel like winners.

Avoids destructive comments about people at work.

Gives Developmental Feedback

Effectively analyzes performance.

Develops specific plans when performance needs improving.

Strives to improve people's performance from acceptable to excellent.

Gives developmental performance feedback in a timely manner.

Encourages Innovative Ideas

Encourages suggestions for improving productivity.

Provides opportunities for others to try out new ideas.

Acts on ideas and suggestions from others in a timely manner.

Avoids taking credit for the ideas of others.

COMMITMENT TO THE TASK
mission

THE EXCELLENT MANANGER:

Keeps the Right Focus

Knows and supports the mission of the overall organization.

Ties individual objectives to larger organizational goals.

Concentrates on achieving what is most important.

Places greater emphasis on accomplishing the mission than following procedures.

Keeps It Simple

Keeps the work simple enough to be understood and implemented.

Breaks work into achievable components.

Encourages efforts to simplify procedures.

Avoids unnecessary complications.

Is Action Oriented

Communicates a positive sense of urgency about getting the job done.

Emphasizes the importance of day-to-day progress.

Encourages taking action to get things done.

Concentrates on meeting deadlines.

Builds Task Importance

Is commited to excellence in task achievement.

Makes the task meaningful and relevant.

Encourages suggestions for improving productivity.

Does not downplay the importance of the work.

the rest appears to be that they simply are made up of a greater number of individual managers acting as models of excellence.

These excellent managers recognize that their own task is to build specific commitments to the customer, organization, key tasks, people, and themselves. For each commitment, this means building proper attitudes and demonstrating positive caring and concern. This becomes the responsibility of every employee, not just the manager. The excellent manager lives by the five commitments and works in concert with others to build commitments. Table 19−2, What Does the Excellent Manager Do? Outlines specific behaviors characteristic of the excellent manager in each of the five commitments. Sustaining and replicating excellence is a reinforcing cyclical process based on the five key commitments. (See Figure 19−7.)

Fundamentally, these commitments are built through dedication and service. When the excellent manager demonstrates genuine dedication and service to subordinates, they demonstrate a dedication and commitment to their tasks. This dedication to task excellence forms the basis for a strong dedication and service to the customer. The net result is that the customer benefits. As the customer profits, so does the organization. Customers maintain the organization's health and vitality through the same kind of dedication and loyalty to the organization. An organization experiencing continued customer loyalty is then in a position to build loyalty and dedication to its management by providing the tools for management's continued success. Long-term excellence is not a mystery. It is the result of building commitments.

Figure 19−7   The commitments as a reinforcing cycle

CUSTOMER
internal and external

| TASK | ORGANIZATION |
| mission | and its management |

PEOPLE   SELF
individuals and the work team   as a manager

This concludes the four chapters focusing on implementing Situational Leadership. We have attempted to give you several specific examples of how Situational Leadership and One Minute Management interrelate and how these powerful behavioral science techniques can make measurable improvements in productivity. In Chapter 20 we will illustrate how several of the motivational and organizational theories we have discussed can be directly related to the Situational Leadership model.

NOTES

1. Louis E. Boone, C. Patrick Fleenor, and David L. Kurtz, "The Changing Profile of Business Leadership," *Business Horizons*, 26, No. 4, pp. 43–46.

2. Mohammad A. Yaghi, "The Behavioral Model: A New Approach to Decision Making," *Pakistan Management Review*, 23, No. 2 (Fall 1982), pp. 39–49.

3. Joseph Steger, George Manners, and Thomas Zimmerer, "Following the Leader: How to Link Management Styles to Subordinate Personality," *Management Review*, 71, No. 10 (October 1982), pp. 22–28.

4. Waldon Berry, "Group Problem Solving: How to Be Efficient Participants," *Supervisory Management*, 28, No. 6 (June 1983), pp. 13–19. See also Edwin A. Locke, David M. Schweiger, and Gary P. Latham, "Participation in Decision Making," *Organizational Dynamics*, 14, No. 3 (Winter 1986), pp. 65–79.

5. Col Eden and John Harris, *Management Decision and Decision Analysis* (New York: Wiley, 1975). See also Robert Hollmann and Maureen F. Ulrich, "Participative and Flexible Decision Making," *Journal of Small Business Management*, 21, No. 1 (January 1983), p. 1–7.

6. Patrick J. Montana and Deborah F. Nash, "Delegation: The Art of Managing," *Personnel Journal*, 60, No. 10 (October 1981), pp. 784–787. See also Charles D. Pringle, "Seven Reasons Why Managers Don't Delegate," *Management Solutions*, 31, No. 11 (November 1986), pp. 26–30.

7. Robert R. Blake, Jane S. Mouton, and Mian A. Ghani, "Situationalism vs. One Best Style: A Brief Study of Two Controversial Styles of Managerial Leadership in Pakistan and U.S.A.," *Pakistan Management Review*, 23, No. 2 (Fall 1982), pp. 70–91.

8. Louise Boone and James C. Johnson, "Profiles of the 801 Men and 1 Woman at the Top," *Business Horizons*, 23, No. 1 (February 1980), pp. 47–52. See also Robard Y. Hughes, "A Realistic Look at Decision Making," *Supervisory Management*, 25, No. 1 (January 1980), pp. 2–8.

9. Saul W. Gellerman, *Managers and Subordinates* (Hinsdale, Ill.: Dryden Press, 1976). See also Loretta M. Church and Raymond E. Alie, "Relationships between Managers' Personality Characteristics and Their Management Levels and Job Foci," *Akron Business and Economic Review*, 17, No. 4 (Winter 1986), pp. 29–45.

10. Andrew M. McCosh, *Management Decision Support Systems* (New York: Wiley, 1978).

11. J. Keith Murnighan, "Group Decision Making: What Strategies Should You Use?" *Management Review*, 70, No. 2 (February 1981), pp. 55–62.

CHAPTER 20

SYNTHESIZING MANAGEMENT THEORY: A Holistic Approach

All the theories, concepts, and empirical research presented in earlier chapters have made a contribution to the field of management. They seem to have some relevance in diagnosing an environment, in making some predictions, and in planning for changes in behavior. These viewpoints have often appeared to be like threads, each thread unique to itself.

Our attempt in this book has been to weave these independent viewpoints into a holistic fabric to increase significantly the usefullness of each in diagnosis and prediction. In this last chapter we will attempt to integrate these theories, using Situational Leadership (discussed in Chapter 8) as a synthesizing framework to portray their compatibilities rather than their differences.

SITUATIONAL LEADERSHIP AND MOTIVATION

In developing the model of the motivating situation (Chapter 2) it was contended that motives directed toward goals result in behavior. One way of classifying high strength motives is Maslow's hierarchy of needs[1] (Chapter 2); goals that tend to satisfy these needs can be described by Herzberg's hygiene factors and motivators[2] (Chapter 3). Both these frameworks can be integrated in Situational Leadership in terms of their relation to various readiness levels and the appropriate leadership styles that have a high probability of satisfying these needs or providing the corresponding goals, as illustrated in Figure 20–1.

It should be stressed that the relationship of theories (Maslow and Herzberg) to readiness levels in Situational Leadership are not necessarily absolute, direct correlations: they are integrative bench marks for practitioners to use in attempting to make better decisions for managing human resources. As a result, styles suggested as appropriate for one concept might not be exclusively for that concept; other styles may also satisfy these needs or goals to some degree. This caution will hold true throughout our discussions in this chapter.

Upon examining Figure 20–1, one can begin to plot the styles that tend to be appropriate for working with people motivated by the various

Figure 20–1 **Relationship between Situational Leadership and Maslow's hierarchy of needs and Herzberg's motivation-hygiene theory**

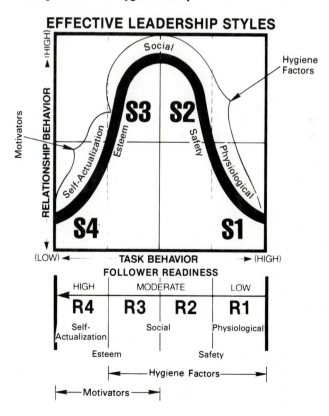

high strength needs described by Maslow. At the same time, leadership styles S1, S2, and S3 tend to provide goals consistent with satisfying hygiene factors, whereas styles S3 and S4 seem to facilitate the occurrence of the motivators.

SITUATIONAL LEADERSHIP, MANAGEMENT STYLES, AND HUMAN NATURE

McGregor's Theory X and Theory Y,[3] Likert's management systems,[4] and Argyris's immaturity−maturity[5] continuum (Chapter 3) blend easily into Situational Leadership, as illustrated in Figure 20−2.

In essence, Likert's System 1 describes behaviors that have often been associated with Theory X assumptions. According to these assumptions,

Figure 20−2 Relationship between Situational Leadership and McGregor's Theory X and Theory Y, Argyris's maturity−inmaturity continuum, and Likert's management systems

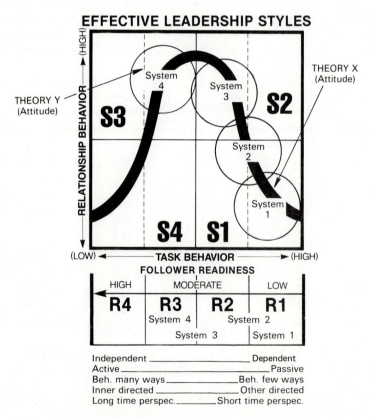

most people prefer to be directed, are not interested in assuming responsibility, and want security above all. These assumptions and the corresponding System 1 behaviors seem to be consistent with the immature end of Argyris's continuum. System 4 illustrates behaviors that have often been associated with Theory Y assumptions. A Theory Y manager assumes that people are *not* lazy and unreliable by nature, and thus can be self-directed and creative at work if properly motivated. These assumptions and the corresponding System 4 behaviors seem to relate to the mature end of Argyris's continuum. System 1 is a task-oriented, highly structured authoritarian management style. System 4 is based on teamwork, mutual trust, and confidence. Systems 2 and 3 are intermediate stages between these two extremes.

In general, the tendency among people is to consider Theory X managers as engaging primarily with task behaviors in highly structured ways and Theory Y managers primarily as using relationship behaviors. This is not always accurate. Theory X and Theory Y are managers' *assumptions* about the nature of people and do not necessarily translate directly into leader *behaviors*. There are examples of both Theory X and Theory Y managers who use all of the four leadership styles.

In one example, a Theory X manager calls a staff meeting and asks for participative (S3) solutions to a problem. In reality, though, he may keep everyone at the table until they agree with his own *predetermined* ideas for a solution. His behavior is participative in nature, but his assumptions are that only his own answer is acceptable.

In another instance, a Theory X manager with a wide span of control does not have sufficient time to supervise closely all the people who report to him. Therefore he uses close supervision (S1) with those people he perceives as major problems and by necessity leaves the others on their own (S4).

In a third example, a Theory X manager may demonstrate support (S2) behaviors in explaining his decisions to his subordinates. However, his behavior may be manipulative rather than "selling" and may be related more closely to his personal objectives than to the goals of the organization or his subordinates.

On the other hand, a Theory Y manager who has learned to diagnose subordinate levels of readiness may be found using all four leadership styles effectively. With people at below-average levels of readiness, he provides the necessary guidance and close supervision (S1). He gives support to people whose abilities are improving but who still need encouragement (S2 and S3). And he delegates appropriately to confident and competent employees who are capable of functioning on their own (S4).

As illustrated in Figure 20–3, Argyris's concept of examining A behavior (structured) and B behavior (unstructured) patterns with Theory X and Theory Y,[6] Schein's four assumptions about human nature and their implied managerial styles,[7] and McClelland's achievement motive[8] can also be integrated into Situational Leadership. Argyris contends that most often structured, controlling A behavior patterns are associated with Theory X assumptions about human nature and that unstructured, nondirective B behavior patterns are associated with Theory Y assumptions. But, as discussed in Chapter 3, there is an important difference between attitude and behavior, and therefore the relationship between Theory X and Theory Y assumptions and A behavior and B behavior patterns is not necessarily a one-to-one relationship. Thus, as Argyris points out, you can find a number of managers who have the predictable XA combination, but there are also some YA managers. Although both types of managers will tend to use styles S1 and S2, their assumptions or attitudes are not the same. The same holds true for YB and XB managers. Their behavior is similar (S3 and S4), but their assumptions are different.

In his book *Organizational Psychology*, Schein discusses four assumptions about people and their implied managerial styles: (1) rational-economic man, (2) social man, (3) self-actualizing man, and (4) complex man. These assumptions can help us further to integrate the work of Argyris, Likert, and McGregor into Situational Leadership, as seen in Figure 20–3.

The assumptions underlying *rational-economic* people are very similar to those depicted by McGregor's Theory X. In essence, people are seen as primarily motivated by economic incentives; passive beings to be manipulated, motivated, and controlled by the organization; irrational beings whose feelings must be neutralized and controlled. These assumptions imply a managerial strategy that places emphasis on efficient task performance and would be consistent with styles S1 and S2.

With *social* people come the assumptions that human beings are basically motivated by social needs; they seek meaning in the social relationships on the job and are more responsive to these than to the incentives and the controls of the organization. The managerial strategy implied for social people suggests that managers should not limit their attention to the task to be performed, but should give more attention to the needs of the people. Managers should be concerned with the feelings of their subordinates, and in doing so, must often act as the communication link between the employees and higher management. In this situation, the initiative for work begins to shift from leader to follower, with the leader tending to engage in behaviors related to styles S2 and S3.

Self-actualizing people are seen as seeking meaning and accomplishment in their work as their other needs become fairly well satisfied. As a result, these people tend to be primarily self-motivated, capable of being very self-directed, and willing to integrate their own goals with those of the organization. With self-actualizing people, managers need to worry less about being considerate to them and more about how to enrich their jobs and make them more challenging and meaningful. Managers attempt to de-

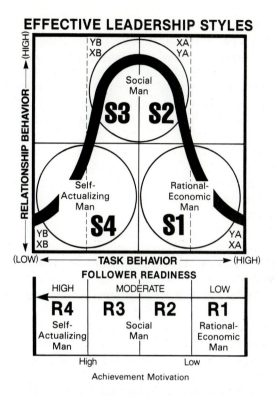

EFFECTIVE LEADERSHIP STYLES

Figure 20−3 Relationship between Situational Leadership and Argyris's A and B behavior patterns, McGregor's Theory X and Theory Y, Schein's four assumptions about people and their implied managerial strategies, and McClelland's achievement motive

termine what will challenge particular workers—managers become catalysts and facilitators rather than motivators and controllers. They delegate as much responsibility as they feel people can handle. Managers are now able to leave people alone to structure their own jobs and to provide their own socioemotional support through task accomplishment. This strategy is consistent with an S4 style appropriate for working with people of high levels of readiness (R4).

According to Schein, people are really more complex than rational-economic, social, or self-actualizing. In fact, people are highly viable, are capable of learning new motives, are motivated on the basis of many different kinds of needs, and can respond to numerous different leadership styles. Complex individuals tax the diagnostic skills of managers, and as Situational Leadership implies, effective managers must change their style appropriately to meet various contingencies.

According to McClelland, achievement-motivated people have certain characteristics in common. They like to set their own goals, especially moderately difficult but potentially achievable ("stretching") goals. In addition, they seem to be more concerned with personal achievement than with the rewards of success. As a result, they like concrete task-relevant feedback. They want to know the score. As illustrated in Figure 20−3, high achievement motivation tends to be associated with readiness levels R3 and R4, and low achievement motivation tends to be associated with readiness levels R1 and R2.

SITUATIONAL LEADERSHIP AND TRANSACTIONAL ANALYSIS

As discussed in Chapter 3, two concepts from transactional analysis (TA) and the work of Berne[9] and Harris[10] are ego states and life positions. As illustrated in Figure 20−4, these concepts can be integrated into Situational Leadership.

The three ego states in TA are Parent, Adult, and Child. An individual whose behavior is being evoked from the Child ego state can be either a destructive Child or a happy Child. The destructive Child seems to be associated with readiness level R1 and, therefore, the leadership style that is necessary with that Child ego state is S1. Low "strokes" are appropriate because too much socioemotional support along with the high structure may be viewed as permissiveness and support for the destructive behavior. If you are interacting with a happy Child, movement is toward readiness level R2, and thus the style that seems to be more effective is S2. Now there is a need for more two-way communication, socioemotional support and facilitating behavior along with the structure.

An individual whose behavior is being evoked from the Parent ego state can be either a nurturing Parent or critical Parent. The nurturing Parent seems to be associated with R2, and, therefore, the leadership style that is necessary with that Parent ego state, as illustrated in Figure 20−4 is S2. Any role defining or structuring has to be done in a supportive way. Too much task behavior without corresponding relationship behavior might suggest to nurturing Parents that the person trying to influence them does not care for them, and this might move their ego state more toward a critical Parent. That form of Parent ego state tends to be associated with readiness level R3 because Style S3 tends to work best when trying to work with a critical Parent ego state. If leaders use a high task style with critical Parents, it just tends to evoke more critical Parent "tapes," and soon these leaders may find themselves in a win−lose, Parent/Parent power struggle. To work with individuals with a critical Parent, leaders first must try to develop a good personal relationship with them before being able to use either of the high task styles (S1 and S2) effectively.

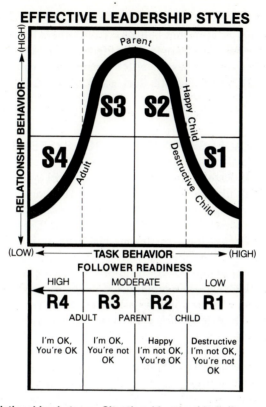

EFFECTIVE LEADERSHIP STYLES

Figure 20−4 Relationships between Situational Leadership and ego states and life positions associated with transactional analysis

In working with people whose behavior is being evoked from their Adult ego state, leaders can use an S4 style and leave them alone. These people are already thinking in rational, problem-solving ways and, provided they have the competence to do their jobs, tend to prefer to be left alone.

As illustrated in Figure 20−4, individuals with an "I'm not OK, you're not OK" life position tend to be associated with readiness level R1 and thus need high direction and close supervision. People who feel "I'm not OK, you're OK" are related to readiness level R2 and thus need both direction and socioemotional support. They will appreciate direction from leaders because they think these people are "OK" but also need high relationship behavior to help increase their "OK" feelings about themselves. People who feel "I'm OK, you're not OK" tend to be associated with readiness level R3. (Remember we are talking about normal people with this ego state and not mentally disturbed people, to whom psychiatrists like Berne would be referring in their discussions of transactional analysis.) Since people with this life

437

position are often covering up "not OK" feelings about themselves, they tend to require high relationship behavior from others before feeling "OK" about them or themselves. People with life positions of "I'm OK, you're OK" seem to relate to readiness level R4 because they can be given responsibility and be left alone and still feel good about themselves and other people.

SITUATIONAL LEADERSHIP AND CONTROL SYSTEMS

In Chapter 7 we discussed three fundamental control systems: Type I is the most structured and like an assembly line, Type II involves job enlargement but still requires manager control, and Type III is the least structured and involves job enrichment and little manager control. The impact that these various control systems have on leadership style is illustrated in Figure 20−5.

As is evident in Figure 20−5, the appropriate style to use with a Type I control system is high task/low relationship, Type II needs a high task/high relationship or high relationship/low task style, and Type III requires a low relationship/low task style. Relationships between control systems and ap-

Figure 20−5 Structural impact of control system on leadership style

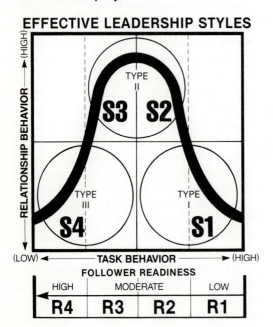

propriate leadership style are supported by the research of Stinson and Johnson.[11]

SITUATIONAL LEADERSHIP AND POWER BASES

In Chapter 9 we discussed seven power bases: coercive, connection, reward, legitimate, referent, information, and expert. As illustrated in Figure 20−6 and supported by the work of Hersey, Blanchard, and Natemeyer,[12] Situational Leadership can provide the basis for understanding the potential impact of each power base. In fact, in Chapter 9 it was argued that the readiness of the follower not only dictates which style of leadership will have the highest probability of success, but that the readiness of the follower also determines the power base that the leader should have in order to induce compliance or influence behavior.

As is suggested in Figure 20−6, a follower low in readiness (R1) generally needs strong directive behavior in order to become productive. To engage effectively in this S1 style, coercive power is often needed. As a follower begins to move from readiness level R1 to R2, directive behavior is

Figure 20−6 Relationship between Situational Leadership and power bases

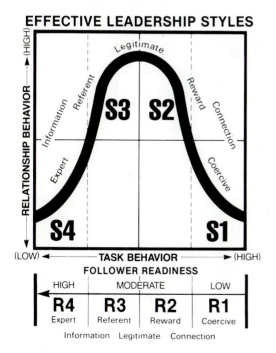

still needed and increases in supportive behavior are also important. The S1 and S2 leadership styles appropriate for these levels of readiness may become more effective if the leader has connection power and reward power. Legitimate power seems to be helpful to the S2 and S3 leadership styles that tend to influence moderate levels of readiness (R2 and R3). Referent power enhances the high supportive but low directive S3 style required to influence a moderate to high level of readiness. Information and expert power seem to be helpful in using the S3 and S4 styles that tend to motivate followers effectively at above-average readiness levels (R3 and R4).

SITUATIONAL LEADERSHIP AND PROBLEM OWNERSHIP

As discussed in Chapter 2, the work of Thomas Gordon[13] on parent effectiveness training (translated into leader/follower terminology) and the William Oncken, Jr., and Donald L. Wass[14] "monkey-on-the-back" analogy integrate well into Situational Leadership, as illustrated in Figure 20−7.

Figure 20−7 Situational Leadership and its relationship to concepts associated with parent effectiveness training

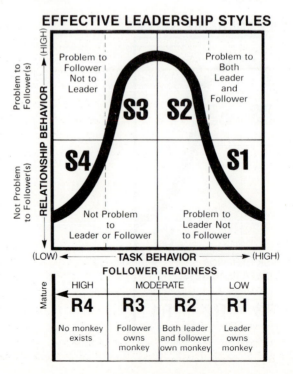

In working with people, Gordon suggests that people's behavior can either be acceptable or unacceptable to leaders. If the behavior of the follower is acceptable to the leader, the leader can use an S3 or S4 style. If the behavior of the follower is unacceptable to the leader, an S1 or S2 leadership style is appropriate. To differentiate further among S1 and S2, and S3 and S4 styles, a leader needs to determine who owns the problem, or in Oncken and Wass's terms, "who owns the monkey." As Figure 20–7 illustrates, if the behavior of the follower is acceptable and not a problem to either the leader or the follower (no monkey exists), then an S4 style is appropriate. If that same acceptable behavior is a problem to the follower—that is, the follower lacks understanding or motivation to continue the acceptable behavior for long periods of time but not the leader (the follower owns the monkey)—the appropriate leadership style to be used with that follower is S3. If a follower's behavior is unacceptable and a monkey to both follower and leader, then an S2 style should be used. And, finally, when the follower's behavior is unacceptable and a problem to the leader but not a problem to the follower (the leader owns the monkey), an S1 leadership has the highest probability of changing that behavior.

SITUATIONAL LEADERSHIP AND ORGANIZATIONAL GROWTH

As suggested in Chapter 15, organizations might be able to grow and develop over time without the crisis or revolutionary phases discussed by Greiner.[15] This could occur if after the phase of creativity managers moved their organization through the growth phases in an order consistent with Situational Leadership.

As illustrated in Figure 20–8 on page 442, the crisis of leadership might be averted by moving from the phase of creativity right into the phase of direction; the crises of autonomy, control, and red tape might be averted by moving from the direction phase right into the coordination phase, then into the collaboration phase, and finally into delegation.

SITUATIONAL LEADERSHIP AND CHANGE

Whenever you talk about initiating change (Chapter 15), a first step is determining the readiness level of the people with whom you are working. If they are low in readiness—dependent and unwilling to take responsibility for the change—they will tend to require more unfreezing (Lewin[16]) than if you are working with people who are moderate or high in their readiness levels. As illustrated in Figure 20–9 on page 442, leadership styles S1 and S2 tend to play a major role in terms of unfreezing; the emphasis in S2 and S3 styles is on the change process; and S3 and S4 stress the refreezing process.

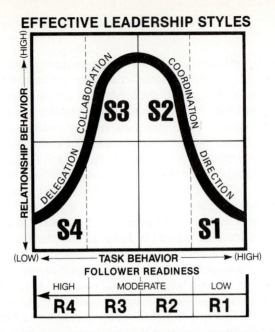

Figure 20–8 Situational Leadership and the evolutionary and growth phases of organizations discussed by Greiner

Figure 20–9 Relationship between Situational Leadership and the process of change

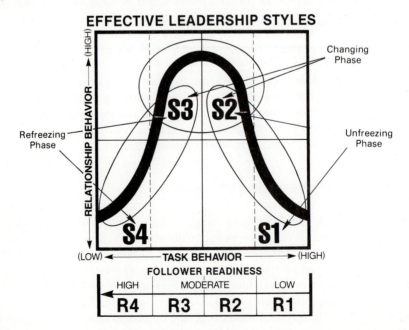

One of the techniques used to increase readiness is behavior modification[17] (Chapter 10), as illustrated in Figure 20–10. When working with people at low readiness levels, at first leaders tend to cut back on structure, giving individuals an opportunity to take some responsibility. When leaders get the smallest approximation of higher levels of readiness, they must immediately increase the socioemotional support as positive reinforcement. This stairlike process (cut back on structure and then increase socioemotional support) continues until the change or changes start to become a habit as the people develop. At that point, leaders tend also to cut back on reinforcement as they move toward S4 and a low relationship/low task style. If done earlier, this cutback on socioemotional support would have appeared as punishment to people at low or moderate levels of readiness. But to people of high readiness, the fact that their leader tends to leave them alone is positive reinforcement not only in terms of the task but also in terms of socioemotional support. As discussed in Chapter 10 and depicted in Figure 20–10, Homme's concept of contingency contracting[18] illustrates the gradual developmental movement (associated with behavior modification) from leader control (S1) to partial control by follower (S2) to equal control (S2 and S3) to partial control by leader (S3) and finally to follower control (S4).

As illustrated in Figure 20–11, S1 and S2 styles seem to be consistent with the behaviors associated with a directive change cycle, while S3 and S4

Figure 20–10   Situational Leadership and behavior modification

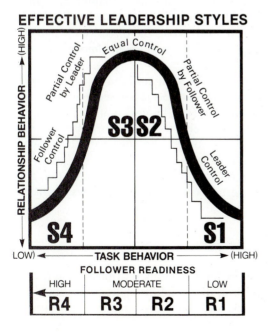

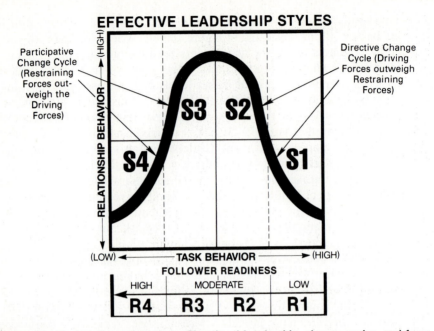

EFFECTIVE LEADERSHIP STYLES

Participative Change Cycle (Restraining Forces outweigh the Driving Forces)

Directive Change Cycle (Driving Forces outweigh Restraining Forces)

RELATIONSHIP BEHAVIOR (HIGH)

S3 S2

S4 S1

(LOW) ◄── TASK BEHAVIOR ──► (HIGH)

FOLLOWER READINESS

HIGH	MODERATE		LOW
R4	R3	R2	R1

Figure 20–11 Relationship between Situational Leadership, change cycles, and force field analysis

are more representative of a participative change cycle (Chapter 2).[19] In a participative change cycle, the change begins at the knowledge level and eventually moves to the organizational level, while the directive change cycle starts with changes in the organization and gradually moves toward changes in knowledge and attitudes.

As also shown in Figure 20–11, S1 and S2 styles tend to be appropriate for building on strong driving forces; S3 and S4 styles seem appropriate for attempting to overcome restraining forces (Chapters 6 and 15).[20] In increasing the driving forces, the emphasis seems to be on short-term output; when attempting to eliminate restraining forces, the concern is more with building intervening variables and concentrating on long-term goals. It should be emphasized that these are only tendencies and bench marks, and it should be recognized that under certain conditions other styles might be appropriate.

SUMMARY

Table 20–1 integrates the summary material presented in this chapter. The table indicates how many of the theories discussed throughout this book are related to the various readiness levels and their corresponding appropriate leadership style.

TABLE 20-1 Relationship Between Leadership Styles, Readiness Levels, and Other Organizational Behavior Theory, Concepts, and Research

Readiness of followers (therefore high probability)	STYLE of Leader
(R1) Low Readiness "Unable and insecure or unwilling . . ." Physiological/safety hygiene factors Rational-economic man Low achievement motivation Child (destructive) ego state I'm not OK, you're not OK Unacceptable behavior Leader "owns the monkey"	**(S1) HT/LR Telling** "Provide specific instructions and closely supervise . . ." Theory X (attitude) XA/YA System 1/System 2 Coercive and connection power Type 1 control system Leader control contracting Direction growth stage Unfreezing, changing (coercion) Directive change cycle
(R2) Low to Moderate Readiness "Unable but confident or willing . . ." Safety/social hygiene factor Rational-economic man/social man Low achievement motivation Child (happy)/Parent ego state I'm not OK, you're OK Unacceptable behavior Both leader and follower "own the monkey"	**(S2) HT/HR Selling** "Explain your decision and provide opportunity for clarification . . ." XA/YA System 2/System 3 Connection, reward, and legitimate power Type 2 control by follower/ equal control contractor Coordination growth stage Unfreezing, changing (identification) Directive/participative change cycles
(R3) Moderate to High Readiness "Able but insecure or unwilling . . ." Social/esteem Hygiene factors and motivators Social/self-actualizing man High achievement motivation Parent and Adult ego states I'm OK, you're not OK Acceptable behavior Follower "owns the monkey"	**(S3) HR/LT Participating** "Share ideas and facilitate decision making . . " Theory Y (attitude) YB/XB System 3/System 4 Legitimate, referent, information power Type 2 control system Equal control/partial control by leader contracting Collaborative growth stage Changing/refreezing (internalization) Participative/directive change cycles

(continued)

TABLE 20-1 (*continued*)

Readiness of followers (therefore high probability)	STYLE of Leader
(R4) High Readiness "Able and confident or willing . . ." Esteem/self-actualization motivators Self-actualizing man High achievement motivation Adult ego state I'm OK, you're OK Acceptable behavior No monkey exists	(S4) LR/LT Delegating "Turn over responsibility for decisions and implementation . . ." Theory Y (attitude) YB/XB System 4 Information, expert power Type 3 control system Follower control contracting Delegation growth stage Refreezing Participative change cycle

CONCLUSIONS AND REFLECTIONS

There is still much that is unknown about human behavior. Unanswered questions remain and further research is necessary. Knowledge about motivation, leader behavior, and change will continue to be of great concern to practitioners of management for several reasons: it can help improve the effective utilization of human resources; it can help in preventing resistance to change, restriction of output, and personnel disputes; and often it can lead to a more productive organization.

Our intention has been to provide a conceptual framework that may be useful to the reader in applying the conclusions of the behavioral sciences. The value that a framework of this kind has is *not* in changing one's knowledge but in changing one's behavior in working with people.

We have discussed three basic competencies in influencing: *Diagnosing*—being able to understand and interpret the situation you are attempting to influence; *Adapting*—being able to adapt your behavior and the resources you control to the contingencies of the situation; and *communicating*—being able to put the message in such a way that people can easily understand and accept it. Each of these competencies is different and requires a different developmental approach. For example, *diagnosing* is cognitive in nature and requires thinking skills; *adapting* is behavioral in nature and requires behavioral practice; and *communicating* is process oriented and requires learning and interrelating the key steps in the process. Since these three competencies require different knowledge and skills, how do we continue the process that we started with this book?

The key to starting the process of changing behavior is sharing the theories that you have read about in this book with other people in your own organization. Two things occur when people who work together all have a common language. First, they are able to give each other feedback and help in a very rational, unemotional way that affects behavior. For example, we once worked with an autocratic manager, "Bill," who was noted for his Theory X memos, such as, "it has come to my attention, and, therefore, as of Monday all personnel will be required to . . . " Shortly after exposing this manager and his staff from two levels below him on the management hierarchy to Situational Leadership model, the manager sent out one of his "famous" Theory X memos. Several days later when we talked to him, he related that he had received a number of written (unsigned) comments on the memo. The comments included such remarks as "a little Theory X today, don't you think?" Do you have anything else in your repertoire besides S1 style?" "Are we really that unwilling?" This feedback had a real impact on the manager as he reexamined his memo and his approach. It was difficult for him to rationalize away the feedback, because like R. D. Laing's *Knots*[21] "he knew that they knew that he knew the theory" and "they knew that they knew that he knew the theory." As some of the managers suggested, this was one of the first times he had really "heard" feedback. As a result of this incident and use of the language in meetings, everyone started helping each other (not just the manager) make changes in their behavior so they could become a more effective working team.

Second, subordinates start to realize that if their manager is using Situational Leadership it is not the manager but *their* behavior that determines the leadership style to be used with them. For example, if everyone knows the theory in a family, the children (especialy teenagers) realize how they can keep their parents off their backs. All they have to do is behave in solid, responsible ways, which everyone has agreed are appropriate, and their parents will be supportive (S3) or leave them alone (S4). But if they want to get hassled and closely supervised by their parents, all they have to do is misbehave and be irresponsible. Thus, theory is a vehicle to help people understand and share expectations in their environment so that they can gradually learn to supervise their own behavior and become responsible, self-motivated individuals. An observation on leadership by the Chinese philosopher Lao-Tse[22] sums it up well: "Of the best leaders, when their task is accomplished, the people all remark, 'We have done it ourselves.'"

We have provided many examples and illustrations throughout this book showing how the behavioral sciences can make a positive difference in the performance of both individuals and organizations. But perhaps our primary objective in writing this book is to make a contribution to world peace. We believe that significant contributions to human well-being will *not* come primarily through economic, military, political, or technological decisions. If we are going to achieve our long-sought goal of world peace, it must come through improved utilization of our human resources—toward helping people become more productive and to have a greater share of the benefits that human productivity can achieve. Our outlook is a world outlook for practical applied behavioral science—an outlook that sees all peoples sharing in the benefits that technology can bring, a world of people living and working in an environment that contributes to their personal well-being, a world of peace. We invite you to join us in working toward this goal.

NOTES

1. Abraham Maslow, *Motivation and Personality* (New York: Harper & Row, 1954).
2. Frederick Herzberg, *Work and the Nature of Man* (New York: World Publishing, 1966).
3. Douglas McGregor, *The Human Side of Enterprise* (New York: McGraw-Hill, 1960).
4. Rensis Likert, *The Human Organization* (New York: McGraw-Hill, 1967).
5. Chris Argyris, *Personality and Organization* (New York: Harper & Row, 1957). See also Chris Argyris, Robert Putnam, and Diana M. Smith, *Action Science* (San Francisco: Jossey-Bass, 1985).
6. Chris Argyris, *Management and Organizational Development: The Path From XA to YB* (New York: McGraw-Hill, 1971). See also Chris Argyris and Donald A. Schon, *Organizational Learning: A Theory of Action Perspective* (Reading, Mass.: Addison-Wesley, 1978); Chris Argyris, *Reasoning, Learning, and Action: Individual and Organization* (San Francisco: Jossey-Bass, 1982).
7. Edgar H. Schein, *Organizational Psychology*, 2nd ed. (Englewood Cliffs, N.J.: Prentice-Hall, 1970), pp. 50–72. See also Edgar H. Schein, *Organizational Culture and Leadership* (San Francisco: Jossey-Bass, 1985); Edgar H. Schein, *Career Dynamics: Matching Individual and Organizational Needs* (Reading, Mass.: Addison-Wesley, 1978).
8. David C. McClelland, J. W. Atkinson, R.A. Clark, and E. L. Lowell, *The Achievement Motive* (New York: Appleton-Century-Crofts, 1953); and *The Achieving Society* (Princeton, N.J.: D. Van Nostrand, 1961). See also David C. McClelland, *Motivation and Society* (San Francisco: Jossey-Bass, 1982); David C. McClelland, *Motives, Personality, and Society: Selected Papers* (New York: Praeger, 1984).
9. Eric Berne, *Games People Play* (New York: Grove Press, 1964). See also Eric Berne, *Beyond Games and Scripts* (New York: Grove Press, 1976); Eric Berne, *Transactional Analysis in Psychotherapy* (New York: Grove Press, 1961).
10. Thomas Harris, *I'm OK—You're OK: A Practical Guide to Transactional Analysis* (New York: Harper & Row, 1969). See also Thomas A. Harris and Amy Bjork, *Staying OK* (New York: Harper & Row, 1985).
11. John E. Stinson and Thomas W. Johnson "The Path-Goal Theory of Leadership: A Partial Test and Suggested Refinement," *Academy of Management Journal*, 18, No. 2 (June 1975), pp. 242–252.
12. Paul Hersey, Kenneth H. Blanchard, and Walter E. Natemeyer, "Situational Leadership, Perception, and the Impact of Power" *Group and Organizational Studies*, 4, No. 4 (December 1979), pp. 418–428.
13. Thomas Gordon, *P.E.T. (Parent Effectiveness Training)* (New York: Peter H. Wyden, 1970). See also Thomas Gordon, *T.E.T. (Teacher Effectiveness Training)* (New York: Peter H. Wyden, 1974).
14. William Oncken, Jr., and Donald L. Wass, "Management Time: Who's Got the Monkey?" *Harvard Business Review*, November–December 1974, pp. 75–80.
15. Larry E. Greiner, "Evolution and Revolution as Organizations Grow," *Harvard Business Review*, July–August 1972, pp. 37–46.
16. Kurt Lewin, "Frontiers in Group Dynamics: Concept Methods, and Reality in Social Science; Social Equilibria and Social Change," *Human Relations*, 1, No. 1 (June 1947), pp. 5–41.
17. B. F. Skinner, *Science and Human Behavior* (New York: Macmillan, 1953). See also A. Bandura, *Principles of Behavior Modification* (New York: Holt, Rinehart & Winston, 1969); B. F. Skinner, *About Behaviorism* (New York: Knopf, 1974); A. Bandura and D. Cer-

vone, "Self-evaluative and Self-efficacy Mechanisms Governing the Motivational Effects of Goal Systems," *Journal of Personality and Social Psychology*, 1983.

18. Lloyd Homme, *How to Use Contingency Contracting in the Classroom* (Champaign, Ill.: Research Press, 1970).

19. Paul Hersey and Kenneth H. Blanchard, "Change and the Use of Power," *Training and Development Journal*, January 1972.

20. Lewin, "Frontiers in Group Dynamics."

21. R. D. Laing, *Knots* (New York: Pantheon Books, 1970).

22. Lao-tsu, *The Way of the Ways: Lao-tsu, Translated and with a Commentary by Herrymon Maurer* (New York: Schocken Books, 1985), p. 52.

RECOMMENDED SUPPLEMENTARY READING

ACKERMAN, LEONARD, and JOSEPH P. GRUENWALD. "Help Employees Motivate Themselves," *Personnel Journal*, 63 (July 1984).

ADAIR, JOHN ERIC. *The Skills of Leadership*. New York: Nichols Pub., 1984.

ADAMS, JEROME B. *Effective Leadership for Women and Men*. Norwood, N.J.: Alblex Pub., 1985.

———. "Effects of Perceived Group Effectiveness and Group Role on Attributions of Group Performance," *Journal of Applied Social Psychology*, 15, No. 4 (1985), 387–398.

ALDEFER, C. P. *Existence, Relatedness, and Growth: Human Needs in Organizational Settings*. New York: Free Press, 1972.

ALLESSANDRA, ANTHONY J., PHILLIP S. WEXLER, and JERRY D. DEEM. *Non-Manipulative Selling*. Reston, Va.: Reston, 1979.

AMADO, FAUCHEUX, G. AMADO, and A. LAURENT. "Organizational Development and Change," M. R. ROSENZWEIG and L. W. PORTER (eds.), *Annual Review of Psychology*, Vol. 33, pp. 343–370. Palo Alto, Calif.: Annual Reviews, 1982.

APPELL, ALLEN L. *A Practical Approach to Human Behavior in Business*. Columbus: Merrill, 1984.

ARGYRIS, CHRIS. *Personality and Organization*. New York: Harper & Row, 1957.

———. *Understanding Organizational Behavior*. Homewood, Ill.: Irwin, Dorsey Press, 1960.

———. *Organization and Innovation*. Homewood, Ill.: Irwin, Dorsey Press, 1965.

———. "Beyond Freedom and Dignity by B. F. Skinner: A Review Essay." *Harvard Educational Review*, 41 (1971), 550–567.

———. *Reasoning, Learning, and Action: Individual and Organization*. San Francisco: Jossey-Bass, 1982.

———. *Increasing Leadership Effectiveness*. Malabar, Fla.: Krieger, 1984.

———. *Strategy, Change and Defensive Routines*. Belmont, Calif.: Pitman Pub., 1985.

ARGYRIS, CHRIS, and RICHARD M. CYERT. *Leadership in the Eighties: Essays on Higher Education.* Cambridge, Mass.: Inst. Ed. Management, 1980.

ARVEY, R. D., and J. M. IVANCEVICH. "Punishment in Organizations: A Review, Propositions, and Research Suggestions," *Academy of Management Review,* 5 (1980), 123–132.

ASCH, S. E. *Social Psychology.* Englewood Cliffs, N.J.: Prentice-Hall, 1952.

———. "Effects of Group Pressure upon the Modification and Distortion of Judgments," in Dorwin Cartwright and Alvin Zander, eds., *Group Dynamics,* 2nd ed., pp. 189–200. Evanston, Ill.: Row, Peterson, 1960.

ATKINSON, JOHN WILLIAM. *Motivation and Achievement.* New York: Halsted Press, 1974.

BACHMAN, J. G., D. G. BOWERS, and P. M. MARCUS. "Bases of Supervisory Power: A Comparative Study in Five Organizational Settings," in Arnold S. Tannenbaum, *Control in Organizations.* New York: McGraw-Hill, 1968.

BALES, R. F. "Task Roles and Social Roles in Problem-Solving Groups," in N. Maccoby et al., *Readings in Social Psychology,* 3rd ed. New York: Holt, Rinehart & Winston, 1958.

BANDLER, RICHARD, and JOHN GRINDER. *Frogs into Princes: Neuro-Linguistic Programming.* Moab, Utah: Real People Press, 1979.

BANDURA, A. *The Social Foundations of Thought and Action: A Social Cognitive Theory.* Englewood Cliffs, N.J.: Prentice-Hall, 1986.

BANKART C. P., and S. W. POWERS. "Individual Decisions and Group Consensus," *Journal of Social Psychology,* 126 (June 1986), 369–374.

BARNARD, CHESTER I. *The Functions of the Executive.* Cambridge, Mass.: Harvard University Press, 1938.

BASS, BERNARD M. *Stogdill's Handbook of Leadership,* 2nd rev. ed. New York: Free Press, 1981.

———. *Organizational Decision Making.* Homewood, Ill.: Irwin, 1983.

———. "Leadership: Good, Better, and Best," *Organizational Dynamics,* Winter 1985.

———. *Leadership and Performance beyond Expectations.* New York: Free Press, 1985.

BATTEN, J. D. *Beyond Management by Objectives.* New York: American Management Association, 1966.

———. *Tough-Minded Management.* New York: AMACOM, 1984.

BAVELAS, A. "Communication Patterns in Task-Oriented Groups," in Dorwin Cartwright and Alvin Zander, eds., *Group Dynamics,* 2nd ed. Evanston, Ill.: Row, Peterson, 1953.

BAVELAS, A., and R. T., HARRIS. *Organizational Transitions: Managing Complex Change.* Reading, Mass.: Addison-Wesley, 1977.

BAVELAS, A., and G. STRAUSS. "Group Dynamics and Intergroup Relations," in K. Benne and R. Chin, eds., *The Planning of Change.* New York: Holt, Rinehart & Winston, 1962.

BEAL, G. M. *Sociological Perceptives of Domestic Development.* Ames: Iowa State University Press, 1971.

———. *Knowledge Generation, Exchange and Utilization.* Boulder: Western Press, 1986.

BEAL, G. M., J. BOHLEN, and N. RAUDABAUGH. *Leadership and Dynamic Group Action.* Ames: Iowa State University Press, 1962.

BECK, DON EDWARD. "Beyond the Grid and Situationalism: A Living Systems View," *Training and Development Journal,* 36 (August 1982), 76.

BELLMAN, GEOFFREY M. *The Quest for Staff Leadership.* Glenview, Ill.: Scott, Foresman, 1986.

BENFIELD, CLIFFORD J. "Problem Performers: The Third-Party Solution," *Personnel Journal,* 64 (August 1985), 96–101.

BENNIS, WARREN G. *The Unconscious Conspiracy: Why Leaders Can't Lead.* New York: AMACOM, 1976.

———. "Where Have All the Leaders Gone?" *Technology Review,* 758, no. 9 (March–April 1977), 3–12.

———. "The 4 Competencies of Leadership," *Training and Development Journal,* 38 (August 1984), 15.

————. *The Planning of Change*. New York: Harper & Row, 1985.

BENNIS, WARREN, and BERT NANUS. *Leaders: The Strategies for Taking Charge*. New York: Harper & Row, 1986.

BENSON, GARY L. "On the Campus: How Well do Business Schools Prepare Graduates for the Business World?" *Personnel*, 60 (July–August 1983), 63–65.

BENZIGER, KATHERINE. "The Powerful Woman," *Hospital Forum*, May/June 1982, pp. 15–20.

BERNE, ERIC. *Transactional Analysis in Psychotherapy*. New York: Grove Press, 1961.

————. *Games People Play*. New York: Grove Press, 1964.

BERNE, ERIC, and C. STEINER. Beyond Games and Scripts. New York: Ballantine, 1978.

BERNE, ERIC, et al. *Transactional Analysis Bulletin: Selected Articles from Volumes 1-9*, Paul McCormick, ed. San Francisco: TA Press, 1976.

BERRY, WALDON. "Group Problem solving: How to Be Efficient Participants," *Supervisory Management*, 28, No. 6, (June 1983), 13–19.

BISSELL, CHARLES BEN. "Diffusing the Difficult Employee," *Management World*, February 1985, pp. 30-31.

BITTEL, LESTER R. *Leadership: The Key to Management Success*. New York: Franklin Watts, 1984.

BLAIR, JOHN D., and CARLTON J. WHITEHEAD. "Can Quality Circles Survive in the United States?" *Business Horizons*, 27 (September–October 1984), 17–23.

BLAKE, ROBERT R. *Executive Achievement*. New York: McGraw-Hill, 1986.

BLAKE, ROBERT R., and JANE S. MOUTON. *The Versatile Manager: A Grid Profile*. Homewood, Ill.: Irwin, 1982.

————. *The Managerial Grid III*, 3rd ed. Houston, Tex.: Gulf Publishing, 1984.

————. "The Managerial Grid III," *Personnel Psychology*, 39 (Spring 1986), 238–240.

BLANCHARD, KENNETH H. "College Board of Trustees: A Need for Directive Leadership," *Academy of Management Journal*, 10 (December 1967).

————. *Leadership and the One Minute Manager*. New York: Morrow, 1985.

————. *The One Minute Manager Gets Fit*. New York: Morrow, 1986.

BLANCHARD, KENNETH, and SPENSER JOHNSON. *The One Minute Manager*. New York: Morrow, 1982.

BLANCHARD, KENNETH, and ROBERT LORBER. *Putting the One-Minute Manager to Work: How to Turn the Three Secrets into Skills*. New York: Morrow, 1984.

————. *Putting the One Minute Manager to Work*. New York: Berkley Pub., 1985.

BLANCHARD, KENNETH, and DREA ZIGARMI. *Leadership and the One Minute Manager*. New York: Morrow, 1985.

BOGUE, E. GRADY. *The Enemies of Leadership*. Bloomington, Ind.: Phi Delta Kappa Educational Foundation, 1985.

BOLMAN, LEE, and TERRENCE DEAL. *Modern Approaches to Understanding and Managing Organizations*. San Francisco: Jossey-Bass, 1984.

BOONE, LOUIS E., C. PATRICK FLEENOR, and DAVID L. KURTZ. "The Changing Profile of Business Leadership," *Business Horizons* 26, No. 4, 43–46.

BOONE, LOUIS E., and DAVID L. KURTZ. *Management*, 2nd ed. New York: Random House, 1987.

BORGATTA, EDGAR F., ROBERT F. BALES, and ARTHUR S. COUCH. "Some Findings Relevant to the Great Man Theory of Leadership," *American Sociological Review*, 19 (1954), 755–759.

BOWERS, D. G. "Organizational Development: Promises, Performances, Possibilities," *Organizational Dynamics*, Spring 1976, pp. 50–62.

BOWERS, D. G., and S. E. SEASHORE. "Predicting Organizational Effectiveness with a Four-Factor Theory of Leadership," *Administrative Science Quarterly*, 11, no. 2 (1966), 238–263.

BRADFORD, DAVID L. *Managing for Excellence*. New York: Wiley, 1984.

BRADFORD, Leland P. National Training Laboratories: Its History 1947–1970. Bethel, Maine: National Training Laboratories, 1974.

————, ed. *Group Development*, 2nd ed. San Diego: Univ. Assoc., 1978.

BRADFORD, LELAND P., JACK R. GIBB, and KENNETH D. BENNE. *T-Group Theory and Laboratory Method*. New York: Wiley, 1964.

BRADLEY, RAYMOND TREVOR. *Charisma and Social Structure.* New York: Paragon House, 1987.

BRASS, DANIEL J. "Being in the Right Place: A Structural Analysis of Individual Influence in an Organization," *Administrative Science Quarterly,* 29 (1984), 518.

BROWN, JANE COVEY, and ROSABETH MOSS KANTER. "Empowerment: Key to Effectiveness," *Hospital Forum,* May/June 1982, pp. 6–12.

BRYMAN, ALAN. *Leadership and Organizations.* London & Boston: Routledge & Kegan Paul, 1986.

BUCKMAN, STEVE. "Finding Out Why A Good Performer Went Bad," *Supervisory Management,* August 1984, pp. 39–42.

BURNS, JAMES MACGREGOR. *Leadership and Values.* Menlo Park, Calif. SRI International, Values and Lifestyles Program, 1984.

BURNS, T., and G. M. STALKER. *The Management of Innovation.* London: Tavistock Publications, 1961.

CAMPBELL, DAVID N., R. L. FLEMING, and RICHARD C. GROTE. "Discipline Without Punishment—At Last," *Harvard Business Review,* 64 (July–August 1985), 162–164.

CAREW, D. W., et al. "Group Development and Situational Leadership: A Model for Managing Groups," *Training and Development Journal,* 40 (June 1986), 46–50.

CARROLL, STEPHEN J., and HENRY L. TOSI. *Management by Objectives: Applications and Research.* New York: Macmillan, 1973.

CARTWRIGHT, D. "Achieving Change in People: Some Applications of Group Dynamics Theory," *Human Relations,* 4 (1951) 381–392.

CARTWRIGHT, D., and A. ZANDER, eds. *Group Dynamics: Research and Theory,* 2nd ed. Evanston, Ill.: Row, Peterson, 1960.

CARUTH, DON, and ROBERT M. NOE. "Motivate! Six Dynamic Solutions to an Age-Old Challenge," *Management Weekly,* June 1984, pp. 14–15.

———. "How Not to Motivate," *Management World,* October 1985, pp. 19–20.

CERTO, S. *Principles of Modern Management Functions and Systems.* Dubuque, Iowa: Brown, 1983.

CHANDLER, A. D., JR. *Strategy and Structure.* Cambridge, Mass.: MIT Press, 1962.

CHRISTNER, CHARLOTTE A., and JOHN K. HEMPHILL. "Leader Behavior of B-29 Commanders and Changes in Crew Members' Attitudes toward the Crew," *Sociometry,* 18 (1955), 82–87.

CHRISTOPHER, ELIZABETH M. Leadership Training through Gaming. New York: Nichols Pub., 1987.

CLARKE, CHRISTOPHER, and SIMON PRATT. "Leadership's Four-Part Progress," *Management Today,* March 1985, pp. 84–86.

COCH, L., and J. R. P. FRENCH, JR. "Overcoming Resistance to Change," *Human Relations,* 1, No. 4 (1948), 512–532.

COFER, C. N., and M. H. APPLEY. Motivation: Theory and Research. New York: Wiley, 1964.

CORNELISSEN, MICHAEL. "Management Trends: People and Technology Are Key," *Business Quarterly,* 50, No. 1 (Spring 1985), 84–88.

CORNELL, RICHARD D. "The 'Age of Entrepreneurialism'—What It Means to You," *Supervisory Management,* January 1985, pp. 22–24.

CRIBBIN, JAMES J. *Leadership, Your Competitive Edge.* New York: AMACOM, 1984.

CROSBY, PHILIP B. *Running Things.* New York: McGraw-Hill, 1986.

CULLINAN, TERRENCE. "Women's Needs Will Continue Job Impact," *California Business,* August 1985, pp. 100–101.

CUMING, PAMELA. *The Power Handbook.* New York: Van Nostrand Reinhold, 1984.

CYERT, RICHARD M., and JAMES G. MARCH. *A Behavioral Theory of the Firm.* Englewood Cliffs, N.J.: Prentice-Hall, 1963.

DALTON, GENE, and PAUL H. THOMPSON. *Novations: Strategies for Career Management.* Glenview, Ill.: Scott, Foresman, 1985.

DeBOARD, ROBERT. "Bridging the Culture Chasm," *Management Today,* March 1985, pp. 88–92.

DIBOLD, JOHN. *Making the Future Work.* New York: Simon & Schuster, 1984.

DILTS, ROBERT, JOHN GRINDER, RICHARD BANDLER, LESLIE C. BANDLER, and

JUDITH DeLOZIER. *Neuro-Linguistic Programming: Volume I—The Study of the Structure of Subjective Experience*. Cupertino, Calif.: Meta Publications, 1980.

DIMOCK, HEDLEY G. *Groups*. San Diego, Calif.: University Associates, 1987.

DOUGLASS, L. M. *Review of Leadership in Nursing*. St. Louis, Mo.: Mosby, 1977.

DRUCKER, PETER F. *The Practice of Management*. New York: Harper & Row, 1954.

———. "The Discipline of Innovation," *Harvard Business Review*, 64 (May–June 1985), 67–72.

———. *Effective Executive*. New York: Harper & Row, 1985.

———. *Managing in Turbulent Times*. New York: Harper & Row, 1985.

DUBLIN, R. "Work in Modern Society," in R. Dublin, ed., *Handbook of Work, Organization, and Society*, Chicago: Rand-McNally, 1976.

EDWARDS, MARK R., WALTER C. BROMON, and J. RUTH SPROULL. "Solving the Double Bind in Performance Appraisal: A Saga of Wolves, Sloths, and Eagles," *Business Horizons*, 28, No. 3 (May/June 1985), 59–68.

EDWARDS, MARK R., and S. RUTH SPROULL. "Making Performance Appraisal Perform: The Use of Team Evaluations," *Personnel*, 62, No. 3 (March 1985), 28–32.

Effective Leadership in Action. Chicago, Ill.: American Marketing Association, 1987.

EINHORN, JAY. *Leadership in Health Care and Human Service Organizations*. Springfield, Ill.: Thomas, 1986.

Essentials of Supervision. Malvern, Pa.: Insurance Institute of America, 1985.

ETIZIONI, AMITAI. *Complex Organizations*. New York: Holt, Rinehart & Winston, 1961.

FERSTER, C. B., and B. F. SKINNER. *Schedules of Reinforcement*. New York: Appleton-Century-Crofts, 1957.

FESTINGER, LEON. *A Theory of Cognitive Dissonance*. Stanford, Calif.: Stanford University Press, 1957.

———. *The Human Legacy*. New York: Columbia University Press, 1983.

FIEDLER, FRED E. "Engineer the Job to Fit the Manager," *Harvard Business Review*, 51 (1965), 115–122.

———. *A Theory of Leadership Effectiveness*. New York: McGraw-Hill, 1967.

———. *Improving Leadership Effectiveness*. New York: Wiley, 1984.

———. *New Approaches to Effective Leadership*. New York: Wiley, 1987.

FIEDLER, FRED E., and MARTIN M. CHEMERS. *Improving Leadership Effectiveness: The Leader Match Concept*. New York: Wiley, 1984.

FILLEY, ALAN C. *Interpersonal Conflict Resolution*. Glenview, Ill.: Scott, Foresman, 1975.

———. *The Compleat Manager: What Works When*. Middeton, Wisc.: Green Briar Press, 1985.

FILLEY, ALAN C., and ROBERT J. HOUSE. *Managerial Process and Organizational Behavior*. Glenview, Ill.: Scott, Foresman, 1969.

FINE, DORIS R. *When Leadership Fails*. New Brunswick, N.J.: Transaction Books, 1986.

FITZGERALD, P. E. "How to Play Catch—and Be a Better Communicator," *Supervisory Management*, 30, No. 1, (1985), 27–31.

FLEISHMAN, E. A. "Twenty Years of Consideration and Structure," in E. A. Fleishman and J. G. Hunt, eds., *Current Developments in the Study of Leadership*. Carbondale, Ill.: Southern Illinois University Press, 1973.

FRENCH, J. R. P., JR., JOACHIM ISRAEL, and DAGFINN ĀS. "An Experiment on Participation in a Norwegian Factory," *Human Relations*, 13, No. 1 (1960), 3–19.

FRENCH, J. R. P., and B. RAVEN. "The Bases of Social Power," in D. Cartwright, *Studies in Social Power*. Ann Arbor: University of Michigan, Institute for Social Research, 1959.

FREUD, SIGMUND. *New Introductory Lectures on Psychoanalysis*. New York: Norton, 1933.

FROMM, ERIC. *The Sane Society*. New York: Rinehart, 1955.

GARDNER, JOHN WILLIAMS. *Excellence*. New York: Norton, 1984.

GARDNER, MERYL P. "Creating Corporate Culture for the Eighties," *Business Horizons*, 50, No. 1 (Spring 1985), 84–88.

GELLERMAN, SAUL W. *Management by Motivation*. New York: American Management Association, 1968.

———. *Managers and Subordinates*. Hinsdale, Ill.: Dryden Press, 1976.

GEVANS, MARTIN. "Organizational Behavior: The Central Role of Motivation," *Journal of Management*, 12, No. 2, (Summer 1986), 203–222.

GHISELLI, EDWIN E., and R. BARTHOL. "Role Perceptions of Successful and Unsuccessful Supervisors," *Journal of Applied Psychology*, 40 (1956), 241–244.

GIBB, CECIL A. "The Principles and Traits of Leadership," *Journal of Abnormal and Social Psychology*, 42 (1947), 267–284.

———. "Leadership," in Gardner Lindzey, ed., *Handbook of Social Psychology*, Cambridge, Mass.: Addison-Wesley, 1954.

GIBB, JACK R. *A New View of Personal and Organizational Development*. La Jolla, Calif.: Omicron Press, 1978.

GIBSON, JAMES L. *Organizations*. Plano, Tex.: Business Publications, 1985.

GINSBURG, SUSAN G. "Diagnosing and Treating Managerial Malaise," *Personnel*, 61 (July–August 1984), 34–46.

GLANZ, E. Foundations and Principles of Guidance. Boston: Allyn and Bacon, 1964.

GODDARD, ROBERT W. "The Rise of the New Organization," *Management World*, January 1985, p. 9.

GORDON, T. *Group-centered Leadership*. Boston: Houghton Mifflin, 1955.

GORDON, THOMAS. *Leader Effectiveness Training*. New York: Bantam, 1980.

———. *P.E.T., Parent Effectiveness Training*. New York: Wyden, 1970.

———. *T.E.T. (Teacher Effectiveness Training)*. New York: Wyden, 1974.

GORN, G. J., and R. N. KANUNGO. "Job Involvement and Motivation: Are Intrinsically Motivated Managers More Job Involved?" *Organizational Behavior and Human Performance*, 26 (1980), 265–277.

GOWEN, CHARLES R. "Managing Work Group Performance by Individual Goals and Group Goals for an Interdependent Group Task," *Journal of Organizational Behavior* 7, No. 3 (Winter 1986), 5–27.

GRANT, PHILIP C. "Why Employee Motivation Has Declined in America," *Personnel Journal*, 61 (December 1982).

GREINER, LARRY E. "Evolution and Revolution as Organizations Grow," *Harvard Business Review*, 51 (July–August 1972), 37–46.

GRIFFIN, RICKY. *Management*. Boston: Houghton Mifflin, 1984.

Group Plannings and Problems—Solving Methods in Engineering Management, ed. by Shirley A. Olsen. New York: Wiley, 1982.

GUEST, ROBERT H. *Innovative Work Practices*. New York: Pergamon, 1982.

———. Robotics: *The Human Dimension*. New York: Pergamon, 1984.

GUEST, ROBERT H., PAUL HERSEY, and KENNETH H. BLANCHARD, *Organizational Change Through Effective Leadership*, 2nd ed. Englewood Cliffs, N.J.: Prentice-Hall, 1986.

———. *Work Teams and Team Building*. New York: Pergamon, 1986.

HACKMAN, J. R., and G. R. OLDHAM. *Work Design*. Reading, Mass.: Addison-Wesley, 1979.

HAGBERG, JANET. "The Good, the Bad and the Ugly: Understanding Power Styles," *Working Women*, 12 (1984), 124–178.

HAGGAI, TOM. *How the Best Is Won*. Nashville: Nelson, 1987.

HAIRE, M. "Psychological Problems Relevant to Business and Industry," *Psychological Bulletin*, 56 (1959), 169–194.

HALE,RANDOLPH M. "Managing Human Resources: Challenge for the Future," *Enterprise*, June 1985, pp. 6–9.

HALL, D. T. *Careers in Organizations*. Santa Monica, Calif.: Goodyear, 1976.

HALPIN, ANDREW W. *The Leadership Behavior of School Superintendents*. Chicago: Midwest Administration Center, University of Chicago, 1959.

HALPIN, ANDREW W., and BEN J. WINER. *The Leadership Behavior of Airplane Commanders*. Columbus: Ohio State University Research Foundation, 1952.

HAMBLIN, ROBERT L. "Leadership and Crises," in Dorwin Cartwright and Alvin Zander, eds., *Group Dynamics: Research and Theory*, 2nd ed. Evanston, Ill.: Row, Peterson, 1960.

HANNEMAN, GERHARD J., and WILLIAM J. McEWEN. *Communication and Behavior*. Reading, Mass.: Addison-Wesley, 1975.

HARRIS, PHILIP R. *Management in Transition*. San Francisco: Jossey-Bass, 1985.

HARRIS, T. *I'm OK—You're OK: A Practical Guide to Transactional Analysis*. New York: Harper & Row, 1969.

HARRIS, THOMAS A., and AMY BJORK. *Staying OK*. New York: Harper & Row, 1985.

HARRISON, EDWARD L. "Why Supervisors Fail to Discipline," *Supervisory Management*, April 1985, pp. 18–22.

HAYAKAWA, S. I., ed. *The Use and Misuse of Language*. New York: Fawcett, 1962.

HAYES, ROGER. *Corporate Revolution*. New York: Nichols Pub., 1986.

HEMPHIL, JOHN K. *Situational Factors in Leadership*, Monograph No. 32. Columbus: Bureau of Educational Research, Ohio State University, 1949.

———. *Leader Behavior Description*. Columbus: Ohio State University, 1950.

———. "Why People Attempt to Lead," in Luigi Petrullo and Bernard M. Bass, eds., *Leadership and Interpersonal Behavior*. New York: Holt, Rinehart & Winston, 1961.

HERSEY, PAUL. *The Situational Leader*. Escondido, Calif.: Center for Leadership Studies. 1984.

———. *Situational Selling: An Approach for Increasing Sales Effectiveness*. Escondido, Calif.: Center for Leadership Studies, 1985.

HERSEY, PAUL, and KENNETH H. BLANCHARD. "Life Cycle Theory of Leadership," *Training and Development Journal*, 23 (May 1969).

———. "Cultural Changes: Their Influence on Organizational Structure and Management Behavior," *Training and Development Journal*, 24 (October 1970).

———. "So You Want to Know Your Leadership Style?" *Training and Development Journal*, 28 (February 1974).

———. "What's Missing in MBO?" *Management Review*, October 1974.

———. *The Family Game*. Reading, Mass.: Addison-Wesley, 1978.

———. "Grid Principles and Situationalism: Both! A Response to Blake and Mouton," *Group and Organizational Studies*, June 1982, pp. 207–210.

HERSEY, P., K. H. BLANCHARD, and W. E. NATEMEYER. "Situational Leadership, Perception, and the Impact of Power," *Group and Organizational Studies*, 4, No. 5 (December 1979), 418–428.

HERSEY, PAUL, and DOUGLAS SCOTT. "A Systems Approach to Educational Organizations: Do We Manage or Administer?" *OCLEA*, publication of the Ontario Council for Leadership in Educational Administration, Toronto, Canada, pp. 3–5.

HERSEY, PAUL, and JOHN E. STINSON. *Perspectives in Leader Effectiveness*. Columbus: Ohio University Press, 1980.

HERZBERG, FREDERICK. *Work and the Nature of Man*. New York: World Publishing, 1966.

———. "One More Time: How Do You Motivate Employees?" *Harvard Business Review*, 46, 1 (January–February 1968), 53–62.

———. *Motivating People*, in P. Mali (ed.). *Management Handbook*. New York: Wiley, 1981.

HERZBERG, FREDERICK, B. MAUSNER, and BARBARA SNYDERMAN. *The Motivation to Work*, 2nd ed. New York: Wiley, 1959.

HESHIZER, BRIAN. "An MBO Approach to Discipline," *Supervisory Management*, March 1984, pp. 2–7.

HILL, NORMAN C. "The Need for Positive Reinforcement in Corrective Counseling," *Supervisory Management*, 29 (December 1984), 10–11.

HOBSON, C. J., R. B. HOBSON, and J. J. HOBSON. "Why Managers Use Criticism Instead of Praise," *Supervisory Management*, 30, No. 3 (1985), 24–31.

HOFEREK, MARY J. *Going Forth*. Princeton, N.J.: Princeton Book, 1986.

HOLLANDER, EDWIN P. *Leadership Dynamics: A Practical Guide to Effective Relationships*. New York: Free Press, 1978.

HOLLMAN, ROBERT, and MAUREEN F. ULRICH. "Participative and Flexible Decision Making," *Journal of Small Business Management* 21, No. 1 (January 1983), 1–7.

HOLT, DAVID H. *Management: Principles and Practice*. Englewood Cliffs, N.J.: Prentice-Hall, 1987.

HOMANS, G. C. *The Human Group*. New York: Harcourt, Brace & World, 1950.

HORNSTEIN, HARVEY A. *Managerial Courage*. New York: Wiley, 1986.

HORTON, T. R. "The Style and Substance of Leadership," *Management Review*, 74 (August 1985).

HOSKINGS, D., and C. SCHRIESHEIM. "Review of Fiedler et al., *Improving Leadership Effectiveness: The Leader Match Concept*," *Administrative Science Quarterly*, 23 (1978), 496–504.

HOUSE, ROBERT J. "A Path-Goal Theory of Leader Effectiveness," *Administrative Science Quarterly*, 16 (1971), 321–338.

HOUSE, ROBERT J., and MITCHELL, TERENCE R. "Path-Goal Theory of Leadership," *Journal of Contemporary Business*, Autumn 1974, pp. 81–98.

HUMBLE, JOHN W. *Management by Objectives in Action*. New York: McGraw-Hill, 1970.

HUNT, J. G. "Personal Factors Associated with Leadership: A Survey of the Literature," *Journal of Psychology* 25 (January 1982), 35–71.

———. *Leadership and Managerial Behavior*. Chicago: Science Research Associates, 1984.

HUNT, J. G., and L. L. LARSON, eds. *Contingency Approaches to Leadership*. Carbondale: Southern Illinois University Press, 1974.

JAGO, A. G. "Leadership: Perspectives in Theory and Research," *Management Science*, March 1982, pp. 315–336.

JAMES, MURIEL, and LOUIS SAVARY. *A New Self: Self Therapy with Transactional Analysis*. Reading, Mass.: Addison-Wesley, 1977.

JAMISON, KALEEL. *The Nibble Theory and the Kernel of Power*. New York: Paulist Press, 1984.

JANIS, I. L. *Victims of Group Think*. Boston: Houghton-Mifflin, 1972.

JANIS, I. L., and L. MANN. *Decision Making*. New York: Free Press, 1977.

JENNINGS, EUGENE E. "The Anatomy of Leadership," *Management of Personnel Quarterly*, 1, No. 1 (Autumn 1961).

———. *An Anatomy of Leadership: Princes, Heroes and Supermen*. New York: McGraw-Hill, 1972.

JOHNSON, DAVID W. *Joining Together*. Englewood Cliffs, N.J.: Prentice-Hall, 1987.

JOINER, CHARLES W. *Leadership for Change*. Cambridge, Mass.: Ballinger Pub., 1987.

JONGEWARD, DOROTHY. *Everybody Wins: Transactional Analysis Applied to Organizations*. Reading, Mass.: Addison-Wesley, 1974.

JONGEWARD, D., and P. C. SEYER. *Choosing Success: Transactional Analysis on the Job*. New York: Wiley, 1978.

JOSEFOWITZ, NATASHA. *You're the Boss!: A Guide to Managing People with Understanding and Effectiveness*. New York: Warner Books, 1985.

KAHN, R. L. "Productivity and Job Satisfaction," *Personnel Psychology*, 13, No. 3 (1960), 275–278.

KAMP, G. *Perspectives on the Group Process: A Foundation for Counseling with Groups*. Boston, Massachusetts: Houghton Mifflin, 1964.

KANTER, R. M. *The Changemasters*. New York: Simon & Schuster, 1983.

KAPLAN, STEPHAN. *Cognition and Environment: Functioning in an Uncertain World*. New York: Praeger, 1982.

KATZ, DANIEL, and ROBERT L. KAHN. *The Social Psychology of Organizations*, 2nd ed. New York: Wiley, 1978.

KATZ, R. "The Influence of Group Conflict on Leadership Effectiveness," *Organizational Behavior and Human Performance*, 20 (1977), 265–286.

KEMP, GEOFFREY. *Projection of Power: Perceptives, Perceptions, and Problems*. Hamden, Conn.: Archon Books, 1982.

KEPNER, C. H., and B. B. TREGOE. *The Rational Manager*, New York: McGraw-Hill, 1965.

KERR, STEVEN. "On the Folly of Hoping for A While Rewarding B," *Academy of Management Journal*, 4 (1975), 76–79.

KLIEN, J., and W. CONRAD. "The Right Approach to Participative Management," *Working Woman*, May 1985, pp. 29–39.

KNAPP, MARK. *Nonverbal Communications in Human Interacting*, 2nd ed. New York: Holt, Rinehart & Winston, 1978.

KNOLL, MARK J., and CHARLES D. PRINGLE. "Path-Goal Theory and the Task Design Literature: A Tenuous Linkage," *Akron Business and Economic Review*, 17, No. 4, (Winter 1986), 75–83.

KOESTENBAUM, PETER. *The Heart of Business*. Dallas: Saybrook Pub., 1987.

KOONTZ, HAROLD, and CYRIL O'DONNELL. *Essentials of Management*, 4th ed. New York: McGraw-Hill, 1986.

KORMAN, A. K. "Consideration, Initiating Structure, and Organizational Criteria—A Review," *Personnel Psychology: A Journal of Applied Research*, 19, No. 4 (1966), 349–361.

KOTTER, J. P. *Organizational Dynamics: Diagnosis and Intervention*. Reading, Mass.: Addison-Wesley, 1978.

———. *Power and Influence*. New York: Free Press, 1985.

LaBORDE, GENIE A. *Influencing with Integrity: Management Skills for Communication and Negotiation*. Palo Alto, Calif.: Science and Behavior Books, 1983.

LAMONICA, ELAINE L. *Nursing Leadership and Management*. Boston: Jones and Bartlett, 1986.

LAO-TSU. *The Way of the Ways: Lao-tsu*; translated and with a commentary by Herrymon Maurer. New York: Schocken Books, 1985.

LARSON, L. L., J. G. HUNT, and R. N. OSBORN. "The Great Leader Behavior Myth," *Proceedings of the Academy of Management*, 1975, pp. 170–172.

LAWLER, EDWARD E., III, and SUSAN A. MOHRMAN. "Quality Circles after the Fad," *Harvard Business Review*, 63 (January–February 1985), 64–71.

LAWRENCE, P. R., and J. W. LORSCH. *Developing Organization: Diagnosis and Action*. Reading, Mass.: Addison-Wesley, 1969.

LAWRIE, JOHN. *You Can Lead*. New York: AMACOM, 1985.

Leadership in Organizations. West Point, N.Y.: Associates, Dept. of Behavioral Sciences and Leadership, U.S. Military Academy, 1985.

LEAVITT, H. J. *Managerial Psychology*. Chicago: University of Chicago Press, 1958.

———. *The Social Science of Organizations: Four Perspectives*. Englewood Cliffs, N.J.: Prentice-Hall, 1963.

LeBOEUF, MICHAEL. *The Productivity Challenge: How to Make It Work for America and You*. New York: McGraw-Hill, 1982.

LEVINSON, H. *The Exceptional Executive: A Psychological Conception*. Cambridge, Mass.: Harvard University Press, 1968.

———. *CEO*. New York: Basic Books, 1984.

LEWIN, K. "Frontiers in Group Dynamics," *Human Relations*, 1 (1947), 5–41.

LEWIN, K., R. LIPPETT, and R. WHITE. "Leader Behavior and Member Reaction in Three Social Climates," in D. Cartwright and A. Zander, eds., *Group Dynamics: Research and Theory*, 2nd ed. Evanston, Ill.: Row, Peterson. 1960.

LEWIS, BYRON A., and FRANK R. PUCELIK. *Magic Demystified: A Pragmatic Guide to Communication and Change*. Lake Oswego, Ore.: Metamorphous Press, 1982.

LIKERT, RENSIS. *New Patterns of Management*. New York: McGraw-Hill, 1961.

———. *The Human Organization*. New York: McGraw-Hill, 1967.

LIPPETT, GORDON. *Organizational Renewal*. New York: Appleton-Century-Crofts, 1969.

LITTERER, J. A. *Analysis of Organizations*. New York: Wiley, 1965.

LIVINGSTON, J. STERLING. "Pygmalion in Management," *Harvard Business Review*, 48 (July–August 1969), 81–89.

LOCKE, EDWIN A., DAVID M. SCHWEIGER, and GARY P. LATHAM. "Participation in Decision Making," *Organizational Dynamics*, 14, No. 3 (Winter 1986), 65–79.

LODEN, MARYILYN. *Feminine Leadership, or, How to Succeed in Business without Being One of the Boys*. New York: Times Books, 1985.

LOMBARDO, MICHAEL. "The Intolerable Boss," *Psychology Today*, January 1984, pp. 44–48.

LOSONCY, LEWIS E. *The Motivating Leader*. Englewood Cliffs, N.J.: Prentice-Hall, 1985.

LUNDY, JAMES L. *Lead, Follow, or Get Out of the Way*. San Diego: Avant Books, 1986.

LUTHANS, FRED. *Introduction to Management: A Contingency Approach*. New York: McGraw-Hill, 1976.

MACHIAVELLI, NICCOLO. *The Prince and the Discourses*. New York: Random House, 1950.

MACKENZIE, K. D. "Virtual Position and Power," *Managerial Science*, 32 (May 1986), 622–624.

MacMILLAN, IAN C., and RANDALL S. SCHULER. "Gaining a Competitive Edge through Human Resources," *Personnel*, 62 (April 1985), 24.

MAIER, NORMAN R. F. *Psychology in Industry*, 2nd ed. Boston: Houghton Mifflin, 1955.

———. *Frustration*. Ann Arbor: University of Michigan Press, 1961.

————. *Psychology in Industrial Organizations*. Boston: Houghton Mifflin, 1973.

MAIN, JEREMY. "The Trouble with Managing Japanese-Style," *Fortune*, April 2, 1984, pp. 50–52.

MANN, F. C. "Changing Superior-Subordinate Relationships," *Journal of Social Issues*, 7, No. 3 (1951), 56–63.

MANSKE, FRED A. *Secrets of Effective Leadership*. Memphis: Leadership Education and Development, 1987.

MARCH, J. G., and H. A. SIMON. *Organizations*. New York: Wiley, 1958.

MARROW, ALFRED J. *Behind the Executive Mask*. New York: American Management Association, 1965.

MARTEL, MYLES. *Before You Say a Word: The Executive to Effective Communication*. Englewood Cliffs, N.J.: Prentice-Hall, 1984.

MARTIN, PETER, and JOHN NICHOLLI. "How to Manage Commitment," *Management Today*, April 1985, pp. 56–57.

MASLOW, ABRAHAM H. *Toward a Psychology of Being*. Princeton, N.J.: Van Nostrand, 1962.

————. *Eupsychian Management*. Homewood, Ill.: Irwin, 1965.

————. *Motivation and Personality*, 2nd ed. New York: Harper & Row, 1970.

MAYO, ELTON. *The Human Problems of an Industrial Civilization*. Salem, N.H.: Ayer Company, 1977.

MCCALL, MORGAN W., JR., and MICHAEL M. LOMBARDO. "What Makes a Top Executive?" *Psychology Today*, February 1983, pp. 26–31.

McCLELLAND, DAVID C. *The Achieving Society*. Princeton, N.J.: Van Nostrand, 1961.

————. *Motivation and Society*. San Francisco: Jossey-Bass, 1982.

————. *Motives, Personality, and Society: Selected Papers*. New York: Praeger, 1984.

McGREGOR, DOUGLAS, *The Human Side of Enterprise*. New York: McGraw-Hill, 1960.

————. *Professional Manager*. New York: McGraw-Hill, 1967.

McPHERSON, R. "The People Principle," *Leaders*, January–March 1982, p. 52.

MEDLIN, WILLIAM A. "Managing People to Perform," *The Bureaucrat*, Spring 1985, pp. 52–55.

MEYERS, SCOTT. *Every Employee a Manager*. New York: McGraw-Hill, 1970.

Military Leadership. Boulder, Colo.: Westview Press, 1984.

MINER, JOHN. *Theories of Organizational Behavior*, Hinsdale, Ill.: Dryden Press, 1980.

MINTZBERG, H. *The Nature of Managerial Work*. New York: Harper & Row, 1973.

————. *Power in and Around Organizations*. Englewood Cliffs, N.J.: Prentice-Hall, 1983.

MISUMI, JUJI. *The Behavioral Science of Leadership*. Ann Arbor: University of Michigan Press, 1985.

MITCHELL, TERENCE R. "Motivation: New Directions for Theory, Research, and Practice," *Academy of Management Review*, 25 (January 1982), 80–88.

MORTENSEN, C. DAVID. *Basic Readings in Communication Theory*, 2nd ed. New York: Harper & Row, 1979.

MURNIGHAN, J. KEITH. "Group Decision Making: What Strategies Should You Use?" *Management Review*, 70, No. 2 (February 1981), 55–62.

NAISBITT, JOHN. *Megatrends*. New York: Warner Books, 1982.

NATEMEYER, W. E. "An Empirical Investigation of the Relationships between Leader Behavior, Leader Power Bases, and Subordinate Performance and Satisfaction," an unpublished dissertation, University of Houston, August 1975.

————. *Classics of Organizational Behavior*. Oak Park, Ill.: Moore Publishers, 1978.

NICHOLLS, J. R. "Congruent Leadership," *Leadership and Organization Review Journal*, 7, No. 1 (1986), 27–31.

NIEHOUSE, OLIVER I. "Controlling Burnout: A Leadership Guide for Managers," *Business Horizons*, July–August 1984, pp. 81–85.

————. "Measuring Your Burnout Potential," *Supervisory Management*, July 1984, pp. 27–30.

ODIORNE, GEORGE S. *Management by Objectives*. New York: Pitman Pub., 1965.

O'DONNEL, MERLE, and ROBERT J. O'DONNELL. "Quality Circles: Latest Fad or Real Winner?" *Business Horizons*, 27 (June 1984), 48–52.

PARKINSON, C. NORTHCOTE. *Parkinson's Law*. Boston: Houghton-Mifflin, 1957.

PATRELLIS, A. J. "Using Power in Interactions with Peers," *Supervisory Management*, February 1985, pp. 18–24.

———. "Producing Results: Using Power with Your Employees," *Supervisory Management*, March 1985, pp. 32–37.

———. "Your Power as an Employee," *Supervisory Management*, April 1985, pp. 37–41.

PATTON, BOBBY R., and KIM GIFFIN. *Interpersonal Communication in Action: Basic Text and Readings*, 3rd ed. New York: Harper & Row, 1977.

PENNAR, KAREN, and EDWARD MERVOSH. "Women at Work," *Business Week*, January 28, 1985, pp. 80–85.

PERROW, CHARLES. *Organizational Analysis: A Sociological View*. Belmont, Calif.: Wadsworth Publishing, 1970.

PETER, LAURENCE J. *Peter's Quotations: Ideas for Our Time*. New York: Morrow, 1977.

PETERS, THOMAS J., and NANCY K. AUSTIN. *A Passion for Excellence—The Leadership Difference*. New York: Random House, 1985.

PETERS, THOMAS J., and ROBERT H. WATERMAN, JR. *In Search of Excellence: Lessons from America's Best-Run Companies*. New York: Warner Books, 1982.

PFEFFER, JEFFREY. *Power in Organizations*. Marshfield, Mass.: Pitman Publishing, 1981.

PHILLIPS, JACK J. *Improving Supervisors' Effectiveness*. San Francisco: Jossey-Bass, 1985.

PIGORS, P., and C. A. MYERS. *Personnel Administration*, 8th ed. New York: McGraw-Hill, 1977.

PINDER, CRAIG C. *Work Motivation: Theory, Issues, and Applications*. Glenview, Ill.: Scott, Foresman, 1984.

PORTNOY, ROBERT A. *Leadership*. Englewood Cliffs, N.J.: Prentice-Hall, 1986.

PRINGLE, CHARLES D. "Seven Reasons Why Managers Don't Delegate," *Management Solutions*, 31, No. 11 (November 1986), 26–30.

PULICH, MARCIA ANN. "What Supervisors Should Know About Discipline," *Supervisory Management*, October 1983, pp. 20–24.

QUINN, JAMES BRIAN. "Managing Innovation: Controlled Chaos," *Harvard Business Review*, 64, No. 3 (May–June 1985), 73–84.

REDDIN, WILLIAM J. *Managerial Effectiveness*. New York: McGraw-Hill, 1970.

———. *Effective Management by Objectives: The 3-D Method of MBO*. New York: McGraw-Hill, 1971.

———. "The 3-D Management Style Theory," *Training and Development Journal*, 21 (April 1967), 8–17.

REYNOLDS, PAUL D. "Leaders Never Quit," *Small Group Behavior*, 15, No. 3 (August 1984), 404–413.

RICHARDSON, PETER R. "Courting Greater Employee Involvement through Participative Management," *Sloan Management Review*, (Winter 1985).

ROBBINS, STEPHEN P. *The Essentials of Organization Behavior*. Englewood Cliffs, N.J.: Prentice-Hall, 1983.

ROETHLISBERGER, F. J., and W. J. DICKSON. *Management and the Worker*. Cambridge, Mass.: Harvard University Press, 1939.

ROGERS, C. R. *Freedom to Learn*. Columbus, Ohio: Merrill, 1969.

———. *Client-centered Therapy*. Boston, Mass.: Houghton Mifflin, 1951.

———. *On Becoming a Person*. Boston: Houghton Mifflin, 1961.

ROHAN, T. M. "Management by Magic?" *Industrial Week*, 230 (Spring 1986), 56–57.

ST. JOHN, WALDET D. "You Are What You Communicate," *Personnel Journal*, 64 (October 1985).

SANDEMAN, HUGH. "The U.S. Management Evolution," *World Press Review*, March 1985, pp. 27–28.

SANFORD, FILLMORE H. *Authoritarianism and Leadership*. Philadelphia: Institute for Research in Human Relations, 1950.

———. "Leadership Identification and Acceptance," in Harold Guentzkow, ed., *Groups, Leadership and Men*, Pittsburgh: Carnegie Press, 1951.

SASHKIN, MARSHALL. "Participative Management is an Ethical Imperative," *Organizational Dynamics*, 12 (Spring 1984), 5–22.

SCHACTER, STANLEY. *The Psychology of Affiliation*. Stanford, Calif.: Stanford University Press, 1959.

SCHEIN, EDGAR H. *Organizational Culture and Leadership*. San Francisco: Jossey-Bass, 1985.

SCHNAKE, M. E. "Vicarious Punishment in a Working Setting," *Journal of Applied Psychology*, 71 (May 1986), 323–325.

SCHRIESHEIM, C. "The Great High Consideration—High Initiating Structure Myth," *Journal of Social Psychology*, April 1982.

SEASHORE, STANLEY E., ed. *Assessing Organizational Change: A Guide to Methods, Measures, and Practices*. New York: Wiley, 1983.

SEGAL, ERICH. *Love Story*. New York: Harper & Row, 1970.

SHAPIRO, IRVING S. "Managerial Communication: The View from Inside," *California Management Review*, 27 (Fall 1984), 157.

SHEA, GORDON F. *Building Trust for Personal and Organizational Success*. New York: Wiley, 1987.

SHINN, GEORGE. *Leadership Development*. New York: McGraw-Hill, 1986.

SKINNER, B. F. *Science and Human Behavior*. New York: Macmillan, 1953.

———. *About Behaviorism*. New York: Knopf, 1974.

SMITH, JONATHAN E., KENNETH P. CARSON, and RALPH A. ALEXANDER. "Leadership: It Can Make A Difference," *Academy of Management Journal*, 27 (December 1984), 765–776.

SMITH, PERRY M. *Taking Charge*. Washington, D.C.: National Defense University Press, 1986.

SNYDER, N. H. "Leadership: The Essential Quality for Transforming United States Business," *Advanced Management Journal*, 51 (Spring 1986), 15–18.

SOLOMON, R. L. "Punishment," *American Psychologist*, 19 (1964), 239.

STANTON, ERWIN S. "A Critical Revaluation of Motivation, Management, and Productivity," *Personnel Journal*, 64 (March 1985).

STARR, MARTIN. "The Adaptability of Management: Winners and Losers," *Government Executive, NASA Special Report*, September 1985.

STEGER, JOSEPH, GEORGE MANNERS, and THOMAS ZIMMERER. "Following the Leader: How to Link Management Styles to Subordinate Personality," *Management Review*, 71, No. 10 (October 1982), 22–28.

STEIL, LYMAN K. "On Listening and Not Listening," *Executive Health*, December 1981, pp. 30–35.

STEVENSON, HOWARD H., and DAVID E. GUMPERT. "The Heart of Entrepreneurship," *Harvard Business Review*, 64, No. 2 (March–April 1985), 85–94.

STOGDILL, R. M. "Personal Factors Associated with Leadership: A Survey of the Literature," *Journal of Psychology*, 25 (1948), 35–71.

———. *Individual Behavior and Group Achievement*. New York: Oxford University Press, 1959.

———. *Handbook of Leadership*. New York: Free Press, 1974.

STOGDILL, R. M., and ALVIN E. COONS, eds. *Leader Behavior: Its Description and Measurement*, Research Monograph No. 88. Columbus: Bureau of Business Research, Ohio State University, 1957.

STRANG, T. S. "Positive Reinforcement: How Often and How Much," *Supervisory Management*, 30, No. 1 (1985), 7–9.

SULLIVAN, J. J. "Human Nature, Organizations, and Management Theory," *Academic Management Review*, 11 (July 1985), 534–549.

TANNENBAUM, ROBERT. *Leadership and Organization*. New York: Garland, 1987.

TANNENBAUM, ROBERT, and WARREN H. SCHMIDT. "How to Choose a Leadership Pattern," *Harvard Business Review*, 37 (March–April 1958), 95–102.

TAYLOR, ROBERT L., and WILLIAM E. ROSENBACH, eds. *Military Leadership*. Boulder, Colo.: Westview Press, 1984.

THEOBALD, ROBERT. The Rapids of Change. Indianapolis, Ind.: Knowledge Systems, 1987.

TICHY, NOEL M. *The Transformational Leader*. New York: Wiley, 1986.

TRICE, HARRISON M., and JANICE M. BOYER, "Studying Organizational Cultures through Rites and Ceremonials," *Academy of Management Review*, 9, No. 4 (1984).

TRIST, E. L., et al. *Organizational Choice*. London: Tavistock Publications, 1963.

URWICK, LYNDALL F., *The Theory of Organization*. New York: American Management Association, 1952.

VAN FLEET, DAVID D. *Military Leadership*. Greenwich, Conn.: JAI Press, 1986.

VAN LARE, JAMES. *Supervisory Leadership*. New York: Training By Design, 1984.

VROOM, V. H. "Can Leaders Learn to Lead?" *Organizational Dynamics*, Winter 1976, pp. 17–28.

VROOM, V. H., and PHILIP YETTON. *Leadership and Decision Making*. Pittsburgh, Pa.: University of Pittsburgh Press, 1973.

WAGNER, ABE. *The Transactional Manager: How to Solve Problems with Transactional Analysis*. Englewood Cliffs, N.J.: Prentice-Hall, 1981.

WALL, JAMES A. *Bosses*. Lexington, Mass.: Lexington Books, 1986.

WALTON, RICHARD E. "From Control to Commitment in the Workplace," *Harvard Business Review*, 64 (March–April 1985).

WALTON, WILLIAM B. *The New Bottom Line*. New York: Harper & Row, 1986.

WEBER, MAX. *The Theory of Social and Economic Organization*, trans. by A. H. Henderson and ed. by Talcott Parsons. New York: Oxford University Press, 1946.

WEINBERG, GERALD M. *Becoming a Technical Leader*. New York: Dorset House, 1986.

WHITE, ROBERT W., and R. LIPPITT. *Autocracy and Democracy: An Experimental Inquiry*. New York: Harper & Row, 1960.

WHYTE, WILLIAM FOOTE. *Pattern for Industrial Peace*. New York: Garland 1987.

WILLIAMS, LOUIS C., JR. "What 50 Presidents and Chief Officers Think about Employee Communication," *Public Relations Quarterly*, Winter 1978, p. 7.

WRIGHT, N. "Leadership Styles—Which Are Best When," *Business Quarterly*, Winter 1984.

WRIGHT, PETER L. *Improving Leadership Performance*. Englewood Cliffs, N.J.: Prentice-Hall, 1984.

YELSEY, ALAN A. "Strategies and Actions for Improving Organizational Performance," *Academy of Management Review*, 9 (June 1984), 25.

YUKL, GARY A. *Leadership in Organizations*. Englewood Cliffs, N.J.: Prentice-Hall, 1981.

ZALEZNIK, ABRAHAM. *Power and the Corporate Mind*. Chicago: Bonus Books, 1985.

ZENGER, JOHN H. "Leadership: Management's Better Half," *Training*, 22, No. 12 (December 1985), 44ff.

INDEX

Contents

PART FOUR: FINAL THOUGHTS

Preface

The purpose of this book is to familiarize you and your advisors—perhaps even your children—with a *will, estate administration,* and *estate taxation.* It explains how a variety of laws affect you or someone close to you.

These subjects are discussed in clear terms: I avoid using technical language except where absolutely necessary. This book is the product of fourteen years of legal practice during which I listened to questions posed by average people—like you—some of whom had a net worth of five hundred dollars, while that of others exceeded a few hundred thousand. In these pages you will become acquainted with their questions and my answers.

Other books have been written on this subject. They describe how to write your will and how to administer an estate without an attorney's advice. Many contain charts and forms and suggestions for readers who want to avoid an attorney's fee. What I offer is general information; whether you choose to seek the services of an attorney is your decision. It is my opinion, however, that you should not consider my summary of ideas as a substitute for the advice of your own attorney. Laws are technical, they vary from state to state, and they change from time to time.

This book teaches you how to talk to your attorney, your family, and anyone else who might be helping you with your finances or with the many other concerns that older people confront. It also teaches children and caregivers how to advise their elder parents or clients.

You will learn what happens to your possessions after your death, how a will allows you to determine who will receive those possessions, and the extent of your power to appoint the person who will supervise

your estate after you are gone. You will also learn about the work that has to be performed by those who are chosen to supervise an estate.

In addition, as a result of my discussion of the living will, you will learn what choices you have regarding a dignified death. Also, you will learn what taxes your estate must pay.

How will you learn all of these things? By reading about the successes and misfortunes of others. I have analyzed the experiences of many clients, and will share these experiences with you.

May this book enrich your life, not only by saving you money, but by helping you solve a few worrisome problems.

Acknowledgments

Writing this book would have been impossible if not for the constant patience and encouragement of my dear wife, Joan. Thank you so much.

However, near the end of the project, I became acutely aware of the closeness of my readers. Knowing these wise and kind people gave my confidence a boost: my friends Philip J. Trabulsy, Jr., and Patrick A. Naughton, who have helped me to believe in my legal ability; the maternal optimist Lillian E. McGowan, who convinced me not to abandon this book; the philanthropic fundraiser Eileen F. Smith, who has consistently asked me to address her audiences of potential donors; and attorneys Richard B. Covey, William R. Dunlop, and Evan R. Dawson, who offered suggestions on how a general audience book on technical subjects balances accuracy and readability. To them, my sincerest gratitude.

My thanks to Steven L. Mitchell, editor of the Golden Age Books series for Prometheus; he personally edited and enthusiastically published my first book. The tireless assistance of my associates, Teri Lombardi and, especially, Elaine Dolan, is also much appreciated.

I want to mention my recently departed legal mentors, Edward M. and Esther K. Benton. They shared with me what they learned in their combined total of almost 120 years of writing wills and administering estates. I miss their friendship and, particularly, their Friday night open house.

To my clients over the years, thank you for telling me, teaching me, and trusting me. To you I offer this book in tribute.

Part One

Preparing Your Will

1

Introduction

DYING WITHOUT A WILL

Dying without a will is known as *dying intestate*. If you die without a will, the state does not take your property. Instead, it will go to your next of kin, what attorneys call your *distributees* or *heirs-at-law*. Each state has its own law defining the next of kin, but here are some general guidelines, typical of the law in most states, to help you identify these persons.

If you are survived by a *spouse* (and not survived by a child or parent), your spouse receives all your property.

If you are survived by *a spouse and a parent* (and not survived by a child), your spouse and your parent share your property.

If you are survived by *a spouse, a child, and a parent,* your spouse and your child share your property, and your parent receives nothing.

If you are *not* survived by *a spouse or a child or a parent,* your brothers and sisters, and the children of your deceased brothers and sisters, share your property.

If you do not desire your property to be distributed to those who would receive it if you were to die intestate, *have a will prepared.* Perhaps you are hesitant to execute a will because of one or more of the following mistaken ideas:

a superstition that if you draw up a will, you are *soon to die;*

an expectation of paying an *exorbitant attorney's fee;*

a theory that if you die after having made a will, a court will *entangle your finances;*

a misconception that if a will exists, the *estate tax will be increased;*

a fear that if you name someone in your will to receive your possessions, *you will not really remain the owner;*

an "I don't" attitude: "I don't have anything to leave anyone"; "I don't have any family or friends"; "I don't care if they fight over my possessions" (a variation of "I don't believe my children will have any problem dividing my possessions"); "I don't worry about it because I will be gone." It is this last depressing "I don't" proclamation that is most frequently heard.

Many people die without a will. But it is within *your* power to determine who receives *your* assets. My goal, which I hope to achieve, is to convince you to have a will.

Sample Situation

Mary and her sister Margaret have lived together and have shared their lives and fortunes. They worked hard and saved their money. Although they consider themselves poor, they have accumulated a substantial amount of money. Their parents are dead, neither sister has married, and neither has had a child. They do have a brother, Charlie, whom neither sister has seen since he ventured off at age sixteen to seek his fortune. When Mary or Margaret dies, the surviving sister and Charlie will split the deceased sister's estate if there is no will. *Charlie will then have found his fortune.*

Executing a will prevents this unfortunate distribution of the deceased sister's estate. Each sister has the right to direct that her sister is to receive everything, and her brother is to receive nothing. Another situation requiring a will, though perhaps not as dramatic but still significant, is your right to choose the recipient of an heirloom or any other possession you might own. Perhaps Margaret *does want* Charlie to receive a particular item. If so, it should be so stated in Margaret's will. *Each of us has the right to select those who are to receive our property.* Do not let the law make this decision for you; do not die without a will.

Money-Saving Suggestions

When your will is prepared, you benefit as well as the survivors who inherit your possessions. The preparation of a will is an ideal time to review your investments, *a time to learn something about your financial health.* Often changes in investment strategies result. I call this the *living motive* for a will.

In addition to reviewing existing investments, preparing a will provides the perfect opportunity to inventory your possessions: a list of all bank accounts, including Individual Retirement Accounts (IRAs) and certificates of deposit (CDs); employee benefits; stock certificates; and any debts owed *to* you. The location of your *safe deposit box* (if you have one) should definitely be included in your inventory. If you own a home, a copy of the *deed* should be inventoried, along with deeds to other real estate holdings, including your cemetery plot.

There are two reasons for reviewing and inventorying your assets. When you die, your inventory will make it easy for your heirs to locate these assets. But more importantly, you now have *greater control* over your possessions because you have an *orderly record* and a *sharper understanding* of what you own.

When your will is prepared, you might also want to consider talking with your attorney about a "living will." Age brings a variety of health concerns, including the fear that a medical emergency or a prolonged illness could arise in which a decision would have to be made regarding life-saving or life-sustaining measures. The living will (about which more will be said in chapter 8) would outline your wishes. Though older persons are more likely to concern themselves with such an eventuality, the living will is a document to consider no matter how old you are. Accidents and medical tragedies know no age boundaries.

WHY HAVE A WILL?

Your ownership of property exists not only during your lifetime, but also after your death. Your will is your hand from the grave, so to speak, a hand that conducts the distribution of your property. A person who makes a will is called a *testator.* Why is it better to be a testator than to die intestate?

You select who will receive your property (called your *estate*) after your death.

You determine whether your estate is left in a *trust,* and you will learn how this gives the designated recipient the benefit of the money, but denies the recipient the control of the money.

You select the person or bank (called an *executor*) who will supervise your estate.

You leave money to your favorite *charity.*

You select who will receive your furniture, clothing, jewelry, and other *personal effects.*

You select who will *enforce any legal rights* that you may have had at the time of your death.

You plan your estate so there will be a *minimum of tax.*

You give advice on your *burial wishes* (but be sure to tell a close relative or friend about your burial preference).

As I mentioned above, you have a will for what I call the *living motive* —it is a time to review your assets and to organize your financial life.

I offer a word of caution. Do not use a will to hurt someone, or to have the last nasty word. The person will never hear it, *because only on television and in the movies is there a reading of the will.* In the real world, people learn about being named in a will when the attorney for the deceased person's executor notifies them of their good fortune.

Sample Situation

John says that his mother, Gladys, does not need a will; she is not *rich* and her financial affairs are *simple.* What John's mother *should have* is a *simple will.* Though she may not be rich, she's probably not poor either. In all likelihood, her financial affairs are not so simple.

Many people *underestimate* their net worth and the net worth of others. They *overestimate* their ability to handle money, as well as the ability of others to handle financial matters. For many older people the denial of wealth avoids *guilt,* and the denial of financial confusion avoids an *admission of inadequacy.* These defenses lead to the unfortunate conclusion that a will is not necessary, either for yourself or for someone you love.

If Gladys is one of the many people who die without a will, the law determines who receives her property and who is appointed to supervise the distribution of that property. Perhaps the people who receive her property, if she dies intestate, are not the people Gladys would have chosen; perhaps the person appointed to supervise the distribution of her property is not the person she would have chosen. Our system allows individuals to own property, and control its destination after the owner's death. *You cannot take it with you.* So exercise your right to choose who receives what you leave behind, and who is to represent your estate. *You should have a will, and you should suggest that those you love consider making a will as well.*

Money-Saving Suggestions

It is false to say that only a millionaire needs a will. Those who are not so rich also need a will to select the people who are to receive whatever property is owned at the time of death. Don't be put off by rumors that wills cost a lot to prepare. Having a will drawn up should not be expensive (anywhere from one hundred to a few hundred dollars, depending on its extent and complexity). I suggest you have a will so that *your survivors will save time and energy after your death since your affairs will then be in order.*

As for the more well off among us, it is through a will that tax-saving techniques are implemented. In Part Three, I will analyze these techniques and demonstrate how "trusts" can save *estate taxes.* Wills that contain a trust can be more expensive due to their complicated structure. The cost can differ depending upon where the attorney is located: usually, attorneys in larger cities are more expensive because their cost of doing business is greater. As with any fee for services rendered (whether it be a doctor, attorney, or a plumber), consumers should learn as much as they can and even do some comparison shopping before committing themselves.

But let us now take a look at the requirements for a will, what comprises an estate, and what role an executor performs.

2

An Overview of Your Will

PREPARING THE WILL

There is a uniform probate law in the United States upon which most states model their legislation concerning wills. Laws differ from state to state; consequently, there may be some requirements peculiar to your state, and your attorney can explain them. Here are some general legal requirements for a will:

Know what you own and to whom you are leaving your property. This is *testamentary capacity,* which is the minimum amount of intelligence a person must possess to have an enforceable will.

Sign and *date* your will at the end.

Sign your will *voluntarily* thereby asserting that no fraud, duress, or undue influence has been exerted. To be more precise, you have not been tricked or deceived when developing it; no one has threatened you with harm if one or more provisions are not included; and you have not been excessively flattered or pressured into incorporating specific provisions to the benefit or detriment of some third party.

Sign your will in the *presence of witnesses.* Most states require two witnesses; a few states require three. Have the witnesses print their names (in addition to their signatures) and include their addresses. The reason for including the printed name and address is to identify each witness clearly. This is crucial information if witnesses have to

be produced in court to testify. More will be said in chapter 3 about witnessing a will.

State to the witnesses that the document is your will and ask them to witness it. This is called *publication.*

The witnesses must be *disinterested,* which generally means that they are not left anything through your will. They must be *adults,* have a reasonable ability to *comprehend* what is happening, and be able to *relate* what is happening.

The *witnesses also must witness each other signing* as witnesses.

Sample Situation

Although a person may dispose of his or her estate in any manner, *there are limits.* Here is a Connecticut case that resulted in a limitation on how an estate could be distributed.

A woman left her estate to a man named John Gale Forbes. She believed he had appeared to her from space when she played with her Ouija board. The evidence showed that she believed Mr. Forbes existed, despite the fact that she knew nothing about him. Her papers made numerous references to him and described the help he had given her during their twenty years of communication. Her executor unsuccessfully tried to establish the existence of John Gale Forbes.

The court decided that the mystical Mr. Forbes was the product of a mental delusion and concluded that the woman lacked testamentary capacity. The will, therefore, was of no consequence (declared null and void). The woman's next of kin received her estate.

Money-Saving Suggestion

Do not try a *do-it-yourself will.* Is a will form purchased at a stationery store sufficient guidance to prepare a will? In some situations it is sufficient; but when it does not work, a major catastrophe can result. *The serious issue of who gets the monetary results of your life requires a visit to an attorney.*

Your visit will save you and your estate more money than the amount of the attorney's fee. There is too much at stake to rely on a standard form. Think of the money the attorney is going to charge your survivors if there is a legal question raised as to whether the will was properly exe-

cuted and witnessed, and whether those inheriting your assets were clearly identified, or whether a particular asset specifically left to someone was clearly identified. *The cost of preventive law is less than the cost of corrective law.*

A doctor's hope should be that illness is eliminated, and the plumber's hope should be that the pipes do not leak. Similarly, an attorney's hope should be that you do not need an attorney. But when you do need a doctor or a plumber or an attorney, go hire one! *This suggestion will in the long run save you both money and headaches, not to mention relieving survivors of unnecessary frustration.*

YOUR ESTATE

You are reading this book either because you are concerned about what happens to *your* possessions after you are no longer here or because you are concerned about what happens to *someone else's* possessions after he or she is no longer here. No one can be sure that there is life after death. But you can be sure that, wherever you go, *you cannot take your property with you.* You can, however, *determine where your estate goes.*

Thus far, we have learned who receives your estate after you die: *either your next of kin, as defined by state law,* or *those named in your will.* We have also learned the requirements for a will. Now let us consider what comprises an estate.

Here is a list of assets commonly owned: real estate, stocks, bonds, cash, bank accounts, certificates of deposit (CDs), life insurance, retirement benefits, jewelry, furniture, clothes, automobiles, art works, and perhaps a business. Your estate may also include other assets, such as: an income tax refund that you have not yet received, a lease (to an apartment, an automobile, etc.), or a debt someone *owes you. Your estate includes everything you own.* Also, *whatever debts you owe* are part of your estate.

Be sure to discuss with your attorney every possible asset you might own. *Review your ownership documents (titles, bills of sale, mortgages, etc.) with the attorney* (and married couples should review these documents with each other). Keep the originals in a safe deposit box, but be sure that a reliable person close to you knows its location. Make photocopies of these documents and keep them at home. When photocopying the will, *do not* remove the staples. (By removing staples, you open the door to a claim by a disinherited distributee that a page of the original will was removed and a new one was inserted.)

This discussion of estates is a good time to introduce the often confusing subject of *joint ownership* of assets. Consider this frequently asked question: "If my will leaves everything to my sister, *but I have our mother's name on my bank account as a joint owner with the right of survivorship,* then at the time of my death who will receive the bank account?" Your mother will receive the bank account. The ownership of the account, in addition to being a present joint ownership by you and your mother, is also a *future ownership* of the entire account by the eventual survivor of the two joint owners. Therefore, at your death, this *joint account is not distributed by your will,* because you gave the future sole ownership to the other person on the account, namely, your mother. This idea of joint ownership will be reviewed on various occasions throughout this book. But let's take another quick look at this situation.

Sample Situation

The only asset comprising John's estate is a money market account of about $50,000. His will divides his estate evenly between his sisters, Teresa and Mary. However, because John is getting quite frail and has difficulty getting to the bank, he puts Teresa's name on the account as a joint owner. Upon John's death, the money market account probably goes to Teresa, *unless Mary can convince a court that John did this for convenience only.*

Money-Saving Suggestions

After reviewing your estate with an attorney, *you should review your insurance coverage on these items:* Review your *homeowner's insurance* policy. Has it kept up with inflation? Do you need a *valuable items* rider to your policy? This covers items, such as jewelry, which are excluded from homeowner's insurance coverage. Also, review your *automobile insurance.*

Check with your employer to see if you have insurance to cover disability. If you are self-employed, you will most probably want to purchase this insurance. Do you have adequate *health insurance,* including major medical insurance coverage? Do you understand *exactly what this health insurance covers?* Also, reevaluate the amount of *life insurance* to determine if you have ample coverage. Not only will you be missed by those who loved you, but your income will be missed if your loved ones relied on you for financial support. Incidentally, review not only your own life insurance, but also that of the person *you rely upon* for support. Speak

to your insurance agent before you have your will prepared. This is the time to obtain answers to all your insurance questions.

Some individuals have too much insurance. Each time they receive information on coverage, especially information about health insurance, they immediately decide to buy it. Exercise your freedom of choice; learn about the coverage before deciding to purchase it. If necessary, have someone review your options with you. Remember, *you have the final word.*

THE PERSONAL REPRESENTATIVE OF THE ESTATE (EXECUTOR OR ADMINISTRATOR)

You have learned of your right to select the person (or bank) who will supervise your estate. *The executor is the person (or bank) named in your will who, after your death, gathers and distributes your assets as directed by your will.* If you die without a will, the court appoints the personal representative of your estate. This is usually your closest relative, and this person is called, not an executor, but an *administrator.*

Although an executor is named in your will, this person (or bank) does not automatically become executor upon your death. The probate court must first determine that your will is a legally valid document. After this occurs, the executor is then authorized to supervise your estate. The court gives the executor a document that in most states is called *letters testamentary* (although referred to in the plural, it is only one piece of paper). The letters testamentary allows the executor to gather the deceased's assets. If you die *without* a will, the person appointed as the administrator of your estate is given *letters of administration.*

Through your executor your wishes are carried out. Whom should you select as executor? This person might be the individual designated to receive the *largest portion* of your estate. If this person is not capable of handling the responsibility, then select some other trusted person as the executor. You could select *someone else who is receiving a legacy,* or your *spouse,* or your *attorney,* or your *bank.* When should there be more than one executor? There is nothing wrong with having two or more executors, who are called *co-executors,* but are they necessary? Co-executors might be necessary if the estate is large (over a few hundred thousand dollars) or unduly complicated (perhaps a business owned by the deceased must be protected by the estate).

Your executor must be honest, efficient, and competent. This person will be your employee after you are dead and will receive a payment called

an *executor's commission*. But even though this individual will be paid, as a courtesy you should ask the person if he or she is willing to take the job. Some states (Florida for instance) require an executor to be a state resident. However, there is an exception that allows a close relative, although living in some other state, to serve as executor. The decision on naming your executor is an important one, so give it some serious thought. Remember, a person might be so involved with his or her own life that there is just no time or energy left to be an executor. Part Two discusses the executor's duties (what is called the administration of the estate).

Sample Situation

Joseph's mother has been dead for a while but her estate has dragged on for years. The estate is beset with confusion; friends and relatives are dismayed and angry. Perhaps the estate has an executor who is lazy, incompetent, or devious. Cases like this do occur. *Choose your executor carefully*. Remember, the recalcitrant executor will make life frustrating for those you love—the people named in your will to receive your estate.

Money-Saving Suggestion

Have a successor executor named in your will. If your first choice predeceases (dies before) you or later decides not to take on the responsibility, this suggestion can save you the expense of a *new will*. (A new will must be drawn if *any* change is made in the existing will. Alternatively, a codicil, an amendment to a will, can be drawn, but it, too, requires all of the same formalities as a will.) Here is how my suggestion of a successor executor can be expressed in a will:

> I appoint my uncle JOHN SMITH (give his current address) as my executor. If he predeceases me or is otherwise unable to act as my executor, I appoint my cousin JAMES SMITH (give his current address) as successor executor.

Be mindful that a co-executor is not the same as a successor executor: the former serve together, while a successor executor takes the place of an executor who had died or is otherwise unable to act as executor. Here is an example of *co-executors* and a *successor executor* expressed in a will:

> I appoint my uncles JOHN SMITH (give his current address) and WILLIAM SMITH (give his current address) as my co-executors. If either one predeceases me or is otherwise unable to act as my executor, I appoint my cousin JAMES SMITH (give his current address) as successor executor.

Before considering whether you should appoint a bank as your executor, here is a suggestion about something that, although quite obvious, is sometimes overlooked. If you decide to have co-executors, *choose people who can work together.* Most people know a great deal about their potential executors, through long associations, family ties, or strong friendships. Therefore, when considering co-executors, it should be easy to determine if the candidates will be compatible. Co-executors who fail to cooperate often find themselves embroiled in lengthy and costly court battles.

A BANK AS EXECUTOR

I like the idea of a bank as executor, especially when there are substantial assets. But even when large estates are not involved, there are still sound reasons for using a bank. Here are some reasons given by my clients over the years: (1) to preserve a business after death; (2) no close relative or friend is willing to serve in the capacity of executor; (3) potential conflict might arise between those designated to receive assets; (4) a testamentary trust is involved [see the end of Part One]; (5) preservation of the estate's assets requires constant supervision; (6) grandparents are leaving their estate to grandchildren; (7) assets are being left to a resident of a foreign country; and (8) a bank's estate and trust department has the necessary experience to accomplish the job in an *efficient* and *competent manner.*

The executor represents all who may claim an interest in the deceased's estate, including the *creditors* of the deceased and also those named as the *recipients of your property.* The executor represents the total mass of interests and not one against the other. Therefore, a bank might be better suited to this job than a relative, who may find it difficult dealing with the various people interested in your estate.

The bank, like any other executor, *receives a fee* for serving in this capacity—as well it should. Often it is the same fee an individual executor receives; in some cases the fee is slightly higher. The executor's fee is usually a percentage of the estate, and is in the range of four percent for estates valued at under one million dollars. As with anything else, be a smart consumer. First, determine whether your spouse, adult child,

To my nephew JOHN SMITH (give his current address) I bequeath my Steinway piano. If he predeceases me, I bequeath my Steinway piano to my niece MARY SMITH (give her current address).

At the time the will is being drafted, some people are only conscious of their own death; they hesitate to name successor legatees. These people believe that they are going to die soon, or at least *sooner than those named as legatees in the will.* But most people live many years after executing a will, and *the probability of outliving one or more of the legatees is quite high.* This is clearly apparent if you imagine a family gathering in honor of the ninety-year-old patriarch, and many of the people at the gathering are the patriarch's legatees. Although the patriarch has the *shortest* life expectancy, surely it is not certain that he will be the *next* family member to die. I recommend that for each legatee named in your will, you consider naming a successor legatee.

This suggestion saves you the cost of revising your will each time a legatee predeceases you. But what happens if you leave your diamond necklace to Mary, and you do not name a successor legatee to receive the necklace if Mary predeceases you? Then, if Mary *does predecease you,* this diamond necklace will be part of your residuary estate, which is the next topic we will discuss.

Before moving on, here is another thought. This suggestion—naming successor legatees in the event that *you outlive some or all of those whom you designated as primary legatees*—should remind you of the obvious reality of the situation. It explodes the myth that preparing a will somehow *hastens your death.*

THE MOST IMPORTANT CLAUSE (RESIDUARY CLAUSE)

Wills have a residuary (or remainder) clause, *which distributes estate assets not otherwise left to someone.* It may be the most important clause in the whole document, because it could distribute the bulk of a person's assets. Perhaps you are familiar with the expression, "All the rest, residue, and remainder of my estate I give, devise, and bequeath to. . . ." In the language of a will, this is how the residuary clause begins. Attorneys sometimes use many words where a few would suffice. The same direction could be expressed, "I give the rest of my estate to. . . ." (Incidentally, land and buildings are *devised;* everything else is *bequeathed.*)

Suppose you want your nephew, your niece, and your friend to share

in your estate equally; if one of them predeceases you, *you want the remaining two to share your estate equally;* if two of them predecease you, *you want the survivor to receive it all.* Here is how you express this intent in your residuary clause:

> All the rest, residue, and remainder of my estate I give, devise, and bequeath in equal shares to the following individuals *who survive me:* my nephew (give name and address), my niece (give name and address), and my friend (give name and address).

If you *fail to have a residuary clause* in your will, then all of your estate assets are not distributed through your will. Suppose, for example, that you leave $25,000 to your sister Mary, that you have no residuary clause, and at your death you are worth $100,000. Who receives the $75,000? It is received by your next of kin. Perhaps the good sister Mary and brother Charlie share the $75,000.

Remember to have a residuary clause. In general, you name your most loved person or persons in the residuary clause. Your wealth may substantially increase between the time you write your will and the time of your death. It is this residuary clause that distributes these estate assets. The importance of naming your most loved person(s) in the residuary clause is shown in the following sample situation. Sometimes naming someone who is not close to you as residuary legatee *is even worse than having no residuary clause.*

Sample Situation

Margaret has a net worth of about $100,000, and in her will she leaves this sum to good sister Mary. She has a brother, evil Charlie, and she wants to leave him the *current miniscule balance* of her assets—maybe a few hundred dollars. Margaret, mistakenly, *names her brother as the residuary legatee.* Ten years later Margaret dies; her estate is worth $300,000. Her sister receives $100,000; her evil brother receives $200,000!!

This was not Margaret's intent. Her mistake was in not naming the most loved person(s) in the residuary clause. Remember that the residuary clause distributes the *additional estate assets you obtained after you signed your will.* Therefore, do not use this residuary clause to distribute the small current balance of your estate assets not otherwise distributed through your will. You may win a lottery, and what remains of this additional wealth at the time of your death goes to your residuary legatee(s).

Money-Saving Suggestion

Suppose you leave your residuary estate to your nephew, your niece, and your friend. If your nephew predeceases you, do you want your niece and your friend to share your entire residuary estate, as in the earlier example? Or do you want your nephew's share to go to someone else? If you want it to go to someone else, this can be handled by naming a *successor residuary legatee*. This can be accomplished by using the following clause:

> All the rest, residue, and remainder I leave as follows: *one-third* to my nephew (give name and address), but if he predeceases me, this one-third is to go to my brother (give name and address); *one-third* to my niece (give name and address), but if she predeceases me, this one-third is to go to ABC charity (give address), for its general purposes; *one-third* to my friend (give name and address), but if my friend predeceases me, this one-third is to go to another friend (give name and address).

Remember, you have these two choices: you can name *successor residuary legatees,* as in the above example, or you can decide to have the *surviving residuary legatees* share your residuary estate, as in the earlier example. Decide now what you want, and express this decision in your will. This decision might save you the expense of a new will (or codicil) if a residuary legatee predeceases you.

Our discussion of legatees and your residuary estate is now complete. But what of all those potential legatees who didn't find their way into your will?

DISINHERITED RELATIVES

In many states a spouse cannot be disinherited, and must receive a mandated minimum share of the deceased spouse's estate. Many states call this minimum share the *spouse's elective share,* which could be, for example, one-third of the deceased spouse's estate, or one-half of the deceased spouse's estate, or whatever the state law stipulates. The spouse can elect to take this mandated minimum share and thus not be limited to the amount left as a legacy. *Find out what protection surviving spouses are offered by your state.* Be aware that the surviving spouse's elective share is reduced if the deceased spouse is survived by children.

Notice that *elective share* and *intestate share* refer to entirely different situations. *Elective share* is what a surviving spouse receives if the deceased husband/wife dies *with a will* that leaves less to the survivor than is guaranteed by state law. The surviving spouse then *elects* to take the higher alternative amount guaranteed by state law. An *intestate share* is what the surviving husband/wife receives when the deceased spouse dies *without a will*. Often, however, the elective share and the intestate share are the *same percentage* of the deceased spouse's estate, although they refer to two entirely different situations.

Perhaps you have heard of a *postnuptial (or prenuptial) agreement*. In this agreement between husband and wife (or entered into by those who are soon to become husband and wife), each can agree to give up this elective share protection. The result of this voluntary waiver of the protection of state law is that *a spouse can then be disinherited*.

Now what about disinheriting the rest of the world other than your spouse? In just about all state jurisdictions, there is no problem in disinheriting a child, a parent, or any other relative. Should you specifically mention a disliked relative and then leave that relative nothing, or perhaps the sum of one dollar? I advise that you do so only if your state requires that your child must be specifically excluded or, if not so excluded, will otherwise share in your estate. *In any other situation it is not necessary to leave someone a dollar*. It does, however, answer a potential challenge that some page of the will has been lost and that is why the challenger is not mentioned. This lost page argument is so weak that it does not need a response. But by leaving a person the sum of one dollar, however, you answer the challenge. There is no need to state the reason for bequeathing only one dollar (or nothing) to one or more people, but some persons like to give a lengthy explanation. Be careful, however, that you do not libel the person receiving the one dollar. (We will look at libel in chapter 8.) In summary, in most situations, the legacy of one dollar is merely an attempt to write *a few piercing final comments*.

Sample Situation

Have you heard the story of the man who asked a relative to remember him in the will? The will had the following provision: "To my relative who asked to be remembered in my will, *I remember you;* this is the reason why I leave you nothing." Nasty, but subtle last words.

The more serious situation is *your rights* upon death of your spouse (or upon divorce). The law in each state is different, particularly in states

known as community-property states. So check with your attorney to find out what protection is provided by your state.

Money-Saving Suggestion

A *nuptial agreement* should include the following statements: each spouse is familiar with the other spouse's assets (which should be listed); each spouse is aware of what *protection* state law gives to a spouse; each spouse enters into the agreement *voluntarily; each spouse waives a minimum share of the other's estate* (although each spouse may voluntarily leave the other spouse a legacy). Each party to such an agreement should have a different attorney review the document before it is signed. This avoids the future claim that an attorney, if shared by the couple, did not fairly represent both parties. Often this claim has merit, particularly if the attorney, shared by the couple, has had a long and close relationship with one spouse and is paid by that spouse.

For a late-in-life marriage, especially where there are children from previous marriages, a nuptial agreement can prove useful. It helps to prevent future family fights, including a potential court battle over a will. *Adult children from the earlier marriages are much more receptive to a parent's impending marriage when there is a nuptial agreement.* It is also a practical arrangement; partners in a late-in-life marriage often decide to keep their first fortunes totally separate from the finances of the new marriage.

Some elderly clients have asked for my thoughts regarding their children's or grandchildren's nuptial agreement. When asked, I offer two opinions:

First, I am not too enthusiastic about a nuptial agreement between younger people. In some situations, no agreement is needed; the pending marriage should be delayed or cancelled. This becomes apparent when the young, poor couple begins to fight over who is to retain possession of items (some of which are not yet owned) *when* they get divorced. The anticipated short duration of the commitment is revealed by the frequency of the use of the word "when."

Second, I often suggest that these older clients stop worrying about their children and grandchildren and concentrate on their own well-being. It is time for elderly adults to look after their own affairs; their good job of raising and seeing to the needs of their children is over. In turn, these children will do the same good job in nurturing the grandchildren. Sometimes the elderly client is so happy with my first opinion (because the client shares it) that my second opinion is embraced wholeheartedly.

From executor and legatees we now move on to those who will attest to the existence of this, your will. These are the *witnesses*.

3

Witnesses to Your Will

THE FUNCTION OF A WITNESS

A will must be witnessed. *In most states two witnesses are required;* in a few states three witnesses are needed. The witnesses must be adults with a *minimum standard of intelligence;* they must be aware that a *will is being signed,* and they must be able to *relate what happened.* The witnesses are witnessing that

(1) the person is *signing* the will;

(2) the person signing the will is signing it *voluntarily;* that is, no fraud, duress, or undue influence is being exerted on the person signing the will;

(3) the person signing the will appears to know the nature and the consequences of the document (as you know, this is called *testamentary capacity*);

(4) the person signing the will says to the witnesses that the document being signed is a will and asks the witnesses to witness the signature (as you know, this is called *publication*);

(5) the *other witnesses* are signing as witnesses.

The signatures of the testator and the witnesses are not notarized. However, there is another document that some states require at the testator's death. It is a notarized statement, signed by the witnesses, that summarizes

what was observed. This notarized statement is called the *affidavit of the witnesses*. In some states the testator also signs this document. A will with this affidavit is called a *self-proved will*.

Although this affidavit of the witnesses does not have to be produced until the time of the testator's death, some states, including Connecticut, Florida, New Jersey, and New York, allow it to be obtained at the time the will is signed. This is very convenient, because if the affidavit of the witnesses is obtained when the will is signed, then after the testator's death the witnesses do not have to be located.

Death, hopefully, will be in the distant future. Therefore, it is desirable to obtain this affidavit of the witnesses at the same time the will is signed, rather than waiting until the testator's death. Even if the executor then finds the witnesses, there is the possibility they *might not remember what happened:* Did they witness the testator signing the will? Did they witness each other signing the will as witnesses? Did the testator have testamentary capacity, and did he or she sign the will voluntarily (without fraud, duress, or undue influence)? Was the will published: did the testator advise the witnesses that the document is the testator's will, and did the testator request the witnesses to witness the signing?

Here are some additional thoughts on your witnesses:

(1) A person who is left a legacy by you cannot be a witness to your will.

(2) Your executor can be a witness to your will.

(3) It is advisable (because it is an important legal document) for you to have not only the minimum two or three witnesses that your state requires, but also one additional witness.

(4) Your witnesses *do not have to know your financial situation or the contents of your will.*

I stated that a person who is left a legacy cannot be a witness to your will. There might be an exception to this rule in your state, and the explanation that follows will also help you become familiar with the legal terminology learned thus far.

Let us assume that Peter witnesses his widowed father's will, that he is his father's only distributee, and that the will leaves everything to him—except $10,000, which has been left to charity. In this situation, Peter, a legatee, can be a witness to the will. Why? If the amount a legatee

receives through a will is *less than the potential intestate share* (the share the legatee is likely to receive if no will existed), then the legatee can be a witness. Peter does not benefit from the will's existence; in fact, he is financially deprived by it. (He would have gotten more from his father's estate had no will existed.) Despite this possible exception, I advise that you *have neither legatee(s) nor distributee(s) as witnesses to your will.*

Sample Situations

Mary has died, but the witnesses to her will have also died. They had not signed an affidavit of the witnesses when they witnessed Mary's will many years ago. Is Mary's will still legally effective? Yes. The validity of the signature of each witness can be verified, one hopes (perhaps by comparing the signature of the witness with another signature that a bank might have on file). But if that will is challenged by the next of kin, the attorney for the estate will be wishing he had *a witness to the event or an affidavit of the witnesses.*

There is a short sample will in the appendix to this book. At the end of it is an affidavit of the witnesses (see p. 217). Take a look at these legal documents. Some words of caution, however: *do not use them as a sample for a homemade will or an affidavit of witnesses.* I include them only to make this book more understandable. Remember that not only do laws differ from state to state, but individual needs differ as well. Wills should be custom-made to fit the special circumstances of the testator.

Money-Saving Suggestion

Make sure you have the affidavit of the witnesses to your will. Not only does this save your executor the time and the expense of locating the witnesses years later, it also avoids the problems of the dead witness and the forgetful witness, neither of whom can give credibility to the will.

If you do not have the affidavit of the witnesses, write to your attorney today and ask why you do not have it. If you are a resident of a state that requires this affidavit and allows it to be signed before your death, *then have this document signed now. Years from now it will save your estate time and money.* It is also a convenience to the witnesses. They can witness a will and not have to travel to court, perhaps from a distant location, at some time in the future.

Let us now discuss having your *attorney as a witness.*

THE ATTORNEY AS A WITNESS

The attorney is not a witness unless he or she specifically signs the will as a witness. Let us assume that the attorney is standing in the office with the testator and two secretaries; the testator is signing the will, and the two secretaries are signing as witnesses. In this example, the attorney is not considered to be a witness, because the attorney does not sign the will as a witness to the document. *Nothing prohibits an attorney from being a witness to a will that he or she has prepared;* however, the attorney must sign the will as a witness.

It is customary for the attorney to provide the witnesses to your will; usually it is the attorney and members of his or her staff. There is no need for you to impose upon your neighbors by asking them to be witnesses; furthermore, it is none of their business that you are executing a will.

Sample Situations

I mentioned that an attorney should know a great deal about clients who ask to have a will prepared. Be candid with your attorney regarding your net worth. *Do not exaggerate or underestimate your assets.* The attorney should know not only your *general financial situation,* but also any particular problems or unusual circumstances surrounding your finances, so that these situations can be properly resolved. I mention this because some people still think that attorneys will charge wealthier clients more than those persons who are less well off. At the time your will is prepared, tell the attorney your actual net worth and ask about the lawyer's fee for drawing up the document. If you do not like the fee, go to someone else. Full disclosure is in your best interest: terrible mistakes can be made in situations where people underestimate their net worth. *Tax planning is then made on the basis of erroneous information.* An even worse situation is where there is no tax planning, because the attorney is not aware that the net worth exceeds the amount that can be left free of tax at death. The risks of being less than candid may be far greater than you ever expected. *Do not hide anything.*

Also be candid with your attorney on any particular family problem. What you tell the attorney is kept in confidence. Do not hestitate to tell the attorney (if applicable) that you have a few extra spouses or a few extra children. Perhaps there are relatives who are indebted to you, or you to them. It is appropriate and necessary for the attorney to learn about these situations now, because they can affect your eventual estate and the estate plan now being formulated.

Money-Saving Suggestion

There are legal methods to reduce the various taxes that confront estates and legatees. For this reason, the topic of taxation will be brought up occasionally, as the need arises, throughout Parts One and Two of this book. Then in Part Three the subject of taxation will be explored in further detail. At this point, however, I want to familiarize you with the various *categories of taxes* that might be encountered:

1. the deceased's *federal individual income tax* for the year of death (and perhaps the previous year if, for example, the death occurred before April 15th);

2. the *state individual income tax* if the deceased was domiciled in a state that taxes income (some states, like Florida, do not have an income tax);

3. the *federal estate tax,* which happens when the taxable estate of the deceased *exceeds $600,000;* but *everything left to a surviving spouse is exempt from estate tax;* [To any married reader who is a noncitizen of the United States or whose spouse is a noncitizen: Our tax law discriminates against noncitizen spouses who receive property from their spouse (whether through a gift or at time of death). So keep in mind that whenever I make a reference to married people, I am assuming that the receiving spouse is a United States citizen. Let me also point out that this discrimination can be alleviated by establishing a Qualified Domestic Trust (QDT). Although I will not be discussing it here, you might want to ask your attorney about a QDT.]

4. a *state estate tax* based on the value of the estate's assets; [This tax is triggered in some states at a much lower valuation than the federal estate tax.]

5. an *inheritance tax* on *those who receive a deceased's assets;* [However, these states generally exempt, in whole or in part, property received by spouses, children, and grandchildren.]

6. if the estate generates income during its administration, a *federal estate income tax;*

7. if the state has an income tax, a *state estate income tax;*

8. the *gift tax,* which is a tax paid by the person *making the gift* (for gifts in excess of $10,000); [The reason for this tax is to prevent an avoidance of estate tax.]

9. an income tax that the legatee(s) or distributee(s) might have to pay on income earned by the estate during administration and distributed to them.

With this general idea of taxes, let us return to wills and take a look at some of the problems to avoid.

4

Problems to Avoid

SOME DRAFTING PITFALLS

A will communicates the testator's intentions. Here are some pitfalls to avoid.

If you leave something to *someone's spouse,* be specific as to the person in question: Do you mean the current spouse or perhaps a later one? This confusion occurs in the following bequest: "I leave $10,000 to my friend Harry Friendly's wife." If you want to leave something to Harry Friendly's wife, let us call her Bertha, then refer to her as Bertha and not chauvinistically as Harry Friendly's wife. Alternatively, if you want to leave something to the person married to Harry Friendly at the time of your death (whether Bertha or someone else), then refer to this person as "the person married to Harry Friendly at the time of my death."

If something is left to a *named employee,* must this person be in the testator's employ at death? For example, it would be very confusing if your will read: "I leave $10,000 to Harry Friendly, who has been and always will be my loyal employee." If he *does* have to be your employee at the time of your death to inherit the $10,000, then say so, like this: "I leave $10,000 to Harry Friendly, but only on the condition that he is employed by me at the time of my death." If he *does not* have to be your employee at your death to inherit, make this clear by not mentioning that "he has been and always will be my loyal employee."

Never leave "my cash on hand" to someone, because few people will know what you mean. Does this include bank accounts? Does it include cash in the cash register of your store? Does it include cash in a safe

44

deposit box? Who knows? "Contents of my home" is also unnecessarily vague. Does this phrase include a painting on the wall? Probably. Does it include your General Motors stock certificates located in the bureau drawer? Probably not. It is confusing.

Do not leave your 1991 Chevrolet to someone; refer to it as the "automobile owned at my death." Otherwise, if you die several years from now, unless you still own the 1991 Chevrolet, your named legatee will not receive it. Even worse, your named legatee will not receive the 2021 Chevrolet you might own at your death.

Sample Situation

Wirsig's estate, a case litigated in Nebraska, is about a will with a serious omission. Twenty dollars was bequeathed to an individual. But the will also contained this direction: "I hereby bequeath and devise all my personal property and all my real property with the exception of twenty dollars." This is an *incomplete sentence;* the will does not identify who receives everything else *other than* the twenty dollars. Who receives the balance, or residue, of the estate?

The court decided that where a testator fails to identify a beneficiary in the will, the court cannot review any additional evidence to determine the identity of a beneficiary. The court reached this decision despite evidence from sources outside the will that the testator's intent was to leave all his property, except the twenty dollars, to his wife. An unfortunate result: make sure your will does not have a similar drafting error.

Money-Saving Suggestion

If you do not understand your will, do not expect other people to understand it. If other people do not understand your will, then after your death a court will attempt to construe what you meant. This court proceeding is called a *construction proceeding,* in which the court looks only at the will to decide what you meant when you created the will. Thus, you cannot rely on the court to correct omissions in your will; moreover, this court proceeding is costly because it can be quite time-consuming.

There are two general areas in which a will might be unclear: (1) the description of the *person* who is to receive something, or (2) the description of the *something* that is to be received. Make sure that *everyone* and *everything* in the will is clearly identified. Only attorneys benefit from a construction proceeding. Do not let it happen to your estate. You have

learned the importance of discussing family and personal affairs with your attorney. You have also learned the importance of *making sure you understand each sentence, word, and paragraph of the document*. Do not have these efforts go to waste by signing a will that contains obvious oversights.

MORE DRAFTING PITFALLS

Leaving someone all the AT&T stock you own at the time of your death might someday cause a problem. Does this person receive the corporate stock in an AT&T spin-off company, shares of whose stock you might own at the time of your death? Not necessarily. Although you can leave stock in specific companies to a legatee, future corporate reorganizations (or your sale of the stock) might result in your legatee receiving a dramatically diminished legacy (or none at all). We will take a further look at this situation in chapter 14, in our discussion of "Too Few Assets."

Leaving someone your certificate of deposit at Chase Manhattan Bank is a similar potential pitfall. Suppose you transfer these funds to Chemical Bank. The legatee who is left the Chase Manhattan Bank certificate of deposit does not receive it if you do not own a Chase Manhattan Bank certificate of deposit at your death. It is better to leave a *specific dollar amount,* rather than a particular certificate of deposit.

Leaving *less than or more than one hundred percent of your residuary estate* is carelessness. If your residuary estate is divided into percentages, make sure they add up to one hundred percent. Avoid a mistake such as leaving eighty percent to Mary and thirty percent to William. Two similar mistakes—the *missing paragraph* and the *missing page*—also occur. These are the subjects of the next sample situations.

Leaving something to your friend without further identifying the friend, perhaps by listing the individual's current address, is a drafting pitfall that could have chaotic results. Suppose, for example, that two individuals with the same name claim to have been the friend or relative named in your will? Without an address to verify the correct legatee, it might be difficult to determine the identity of this person.

Leaving money to a *group of people*—the specific members of which are bunched in a confusing sentence—often has problematic results. Here is an example of such a confusing sentence: "I leave $10,000 to the following: *the children of my brother Robert, and my brother John.*" There are two problems here: is $10,000 the total amount to go to the group, or is $10,000

to go to each member of the group? Is money being left to John or to the children of John (the comma after Robert is crucial)? Read the confusing sentence again, and you will recognize these two pitfalls.

Sample Situations

Court cases describe basic oversights that appear in wills. These oversights include a *missing paragraph* or a *missing page* of the document.

The example of a missing paragraph can be found in a will in which each paragraph is numbered, but one paragraph number is missing. Perhaps paragraph THIRD is followed by paragraph FIFTH. The relative not named in the will may claim that paragraph FOURTH is devoted exclusively *to lovable him or her.*

The example of a page being absent in a will may occur when the document has each page numbered, but one number is missing. Perhaps page THREE is followed by page FIVE. If the text flows clearly from page THREE to page FIVE, this is evidence that a page has *not* been removed from the will; the pages are simply misnumbered. Again, however, the lovable one can now claim that a full page is devoted exclusively *to him or her.*

Try explaining to a relative who has been left out of the will that these inaccuracies are only insignificant oversights by the proofreader. The forgotten relative will forever believe that his or her legacy was contained in missing paragraphs or pages. The court will probably not listen to the cry of this disinherited person; it will probably agree with the nominated executor that the will is complete. But why risk the cost of a court proceeding? Careful proofreading is a must.

Money-Saving Suggestion

Do not rush any stage of the will-preparation process. It is an important document. That one final office conference may be crucial to assure a properly prepared will. While word-processing equipment makes it easier to revise drafts of a will, this technological advance has brought with it a drawback. Suppose you are at the attorney's office and are ready to sign your will, but decide suddenly to make a last-minute change. These quick revisions are just the occasions when mistakes can be made. I suggest that if you make a last-minute change, delay signing your will; take the new draft home with you and take a day or two to make sure that the revised will expresses your intentions. When you are sure, return to the

attorney's office for the signing and witnessing of the will. But do not let too much time elapse between office visits. Remember that during the interval either *no will exists* or *some prior will is still in force*—a will that may not reflect your current wishes for the distribution of your assets.

Perhaps the reason you decided on a last-minute change was because you had not given enough thought to including some instructions in your will the first time it was drawn—for example, the disposition of your household furniture. The next chapter will consider some of these instructions.

5

Special Instructions

FURNITURE AND PERSONAL EFFECTS

In your will there should be a paragraph, or perhaps a few paragraphs, stating who receives your clothing, furniture, books, paintings, jewelry, silverware, automobile, and other personal items. I find this clause useful:

> I give and bequeath all my tangible personal effects, *including* clothing, furniture, books, paintings, silverware, (and whatever else you want to *include*), but *excluding* cash, securities, any other monetary instruments, jewelry, automobiles, (and whatever else you want to *exclude*) to (name the person), now residing at (person's address), if this person survives me. My estate shall pay the reasonable cost of moving these items. (In another paragraph, name the people who are to receive the jewelry, automobiles, and whatever other items have been excluded from this clause.)

The law of your state may require that some of these items be left to a surviving spouse as part of what is called a *homestead right*. Otherwise, you have flexibility. But spell out who gets what.

What about leaving items such as furniture or jewelry *equally* to two individuals, perhaps your two children? In such a case, consider giving your executor the authority to make the final decision in the event that the two individuals cannot agree on a fair division of the items. Alternatively, consider leaving items such as furniture or jewelry to just one individual to avoid a division problem. Of course, if you want a particular person to receive a valuable item, such as a ring, clearly identify it and who gets

it. To avoid confusion, be sure the identification is sufficient *to distinguish the item in question from any similar items.*

I recommend that you try to *limit the number of people* who are to receive your furniture and other personal effects. As the number of recipients increases, your executor is burdened with the responsibility of attempting to place the objects with those for whom they are intended. Naming so many people is an indication that you are *trying too hard* to have a will that is *perfectly fair*—an impossible goal to achieve.

Sample Situations

A judge, so the story goes, could not get two brothers to agree to an equal distribution of furniture. The disagreement revolved around an antique rocking chair. Neither brother was willing to sell his half of the rocker to the other. The judge brought the matter to a conclusion when he threatened to *break the antique rocker in half.* The brothers quickly found a way to settle their disagreement.

A less intimidating way of settling this type of dispute is to agree on the value of a contested item. Then, by the flip of a coin, decide who is to be the seller. This is a variation of the device used by a parent whose two children argue over the relative sizes of cake slices. The parent tells one child to cut the cake and allows the other child to get the first choice.

The expense of shipping furniture to a legatee can also cause a problem. The legatee usually bears the expense of insuring and shipping the furniture. But to avoid any controversy, *the will should state whether the estate or the legatee is to pay the expenses incidental to delivering the furniture to its final destination.*

Money-Saving Suggestion

In preparing your will you should give serious consideration to *not* identifying each item of jewelry, clothing, and furniture. An identification could result in a higher appraisal value of your estate, thereby triggering a higher estate tax. There is a natural tendency to presume a high value for items specifically described in your will. When the executor then submits a low valuation to the taxation authority, it is suspect. I am not advising tax fraud, just common sense. *Costume jewelry should not be identified in the will;* if it is, no one can fault the state or federal tax auditor for being suspicious of a low valuation.

Items of small economic value (although of high emotional value)

should perhaps be left to one person. You can then leave a note (which I refer to as a *letter of intent*) to this person, and suggest how you would like these items distributed. Even better, you could make a gift of these items now, *so that both you and the recipient can share this pleasure of giving and receiving.* There is also the additional incentive of reducing the value of your eventual estate, thereby saving the estate some tax. But more on this in Part Three on taxation.

Let us take a look at this *letter of intent.*

LETTER OF INTENT

Have you written a *letter of intent* to your son or daughter, the contents of which are to be read after your death? Perhaps the letter advises your child on how to spend the legacy; perhaps it suggests that some small item received by the legatee be given as a gift to a third party. Whatever its content, this letter is *not legally binding.* Generally, I do not recommend letters of intent to my clients. If what you have to say is important, then put it in the will. I *do recommend its use,* however, in *two situations.*

The first is where there are a few pieces of *jewelry,* none very expensive, but each with sentimental value. Consider leaving all the jewelry to one person and then, through a letter of intent, suggest who are to receive the various pieces. The benefit of this approach is the *ease with which the executor can distribute the jewelry* to the one person named in the will.

The other situation is that of a *legacy to children.* Suppose Grandma has collectibles, e.g., silver coins, and she wants each grandchild to receive an equal share of the coins. If Grandma leaves the coins "to her grandchildren," two problems could arise. The first and more serious problem occurs if any of the grandchildren are minors. In probating the will, the court may appoint a guardian, perhaps *a different guardian for each minor grandchild,* to assure that the child receives the legacy. This results in unnecessary expenses for the estate and intrusion of a stranger into the family's finances. We already know the second difficulty, which I call the rocking chair problem: *dividing these coins evenly among the grandchildren.* Perhaps Grandma should leave the silver coins to her most trustworthy child, with a letter of intent stating that she hopes these coins will be distributed equally among her grandchildren. This advice is given to save unnecessary legal fees.

The following suggestion is offered in the hope of saving survivors some anguish. Do not leave a letter of intent that recites why you love or hate

someone, or a letter that explains some pleasant or painful experience. It is unfair to your survivors, because they cannot respond. There is a poignant scene in Neil Simon's play *Broadway Bound* about such a letter from a father to his son. The father wanted to explain everything; the son reads the letter and disdainfully announces that the letter explains nothing.

Sample Situation

A client enters an attorney's office with a look of anticipation. A happy look! After all, he has his grandmother's letter, which clearly states, "I love you; I leave you everything; this letter is to be considered my will." The letter clearly has helped him get over the grief caused by her recent demise. Oh, she was so rich, and he is so glad she did not suffer through a long (and *expensive*) final illness. *Both of them are now in a much higher state of being.*

The attorney confirms the good news—your grandmother loved you. But then comes the bad news—in this jurisdiction (as in most states) *Grandma's letter of intent is not a will.* The crestfallen client barely hears the attorney describe what you have already learned. To be a will, the document must be signed in the presence of witnesses; the witnesses must observe that the testator has testamentary capacity and that no fraud, duress, or undue influence has been exerted on the testator; the witnesses must be told by the testator that this is the testator's will; the witnesses must be asked by the testator to witness the testator's signature; in addition to witnessing the testator's signature, the witnesses must witness each other signing as witnesses. Because Grandma's letter of intent has *none of these characteristics,* it is not and cannot be considered a will. Also, the distraught "heir" usually makes the futile and expensive attempt to convince a court that the letter of intent is indeed a will. May you never be left such a letter unless, of course, there is a will to back up your Granny's intentions.

Money-Saving Suggestions

If a legacy to a minor is not of great economic value, leave it to an adult and use a letter of intent to disclose your wishes. *This avoids the expense of a court supervision of the legacy until the child reaches adulthood.*

I also suggest that if you ever receive a letter of intent stating that you are to inherit everything, immediately tell the sender that the letter is appreciated. Then, strongly urge your well-intentioned benefactor to contact an attorney to learn about the document's legal limitations.

DIRECTIONS TO PAY DEBTS

The following is a typical clause in a will directing that the debts of the deceased are to be paid by the executor:

> I direct that all my *enforceable unsecured* debts, funeral expenses, the expenses of my last illness, and the administration expenses of my estate be paid by my executor as soon after my death as possible.

When using such a clause, here are two problems to avoid:

Do not use terms that may revive a debt you are no longer obliged to pay. An example is a debt that has been discharged in bankruptcy; another example is a debt that cannot be collected because the time when the creditor could bring a lawsuit has expired (this is called the expiration of the *statute of limitations*). Here is a debt-payment clause that might revive a bankruptcy debt or a debt barred by the statute of limitations: "I direct my Executor to pay all debts and claims *that are fair.*" Refrain from using such ambiguous language. In the typical clause, the adjective *enforceable* describes *debts,* thus preventing the revival of debts that have been extinguished by bankruptcy or the expiration of a statute of limitations.

Do not use words that could be construed to require payment of a debt secured by a mortgage. (As you probably know, a mortgage is a debt *secured* by real estate.) Suppose, for example, that a person dies at a time when his home has a mortgage balance of $80,000. Assume also that the home has been left to Mary. Is the $80,000 debt to be paid before Mary receives the home? No. However, if the debt-payment clause says that the executor must pay *all my debts,* Mary could argue that she is entitled to have the $80,000 debt paid, thereby receiving the home *without* a mortgage. In the typical clause, the adjective *unsecured* describes *debts,* thereby expressing the intention that the debt secured by the home is not to be paid by the executor. The sentence leaving the home to Mary should also specifically express your intention that the debt secured by the home is not to be paid by the estate; alternatively, if you want the debt paid off, then clearly state this intention.

Sample Situation

Whether or not your will states that debts are to be paid, believe me, they will be paid. Your creditors will not let the debt(s) be forgotten. But

suppose the debts exceed assets. There is a priority in the payment of debts, and most states generally follow this order of payment: *secured claims,* family allowance, reasonable funeral expenses, necessary medical and hospital expenses of the last illness, costs and expenses of administering the estate, taxes, judgment debts, and then all other debts.

First on this above list are *secured claims.* A claim is secured if a court has on record that certain property is to be the source of payment of a particular debt. Examples include a mortgage on real property (which is land or a building) and a lien on personal property (which is everything else, e.g., cars, books, furniture, etc.). These secured claims are in a category by themselves because, generally, they are given a payment priority over other debts. They are *not subject to a proportional reduction where the total debts of the estate exceed the total assets of the estate.*

Here is an example of proportional reduction: Suppose the deceased left an estate consisting only of his home, valued at $50,000. Further suppose that the deceased's total debt was $100,000—owing $50,000 to a bank and $25,000 to each of two people. Therefore, the $50,000 in assets would pay only half the debts. The bank would receive $25,000, and each individual creditor would receive $12,500. However, if the bank had a mortgage (a secured claim) on the deceased's home, the bank would receive the full $50,000.

Money-Saving Suggestions

To the reader who may be a *creditor* of an estate, I stress the importance of bringing the debt—whether secured or unsecured—to the attention of the estate. Do this as soon as possible, and you should have an attorney represent you in your legal proceeding against an estate. A quick notification is important, because some states *allow only a short period of time* for creditors to present their claims. If you fail to act within this period of time, most likely the debt will not be paid.

To the reader who may be a *debtor,* I have this suggestion. If you have a favorite creditor, you might discuss with your attorney the possibility of giving this creditor a *security interest.* This way, the creditor receives priority over other creditors, either in the event of your bankruptcy or in the event of your death.

BURIAL DIRECTIONS

There is nothing wrong with having directions in your will that outline how you desire to be buried or how your physical remains are to be handled (e.g., cremation, donation for scientific purposes, or some special service). *But be sure that someone you trust is aware of these directions.* It is especially important that individuals who choose cremation express this desire not only in the will but also to a friend or relative who is likely to be in the position to carry out these wishes. Probably this friend or relative is the executor. The will might not be discovered *until after the family reconvenes from the burial at the cemetery.* So, to repeat, share your thoughts with a person close to you, and do it now. Incidentally, at one time religious teaching opposed cremation. This idea has been significantly modified, and few religions now oppose the practice.

At the time your will is drawn (better still, do it today), find out if there is a family *cemetery plot;* if so, who has the deed, and who is to be buried there. Families often find themselves searching for the deed when a relative dies. Usually the deed is located, but even if it cannot be found, the problem does eventually get resolved. The name of the cemetery is remembered, the cemetery finds its record of the plot location and identifies the owner, who then gives consent to the burial. But it is something that should not be left to the last minute; this is a time when family and friends should not be forced to undergo additional stress.

You may decide to have parts of your body used for *anatomical gifts,* or your entire body used for *medical research.* Eye banks, hospitals that perform organ transplants, and medical schools are frequently in need of these gifts. Many states have a section on driver's licenses where residents can express their desire to donate one or more body parts or their entire body for medical purposes.

Be sure to leave directions as to whether there is to be a traditional wake. Perhaps your preference is a *memorial service.* Opinion is mixed as to which of these offers the greater benefit to survivors. Some people are of the opinion that viewing the body is important, because it forces survivors to accept the death of a loved one. My preference is the memorial service, because the body is no longer as important as the type of life that was led. These are not pleasant thoughts, but if your survivors know your wishes, *the emotional stress on them can be significantly reduced.*

Sample Situation

You have the right to decide the manner in which your body is to be disposed. Put these instructions in your will and tell your decision to your executor (and perhaps another trusted person). When this has been done, you do not have to think further on the subject. At your death, the person to whom you have confided this information will follow your instructions.

Money-Saving Suggestions

To the person making the funeral arrangements, *be a smart shopper*. Never waste money; more importantly, never waste someone else's money! This someone else is the residuary legatee, whose legacy is decreased by the amount spent on the funeral (and who might advise the executor not to reimburse the person who orchestrated and paid for the lavish send-off of the deceased). Avoid the urge to go overboard; it is a meaningless effort to use a funeral to show the deceased the extent of your love. *If you are too confused or miserable to make wise choices, then ask someone to make these choices for you.*

Now a few words on planning for yourself. The least expensive alternative regarding body disposal is cremation with a memorial service. The expenses of embalming and renting a room in the funeral home are eliminated. Also there is no need for the purchase of an expensive casket or a gravestone. But it is your decision. *Whatever you decide, however, state your decision in your will and advise your executor accordingly.*

Suppose you change your mind after the will has been signed? *Do not make a change on your will.* Instead, have a new will drawn up or have a codicil prepared.

6

The Codicil

AMENDMENT TO A WILL

A *codicil* is an amendment to a will. Even though amended, the will remains valid; only those parts that are changed by the codicil are revoked. A codicil has the same requirement of legal formality as does a will: it must be *signed* and *dated;* the person must have testamentary capacity and must be signing the codicil *voluntarily;* the witnesses must be told that the document being signed is a codicil to a will and asked to witness the signature (as you know, this is *publication*); the codicil must be *witnessed* in the same manner as a will. A person's will, along with accompanying codicils, is presented to the court at the time of death.

I do not recommend a codicil, and my reasons are both procedural and substantive. It results in too many papers, too many affidavits, and possible confusion. When a codicil amends an earlier codicil, you then realize the problems of this shortcut. These are the *procedural reasons.*

An important *substantive* reason to avoid a codicil is the following. *Your will shows your intention before the codicil was executed.* Therefore, someone will clearly know that his or her legacy was diminished or eliminated by the codicil (just as someone will know that his or her legacy was enlarged by the codicil). *Why invite trouble for your estate from the person whose legacy was diminished?* That person may decide to challenge the codicil.

But even if a codicil is not an incentive to challenge, I still do not recommend it. If information serves no useful purpose, do not reveal it. Why let cousin Harry know that you had initially left him $10,000, but

changed your mind and left $10,000 to cousin Susie instead? If you make this change with a *new will*, cousin Harry will probably never learn of the change. With a *codicil* cousin Harry knows he came close, but receives nothing. Even if he does not challenge the change, no purpose is served by letting him know what might have been?

Here is a quick question for you to consider. Recall that only the distributees can challenge a will. Who do you think is entitled to challenge a codicil? That's right—*the same distributees*. But now let me add something to your rapidly increasing knowledge: *Anyone whose legacy has been diminished by the codicil (or a later will) can challenge it.* For example, John, a friend of Mary, is bequeathed $40,000 through Mary's will. Her codicil eliminates his legacy. John, although not a distributee of Mary, can challenge her codicil.

Sample Situation

A few years ago, a client asked me to prepare a third codicil to his will. In this codicil was an amendment to the second codicil, an amendment to the first codicil, and an amendment to the original will. A new will turned out to be easier to prepare, and easier for my client to understand. Since then, I have prepared only a few first codicils, and I have not prepared any second codicils.

Money-Saving Suggestions

Tell your attorney to redraft the will rather than prepare a codicil, which is often confusing and no less expensive than redrafting an existing document. Many attorneys use word processors, so the typing task is now less burdensome. It is much easier for you to have your will contained in one document, instead of having numerous amendments. I repeat, the primary reason for having a new will prepared, rather than a codicil, is that a will *and* a codicil reveal too much. *The codicil antagonizes the person whose inheritance has been diminished by the change.*

If you feel that a codicil is the best approach for you, then *carefully* read your will and its codicil(s). Make sure the legal documents are clear to you; make sure they are not contradictory, and that there is no inconsistency between them; make sure each codicil is signed, dated, published, witnessed, and that the affidavit of the witnesses is obtained.

If your codicil was prepared for the purpose of leaving something to a charity, the following discussion in chapter 7 may offer some helpful advice, along with some useful suggestions.

7

Charities and Children

LEAVING A LITTLE SOMETHING TO CHARITY

If you have a favorite charity, perhaps you want to leave it something in your will. While there is no guarantee that such philanthropy will secure a place for you in heaven, what you leave to a charity brightens the lives of other people.

Some states impose a *limitation* on how much can be left to a charity. There might be a law that does not allow an amount over a specific percentage of your assets to be left to a charity; however, the law is perhaps applicable only if there is a surviving spouse or a surviving child to protect. Most states, however, do allow you to leave everything to a charity. But, again, perhaps there is an exception, such as: if you leave everything (or even something) to a charity and *die shortly thereafter*. The charity might be prohibited from receiving this legacy (or the court might inquire as to whether any undue influence was exerted on the testator).

Your attorney can advise you on any particular limitation that your state imposes upon charitable legacies, but here are some further thoughts on charities that are applicable *everywhere:*

Make sure that you clearly identify the charity. Write to the charity and request its *legal name.*

What happens if at your death the charity named in your will *is not in existence?* Perhaps a *successor charity* should be named in the event that this happens.

Charities must meet various state and federal requirements to remain tax exempt. But suppose at your death the charity is no longer a qualified charity as determined by the Internal Revenue Service. Since contributions only to a qualified charity are allowable as tax deductions, perhaps a successor charity should be named in your will in the event this happens (so that your estate receives a tax deduction for the amount of this legacy).

Be alert in choosing your favorite charity. There are some wonderful organizations, and some not so wonderful ones. Familiarize yourself with the leadership, finances, purposes, and effectiveness of your chosen charity.

Sample Situations

A major source of funding for most charities consists of legacies in the wills of generous benefactors. If you decide to leave money, stocks, bonds, etc., to a charity, give the organization *discretion regarding how to use the legacy.* If you follow this suggestion, the words "for its general purposes" should be included, along with the name of the charity and the amount of the legacy. This helps the organization in two ways: it gives the charity flexibility and it reduces the charity's bookkeeping chore.

Allowing a charity to use the legacy for its general purposes avoids the following problem. Suppose a legacy is limited to a particular purpose, and the purpose is obsolete at the time the charity is to receive the legacy. A case that comes to mind is the gift of money to a medical charity, but the legacy is limited to *research on a specific disease.* Suppose the disease is already eliminated (cured) by the time the benefactor dies. The broader directive "for its general purposes" may be more appropriate.

Another case where the stated particular purpose of a legacy can become a problem is when the gift is intended for the construction of a *new building.* Suppose the charity does not need a new building at the time of your death? Again, I suggest the broader directive "for its general purposes."

Here is an alternative approach: Again, suppose you want the charity to use the money for scientific research on a specific disease (or for the construction of a new building, etc.). State this purpose but add a clause that *if this purpose is not feasible, the charity may use this money for its general purposes.*

Money-Saving Suggestions

If you want your estate to obtain a charitable tax deduction, you are required to *leave the legacy to the entire charity and not just to a specific division.* For example, your estate could have a problem if you chose to leave a legacy to *the library* of ABC Charity, because the library is neither a legal entity nor a charity. You should state your intention: "I leave this legacy to ABC Charity, to be used, if possible, for its library; otherwise, the legacy is to be used by ABC Charity for its general purposes."

As for choosing a charity, I suggest this approach. *Volunteer to do some work for the charity.* This is a great way to learn about the organization, to help others, and to help yourself. You will receive that wonderful feeling of accomplishment when you make a meaningful contribution to those who truly need it. If you have questions about charities, contact your state attorney general's office for information pertaining to investigations of fraud.

CHILDREN

The loss of a parent is painful, but being disinherited is also painful. If the child believes the exclusion from a parent's will is the result of a loosely worded document, this can be devastating. Make your intentions clear if you have (or acquire) a child. A child can be legally classified in a variety of ways:

the *traditional* child, resulting from the union of a married man and woman or a marriage-like relationship (e.g., common law marriage);

the *adopted* child, whose legal status has been confirmed by an adoption proceeding;

the *stepchild,* whose parent has remarried and the new spouse has not legally adopted the child;

the *surrogate* child, born to a mother who, before the nonsexual conception occurred, relinquished custody of the child to the biological father;

the *out-of-wedlock* child, also called a biological child, whose parents brought it into the world in a traditional manner, but the father and mother were not married when the child was born;

the *posthumous* child, born after the father's death; and

the *after-born* child, also called the pretermitted child, who is born after the parent signed a will.

This last category, the child born to the testator after the will is written, is protected by statute in many states. This child can also be protected by stating *in your will* what legacy (if any) is to be received by a child, *of whatever type,* who comes into your life after you sign your will. You can also have a new will prepared after the arrival of a child.

This subject of identifying various categories of children is important to older persons, even if the elderly leave everything to their adult children. Successor legatees might be grandchildren (in the event that the older person is predeceased by his or her children). For example, if your son predeceases you, do you want his adopted child to share your estate? Whether you do or not, spell it out.

Sample Situation

With your will there is an element of suspense; until the time of your death, perhaps only you and your attorney know for sure what has been set forth in the document and how your wishes are to be carried out. Two dramatic changes are taking place in our society: there is a *breakdown of the family structure,* and people are *living longer.* I have no idea if these two changes are interrelated, but I do know that these changes have resulted in children being disinherited. Families are scattered all over the United States, if not the world. With increased longevity, this separation of parents from their children can often be a long one. The parents may be far away, emotionally as well as geographically; they may have established new friends and new lives. The cases are numerous where children are not left a legacy by either the first parent to die or the second. *Again, there is nothing wrong in disinheriting a child.* But most elders do leave their fortunes to their children. However, *you are in control regarding this matter,* so make up your own mind.

Money-Saving Suggestions

Whether you plan to disinherit or to leave a legacy to a child, make sure you clearly identify both your *intent* as well as the *identity* of the child(ren). If you are leaving something to a child who is adopted, state the name

of your child. If you have another child, or adopt a child, or marry some-one with a child, take the time to read your will; perhaps you might want to speak to your attorney to learn if your current will provides for this new child. *If you so desire, have a provision in your will to address the possibility of a child who might be born or adopted after you have executed the document.*

If you are leaving something to your friend, and you direct that if this friend predeceases you then the legacy goes to your friend's children, be sure to state the name(s) of the child(ren); you might even want to add the following clause to protect any after-born or adopted children: "and to any other children who are born or adopted."

NAMING A GUARDIAN

It is important for a parent (or perhaps a grandparent who has legal custody) of a young child to plan for the possibility that the child will be an orphan. You can appoint in your will the person who will be legally responsible for your child. This person is called a *guardian.*

In Part Four of this volume, I will discuss topics similar to that of "guardian": namely, *conservators* and *committees.* The conservator is an individual who is appointed by a court to manage an adult's property (which, of course, includes money). A committee is an individual appointed by a court and entrusted with the total care of the adult—*both the person and his or her property.* The concept of a guardian is discussed here in Part One because, unlike a conservator or a committee, *the guardian of a minor is appointed through a will.*

You must decide who is best qualified to take care of the child in the event of your death, and then ask yourself whether the person would be willing to assume this responsibility. If you think this qualified person would be willing, approach the person with your proposal. If the person expresses a willingness, then *name this person in your will* as the guardian. Consider having an alternate guardian named in your will, in case your first choice is unavailable or unwilling, if the need arises, to serve as guardian. Here is a sample clause appointing a guardian:

If my spouse, (give name), predeceases me, and any child of mine is under the age of majority at my death, or if my spouse survives me and dies, while any child of mine is under the age of majority, without having nominated a guardian of each child of mine, I hereby nominate,

constitute, and appoint my friend (give name), currently residing at (give address), as the guardian of each child of mine. If this person for any reason, shall fail to qualify or cease to act as such guardian, I hereby nominate, constitute and appoint my friend (give name), currently residing at (give address), as successor guardian. I expressly direct that no bond or security of any kind shall be required of any guardian in any jurisdiction to secure the faithful performance of duties and, to the extent legally permissible, I hereby relieve the guardian from filing accounts of the guardianship in any court.

The real benefit to naming a guardian in your will is the *planning that accompanies your choice*. The fact that the person you selected has expressed a willingness to serve is also a benefit.

Sample Situations

Whenever there is placement of a child—whether into a foster home, an adoptive home, with one of the divorced parents, or with a guardian after the child has been orphaned—the court usually interviews the child. Sometimes the child is also interviewed by social workers and psychiatrists.

I vividly remember a case in which I expressed to the court one of the relevant factors on child placement—*the wishes of the nine-year-old child.* The judge indignantly responded that the decision in the case should not be made by a nine-year-old. Although the child should not decide with whom placement is to be entrusted, in my opinion *the child's wishes surely should be considered.* In selecting the appropriate guardian, listen to what the child says about the person you plan to appoint as guardian and include this input with your own ideas.

Money-Saving Suggestion

Consider entrusting the legacy you leave your child to a person *other than* the child's guardian. Perhaps your sister could be the person entrusted with your child's legacy, and you would name her as *guardian of the child's property*. At periodic intervals she could provide money to your brother, who could be the *guardian of your child*. This way you have an extra pair of eyes watching your child and your child's money. Of course, if you are thinking of choosing different people for these separate roles, consider whether they get along with each other. One other point: you do not have to choose a family member to be the guardian.

I have already suggested that you listen to the opinion of the person for whom a guardian is to be appointed. Some people, however, are hesitant to discuss death, especially their own. I agree, there should be a hesitancy. *Death is difficult to contemplate, whether you are nine or ninety.* However, the subject of death can and should be discussed, but with an awareness that the possibility of the loss of a loved one—especially when there is a reliance upon this loved one—is a frightening concept to everyone.

Planning for the future of your potential orphan or your elderly parent avoids two extreme situations. There is the survivor who is *loved too much;* ironically, family members fight to show their love. The other extreme is the *unloved survivor,* who gets bounced from family to family because no one wants to assume this responsibility.

Now that you have taken the time to plan for the well-being of people in your care, it's time once more to consider the most important person in your will—you.

8

Some Final Thoughts

YOUR INVENTORY

I have already suggested the need for an inventory, a simple list, of what you own. Here are three reasons for having an inventory: it makes your life more *orderly,* it makes your *financial assets more understandable,* and it makes your *survivors' job easier.* But I really want you to have an inventory *in order to prevent your state government from receiving your assets.*

My concern is not so much with your household items (although you should have a list of the contents of your home and give a copy of it to your home insurance agent), but with your *money assets.* Assets that are owned by you at the time of your death—but unknown to your executor and therefore never collected and distributed to your legatees—will be turned over to the state as property that has been abandoned by the owner. If you want your assets distributed to those you love, then you *must let your executor know what you own through your inventory.* I also advise married couples to review their asset inventory; both parties should know and understand their combined finances. There are too many unfortunate situations where the surviving spouse does not know the total assets owned by the deceased spouse.

With the proliferation of certificates of deposit (CDs), tax-deferred investments, tax-exempt investments, zero-coupon bonds, mutual funds, Individual Retirement Accounts (IRAs), and so on, it is possible that you will lose—or your executor will never locate—one or more of your investments. Look at the long lists of names that local banks periodically publish in newspapers. The lists contain names of depositors whose accounts have

been inactive for a number of years, and the banks are attempting to locate the holders of these accounts. It is a fact that many of these depositors are dead. It is also a fact that *the money in these accounts will eventually be owned by the state government if the funds go unclaimed.* The legal term describing this transfer of abandoned assets to the state is *escheat.*

At the time your will is drafted, make an *inventory* of all your assets. For your bank accounts, include the account number along with the address of the bank; for your shares of corporate stock, include the name of your stockbroker if these shares of corporate stock are held in a brokerage account. Update your list annually; your list does not have to be typed. Each year you can just cross out those assets you no longer own and add the new assets. A convenient time for the annual update is after the April 15th filing of your income tax return. Your attorney should see this inventory, and *your executor should know where your inventory is located.* Your insurance broker should be consulted as to whether all the items on your list are adequately insured.

I cannot emphasize enough the need for this inventory; bank accounts and other financial accounts do get lost—in some cases forever. Elderly citizens are at particular risk because other problems, such as illness, might distract them from keeping their financial affairs in order.

Sample Situation

Estates frequently have this significant problem: difficulty in discovering what the deceased owned. This problem can be easily prevented.

Schedule B from your federal individual income tax return is a good starting point for your inventory. This schedule lists all your taxable interest and dividends. I advise clients to ask their tax preparer to list the account number after the source of the income: for example, ABC Bank, Account Number 01–117,003. Photocopy this schedule and you have most of your financial inventory completed.

Not only is this an easy way to prepare your inventory, but it also helps if an income tax audit occurs. If the Internal Revenue Service's computer beeps when it scans your return, perhaps the account number will clarify the situation when a human being examines your return. If it does not clarify the situation, you may be required to meet with an Internal Revenue Service auditor. At this stage of the audit, your records can save you dollars that otherwise might be assessed by the tax auditor.

Money-Saving Suggestion

You, not just your heirs, benefit from this list of assets. You may learn that *some investments are doing better than others,* and you may decide to make some investment changes. For example, make a comparison between *the after-tax money in your pocket from taxable income and the money in your pocket from tax-exempt income.* A tax-exempt income yield of eight percent interest is better than a taxable income yield of ten percent interest for those in the higher income bracket who are taxed at a twenty-eight percent rate. The inventory therefore becomes far more than a list; it comprises many facts that can be used to evaluate your investments. The inventory makes your life more *organized.*

LIBEL AND PROVISIONS AGAINST PUBLIC POLICY

The existence in a will of *a provision that is offensive to someone may be the source of a lawsuit.* The offended person could prevail in a suit based on *libel,* a legal action for damage done to a person's reputation.

As I mentioned earlier, try not to be humorous or sarcastic in describing someone in your will. Most definitely, do not have your will become the foundation for a libel lawsuit. Refrain from describing someone as a thieving scoundrel. While some courts might say that the scoundrel in question has no action against your estate, other courts might well hold your estate liable for the injury that your will has inflicted on this *thieving scoundrel's reputation.* Resist the urge to have the last word, because, in the end, the person you libel may get your last penny.

Another reason for urging you to refrain from writing humorous or nasty words in your will is the concept of *testamentary capacity,* a fundamental feature of any valid will. If you attack someone in your will, the opportunity presents itself for the injured party to question your state of mind when you signed the will. It would be ironic if the final consequence of those well-placed nasty words is a court determination that you lacked testamentary capacity.

A situation similar to the libelous statement is that known as the *provision against public policy.* For example, a father leaves his daughter the whole of his estate, but imposes a condition that *first she must get divorced.* This is a provision against public policy and will not be enforced. This subject is further discussed in the next sample situation.

Sample Situation

Just as the law does not permit you to use your will as an instrument to destroy a person's character or reputation, *a provision in your will that is against public policy will not be recognized by the court.* There are cases of a legacy being left to an individual, but only if that individual does something. If the required action is against public policy, the court can *disregard the provision.* The example above is a case in point: a legacy to a person is conditioned on the provision that the person *must get divorced* before the legacy can be received.

One case where the legacy was conditioned on the provision that the person *must get married* supposedly can be found in the will of George Bernard Shaw. The story is told that he intended to leave everything to his wife on the condition that she remarry within one year after his death. He wanted to be sure at least one person would grieve his passing.

Do not have this type of provision in your will. After the laughter subsides, your will may be denied probate, or the legatee may not get the legacy, or the legatee may get the legacy without the provision being enforced. The provision is, at best, *meaningless;* at worst, it *denies all your legatees their legacies.*

Money-Saving Suggestions

Neither libel someone in your will nor impose a condition on a legacy that is against public policy. Your will is a serious legal document. Its purpose is to distribute your assets to those whom you wish to receive them. This purpose can be defeated if you write your will in a frivolous fashion; your estate will also incur unnecessary legal fees.

Here is a practical suggestion. Why wait until you are dead to tell a person how upset you are about something the individual said or did? Tell the person now; you might be pleasantly surprised at the result. Even if the problem remains unresolved, you have had the satisfaction of expressing your displeasure.

A LIVING WILL

A *living will* is a document outlining how a person wants to be medically treated in the event of a terminal illness or a condition that requires decisions about the use of life-sustaining procedures. If the person is later rendered

unable to communicate a medical treatment decision, then the desires expressed in the living will are what society is asked to recognize.

The living will is used by an individual who does not want to be subjected to a futile prolongation of the dying process. Your living will can state a desire that life support systems, feeding tubes, and heroic measures are not to be used when there is no chance of recovery. It is not the expression of a desire to end life; it is an appeal that medical technology not be used to *prolong the dying process if no reasonable chance of recovery is likely.*

The living will is an assertion of a person's right to *self-determination.* Some people are in favor of it as an expression of personal autonomy and thus conclude that it is a means to *allow* death to take place. Others, most particularly those opposed to the living will, are of the mind that it is a means to *cause* death. What do you think? Here is a wallet-size summary of the living will:

TO MY FAMILY, PHYSICIAN, AND HOSPITAL: If there is no reasonable expectation of my recovery from extreme physical or mental disability, I direct that I be allowed to die and not be kept alive by artificial means and heroic measures. I ask that medication be mercifully administered to me for terminal suffering even though this may shorten my life.

I hope that you who care for me will feel morally bound to act in accordance with this urgent request. *(This wallet-size summary is distributed by the organization called Concern for Dying.)*

After you sign your living will, it is signed by witnesses. Suggested witnesses are your doctor, attorney, or executor, although any competent person can be a witness.

Sample Situation

All of us have read in the newspaper or seen on television the story of the terminally ill comatose patient kept alive by so-called heroic measures. In many of these cases there is confusion among those who love the person. The question is repeated: "What does my sick friend want?" A living will provides the answer; it helps both you and those you love in times of great despair. The vast majority of states now recognize the living will.

A real benefit of the living will is that your family, attorney, executor, doctor, and hospital know your thoughts and wishes on the subject of

heroic medical treatment. But most importantly, your acceptance or rejection of the living will *forces you to reach a decision regarding extraordinary medical procedures.* Make up your mind on this subject and let your wishes be known. Have a living will prepared if you want to exercise this self-determination.

Money-Saving Suggestions

Unnecessary, unwanted, painful, and expensive medical treatment may be eliminated by signing a living will. If you have a living will, make sure that your *doctor* is aware of it and insist that the document be shown to any *hospital* that ever admits you as a patient. (To receive more information on the living will, write to Concern for Dying, 250 West 57th Street, New York, New York 10107. This organization has distributed millions of copies of the living will since it began educating the public in 1967.)

Here is another suggestion: If you have a problem distinguishing between a living will and euthanasia, discuss this subject with someone. Perhaps your doctor, minister (rabbi or priest), or attorney can provide some direction. Although they can help you prepare to reach your decision, they cannot make these choices for you. *It is your responsibility to decide what is best for you.*

Allow me to give you my rebuttal to one of the arguments against a living will. The argument is that the doctor might withhold treatment in a case where the patient *clearly has a chance of recovery.* My answer: in this hypothetical case the doctor is incompetent; seeking a second opinion, not the rejection of a living will, is how to *limit the possibility of a medical mistake.*

UPDATING A WILL

If you decide to change your will, see your attorney and have a new one prepared. Remember that the will is dated; the document with the most recent date is your *last will and testament.* What should you do with your old will? Save it, because it serves as a good record of your desires over the years. Your attorney should be the one to save it, so that the prior wills are not available after your death to the casual observer of your personal papers. Here are some thoughts on when a will should be updated:

when your wealth increases: perhaps as a result of having received a legacy;

when you get married, become a parent (or a grandparent), or get divorced;

when a person named in your will dies, and you have changed your mind about the successor named to receive the legacy;

when any person named in your will falls out of your favor;

when a legatee becomes profligate and you want to leave the legacy in a trust to protect the wealth from being improperly spent;

when your opinion of your executor changes; and

when you become aware of an estate tax law change.

The cost of a legal consultation or preparing a new will is far less than the amount that can be saved by sound planning.

Do not make any changes to your existing will without consulting your attorney. Suppose you cross out something in a will. What you might have done is destroy the whole will; in some states you have done nothing, that is, the part you thought you deleted remains as part of the will. If a court has to determine the legal effect of your crossing out, this future cost to your estate will significantly exceed the present cost to you for preparation of a new will. *To change your will requires either a new will or a codicil. In either case, the legal formalities (witnessing, etc.) are the same.* Also, remember what you have learned about codicils. I do not recommend this shortcut; have a new will prepared and it should be no more expensive than the amendment you contemplated.

Sample Situations

Generally, the law considers your will to have been revoked if you destroy the document. Furthermore, the law presumes that a missing will was destroyed *by you,* the testator, if it was in your possession and cannot be found. "Presumes" here means what is accepted as fact, unless contradictory evidence is provided. So, if you *accidentally* lose the original of your will, upon your death the law considers your will to have been revoked by you, *unless proven otherwise. To prove otherwise is difficult,* because your executor (who will bear this burden of proof) will not know whether you ripped it up *deliberately* or threw it out *accidentally.*

Here is another reason *not* to keep your original will at home. After your death, someone not named in the will might be the person who discovers the existence of the will and then destroys it. Therefore, you might want to consider having someone safeguard this important document.

Should your attorney hold the original will while you retain a copy? It might be safer to proceed in this fashion. But be aware that some attorneys desire to hold the original of the will in order to increase the chance of eventually *representing the executor of your estate.* This presumes that the executor will hire the attorney who prepared and safeguarded the will (and also presumes that the attorney will outlive the testator). Both presumptions are speculative and perhaps not all that significant, but there is no harm in sharing these ideas with you. If the attorney who holds your will happens to die before you do, then contact the attorney's office (frequently the law office will contact all of the attorney's clients in such cases) and either retrieve the will or select some other attorney in the firm to be the person responsible for safeguarding your last will and testament.

Two other places to keep your original will are: (1) with your executor (or some other trusted person) or (2) in your safe deposit box. However, if the latter option is used, be sure that directions contained in the original will pertaining to such matters as your burial have been unequivocally stated by you to your most trusted person (probably your executor), who in this instance should be in possession of a copy of the will. Your executor should have no problem gaining access to your safe deposit box at the time of your death.

Money-Saving Suggestion

While I believe attorneys are necessary in preparing wills, do not become what I refer to as a *will groupie.* This is a person overly preoccupied by the will, and who pays unnecessary attorney's fees. Some people do this because they enjoy talking with the attorney about who is getting what, who is not getting what, and how their legatees (and nonlegatees) may react. A tip-off on whether you are a will groupie is if you are overly concerned about the *reading of the will.* Remember that there is no such thing. A will that is carefully prepared by your attorney should not have to be changed more than a few times in your lifetime. Perhaps your will can last for your entire life. *But take a look at your will each year at about tax time,* perhaps when you update your inventory of assets. If there has been a significant change in your life, then go see an attorney.

AN ATTORNEY IS NECESSARY

Yes, an attorney *is necessary* to advise you on every area covered in this book. But do not hire the first attorney you interview; comparative shopping is a good way to educate yourself. Listed below is a four-step approach to your first encounter with an attorney. Discuss *experience, speed, outcome,* and *fee,* as follows:

Ask questions about the attorney's *experience* with the particular legal matter. Spend time getting to know the attorney; allow this person to get to know you.

Ask *how long* it is going to take the attorney to solve your problem. An attorney who does this for a living should know the answer.

Obtain the attorney's prediction on the *outcome* of the legal problem. Perhaps you will learn that the attorney *cannot* solve your problem.

Discuss the *fee.* The attorney may not be able to give an exact fee, but you should at least receive a clear estimate of the approximate amount to be charged. Learn how the attorney has calculated this amount. Is it based on the size of the estate? Is it based on the estimated number of hours of work? Also, you should know at what time payment is due. If you hire the attorney, have this fee agreement clearly stated in a follow-up letter (written either by you or the attorney). The disbursement costs, such as court filing fees and other expenses, also should be explained to you.

In summary, whether you are dealing with an attorney, a doctor, an automobile mechanic, or a plumber, you should ask about the *experience* of the person providing the service, *how long* it will take, what is the anticipated *outcome,* and what is the *fee.*

Shakespeare wrote that *all attorneys should be killed.* Try these more moderate alternatives: when you need an attorney, hire one; but before you hire an attorney, be careful and *ask questions.* If the relationship becomes unsatisfactory to you, *put an end to it (the relationship, not the attorney's life).*

Sample Situations

Some people consider attorneys to be rascals, while others see them as heroes. Perhaps it started when Aaron represented Moses before the phar-

aoh and *lost his case*. Perhaps it started when Thomas More represented the pope before King Henry and *lost his case*. Most attorneys are neither heroes nor rascals. *They are people providing a service on a subject matter known to them*. Sometimes they win, sometimes they lose, and sometimes *the distinction between victory and defeat is somewhat unclear*.

A mistaken view is that attorneys are *all-powerful*. Not true. Attorneys are like *jockeys:* they provide direction within defined boundaries, guide the matter to a conclusion, and try to have the results pay off for the client. Perhaps a perfect solution to the legal problem does not exist and compromise is the alternative. Most troublesome, however, are the cases in which the attorney does not advise the client at the outset of what can and cannot be achieved. The client has high expectations; the attorney hesitates to be the bearer of bad news; and when the client's expectations are not realized, the client justifiably feels that the attorney did not perform satisfactorily.

A final observation is that attorneys are not *psychiatrists*. Particularly with family problems, your attorney should not be expected to solve the nonlegal aspects of these disputes. Your legal counsel, however, can give guidance as to how you can solve the problems, or at least he can listen as you articulate and clarify the problems. Conversely, *if the attorney increases the family's problems, then hire another lawyer*.

Money-Saving Suggestions

Good legal advice can save a substantial amount of money. You should hire an attorney to plan your estate and to advise you on those few major legal decisions that confront each of us. We have all heard stories about the terrible attorney (doctor, auto mechanic, plumber). *If you have a problem with an attorney, then hire a more qualified legal counsel*.

Here is some advice that is simple but often disregarded: *good communication* solves a lot of problems. Your relationship with your attorney should be a close one, so talk with your lawyer.

THE ATTORNEY'S JOB

Words that have a specific legal meaning should be used only if both you and your attorney understand them. Helping you to understand in a general way every *word,* every *sentence,* and every *paragraph* in your will is one of your attorney's most important jobs. Your attorney's function also includes:

Helping you understand what you own. This might require an appraisal of your business, an explanation of the death benefits available from your employer, an evaluation of your life insurance, or confirmation of your ownership interest in a particular parcel of real estate.

Advising you on estate taxes that might be owed by your estate and suggesting ways to lessen them.

Listening patiently and asking you to express your thoughts and feelings as to why someone should or should not be in your will. This is the extent of the direction the attorney should give in responding to the question, "Do you think I should leave her anything?"

Assisting you in the preparation of a will.

Assuring you that your will conforms to the laws of your state.

Giving you advice on related subjects, such as: medicare and medicaid, private health insurance, social security, the income tax treatment of any lump-sum pension distributions, and addressing all the legal issues now confronting you or eventually confronting your estate. Perhaps the best job the attorney can perform in some of these areas is to refer you to an attorney who specializes in the particular subject of concern.

The relationship between an attorney and a client is a close one, especially in this area of will preparation. *Be candid with your attorney.* What you tell your attorney is held in confidence. The attorney cannot repeat information to anyone without your consent.

Sample Situation

Real property includes land and buildings; everything else is *personal property.* Therefore, your *shares of stock,* your car, your furniture, your jewelry, your clothing, and your bankbooks are all *personal property.* Suppose your will directs that someone is to receive *all your personal property.* You now know that any shares of stock you own in General Motors Corporation, in your cooperative apartment, or in your family-owned corporation will go to this person receiving *all your personal property.* It is your attorney's job to advise you on the importance of every word in your will, *particularly if the word has a legal meaning.* Otherwise, your will might be expressing something contrary to your wishes.

Money-Saving Suggestion

Be safe, spell out the items you intend to leave to various people. Do not rely on confusing general terms such as *personal property, tangible personal property,* and *personal effects.* These expressions may sound similar, but they have entirely different meanings.

Personal property is a broad category and includes everything other than land and buildings. As explained in the sample situation, it includes shares of stock in a corporation.

Tangible personal property distinguishes tangible items, which are items that can be felt (an example is your jewelry), from things that are symbolic of something (an example is your bankbook, which is symbolic of the money in the account). So the person receiving your tangible personal property will receive your jewelry but not your bankbook.

Personal effects means your clothing and other items that are closely connected with you. Obviously this definition is quite vague. Does it include your pants? Yes. Does it include your wallet? Yes. Does it include the money in your wallet? No. Does it include the contents of a safe deposit box if the key to the box is in your wallet? No.

GUILT, GREED, EXPLOITATION, AND UNDUE INFLUENCE

Oh, what emotions a will stirs! If a friend or relative asks your advice on whether a will is necessary, say yes. I have heard many people recount a tale similar to the following:

> My ninety-six-year-old aunt said, "I think I should put my affairs in order, please help me." So as not to appear greedy, I responded, "Oh, there's no rush, *you're not going to die.*"

The person asking for your advice is most likely thinking of leaving you money, appointing you as executor, or both. *You can help that person and also help yourself.* Do not feel guilty, greedy, unworthy, or anything of the kind. On the other hand, do not let that person exploit you. Do not bank on the promise that *you are in my will.* Maybe you are the potential legatee; but there is also the possibility that you are being exploited.

Remember reading about undue influence? You learned that a person's will must not be the result of undue influence having been exerted. However, *good salesmanship is not undue influence.* But those who can

talk a person into leaving them some money are unique indeed. My experience is that people can see through the various ploys and cajolings, and are offended by someone asking for a legacy. The request for a legacy usually results not only in a strained relationship but in no legacy. *Suggest the importance of a will;* this is the best salesmanship.

Most individuals die without a will, and thus do not exercise their right to choose who receives their property, however large or small it may be. We are complex creatures: our lives, our relationships, our finances, and the reasons some give for having wills (and others for not having them) are probably just as complicated. It is my opinion, however, that *a person without a will is a person who avoids thoughts of death,* those vague thoughts of nothingness, of being a flicker in the galaxy, of judgment, of perfect happiness. Whether or not you think about it, however, death is inevitable. But your will, unlike your death, is something within your control. So think about your will, plan your estate, and stop thinking about death, and . . . *thy will be done.*

Sample Situations

The cases of disappointed heirs are sad stories. These people were told they would get the booty. Perhaps they were told the truth, but a later will then knocked them out. Or perhaps they were being fooled, and learned the sad truth upon the death of the person who lied to them. Another case that frequently occurs is the rich relative who honestly alerts the legatees of their potential good fortune, but the high cost of medical care, perhaps nursing home care, *depletes the assets of this relative who had once been rich.*

Do not exploit others, and do not let anyone exploit you. It serves no purpose to tell someone that there is a legacy for them in the future. *Most people do not reveal the names of the legatees. This is what I advise.* Although you should not tell your legatees that they are in your will, I again advise you to *ask* your executor if he or she will serve in that capacity. I suggest this for the following reasons: Not only is it a courtesy that should be extended to the potential executor, it gives you the opportunity to tell this person where your will and asset inventory are kept. Most importantly, it is the only way to find out if the person is willing to serve as your executor.

Money-Saving Suggestion

Some people feel uncomfortable when told by a friend or relative that they are named in the will. I repeat, do not feel guilty, greedy, unworthy, or obligated to act differently toward your potential benefactor. Continue the same relationship you enjoyed before you were informed. *This suggestion can save you the energy and expense of caring for someone who is exploiting you.* Ask yourself if you would otherwise render this care. Do not think that if you help someone, then you will be rewarded with a legacy. There are legions of disappointed people who mistakenly believed they were the heirs apparent. Keep in mind, care and concern should be *motivated by love, not by money.*

A LIVING (INTER VIVOS) TRUST

No treatment of wills is complete without a discussion of trusts. This section on a living trust introduces the subject. *Testamentary trusts* are discussed in the next section.

A *trust* is a contract between a person and a trustee, whereby the person transfers money or other property to the trustee, who holds the property for the benefit of someone else. There are three parties involved: the person with the money is called the *settlor* (or the *grantor*); the person entrusted with possession of the money is called the *trustee;* and the person benefiting from the money is called the *beneficiary.*

An *inter vivos* trust is made by a *living person.* (Incidentally, *inter vivos* is Latin for "between the living," and most people refer to this type of trust as a *living trust.*) A *testamentary trust* is the same as a living trust, except that the trust is established *in a person's will,* and it thus takes effect upon the person's death.

A trust agreement, like any contract, gives you flexibility as to what terms and conditions are agreed to by the settlor and the trustee. For example, the settlor can require the trustee to give the income annually to the beneficiary, or the settlor can require that the trustee accumulate the income and delay giving any money to the beneficiary until a later time. The settlor can establish guidelines as to how the trustee is to invest the trust funds, specify when the trustee is to terminate the trust, and direct how the trustee is to distribute the balance of the trust funds when the trust is terminated.

The settlor, by appointing someone to control the money, is exerting

a control over the beneficiary. When you think of a trust, whether a living trust or a testamentary one, think of *control.*

One trust provision I favor is called a *sprinkling income provision.* It gives the trustee the power to distribute income among a few beneficiaries, and not necessarily in equal shares. From year to year the trustee can decide which beneficiary (or beneficiaries), is (are) to receive the income. The trustee can also decide the amount of income that is to be received by each beneficiary.

Sample Situation

A client once asked me why living trusts are used in cases where a lot of money is involved. Administrative and legal costs make trusts impractical for the less well-off person. If the individual setting up the trust is not well off, the tax savings are small or nonexistent. You will learn more about tax savings in Part Three, but let us take a quick look at taxes right now.

Money-Saving Suggestion

Income tax savings and *estate tax savings* can result from the use of a living trust.

Suppose mother puts $10,000 into a living trust for the benefit of her twenty-year-old son. *Income tax savings* are realized, assuming that the yield (the interest income) from the money is likely to be taxed at a lower rate for the son, rather than at the possibly higher rate the mother might be required to pay on similar income. The *estate tax savings* arises because she has reduced her taxable estate by at least a portion of the amount of the trust. In addition, there is the estate tax savings on the amount which the $10,000 might have increased over the remainder of the mother's life.

However, savings on income and estate taxes would have resulted even if she had given the money *outright to the son.* But a trust has the *additional* tax benefit of keeping this money *out of the son's eventual estate,* as we will see by once again looking at this example of a living trust:

Wealthy Mother delivers $10,000 to the ABC Trust Company. It is to be held in trust for her son. Mother is the *settlor;* ABC Trust Company is the *trustee;* the son is the *beneficiary.* The trust company is to invest

the money and distribute the income annually to the son. Upon the son's death, the trust company is to end the trust and *distribute the principal in the trust to her other children surviving her son. The principal in this trust is not included in the taxable estate of the son.*

The mother can decide to give the trustee discretion to distribute some of the *principal* (the $10,000) to the son at whatever time the trustee so decides. She also can decide to have the trustee retain the income until the son reaches a certain age, and then start to make distributions to him. There are practically no limits on the terms the mother can include in the trust.

A TRUST IN THE WILL (TESTAMENTARY TRUST)

A testamentary trust is the same as a living trust, except *it is contained in a will and takes effect when the testator dies.* It is a way to leave a legacy to someone and at the same time *control* the timing of the distribution to the legatee. Furthermore, it is a way to *control* where that legacy will go when the legatee dies. You might want to establish a testamentary trust in these situations:

money is left to a *minor child;*

money is left to a profligate adult who is likely to *squander* it if the legacy is not protected;

money is left to an adult who is unable to *manage* it;

money is left to someone who is *mentally incompetent;*

you want to exert *control* over the funds for a period of time (i.e., you want to exert control over the person's use of the money for that person's lifetime, and upon that person's death you want to exert control over the choice of the eventual recipient of the money—in which case, your trustee is your *controlling hand from the grave*); or

you want the *estate of the person receiving your money to avoid future estate taxes* (and my next money-saving suggestion explains this idea).

A trust, whether *living* or *testamentary,* offers you flexibility; your attorney can custom prepare it to fulfill your wishes. *The power of the trustee can be extensive or quite limited.* I caution you to avoid being too rigid or too vague in your directions to the trustee.

One example of being *too rigid* would be an absolute direction to the trustee that the trust principal always consist of fifty percent stock and fifty percent tax-exempt bonds. This instruction would have an ironic result. When the stock comprising fifty percent of the trust principal is doing poorly and decreases in value, some of the tax-exempt bonds would have to be sold to buy more stock to maintain the equal value of stocks and tax-exempt bonds in the trust.

An example of being *too vague* is an absolute direction to the trustee that the trust principal is never to be invested in companies that are *antisocial.* Would this vague standard allow a trustee to invest in a company that makes military equipment? Could the trustee invest in a company that produces food high in cholesterol?

Try to strike a balance between *rigid instructions* and *vague instructions* to the trustee.

Sample Situation

As with *living* trusts, *testamentary* trusts are generally used only by the wealthy. That is, the person establishing the trust is wealthy; the beneficiary may or may not be. Can the beneficiary, who but for the trust is poor, qualify for social welfare benefits such as medicaid? Maybe.

The trust document should direct that the trustee has total discretion as to whether any income is to be distributed, with a further direction that the principal is not to be distributed. It can also stipulate that a trustee should *withhold income if the result would be the disqualification for government benefits.* Speak to your legal advisor about this, since some government agencies frown on using this method to qualify for benefits.

Money-Saving Suggestion

In the following example of a *testamentary trust,* it is the *later* estate of John (the beneficiary) that avoids estate tax:

I, JAMES SMITH, give and bequeath $100,000 to my trustee, XYZ Trust Company, IN TRUST NEVERTHELESS, and XYZ Trust Company is annually to distribute the income to my brother, JOHN

SMITH. Upon JOHN SMITH'S death, the XYZ Trust Company is to distribute the principal equally to the children of JOHN SMITH then surviving him.

(IN TRUST NEVERTHELESS means "in spite of that." So the possession of the money is given to the trust company but, in spite of that possession of the money, it is holding that money for the benefit of others, in this instance, John and his children.)

The estate of *James* does not save any money as a result of this testamentary trust. But upon the subsequent death of *John,* there is a double savings. First, the $100,000 does not pass through John's estate, so there is a *reduction in the executor's fee* because it is the trustee, not the executor, who distributes this trust principal upon John's death. Second, this $100,000 is *not included in the John's taxable estate,* because he did not really own the $100,000; he had a limited use of the money (only the income derived from the principal).

One cost of having a testamentary trust is the fee paid annually to the trustee. Although this fee is an income tax deduction, I suggest you consider a testamentary trust only if there is a significant reason for its use. *The reason I find quite compelling is when the beneficiary of the trust would otherwise squander the inheritance if it were not supervised by a trustee.* But balance the benefits of using a trust with the possible economic frustration the beneficiary may feel because of the restricted availability of these funds. Emotional frustration is also experienced because the beneficiary feels inept, untrustworthy, and still *controlled by the deceased.*

YOUR ESTATE PLAN

All of us should think about our own death and the *disposition of our possessions after we are gone.* What is most important is our concern for those who survive us. If someone's survival has been dependent upon your economic assistance, you want that person to be able to continue without you. You also want those you leave behind to be able to spend their time in productive and enjoyable pursuits, not in long and involved attempts to complete the puzzle of your economic life.

In concluding Part One, let us review some of the major points discussed. An estate plan has been put together, and here is a summary:

You have gathered together all your important *legal documents.*

You have evaluated all your *insurance coverage.*

You have reviewed all your *investments,* and have created an *inventory of all your assets.*

You have chosen an *executor* to handle your estate.

You have chosen a *guardian* if you have a dependent child.

You have decided who are to be your *legatees.*

You have determined whether you want a *living will.*

You have located the deed to the *cemetery plot,* given directions for burial (and these directions might be included in your will), and you definitely have *discussed these directions with someone.*

You have signed your will and have told your executor where it is located.

Where do we go from here? Part Two will focus on *administering your estate,* which is the procedure for gathering and distributing your assets after you have died. In Part Three, the estate plan will be completed by reviewing the various *taxes* that must be paid by an estate. In Part Four, we will conclude our discussion by tying up loose ends regarding matters of life and death.

Sample Situation

Although the gathering together of your important documents might not be of great benefit to *you* (but it will make it easy for you to locate the information when you need it), in every case where the decedent had all the important documents in a safe place, the *executor's job* of administering the estate was always easier.

Money-Saving Suggestion

Here is a list of important documents and other vital information the originals of which should be kept in a safe place, perhaps in a safe deposit box, with photocopies at home:

your will

your tax returns for the past three years

your financial records for the past three years

the deed for your cemetery plot

the deed for your home

an inventory of your assets

your passport

life insurance policies

home insurance policy

bankbooks

Individual Retirement Accounts (IRAs)

certificates of deposit (CDs)

the name of the bank where your social security check is deposited

stock certificates

statements of employee benefits

statements of accrued sick leave

statements of accrued vacation

death certificates of close family members

your family tree

your birth certificate

military discharge papers

divorce decree(s)

your completed living will

trust agreements

the location of your safe deposit box

proof of any debt owed to you (IOUs, contracts, letters of agreement, liens, etc.)

proof of any debt you owe (invoices, contracts, IOUs, letters of agreement, etc.)

a list of credit card accounts

the names and addresses of your doctor, lawyer, and accountant.

I include military discharge papers on my list because your executor might refer to them if your burial is to be in a national cemetery, or if your survivors want to receive a flag in tribute to your military sacrifice.

Why do I advise you to retain copies of the death certificates of close family members? As you will learn in Part Two, some states require your executor to contact your next of kin at the time of your death in order to give them an opportunity to question the legality of your will. Therefore, by having copies of death certificates for departed close family members, it will be an easier job for your executor to show the court how the identity of your surviving next of kin was determined.

If you cannot find any of the information on this list, locate it (or replace it) immediately. Keep in mind that almost everyone knows where most of this information can be found. But it is those few missing items that will cause problems. *Find (or replace) them now!*

Let us now see what happens in the administration of a deceased person's estate.

Part Two

After Death

9

Introduction

PROVING THE WILL (PROBATE)

A general understanding of the probate process is necessary because this is the first legal activity in the administration of an estate. Here is an overview, which will be expanded upon in chapter 11.

The probate process, undertaken by the person named in the will as executor, consists of (1) filing the will and the affidavit of the witnesses in court; (2) producing the death certificate; (3) notifying the legatees and all those who would inherit (the next of kin) if the will were successfully challenged; and (4) *concluding with the court's decision that this document is the deceased's will* or, alternatively, that the document is not a legal will. Through probate—and the court's approval of the will—the named executor is authorized to begin to administer the estate. The executor's seal of approval, issued by the court, is a legal document known in most states as *letters testamentary*.

Probate can be delayed by either of two occurrences: the will is *challenged* by the next of kin, or the executor *cannot locate* the next of kin. In either of these sources of probate delay the court can grant a preliminary authorization that allows the named executor to act on the testator's behalf. Permission is granted to the executor named in a will, which has not yet been approved by the court, to safeguard the estate's assets. This preliminary authorization, however, does not allow the executor to distribute any assets to the legatees. This preliminary authorization is aptly referred to as *preliminary letters testamentary*.

Keep in mind the distinction between probate assets and gross assets

of the deceased. *Probate assets* include only those *assets distributed by the will*. *Gross assets* are the *total assets* owned by the deceased. Therefore, gross assets include not only the probate assets but also many nonprobate assets (assets that pass by right of survivorship) such as: joint bank accounts, insurance policies with a named beneficiary, jointly owned real estate, and "in trust for" (or "payment on death") accounts. Later in this chapter we will take a look at joint bank accounts and "in trust for" bank accounts.

Sample Situation

During probate, problems sometimes arise between the person named as the executor and the attorney he or she has chosen. Predictably, these problems are about money, namely *the attorney's fee*.

The question of fees should be resolved at the first meeting between the executor designate and the attorney who is being interviewed. This meeting should take place shortly after the testator's death. The decision on the fee should be confirmed in writing, and both people should sign it. The designated executor should remember to sign the agreement, not as an individual, but on behalf of the estate. Then, shortly after being appointed as the executor, this employment contract can be reaffirmed.

The amount of the attorney's fee varies from state to state. But even individual attorneys within the same community have different fees. The fee, however, is generally about two to four percent of the value of the estate.

Money-Saving Suggestion

At the meeting scheduled by the person named in the will (but not yet appointed by the court) as executor, perhaps a next of kin or a major legatee should also attend. He or she might be a good source of information.

At this meeting try to spend a couple of hours in presenting information to the attorney such as: income tax returns, the names and addresses of next of kin, whether any assets require special safeguarding, and a general review of the deceased's asset inventory. *Discuss possible problems,* such as the survivors' immediate need for cash. If the estate gets off to a good start, there is usually clear sailing ahead. The opposite, unfortunately, is also true.

Avoid the pitfall of trying to do too much at this first meeting. Your goal should be to identify and discuss possible problems, rather than attempting to resolve them. The initial meeting should last no longer than

two hours. *If it is well organized by the attorney, a lot of information can be communicated.* Survivors are tense and upset after a loved one's death, and a two-hour meeting is long enough. Also, remember that the attorney is only being interviewed; there is no need for you to hire this particular lawyer.

ADMINISTERING AN ESTATE

After the will is probated, the property of the deceased is gathered; any debts owed by the deceased are paid; and the remaining assets are then distributed to the legatees. This process—gathering and distributing the assets of the deceased—is called *administering an estate,* which can be accomplished in as little as a few months, or it could take years.

When administering the estate, it is important to know who is in charge. If there is a will, then the *executor* is in charge of gathering and distributing the deceased's assets. If there is no will, then the court appoints an administrator (usually the closest relative of the deceased or the closest relatives of the deceased if they are of equal degree of kinship) who is responsible for performing these tasks. No one can force you to become the administrator; but, as next of kin, you have the legal right to ask the court to appoint you as the administrator. The executor or the administrator (if there is no will) is referred to as *the personal representative of the estate.* As you know, the executor's identification is *letters testamentary;* the administrator's identification is *letters of administration.*

Which debts must the estate pay? Only those debts that the deceased would have had to pay, along with those necessary debts incurred by the estate, are paid by the personal representative out of the deceased's assets.

So who gets what's left? An asset of the deceased is distributed in one of four ways: (1) If the deceased had a will, assets owned go to the legatees named in the will. (2) If the deceased did not have a will, assets owned go to the next of kin. (3) If the deceased owned an asset jointly with someone and there is the right of the survivor to own the entire asset (for example, if John and Mary owned a bank account jointly with a right of survivorship), then the surviving owner receives the asset. (4) If an asset was owned by the deceased but was in trust for someone (for example, John had a bank account in trust for Mary), then the person it is in trust for receives the asset. We will learn more about *joint ownership* and *in trust for ownership* later in this chapter. But for now let me stress one idea on joint ownership: I recommend that the document setting out

such joint ownership state that there is *a right of survivorship,* thus making your intention absolutely clear to everyone that, when one owner dies, the survivor will own the entire asset. If you do not want the other person on the account to own it when you die, then use neither joint ownership nor name a beneficiary on an "in trust for" account. Unfortunately, sometimes there is confusion as to the legal effect of a joint account. A person might put a trusted person's name on an account just for the convenience of having that person available to make a withdrawal, *not knowing that upon death the other person has a claim to the entire account.*

Sample Situation

How long does it take to administer an estate? A recent report from the Office of the Attorney General of New York State gives case histories of estates that have continued for more than a quarter century. But don't despair. Most estates are administered within a year or two, and there is no need for this to be a traumatic experience.

Some states have a requirement that legacies be paid within a short time after death. However, even if the state of domicile of the deceased does not have this requirement, the executor should try to distribute the assets within a year after death. There is the procedure whereby a partial distribution of the legacy can be made, and a portion can be retained for contingencies such as debts and taxes. Those who have been waiting for more than a year for an executor to make a distribution to them from an estate should get on the telephone right away and arrange to meet with the executor and with the attorney for the estate. *Find out the cause of the delay.*

Money-Saving Suggestions

Your state might have an expedited procedure for small estates. It involves less paperwork, is less costly, and is quicker. You do not need an attorney. Find out the dollar amount in your state's definition of a small estate. It can be anywhere from a couple of thousand dollars up to almost one hundred thousand dollars.

Keep in mind that the amount refers to those assets owned solely by the deceased and without a named beneficiary. An estate with hundreds of thousands of dollars in assets, such as joint accounts, but only a few thousand dollars of assets in the sole name of the deceased, is eligible for the small estate procedure. Use of this expedited procedure, if applicable,

a wealthy individual, the reduced probate costs are small when compared to the benefits of using a testamentary trust. In the above sample situation, James possibly concluded that it is better not to have his estate avoid the probate costs because he wanted the legacy to John to be *controlled* by a trustee.

Now that these preliminary introductory matters have been put behind us, we can begin our discussion of administering an estate.

10

Preliminary Activities

OBITUARY; SECURING THE HOME

Is it a good idea to publish the obituary of a loved one? It is a personal decision that has to be made by the person closest to the deceased, probably by the person who will be the executor. But here are four reasons for doing so. The main reason is to *advise people of the death*. However, close friends and relatives should be telephoned, because many people do not read the obituary page of the newspaper. The second reason is to *honor the deceased*. Surely, however, it is better to have said nice things directly to the person rather than wait until after the person is dead; only the survivors hear the kind words extolling the virtues of the deceased's life. The third reason is that *a charity can be suggested as the recipient of contributions*. The fourth reason is that it may be a good research source for an executor in some future estate *seeking the identity of a deceased's next of kin* (the subject of the next money-saving suggestion). Share your own thoughts on the subject of an obituary with your executor.

Be aware that an obituary advises criminals in our society that a home may be standing vacant, particularly at the time of burial. Valuable possessions (jewelry and the like) should not be kept in the deceased's empty home. Safeguard the home; for security reasons some families arrange for a house sitter during the funeral.

In addition to potential burglary, some families have expressed other reasons for not publishing an obituary. Unscrupulous people sometimes use an obituary column as a referral source for business. Estates have been preyed upon by real estate brokers, appraisers, attorneys, investment

advisors, charities, merchants, stock brokers, creditors, and others. Be *cautious* in dealing with every provider of service who solicits your business after the death of a loved one. Better yet, have *no dealings* with these people. If you are contacted by someone you do not know, most likely your name was obtained from the obituary. Try not to make any major decisions at this time; but if you do, consult only *trusted friends and advisors.*

Sample Situation

It is a sad fact that many homes are burglarized during a funeral service. The criminal reads the obituary and notes the time of burial. In the case of the deceased who lived alone, this threat continues for as long as property remains in the deceased's last residence. Many people are aware that there is now a permanently vacant home.

As I tell my clients, be careful! *Make sure the home is secured.*

Money-Saving Suggestion

As you know, when a person dies, the next of kin are sought for one of two reasons: either the deceased did have a will, and they are the people who might possibly contest it; or the deceased did not have a will, and they are the people who are entitled to inherit the deceased's property.

Obituaries are a good vehicle for *locating the next of kin.* Suppose the deceased had *no immediate family.* Further suppose that both the mother and father of the deceased had numerous brothers and sisters, but the identities of most of them are unknown. All these maternal and paternal aunts and uncles are the deceased's next of kin. If the dates of death for some of these relatives are known, I suggest that the personal representative of the estate *research the local newspapers in the communities where these deceased persons last resided.* New family information can be discovered through obituaries of other family members. (An outstanding source for locating obituaries is the Genealogical Society of the Church of Jesus Christ of Latter-Day Saints. Its catalogues contain literally millions of obituaries.)

FUNERAL EXPENSES

Part of the job of administering an estate is arranging for the disposal of the body. Cremation is an alternative to a more costly funeral. Through-

out history, some organized religious groups have opposed cremation, but these barriers have essentially disappeared. If cremation was not the deceased's preference (and the executor should know this), I give you the following list of goods and services provided by a funeral home:

Minimum Services:

> Personnel available twenty-four hours a day.

> Coordinating plans with the cemetery.

> Completion of the required forms to obtain the death certificate and the permit for the disposition of the body.

Additional Services:

> Coordination of the funeral ceremony.

Preparation of Remains:

> Embalming

> Cosmetic preparation

Facilities:

> Use of facilities for viewing.

Other Goods:

> Acknowledgment cards

> Prayer cards

Casket:

> In addition to the casket there might be an outer burial container.

Other Charges:

> Transportation

> Cemetery fee

> Pallbearers

> Musicians

> Gratuities

> Obituary notice

> Certified copies of the death certificate

Sample Situation

You—not your surviving spouse, executor, relative, or friend—must decide about the funeral. It is appropriate for everyone—not just for the person who is seriously ill—to tell the executor, spouse, friend, or close relative what funeral arrangements are desired. I know this is a difficult topic, but having this discussion makes the survivor's job somewhat easier.

Money-Saving Suggestion

If you are the person entrusted with the funeral arrangements, be sure you know what it is that you are purchasing and what alternative choices are available. Be a smart shopper, even in time of tragedy.

You have learned that probate means "proving the will." Let us look at the procedure this "proving" entails.

11

Probate Procedure

LOCATING THE WILL

The person has died, the obituary has been published, and the burial has taken place. What next?

Is there a will? If the deceased was careful about preparing and planning the estate, someone would have been told the location of the will (and also the location of all the other important papers). But if it is not known whether the deceased had a will (or if it is known that a will does exist, but no one is sure where it is), here are some suggestions on how best to go about searching for the will:

Ask *relatives* of the deceased if they have any knowledge of a will. While difficult to do during the time of burial, this is nevertheless the best opportunity you'll have, because the clan is all gathered together.

Search the *house* of the deceased. Do not discard anything.

Find out if the deceased had a *safe deposit box*. One way to do this is to review the *cancelled checks* of the previous year in search of the annual payment for the safe deposit box rent. Since the safe deposit box rental payment is a miscellaneous itemized deduction, look at the previous year's tax return and accompanying records to find out whether the deceased rented one.

Find out if the deceased had an *attorney*. Look again through the cancelled checks to see if an attorney's fee was paid.

Check the *courthouse;* perhaps the will is on file. In most states a will can be placed in the safekeeping of the court during the testator's lifetime.

Visit the local *banks;* perhaps a bank is named as executor and is holding the will.

An easy way to go about searching for the will is to go *where the testator told you the will is kept.*

Another easy way is to look at the *testator's inventory,* which should identify the location of the will. You, as testator, can make it easy for your executor to locate your will.

It is a crime to hide or destroy the will of a deceased person. Obviously this is a difficult law to enforce, and violations often go undetected. Therefore, when making a will, *give serious consideration to having your executor retain possession of the document—or at least a copy.* (An exception to this would be an executor who is receiving *less through your will* than the person would receive *if you died without a will.* Do not offer this temptation to your executor: *the temptation to destroy the will.*) Also, your *attorney's vault* is a possible depository for your will.

Sample Situation

Most states have laws that provide a procedure whereby a person who possibly has possession of a deceased's will can be forced to appear in court. This person is then required to give sworn testimony as to whether he or she has the will or knows its whereabouts. If this testimony reveals the existence of a will, then it must be produced for probate.

Many times the situation of the recalcitrant person who has the will is quickly resolved by this court proceeding. Often the person just keeps putting off bringing the will to the court's attention, *without intending to conceal the document.* Sadly, however, I am sure there are cases where a person dies, someone has the deceased's will, and the document is never produced. If no one else knows that there is a will, then the deceased's estate is administered as if the person had died intestate.

Money-Saving Suggestions

Do not sign duplicate copies of your will. All signed copies must be produced in court. (Keep in mind that a photocopy is not a signed copy; there is nothing wrong in having photocopies of your original will, but be sure the person doing the photocopying *does not remove the staples.*) If a *signed copy* that was in the testator's possession cannot be produced, *the law presumes that the testator revoked the will by destroying it.* Therefore, *by not signing duplicate copies,* you save the executor the trouble of searching for all the signed duplicates. Furthermore, you will have avoided the calamity of your last will and testament being denied probate because of the mistaken belief that you had revoked any one of these signed duplicates by destroying it.

As you already know, you are always free to have a *new will* prepared. If you do, the old will is automatically revoked in favor of the new will, whose later date makes *it* the document to be probated. (What I do not recommend is *multiple signed originals of the same will;* one is enough. If someone knows that you had in your possession *multiple* signed originals of the same will, your executor will be *required to produce all of them.*)

I also suggest that when you ask the person close to you to be your executor, tell that person where you keep all your important papers, including your will.

DETERMINING THE DOMICILE

As you know, the person named in a will as executor petitions the court to obtain letters testamentary. This process of probating the will is undertaken in the *state where the deceased was domiciled.*

The word *domicile* is derived from the Latin word for home. *Domicile is the place where a person has a permanent home.* A person acquires a domicile by living there and having no definite present intention of later moving from there. Domicile entails not only residence in fact but also intent to make that residence one's home. Do not be confused by these definitions of domicile, because, for most of you, your domicile is *where you live.* The problem arises either when you are in the middle of a move or when you have two or more houses.

In which state are *you* domiciled? If you are not sure of the answer (perhaps you have homes in Michigan and Florida), you can be sure that

the various states where you now live will someday be fighting over the question of your domicile. The answer has *estate tax consequences,* in that either or both states might attempt to impose an estate tax. The answer to the domicile question also determines which state law controls these issues: e.g., what are the *requirements for a valid will,* who are your next of kin, what protection from disinheritance is given to a spouse, what rights are given to creditors of the estate, and so on. The first issue—*requirements for a valid will*—is a most important one. If your domicile changes to another state, then your will should be *reviewed by an attorney in your new state to assure that it meets the new state's requirements.*

I am not suggesting anything so drastic as selling your vacation home in order to eliminate any question about your domicile. But you should decide which home is your *permanent* home, then be consistent. The following should be concentrated in your state of domicile: voter registration, driver's license, automobile registration, recorded place of residence for federal tax return purposes, residence as indicated on employer records, the address at which you receive your pension check(s) and social security checks, and the location where you serve on jury duty.

The problem arises when two or more states have a claim that you *permanently reside within their borders.* Take the example of a retired automotive employee who votes in Florida and lists a Florida address on his federal tax return; but perhaps this same person registers his automobile and obtains his driver's license in Michigan, has General Motors pension checks and social security checks sent to his Michigan address, and is on the Michigan jury roster. At the time of death, both states will feel compelled to claim the person as a resident, since each state has what it believes to be firm grounds for doing so. You can avoid this problem if you decide which is your state, that is, where you have your permanent home. After your choice has been made, be consistent in listing this state on all vital records.

Sample Situation

Even where questions of domicile do not arise, two states may be involved in the administration of an estate. This occurs when a deceased owned real property (land, a home, or other building) in a state other than the domiciliary state, because *after an owner's death, the transfer of any real property is affected by the law of the state where it is located.* Take, for example, the situation of a person who had a permanent home in Michigan, but owned a winter home in another state. The will is probated in Michigan,

the state where the deceased was domiciled. The other state then requires what is called an *ancillary probate proceeding*. Normally the state where real property is owned accepts *the will admitted to probate in the domiciliary state,* and issues ancillary letters testamentary to the executor. Ownership of the real property then is transferred to the person named in the will. The transfer of personal property—anything other than real property— (such as your bankbook, bonds, jewelry, etc.) is controlled by the state where you were domiciled. This is true even if you own bonds issued by, have a bank account in, or possess any other property (other than real property) connected to another state.

Money-Saving Suggestions

In almost all cases where there is a question of the deceased's domicile, the issue arises because the *deceased* never decided which state would be the home state. *State your domicile at the beginning of the will.* This is done simply by listing your address. While this does not prevent the problem of two state jurisdictions doing battle over tax dollars, my suggestion will cause *you* to analyze *the question of domicile* and clearly decide which state is the domiciliary state. Then be *consistent*.

To those of you who plan to buy real property in a state other than your domiciliary state, consider having a *joint owner (with the right of survivorship)* on the deed. This avoids an ancillary probate proceeding in the nondomiciliary state, although it does not avoid the payment of that state's estate tax based on the value of the land, the house, or other building owned there.

LOCATING THE NEXT OF KIN

In some jurisdictions, the person named in the will as executor has to prove to the court that *all the next of kin have been notified* and that none of them are contesting the will. The proof is a statement, signed by the next of kin and submitted to the court, waiving the rights of these persons to contest the will. A next of kin who does not waive this right is advised by the court of the date when a challenge to the will must commence. In other jurisdictions *the will is just filed in court,* and the court waits a short period of time to see if anyone comes forward to challenge the document. These other jurisdictions are, obviously, less protective of the rights of the next of kin.

Notification of the next of kin, those who would receive the deceased's probate assets if the will is denied probate, prevents bogus wills from being probated. Who else is better motivated to assure the legality of the will than those who would most benefit from the court's rejection of the document? Do not get confused about this notification process. This confusion can best be illustrated by a brother who had survived his two sisters: one sister died *with* a will, and the court notified him; another sister died *without* a will, and the court also notified him. That's right. In the first case he was notified that, as next of kin, he has a right to *challenge the sister's will;* in the second case he was notified that, as next of kin, he is to *receive the sister's estate assets.*

Locating the next of kin is quite simple in most situations. However, it can be complicated when the deceased *is not survived by any close relatives.* Many families have not been in this country for more than two generations, so the search for the next of kin often takes the executor to some far-off lands. The typical search procedure for the next of kin of one who is *not survived by any close relatives* is to trace the brothers and sisters of both parents of the deceased, and if all these aunts and uncles are deceased, then look for the children and grandchildren of these aunts and uncles. As you know, the children of your aunts and uncles are your first cousins. Perhaps you do not know that the *children of your first cousins are called your first cousins once removed* and, furthermore, you might not know of their existence.

Let me restate this while you think of your own family tree, but with some adjustments. *Assume you do not have an immediate family, and you never met any of your aunts or uncles.* Their children are your first cousins, and your first cousins' children are your first cousins once removed. So, if you have no close family members, and your aunts and uncles stayed in a foreign country, it could be difficult to locate all your next of kin, because you may be looking for your first cousins once removed. However, in most situations a person's next of kin are quite easy to determine, and you might want to refer to the first chapter of this book to refresh your memory about the guidelines for who is your next of kin.

Sample Situation

One case that comes to mind is that of an elderly woman whose husband had predeceased her. The woman had no children and no brothers or sisters; both of her parents had come from Europe, and they had *numerous brothers and sisters, all of whom were deceased.* They had a number

of children (her first cousins). It was difficult to locate all these children; however, it was necessary because they were the next of kin.

What is interesting about this case is that both sides of the elderly woman's family tree *(her mother's side and her father's side)* were missing, making it doubly difficult to locate the next of kin. Notice, when I refer to both sides of a person's family tree, I refer to the person's *parents*. Do not confuse this with in-laws; *your spouse's family are not your next of kin.* But relatives, both on your mother's side of your family and on your father's side of your family, may be your next of kin (as in the above situation). If you do not have parents, spouse, children, brothers or sisters, nieces or nephews, aunts or uncles, then your next of kin are your first cousins. Your first cousins on your father's side of the family are the same relationship to you as your first cousins on your mother's side of the family. In some families, identifying all these first cousins can take some time. There are companies that specialize in locating relatives. These genealogical searches can be expensive; therefore, I recommend that you carefully check the credentials of the company you hire, and consult with your attorney before you engage its services.

Money-Saving Suggestions

If out-of-town legatees and distributees visit for the funeral, the executor should obtain their names and addresses so as to have this information when it comes time to notify them that a will is offered for probate. They are also good sources of information in locating any other relatives who may be the legatees or next of kin of the deceased.

Again, keep in mind that instances of no close next of kin *do not occur too frequently.* Even when the situation does occur and the next of kin are as remote as first cousins once removed, *often the identity of these individuals is known.* If this is your situation, here is my suggestion: give their names and addresses to your executor. It is unfortunate indeed when a person *knows that his or her next of kin are distant relatives, knows their identity and location, but takes this information to the grave.*

CHALLENGES TO A WILL

If your will has been prepared carefully by you and your attorney, then the chance of anyone contesting it is remote. Your next of kin, neverthe-

less, may still challenge the will. A legatee named in an earlier will also has the right to contest a later will (or codicil) if the legacy to be received was more under the earlier document. This is fair. How else can society assure that bogus wills are not being presented for probate? Our laws, therefore, allow a challenge by those who would receive the assets of the deceased if the will is not valid.

If someone does choose to challenge the will, there are a few possible resolutions to this problem. The challenger (known as the *contestant*) and the executor may seek to *settle* the will dispute, wherein the contesting next of kin receives something in return for withdrawing the claim that the will is not valid. This would occur in a situation where the deceased's testamentary capacity was marginal, and the legatees and the next of kin—the adversaries in the proceeding—decide to *compromise*. Alternatively, the probate judge may *dismiss* the contestant's challenge because it has no merit. The final possibility is to have all questions presented and argued in a *trial*. Incidentally, if there is a trial, the right to a jury depends on the law of the domiciliary state of the deceased. The U.S. Constitution does not guarantee a jury trial to those contesting a will; however, some states have a statutory provision allowing for such jury trials.

Here are two suggestions that might help avoid challenges to a will. *Do not tell* your potential legatees that they are to receive something from your estate. If you do and then later change your mind and execute a new will, those people given an unfulfilled promise of a legacy may express their disappointment by challenging the will.

My second suggestion is that you *clearly express your intentions in your will*. Remember my earlier suggestion that if you leave your automobile to a particular legatee, the will should identify the automobile as the one you own at the time of your death. Do not leave a legatee your 1991 Chevrolet. When you die you may own the year 2021 model. If the "almost owner" of the automobile is also a next of kin, then this type of ambiguity may be enough to enrage the person, who then challenges the will.

There are relatively few challenges to a will. It may appear, however, that there are many will contests due to the publicity given to the occasional one. As for the outcome of such challenges, most are settled before going to trial.

Sample Situation

The most expensive probate occurs when some one or more persons contest the will. Probably the longest and most expensive challenge in history was over the will of Matthias, the Hapsburg Emperor. Bohemia rejected the heir, Ferdinand II, named in Matthias's will. The challenge resulted in the Thirty Years War.

The following situation is the most bizarre will contest that has come to my attention. The next of kin of the deceased were his three siblings: a disinherited brother who challenged the will and two sisters who were bequeathed the entire estate. The two sisters, aware that their deceased brother probably lacked testamentary capacity, *graciously decided to divide the small estate equally among all three surviving siblings.* Although a total victory for the brother who had been disinherited, *he was not happy with this generous settlement.* From this situation I learned that there is a thrill to attacking a will and that such thrill can be as pleasurable as gaining a financial reward.

Money-Saving Suggestions

In many cases where a will is contested, the argument raised by the next of kin is that the deceased lacked the testamentary capacity necessary to execute the document. Here it is imperative that the *executor act quickly to obtain statements from those who knew the deceased.* Doctors, household help, friends, and relatives are good sources of statements. The reason I suggest that the executor act quickly is because *you want to be the first person obtaining the statements of those who knew the deceased.* I have found that people sometimes answer questions based on how a question is asked. I am not suggesting that such people are lying, but pollsters know that *people express satisfaction when asked to tell some good things about someone,* and they express dissatisfaction when asked to tell some bad things about someone.

Do not allow the fear of a challenge by a next of kin to prevent you from having a will prepared. To permit this fear to prevent you from having a will drawn *allows your next of kin to receive your estate.*

RENUNCIATION BY THE EXECUTOR

If you are named the executor in a will, the first decision you have to make is whether or not you want to serve in this capacity.

Some reasons for *not wanting to serve* (and thus *renouncing* appointment as executor) are that you do not have the *time,* the *energy,* the *talent,* or the *patience* required to administer an estate; perhaps it is too *depressing* a job; possibly you *dislike* the next of kin or those named as legatees in the will. Whatever your reason, *you can renounce.* However, *it is better to say no when asked by the testator,* rather than exercising your right to renounce sometime later after the testator's death. Keep in mind that if you decide to renounce your appointment as executor, *you still have the obligation to bring the will to the court's attention.*

One reason you might *want to serve as executor* is because you *loved* the deceased and want to see the person's life's work brought to a smooth conclusion. Another reason is because you receive a *fee* for this service. Your fee, although varying from state to state, is approximately three to four percent of the value of the assets you administer. A third reason to serve is because you may be receiving a significant *legacy,* and you want to see that things are done right.

While you are serving as executor, you might decide to *resign* before you complete the job of administering the estate. Upon resigning, you must usually account to the court for the estate assets you have gathered and distributed. Another situation that can occur is the *death* of an executor before the end of the administration of the estate. In this instance, the *deceased executor's executor* files an account with the court, and a successor is appointed.

Assume you have neither initially renounced your appointment nor resigned or died during your service as executor. There is still another possibility. While you are serving as executor, a person interested in the estate can petition the court for your *removal.* Reasons for this move might be alleged negligence, conflict of interest, or lack of activity in the administration of the estate.

If the executor named in the will *renounces, resigns, dies while serving, or is removed, who becomes the new executor and, therefore, the new holder of letters testamentary?* A carefully drawn will provides for this contingency. Do you remember my suggestion that your will should name a person or bank as the *successor executor?* If the primary executor fails to become the executor (or after assuming the role ceases to function due to death, resignation, or removal), *this successor executor becomes*

the new executor and receives letters testamentary. If a successor executor is not named in the will, then the court appoints someone to administer the estate. The next of kin or one of the legatees named in the will is the likely person to be appointed.

Sample Situations

There are two cases in which an executor is advised to waive the fee for performing this function. In cases where a surviving spouse serves as executor, if the executor's fee is not waived, it is subject to income tax. To illustrate, let us assume that a wife's net estate is worth $100,000, and she leaves all of it to her husband, who is designated the executor. Let us further assume that the state law provides for an executor's fee in the amount of three percent of the probate estate. Thus the husband receives a $97,000 legacy free of federal estate tax, because *what a spouse receives is free of any federal estate tax as a result of the estate tax marital deduction.* The husband also receives a $3,000 executor's fee, which is subject to federal income tax. But by waiving the executor's fee, the husband receives $100,000 completely free of any federal *estate* or *income* tax.

The second situation is similar but with a different family relationship. Assume a widow has a net estate of $100,000, and she leaves it all to her son, who has been designated the executor. As in the above case, let us assume that the state law provides for an executor's fee in the amount of three percent of the probate estate. Thus the son receives a $97,000 legacy free of federal estate tax, *because there is no federal estate tax on estates up to $600,000 (in addition to any amount a spouse receives).* The son also receives a $3,000 executor's fee, which is subject to federal income tax. But again, by waiving the executor's fee, the son receives $100,000 free of any federal *estate* or *income* tax.

Keep in mind, however, that if an estate *is* subject to an estate tax (for example, if it exceeds $600,000), there is likely to be a tax savings by *accepting this commission.* Consider the following: John is the *executor and sole legatee* of an estate with substantial assets. If John's individual income tax on this commission is 28 percent of the commission *received by him,* and the estate tax savings is 40 percent of this expense *paid by it,* then John *should receive* the commission. Why? Because the tax *legally avoided* by the estate *exceeds the income tax owed by John.*

Money-Saving Suggestion

You may decide at the time you are having your will prepared that it is tax-wise to have your executor serve without a fee, and you can state so in your will. Here is a will clause that implements this suggestion:

> I expressly direct that my executor (or my successor executor, if serving) is not to receive any fee or commission.

This clause eliminates the need for the executor to waive the fee.

The obituary has been published, the funeral has been conducted, the will has been located and presented to the court in the jurisdiction where the deceased was domiciled, the next of kin have been contacted, the will has not been contested, and the executor has accepted his or her appointment. How does an executor prove this status?

12

Results of Probate

IDENTIFICATION OF THE PERSONAL REPRESENTATIVE

Probate results in the issuance of a document to the executor. In many states this document is called *letters testamentary.* You already know about this document; it was introduced in Part One, in our discussion of whom to choose as executor; it was again explained during our discussion of probate. As you also already know, if a person dies *without a will,* the relative appointed by the court to administer the estate (*the administrator*) receives a document similar to letters testamentary. In many states this document is aptly called *letters of administration.* Whether an executor or administrator, this person is called the *personal representative of the estate.*

A copy of the letters testamentary or the letters of administration must be produced to those individuals transacting business with the personal representative of the estate. For example, a bank holding money in the name of the deceased never releases this money to the personal representative of the estate without first receiving a copy of either the letters testamentary or the letters of administration. Also, if real estate owned by the deceased is to be sold, a buyer of the real estate never accepts a deed signed by the personal representative of the estate without first receiving a copy of the letters testamentary or the letters of administration. Such letters attest that the executor or administrator is empowered to act on behalf of the estate.

After the court has issued letters testamentary or letters of administration, the actions of the executor or administrator are supervised by the court. This supervision has come under criticism in recent years for

114

being unnecessarily *complicated* and *expensive*. Since many estates are resolved in a friendly fashion, this supervision *often is unnecessary*. In my opinion, however, it serves a good purpose, even though it is not needed for every estate. Even if court supervision is proven to be *unnecessary* in nine out of every ten estates, it would be an impossible job for the court to formulate the criteria that would allow *the nine estates to be handled informally*. Furthermore, even if supervision is shown to be unnecessary in many cases, *perhaps it is this supervision that lessens or prevents problems such as dishonesty and carelessness.*

Sample Situation

Some have written that attorneys are made rich by the probate process. I have tried neither to praise nor criticize attorneys. However, as with all your concerns, you only have two sources of information: yourself and some trusted person. Some similar situations come to mind: if you want to sell your home, you can decide to seek the assistance of a *real estate broker* or sell it yourself; if you want to invest in the stock market, you can hire a *full-service brokerage firm* that advises you on your transactions or you can advise yourself (and just have a discount brokerage firm place your orders); if you are preparing your tax return, you can go to an *accountant* or you can do it yourself. No real estate manual, investment literature, tax return instruction guide, or book on wills can give you the clear and relevant advice that can be obtained from your own personal advisor. But some people decide not to seek personal professional help. Although independence is a sign of wonderful emotional maturity, *sometimes people do need assistance.*

Money-Saving Suggestions

How many copies of the letters testamentary should initially be ordered? Count the depositories holding assets of the deceased; each will require one copy. Do not order too many copies, however. Someone later on who seeks proof of your identity will require a copy that is recently dated. (This does not mean that probate is undertaken all over again. It just requires a trip to the courthouse to obtain a copy of the letters testamentary, stamped with the date of your trip; or telephone your attorney, who can obtain it quite readily.)

Another suggestion is to remember that the court can issue *preliminary letters testamentary*. Essentially it is permission granted to the exec-

utor named in a will, which has not yet been approved by the court, to *safeguard* the estate assets, but without the authority to *distribute* these assets to the legatees. This is useful in those situations where either the next of kin is being located or happens to be challenging the will.

THE COSTS OF DYING

The doctor's bill and the funeral bill are obvious costs of dying. There are also taxes. But there are other costs of dying. Probate results in the additional costs of the *court filing fee, the executor's bond, the attorney's fee, and the executor's fee.*

General estimates of these costs can be stated as a percentage of the value of the estate: the court filing fee and the executor's bond are less than one percent; the attorney's fee is approximately two to four percent; and the executor's fee is approximately three to four percent.

These administrative costs can be *avoided through joint ownership of assets with a right of survivorship.* But remember the problems of joint ownership: there may be a gift tax triggered at the time of the creation of the joint ownership; the joint asset is a target of creditors of either owner; if held jointly with a spouse, a divorce settlement may be affected by a joint ownership; if the intended joint ownership is not properly recorded as such, the asset will eventually be owned by distributees if there is no will.

Here is an example of this last problem. Margaret and Mary, who are sisters, have a joint certificate of deposit; upon expiration it is renewed, but (either mistakenly or deliberately) Mary's name is omitted. When Margaret dies, the certificate of deposit goes to the residuary legatee in her will. If Margaret has no will, the certificate of deposit goes to her distributees. This can prove to be quite unfortunate *if some undesirable relative is one of the distributees.*

Some people complain about the costs of probate and estate administration. Bear in mind, however, that the purposes of probate and estate administration are to evaluate any claims against the estate and then to distribute to the legatees the property of the deceased free of any claims of creditors. These purposes are important to both the *creditors* and the *legatees.* Therefore, it is a court-supervised estate and, yes, it is expensive. It is also time-consuming. But rather than having a society hell-bent on avoiding court supervision and its costs, in my opinion a better

solution is to *streamline the whole process of probate and administration of an estate.*

Many states are reacting to the outcry that the legal costs of dying are too high. The best development so far is the previously mentioned streamlined procedure most states now have for the administration of smaller estates (a procedure similar to Small Claims Courts).

Sample Situation

Probate can be avoided by transferring all your assets to a trust. In many states you can be the trustee of the trust and also the beneficiary. You name a successor trustee who is to take your place upon your resignation (perhaps due to illness) or your death. *The trust instrument determines to whom the assets are to be distributed upon your death.* If you follow this approach, make sure all your assets are legally owned by the trust. (For example, John Jones's bank account would now be owned by the Revocable Grantor Trust of John Jones dated November 11, 1991.) Benefits of this trust are that you *retain control* of your assets, you *can revoke* the trust at any time, someone is there to handle your affairs if you cannot continue to be trustee, and there can be a *savings in probate costs* at the time of your death.

Note that the trust is *revocable:* you reserve the right to make changes. If it is not revocable, there can be problems. First of all, *you cannot change it.* Also, there is a *gift tax consequence* because you have made a gift (to take effect in the future) to those receiving the assets upon your death.

Should you set up this type of trust and avoid probate? The trade-off is that while the cost of the future probate might be reduced because the assets avoid probate, there is still the legal expense of establishing the trust. Also a trust is informal and assets will be transferred at the time of your death without court supervision. Proceed cautiously whether you set up a revocable or irrevocable trust, and sign the trust instrument only after it has been thoroughly explained and you understand it (*particularly the tax consequences*).

Money-Saving Suggestion

Unless you think your executor is an incompetent or a crook (and therefore you would not name this person), *why have the estate pay for an executor's bond?* A bond is a promise made to the court by a bonding company that it will pay any losses caused by the executor's negligence

or dishonesty. The bond usually costs between a few hundred and a few thousand dollars, and this amount is saved by your estate if your will states that a bond is not necessary. It is a simple statement that can be expressed in your will quite clearly, like this: "My executor (or successor executor, if serving) shall not be required to post a bond in any jurisdiction." This waiver of the bond does not lower the standard of care required by an executor. He or she is still required to be honest and competent, which is the subject of chapter 15.

In the next chapter, we will explore the gathering of assets, particularly the deceased's safe deposit box; the deceased's business; and the deceased's home and its contents.

13

Gathering Assets

GATHER, APPRAISE, AND SAFEGUARD

In most situations, it is easy to gather the deceased's assets. They consist of furniture, clothing, jewelry, household articles, and money. Perhaps the assets also include a house, an automobile, the value of a life insurance policy if owned by the deceased (and without regard to whom it is payable or whose life is insured), and employee benefits. Gathering the assets usually presents no major problems, although some assets are more obvious than others. One not so obvious asset is any legal claim that the deceased, if still alive, could assert; perhaps it is a claim against the person who caused the death (e.g., the driver of an automobile). Another less obvious asset is insurance reimbursement for medical expenses paid by the deceased. One problem in gathering assets is encountered in every estate: *How is the executor sure that all the assets have been gathered?* He or she must go through all the deceased's papers, thoroughly search the house, look at recent tax returns, and review all mail sent to the deceased after death. The ideal situation occurs, of course, when the *deceased has left the inventory of assets that I have so often stressed throughout this book.*

An appraisal of some assets may be needed. Real estate, works of art, furniture, and jewelry are four examples of items requiring appraisal. To have a record of the value of decedent's *shares of corporate stock* at the time of death, consult the *Wall Street Journal.*

Most importantly, immediately following the death, the personal representative of the estate must *safeguard* these assets until they are

119

distributed. If the deceased lived alone, change the lock on the apartment or house. Be sure that home-owner's or tenant insurance is still in force. Deposit the money assets you gather, such as bank accounts, in an interest-bearing estate account and be sure that the estate account is protected by the Federal Deposit Insurance Corporation (F.D.I.C.). If the estate account exceeds the maximum amount covered by the F.D.I.C., then invest the excess amount in United States Treasury Department securities (preferably the short-term bills so that the money is quickly available for distribution). If the estate owns corporate stock, exercise extreme caution. Ideally, the assets should be distributed as quickly as possible.

Sample Situations

In gathering assets, I send the following letter to banks where the deceased might have had an account:

> As the attorney for the Estate of Michael Testator, I represent Michael Testator, Jr., the Executor, and enclose his certificate of Letters Testamentary. Also enclosed is a notice from your bank, found in the home of the deceased, that refers to account #500681. Please give me a written response to these four questions:
>
> What was the balance in account #500681 on (give date of death)?
>
> Is any other name listed on this account? If so, advise me if there is a right of survivorship and provide me with documentation.
>
> Are there any certificates of deposit or other accounts in Michael Testator's name? If so, what are the account numbers and balances as of (date of death)? Are any other names listed on these accounts and, if so, is there a right of survivorship?
>
> Is there a safe deposit box?

You should always include the question on the existence of a safe deposit box. Sometimes a person has more than one safe deposit box, so be on the lookout for a second or even a third such depository by following my earlier suggestions with respect to reviewing the deceased's cancelled checks for the previous year, and by asking each bank that has money assets of the deceased. Also, do not assume that a bank will auto-

matically notify you of the existence of a safe deposit box; you must ask this question.

In collecting money assets, it has been my experience that telephone calls and exchange of correspondence with the bank or brokerage firm are not the best methods of communication. If possible, *go to the depository.* Personal contact, whenever possible, results in a faster and more efficient gathering of assets.

Money-Saving Suggestion

A suggestion to executors, relatives, and friends of the deceased: do not go through the deceased's papers and other personal items *without a witness.* This avoids the accusation that you stole money, jewelry, or other items of value.

THE SAFE DEPOSIT BOX

Even if there are joint owners of the safe deposit box, the survivor is not allowed access to it. *The law of most states directs that the safe deposit box of a deceased person is to be sealed.* It is to be opened only by the personal representative of the estate who, in many states, is accompanied by a representative of the state's taxation department.

One way that a surviving owner of a safe deposit box can illegally gain access is by pretending that nothing has happened to the now deceased co-owner. Another subterfuge is to have a box, held in the name of a corporation, contain assets owned by an individual; upon the individual's death, a surviving corporate officer can gain access. I do not advise either tactic. The "let's get to the box" attitude is motivated by an attempt to escape estate taxation. It usually results in tax evasion of an inconsequential amount that is usually less than the *value placed on the energy that went into this improper activity.*

Cash should not be stored in a safe deposit box. First, if cash is discovered by a taxation official, an income tax might be levied upon this asset. Why? Because the taxation official might presume that tax evasion has occurred. Second, someone in a cash business who evades tax and stores the cash in a safe deposit box is losing the investment income this money would yield. This income from investments would soon exceed the amount of income tax evaded.

Here is the major problem with joint ownership of the safe deposit

box. Suppose the survivor of the two owners gets to the bank *after* the bank has discovered the death of the other owner. The safe deposit box will have already been sealed. Then, when the state tax official inventories the box, the *survivor's items* in the box, along with the deceased's items in the box, are presumed to be the property of the deceased's estate. This can result in a higher estate tax. If you do share a safe deposit box, then have a note in the box, signed by both owners, stating who owns what.

In times past, safe deposit boxes were quite popular because bonds payable to the bearer were an investment held by many people. Upon the owner's death, the heir (or a thief) would go to the box and become the new bearer, and estate tax was thereby evaded. Today, bearer bonds are virtually nonexistent. A safe deposit box should be used to *safeguard your valuable items,* and not for the purpose of *tax evasion.*

Sample Situation

A safe deposit box is not the best place for important papers such as your burial instructions or a cemetery deed. If you want to be cremated, or if you have other instructions that need immediate action, make sure these instructions are known by someone who cares, and that the instructions are not hidden away in a safe deposit box. *The safe deposit box will not be opened in time to fulfill your wishes.* Perhaps you are aware of cases where these situations occurred, and how frustration and guilt resulted because the dead person's wishes were not fulfilled. Spare your family and friends the embarrassment of finding out too late what your last wishes were regarding the disposal of your physical remains.

If all your important papers, including burial instructions, are in your safe deposit box, here is a way to avoid the case of the *cremation that did not occur.* Keep *photocopies* of these papers at home and, most importantly, tell someone (your executor is a good choice) of your wishes.

Money-Saving Suggestions

Rather than two people jointly owning a safe deposit box, I suggest they rent separate ones. However, each can have a *power of attorney* for the other's safe deposit box. Consider this example: Mary and Sue each has her own safe deposit box and each has a power of attorney for the other person's box. If either one of them is sick and unable to go to their respective safe deposit boxes, the other one can go even though she is not a co-

owner. Then, when either Sue or Mary dies, *only one safe deposit box is sealed.* The survivor's is unknown to the tax authorities. This suggestion is preferable to what often happens: two people have a jointly held safe deposit box; their jewelry, cash, bearer bonds (if any), and other items are in the one box; the survivor is to go to the box as soon as possible; however, the grieving survivor forgets to do this and the box is sealed by the bank. The tax authority then claims that all the items in the safe deposit box were owned by the deceased person.

A final suggestion deals with the *need* for a safe deposit box. Unfortunately, due to the prospect of burglary, such a precaution is needed to safeguard valuable items, including legal documents and jewelry. Consider whether or not you have a need for a safe deposit box. *Most people do need one.*

THE DECEASED'S BUSINESS

The owner(s) of a business, including partnerships and corporations, should plan for the inevitability of death. It is a good idea for the owners to discuss with each other the consequences of the death of either or all of them. If the business has only one owner, this owner should educate a successor or two, and thus assure the continuation of the business after the owner's death.

What happens to a business when the owner dies? The personal representative of the estate continues the business until it is transferred to the new owner. It is an important job, because the business may be the most valuable asset in the estate.

Here are five suggestions I give to a personal representative of the estate in such situations: (1) *Read the deceased's will* to find out if there are any instructions concerning the business. (2) Remember that you *act at your peril* in continuing the business. (3) Continue the business only until you are legally able to *transfer it* to the person or persons who inherited it. (4) *Consult with the eventual owners* before each and every decision regarding the business. (5) Do not use *other assets of the estate* to pay any expenses of the business.

Perhaps the executor is authorized by the will to sell the business. If so, be sure that a qualified appraiser establishes the company's value. The executor should invite input from the legatees before a contract of sale is signed. Give the legatees an opportunity to bid more for the business than the prospective buyer has offered. Also, be sure that there are no

other interested buyers who are willing to offer more than the price you are about to accept.

If a business is sold after the death of the owner, then most likely *the deceased had not adequately planned for the eventuality of death.* The product of a lifetime of hard work should not be terminated by death, but should be continued by a legatee chosen and trained by the owner.

Sample Situations

There are many cases of a small business losing all its value during the administration of an estate. If the testator has not trained a successor, and if the personal representative of the estate is not a good manager, then chaos results.

During the administration of an estate, a business can lose its value for a variety of reasons, including: loss of *customers*, loss of *employees*, loss of *suppliers*, a lost *lease*, and lost (or stolen) *inventory*. Whether a business is to be continued by an heir or eventually sold, it is the job of the personal representative of the estate to preserve its value during the administration of the estate.

Whether to sell or keep the business is too broad a question on which to generalize. *Keep in mind that retaining the business might be the riskier choice,* when compared to the stability of conservatively investing the proceeds from the sale of the business. On the other hand, it is sad to see it sold if the reason for the sale is that *no one knows how to run the business.*

Money-Saving Suggestion

Owners of a business should acquaint themselves with a buy-sell agreement. The co-owners might decide among themselves the value of each owner's interest in the company, and agree that, upon the death of an owner, the deceased owner's share is to be acquired by the other owner(s). The cost of this acquisition can be funded by life insurance.

In the situation where *there is only one owner of the business,* an arrangement might be made with a prospective buyer, perhaps an employee. An agreed upon value of the business is determined, and upon the owner's death the business is sold. *Be sure to update annually any agreement that states the value of the business.*

A benefit of such an agreement—perhaps the best benefit of all— is that it forces an owner to *plan for the consequences of death.* Be aware,

however, that your personal advisor must grapple with the tax consequences, particularly the effect of Section 2036(c) of the Internal Revenue Code (which is beyond the scope of this volume).

THE HOUSE AND ITS CONTENTS

Here is a warning to the personal representative of the estate and close relatives: *do not discard anything* without first giving serious thought to its possible value. What appears to you to have little or no value may have great value to some other person. If that other person is to inherit what you just discarded, then you are in trouble. Have witnesses, and ask the legatees for input. *Also, do not overlook anything.* Look carefully in drawers, under the mattress, and in places where the deceased may have hidden something; sometimes you can find hidden treasures. These hidden treasures, of course, will be part of the estate and not the property of the finder. Be optimistic: search the attic because that is where the old paintings, first editions, and antiques are found. *Old does not mean worthless, whether it is a painting, a book, an antique, or a person.*

If the deceased lived alone, whether in an apartment or a private home, I again advise you to be sure that the dwelling is insured and secured. Be sure that jewelry and other valuable items are removed from the dwelling before the moving company arrives. The post office should be advised to forward mail to the personal representative of the estate. Make sure no one other than the personal representative of the estate or a chosen family member is allowed access to the dwelling. As for the furniture of a deceased person who lived alone, perhaps the person who inherits the furniture wants to donate some or all of it to a charity. Similarly, the person who inherits the clothing may also want to donate it to a charity. If there is a lease to an apartment occupied by a deceased who lived alone, the attorney for the estate can advise on the possibility of terminating it. Alternatively, the continuation of a favorable lease can be a valuable asset of the estate (and this is the subject of the next sample situation).

As for the accumulated mail and other miscellaneous papers, I recommend that after they are reviewed, retain them. Hidden among these assorted papers may be a will, the address of a next of kin, a bank statement, a letter from a creditor that a debt was cancelled or paid, a suggestion of the location of a safe deposit box, a deed, a lease, or some other important document. When the estate is closed, undertake a final review

of these papers. If need be, at this time *they can be discarded.* Why hoard papers that have no worth? If you are in doubt as to what you should retain, consult with the attorney for the estate.

Sample Situation

The rent a landlord charges on an apartment is controlled in some communities by the local government. This often results in a rent that is *significantly less* than what it would be in a free enterprise system, where rent is set at whatever the market will bear. Rent control protects senior citizens living on a fixed income, and in such instances it is a wonderful idea. I oppose it when wealthy individuals, of whatever age, reap its benefits.

A result of this *rent control* is the situation of a family member who *claims to have been living in the apartment and therefore should be allowed to continue renting it at an artificially low rent.* Sometimes this is a valid claim. But whether the landlord or the tenant should prevail is not as important as my concern that the personal representative of the estate does *not quickly surrender possession of the apartment.* Find out what choices the law allows, what the interested family members want to do, and then make your decision. A premature surrender of the lease may turn out to be the *surrender of the estate's most valuable asset.*

Money-Saving Suggestions

Suppose you inherit your aunt's furniture, and further suppose that you have no use for it. I suggest that this used but usable furniture can be given to a charity. Both you and the charity are richer for this gift, and you do not have to wait long for your reward—just until April 15th when you list the value of this gift as an income tax deduction. An asset received from an estate has a date-of-death value for tax purposes, and this is the value placed on a charitable gift of the asset. So be sure that the furniture is appraised for these two reasons: it is needed for the *estate tax return,* and it is needed to substantiate the amount of the charitable deduction taken on the *individual income tax return* of someone who has made a charitable gift of property received from an estate.

I further suggest that you consider *disclaiming* this legacy, perhaps to allow your successor, who then receives it, to give it to a charity. Your decision depends on whether you or the successor legatee is in the higher income tax bracket; that is, which of you has the greater income tax savings as a result of the charitable gift. But balance this tax advice with

the practical decision as to whether you want someone to get richer at your expense. Let us now take a closer look at this technique called *disclaimer* and learn who receives a legacy that has been disclaimed.

14

Distributing Assets

REFUSING AN INHERITANCE (DISCLAIMER)

A person is allowed to refuse a legacy, or to refuse a portion of a legacy. This is called *disclaimer,* or *partial disclaimer.* Why does someone disclaim? Perhaps there is a successor legatee named, and the person disclaiming wants this successor legatee to receive the legacy. For example, suppose James is entitled to receive a legacy of $50,000, and the deceased's will further states: "If James has predeceased me, this $50,000 goes to his son, John." If James disclaims the legacy, he is considered to have predeceased the testator, and his son, John, then receives the legacy.

But why would James want his son John to receive the legacy? One reason might be that James is *terribly in debt;* he knows that if he accepts the $50,000, then his creditors will quickly grab it. Another reason might be that James is *rich* and old, and his eventual estate faces a high estate tax. By disclaiming this legacy, he passes this property on to his son, without the property eventually being included in his own estate. Caution must be taken that the disclaimer is properly made, so as not to be treated as a gift made by the person disclaiming the legacy to the person receiving the legacy, and thereby subject to a gift tax (which you will learn about in Part Three).

Notice that in my example *there is a successor legatee named in the will.* If no successor legatee is named, then the disclaimed legacy *goes to the residuary legatee(s) or their successors.* If they also disclaim, then the distributees receive the disclaimed legacy. But even a distributee can disclaim. If this occurs, the other distributees receive the disclaimed legacy.

If you are thinking of disclaiming a legacy, be aware of the *time period* in which your state requires that a disclaimer must be made, and also be aware of the *identity* of the lucky recipient of what you disclaim.

A disclaimer is a *post-mortem estate planning tool.* Perhaps something is *overlooked* when the testator's will is prepared; alternatively, something happens *after* the will is prepared. But if there is to be an oversight, it is always better to have one that can be corrected. It is also possible that some post-mortem planning is not a corrective measure; it merely implements an idea that was not relevant prior to the testator's death, *but is now relevant, perhaps due to a change in the legatee's life.*

Sample Situations

Any estate asset received by a surviving spouse is *free of federal estate tax* (but only if the surviving spouse is a United States citizen). Therefore, the child of a decedent might choose to disclaim a legacy if the surviving parent would then become the recipient of the legacy. *This avoids estate tax.* For example, if a husband leaves one-half of his estate to his wife and the other half to his child, then the child might elect to receive only so much of the legacy that is free of estate tax and disclaim the balance. This occurs only in estates of substantial value (as you will learn in Part Three, up to $600,000 worth of assets—in addition to any assets received by a surviving spouse—can pass free of federal estate tax). But if the father leaves an estate of *$2 million equally to his wife and his child,* perhaps the *child might disclaim* $400,000. The child then receives $600,000 (and this amount is free of estate tax), and the surviving spouse receives $1,400,000 (which is also tax free).

Sometimes the reverse situation occurs. Suppose a husband and wife are each worth $1 million. If the husband dies first and has left *everything* to his wife, perhaps the *wife might disclaim* $600,000. Whether or not she disclaims, there is no estate tax on the husband's estate. But the wife knows there is going to be a substantial estate tax *on her eventual estate.* If her children are the successor legatees, she might decide to disclaim, and have some of the assets now pass *directly from the husband's estate to the children, thus avoiding eventual inclusion in her taxable estate.*

Money-Saving Suggestion

You have learned that a disclaimer can save taxes, or it can protect money from the creditor(s) of a legatee. But the legatee who is contemplating a disclaimer must make a practical decision. Is the tax that is saved or the creditor's claim that is avoided *worth the loss of the legacy?* The child of the wealthy deceased person may decide to accept the legacy, even if it results in the payment by the estate of an estate tax. The child has no assurance that the surviving parent will reward a tax-wise disclaimer. (In fact, a too obvious reward, such as an immediate gift to the disclaiming person, may disqualify the tax benefit of the disclaimer.) So, too, a debt-ridden legatee may decide to accept the legacy, pay off the creditor, and face the world without the burden of a stalking creditor. The question of whether or not to disclaim is a difficult one to answer. *Once disclaimed, the legacy cannot be reclaimed.*

PRELIMINARY CONSIDERATIONS

After the assets of an estate have been gathered, it is then time for the personal representative of the estate to distribute them. Here are some considerations:

Early distribution should be the goal. This is a courtesy to those who are to receive the property. Remember to obtain a receipt from the recipient of an estate distribution. Also, remember to retain sufficient assets to pay any debts of the estate that might eventually be incurred.

Find out if an advancement of a legacy has been made by the deceased. An *advancement* is a gift that was made by the now deceased person, with the intention that the gift reduces what the recipient would otherwise receive as a legacy. If an advancement of a legacy was made by a deceased, the personal representative of the estate *must* reduce the legacy by the amount of the advancement.

Where any real property (land, a house, or other buildings) is an estate asset, the *real property is sold* only *in extraordinary circumstances.* A situation where it could be sold is where there is insufficient cash to pay a creditor of the estate. However, even in this situation, the person entitled to the real property has the opportunity to take the property and reimburse the estate. A quick example of this situation:

Mary leaves her house, worth $100,000, to nephew John; Mary dies with no other assets and $10,000 of unpaid bills. John has the right to take the house and pay the estate $10,000.

If a *legatee has predeceased* the person whose estate is being administered, be certain as to what happens to this legacy. It may go to the *surviving children* (or grandchildren) of the predeceased legatee, and this situation can occur *when the predeceased legatee is closely related to the decedent,* such as a legacy left to the testator's now predeceased brother.

If you are the personal representative of an estate, you should review with your attorney any problem about the distribution of assets *before* making the distribution. If an item has been improperly distributed, it may be hard to retrieve; if money has been improperly distributed, it might have been spent by the recipient who now has no money to make repayment.

A legacy of a *specific item* carries with it any *increase* in the item's value. However, a bequest of money earns interest only in some state jurisdictions. This is the subject of the sample situation.

Sample Situation

Suppose a legatee is left $10,000. Does the legatee receive interest income on the $10,000? In many states the legatee does not earn interest income on the legacy. However, in some states a legacy does earn this interest income, but not until after a specific period of time has elapsed (approximately one year) from the date of death. Where interest on the legacy is required to be paid, *it is paid even if the personal representative of the estate has not invested the deceased's money,* and the amount is based on the prevailing rate of interest. For the oversight of not investing the estate assets, the personal representative of the estate is *surcharged,* which means making payment from his or her own funds to the estate for the loss incurred. This will occur even if the executor *does not know that estate assets should be prudently invested.* The executor is *still liable* (as you will learn in chapter 15 in the discussion on liability of the personal representative).

Money-Saving Suggestions

You may receive income from your legacy in either of two situations. The first situation I just described: there is an inordinate delay in receiving the legacy and the legatee receives interest on this legacy. The second, and much more frequently encountered situation, is the *receipt by the residuary legatee(s) of the income*—including interest or dividend income not otherwise paid to another legatee—that was earned while the estate was being administered.

I suggest that if you do receive income from the legacy, then fulfill your obligation to *pay any income tax that is due on it.* (Do not confuse *income* from a legacy and a *legacy*—you do not pay any *income tax* on the *legacy itself.*) Just as your employer sends to you and the government a W-2 form that states your taxable wages, and just as your bank sends to you and the government a 1099 form that states your taxable bank account interest income, the executor sends to you and the government a K-1 form. *This form states the taxable amount of interest, dividends, and other income that you have received from the estate.* Unlike the small W-2 and 1099 forms, the K-1 form is a full-size sheet of paper.

I have two suggestions concerning any K-1 form you might receive. First, *report as taxable income* on your individual income tax return the amount stated on the K-1 form as taxable to you. This you should do not only to fulfill your obligations as a citizen, but also to avoid the assessment of interest and penalties on any tax assessment on this income. Second, you may have a *deduction* stated on the K-1 form, so be sure you take advantage of this deduction on your individual income tax return.

TOO FEW ASSETS

Ademption and *abatement* are legal terms often used when discussing an estate. They describe situations in which the optimistic deceased leaves more through the will than is eventually available to be distributed. The easiest way to explain these words is through examples.

Suppose Grandmother's will provides that Mary is to receive all her General Motors stock. After signing her will, however, Grandmother sells the stock, and upon her death there is no General Motors stock among the estate assets. This is an example of *ademption,* which simply means that a legatee would have gotten something if it were there to get. The legatee does not get it, however, because the *deceased did not own it*

at the time of death. Not too much has to be discussed about ademption. If you leave a specific item to someone, and then you dispose of the item, you may want to have a new will prepared and leave some other item to the person whose legacy has been lost through ademption.

Now a few words about abatement. Suppose that Grandmother's will provides that person A is to receive $20,000, person B is to receive $40,000, and person C is to receive $60,000. Grandmother dies and leaves an estate of only $60,000, despite her optimism that her net worth would be $120,000 at death. Through abatement, person A receives $10,000, person B receives $20,000, and person C receives $30,000. *Abatement* simply means *a proportional reduction* in each legacy when the estate has insufficient assets to pay all the legacies.

To avoid abatement, you should clearly express in your will the priority of legacies. If you are leaving money to a number of people, you can express your desire as to which legacies are to be paid first. Therefore, if your net worth declines, your will has covered this situation, and the preferred legacies are not reduced by abatement. Another way of avoiding abatement is to use a *fractional formula* in the residuary clause. In the above example, Grandmother really wants to leave *one-sixth* to person A, *two-sixths* to person B, and *three-sixths* to person C. Perhaps this is the preferred way for Grandmother to express her intent, rather than by giving specific amounts to the three legatees.

Sample Situations

It is confusing to read legalese, the technical language of attorneys. Ideas should be expressed in understandable language. Imagine an attorney telling a person who had been bequeathed $60,000 by Grandmother's will that this amount is now *subject to an abatement.* The person's immediate thought might be that this abatement is a bonus. The person will be enraged when told that the legacy is to be reduced. An attorney's scholarly lecture on the legal development of the abatement doctrine will only heighten the rage.

I present these legal terms, ademption and abatement, not only because of their impact on estates, but also to show you that *the ideas expressed in the administration of an estate are not extremely complex.* Word usage, however, sometimes makes the subject difficult. Estate planning, estate administration, and taxation should be expressed in plain language whenever possible, because they are subjects of importance to everyone. Legislators and attorneys should heed this advice.

Money-Saving Suggestions

Some of you really like the idea of leaving your shares of stock in General Motors or AT&T to your legatees, so here is another idea.

Suppose you own General Motors stock that is now worth $50,000, and you want your favorite niece to receive it. In order to protect your niece's legacy in the event you sell your General Motors stock or it declines dramatically in value, I suggest you consider the following. Leave her all the shares of General Motors stock you might own at the time of your death, but add: "If the value of this stock is less than $50,000 at that time, I leave her a cash bequest of the amount by which $50,000 exceeds the value of all my shares of General Motors stock." Therefore, if the General Motors stock is worth $30,000 when you die, your niece will receive this stock plus $20,000. If your General Motors stock is worth $100,000, then that is what your niece receives. *This suggestion might save you the cost of having a new will or codicil prepared.*

On the other hand, maybe you just want to leave her the General Motors stock. If you do not own it at your death, then she doesn't receive it; or if you do own it but it is only worth $30,000, then that's what she receives. *You decide.* These are just various *options available to you.*

Here is another thought on this subject. I am sure there are readers who have wills that leave shares of stock in the AT&T Corporation to someone, and these wills were written before the federal government reorganized AT&T. Do you want the legatee to receive the shares of stock in the spin-off Baby Bell Corporations? Your will should be updated if you want the legatee to receive the spin-off corporation shares; otherwise, *NYNEX and her orphan sisters might go to the residuary legatee.*

CREDITORS OF THE ESTATE

The distribution of the deceased's assets is made to the legatees and the creditors of the estate. Paying the creditors is a major job of the personal representative of the estate, and it is more complex than distributing the legacies. The creditors of the estate include those who are owed money *by the deceased* and also those who are owed money *by the estate.*

Two likely creditors of the estate are the *doctor* who treated the deceased during the final illness and the *funeral home.* Many times these bills are paid by close family members who then become the creditors

of the estate. The personal representative of the estate should reimburse these people, but only after receiving proof of payment of the medical bills and the funeral bill.

Other major creditors of the estate are the *tax collectors*. As you will learn in Part Three, the taxes could be for the *current year's federal and state income tax,* or perhaps tax owed on *prior years' income* (due to an audit or maybe tax returns were never filed), or the *federal and state income tax on the income generated by the estate during its administration,* or any *estate taxes*.

Keep in mind that the personal representative of the estate can be personally liable to the creditors of the estate. This can occur if *all the assets of the deceased are distributed to the legatees before the legitimate creditors of the estate are paid.* In this instance, the *creditors* can sue the personal representative of the estate. The personal representative is also in trouble if *debts that are NOT legally enforceable ARE paid;* in this instance, the *legatees* can sue the personal representative of the estate.

The personal representative should read the will; sometimes it contains information regarding a decedent's debts.

Personal representatives should be on the lookout for fraudulent creditors. Occasionally the media report on bogus bills sent to a deceased with a claim that services were rendered or products were sold to the decedent. *Beware.*

In some states, the *creditors* are required, within a specified time period, to file a notice of claim; in other states, the *personal representative of the estate* needs to publish a notice of his appointment. Through these procedures, the personal representative of the estate is alerted to the existence of claims. In practice, however, the personal representative usually becomes aware of the deceased's debts *through the receipt of bills mailed to the deceased's last known address.*

Sample Situation

A creditor claims he is owed money by the deceased, but there is no solid evidence of this debt. Although not certain of the validity of the claim, the personal representative of the estate pays the debt. The residuary legatee then sues the personal representative. The result might be a *surcharge* and, as you know, this means the personal representative is required to reimburse the estate for the cost of the error. In this case, the amount of the surcharge would be the *amount erroneously paid to the creditor.*

These sad cases always occur. If you are the personal representative of an estate, do not pay claims of creditors unless you are *absolutely certain that there is a legal obligation to pay.* On this your attorney can advise you.

Money-Saving Suggestions

In some situations it is advisable to settle a creditor's questionable claim. This suggestion should be considered with an awareness of the *costs of litigation that can be avoided if a claim is settled.* This compromise should be approved either by the court or the legatees—ideally, by both. Until such time as the situation is resolved, the personal representative of the estate must retain in the estate account an amount equal to the amount of the claim. If all the assets of the estate have been distributed and the creditor then prevails in its claim against the estate, the personal representative of the estate is most likely *personally liable* for payment.

For *creditors of an estate,* here is a suggested statement of a claim, precise and uncomplicated, filed by a creditor: "To the Estate of John Testator: there is due to me from the Estate of John Testator the sum of $3,000, for medical services rendered to John Testator during the two months preceding his death." Have your attorney review this statement, serve it upon the estate, and file it in court.

15

Final Thoughts on Estate Administration

LIABILITY OF THE PERSONAL REPRESENTATIVE

In fulfilling the wishes of the deceased as expressed in the will, *the personal representative of the estate should not attempt to implement personal ideas as to what is fair.* Ask the attorney for the estate to advise you on the proper legal solution to a problem. The personal representative is liable for mistakes made in administering the estate, so be careful. Let us review a few of the areas where caution should be exercised.

Make sure that all *tax audits have been completed* before distributing all the estate assets. You can ask the Internal Revenue Service to expedite its review of tax returns. If an audit determines that tax is owed, and *assets which could have been available for taxes have been distributed,* then the personal representative of the estate *might* be liable for the payment of the tax.

Caution must be exercised in the areas of *sale of assets* and *payment of claims.* If it is necessary to sell any asset of the estate, then the representative is required to obtain the best possible price and to substantiate why this price is the best possible price obtainable. Appraisals by experts, bidding, and comparable sales are ways to meet this requirement of price substantiation. As for payment of claims, *do not pay* any claim against the estate unless you are certain that there is a legal obligation to pay. On the other hand, make sure that you *do pay* the claims of the estate that are legally enforceable against it.

Receive consents from interested parties, whenever possible, regarding those difficult decisions pertaining to the distribution of assets. A decision

is difficult when there exists the possibility that a reasonable person could question your judgment. I know this advice is vague, but an executor needs his or her own attorney to render an opinion on the variety of problems that can arise with respect to asset distribution, and what decisions by an executor a "reasonable person could question."

Also *receive a final release,* signed by each legatee, attesting that the distribution of assets has been made. To the residuary legatee's release, attach *a copy of your accounting* of all the estate funds that you received and disbursed (otherwise, the person signing the release may claim that he or she was not fully informed). Receive the release (and the approval of the accounting from the residuary legatees) before the legacy is distributed.

The personal representative of the estate cannot delegate to others the jobs entailed in administering an estate; it is a hands-on operation. Clerical tasks obviously can be delegated. But I cannot overemphasize that each decision involved in handling estate assets has to be made by the personal representative, because he or she is answerable to any claimant for each decision.

Sample Situation

There are cases where the personal representative of the estate is criticized, sued, and surcharged for being too extravagant. This occurs when the funeral costs are excessive or payments are made to questionable creditors. Be careful, and consult the attorney for the estate frequently during the administration of the estate. The personal representative, whether as executor or as administrator, is personally liable for errors made and may be *required by the court to reimburse the estate for these errors.*

The standard that is demanded of the personal representative is a *reasonable business person's standard of care: how a reasonably smart business person would handle a similar situation.* If this general level of care is not achieved, then watch out. Surcharge may result. Being a personal representative can be a rewarding job, financially and emotionally. But it is difficult. Be careful, honest, and thorough; *things will work out all right.*

Money-Saving Suggestion

The most costly mistake a personal representative of the estate can make (although often undetected) is not collecting all the deceased's assets. In many cases elderly people are circumspect about how much or how little they have. Sometimes they are downright misleading. Therefore, do not

rely on a testator's sympathy-evoking statement that there will *not be much in my estate*. There might be a whole lot in the estate, so search thoroughly.

Furthermore, the personal representative should use a *checklist* to avoid careless oversights that might lead to a lawsuit. The result of this lawsuit might be that the personal representative reaches into his or her own pocket, removes money, and gives it to the estate. How much money is given to the estate? It is the amount that the court determines is fair restitution for losses caused by carelessness or extravagance.

A CHECKLIST FOR THE PERSONAL REPRESENTATIVE

The job of the personal representative of the estate, whether as an executor or an administrator, is all-encompassing. Here is a summary of the personal representative's responsibilities:

Secure the home; arrange the funeral; order the death certificates.

Arrange for the mail of the deceased to be held at the post office, and upon your appointment as the personal representative, have the mail forwarded to you.

Locate the will. Select the attorney to represent the estate, unless it is a small, uncomplicated estate that you have decided to handle yourself.

Review all the insurance policies of the deceased; suggest to the survivors that they review their own insurance policies.

Contact the employer of the deceased (or the former employer of a retiree) and learn what death benefits are owed to the estate.

Send a copy of the will to any interested party who requests it. (However, do not remove the staples from the will when photocopying it.)

Locate all the next of kin. Do not be secretive with any legatees or next of kin.

Review all the deceased's records in order to determine the assets and the liabilities of the estate.

Gather all the assets; enter the safe deposit box; and continue running the deceased's business, if necessary.

Obtain an appraisal of property.

Notify the Social Security Administration of the death.

Review the tax returns for the three years prior to death.

Determine the rights of creditors.

Open up an estate checking account.

Pay all estate taxes and all income taxes.

Sell assets, but only if this is allowable and necessary.

Distribute all the legacies.

Receive releases from all the legatees.

File the accounting in court, if necessary, and then your job is over.

The personal representative of the estate needs the advice of an experienced estate attorney, particularly in the areas of obtaining court appointment, paying taxes, resolving adverse claims, distributing assets, and filing an accounting. This might not be necessary, however, in a small, uncomplicated estate. The trick is to estimate accurately, at the outset, the *size and complexity of the estate* (which, once again, could be made infinitely easier if an asset inventory were available).

Sample Situation

I am aware of an estate in which nothing has been done in the two years since the date of death. The court, legatees, creditors, and taxation authorities have been exceptionally quiet. Any year now there will be a crisis, and most likely it will be precipitated by the Internal Revenue Service, looking for income tax returns. The case of the lazy personal representative is a sad one because when things heat up, *the job is a nightmare.* Therefore, if you are a personal representative of an estate and cannot handle the job, then go to court and obtain permission to resign. Do not put this off just because your inactivity has not yet been questioned. At some point it will be questioned, and then you will have a *major problem on your hands.*

Money-Saving Suggestion

Prior to your appointment as the personal representative of an estate, do not sign any contracts on behalf of the estate. If a contract must be

signed, then it must be conditioned on being ratified after your appointment as executor or administrator. There also should be an express provision in the contract that you have not yet been appointed as the personal representative of the estate, and that you are not personally liable for the performance of the obligations stated in the contract. This was mentioned at the outset of Part Two in the discussion of the agreement made with an attorney prior to an individual's official appointment as executor. This suggestion applies to *all agreements* entered into by a named executor not yet appointed.

With regard to handling money: buy a simple ledger book and record in it every dollar you *receive* and every dollar you *spend.* Then buy two manila envelopes: in one, file proof of assets received, such as closed-out bank account books; in the other, file bills paid and receipts for payment. It is uncomplicated if you follow these suggestions. When the estate is ready to be wrapped up, the information for your accounting is efficiently organized. The main reasons for problems in preparing an accounting are (1) *the failure to record a transaction* and (2) *the failure to save documentation.* Accounting for money received and paid out is the major responsibility of the personal representative of the estate.

As for your other responsibilities, prepare a checklist. I offer this suggestion because I know that more mistakes are made by a personal representative who knows something has to be done but *forgets* to do it, than by a personal representative who does *not know* that something has to be done.

At the end of Part One you were presented with a long list of important documents and personal information that should be *located and safeguarded* at the time your will is prepared, and you have just reviewed a checklist for the *personal representative of an estate.* Now let us look at some *general reminders applicable to all who have a will prepared.*

A CHECKLIST FOR EVERYBODY

Does your executor know *where your will is located?* Does your executor know the names and addresses of your *next of kin?*

Do you have a *living will?* Does your doctor know you have it? Does a trusted person, such as your executor, know you have it?

Does your executor know if you have a *safe deposit box?* Does the executor know *where it is located?*

Have you discussed *funeral arrangements* with your executor or some other person close to you? If you own a cemetery plot, do you have the *deed?*

Do you know what property of yours is held in *joint ownership* with right of survivorship, and what bank accounts are *in trust for* someone?

Are all the insurance policies you own, bank accounts, and other investments included on *your inventory?* Do you know whether you have named someone as the beneficiary upon your death, or have you decided to have these assets distributed as part of your probate estate?

Is your Individual Retirement Account (IRA) included on your inventory? Do you have more than one account? Have you named someone as the beneficiary of these accounts upon your death? Alternatively, you might have decided that these accounts are to be distributed as part of your probate estate.

Do you know the death benefits provided by your *employer,* or *previous employer,* if retired, *and who will receive them?*

Is it clear which state is your *domiciliary state?* If you have real estate in another state, have you decided whether or not to name a joint owner with the right of survivorship so as to avoid ancillary probate in that state?

Do you have your *tax returns* (and supporting data) for the last three years?

Sample Situation

Your survivors will miss you, and they might not be emotionally able to sort through mountains of papers that have accumulated in your closets and drawers over the years. *Try to make things easy for them.*

The doubts of those who survive disorganized testators are consistent and constant: What were the wishes of the deceased? Were annual income tax returns filed? Did the deceased have a life insurance policy? Were out-of-state investments owned by the deceased? Where did the deceased want the family heirloom to go? Did the deceased have many debts? Did the deceased have a will, a safe deposit box, or a receipt for prepayment of funeral expenses? *What else should be done?* This agonizing can be

extremely troublesome to those you love. If you have organized your estate, the burden of the personal representative will be significantly lighter.

Money-Saving Suggestion

Here is a summary of good reasons for having your affairs in order:

> to make *your life* easier;

> to assure that you and your possessions are adequately *insured;*

> to clarify whether or not your cash assets are properly *invested;*

> to secure the future of your *business;*

> to assure that your assets are not *lost,* and thereby given to your state;

> to help you (or, after your death, your executor) survive a *tax audit;*

> to avoid the misfortune of the personal representative of your eventual estate paying a *debt* that you did not owe, or failing to collect a *debt owed to you;*

> to lessen the cost of *probate;*

> to assist your executor because, if you are organized, your estate will be *easier to administer.*

Put your affairs in order today!

PSYCHOLOGICAL ASPECTS

Let us conclude our journey through the administration of an estate by spending a few minutes on the psychological aspects of death. Those who lose a loved one experience shock, grief, and maybe guilt. But most of all the biggest hurt is the loneliness. Remember, too, the lives of the survivors now become more complicated. Some of the tasks performed by the deceased are now assumed by the survivors. The breakdown of the nuclear family—relatives scattered throughout the country—makes the loneliness and these new responsibilities even more poignant.

I have written this book because I want you to know how a deceased's assets are transferred after death, so that *you can control this aspect of death* by making things less complicated for your executor and other survivors.

Sample Situations

There are many cases of inheritances being squandered by the recipients. Bad investments, reckless spending, succumbing to the wiles of the con artist—these things can happen. One reason for these unfortunate occurrences is that perhaps the recipient of the windfall legacy *feels that it is undeserved*. Possibly this is an aspect of *guilt*. Whatever the reasons, there are many cases of money virtually being thrown away. Another reason for a squandered legacy is that the recipient has neither the *prior experience of handling money* nor the development of an *attitude about money*.

One way to avoid these unfortunate occurrences is for the testator to consider using a testamentary trust, which empowers a trustee to supervise the recipient's legacy thus preventing the legacy from being squandered.

But here is another way to avoid the tragedy of the squandered inheritance, and it avoids the costs of a trustee. The legatee should invest the inheritance in the safest investment—perhaps a money market account, a certificate of deposit, or a United States Treasury security. Then wait about a year before buying any big-ticket items, before undertaking any innovative investments, before spending even a penny of the legacy. However, your legatee may not be this prudent, so do give some thought to a testamentary trust.

Money-Saving Suggestion

Make only the most necessary decisions after a loved one's death. Seek the counsel of others but *be careful in your choice of a strong shoulder*.

Part Three

Taxation

16

Introduction

People die, but state and federal governments live on. Death does not abate their appetites for taxes; their fat budgets need constant feeding. The personal representative of an estate has quite a few tax returns to file and taxes to pay. This is the subject we will now tackle. It is the most difficult part of the book, *but you can handle it.* You will soon find out that taxation is not nearly as intriguing a subject as either your will or the administration of an estate.

The discussions on *income taxation of the estate, progressive tax rates, the decedent's final income tax return, a tax audit, and stepped-up basis at time of death* apply to the average person. But keep in mind that at least some of the discussion in this part of the book applies only to estates with substantial assets—about three percent of all estates. However, also keep in mind that many older people are wealthier than they might realize, due to appreciation in the value of their homes, the value of pension benefits, legacies received from other people's estates, investments that have grown, and so on. So look at your *asset inventory.* You might discover that all of Part Three is of great significance to you. Whether all or part of this section of the book applies to you, the material is included in order to offer you a *general overview* of wills, estate administration, and estate taxation.

OVERVIEW OF TAXATION

An estate has quite a few tax returns to file. Here is a summary of these returns, which we will look at more closely in the following chapters.

The *federal individual income tax return* (Form 1040) has to be filed for the person's year of death. If the person has died before April 15th, and the previous year's return has not been filed, then this return also has to be filed. Similarly, if the deceased's state has a state income tax, the *state individual income tax return* for the year of death has to be filed, and perhaps the state income tax return for the previous year also has to be filed.

Any other previous years' *federal individual income tax returns that have not yet been filed* must now be submitted. Also, any *federal individual income tax returns under audit* (or that may soon come under audit) may result in the assessment of an additional federal individual income tax. Similarly, any other previous years' *state individual income tax returns that have not yet been filed,* should now be filed. Also, any *state individual income tax returns under audit* (or that may soon come under audit) may result in the assessment of an additional state individual income tax.

A *federal estate income tax return* (Form 1041) has to be filed by the estate, to report the *income* generated *by the estate* during its administration. Similarly, a *state estate income tax return* must be filed, to report the *income* generated *by the estate* during its administration. The latter, of course, is required only if the deceased's state has an income tax.

A *federal estate tax return* (Form 706) might have to be filed. The tax paid is not an income tax; it is a tax on the *estate assets.* You will learn that the taxable estate of the deceased must exceed $600,000 before this tax is triggered. A *state estate tax return* might have to be filed, and you will learn that, unlike the federal government, some states impose an estate tax on relatively small estates.

Finally, in some states a *state inheritance tax* is owed by *recipients* of estate assets, but closest relatives of the deceased are often exempt from this inheritance tax.

Sample Situation

Tax law is a balancing act between *simplicity* and *fairness.* The simpler tax law is usually the less fair law. An example of a *simple tax law that is not fair* is this hypothetical law of one sentence: "Everyone must pay $8,000 tax per year." Quite simple.

The reverse is also true: the *more complex tax law is usually the fairer law*. The example I have chosen of a complex tax law is not hypothetical. It is an income tax law with which you might have some familiarity: *the tax treatment of Social Security benefits*.

If a Social Security recipient has more than $25,000 of income (or more than $32,000 of income if married and filing jointly), then a portion of social security is subject to income tax. Simple so far. But here the computation headaches begin: To determine whether this $25,000 (or $32,000) threshold amount is exceeded, even tax-exempt income is included (and also *one-half* the social security amount is included); but only *one-half* of the amount by which the $25,000 (or $32,000) is exceeded is taxed; and this amount that is taxed cannot exceed *one-half* the social security benefit, etc. Is this law *fair?* Who knows; fairness is so hard to define. Is it *complex?* Millions of older Americans know the answer. Is it *confusing?* Yes!

So that I do not add to the confusion, I want to distinguish this tax treatment of Social Security benefits from another important question: How much are you permitted to earn without having to *forfeit receiving some of your Social Security?* The answer to this question is neither complex nor confusing. But the answer changes each year.

Money-Saving Suggestion

There are many cases of wealthy people who do not worry about estate tax. After all, the person will be dead when it is time for the estate to pay the tax. *I suggest, however, that you learn how tax dollars can be saved, both income tax dollars and estate tax dollars.* After all, taxation is not a voluntary contribution; the government forces you to pay. A practical attitude is to *balance the amount of tax that legal strategies can avoid with the degree of inconvenience these tax strategies impose.* Keep in mind that an evaluation of tax risks inherent in your personal situation *requires the assistance of a skilled tax consultant.*

17

Estate Taxation

THE TAXABLE ESTATE

The answer to the question "What comprises a taxable estate?" is found in the Internal Revenue Code. The relevant provisions in the code are summarized by this all-encompassing statement: *everything owned by the deceased* is included in the taxable estate.

Form 706, which is the federal estate tax return form, is currently divided into nine sections. It groups your assets as follows:

Schedule A—Real Estate
Schedule B—Stocks and Bonds
Schedule C—Mortgages, Notes, and Cash
Schedule D—Insurance on the Decedent's Life
Schedule E—Jointly Owned Property
Schedule F—Other Miscellaneous Property
Schedule G—Transfers During the Deceased's Life
Schedule H—Powers of Appointment
Schedule I—Annuities

The value of the deceased's estate is the total value of the person's property *at the time of death*. But there is a choice available to the personal representative of the estate; he has the option to value all the assets either as of the date of death or, if lower, as of the date *six months after death*. The rules on this so-called alternate valuation choice are beyond the scope

of this volume, but do be aware of the choice. If you have questions, ask your attorney.

From the total value of the deceased's assets certain deductions are made, including: the *administration expenses,* the value of *what is left to a spouse,* and the value of *what is left to a charity.*

The total value of the deceased's assets (valued at the time of death or at the alternate valuation date six months from the date of death), minus allowable deductions, results in the value of the *taxable estate.* The next chapter will outline how much tax is paid on this taxable estate, *payment of which is due nine months after the date of death.*

Notice that the taxable estate includes jointly owned property, which is listed in Schedule E of the tax form. *Many people incorrectly assume that if they put someone else's name on the bankbook, the estate saves taxes.* But, as we have already learned, a joint account *does not reduce the estate tax.* What happens is that the *other person on the account receives the account,* the *will has no effect* on this account, and *probate costs are reduced.*

Sample Situations

Some years ago, a judge with the interesting name of Learned Hand wrote these often-quoted words in his decision on a tax case:

> Over and over again the courts have said that there is nothing sinister in so arranging one's affairs as to keep taxes as low as possible. Everyone does so, rich or poor: and all do right, for nobody owes any public duty to pay more tax than the law demands. *Taxes are enforced exactions, not voluntary contributions.*

Keep in mind the distinctions between *tax avoidance, tax deferral,* and *tax evasion.* There is nothing wrong with avoidance or deferral (it is at least one reason you picked up this book); but tax evasion is a crime. Here are some examples of *avoidance, deferral,* and *evasion;* I have chosen income tax examples with which you might already be familiar: (1) investing in municipal bonds that yield tax exempt interest income is *tax avoidance* (which means you have *legally avoided* the payment of an income tax); (2) investing in an aptly named tax-deferred annuity, where tax on the interest income is not taxed until money is withdrawn, is *tax deferral* (which means a *legally permissible delay* in paying the tax); (3) investing in a money market account at your local bank and not disclosing the

taxable income is *tax evasion* because the tax law requires it to be reported and this act of nonreporting, an attempt to escape this law, is the crime of tax evasion.

Money-Saving Suggestion

Find out what tax will be levied on your eventual estate; then seek suggestions from an expert on how to plan your affairs so that this tax can be lessened. Two major areas of tax planning are *gift-giving* and the *maximum use of the marital deduction.* Both of these ideas will be discussed shortly.

Personal representatives can save their respective estates money by seeing that an accurate appraisal report has been made on assets such as real estate and jewelry as soon after death as possible. If there is an audit, it is absolutely necessary to have your valuation expert defend the appraisal value of the property in question. This is the only way to rebut an exorbitant appraisal by the government.

FEDERAL ESTATE TAX

What is the fare paid to the federal government for your final journey? It could be an expensive departure, but one due only from the estates of the rich. If the deceased's net worth is less than $600,000, no federal estate tax is due. In addition to this figure, any amount left to a spouse is free of any federal estate tax. (Keep in mind that the surviving spouse must be a United States citizen.) For example, a married person can leave an estate of $2 million, free of any estate tax, simply by leaving the spouse $1,400,000, and a child $600,000. After all this good news, what is the bad news, you ask? It comes in the form of the *estate tax rate.* For those estates that do owe an estate tax, the rate will be at least a hefty *37 percent.*

Here are some estate tax concepts that may be relevant to your situation; your advisor can discuss them further with you. The estate might be allowed to pay the tax in *installments* over a period of fifteen years. Also, if property in the deceased's estate has been (or will be) *taxed in someone else's estate* within the recent past (or very near future), there is a reduction in the estate tax. (For example, John dies and leaves his estate to Mary; an estate tax is paid; then Mary dies three years later.) If a substantial amount is left to someone who is more than one generation younger than the deceased (for example, a grandfather leaves a legacy to a grandchild), there may be a separate tax called a *generation-skipping tax.*

The personal representatives of estates *should not attempt to complete the federal estate tax return (Form 706)*. Unlike an individual income tax return (the standard Form 1040), which the uninitiated may be able to complete, only experts should grapple with the federal estate tax form. Not only can it be tricky, but a lot of money could be at stake. Once the estate tax form has been completed, be sure that *timely payment* is made to avoid interest and/or penalties to the Internal Revenue Service. In order to prove that payment and filing have been made, send the check and the tax return by *certified mail* with a *return receipt requested*.

Sample Situations

Many estates have not been planned for the purpose of saving estate tax dollars. The federal estate tax could have been reduced if only certain changes in asset ownership had been implemented. In those cases where federal taxes are avoided, two techniques frequently appear: *testamentary trusts and gifting assets*. The former saves estate tax in the estate of the beneficiary of the trust. An example of a testamentary trust is presented in the money-saving suggestion that follows. The latter technique of gifting is described in the next section.

Money-Saving Suggestion

Let us take the situation of two sisters, Joan and Mary. Each has a net worth of $600,000, and their one relative is nephew Paul. Joan wants to leave everything to Mary; Mary wants to leave everything to Joan. When they are both gone, Paul is to receive their fortunes.

I suggest that Joan leave her estate in a testamentary trust, from which Mary can draw income annually. Upon Mary's later death, Mary's assets, and the principal of the testamentary trust established in Joan's will, are distributed to Paul.

As for Mary's will, it can be a mirror-image of Joan's. If Mary dies first, then Joan receives the income from the testamentary trust in Mary's will. Upon Joan's later death, Joan's assets, and the principal of the trust established in Mary's will, are distributed to Paul.

No federal estate tax is paid by either estate. However, if the first to die had left the $600,000 outright to her sister (rather than to a testamentary trust for the benefit of her sister), *when the survivor dies there is a taxable estate of $1,200,000, with a tax that could be as high as $240,000.* However, with my testamentary trust suggestion, the *survivor*

of the two sisters leaves a $600,000 taxable estate, because the "other" $600,000—*the money left in a trust by the first sister to die*—is not taxed in the surviving sister's estate. For wealthy readers, this suggestion can save your estate a *bundle*.

GIFT TAX

The federal government has (and a few states, including New York, have) a gift tax so that people cannot escape the estate tax by giving away their money, stock, or real estate, etc., thus dying without any estate (or with an estate that has been substantially reduced). *A gift tax is a tax paid by a person who gives a large gift.* It is a tax that supplements the estate tax. People who receive the large gifts do not pay any tax on the amount of these gifts. The person making the gift reports this transfer of assets on IRS Form 709. In general, this form must be filed by April 15th after the calendar year in which the gift was made.

How large is a "large gift"? For the federal government, large means over $10,000. So, if you give your nephew a $9,000 gift, there is no worry about taxes for you or him—no estate tax, no gift tax, and no income tax. *Gifts of amounts up to $10,000 to each recipient during a calendar year, to as many people to whom you want to make a gift, year after year, are not subject to a gift tax.* This $10,000 limitation is called the *annual exclusion amount,* that is, the maximum amount that can be given annually to any number of recipients without any worry of gift taxes. (Some of you might remember when this amount was $3,000.)

If a gift of money is given, it is easy to determine how much $10,000 is. But suppose stock that cost $5,000 is given as a gift when it is worth $10,000? This is a $10,000 gift—the value at the time the gift is made.

In the last section, we learned that an individual can leave $600,000 without the estate being taxed by the federal government. Let me expand a bit on this. Since the gift tax is supplementary to an estate tax, the $600,000 amount is the *total untaxed amount that either can be given away as a gift during your life or left in your estate.* Therefore, you can give a gift of a few hundred thousand dollars during your lifetime and not have to pay any federal gift tax. At the time of death, however, the amount *free of federal estate tax* is reduced by the total amount of your taxable gifts. Perhaps the following example will help to explain this law:

John gave his son $210,000 in 1984. John dies in 1990 leaving an estate of $500,000. *There is a federal estate tax on $100,000, and the amount of tax is $37,000.* Why? Because $10,000 of the $210,000 gift does not enter into the computation (recall the $10,000 annual exclusion); the $200,000 portion of the gift plus the $500,000 estate equal $700,000; but only a total of $600,000 of gifts and estate is free of tax; this leaves $100,000 upon which a tax is levied; the federal estate tax on this amount is currently $37,000 (37 percent of the taxable $100,000).

A final point: If a husband and wife *join* in giving a gift, a gift of up to $20,000 per year can be given to each recipient, and repeated year after year. It can be given to as many people each year to whom this couple wishes to make a gift, and there are no gift tax consequences. The $600,000 amount is not reduced. The reason a husband and wife can jointly give up to $20,000 is because each can be considered the giver of one-half, or $10,000, which is the amount of the *annual exclusion* discussed earlier.

Sample Situation

Telling a wealthy person to give away money to save estate taxes is like telling an incorrigible ninety-three-year-old to stop smoking cigars, to abstain from drinking, and to cease carousing. It is a justifiable attitude for the elder person to conclude that the estate tax—like cigars, liquor, and carousing—does not have any adverse personal effect. *It is the estate that pays the tax.* This attitude has been expressed by many people, and there is nothing wrong with it. I have presented options so that you can make an informed decision. *What is right for you should not be questioned or judged by anyone.*

Money-Saving Suggestion

A wealthy individual is advised to consider giving property worth $10,000 each year to many people, year after year, to reduce the eventual estate tax. The estate will have a substantially reduced estate tax, although it means that the benefactor has deprived himself of the enjoyment of the gift property by having given it away.

Let us review the tax consequences when a mother gifts $10,000 to her child:

Mother does not pay any federal gift tax on this gift, because it does not exceed $10,000. The child pays neither a federal gift tax nor a federal income tax on this gift. When Mother dies, the government has lost the opportunity to impose an estate tax on the $10,000. Additionally, the government has lost the opportunity to impose an estate tax on *the amount by which the $10,000 might have appreciated from the time of the gift to the time of the mother's death.* For example, if she had not made the gift and then lived many more years, the $10,000 amount could be worth much more at the time of her death.

The $10,000 gift does not appear on the mother's individual income tax return. *But future income tax might be saved,* because the tax on the annual interest from this $10,000 gift will be paid by the child, who possibly is taxed at a lower tax rate than the wealthier mother. This idea requires us to take a look at *progressive tax rates.* Let us do so.

PROGRESSIVE TAX RATES

A *progressive tax rate* increases as the amount to be taxed increases. But the increased tax rate affects only the *additional dollars.* For example, let us look at the progressive estate tax rates imposed on taxable estates over $600,000. The tax on an estate valued between *$600,000 and $750,000* is 37 percent of the amount over $600,000. The tax on an estate valued between *$600,000 and $1,000,000* is also *37 percent* of the amount between $600,000 and $750,000, *plus* a tax of *39 percent* on the amount between $750,000 and $1,000,000. This *progression of increasing rates* continues until the maximum rate, which has been as high as 55 percent, is reached. (The 55 percent has been applied to the portion of an estate that exceeds $3,000,000.) Keep in mind that these rates may change from time to time, through amendment of federal tax laws by Congress.

Sample Situation

Here is a situation that demonstrates how *progressive tax rates* affect not only estate tax planning, but also *income tax planning:*

Facts: John is married and files a joint income tax return. His total taxable income for the year will be $50,000. He has $100,000 to invest. His bank is offering a certificate of deposit *yielding 7 percent taxable*

interest income. His alternative investment is a municipal bond *yielding 6 percent tax exempt interest income.* Assume that John's tax bracket, the percentage of tax on his highest taxed dollar, is *28 percent* (keeping in mind that this tax bracket can vary from year to year, depending both on *John's income* and the *tax rates* for that year).

Question: Which investment will yield the greater "after tax" amount, the investment yielding the *7 percent taxable interest income* or the investment yielding *the 6 percent tax exempt interest income?*

Answer: The 6 percent tax exempt investment will put $6,000 in his pocket, as compared to the *after tax* amount of only $5,040 from the 7 percent taxable investment.

Explanation: The $7,000 yield from the 7 percent taxable investment will have a tax of $1,960 (28 percent of $7,000). Therefore, the $7,000 taxable yield will net John $5,040 after the federal tax is paid ($960 less than the income from the tax exempt investment).

Conclusion: John should consider purchasing the tax exempt investment.

Money-Saving Suggestion

Tax planning is important for wealthy individuals, because their potential tax—both estate tax and income tax—can be a substantial amount. Remember once again what you have learned throughout this book about the need for an asset *inventory;* sometimes people do not realize that with the passage of time their assets have grown just like inflation has grown. A person, although surely not wealthy, may have a home that has quite dramatically appreciated in value. Remember, too, that everything you own at the time of death is included in your gross estate, including all your bankbooks (even those that list your favorite niece as a joint owner or as the "in trust for" beneficiary).

As for the federal estate tax, someone with a net worth of under $600,000 would probably have only minimum benefit from estate tax planning. But the estate of someone with assets of over $600,000 will save (under current law) at least thirty-seven cents for each dollar that is removed from the eventual taxable estate. This amount of potential savings increases as the value of the estate increases, due to the progressive tax rates. The eventual estate of a multi-millionaire can *save a fortune through estate tax planning.*

STATE DEATH TAXES

State death taxes are of two varieties: an *inheritance tax* and a *state estate tax.*

About fifteen states have an inheritance tax. This tax is imposed upon *those who receive the deceased's assets.* Fortunately, surviving spouses, children, and grandchildren are either totally or partially exempt from this inheritance tax in most of these states. However, other individuals (often including brothers and sisters of the deceased) who inherit the deceased's assets have to pay the inheritance tax in those fifteen or so states that levy it. A state where this tax is particularly severe is Iowa.

Every state has a *state estate tax* (now that Nevada has adopted it). There are three ideas about a state estate tax that might be of interest to you: (1) Some states impose this tax even on relatively *small estates* (for example, an estate of $100,000); however, the tax is *much lower* than the federal estate tax (for example, the tax might be 5 percent of the estate value). (2) Various states only impose this tax on large estates—those valued at more than $600,000. (3) In some of the states that only impose the tax on large estates, the state estate tax is eliminated by the *federal estate tax credit* for all or a portion of any state estate tax paid by the estate.

A *tax credit* reduces *a tax* by the amount of the credit. This can be contrasted to a tax deduction, which reduces *the amount which is taxable.* For example, a tax credit of one dollar reduces a tax by one dollar; a tax deduction of one dollar is less valuable, because it only *saves what would have been the tax* on that one dollar.

Returning now to the federal estate tax credit for state estate taxes, there is a *limit on how much of a state death tax* (whether an inheritance tax or an estate tax) is allowed as a federal estate tax credit. This limit depends on the total value of the estate, and is stated in an Internal Revenue Service chart (see Appendix B). For example, if an estate is valued at $1,100,000, the amount of the state death tax paid—up to a maximum amount of $38,800 (the Internal Revenue Service chart gives me this amount)—is the amount allowed as a federal estate tax credit. From this flows the following two examples: First, if the state death tax on a $1,100,000 estate is $20,000, then the federal estate tax credit (or reduction) is $20,000 and, therefore, the federal government has indirectly paid the estate's state death tax. Second, if the state death tax on a $1,100,000 estate is $40,000, then the federal estate tax credit (or reduction) is *limited to* $38,800 (the amount in the IRS chart for estates of $1,100,000).

If the federal tax credit for state death tax paid is still a bit confusing, talk to your attorney or tax consultant. What is within your control is your ability to establish which state is your state of domicile. *You do not want two states fighting over who receives the state death tax.*

Sample Situations

Suppose John is a resident of a state that has an inheritance tax that is paid by *someone* (other than a spouse, children, and grandchildren) *receiving assets from the estate.* It also has an *estate tax* that taxes only estates of substantial value. John leaves his son $125,000 and his brother $30,000. John's estate *pays no federal or state estate tax;* his brother *pays an inheritance tax;* his son *does not pay an inheritance tax.*

Here is another sample situation: John is a resident of New York State, a state that has *no inheritance tax* but does have *an estate tax* (on an estate where a nonspouse receives over $108,343). Again, his son and brother are left $125,000 and $30,000 respectively. The *estate pays an estate tax of about $2,750;* the *son and brother pay no inheritance tax;* there is *no federal tax owed because the estate is less than $600,000.*

Money-Saving Suggestion

If an estate incurs a federal tax, there is a reduction of the federal estate tax by the tax credit for the state death tax. However, the estate might *not* be allowed a federal estate tax credit that equals the *entire amount of the state death tax,* because the credit is subject to the limits outlined in the IRS chart in Appendix B.

WHEN A SPOUSE INHERITS

If you are *married,* then this section is an important one for you. I will repeat the great news for married couples. *Everything you inherit from your spouse is free of any federal estate tax. Any gift you receive from your spouse is also free of any federal gift tax.* (Again, remember that the surviving spouse—the one who receives the inheritance or gift—is assumed to be a United States citizen.)

There is a big problem, however, despite the tax-free treatment of assets inherited by a spouse. *What happens when the surviving spouse dies?* Quite likely, the estate of the surviving spouse will contain all or

a considerable portion of the assets of both husband and wife, resulting in quite a significant tax being levied upon the estate.

Here is an example: Mr. Smith is worth $600,000, and Mrs. Smith also is worth $600,000. There is no estate tax when the first spouse dies. But there will be a huge estate tax (perhaps as high as $240,000) when the remaining spouse dies, *because his or her estate will probably be in excess of $1.2 million.*

Earlier I demonstrated how two sisters, each worth $600,000, could avoid estate tax (and the surviving sister, in addition to her own $600,000, has the use of the deceased sister's $600,000). Similarly, a married couple can avoid an estate tax on a combined estate of $1.2 million. Like the two sisters, Mr. and Mrs. Smith can use a testamentary trust. My next money-saving suggestion shows how a married couple can avoid estate tax on a combined estate of $1,200,000.

Sample Situation

Married couples like to use a testamentary trust to be sure that legacies to the children are protected in the event that the *surviving spouse re-marries.* For some people the tax savings motive is secondary. The following money-saving suggestion explains the twofold purpose of this $600,000 trust: *to assure that the children of the marriage receive a legacy and to save taxes when the widow or widower dies.*

Money-Saving Suggestions

A testamentary trust can have dramatic estate tax savings. *Also, this trust clearly specifies the ultimate recipient of the money.* Mr. and Mrs. Smith, each worth $600,000, can leave a total amount of $1,200,000 without any estate tax in *either* estate. Each will simply states: "I leave $600,000 to my trustee, the XYZ Trust Company, for the benefit of the following people. My trustee is to distribute all the income to my spouse annually. Upon my spouse's death the principal is to be distributed evenly among our three children, and this trust is to terminate."

The $600,000 that the spouse leaves in trust (for the benefit of the *surviving spouse and then for the children*) is not taxable, because $600,000 can be left to anyone free of any estate tax. Therefore, the estate of the first deceased spouse pays no estate tax. This amount held in trust is then free of tax in the surviving spouse's estate, since it is not considered to be the surviving spouse's property (even though the surviving spouse had

substantial use of these funds). In addition, the surviving spouse can then leave the children another $600,000, also free of any estate tax. The children (or any other legatees) of Mr. and Mrs. Smith can thereby receive $1.2 million undiminished by any federal estate tax.

Suppose a spouse has more than $600,000 and has these three objectives: (1) leaving this additional amount to his *spouse;* (2) using a trust, so as to be able to determine the *ultimate recipient(s)* after the surviving spouse's death; and (3) having this bequest *qualify for the marital deduction.* Can these three objectives be realized? Yes, through the use of what is called a QTIP (Qualified Terminable Interest Property) Trust. These trusts obviously are relevant only to the very wealthiest of couples, but I did want to at least mention the QTIP Trust before moving on to a topic relevant to every estate—the *deceased's final income tax return.*

18

Income Taxation

THE FINAL INCOME TAX RETURN

The deceased's final income tax return is filed by the personal representative of the estate. It is the same Form 1040 that would have been filed had the person lived. There are a few decisions that have to be made by the personal representative, including: the choice of *filing status* if the deceased was married, the tax treatment of *medical expenses,* and the tax treatment of income from *United States Savings Bonds.*

A *joint tax return* can be filed for the year of death if there is a surviving spouse. I suggest that three returns be tentatively prepared: one for the *deceased spouse alone,* using the married-filing-separately status; one for the surviving spouse alone, also using the married-filing-separately status; and one for *both husband and wife,* using the married-filing-jointly status. Readers and their tax consultant will have to determine the less costly choice (either *filing jointly* or *married-filing-separately*).

The *cost of medical care* provided to the deceased (paid within a year after death) may be taken as a deduction *either* on the deceased's final year's *federal individual income tax return or* on the *federal estate tax return* (but not on both). Many times there is no tax savings realized, *regardless of which of these two options is chosen.* If the unreimbursed portion of the medical expenses is less than 7.5 percent of your adjusted gross income, it is disregarded on an individual's income tax return. If there is no estate tax owed, the medical expense deduction taken on an estate tax return is meaningless. The choice becomes important when *only* the income tax *or* the estate tax can be reduced by deducting the medical

expenses. Make sure you take it *on the one where tax is reduced.* The choice is also important when *both* the income tax and the estate tax could be reduced by deducting the medical expenses. Make sure you take it *on the one that results in greater tax savings.*

The third decision is the treatment of *United States Savings Bonds* interest, which for many older persons is substantial if it has accrued over a number of years. It can be reported on the *deceased's final income tax return,* on the *estate's income tax return,* or on the *beneficiary's income tax return* (if the bonds are distributed to a beneficiary who sells them). Do some calculating before making your decision.

Sample Situation

Estate executors and/or administrators need to file Form 56 with the Internal Revenue Service. This form is the personal representative's notification to the IRS of his or her appointment to handle the affairs of the deceased. It advises the IRS where to send notices, including any audit notices.

I suggest you file this form. *Otherwise, you are likely to miss an opportunity to question any income tax audit findings of the Internal Revenue Service.* This is because a statute of limitations—the time in which you must challenge the IRS's ruling—could expire *without your even knowing of the existence of an audit.* The statute of limitations begins to run from the time the Internal Revenue Service *mails* a statutory notice to the taxpayer, not when the taxpayer receives it. Keep in mind that the IRS is required to send notices only to the *last known address* of a taxpayer. *The burden is on the personal representative of the estate to let the government know where mail is to be sent.*

Money-Saving Suggestions

In addition to the deceased's final income tax return, there may also be the necessity of filing the deceased's previous year's income tax return. This occurs when a deceased has died early in the year (before April 15th), before having filed it.

In such cases, the personal representative of the estate should take advantage of the *four-month automatic extension of time to file the previous year's tax return by filing Form 4868.* It is this previous year's tax return that sometimes presents some difficulties in fact gathering. This is particularly true when death occurs in late March or early April, close

to the filing deadline. If matters are in a turmoil, it is advisable to obtain this extension so that an accurate tax return can then be prepared. Realize that what you are obtaining is an extension of time to *file* the tax return, not an extension of time to *pay* the tax that might be due. Therefore, estimate the amount owed and mail a check for this amount along with Form 4868. Remember to put the deceased's social security number on the check.

In addition to this automatic four-month extension, a further extension can be requested by filing Form 2688. Although this further extension is not automatically granted, a reason such as the death of the taxpayer or incomplete records is usually sufficient for the IRS to grant this additional extension of time to file. I do not recommend seeking this additional extension. Why delay matters so long?

INCOME TAXATION OF AN ESTATE

An estate generates income during the time it is administered, and thus *an estate might have to pay an income tax just like a person would.* Here are two examples of how an estate generates income during its administration: stocks owned by the deceased pay dividend income; bank accounts owned by the deceased generate interest income. The estate income tax return is Form 1041, similar to the individual income tax return (the Form 1040).

The estate income tax return must give the estate's identification number. (As soon as the executor is appointed, he files Form SS-4 with the Internal Revenue Service to obtain this identification number.) The income received by the estate is listed, the allowable deductions are subtracted from the income, the tax is computed, and the return is signed and filed by the personal representative of the estate.

In addition to reading the instructions carefully, here are a few tips: (1) decide whether to elect a calendar year or a fiscal year; (2) funeral expenses are not deductible on the estate's income tax return (but remember to deduct these expenses on the estate tax return); (3) administration expenses (such as executor's commission and attorney's fee) can be taken *either* on the *estate's income tax return* or on the *estate tax return;* (4) distributions from the estate (generally up to the amount of the income) to beneficiaries are deductions on the estate's income tax return.

The estate income tax return is more complex than your individual income tax return. However, if you can do your own taxes, *you can possi-*

bly do an estate income tax return. Realize that you might be adept at doing your own income tax return only because you have been *doing it for years;* the Form 1041 is a *new experience for the executor.*

Taxes might be saved if the assets of an estate are distributed slowly. This is because the income tax on the yield from these assets may be less if this yield is taxable on the estate income tax return rather than taxable on the recipient's income tax return. The following sample situation demonstrates how slowness is sometimes tax-wise.

Sample Situation

John is a successful salesman and his taxable income is about $100,000 each year. His elderly aunt dies and John is her only legatee (he is the residuary legatee). John is to receive the only asset she owned, a $50,000 certificate of deposit yielding 10 percent interest income annually ($5,000 each year). If there is a delay in distributing the legacy, the $5,000 interest income is taxable to the estate (and is taxed at the rate applicable for $0 to $5,000 of income). This happens because the estate has not made a distribution to John and, therefore, the estate has not received an income distribution deduction. The estate (which earned the income) pays a *lower estate income tax* on this yield than John, who might be in a *higher income tax bracket* (quite likely, since in this sample situation John has taxable income of $100,000, so the additional $5,000 of taxable income would be taxed at the rate applicable for $100,000 to $105,000 of income). But *be reasonable in how long you delay distribution.*

Money-Saving Suggestion

Here is a suggestion (and a warning) to personal representatives of estates. You could be *personally liable* for taxes owed and unpaid by an estate— the income taxes (the tax computed on the federal individual income tax Form 1040 and the federal estate income tax Form 1041) and the estate taxes (the tax computed on the federal estate tax Form 706). This would occur if the personal representative of the estate distributes all the estate's assets before paying all these taxes. Then the government could reach into the pocket of the personal representative (executor or administrator).

In addition to the possibility of personal liability if all taxes are not paid, a raft of letters will be forthcoming from the Internal Revenue Service, your state tax people, and the legatees. To sort it all out a few years later is an expensive and frustrating exercise. The timely filing of all tax

returns and the payment of all the taxes that are due are essential responsibilities, but be sure that the estate is not paying more than necessary to the government. What happens if too little is paid to the government? Let us take a look at a tax audit.

TAX AUDIT

A tax audit is not the terrifying experience one so often imagines. Personal representatives of estates should stay calm if an audit is announced. The auditor *requests* information; you *provide* the information; the auditor *decides* whether the tax return accurately computes the tax owed; the auditor may *assess* an additional tax on the estate; if the assessment is correct, an additional tax is *paid*.

If you are *worried* about the audit, then go to the audit with an attorney, an accountant, or a person qualified by written examination to represent taxpayers before the Internal Revenue Service. If you are *terrified* about the audit, then stay home and put your trust completely in the hands of a competent representative.

But if you follow these suggestions, you will have a worry-free tax life: *report* all the deceased's assets on the *estate tax return,* and all the income from the estate on the *estate income tax return;* on these returns *deduct only* those expenses that were incurred and are allowable as deductions; *be assertive,* however, and even when in doubt do not be intimidated by the auditor.

Suppose you disagree with the auditor's decision. You have a right to appeal within the Internal Revenue Service itself. After that appeal, your ultimate relief is to take one of two approaches: either pay the additional tax and then institute a lawsuit for a refund in the Federal District Court (or the Federal Court of Claims); or, alternatively (and the more practical approach), do not pay the additional tax and immediately start a lawsuit in the United States Tax Court. Be aware of the statute of limitations (the time in which a lawsuit must be commenced) for a lawsuit begun in the United States Tax Court. It must commence within *ninety days* from the date on the *notice of deficiency* that candidly advises you that *you have ninety days to petition the United States Tax Court.* The lawsuit is started by the taxpayer, who files a legal document, called a petition, with the United States Tax Court.

Sample Situation

Experience teaches that *the less said at an audit the better the results.* It is better to let your records speak for themselves whenever possible, so be sure to keep accurate and complete records.

Here are some of the items that are frequently requested at the audit of an estate tax return: (1) the deceased's Form 1040 individual income tax returns for the past three years, (2) all Form 1041 estate income tax returns, (3) bank and brokerage statements for the three years prior to death and the entire period of the estate administration, (4) all life insurance policies, (5) any personal property insurance policy, (6) proof of payment of all items deducted on any tax return, (7) the estate checkbook and all the cancelled checks, (8) any gift tax returns, and (9) appraisals of the value of estate assets.

Money-Saving Suggestions

The most important advice I can give is *not to be intimidated* by a tax auditor. Keep in mind these eight suggestions on audit etiquette: *arrive* on time; *bring* the requested information; *listen* carefully; *do not apologize; do not insult the auditor* (it never helps and sometimes hurts); *do not dump* boxes of receipts on the auditor's desk; *do not sign* anything (go home and calmly review the auditor's findings); *do not say* a final nasty remark (the auditor is a taxpayer, too). GOOD LUCK!

Finally, try to make the auditor's job easy by providing requested information promptly. The reason this approach achieves more favorable results is that the auditor has spent less time on the audit than had been anticipated. He need not justify (to himself or his supervisor) the long hours of tedious work *by deciding every questionable issue in favor of the government.*

STEPPED-UP BASIS AT TIME OF DEATH

If you sell real estate, a share of stock, or any other asset at a gain, you are required to pay *income tax on the amount of the taxable gain.* Your *taxable gain* is the amount by which your *selling price* exceeds your *basis;* your *taxable loss* is the amount by which your basis exceeds your selling price. In most situations, *basis* is a tax term that means your *cost, plus* the cost of any *improvements, less* any *tax depreciation.*

With this knowledge, let us now compute the taxable gain on the sale of a plot of land. If you paid $100,000 for the land, spent an additional $10,000 to have the land cleared, and then sold the land for $200,000, *your gain is $90,000.* This is because the *selling price* of $200,000 *exceeds* the *basis* of $110,000 (which is the $100,000 purchase price plus the $10,000 cost of the clearing) *by $90,000.*

But special tax treatment is given to assets received from a decedent's estate (except for appreciated property acquired by gift within one year of the decedent's death). The recipient of the asset receives a basis that is called a *stepped-up basis at the time of death.* This description is appropriate, since the basis (the amount *above which* is the taxable gain) is stepped-up (or increased) to the *value at death.*

The following example, using the same numbers found in the previous illustration, shows the *tax benefit of a stepped-up basis at the time of death:*

John buys a plot of land for $100,000. He has the land cleared for $10,000. Years later he dies and leaves the house to his nephew. The value of the house at John's death is $200,000. The nephew's gain on his ultimate sale of the land is *measured from $200,000* and not from his uncle's $110,000 basis. The nephew has received what tax people call stepped-up basis at time of death. *The $90,000 appreciation during the uncle's ownership is never taxed.*

This is a significant tax benefit for families who own property that has appreciated in value. *Income tax is never paid on the appreciation in value of such property for the period between the time the property was acquired and the owner's death.*

Keep in mind that if property has *declined* in value prior to death, the basis for the person inheriting the property is also the date of death value, which is called a *stepped-down* basis. For example, if you inherited Grandmother's stock, which cost her $60 a share but is only worth $55 per share at the time of her death, your stepped-down basis—used to measure your eventual gain or loss upon sale—is $55.

Sample Situation

If a more well-off taxpayer gives gifts to members of the family, perhaps this taxpayer should give *money rather than stock that has appreciated in value.* Here is a case that helps to explain why:

Father, a widower, has $400,000 in money market accounts. He also has $400,000 worth of stock that years ago only cost him $200,000. Father is giving gifts to his child. Should he give money or stocks? Money. Why?

If he owns the stock until he dies, and his child (or anyone else) then inherits the stock, neither the father nor the child will pay an income tax on any growth from the time the father *bought it until his death.* Why? When the stock is sold by the heir, the gain is measured from the *stepped-up basis at the time of the father's death.*

However, if Father *gives* the stock (rather than willing it), when the child sells the stock, *the gain is measured from the cost at which the father bought it.*

Money-Saving Suggestions

If you possess property that has increased substantially in value (real estate, stock, etc.), *I suggest you do some serious calculating before deciding to sell (or give away) the asset.* If you hold onto it for the rest of your life, your heir can sell the property, and neither you nor your heir incur any income tax on its appreciation in value during the time of your ownership.

The preceding suggestion is unrealistic if you definitely want to sell the property, and particularly unrealistic if you have *a need for the cash proceeds.* Like any suggestion that saves tax dollars, what a person wants or needs is equally as important as the tax-wise suggestion. Some people make decisions that are not the best ones strictly from a tax point of view. But if it is what the person wants, despite a favorable tax alternative, then so be it. You decide, but there is nothing wrong in listening to the advice of others.

19

Family Businesses, and Charities

THE FAMILY FARM AND OTHER FAMILY BUSINESSES

The value of real estate owned by the deceased, including the family farm, is included in the gross estate. The fair market value is determined by an appraiser, and is estimated to be what someone might be willing to pay for the property. Generally the appraiser bases the estimate on recent selling prices of similar pieces of property.

But there is a problem. The Internal Revenue Service requires the appraiser to base the estimate on an assumption that the property is put to its *highest and best use*. A farm, for example, located close to a crowded urban center, might be valued, not as a farm, but as a tract of land that could be a potentially attractive location for commercial or residential use. Big trouble for farmers!

There is, however, a relief provision in the Internal Revenue Code, and farms, as well as other real estate, can be exempt from this highest-and-best-use standard. To obtain this relief, there are various specific tests that must be met. Essentially, *if the farm or business real estate is a substantial percentage of the deceased's estate, and has been used for such purposes for a substantial period of time, then the valuation will be exempt from the highest-and-best-use standard.*

The rationale for this tax-relief provision allowing a lower actual (or special use) valuation is quite understandable. The government considers it unfair to place a heavy tax on the family, *because payment of the tax might require the family to sell or mortgage the farm in order to pay the estate tax.*

The estate tax is normally paid nine months after death. However, another relief provision to help a *family farm or other business* is the availability of *installment payments*. If a family business is a substantial percentage of the deceased's estate, the taxing authorities might permit payment of the tax to be made over a fifteen-year period. Although there is interest charged on this deferred payment, the interest on at least some of this amount is lower than the prevailing rate of interest charged by a bank.

Both of the above-described situations, *special use valuation* and *installment payment of estate taxes,* need careful planning. Keep in mind that the tax benefit is "recaptured" if there is a change of use or ownership *during a substantial period of time after being inherited.*

Sample Situation

A crucial time for a family-owned business is the death of the family member most active in the business. Make sure someone has been educated in every aspect of running the company. Otherwise, the business might have to be *discontinued;* even worse, legal action might be instituted against the estate for *unfulfilled commitments* made by the deceased owner that no one is now available to complete.

Money-Saving Suggestion

So often have I emphasized the importance of *everyone* keeping an *inventory,* and I hope you remember my advice that you *must tell your executor where this inventory and other important papers are kept.*

Business owners have the additional tasks of *choosing a successor* and *keeping this person* continuously updated on such matters as: accounts payable and receivable, existing contracts, recent amendments to pension plans and other employee benefits, and every other aspect of the business. For those readers who do not want to divulge *everything* to the successor, I suggest that at least you tell the successor where this *confidential information is kept.* Perhaps with the passage of time you will entrust your successor with the actual information. But, in the meantime, make sure all your confidential records are *complete* and your successor knows *where they are kept.*

CHARITABLE TRUSTS

We have already discussed the estate tax benefit of leaving money or other property to a charity (see chapter 7): those dollars (or the value of other property) left to a charity are not subject to an estate tax.

We have also discussed the use of a testamentary trust (see chapter 8), whereby a testator leaves money or other property to a beneficiary, but the money or property is to be controlled by a trustee. The reasons a testator might give for doing this are varied, but could include: a lack of confidence in the beneficiary (thereby appointing someone else to control the assets in the trust) or a desire to determine *who receives the assets after the lifetime beneficiary dies.*

Let us combine these two ideas of leaving money to a charity and using a testamentary trust. The following example of a charitable remainder trust demonstrates how they could be combined and expressed in the will of John's father:

> I bequeath the sum of $400,000 to my trustee, ABC Trust Company, in trust nevertheless, for the benefit of my son, John. *My trustee is to distribute annually seven percent of the net fair market value of the trust assets, as valued annually, to my son, John,* and upon his death my trustee is to distribute the principal to DEF Charity and terminate the trust.

The estate is allowed a deduction for the fair market value of what the charity eventually is to receive. The value of what John will receive (which is referred to as his unitrust interest) depends on the age of John when his father dies. If John is young, the value of the charitable deduction is not so great, because the charity receives the money far in the future. Also, notice the words giving John a fixed percentage of the trust annually. The law requires the charitable trust to distribute annually (out of interest or principal or both) a fixed percent of the trust principal (at least 5 percent) in order for the estate to qualify for a charitable deduction. The higher the percentage to John, the lower the charitable deduction. The law *does not allow an estate tax charitable deduction* if what John receives is measured *only* by the income earned annually, even if upon his death the funds in the trust are to be distributed to a charity.

Sample Situation

Joan is in her mid-eighties. She has a net worth of $800,000. Her only relative is her younger and poorer sister, Matilda. Joan wants to leave her entire estate to Matilda. Joan really does not care who receives what is left of the $800,000 after both she and Matilda are dead. Joan, however, has always had an admiration for the good work done by the New York Foundling Hospital. A *charitable remainder trust* might be the appropriate estate plan for Joan. She can help her sister, help a charity, and save her estate some taxes. She can leave the $800,000 to a trustee for Matilda's benefit; Matilda receives a fixed percentage of this amount each year; and upon Matilda's death, the New York Foundling Hospital receives all the assets held by the trust.

Definitely, the estate tax on Joan's estate will be *lower* as a result of the charitable remainder trust because, in addition to the tax-free $600,000 amount, the charitable deduction at least partially wipes out the remaining $200,000 in the taxable estate. *Definitely,* poorer Matilda's estate will have no estate tax for a reason unrelated to the charity being named by Joan as the ultimate recipient. Matilda's estate is not taxed, because *none* of the $800,000 in the trust will be included in Matilda's taxable estate. Why? Because Matilda did not have the right to name the ultimate recipient, a charity or otherwise, upon her death. This ultimate beneficiary, New York Foundling Hospital, was *already chosen by Joan.*

Money-Saving Suggestion

To those who plan on discussing charitable trusts with their attorney, I suggest you read these descriptions of three types of charitable trusts that currently qualify under federal tax law for the estate tax charitable deduction.

A *charitable remainder annuity trust* is required to pay annually to the lifetime beneficiary a definite percentage of the *value of the assets* (the federal tax law establishes the *minimum* percentage, which is currently at 5 percent), *as valued on the day the trust is established,* which for a testamentary trust would be the date of the testator's death.

A *charitable remainder unitrust* is required to pay annually to the lifetime beneficiary a definite percentage of the *value of the assets* (again, the federal tax law establishes the *minimum* percentage, which is currently at 5 percent), *as valued annually.*

The difference between these trusts is the *time* at which the principal of the trust is *valued.* They are similar in that both require a *minimum*

percentage of the trust assets to be distributed annually to the lifetime beneficiary, and the person establishing either trust *chooses the trustee.*

This last aspect distinguishes these two charitable remainder trusts from another type of charitable trust called a *pooled income fund.* With this type of trust, the *charity is the trustee* and the funds are pooled (combined) with funds already contributed by others. The lifetime beneficiary receives a prorated portion of the earnings from the pool of funds.

This brings us to the end of our taxation discussion. We now move on to Part Four to take consider some additional ideas that might be of interest.

Part Four

Final Thoughts

20

Some Additional Ideas

OUR LEGAL SYSTEM

Our legal system has become difficult for the average person to comprehend, and that is why I have tried to explain wills and estate administration in what I hope is an understandable way. But why is the law so complex?

First, our lives are complex and so are the rights and responsibilities we enjoy under the law. Adding to this complexity is the fact that we live under two sets of laws, federal and state. A second reason for the law's complexity is that *we want our rights and responsibilities specifically enumerated.* Therefore, so many legal forms are required for even the simplest of transactions, because people want to be *definite* in their dealings. Third, the law is complex because its goal of *fairness* is reachable only with statutes that try to cover every imaginable situation. This results in laws that are *overprotective,* that might apply to situations where protection is not needed.

From the drawing of a will to the final account prepared by the personal representative of the estate, dozens of documents are written, reviewed, revised, signed, recorded, challenged, and appealed. Time-consuming, yes, but the end result has a dramatic effect on the lives of many people. The best response to this legal bureaucracy is an educated public. If those who are affected by the legal system have a *general understanding of that system,* then the law's complexity will be far less frustrating.

Sample Situation

A woman died and her surviving spouse received all her assets—consisting of real estate, bank accounts, and pension benefits—because they were held in joint ownership with the right of survivorship. An appraisal of the real estate was required. In fact, it was important for the surviving spouse to have this appraisal, and the reason for the appraisal is the subject of this sample situation.

Let us assume that the real estate is valued at $500,000 at the time of the woman's death. Further assume that the real estate originally cost $200,000 some years ago. If there is a valid appraisal showing the $500,000 date-of-death-value, a potential reduction of income tax, upon an eventual sale of this property by the surviving husband, can result. Let me explain.

When a husband and a wife jointly own an asset, the law concludes that one-half is owned by the husband and other half is owned by the wife. The half owned by the now deceased wife receives the stepped-up basis at time of her death, which means that this half has a $250,000 (the value at death) tax basis for measuring gain on the sale. The husband's half has his original basis of one-half of the $200,000 cost, or $100,000. Therefore, if the husband now sells the property for $500,000, the gain on the sale of this property (which only cost $200,000) is $150,000. This $150,000 is the difference between the total basis of $350,000 (the deceased wife's $250,000 stepped-up basis, plus the husband's $100,000 basis) and the selling price of $500,000. Incidentally, of this $150,000, perhaps only $25,000 is taxable; under current law, if the eligibility requirements (including age, ownership, and use) are met, the sale would qualify for exclusion of up to $125,000 of gain.

So, the appraisals were obtained and the federal and state estate tax returns were filed. Although no estate tax was owed, the tax returns established a record of the stepped-up basis at time of death. Some may think this to be a *waste of time*, but there was a *potential future income tax benefit* from documenting the date-of-death value of the portion owned by the deceased spouse (the stepped-up basis at time of death). This made the paper chase necessary and worthwhile.

Money-Saving Suggestion

If you are a surviving spouse, establish the value of your home at the time of your deceased spouse's death by having a realtor give you a written appraisal. This way, if you ever sell the home, you will either not owe

any tax or you will *pay a tax that is no greater than the law requires.*
Do this even if the assets were owned jointly with your spouse; and do
it even though there is no estate tax to pay.

POWERS IN TRUST

Suppose you wish to leave money or other property to someone who
is now an infant? There are a few alternatives.

You can use a *testamentary trust.* In your will you might decide to
set up the trust as follows:

> I leave $100,000 to ABC Bank as Trustee, to hold the money in trust
> for my grandson, John Doe; the ABC Bank is to accumulate the income
> until John Doe is eighteen years old (or whatever age you like); then
> ABC Bank is to distribute the entire amount to John Doe.

Rather than having the income accumulate, you can direct your trustee
to distribute the income, or even the principal, to the minor if he or she
is responsible, or to the parent of the minor, or to anyone who provides
a service to John. Upon your death, the money will be held by the ABC
Bank, as Trustee, until John Doe is whatever age you choose. Suppose
that at the time of your death, John has already reached the age you
specified in the trust? He will receive the legacy, without it ever being
held by a trust.

An alternative is to bequeath the $100,000 *outright* to John Doe,
believing that he will have reached adulthood at the time of your death
(far in the future). But if he is still a minor when you die, then someone
(usually called a *guardian*) will be appointed by a court to supervise the
money. This supervision will continue until John Doe reaches the age
of majority. Be aware of these two points about a guardianship: a guardian
costs money, and the person serving as guardian might be a stranger who
intrudes into John Doe's life.

If the testator neither wants to *establish a testamentary trust in his
will* nor wants *the court to appoint a guardian,* I recommend the following *powers in trust clause* in the will. Your attorney can explain the rules
of your state regarding powers in trust, but this is how it generally works:
You give your executor the power to hold the legacy of a minor until
the minor reaches the age of majority. You also give the executor the
power to apply this money for the benefit of the minor.

I recommend that your will contain a powers in trust clause, even if all your primary legatees are adults. Remember that you have (or should have) alternate legatees named in the will. Although you might leave everything you own to your adult son, John, your will might direct that everything is left to his daughter if he predeceases you. If John, in fact, predeceases you, your legatee may be John's infant daughter. In this case, the powers in trust clause avoids the appointment of a guardian. The upcoming sample situation provides a powers in trust clause.

Sample Situation

Here is a powers in trust clause, which I include in most wills:

> If any person should be under the age of majority when he or she shall become entitled to a legacy or a share of my estate or of any terminating or partially terminating trust, such legacy or share (hereinafter referred to in this Article as the "share") shall vest absolutely in such minor notwithstanding minority. However, my executor may, in his discretion, retain custody of such share until such minor attains the age of majority. My executor, if he decides to retain custody of such share, shall pay or apply so much or all of the income or principal to *or for the benefit of* such minor as he deems necessary or desirable, regardless of any other source or sources of income or support which the minor may have, adding any income not so paid or applied to principal annually. When such minor shall attain the age of majority, the then principal of such share, together with any accumulated income thereon, shall be paid over to such minor. If such minor shall die before attaining the age of majority, then, upon the death of such minor, the then principal of such share, together with any accumulated income thereon, shall be paid over to the estate of such minor.
>
> In making payments to or on behalf of such minor, my executor may make payment directly to such minor if he deems such minor to be of reasonable age and competence, to make application directly to the use of the minor or to make payment to a parent of the minor, to a guardian of the minor appointed in this state or in any other jurisdiction, to a custodian (including any executor hereunder) for such minor under the Uniform Gifts to Minors Act of this state or any other jurisdiction (whether appointed by any executor hereunder or any other person), or to any adult person with whom the minor resides or who has the care or custody of the minor temporarily or permanently.

Money-Saving Suggestion

If you do not want to use a testamentary trust for a legacy to someone who is a minor (perhaps because *you want to avoid the expense of
a trust,* or you think *you will not die before the child reaches majority*),
then consider having a powers in trust clause. This suggestion might save
your estate the cost of an additional court proceeding to appoint a guardian,
and the cost of paying the guardian.

DISINHERITING THOSE WHO OBJECT

You may have a concern that a particular person might attempt to challenge
your will after your death. Unfortunately, there is no sure way to prevent
your will from being challenged; it's one of those "rights" that all distributees
have, and some choose to exercise. One practical way to approach the
question of potential challenges is to forget about it; just have confidence
that your will is legally sufficient to withstand any and all attempts to
contest it.

However, in many states there is something that can be done to
discourage a potential challenger from exerting the right to contest a will.
By inserting a clause such as the following (which is referred to by the
Latin words *in terrorem,* meaning "by way of warning"), the potential
challenger may have second thoughts about contesting the will:

> If any legatee under this my will, or any codicil hereto, shall, in any man-
> ner, directly or indirectly, attempt to contest or oppose the probate or
> validity of this my will, or any codicil hereto, in any court, or commence
> or prosecute any legal proceeding of any kind in any court to set aside
> this my will, or any codicil hereto, then and in that event such legatee
> shall forfeit and cease to have any right or interest whatsoever under this
> my will, or under any codicil hereto, or in any portion of my estate,
> and in such event, I hereby direct that my property and estate shall be
> disposed of in all respects as if such legatee had predeceased me.

Along with this clause, your will leaves the next of kin whom you
dislike (and whom you fear is a potential challenger) a sum of money.
Here is an example to help you undersand why a "sum of money" is
bequeathed: Assume that widow Mary has two next of kin, her good
son George and her bad son Brian. Her total worth consists of a money

market account with a balance of $100,000. She leaves $15,000 to Brian, and includes an *in terrorem* clause in her will. Might Brian contest the will? If he does so and *wins,* he receives his intestate share of $50,000; but *if he loses, he receives nothing* (because the will, now approved by the court, conditions his $15,000 legacy on *his not contesting the will*). The $15,000 is the enticement that might be just enough to dissuade him from contesting the will. Brian might be willing to accept the $15,000, and not contest the will.

However, give careful consideration to using this approach because it is a form of succumbing to blackmail. In my example, the widow Mary has left $15,000 to Brian, hoping that he will accept this legacy rather than try to defeat the will and receive his intestate share of $50,000. Perhaps Mary should not worry so much about Brian—and leave him nothing. I also suggest that widow Mary put good George's name on the money market account as the "in trust for" (i.t.f.) beneficiary; and this money goes to George, even if the will is contested successfully. But Mary should also have a will leaving everything to George, just in case she withdraws the money from the money market account, purchases a certificate of deposit, and *forgets to put George's name on the certificate of deposit.* She should also have a will naming George the residuary legatee, in case she *wins the lottery.*

Sample Situations

Earlier on we learned about living trusts, called *inter vivos trusts* (see chapter 8). Those who anticipate that a disinherited next of kin might be a potential challenger to the will might give some thought to establishing a living trust. A bank (or perhaps even you) can serve as trustee; you can transfer your assets to this trustee; *and* you can be the beneficiary of the trust. The trust instrument names who succeeds you as trustee after your death, and specifies who receives the trust funds at your death. The assets in the trust avoid probate at the time of your death. However, as you have learned throughout this book, these assets in the trust are still included as part of your taxable estate.

Why is this procedure preferred by some people, rather than having the estate distributed by the will? Well, it does eliminate the challenges of lack of testamentary capacity, fraud, duress, and undue influence that can be aimed at a will. If you establish this trust, and you receive distributions of money from this trust until your death some years later, it is difficult for your disinherited heir to argue successfully that you did

not know what you were doing. After all, you were living with this trust from perhaps age seventy until perhaps age ninety-two.

Another way of decreasing the chances of a will challenge is to make gifts of your assets to those you love, thereby *reducing the value of your eventual estate* (although, as you learned in chapter 17, there might be a gift tax owed by you). This is a dramatic approach, because once the gift has been given, you have *no legal right to get it back.* There are cases, however, of people giving away money, motivated by their dislike of a relative who may challenge a will if there is money available in an estate.

Money-Saving Suggestion

Give consideration to establishing a *living trust.* It saves probate costs, and it lessens the chances of aggressive relatives picking over your estate. These trusts are particularly popular in California, Florida, Illinois, Massachusetts, and Ohio. I am only suggesting that you consider this approach; you may decide against it. I do not want to further complicate your life—e.g., by suggesting that you have all your assets in a trust— unless you are certain that your particular situation warrants the paperwork and the attorney's fee. On the other hand, you may want to establish this *living trust.* You *are* in control.

A LEGATEE WHO MIGHT GET DIVORCED

Divorce is a fact of life. Many people, therefore, have the following concern: "I'm leaving my son everything, but I'm so afraid that he and his wife will get divorced after I die; in the divorce settlement she will get half of whatever I might leave my son."

There are a couple of ways to approach this problem. One strategy is to act like an ostrich, put your head in the sand, *and just do not worry about this problem.* I am being completely serious here. Sometimes worrying about your child's possible divorce can actually be a self-fulfilling prophecy. What you are doing is projecting onto your child your dislike of the chosen mate. While parents should not be blamed for everything (and perhaps they should be blamed for nothing), some parents can be blamed for a child's divorce. They convince a weak person that this is the anticipated outcome.

A more profound bit of advice would be to leave your child the legacy *in trust*. Consider giving your trustee the discretion to distribute or withhold income. We will consider this more closely in the next sample situation.

But realize that you can never have a perfect plan for the distribution of your assets after death. I believe that this quest for the perfect distribution of assets is, ironically, part of the reason so many people die without a will. Years of thought and worry result in a paralysis of decision-making ability. Thinking about death is what makes the preparation of a will difficult in itself; do not make matters worse for yourself by seeking perfection. *Structure* a plan, *discuss* it with your attorney, *prepare* the will, *review* it every year or two—this is all anyone can or should do.

Sample Situation

The various states have developed their own laws determining the economic consequence of divorce on concepts of fairness. Alimony, the periodic payment of money from the richer spouse to the poorer spouse, is being supplemented or substituted by equitable distribution. With *equitable distribution,* each spouse can receive one-half of all the assets acquired during the marriage—maybe more or less than one-half depending on the history of the marriage. But what if one spouse is the beneficiary of a trust?

A judge might react unsympathetically to the beneficiary of a substantial trust, and decide that this spouse is not in *need* of support (or perhaps able to *provide greater support* to the other spouse). However, if distributions from the trust are at the discretion of the trustee, the spouse/beneficiary would impress upon the court that future distributions are *not a sure thing*.

Money-Saving Suggestion

Rather than worrying about your legatee's marriage and whether or not this legacy should be put in trust, consider the possibility that your own marriage may disintegrate. A nuptial agreement with your spouse, which we discussed earlier in chapter 2, may be needed. This agreement can cover two situations: *if divorced,* what are the financial obligations of each spouse; if there is a *death* of a spouse, should the surviving spouse receive the minimal spousal share (the elective share that we also discussed in chapter 2), or are the spouses waiving this right. Think about it.

This worry about your legatee who might get divorced centers on a word that often appears in discussions of estate planning—*control.* The

hand from the grave can exercise some control, but there is a limit. My suggestion is that you worry less. Of course, a trust in the will is the control that sometimes is required.

POWER OF ATTORNEY; CONSERVATOR

You are probably familiar with a *power of attorney*. Simply stated, person A gives person B the rights of A, such as the right to withdraw A's money from a bank. It may be a *general power of attorney*, where B is treated in every situation as if B were A. For example, B can sell A's home or withdraw money from A's bank accounts. Or it can be a *limited power of attorney*, where B can legally bind A to just one transaction (or perhaps a few). For example, B is only authorized to have a power of attorney for a particular bank account.

There is a clause, called a *durable power* clause, that can be included with a power of attorney. This clause states that the power will remain in force *even if the person giving the power becomes mentally incompetent*. There is even a clause, called a *springing power* clause, that says the power is only *effective if and when the person giving the power becomes mentally incompetent*. There is no power of attorney, however, that *continues after the death of the person granting the power.*

If you are the person *giving* a power of attorney, be careful. You must have great trust in the person to whom you give your power. Be careful as well if you are the person *receiving* a power of attorney. If an old and sick person gives you a power, realize that you may have to answer for all your actions on behalf of that person. Remember reading in chapter 15 about the responsibility of the executor to act prudently or else risk the consequences of personal financial liability for every imprudence? The same standard applies here. You may be questioned years later; you cannot then say that this old and sick person authorized and supervised all your actions. Even if not actually stated in the power of attorney, implicit in the *authorization* is that you act *prudently*. What is also implicit is that your control of the money was not *supervised;* the enfeebled person gave you this control *only because unassisted financial management was no longer possible.*

A *conservator* is a person appointed by a court to represent a person who cannot manage his or her financial affairs. In some states the conservator goes under another title, such as guardian. A doctor usually is required to testify in court as to whether the person whose affairs are

to be supervised is able to manage alone. The person who petitions to become a conservator is questioned by the court on both motive and ability. A conservator is appointed only after unequivocal evidence has been presented to the court that a conservator is necessary. A *committee* has more extensive legal significance than a conservator. A committee is a person who not only manages the finances but also has the authority and responsibility to act in all matters on behalf of the incapacitated person. The appointment of the committee results in the loss of civil rights of the incapacitated person.

Let us compare the function of a conservator with that of a holder of a power of attorney. It is safer to be a conservator because your actions are reviewed by the court periodically (usually annually). With a power of attorney you are acting all alone, and are a target for those who may later want to question your conduct. This is the subject of our next sample situation.

Sample Situations

Looking at the interests of the *person receiving a power of attorney,* it is better to be appointed a conservator than to control another person's finances with a power of attorney (unless it is just for a short time, such as during a hospitalization). Imagine holding a person's power of attorney for six years, and then having someone ask you to account for every penny of *principal* and *investment income,* including interest, dividends, gains or losses, for the past six years. Someone who possesses a power of attorney for another individual may one day have to present such an accounting on how the incapacitated person's assets were invested and spent. Even if you were bonded, that wouldn't help *you.* Bonding is protection for *the person whose money you are managing.* If the bonding company has to make good on your mistakes, it will. It will then proceed to collect this money from you.

Looking at the interests of the *person giving a power of attorney,* it can be risky since great trust is being placed in another individual. The person you trust might be dishonest or reckless or generally incompetent. Be independent for as long as possible. There are alternatives, like an emergency joint bank account with a friend (which is described in the next money-saving suggestion), to assist in this regard.

The form for transferring power of attorney can be obtained at most stationery stores, but I recommend that you discuss its use with your attorney. In some situations a power of attorney *is appropriate.* But proceed

cautiously. Incidentally, if you want to give someone power over a particular bank account, the bank most likely requires that you use the bank's power of attorney form.

Money-Saving Suggestion

A client of advanced age who lived alone asked me if I had any suggestions on how to assure that her bills would be paid if she were hospitalized for a short period of time. She was particularly concerned about her rent, utility, and medical insurance bills. I advised her to have a joint bank account with a friend or relative and to give this person the right to withdraw funds. Because the friend is able to withdraw money from the account, I advised her to leave only about $2,500 in the account. The friend could then pay the bills with money withdrawn from the joint account. *This procedure avoids the problem of unpaid bills when you are in the hospital for a short stay.* It alleviates the fears that you might be evicted, that your telephone service might be disrupted, or that the grace period for late payment of an insurance premium might expire. In some situations there is no need to transfer power of attorney or establish a conservator *if you follow my joint bank account suggestion.*

MOURNING ACCOUNT

Some elderly folks have a worry about paying their funeral bill. This is a serious worry, one that cannot be put to rest by commenting, tongue in cheek, that the funeral director will not be able to sue you. For those who are concerned about these expenses, here are a few suggestions.

> I recommend that you tell your friend, whose name is on that *small bank account,* that these funds are to be used not only to pay bills during an emergency, such as your hospitalization, but also for funeral expenses. If you are not comfortable with this recommendation, perhaps one of the following suggestions will assist you.

> Since you obviously trust your executor (by giving this person the legal right to control all your assets after your death), consider opening *a savings account in your executor's name.* Deposit enough money in it to cover the anticipated funeral expenses.

Prepay the funeral expenses. This helps to assure that your burial wishes are carried out. However, make sure your executor has the receipt from the funeral home (and, as you first learned in chapter 5, make sure your *executor is fully informed of your burial wishes*). Keep in mind that the amount paid is perhaps just an estimate. But maybe the funeral home will agree to a fixed price, and any increased cost as a result of inflation will be offset by the interest the funeral home will have received on the money you paid.

You might also get some relief by realizing that a funeral home does not always require *instant payment*. It will give your closest relative, or your executor, a short period of time in which to gather the estate's assets and thus have money available for payment of this final bill.

Have you thought of *cremation?* It is not expensive, and it is the funeral of choice for more and more people. Cremation and a memorial service, in my opinion, is an appropriate way to go. A memorial service is a general reaffirmation of the worth of life and a review of the particular individual's basic goodness.

If you have a worry about your funeral bill, then resolve the problem now, and *never let it bother you again.*

Sample Situation

There are cases of people who die and no one knows whom to contact. Perhaps the body is discovered by the superintendent in the building where the deceased resided. Perhaps the person died while living in a shelter for the homeless. In these cases the community's public administrator takes care of the burial. *This is what is feared by some senior citizens.* It is not only the question of the payment for the final disposition of the body, but also whether the body is *claimed and put to rest.*

Families are now spread throughout the country, and even the world. The case of the elderly person who lives alone is not a unique one. However, the problem of claiming the body and putting it to rest is really the least important of quite a few problems that this elderly person encounters. Far more serious are the problems of *loneliness* (which often, but not necessarily, results from being alone), *health maintenance,* and *housing.* I believe that an appropriate standard by which to judge the decency of a society is the manner in which its elderly are treated. It is unfortunate that Congressman Claude Pepper of Florida is no longer with us. I am optimistic, however,

that other members of Congress will champion the cause of senior citizens and that the political power of older persons will continue to grow. Senior citizens are dedicated voters, and if demographic studies are correct, their numbers are dramatically increasing. Eventually, Congress will have to respond.

Money-Saving Suggestion

My suggestions to senior citizens who are alone include: try to develop a *friendship* with someone, perhaps someone who also is alone; join a *social group* in your neighborhood, perhaps at your church or synagogue; express your aloneness to a *relative,* and see if there is any expression of support; explore the possibility of relocating to a *senior citizen* housing development (but not to a nursing home); if you are able, *volunteer* your time to a favorite charity.

Bob Hope, in delivering a commencement address, gave this advice to those going out into the world: *don't go.* To those thinking about entering a nursing home, I give the same advice. The loss of independence is overwhelming; the nursing home alternative should be chosen only after all other reasonable options have been explored and rejected.

LIFE INSURANCE

One purpose of life insurance is to *pay any estate tax.* This is a particular need if an individual owns assets that are not liquid (for example, a building). It may be difficult for an estate to pay the estate tax without selling or mortgaging the asset.

Of course there are other important reasons for life insurance. *Through life insurance, survivors who relied upon a deceased's income can continue to live with financial security.* The period after death is a difficult time for the survivors. Surely it is not the time for them to cope with financial difficulties.

Both spouses should be insured, particularly in double-income families. If there is a dependent child, the amount of insurance needed can be substantial. This is especially true if one spouse has a job involving travel. Imagine if the nontraveling spouse were to die. What would be the cost of an around-the-clock, live-in helper? Maybe the cost of a larger home should also be anticipated, because of the extra space needed for the live-in helper. Explore your insurance needs. The cost of adequate insurance protection is well worth it.

There are two basic types of life insurance: *term insurance* and *whole-life insurance*. With term insurance, you pay the premium, and if you do not die during the term of the policy (usually one year), then you happily have lost your investment. Whole-life insurance, which is more expensive than term insurance, gives you life-insurance protection and a cash build-up in the policy. There are variations on term and whole-life insurance (including survivor whole-life insurance), which your insurance advisor can explain to you. After you have purchased insurance, remember to increase the coverage periodically to keep up with both your higher standard of living and inflation.

Sample Situation

Someone said to me that he was too poor to afford insurance. *The irony is that the poorer you are the greater your need for life insurance.* This is because your survivor will not be receiving any legacy from you, and the loss of your income may be followed by a period of increased expenses. It is difficult to solve the problem of being poor. But life insurance is one way to ease the burden on your survivors. Life insurance should be on your priority list of investments.

Money-Saving Suggestion

Perhaps the *beneficiary* of a life insurance policy should be *the owner of the policy.* Here is one way to keep a life insurance payout free from estate tax:

There is $100,000 of life insurance on Mary's life, and the proceeds are payable to John. *John owns the policy and pays the premium.* This way, Mary's total estate does not include the $100,000.

You can also have a trust own the policy. *This saves estate tax when the insured dies, and also when the primary beneficiary dies.* Here is how you implement this suggestion:

There is $100,000 of life insurance on Mary's life, and the proceeds are payable to *an irrevocable trust that owns the policy (ideally, from its inception) and pays the premium.* The trust receives the $100,000 upon Mary's death. The trust agreement directs that John is to receive the income from the $100,000 for the rest of his life. The trust agreement

also directs who eventually is to receive the $100,000 upon John's death. This way, neither Mary's estate nor John's estate includes the $100,000 of insurance proceeds.

Keep in mind, however, that an insurance policy, such as a whole life policy, has a *value* to it. For example, if *John owns* the policy that *insures Mary's life,* then, upon *John's death,* his estate will include the value of this policy. Consult your insurance advisor. Also, compare the premiums of different companies; there is a difference among carriers. Inquire as to whether the policy is automatically renewed each year, or whether you are required to have periodic physicals. If you are a smoker, I urge that you give it up; not only will you feel better, your life insurance premium is lower because your life expectancy is longer.

COMMON DISASTER

A common disaster is relevant to a discussion of wills because people dying in the disaster may have an interest in each other's estates. These situations are not so unusual; they can occur when there are tragedies such as fires, automobile collisions, or airline crashes, any of which could result in multiple deaths of family members.

Let us take the example of an aunt who is leaving her entire estate to her niece. Perhaps they are the closest of friends, travel extensively together, and generally share their lives. Therefore, there is a chance that they will die together, perhaps when traveling. For the aunt's will, here are two recommendations that might be considered:

As mentioned at the start of this book, it is always good to have a *successor legatee.* Although the aunt's will leaves all the rest, residue, and remainder of her estate to her niece, the will should also state to whom the property goes if the niece predeceases the aunt.

The aunt's will should also have a clause (called a *common disaster clause* or a *simultaneous death clause*) such as the following: "If any beneficiary under this my Will and I should die in a common disaster or under such conditions that it would be difficult or impossible to determine which of us died first, then such beneficiary shall be deemed for the purposes of this Will to have *predeceased me."* This way, if the aunt and niece die together, the aunt's assets go to the successor legatee named in the aunt's will, and not the legatees of the niece.

Suppose the aunt decides to have the simultaneous death clause state the opposite presumption; that is, if she and the niece die together, then the aunt is deemed as having predeceased the niece. The aunt's estate is then distributed to those named in the *niece's will*. If the niece does not have a will, the aunt's estate goes to the *niece's next of kin*. With respect to my example, I know of no reason for the aunt to make this choice.

If you have a common disaster clause in your will, read it. Learn which choice *you* made; find out *why* this choice was made. In summary: you control where your assets go if *your legatee has predeceased you* by having named a *successor legatee;* furthermore, you are also controlling where your money goes if *you and your legatee die together* by having a *common disaster clause* in your will.

Sample Situations

In the case of simultaneous death of a married couple, the common disaster clause is crucial.

The first case to look at is the married couple, *without children from this marriage,* who are killed in an accident. Suppose, for example, that the wife survives the husband by a few minutes. Unless your state has a law dealing with this situation, or unless the *husband's* will has a common disaster clause, those named in the *wife's* will (or in the absence of a will, the wife's next of kin) receive the husband's assets as well as the wife's assets. This is significant for the couple without children, because the *husband's and wife's successor legatees might not be the same people.* It is also significant for a couple where there is a child or children from a *previous marriage.* Although each spouse might leave everything to the other, the wife might leave everything to her nieces and nephews (or a child from a previous marriage), in the event that her husband predeceases her. The husband, on the other hand, might leave everything to his nieces and nephews (or a child from a previous marriage) if his wife predeceases him.

Another case to consider is that of the wealthy couple. For tax reasons, the will of the wealthier spouse might state that the other spouse is the survivor in the event of a common disaster. This is particularly important if only one spouse has assets in excess of $600,000. This couple has to plan this clause carefully, as well as every aspect of the will, to utilize fully the opportunity to have up to $600,000 pass tax free through the *poorer spouse's estate.* Pages could be written about this situation; if it applies to you, I leave it to your attorney to explain how this tax savings is achieved.

Money-Saving Suggestion

Do not rely on state law to cover the situation of common disaster; have a simultaneous death clause in your will. Your legatee may die with you in an accident. In most situations you do not want this legacy ultimately to be distributed to this person's legatees or next of kin.

NONMARITAL RELATIONSHIPS

Suppose you want to leave your estate to someone you love, but you are aware that your closest relatives *do not approve* of this person. Perhaps it is a homosexual relationship, a heterosexual relationship not sanctioned by marriage, or an interracial relationship. Perhaps other people close to you do not believe this person is worthy to live with such *perfection embodied by the one and only you.* Here is what you can do:

> Your bankbooks and other investments can have your friend's name on them; use either the *in trust for* or *joint account with right of survivorship* forms of ownership. (Once again, this assures that the asset goes to the other person on the account and is not distributed through your will. However, it does not remove this asset from your taxable estate.)
>
> Have a *will* prepared; leave your assets to this person if that is your wish.
>
> Have a clause in the will—the *in terrorem clause* discussed earlier — stating that if a person challenges the will, this person receives nothing.
>
> Finally, if you are suffering from a terminal illness, you might want to make a *gift* of your assets to the one you love. File a gift tax return if necessary (as you know, it is necessary if the gift exceeds $10,000). Be sure to unequivocally deliver the gift to the recipient, and make sure the recipient unequivocally accepts the gift. This is how your attorney would advise you. But your attorney would conclude with this serious and practical warning: once the gift is given, *you have no recourse to reclaim it.* The seriousness of this situation is twofold: the gift might be all your money, and it might be money that is desperately needed for medical treatment. *Proceed cautiously.*

Estate problems often occur when the deceased has died of AIDS (Acquired Immune Deficiency Syndrome). Family members are judgmental of the person remembered in the will.

Sample Situation

Do not confuse highly publicized palimony cases with estate cases. Palimony cases occur when former friends split, and they are fighting between themselves. Estate cases on nontraditional relationships occur when *the friend of the deceased receives the deceased's assets, and the family of the deceased questions the will.*

What the will says is almost always what happens. *So make sure there is a will.* Without a will (or an "in trust for" account or "joint account with right of survivorship" or a "living trust"), the most loved person has no chance of receiving a thing.

Money-Saving Suggestion

Severe family disruption can occur over items possessing virtually no economic value. As the combatants often state, it is the principle of the matter that is important. More likely, it is a deep-rooted problem that erupts over a question as trivial as "Who gets the five-cent refundable cans owned by the deceased?" A costly will contest can result.

Furniture is often a contested area. Here is a suggestion for two people living together. Both should have a list of what each owns; the list should state how ownership was obtained and that there is no intention of making a gift of furniture to family members. This helps to avoid two problems: the potential claim of a family member that the furniture of the deceased was never owned by the deceased, but only *loaned* to the person by this family member; and conversely, the potential claim of a family member of the deceased that, during the final illness, the deceased gave the furniture as a *gift* to the family member.

Another suggestion for cases in which a will challenge is imminent is to *videotape the signing of the will.* The film might then be admissible as evidence to show testamentary capacity. However, videotaping the signing of a will is a new development and there are some possible dangers. For example, the terminally ill person might appear so debilitated on film that the videotape might do more harm than good. Nevertheless, videotaping the signing of the will is something to consider.

TOO RICH FOR MEDICAID

The poor qualify for medical assistance through the government program known as Medicaid. "Poor" means "very poor," a net worth of less than approximately $4,750 and minimal income. There is not much you can do about the government's definition of "poor." There is, however, something that you can do to decrease your net worth. *Give gifts!*

The tactic of giving gifts, and thus becoming poor enough to qualify for government assistance, can present a minefield of problems. I recommend legal advice, but here are some things to consider:

Apply for Medicaid no sooner than *two and one-half years* after the gifts are made. You may want to wait three full calendar years so that the tax returns for the previous three years show only minimal income. I recommend that tax returns be filed, even if the income is *below the amount that triggers the filing requirement*. It provides evidence of little or no income. Also, check with your attorney to be sure that the two and one-half year period has remained the minimum interval between gift-giving and qualification for Medicaid.

Most people will not make large gifts, so *proceed diplomatically* if you suggest to an older family member that gift-giving may allow eventual Medicaid eligibility. That person's accumulated money is the product of a lifetime of hard work and is not readily given away.

Some people are happier giving money to a nursing home than to a relative, particularly to a relative who asks for a gift. Some people believe that *better medical and nursing service is rendered* when the patient, rather than the government, is making the payment. Some people also believe that a *stigma is attached to welfare payments,* and thus they will not apply for Medicaid. In most situations the nursing home employees who provide the care *do not know whether the patient or the government is paying.* As for stigmatizing a Medicaid recipient, remember that many of them have paid *quite a lot of taxes over the years* as well as having made *other valuable contributions* to our society. If a society cannot, or worse *will not,* provide for the *poorest* among its *oldest* citizens, then this society will not long endure.

In most if not all states, a person has an obligation to support a spouse, so *gifts of all your assets to your spouse will not enable you to qualify for Medicaid later on.*

Move slowly, carefully, in good taste, and with advice of wise counsel. You may have heard stories where money was given away to meet Medicaid qualifications. Either a crime was committed by defrauding the government with a false answer to the "were gifts made" question on the Medicaid application, or some careful legal planning was successfully implemented.

Sample Situation

Doctors' bills, nursing home charges, home care expenses, medication, and all the other health-related costs incurred by the aged and sick patient may total a tremendous sum of money. Four suggestions might help you avoid this calamity: do your best to *stay healthy,* pay for a very comprehensive medical *insurance policy,* give *gifts* of your money, and consider having a *living will.*

A sample situation on gifts that I remember most vividly concerned a person who asked me if I would speak to his elderly female relative who was leaving everything to him. He wanted her to start making gifts to him, because he was afraid medical expenses would substantially erode, or perhaps even eliminate, her assets. When I asked where the relative lived, he responded, without any embarrassment, "Somewhere in New Jersey, I haven't been out there in quite a while." I advised him that there was no chance of receiving a gift, and that such a request might jeopardize his legacy.

Money-Saving Suggestions

Gifts made by a person who is relatively well off can make that person poor enough to qualify for government aid. I recommend these gifts, however, only where there is a loving family relationship that has existed for many years. The successful instances of this gift-giving technique are where the family member is *presently living with the potential recipients of the gift.* The person making the gift is reciprocating the love already shown by other family members. The eventual qualification for Medicaid is a possible family bonus some years later.

Do not make such gifts when the door of the hospital is being opened. The gifts should be made when the giver is still relatively healthy. A few years should elapse before applying for Medicaid. *The applicant for Medicaid must explain to the government all gifts made within a few years prior to the application.* Unless the explanation shows some extraordinary circumstances for gifts made shortly before applying for Medicaid (and I cannot think of any example), the applicant will not be considered eligible.

SELLING YOUR RESIDENCE

The most valuable asset in many estates is the family residence. There are two concerns associated with the sale of a home, *taxes* and *emotions*.

I offer four ideas on the *tax consequences* of selling your home:

> If you sell your home and *buy (bought) or build (built) a new one within a time period specified in the tax law* (currently *two years,* so I will use two years when referring to this time period), the entire profit from the sale is tax deferred if your replacement residence costs more than the adjusted sales price of your old home. This applies to everyone, regardless of age.

> If you are over the age of fifty-five, up to $125,000 of profit from the sale might be exempt from tax, even if you do not buy or build a new home within two years. *This is a tax break that can be used only once in a lifetime.*

> If you do not buy or build a new residence within two years and you do not qualify for the over age fifty-five treatment, *your profit from the sale is taxed just like regular income.*

> *The stepped-up basis that your heirs will receive at the time of your death might be a tax reason for you to hold onto your home.* This situation exists if the home has appreciated in value by more than $125,000 and also if a new residence is not going to be purchased. Therefore, if you sell it (and do not defer payment of the tax by buying a new home), you will pay a tax on the portion of your gain exceeding $125,000. By holding onto it *until your death,* both you and your heirs avoid any tax on the increase in value in the home.

The *emotional problem* associated with selling a residence is that the home might be too big for its one or two occupants. Some readers may be in the highly emotional state known as the *empty nest syndrome:* the children are grown, and now the big house seems so empty. This loneliness is extremely severe if a loved one has recently died, so the idea of selling the home is considered. *But do not act in haste.* In the next few pages we will explore the emotional and social costs of selling the residence and moving, but first a sample situation and a money-saving suggestion.

Sample Situation

To help you understand the following money-saving suggestion, here is a quick legal description of a cooperative (co-op) apartment and a condominium (condo) apartment.

In a co-op the building is owned by a corporation, and you buy shares of stock in this corporation. You are given a lease (called a proprietary lease) to the apartment you occupy. If the building has a mortgage, you pay a portion of the cost of the mortgage. *In a condo you actually own a piece of real property,* which is your apartment. There is usually no mortgage on the building. It is easier to sell a condo because, unlike a co-op, you do not have to ask the neighbors (serving as the building's directors) to approve a potential buyer.

Money-Saving Suggestion

As you know, if you sell your residence and buy or build a new one within two years, you can defer paying any tax on the entire profit from the sale. However, to defer paying a tax on the entire profit, you must replace your residence with a more expensive home than the one you sold. Here is a thought for someone who has sold a home and has bought a cooperative apartment. The cost of the new apartment includes not only what you pay the seller, but also the *amount of mortgage on the building* attributed to your percentage of ownership of the corporation that owns the building. Here is an example:

A home that was purchased a few years ago for $40,000 is sold at $100,000, for a profit of $60,000. In order to defer a tax on this $60,000 profit, a new home must be bought or built for at least $100,000 within two years. Suppose a new home is bought for only $80,000? Then there is a current tax on $20,000 of the profit. But if a co-op is purchased for $80,000, the portion of the building mortgage assumed by the buyer is added to the purchase price of $80,000, and perhaps this additional amount increases the total cost to $100,000 or more.

With the popularity of co-op apartments, perhaps you will encounter this situation. Since a *condo* usually does not have a mortgage on the building, it is rare that this situation applies.

RELOCATING

States of preference for people who choose to retire have included Arizona, California, Florida, Kentucky, North Carolina, and South Carolina. I advise you to think twice before you move to the promised land of sun and fun for seniors. The best place to retire might be right where you are now living. The emotional trauma of relocating is double-barreled: the upheaval of *making the move* is followed by the uncertainty of *establishing an identity* in the new community.

As for the move itself, it is not the one-day affair when the movers arrive and load the truck. It is many months of sorting out, throwing out, and reliving a lifetime of memories. It is a round of saying goodbye to those who are close to you and, interestingly enough, those you recently discovered are close to you. You are saying goodbye to your roots: friends, shopkeepers, bankers, ministers, and family members who have decided not to relocate. *Any retired person I have ever spoken to about this move has expressed feelings of loss and pain.*

The second part of the trauma is establishing an identity in the new location—different people, different climate, a new and different life. Perhaps this is not the stage of life to start a new existence. Remember the Tom Dooley television advertisement where he exhorted the viewers to come on down. (Where? Florida!) Looking back on this advertisement, I now realize that it was a promise of a fountain of youth; the advertisement showed the youngest retirees I have ever seen. Older Americans went, while younger Americans counted the years until retirement.

Give some thought (and I mean a year of thought) to relocating after a spouse or close relative dies. The time of grief is not the time to make such a dramatic change. Many times we take life's pleasures for granted. The friendly local merchants, the friendships developed over the years, the memberships in a church group or social club, and the characters who bring the community to life—they are all a significant part of your life. For the older person, particularly one who has lost a loved one, the security of familiarity is important. *Relocation can be exhilarating but also traumatic.*

Sample Situation

I was recently told of a couple who had lived in their home for forty-eight years, decided to retire, and purchased a new home *without even seeing it.* They relied on pictures and on the glowing description of the

leisurely life in this retirement heaven. The person telling me the story was surprised and saddened. These were his parents' next door neighbors, and he had known them his whole life, keeping in contact with them even after he married and moved away from home. He said that they were a part of his life, and when they moved he felt sad for them, for his parents, and for himself. To think they moved without even seeing their new home! Surprise was not my reaction.

The retirement move has been reinforced by advertising, which seductively entices retired people to find happiness *elsewhere* by crossing the River Jordan and entering the promised land. When the time comes that the body is older and wearier, there is a greater susceptibility to this preconditioned idea that a different location is what the older body needs. *Perhaps where you are now living is the best location for your retirement.*

Money-Saving Suggestions

Before you make a decision on permanent relocation, *take a vacation for a few months in the retirement community of your dreams.* The extra expense of renting accommodations for this long vacation may prove to be worthwhile. During this vacation you can decide whether the dream is reality. If it really is a dream come true, then relocate; if not, you have saved yourself some heartache and some money.

Here is something I learned from a client who had recently retired. If you live in a large city, *become a tourist in your city:* visit the museums, the stores, and the local attractions. If your city has a sightseeing bus tour, take it. At least get to know your city, or perhaps reacquaint yourself with your city before you relocate. Maybe you will like it. Maybe you will even stay!

ON BEING A WIDOW OR WIDOWER

In some families, one of the spouses is the dominating force on budgeting and investing. My overall experience among clients has been that this chore is pretty much gender neutral. With some older clients, however, this division of labor sometimes slants more to the husband.

Both spouses should understand money. One of the spouses will outlive the other, and it is difficult when the less knowledgeable money manager is the survivor. Therefore, start sharing your knowledge of money with your spouse. Both husbands and wives should know their stockbroker,

their banker, their insurance agent, and their trusted family attorney. Each should know the family's monthly cost of living, and each should know how to manage the family budget. A great development in education has been the proliferation of adult education courses. Take a few of these courses together, particularly on financial management. By planning now, the eventual survivor of your marriage will be able to cope with the return to single life.

You have just been reading about money, and whether a widow or widower can handle money. But the far greater problems encountered by widows and widowers are *emotional in nature*. They have to cope with feelings of anger, regret, and loneliness. The *anger* may be directed at the deceased spouse, God, the physician, relatives, government institutions such as the Social Security Administration, the executor, the attorney, and friends who are perceived as being distant. The plaintive cry is, "Why have I been left alone?" There is *regret* at not having fully shared the good times with the deceased spouse. The survivor wishes that the fulfillment of dreams had not been deferred, because now it is too late. *Loneliness,* along with helplessness, anxiety, and fear, engulfs the surviving spouse, who now must face the future alone. There is also the nagging doubt as to whether solo living is possible.

Sadly, the surviving spouse may try an emotional release through abuse of alcohol or drugs. However, by planning for the eventuality of a spouse's death, you can lessen the pain. Be financially independent; have some individual interests; develop a friendship or two. Most of all, *have confidence that you will survive the pain.* Do not reject a helping hand extended by family members; *you are deserving of this help.*

Sample Situation

There is a story about the married man who had a guilt-provoking clause in his will. He requested to be cremated, to have his ashes mixed in a can full of paint, which would then be used to paint the ceiling of the bedroom.

Perhaps this story elicits a chuckle. But the subject of the story, *guilt,* is both relevant and serious. The guilt felt by the surviving spouse is *self-inflicted* and *unnecessary*. However, it is equally as painful as the guilt-provoking clause in the deceased spouse's will. Often a surviving spouse feels guilty, despite a history of emotional balance. This results from the unanticipated sense of relief that the spouse has died, and this relief is experienced for two reasons. The *surviving* spouse is relieved that the burden of the painstaking care of an ill spouse has finally ended; the surviv-

ing spouse is also relieved that the *deceased* spouse is no longer suffering. Such relief is normal and should not be *a source of guilt*. If the surviving widow or widower rejects the helping hand extended by children of the marriage (or other close family members), guilt is often the culprit. An awareness of this problem might help both the surviving spouse and the rejected family members understand why the survivor is sometimes not too cooperative in accepting advice or assistance.

Money-Saving Suggestions

It is never too early to start planning for retirement and the possibility of being the surviving spouse. Plan for both the *economic* and the *emotional* consequences of widowhood. Plan on living retirement as a couple, but also plan for the possibility that you will be the survivor of the marriage.

Learn to be independent. Start today. A *net worth statement* should be prepared; it allows both spouses a clearer view of their financial picture, and it is also a start for when they begin planning eventual retirement. If the couple does not understand money, they should start to learn about it today. Each partner should also develop an interest in some activity in which he or she participates as a solo, not as a member of a couple. These suggestions will somewhat ease the emotional trauma the survivor will experience when the spouse dies.

AN ESTATE TAX REVIEW FOR WEALTHY SPOUSES

There is no estate tax on *any amount received by a spouse* (again, assuming this spouse a United States citizen). After the death of both spouses, however, there is a federal estate tax on everything over $600,000, and the tax starts at 37 percent. For example, suppose the combined net worth of a couple is $700,000. Here is what happens: a spouse dies, and the surviving spouse can receive everything without the payment of any estate tax. When the surviving spouse then dies, the children (or whoever) get everything, and the estate tax is $37,000. Here is a proposed estate plan for this couple with a *total net worth of $700,000;* it shows how this $37,000 estate tax on the estate of the surviving spouse can be avoided:

Assets in the amount of $500,000 are jointly owned; the husband owns $100,000 individually; and the wife owns $100,000 individually. The husband, through his will, leaves $100,000 to his wife, in trust, and

she will receive the income from this $100,000. The $500,000 belongs to the wife upon the husband's death through the joint ownership. The wife's will is a mirror image of the husband's. The tax benefit is that the $100,000 currently in a trust is not taxed in the eventual estate of the surviving spouse.

Let me repeat the *economic result* of this plan on the *surviving spouse:* the surviving spouse has $600,000 (the $500,000 that had been jointly owned and the $100,000 individually owned), plus the income from the $100,000 trust. Let me repeat the *estate taxation result* on the *estate of the surviving spouse.* This *$100,000* trust is not included in the taxable estate of the second spouse to die, and thus the surviving spouse has a tax-free estate of *$600,000* (the $500,000 that had been jointly owned and the $100,000 individually owned).

As you already learned in chapter 17, a couple can leave up to $1.2 million free of federal estate tax. But how? It is the same trust technique as just suggested to the couple with total assets of $700,000. The husband owns $600,000 individually; the wife owns $600,000 individually; and each leaves everything to the other in a testamentary trust. Upon the death of the first spouse, there is no estate tax; upon the death of the surviving spouse there is no estate tax, because *the $600,000 in the testamentary trust of the first spouse to die is not included in the taxable estate of the surviving spouse.*

Sample Situations

Here are some other estate tax ideas for the wealthy couple who has total assets over $600,000, as learned from case histories of actual couples with substantial assets:

Do nothing. Many spouses want to receive everything; they do not want to be bothered with a trust set up in a will, and they do not worry if there is an estate tax *after they both have died.*

Again do nothing. However, after the first spouse has died, the surviving spouse might consider giving gifts to reduce net worth closer to the $600,000 amount.

Use a trust as explained on the previous page.

A husband and a wife might each consider *increasing the amount left to those other than the spouse,* which is the subject of the following suggestion.

Money-Saving Suggestion

Consider increasing the amount left to *those other than the spouse.* Here is an example:

> A husband and wife have a net worth of $700,000. The problem is that after both have died, there will be a $37,000 estate tax. They could own $500,000 of assets jointly. The wife owns $100,000 of assets in her name only; the husband owns $100,000 of assets in his name only. The wife could then leave $100,000 to their (or her) children; her husband receives the $500,000 of jointly owned property if he survives his wife. Similarly, the husband could leave $100,000 to their (or his) children, and his wife receives the $500,000 of jointly owned property if she survives him.

With this suggestion the *surviving spouse* has $600,000 (the $500,000 that had been jointly owned plus the $100,000 individually owned). This plan, rather than the previous plan, has the benefit that *there is no trust;* the detriment is that money is dropped down to the younger generation *while either the husband or wife is still alive.* Some people like this suggestion; others say, "So what if our children have to pay an estate tax!"

SHOULD SPOUSES OWN ASSETS JOINTLY?

Estate tax consequences for wealthy spouses have just been reviewed. Joint ownership was again mentioned. Let's review this option. It is important, and often misunderstood, which could be costly.

If a couple's total net worth is under $600,000, then I generally recommend joint ownership. This way everything goes to the surviving spouse and there is no need to go to court with the will of the first spouse to die. Succinctly and legally stated, *probate is avoided.* There is no federal estate tax either when the first spouse dies or when the surviving spouse dies.

Here are two situations, however, where joint ownership must be avoided:

First, if some money is left in the will to someone other than the spouse, then that person will receive nothing *if a husband and wife jointly own everything.* This occurs because the surviving spouse receives everything through the joint ownership, and there is nothing left to be distributed through the will. Therefore, if a spouse wants to leave $10,000 to a daughter, make sure that the $10,000 is solely owned, that is, it does not have both spouses' names on the account. Taken one step further, the spouse may want to put *the daughter's name on a $10,000 account as the designated beneficiary* so that this account also avoids probate.

Second, if any trust is used (for example, something left to a spouse in a trust set up in a will to avoid estate tax when both spouses have died), then there must be a solely-owned asset to fund the trust. Otherwise, the surviving spouse gets everything through joint ownership, and there is nothing available to fund the trust set up in the will.

Remember our previous discussions (in chapter 18 and again at the beginning of this chapter) on stepped-up basis at time of death: when spouses own property jointly, one-half is treated as belonging to each spouse. The significance of this fact is brought out in my next money-saving suggestion, and is another reason spouses may decide *against* joint ownership.

Sample Situation

The case for anyone, including husbands and wives, owning assets jointly with right of survivorship is to avoid the costs of probate. For many individuals this avoidance of probate costs makes joint ownership desirable. Be aware, however, that joint ownership lessens your control over the asset and may allow creditors of one owner of the asset to tie up the asset. But the case where it is absolutely essential that spouses, or anyone else, do *not* own all their property jointly is where there are testamentary trusts. Once again I stress this rule: if there are testamentary trusts (established to *avoid estate tax* and to determine who *eventually receives the money* when the surviving spouse dies), there must be assets owned solely by the husband and solely by the wife. Otherwise, *there will be no available funds to be held by the trust.*

Money-Saving Suggestions

When a joint owner dies, the Internal Revenue Service presumes that this deceased owner held the *entire* interest in the property (and although this presumption can be rebutted, it is sometimes a difficult task). However, if the joint owners are husband and wife, the law concludes that each owns half of the asset. You saw this example at the outset of this chapter. Let me show you a situation where it might be advantageous from a tax point of view for either a husband or wife to have *sole* ownership of an asset.

Suppose a husband and wife jointly own an asset that has increased in value. *It might be advisable to have the asset solely owned by the spouse with the shorter life expectancy, rather than jointly owned.* This is particularly true if there is the possibility of the asset being sold by the surviving spouse. For example, suppose a sixty-year-old wife and a seventy-seven-year-old husband own a building. They might decide to have the *husband own the property in his name alone.* Upon his death (which actuarily will occur first), if the property is then sold by the widow, no income tax is owed on the sale. The reason for this tax consequence is that any gain upon sale is measured from the value at the time of the owner's death (the stepped-up basis at time of death which we have already discussed in chapter 18).

However, if jointly owned (which is the example at the outset of this chapter), upon the death of the husband, he is considered to have owned only one-half the asset. Therefore, only his half of the asset receives the stepped-up basis. But remember that decisions are based not *only* on taxation considerations. Perhaps one spouse does not want the *other spouse to have sole ownership of the asset.* Most importantly, do not start transferring ownership of assets without discussing with your attorney *all the ramifications of this generalized summary,* particularly if you live in a community property state.

MORE ON ATTORNEYS

There are many books on the subject of inheritance. Most of them have a clear message—*stay away from attorneys.* Form books, "how to avoid probate" books, and books about how inheritances are dissipated through legal fees are constantly being published. The cry is for joint ownership; the clamor is for living trusts.

But here is something that many of the how-to books overlook. The attorney makes money not in writing wills, not in probating wills, and not in giving legal advice to the personal representative of the estate. These fees only pay the attorney's office expenses. The attorney makes the real money—and a substantial amount of it—*when something goes wrong*. The fees earned when a wealthy person dies can be large, because the problems can involve substantial amounts of money. The legal problems are launched by *aggressive heirs* who realize that the affairs of the deceased are in disarray, or the problems are launched by an Internal Revenue Service agent drooling at the possibility of a *substantial tax.*

My point is that the legal fee resulting from following general advice, which may be incomplete or inaccurate for a particular situation, will be substantially higher than the legal fee that would have been charged at the outset.

Sample Situation

Just as sometimes there is resentment toward attorneys who charge a fee because someone dies and assets have to be distributed, there also is resentment toward those who receive the assets of the deceased. I have witnessed this in so many cases. As one person said to me: "It is so unfair that my dullard relative gets all that money."

Some years ago, this idea was expressed in a more scholarly manner in this excerpt from the *Law Review* of the University of California:

> Inherited wealth is bestowed in an arbitrary fashion which may tend to be inefficient, particularly when compared with the distribution of earned wealth. The latter is generally distributed according to the productivity of the earner. . . . In contrast, inheritance does not tend to flow to those who have proven they can efficiently allocate resources into areas valued by the society. Indeed, bequests are frequently made to those in greatest need—the poorer or the less competent. Hence, there is a tendency for inheritance to flow to those least capable of efficiently employing it. . . . Special problems of efficiency arise when a business is inherited, for the incapable head of an inherited business is much more difficult to get rid of than a hired hand who proves himself incompetent. (22 *UCLA Law Review* 903, 916-917, [1975])

Money-Saving Suggestion

Your need for an attorney is in proportion to your net worth; the wealthier you are, the greater your need to see an attorney. Wealth is a vague standard; however, one yardstick is that $600,000 threshold amount that the federal government has established in the estate tax law. Another standard is your degree of concern that whatever money you have—maybe $20,000—goes to *whom you choose, quickly and inexpensively.* But the *peace of mind* you can experience by discussing your affairs with a trusted attorney should be reason enough for you to consider seeking advice.

INVESTING YOUR LEGACY

Often a legacy is received by someone who is not experienced in handling finances, and there is confusion about how to invest it. Though you should consult your bank or investment counselor, one investment I recommend that is both safe and lucrative is United States Treasury Department securities. I recently read that over the last twenty-five years, these securities outperformed stocks, bonds, gold, silver, oil, coins, and stamps. An additional benefit of Treasury securities is that the yield is free of both state and local income tax.

A question often asked is: Which Treasury security should be purchased, the short-term bill, the intermediate-term note, or the long-term bond? It is a difficult question to answer because it requires a prediction as to where interest rates offered to investors are heading. If you predict a higher rate of return in future years, then purchase a short-term Treasury bill. When it expires you can then buy a treasury security that may have a higher rate of return. If you think rates are now relatively high, perhaps the long-term bond is the choice for you. If you are still in doubt, perhaps the intermediate-term, two-year Treasury note is best.

Keep your recently acquired money *out of the stock market.* If you disagree with me, then consider getting into the stock market gradually, and with the advice of a competent broker recommended to you by a trusted and knowledgeable friend. I give the same advice about *real estate—avoid making a big plunge with those legacy dollars.* If you do, make sure you first educate yourself about real estate. Entry into the real estate market can be financially rewarding (particularly in times of inflation), but it must be done slowly and shrewdly.

If you have received a legacy, be cautious when approached by any investment advisors, certified public accountants, certified financial planners,

insurance agents, salespeople, stockbrokers, real estate brokers, or any other people who contact you about investments within a year of the person's death. *Perhaps these advisors have learned of your legacy through an obituary or through public records in the courthouse.* This is a difficult and emotional time for you, so it is not a good time to hire new advisors. You are vulnerable to get-rich-quick schemes, particularly if your legacy is laden with guilt. Invest your legacy in United States Treasury Department securities. My runner-up investment is a deposit at your local bank—one insured by the federal government (FDIC). With a United States Treasury Department security or an insured bank account, you avoid the difficult analysis that goes into hiring a financial advisor and then evaluating complicated investment alternatives.

Sample Situation

Tax-exempt bonds issued by municipalities have the benefit of being free of any federal tax. If issued by your state, then they are also free of your state tax. But there are three areas of concern that I pass along to you.

The first is straightforward: make sure your tax-exempt bond is, in fact, tax exempt. *The yield on some bonds issued by municipalities may be taxable.* Be sure to discuss any contemplated purchase of tax-exempt bonds with your tax advisor, and determine whether you will be taxed on any of the income.

The second concern rests with the *safety of the investment.* Bonds issued by municipalities, unlike the Treasury securities, are not guaranteed by the federal government. Essentially, with municipal bonds you are relying on the financial stability of the municipality. Some bonds, however, are insured; but the yield is lower than uninsured bonds of comparable quality.

The third concern lies in the *volatility of the value* of the tax-exempt municipal bonds. Keep this rule in mind: *if interest rates go up, the value of your bond goes down.* Suppose your thirty-year bond, in the face amount of $100,000, yields interest of ten percent. Assume that the interest rate offered to investors increases to fifteen percent. Perhaps as little as $66,666 would be paid for your $100,000 bond. This is because $66,666 would yield interest income of $10,000 from an investment yielding fifteen percent, the same yield from your $100,000 bond. This danger of loss of principal is not so acute if you are going to hold your bond until maturity. However, if you hold the bond until maturity, you earn less on your money (in my

example, ten percent rather than fifteen percent) than the investor whose *capital was available for investment in the higher-yielding bond offerings.*

Money-Saving Suggestions

Since no one knows the future, *no one can tell whether today's interest rate is high or low relative to what the unknown future rate will be.* Therefore, I suggest intermediate-term Treasury securities. For those who prefer tax-exempt municipal bonds, I also suggest the intermediate-term bonds.

Another suggestion is that you buy your United States Treasury Department securities directly from any of the twelve Federal Reserve Banks. That way you save the $25 to $50 handling fee charged by many banks and brokerage firms.

LIVING AND DYING

Planning for death is important, and so is understanding money. But ask yourself if you have ever seen an armored truck, laden with money, as part of a funeral procession. I haven't, so I have concluded—like many others before me—you can't take it with you. *The life you live, and hopefully enjoy, is what is most important.*

The generation reaching middle age in the 1990s will have tremendous financial gain from the legacies received from their parents, who were the children of the Depression. But the more valuable legacy we have already received is the example of the lives led by those who are now our elder citizens.

Sample Situations

Robert Louis Stevenson was in poor health the greater part of his life, but everyone knew he was the world's greatest optimist. One day his wife went into his room and saw him cheerfully working on his manuscript. "I suppose you will tell me that it is a glorious day," she said to him. "Yes," he replied, as he looked out at the sunlight streaming through his window, "I refuse to permit a row of medicine bottles to block the horizon."

There is also this story, told by an Alabama attorney, which I read in the *American Bar Association Journal* a couple of years ago. An attorney's mother asked him, "Do you know how to fix it so some other woman won't be able to marry your father for my money after I die?" The attorney

explained to his mother the use of trusts, but his mother was not satisfied. The attorney thought long and hard. When he told his mother that he had a solution, her eyes lit up. "Spend it now," the attorney said. My sad sequel to this story is that she will not spend it now. Like so many elderly people today, she will be afraid her money will run out before she dies.

Money-Saving Suggestion

My suggestion to this woman is to consider purchasing a joint and survivor annuity from an insurance company. In return for her principal amount, she receives a monthly check for as long as she lives, and then her husband, if he survives her, receives a monthly check for the rest of his life. This way Dad is protected from "the other woman."

I end this book with a general observation on money. So many people have extreme attitudes on the subject—either being so *thrifty* that life is not enjoyed to the fullest extent possible, or by being so *profligate* that life is one financial crisis after another. *To the big savers,* I commend your discipline, but I suggest that if you can afford something, like that trip always planned but never taken, then spend the money and enjoy it. Remember that even this book has not taught you how to take it with you. *To the big spenders,* I express my amazement at your inventiveness, but I suggest that the pain of the credit card payments offsets the pleasure of the goods and services purchased on optimism.

I hope that this book has enriched your life, perhaps by showing you ways to save money or, more importantly, by helping you solve a few worrisome problems.

Appendices

Appendix A

A Sample Will

Here is a sample will and an accompanying Affidavit of Witnesses to give you an idea of the form and content of these documents. Because laws differ from state to state and because your particular situation is unique, this sample will is set forth as an example only and thus not intended for use, whether in whole or in part, by the reader. Your will should be prepared by an attorney.

I, THOMAS DOE, residing at (address), do hereby make, publish and declare this instrument to be my Last Will and Testament, hereby revoking any and all wills and codicils heretofore made by me.

FIRST: I direct that all my unsecured enforceable debts and funeral expenses, the expenses of my last illness, and the administration expenses of my estate be paid as soon after my death as may be practicable.

SECOND: I give and bequeath my wearing apparel, jewelry, motor vehicles, household furnishings, books, silverware, glassware, works of art and all other personal and household effects, if I own any of such articles at my death, together with all of my interest in all casualty insurance policies insuring such property against any loss or liability, to my wife, JANE DOE, if she survives me or, if she predeceases me, to my only son, THOMAS DOE, JR.

THIRD: All the rest, residue and remainder of my estate, of whatsoever nature and wheresoever situated, which I may own or to which I may in any way be entitled at the time of my death, including any lapsed

or renounced legacies or devises, is referred to in this my Will as "my residuary estate" and shall be disposed of as provided in Article FOURTH of this my Will.

FOURTH: I give, devise and bequeath ONE HUNDRED PERCENT (100%) of my residuary estate to my wife, JANE DOE, if she survives me or, if she predeceases me, to my only son, THOMAS DOE, JR. If he has also predeceased me, then my residuary estate is to go to his children, including adopted children, in equal shares. If there are no children, then my residuary estate is to go to my distributees.

FIFTH: A. I hereby nominate, constitute and appoint my wife, JANE DOE, as Executor of this my Will, and my son, THOMAS DOE, JR., as Successor Executor.

B. I expressly direct that no bond or security of any kind shall be required in any jurisdiction to secure the faithful peformance of duties by either my Executor or her successor if he serves.

C. I authorize and empower any fiduciary at any time acting hereunder to resign without leave of court. Any such resignation shall be effective upon delivery of a written instrument of resignation, duly signed and acknowledged, to any other then acting fiduciary or, if none, to the fiduciary named or appointed to serve as a successor.

IN WITNESS WHEREOF, I have hereunto set my hand to this, my Last Will and Testament, on (date), no counterpart hereof having been executed by me.

(legal signature) _____

THOMAS DOE

The foregoing instrument was, on the day of the date thereof, signed, sealed, published and declared by THOMAS DOE, the Testator therein named, as and for his Last Will and Testament, in the presence of us, the undersigned, who at his request and in his presence and in the presence of each other, have hereunto set our names as witnesses.

(The signatures, printed names and addresses of the witnesses appear here.)

Affidavit of Witnesses

STATE OF_____)
) SS.:
COUNTY OF _____)

Each of the undersigned _____, who also acted as supervising attorney, _____, and _____, individually and severally being duly sworn, deposes and says:

The within Will was subscribed in our presence and sight at the end thereof by THOMAS DOE, the within named Testator, on the _____ day of (month), (year), at the Law Offices of (name and address of attorney).

Said Testator at the time of making such subscription declared the instrument so subscribed to be his Last Will and Testament.

Each of the undersigned thereupon signed his or her name as a witness at the end of said Will at the request of said Testator and in his presence and sight and in the presence and sight of each other.

Said Testator was, at the time of so executing said Will, over the age of eighteen years and, in the respective opinions of the undersigned, of sound mind, memory, and understanding and not under any restraint or in any respect incompetent to make a Will.

The Testator, in the respective opinions of the undersigned, could read, write, and converse in the English language and was suffering from no defect of sight, hearing, or speech, or from any other physical or mental impairment, which would affect his capacity to make a valid Will. The Will was executed as a single, original instrument and was not executed in counterparts.

Each of the undersigned was acquainted with said Testator at such time and makes this affidavit at his request.

The within Will was shown to the undersigned at the time this affidavit was made and was examined by each of them as to the signature of said Testator and of the undersigned.

The foregoing instrument was executed by the Testator and witnessed by each of the undersigned affiants under the supervision of the above-named attorney-at-law.

_____

(Witness Signature)

_____

(Witness Signature)

_____

(Witness Signature)

Severally sworn to before me this _____ day of (month), (year).

(signature and official seal) _____

Notary Public

Appendix B

INTERNAL REVENUE SERVICE CHART OF MAXIMUM TAX CREDIT FOR STATE DEATH TAXES

From*	To*	Credit = +	%	Of Excess Over
0	$ 40,000	0	0	0
$ 40,000	90,000	0	.8	40,000
90,000	140,000	400	1.6	90,000
140,000	240,000	1,200	2.4	140,000
240,000	440,000	3,600	3.2	240,000
440,000	640,000	10,000	4	440,000
640,000	840,000	18,000	4.8	640,000
840,000	1,040,000	27,600	5.6	840,000
1,040,000	1,540,000	38,800	6.4	1,040,000
1,540,000	2,040,000	70,800	7.2	1,540,000
2,040,000	2,540,000	106,800	8	2,040,000
2,540,000	3,040,000	146,800	8.8	2,540,000
3,040,000	3,540,000	190,800	9.6	3,040,000
3,540,000	4,040,000	238,800	10.4	3,540,000
4,040,000	5,040,000	290,800	11.2	4,040,000
5,040,000	6,040,000	402,800	12	5,040,000
6,040,000	7,040,000	522,800	12.8	6,040,000
7,040,000	8,040,000	650,000	13.6	7,040.000
8,040,000	9,040,000	786,800	14.4	8,040,000
9,040,000	10,040,000	930,800	15.2	9,040,000
10,040,000	. . . .	1,082,800	16	10,040,000

* Adjustable taxable estate amount, which is the decedent's taxable estate less $60,000.

Glossary

Abatement: A proportional reduction of monetary legacies, when the funds or assets out of which such legacies are payable are not sufficient to pay them in full.

Ademption: Extinction of a legacy by a testator's act equivalent to revocation or indicating intention to revoke, i.e., selling or giving away the object during one's lifetime, thus making it unavailable to be distributed at time of death.

Administrator of an estate: A person appointed by a court to administer (i.e., manage or take charge of) the assets and liabilities of a deceased, when such person has died without a will (and therefore without having named an executor).

Advancement (of a legacy): Money or property given to a legatee and intended to be deducted from a legacy stated in the will.

Affidavit(s) of the witness(es): A signed statement made voluntarily by a witness to a will and confirmed by the oath of the witness taken before a notary public. This statement recites the observations of the witness at the time the testator signed the will.

Alimony: Money that a husband or wife by court order pays to the other for maintenance while they are separated or after they are divorced.

Ancillary Letters Testamentary: Authorization by a court, in a state other than where the deceased was domiciled, given to an executor to administer the deceased's real property in this other state.

Ancillary Probate Proceeding: Estate administration in a state, other than the state where decedent was domiciled, where decedent owned real property (land and any structures thereon).

Assets with right of survivorship: An asset having two or more owners, and the survivors among these owners succeed to the deceased owner's interest in the asset.

Basis: Acquisition cost, or some substitute therefor, of an asset, and this basis is used in computing gain or loss on sale of the asset. An example of "some substitute therefor" is the stepped-up basis (or stepped-down basis) which an heir receives for property acquired from a deceased's estate.

Beneficiary: One who benefits from an act of another, such as a beneficiary of a trust or a beneficiary of a will.

Bequeath: To give personal property by will to another. It therefore is distinguishable from "devise," which is a testamentary disposition of real property (land and any structures thereon).

Buy-Sell Agreement: An arrangement, particularly appropriate in the case of a closely held corporation or a partnership, whereby the surviving owner(s) (i.e., shareholders or partners) of the entity (i.e., corporation or partnership), or the entity itself, agree(s) to purchase the interest of a withdrawing or deceased owner (i.e., shareholder or partner).

Charitable Remainder Annuity Trust: A trust that must pay the non-charitable income beneficiary or beneficiaries a certain sum annually, which is not less than a certain percentage (currently 5 percent) of the *initial net fair market value* of all property placed in the trust as valued when the trust is established. Upon the death of the income beneficiary, the charity receives the trust principal.

Charitable Remainder Unitrust: Same as a charitable remainder annuity trust, except the distribution to the income beneficiary is based on the value of the trust as *valued annually*.

Codicil: A separate legal document, signed and witnessed with the same legal formalities of a will, that may explain, modify, add to, subtract from, qualify, alter, restrain or revoke provisions in an existing will. Often simply referred to as an amendment to a will.

Co-executor: One who serves as executor at the same time with one or more other executors.

Common Disaster Clause: See Simultaneous Death Clause.

Conservator: A guardian, protector, or preserver appointed by a court to manage the financial affairs of someone unable to manage his or her financial affairs without some assistance.

Construction proceeding: A court proceeding that interprets an ambiguously worded will.

Creditor: A person to whom a debt is owed by another person (who is called the "debtor").

Death taxes: The generic term to describe all taxes imposed on property or on transfer of property at the death of the owner, including estate and inheritance taxes. See Estate tax; Inheritance tax.

Depreciation: The write-off for tax purposes of the cost, which is subject to certain adjustments, of a tangible (physical) asset over its estimated useful life.

Destroy a will: In relation to wills, the term "destroy" means not only the total physical annihilation of the will into other forms of matter, but a destruction of its legal efficacy, which may be by a written cancellation, obliterating, tearing into fragments, discarding, etc.

Devise: To make a testamentary disposition of land or realty by the last will and testament of the testator.

Disclaimer: The act by which a party refuses to accept an estate, or some part thereof.

Disinherit: The act by which the owner of an estate deprives a person, who would otherwise be his heir, of the right to inherit.

Distributee: An heir; a person entitled to share in the distribution of an estate. This term is used to denote one of the persons who is entitled under the statute of distributions in the state where the deceased was domiciled, to the estate of one who has died intestate (without a will). Also called a next of kin.

Durable Power of Attorney Clause: A clause in a power of attorney document stating that the power remains operative even if the person giving the power becomes mentally incompetent. See Power of Attorney.

Empty nest syndrome: An expression denoting the loneliness parents sometimes feel when their children leave home to pursue their own lives. Opposites are the "return to the nest" or the "never left the nest" syndrome.

Enforceable agreement: An agreement, or contract, that the law recognizes and enforces.

Equitable distribution: Divorce statutes in certain states grant courts the power to distribute equitably, upon divorce, all property legally and beneficially acquired during marriage by husband and wife, or either of them, whether or not legal title lies in the joint or individual names.

Estate: The total property of whatever kind that is owned by a decedent prior to the distribution of that property in accordance with the terms of a will, or, when there is no will, by the laws of inheritance in the state of domicile of the decedent. It means, ordinarily, the whole of the property owned by anyone, the realty as well as the personalty.

Estate tax: A tax imposed on the deceased's estate. Thus, an estate tax is levied on the decedent's estate and not on the heir receiving the property. It is a tax levied on the right to transmit property, while an "inheritance tax" is levied on the right to receive property. See Inheritance tax.

Executor: A person appointed by a testator to carry out the directions and requests in his will, and to dispose of the property according to testamentary provisions after the testator's death.

Executor's commission: A fee the executor receives for administering a deceased's estate.

Generation-Skipping Transfer tax: A tax on the transmission of wealth from older-to-younger generation recipients that would otherwise avoid the transfer tax (estate tax or gift tax) payable by an intervening generation.

Gift tax: A tax imposed on the transfer of property by gift. Such tax is based on the fair market value of the property on the date of the gift. However, under current law gifts of $10,000 or less may be made annually, to an unlimited number of recipients, without incurring a federal gift tax.

Grantor: The creator of a trust is usually designated as the grantor of the trust. See Settlor.

Gross assets of an estate: The property owned or previously transferred by a decedent that will be subject to the federal estate tax. It includes the probate estate, which is property actually subject to administration by the administrator or executor of an estate. It also includes the nonprobate assets of the deceased, such as joint bank accounts and proceeds of life insurance.

Guardian: A person lawfully invested with the authority and charged with the duty of taking care of a person. One who manages the property and rights of another person.

Homestead right: Property set apart by the court for the use of a surviving husband or wife and the minor children out of the commonly owned property or out of the real estate belonging to the deceased.

Inheritance tax: A tax imposed in some states upon *recipients* of estate assets, but close relatives of a deceased are often exempt from this tax.

Insurance: A contract whereby, for a stipulated price, one party undertakes to compensate the other for loss on a specified subject by specified perils.

Disability insurance: Type of insurance protection purchased to cover payments for a work-precluding injury.

Homeowner's insurance: Policy insuring individuals against any, some, or all of the risks of loss to personal dwellings, or the contents thereof, or the personal liability pertaining thereto.

Liability insurance: Insurance that covers suits against the insured for damages such as injury or death to others, or property damage, and the like. It is insurance for those damages for which an automobile driver, for example, can be held liable.

Life insurance: A contract between the holder of a policy and an insurance company (i.e., the carrier) whereby the carrier agrees, in return for premium payments, to pay a specified sum (i.e., the face value or maturity value of the policy) to the designated beneficiary upon the death of the insured.

Term insurance: Form of pure life insurance having no cash surrender value and generally furnishing insurance protection for only a specified or limited period (term) of time. Such policies are usually renewable.

Whole life insurance or **Straight life insurance:** Insurance for which premiums are collected so long as the insured may live and these whole life policies build up cash reserves, whereas term policies do not.

In Terrorem Clause: A clause in a will providing for the revocation of a bequest or devise if the legatee contests the will.

Intestate, (dying intestate): Dying without a will.

Intestate share: The portion of an intestate's estate received by a distributee.

"In Trust For" Account: See Totten Trust.

Joint ownership of assets: An asset with two or more owners, the survivors of whom might succeed to ownership of the deceased's share of the asset, depending upon whether there is the right of survivorship.

Judgment debts: Debts that are evidenced by matter of court or other government agency record. They are debts for the recovery of which judgment has been rendered as the result of a successful legal action.

Legacy: What is received through someone's will.

Legatee(s): The person(s) to whom a legacy in a will is given. The term may be used to denominate those who take under the will without any distinction between land and realty (which is devised) and personalty (which is bequeathed).

Letters of Administration: A formal document issued by a court appointing someone to administer the estate of a person who died without a will.

Letters of Intent: A letter that has no legal enforceability, but merely shows a person's intentions or desires.

Letters Testamentary: The formal instrument of authority and appointment given to an executor by the proper court, empowering him to enter upon the discharge of his office as executor (which is to gather and distribute the assets of the deceased). It corresponds to letters of administration granted to an administrator, appointed when someone dies without a will.

Living (Inter Vivos) Trust: A transfer of property during the life of the owner to a trustee for the benefit of a beneficiary. To be distinguished from a testamentary trust where the property passes at death. (See Testamentary Trust.) Different from a bank account "in trust for" someone, which has no accompanying trust contract. Also different from a Living Will.

Living Will: A document, possessing legal status in most but not all states, signed by an individual stating his or her desires regarding medical treatment in the event of a terminal illness.

Mortgage: An interest in land created by a written instrument providing security for the performance of a duty or the payment of a debt.

Net worth: What remains after deduction of liabilities from assets. Also expressed as the difference between total assets and liabilities of an individual, a corporation, etc.

Nuptial Agreement: See Prenuptial Agreement.

Palimony: Term having a meaning similar to that of "alimony" except that award, settlement, or agreement arises out of the nonmarital relationship of the parties (i.e., nonmarital partners).

Personal effects: Articles associated with a person as property having more or less intimate relation to the person. A broad reference in the context of wills and estate administrations is to the following items owned by a decedent at the time of death: clothing, furniture, jewelry, silverware, china, crystal, cooking utensils, books, cars, televisions, radios, etc. A narrower reference of the term includes only such tangible property as attended the person, or such tangible property as is worn or carried about the person.

Personal property: Everything other than land or realty. See Real property, which is land and buildings.

Personal Representative of the Estate: Term applied to either an executor (when there is a will) or administrator (when there is no will).

Power of Attorney: An instrument authorizing another to act as one's agent or attorney. The agent is attorney in fact and the power is revoked on the death of the principal by operation of law. Such power may be either general or limited. See also Durable Power of Attorney Clause.

General Power of Attorney: Allows another to act in all matters as one's agent.

Limited Power of Attorney: Allows another to act as one's agent in some limited situation(s), such as granting this power to someone to withdraw money from a particular bank account.

Predecease: To die before; the correlative of "succeed."

Preliminary Letters Testamentary: Limited authorization for a person named as executor in a deceased's will to protect the assets of the estate prior to the will being admitted to probate (which results in the issuance of Letters Testamentary).

Prenuptial Agreement: An agreement entered into by prospective spouses prior to marriage but in contemplation and in consideration thereof. By it, the property rights of one or both of the prospective spouses are determined in the event of divorce or death. Called a post-nuptial agreement if entered into during the marriage.

Probate assets: Those assets of the deceased distributed in accordance with the terms of the last will and testament. Property that has a named beneficiary (or jointly owned with right of survivorship) is not probate property.

Probate Court: A court having general powers over probate of wills, administration of estates, and, in some states, empowered to appoint guardians and conservators. A court with similar functions is sometimes called a Surrogate's or Orphan's Court in certain states.

Probate law: The body or system of law relating to all matters of which probate courts have jurisdiction.

Progressive tax rate: A type of graduated tax, as in the case of the federal income tax, which applies higher tax rates as income increases.

Public Administrator: When a person dies without a will (and therefore without an executor), a distributee (or legatee) is appointed to serve as the administrator. If there is no one available to so serve, then a public official of the community serves as administrator. This official is often called the community's public administrator.

Publication: The formal declaration made by a testator at the time of signing a will that it is a last will and testament and the request to witnesses to witness the signing thereof.

QTIP Trust: An abbreviation for Qualified Terminable Interest Property Trust, it is a trust for a spouse's benefit that qualifies for the marital deduction and also allows the spouse establishing the trust to determine the ultimate beneficiary upon the other spouse's death. To qualify for the marital deduction, the trust must distribute all the income to the spouse at least annually, the spouse receiving the income must be a United States citizen, and an election must be made to have this trust treated as a QTIP Trust.

Real property: Land and buildings are real property. The most common example of real property is a person's house. See Personal property, which is everything other than real property.

Renunciation by an executor: The act by which a person abandons a right acquired without transferring it to another. In connection with wills, it is the act of a proposed executor waiving his right to so serve.

Residuary estate: That which remains after debts and expenses of administration and legacies have been satisfied. It consists of all the probate estate that has not been otherwise legally disposed of by the will.

Security interest: A form of interest in property that allows for the property to be sold upon default of the obligation for which the security interest is given. A mortgage is used to grant a security interest in real property (land and real estate). A lien is an agreement between creditor and debtor that grants a security interest in personal property (everything other than real property).

Self-proved Will: A will that contains a notarized affidavit of witnesses.

Settlor: One who creates a trust. Also referred to as a Grantor.

Simultaneous Death Clause: A clause in a will that provides for the disposition of property in the event that there is no evidence as to the priority of time of death of the testator and another. Also referred to as a Common Disaster Clause.

Spouse's Elective Share: The minimum percentage of a deceased's estate, despite the will, that state law mandates must go to the surviving spouse.

Statute of limitations: The period of time in which a legal action must be brought.

Stepped-up Basis: An increase in the income tax basis of property received from an estate to the fair market value at death (or to the alternate valuation, which is the value of the property six months after death).

Successor Executor: An executor who follows or succeeds an earlier executor and who has all the powers of the earlier executor. Wills generally make provisions for appointment of one or more successor executors in the event that the primary executor fails or ceases to act. The major reason for a primary executor to fail to act is that this person has predeceased the testator.

Successor Legatee(s): Alternate person(s) named to receive a legacy in the event the predecessor legatee has predeceased the testator or disclaims the legacy. See Disclaimer.

Successor Residuary Legatee(s): Same as successor legatee(s), except he, she, or they succeed to a residuary share of the estate.

Surviving spouse: The spouse who outlives his/her partner. A term commonly found in statutes dealing with probate, administration of estates, and estate and inheritance taxes.

Survivorship Clause: Survivorship occurs when a person becomes entitled to property by reason of his having survived the death of another person who had an interest in it.

Tangible personal property: Property, such as a chair or automobile, that may be touched or felt. It is in contrast to symbolic property such as a stock certificate that represents ownership of part of a corporation, or a bank account that represents the money in the account, and this symbolic property is intangible personal property.

Taxable estate: The gross estate (all the assets) of a decedent reduced by certain tax deductions, e.g., administration expenses, marital and charitable deductions, etc.

Tax audit: The review and questioning by the government of a tax return.

Tax avoidance: Legally planning your affairs so as to minimize, or avoid, tax.

Tax credit: An actual reduction of tax by the amount of the credit. More valuable than a tax deduction.

Tax deduction: A reduction of the amount to which a tax is applied.

Tax deferral: A legally permissible delay of payment of a tax.

Tax evasion: The crime of not paying tax that is legally owed.

Tax exempt: Free of tax, e.g., the interest income on certain municipal bonds that is not subject to federal income tax.

Tax schedules: A chart showing tax rates.

Testamentary capacity: It is the testator's capacity to know the general nature and extent of property the testator owns and those persons to receive this property at the time of the testator's death. It is a minimum awareness standard required of someone signing a legally enforceable will.

Testamentary Trust: A trust that takes effect at the death of the testator. It is contained within a will. See Living Trust.

Testator: One who makes or has made a will; one who dies leaving a will.

Totten Trust Account: It is created by the deposit by a person of his own money in his own name with a revocable designation of someone who is to receive the amount in the account at the time of the depositor's death. An example of a Totten Trust is a bank account that is owned by John and "in trust for" (i.t.f.) Mary. A "payment on death" (often abbreviated with the capital letters P.O.D.) account is similar.

Trust Agreement: An agreement whereby one person, called a trustee, holds property for the benefit of another, called a beneficiary. See Living Trust; Testamentary Trust.

Trustee: A person holding property for the benefit of a beneficiary in trust. The trustee has the legal title to this property, which is held for the benefit of another.

Valuable Items Rider (to homeowner's insurance policy): A separate insurance agreement, usually associated with a homeowner's insurance policy, whereby items such as jewelry and furs are insured.

Witness to a will: One who has observed the testator signing the will and subscribes his or her own name thereto. Most state statutes require two attesting witnesses, although some states require three such witnesses. In some states the witness is required to witness the other witnesses signing as witnesses.

I dedicate this book to those who survived the Depression and who went on to display the most dedicated work ethic of any generation. Although this book gives you information about what happens to your assets after your death, it also offers information about life. It will save you money and, hopefully, it will make life easier for you and your survivors.

Published 1990 by Prometheus Books
700 East Amherst Street, Buffalo, New York 14215

Copyright © 1990 by Eugene J. Daly

This publication is designed to provide accurate and authoritative information in regard to the subject matter covered. It is sold with the understanding that the author and the publisher are not engaged in rendering legal, accounting, or other professional service. If legal advice or other expert assistance is required, the individual and personal service of a competent professional person should be sought. (From a Declaration of Principles jointly adopted by a Committee of the American Bar Association and a Committee of Publishers.)

Library of Congress Cataloging-in-Publication Data

Daly, Eugene J.
    Thy will be done : a guide to wills, taxation, and estate planning for older persons / by Eugene J. Daly.
        p.   cm. — (Golden age books)
    ISBN 0-87975-591-1 (cloth)
    ISBN 0-87975-586-5 (paper)
    1. Wills—United States—Popular works. 2. Trusts and trustees—
United States—Popular works. 3. Estate planning—United States—
Popular works. 4. Inheritance and transfer tax—Law and
legislation—United States—Popular works. 5. Aged—Legal status,
laws, etc.—United States—Popular works. I. Title. II. Series.
KF755.Z9D35   1990
346.7305′4—dc20
[347.30654]   89-70027
                                                                        CIP

Printed on acid-free paper in the United States of America

Thy Will Be Done

A Guide to Wills, Taxation, and Estate Planning for Older Persons

Eugene J. Daly, Attorney at Law

Golden Age Books

Prometheus Books
Buffalo, New York

14

With her two brothers this fair lady dwelt,
  Enriched from ancestral merchandize,
And for them many a weary hand did swelt
  In torched mines and noisy factories,
And many once proud-quiver'd loins did melt
  In blood from stinging whip;—with hollow eyes
Many all day in dazzling river stood,
To take the rich-ored driftings of the flood.

15

For them the Ceylon diver held his breath,
  And went all naked to the hungry shark;
For them his ears gush'd blood; for them in death
  The seal on the cold ice with piteous bark
Lay full of darts; for them alone did seethe
  A thousand men in troubles wide and dark:
Half-ignorant, they turn'd an easy wheel,
That set sharp racks at work, to pinch and peel.

16

Why were they proud? Because their marble founts
  Gush'd with more pride than do a wretch's
    tears?—
Why were they proud? Because fair orange-mounts
  Were of more soft ascent than lazar stairs?—
Why were they proud? Because red-lin'd accounts
  Were richer than the songs of Grecian years?—
Why were they proud? again we ask aloud,
Why in the name of Glory were they proud?

17

Yet were these Florentines as self-retired
  In hungry pride and gainful cowardice,
As two close Hebrews in that land inspired,
  Paled in and vineyarded from beggar-spies;
The hawks of ship-mast forests — the untired
  And pannier'd mules for ducats and old lies —
Quick cat's-paws on the generous stray-away, —
Great wits in Spanish, Tuscan, and Malay.

18

How was it these same ledger-men could spy
  Fair Isabella in her downy nest?
How could they find out in Lorenzo's eye
  A straying from his toil? Hot Egypt's pest
Into their vision covetous and sly!
  How could these money-bags see east and west? —
Yet so they did — and every dealer fair
Must see behind, as doth the hunted hare.

19

O eloquent and famed Boccaccio!
  Of thee we now should ask forgiving boon,
And of thy spicy myrtles as they blow,
  And of thy roses amorous of the moon,
And of thy lilies, that do paler grow
  Now they can no more hear thy ghittern's tune,
For venturing syllables that ill beseem
The quiet glooms of such a piteous theme.

20

Grant thou a pardon here, and then the tale
  Shall move on soberly, as it is meet;
There is no other crime, no mad assail
  To make old prose in modern rhyme more sweet:
But it is done—succeed the verse or fail—
  To honour thee, and thy gone spirit greet;
To stead thee as a verse in English tongue,
An echo of thee in the north-wind sung.

21

These brethren having found by many signs
  What love Lorenzo for their sister had,
And how she lov'd him too, each unconfines
  His bitter thoughts to other, well nigh mad
That he, the servant of their trade designs,
  Should in their sister's love be blithe and glad,
When 'twas their plan to coax her by degrees
To some high noble and his olive-trees.

22

And many a jealous conference had they,
  And many times they bit their lips alone,
Before they fix'd upon a surest way
  To make the youngster for his crime atone;
And at the last, these men of cruel clay
  Cut Mercy with a sharp knife to the bone;
For they resolved in some forest dim
To kill Lorenzo, and there bury him.

23

So on a pleasant morning, as he leant
  Into the sun-rise, o'er the balustrade
Of the garden-terrace, towards him they bent
  Their footing through the dews; and to him said,
"You seem there in the quiet of content,
  Lorenzo, and we are most loth to invade
Calm speculation; but if you are wise,
Bestride your steed while cold is in the skies.

24

"To-day we purpose, ay, this hour we mount
  To spur three leagues towards the Apennine;
Come down, we pray thee, ere the hot sun count
  His dewy rosary on the eglantine."
Lorenzo, courteously as he was wont,
  Bow'd a fair greeting to these serpents' whine;
And went in haste, to get in readiness,
With belt, and spur, and bracing huntsman's dress.

25

And as he to the court-yard pass'd along,
  Each third step did he pause, and listen'd oft
If he could hear his lady's matin-song,
  Or the light whisper of her footstep soft;
And as he thus over his passion hung,
  He heard a laugh full musical aloft;
When, looking up, he saw her features bright
Smile through an in-door lattice, all delight.

26

"Love, Isabel!" said he, "I was in pain
　Lest I should miss to bid thee a good morrow:
Ah! what if I should lose thee, when so fain
　I am to stifle all the heavy sorrow
Of a poor three hours' absence? but we'll gain
　Out of the amorous dark what day doth borrow.
Good bye! I'll soon be back."—"Good bye!"
　　　　　said she:—
And as he went she chanted merrily.

So the two brothers and their murder'd man
　Rode past fair Florence, to where Arno's stream
Gurgles through straiten'd banks, and still doth fan
　Itself with dancing bulrush, and the bream
Keeps head against the freshets. Sick and wan
　The brothers' faces in the ford did seem,
Lorenzo's flush with love.—They pass'd the water
Into a forest quiet for the slaughter.

There was Lorenzo slain and buried in,
　There in that forest did his great love cease;
Ah! when a soul doth thus its freedom win,
　It aches in loneliness—is ill at peace
As the break-covert blood-hounds of such sin:
　They dipp'd their swords in the water, and
　　　　　did tease

Their horses homeward, with convulsed spur,
Each richer by his being a murderer.

29

They told their sister how, with sudden speed,
  Lorenzo had ta'en ship for foreign lands,
Because of some great urgency and need
  In their affairs, requiring trusty hands.
Poor Girl! put on thy stifling widow's weed,
  And 'scape at once from Hope's accursed bands;
To-day thou wilt not see him, nor to-morrow,
And the next day will be a day of sorrow.

30

She weeps alone for pleasures not to be;
  Sorely she wept until the night came on,
And then, instead of love, O misery!
  She brooded o'er the luxury alone:
His image in the dusk she seem'd to see,
  And to the silence made a gentle moan,
Spreading her perfect arms upon the air,
And on her couch low murmuring "Where?
    O where?"

31

But Selfishness, Love's cousin, held not long
  Its fiery vigil in her single breast;
She fretted for the golden hour, and hung
  Upon the time with feverish unrest—
Not long—for soon into her heart a throng

Of higher occupants, a richer zest,
Came tragic; passion not to be subdued,
And sorrow for her love in travels rude.

32

In the mid days of autumn, on their eves
  The breath of Winter comes from far away,
And the sick west continually bereaves
  Of some gold tinge, and plays a roundelay
Of death among the bushes and the leaves,
  To make all bare before he dares to stray
From his north cavern. So sweet Isabel
By gradual decay from beauty fell,

33

Because Lorenzo came not. Oftentimes
  She ask'd her brothers, with an eye all pale,
Striving to be itself, what dungeon climes
  Could keep him off so long? They spake a tale
Time after time, to quiet her. Their crimes
  Came on them, like a smoke from
              Hinnom's vale;
And every night in dreams they groan'd aloud,
To see their sister in her snowy shroud.

34

And she had died in drowsy ignorance,
  But for a thing more deadly dark than all;
It came like a fierce potion, drunk by chance,
  Which saves a sick man from the feather'd pall

For some few gasping moments; like a lance,
   Waking an Indian from his cloudy hall
With cruel pierce, and bringing him again
Sense of the gnawing fire at heart and brain.

35

It was a vision. — In the drowsy gloom,
   The dull of midnight, at her couch's foot
Lorenzo stood, and wept: the forest tomb
   Had marr'd his glossy hair which once could shoot
Lustre into the sun, and put cold doom
   Upon his lips, and taken the soft lute
From his lorn voice, and past his loamed ears
Had made a miry channel for his tears.

36

Strange sound it was, when the pale shadow spake;
   For there was striving, in its piteous tongue,
To speak as when on earth it was awake,
   And Isabella on its music hung:
Languor there was in it, and tremulous shake,
   As in a palsied Druid's harp unstrung;
And through it moan'd a ghostly under-song,
Like hoarse night-gusts sepulchral briars among.

37

Its eyes, though wild, were still all dewy bright
   With love, and kept all phantom fear aloof
From the poor girl by magic of their light,
   The while it did unthread the horrid woof

Of the late darken'd time,—the murderous spite
　Of pride and avarice,—the dark pine roof
In the forest,—and the sodden turfed dell,
Where, without any word, from stabs he fell.

38

Saying moreover, "Isabel, my sweet!
　Red whortle-berries droop above my head,
And a large flint-stone weighs upon my feet;
　Around me beeches and high chestnuts shed
Their leaves and prickly nuts; a sheep-fold bleat
　Comes from beyond the river to my bed:
Go, shed one tear upon my heather-bloom,
And it shall comfort me within the tomb.

39

"I am a shadow now, alas! alas!
　Upon the skirts of human-nature dwelling
Alone: I chant alone the holy mass,
　While little sounds of life are round
　　　me knelling,
And glossy bees at noon do fieldward pass,
　And many a chapel bell the hour is telling,
Paining me through: those sounds grow strange
　　　to me,
And thou art distant in Humanity.

40

"I know what was, I feel full well what is,
　And I should rage, if spirits could go mad;

Though I forget the taste of earthly bliss,
  That paleness warms my grave, as though I had
A Seraph chosen from the bright abyss
  To be my spouse: thy paleness makes me glad;
Thy beauty grows upon me, and I feel
A greater love through all my essence steal."

41

The Spirit mourn'd "Adieu!"—dissolv'd, and left
  The atom darkness in a slow turmoil;
As when of healthful midnight sleep bereft,
  Thinking on rugged hours and fruitless toil,
We put our eyes into a pillowy cleft,
  And see the spangly gloom froth up and boil:
It made sad Isabella's eyelids ache,
And in the dawn she started up awake;

42

"Ha! ha!" said she, "I knew not this hard life,
  I thought the worst was simple misery;
I thought some Fate with pleasure or with strife
  Portion'd us—happy days, or else to die;
But there is crime—a brother's bloody knife!
  Sweet Spirit, thou hast school'd my infancy:
I'll visit thee for this, and kiss thine eyes,
And greet thee morn and even in the skies."

43

When the full morning came, she had devised
  How she might secret to the forest hie;

How she might find the clay, so dearly prized,
  And sing to it one latest lullaby;
How her short absence might be unsurmised,
  While she the inmost of the dream would try.
Resolv'd, she took with her an aged nurse,
And went into that dismal forest-hearse.

44

See, as they creep along the river side,
  How she doth whisper to that aged Dame,
And, after looking round the champaign wide,
  Shows her a knife. — "What feverous hectic flame
Burns in thee, child? — What good can thee betide,
  That thou should'st smile again?" — The
              evening came,
And they had found Lorenzo's earthy bed;
The flint was there, the berries at his head.

45

Who hath not loiter'd in a green church-yard,
  And let his spirit, like a demon-mole,
Work through the clayey soil and gravel hard,
  To see scull, coffin'd bones, and funeral stole;
Pitying each form that hungry Death hath marr'd,
  And filling it once more with human soul?
Ah! this is holiday to what was felt
When Isabella by Lorenzo knelt.

46

She gaz'd into the fresh-thrown mould, as though
   One glance did fully all its secrets tell;
Clearly she saw, as other eyes would know
   Pale limbs at bottom of a crystal well;
Upon the murderous spot she seem'd to grow,
   Like to a native lily of the dell:
Then with her knife, all sudden, she began
To dig more fervently than misers can.

47

Soon she turn'd up a soiled glove, whereon
   Her silk had play'd in purple phantasies,
She kiss'd it with a lip more chill than stone,
   And put it in her bosom, where it dries
And freezes utterly unto the bone
   Those dainties made to still an infant's cries:
Then 'gan she work again; nor stay'd her care,
But to throw back at times her veiling hair.

48

That old nurse stood beside her wondering,
   Until her heart felt pity to the core
At sight of such a dismal labouring,
   And so she kneeled, with her locks all hoar,
And put her lean hands to the horrid thing:
   Three hours they labour'd at this travail sore;
At last they felt the kernel of the grave,
And Isabella did not stamp and rave.

49

Ah! wherefore all this wormy circumstance?
  Why linger at the yawning tomb so long?
O for the gentleness of old Romance,
  The simple plaining of a minstrel's song!
Fair reader, at the old tale take a glance,
  For here, in truth, it doth not well belong
To speak:—O turn thee to the very tale,
And taste the music of that vision pale.

50

With duller steel than the Perséan sword
  They cut away no formless monster's head,
But one, whose gentleness did well accord
  With death, as life. The ancient harps have said,
Love never dies, but lives, immortal Lord:
  If Love impersonate was ever dead,
Pale Isabella kiss'd it, and low moan'd.
'Twas love; cold,—dead indeed, but not dethroned.

51

In anxious secrecy they took it home,
  And then the prize was all for Isabel:
She calm'd its wild hair with a golden comb,
  And all around each eye's sepulchral cell
Pointed each fringed lash; the smeared loam
  With tears, as chilly as a dripping well,
She drench'd away:—and still she comb'd, and kept
Sighing all day—and still she kiss'd, and wept.

52

Then in a silken scarf,—sweet with the dews
  Of precious flowers pluck'd in Araby,
And divine liquids come with odorous ooze
  Through the cold serpent-pipe refreshfully,—
She wrapp'd it up; and for its tomb did choose
  A garden-pot, wherein she laid it by,
And cover'd it with mould, and o'er it set
Sweet basil, which her tears kept ever wet.

53

And she forgot the stars, the moon, and sun,
  And she forgot the blue above the trees,
And she forgot the dells where waters run,
  And she forgot the chilly autumn breeze;
She had no knowledge when the day was done,
  And the new morn she saw not: but in peace
Hung over her sweet basil evermore,
And moisten'd it with tears unto the core.

54

And so she ever fed it with thin tears,
  Whence thick, and green, and beautiful it grew,
So that it smelt more balmy than its peers
  Of basil-tufts in Florence; for it drew
Nurture besides, and life, from human fears,
  From the fast mouldering head there shut
        from view:
So that the jewel, safely casketed,
Came forth, and in perfumed leafits spread.

55

O Melancholy, linger here awhile!
  O Music, Music, breathe despondingly!
O Echo, Echo, from some sombre isle,
  Unknown, Lethean, sigh to us — O sigh!
Spirits in grief, lift up your heads, and smile;
  Lift up your heads, sweet Spirits, heavily,
And make a pale light in your cypress glooms,
Tinting with silver wan your marble tombs.

56

Moan hither, all ye syllables of woe,
  From the deep throat of sad Melpomene!
Through bronzed lyre in tragic order go,
  And touch the strings into a mystery;
Sound mournfully upon the winds and low;
  For simple Isabel is soon to be
Among the dead: She withers, like a palm
Cut by an Indian for its juicy balm.

57

O leave the palm to wither by itself;
  Let not quick Winter chill its dying hour! —
It may not be — those Baälites of pelf,
  Her brethren, noted the continual shower
From her dead eyes; and many a curious elf,
  Among her kindred, wonder'd that such
        dower
Of youth and beauty should be thrown aside
By one mark'd out to be a noble's bride.

58

And, furthermore, her brethren wonder'd much
  Why she sat drooping by the basil green,
And why it flourish'd, as by magic touch;
   Greatly they wonder'd what the thing
         might mean:
They could not surely give belief, that such
  A very nothing would have power to wean
Her from her own fair youth, and pleasures gay,
And even remembrance of her love's delay.

59

Therefore they watch'd a time when they might sift
  This hidden whim; and long they watch'd in vain;
For seldom did she go to chapel-shrift,
  And seldom felt she any hunger-pain;
And when she left, she hurried back, as swift
  As bird on wing to breast its eggs again;
And, patient as a hen-bird, sat her there
Beside her basil, weeping through her hair.

60

Yet they contriv'd to steal the basil-pot,
  And to examine it in secret place:
The thing was vile with green and livid spot,
  And yet they knew it was Lorenzo's face:
The guerdon of their murder they had got,
  And so left Florence in a moment's space,
Never to turn again. —Away they went,
With blood upon their heads, to banishment.

61

O Melancholy, turn thine eyes away!
  O Music, Music, breathe despondingly!
O Echo, Echo, on some other day,
  From isles Lethean, sigh to us — O sigh!
Spirits of grief, sing not your "Well-a-way!"
  For Isabel, sweet Isabel, will die;
Will die a death too lone and incomplete,
Now they have ta'en away her basil sweet.

62

Piteous she look'd on dead and senseless things,
  Asking for her lost basil amorously;
And with melodious chuckle in the strings
  Of her lorn voice, she oftentimes would cry
After the pilgrim in his wanderings,
  To ask him where her basil was; and why
'Twas hid from her: "For cruel 'tis," said she,
"To steal my basil-pot away from me."

63

And so she pined, and so she died forlorn,
  Imploring for her basil to the last.
No heart was there in Florence but did mourn
  In pity of her love, so overcast.
And a sad ditty of this story born
  From mouth to mouth through all the country
        pass'd:
Still is the burthen sung — "O cruelty,
To steal my basil-pot away from me!"

On Visiting the Tomb of Burns

The town, the churchyard, and the setting sun,
  The clouds, the trees, the rounded hills all seem,
  Though beautiful, cold—strange—as in a dream
I dreamed long ago. Now new begun,
The short-lived, paly summer is but won
  From winter's ague, for one hour's gleam;
  Though sapphire warm, their stars do never
            beam;
All is cold beauty; pain is never done
For who has mind to relish, Minos-wise,
  The real of beauty, free from that dead hue
  Sickly imagination and sick pride
Cast wan upon it! Burns! with honour due
I have oft honoured thee. Great shadow, hide
Thy face—I sin against thy native skies.

Old Meg she was a gipsey

Old Meg she was a gipsey,
  And liv'd upon the moors;
Her bed it was the brown heath turf,
  And her house was out of doors.

Her apples were swart blackberries,
  Her currants pods o' broom,
Her wine was dew o' the wild white rose,
  Her book a churchyard tomb.

Her brothers were the craggy hills,
  Her sisters larchen trees—
Alone with her great family
  She liv'd as she did please.

No breakfast had she many a morn,
  No dinner many a noon,
And 'stead of supper she would stare
  Full hard against the moon.

But every morn of woodbine fresh
  She made her garlanding,
And every night the dark glen yew
  She wove and she would sing.

And with her fingers old and brown
  She plaited mats o' rushes,
And gave them to the cottagers
  She met among the bushes.

Old Meg was brave as Margaret Queen
  And tall as Amazon:
An old red blanket cloak she wore;
  A chip hat had she on.
God rest her aged bones somewhere—
  She died full long agone!

This mortal body of a thousand days

This mortal body of a thousand days
  Now fills, O Burns, a space in thine own room,
Where thou didst dream alone on budded bays,
  Happy and thoughtless of thy day of doom!
My pulse is warm with thine old barley-bree,
  My head is light with pledging a great soul,
My eyes are wandering, and I cannot see,
  Fancy is dead and drunken at its goal;
Yet can I stamp my foot upon thy floor,
  Yet can I ope thy window-sash to find
The meadow thou hast tramped o'er and o'er,—
  Yet can I think of thee till thought is blind,—
Yet can I gulp a bumper to thy name,—
O smile among the shade for this is fame!

There is a joy in footing slow across a silent plain

There is a joy in footing slow across a silent plain,
Where patriot battle has been fought, when glory
      had the gain;
There is a pleasure on the heath where Druids old
      have been,
Where mantles grey have rustled by and swept the
      nettles green:
There is a joy in every spot made known by times
      of old,

New to the feet, although the tale a hundred times
        be told:
There is a deeper joy than all, more solemn in
        the heart,
More parching to the tongue than all, of more
        divine a smart,
When weary feet forget themselves upon a
        pleasant turf,
Upon hot sand, or flinty road, or sea shore
        iron scurf,
Toward the castle or the cot where long ago
        was born
One who was great through mortal days and died
        of fame unshorn.
Light hether-bells may tremble then, but they are
        far away;
Woodlark may sing from sandy fern, — the sun may
        hear his lay;
Runnels may kiss the grass on shelves and shallows
        clear,
But their low voices are not heard, though come
        on travels drear;
Blood-red the sun may set behind black
        mountain peaks;
Blue tides may sluice and drench their time in
        caves and weedy creeks;
Eagles may seem to sleep wing-wide upon
        the air;
Ring doves may fly convuls'd across to some high
        cedar'd lair;

But the forgotten eye is still fast wedded to the
         ground—
As palmer's that with weariness mid-desert shrine
         hath found.
At such a time the soul's a child, in childhood is
         the brain;
Forgotten is the worldly heart—alone, it beats
         in vain.
Aye, if a madman could have leave to pass a
         healthful day,
To tell his forehead's swoon and faint when first
         began decay.
He might make tremble many a man whose spirit
         had gone forth
To find a bard's low cradle place about the
         silent north.
Scanty the hour and few the steps beyond the bourn
         of care,
Beyond the sweet and bitter world—beyond
         it unaware;
Scanty the hour and few the steps, because a
         longer stay
Would bar return and make a man forget his
         mortal way.
O horrible! to lose the sight of well
         remember'd face,
Of brother's eyes, of sister's brow, constant to
         every place;
Filling the air, as on we move, with
         portraiture intense,

More warm than those heroic tints that fill a
        painter's sense,
When shapes of old come striding by and visages
        of old,
Locks shining black, hair scanty grey, and passions
        manifold.
No, no, that horror cannot be — for at the cable's
        length
Man feels the gentle anchor pull and gladdens in
        its strength.
One hour, half-idiot, he stands by mossy waterfall,
But in the very next he reads his soul's memorial:
He reads it on the mountain's height, where chance
        he may sit down
Upon rough marble diadem, that hill's
        eternal crown.
Yet be the anchor e'er so fast, room is there for
        a prayer
That man may never lose his mind on mountains
        bleak and bare;
That he may stray league after league some great
        birthplace to find,
And keep his vision clear from speck, his inward
        sight unblind.

The Eve of St. Agnes

1

St. Agnes' Eve—Ah, bitter chill it was!
The owl, for all his feathers, was a-cold;
The hare limp'd trembling through the
      frozen grass,
And silent was the flock in woolly fold:
Numb were the Beadsman's fingers, while he told
His rosary, and while his frosted breath,
Like pious incense from a censer old,
Seem'd taking flight for heaven, without a death,
Past the sweet Virgin's picture, while his prayer
      he saith.

2

His prayer he saith, this patient, holy man;
Then takes his lamp, and riseth from his knees,
And back returneth, meagre, barefoot, wan,
Along the chapel aisle by slow degrees:
The sculptur'd dead, on each side, seem to freeze,
Emprison'd in black, purgatorial rails:
Knights, ladies, praying in dumb orat'ries,
He passeth by; and his weak spirit fails
To think how they may ache in icy hoods and mails.

3

Northward he turneth through a little door,
And scarce three steps, ere Music's golden tongue
Flatter'd to tears this aged man and poor;

But no — already had his deathbell rung;
   The joys of all his life were said and sung:
   His was harsh penance on St. Agnes' Eve:
   Another way he went, and soon among
   Rough ashes sat he for his soul's reprieve,
And all night kept awake, for sinners' sake
         to grieve.

4

The ancient Beadsman heard the prelude soft;
   And so it chanc'd, for many a door was wide,
   From hurry to and fro. Soon, up aloft,
   The silver, snarling trumpets 'gan to chide:
   The level chambers, ready with their pride,
   Were glowing to receive a thousand guests:
   The carved angels, ever eager-eyed,
   Star'd, where upon their heads the cornice rests,
With hair blown back, and wings put cross-wise on
         their breasts.

5

At length burst in the argent revelry,
   With plume, tiara, and all rich array,
   Numerous as shadows haunting fairily
   The brain, new stuff'd, in youth, with triumphs gay
   Of old romance. These let us wish away,
   And turn, sole-thoughted, to one Lady there,
   Whose heart had brooded, all that wintry day,
   On love, and wing'd St. Agnes' saintly care,
As she had heard old dames full many times declare.

6

They told her how, upon St. Agnes' Eve,
Young virgins might have visions of delight,
And soft adorings from their loves receive
Upon the honey'd middle of the night,
If ceremonies due they did aright;
As, supperless to bed they must retire,
And couch supine their beauties, lily white;
Nor look behind, nor sideways, but require
Of heaven with upward eyes for all that
       they desire.

7

Full of this whim was thoughtful Madeline:
The music, yearning like a god in pain,
She scarcely heard: her maiden eyes divine,
Fix'd on the floor, saw many a sweeping train
Pass by—she heeded not at all: in vain
Came many a tiptoe, amorous cavalier,
And back retir'd, not cool'd by high disdain;
But she saw not: her heart was otherwhere:
She sigh'd for Agnes' dreams, the sweetest of
       the year.

8

She danc'd along with vague, regardless eyes,
Anxious her lips, her breathing quick and short:
The hallow'd hour was near at hand: she sighs
Amid the timbrels, and the throng'd resort

Of whisperers in anger, or in sport;
'Mid looks of love, defiance, hate, and scorn,
Hoodwink'd with faery fancy; all amort,
Save to St. Agnes and her lambs unshorn,
And all the bliss to be before to-morrow morn.

9

So, purposing each moment to retire,
She linger'd still. Meantime, across the moors,
Had come young Porphyro, with heart on fire
For Madeline. Beside the portal doors,
Buttress'd from moonlight, stands he,
        and implores
All saints to give him sight of Madeline,
But for one moment in the tedious hours,
That he might gaze and worship all unseen;
Perchance speak, kneel, touch, kiss—in sooth such
        things have been.

10

He ventures in: let no buzz'd whisper tell:
All eyes be muffled, or a hundred swords
Will storm his heart, Love's fev'rous citadel:
For him, those chambers held barbarian hordes,
Hyena foemen, and hot-blooded lords,
Whose very dogs would execrations howl
Against his lineage: not one breast affords
Him any mercy, in that mansion foul,
Save one old beldame, weak in body and in soul.

11

Ah, happy chance! the aged creature came,
Shuffling along with ivory-headed wand,
To where he stood, hid from the torch's flame,
Behind a broad hall-pillar, far beyond
The sound of merriment and chorus bland:
He startled her; but soon she knew his face,
And grasp'd his fingers in her palsied hand,
Saying, "Mercy, Porphyro! hie thee from
    this place;
They are all here to-night, the whole blood-thirsty
    race!

12

"Get hence! get hence! there's dwarfish
    Hildebrand;
He had a fever late, and in the fit
He cursed thee and thine, both house and land:
Then there's that old Lord Maurice, not a whit
More tame for his grey hairs — Alas me! flit!
Flit like a ghost away." — "Ah, Gossip dear,
We're safe enough; here in this arm-chair sit,
And tell me how" — "Good Saints! not here,
    not here;
Follow me, child, or else these stones will be
    thy bier."

13

He follow'd through a lowly arched way,
Brushing the cobwebs with his lofty plume,

And as she mutter'd "Well-a—well-a-day!"
He found him in a little moonlight room,
Pale, lattic'd, chill, and silent as a tomb.
"Now tell me where is Madeline," said he,
"O tell me, Angela, by the holy loom
Which none but secret sisterhood may see,
When they St. Agnes' wool are weaving piously."

14

"St. Agnes! Ah! it is St. Agnes' Eve—
Yet men will murder upon holy days:
Thou must hold water in a witch's sieve,
And be liege-lord of all the Elves and Fays,
To venture so: it fills me with amaze
To see thee, Porphyro!—St. Agnes' Eve!
God's help! my lady fair the conjuror plays
This very night: good angels her deceive!
But let me laugh awhile, I've mickle time
        to grieve."

15

Feebly she laugheth in the languid moon,
While Porphyro upon her face doth look,
Like puzzled urchin on an aged crone
Who keepeth clos'd a wond'rous riddle-book,
As spectacled she sits in chimney nook.
But soon his eyes grew brilliant, when she told
His lady's purpose; and he scarce could brook
Tears, at the thought of those enchantments cold,
And Madeline asleep in lap of legends old.

16

Sudden a thought came like a full-blown rose,
Flushing his brow, and in his pained heart
Made purple riot: then doth he propose
A stratagem, that makes the beldame start:
"A cruel man and impious thou art:
Sweet lady, let her pray, and sleep, and dream
Alone with her good angels, far apart
From wicked men like thee. Go, go!—I deem
    Thou canst not surely be the same that thou
        didst seem."

17

"I will not harm her, by all saints I swear,"
Quoth Porphyro: "O may I ne'er find grace
When my weak voice shall whisper its last prayer,
If one of her soft ringlets I displace,
Or look with ruffian passion in her face:
Good Angela, believe me by these tears;
Or I will, even in a moment's space,
Awake, with horrid shout, my foemen's ears,
    And beard them, though they be more fang'd than
        wolves and bears."

18

"Ah! why wilt thou affright a feeble soul?
A poor, weak, palsy-stricken, churchyard thing,
Whose passing-bell may ere the midnight toll;
Whose prayers for thee, each morn and evening,

Were never miss'd." — Thus plaining, doth
     she bring
A gentler speech from burning Porphyro;
So woful, and of such deep sorrowing,
That Angela gives promise she will do
Whatever he shall wish, betide her weal or woe.

19

Which was, to lead him, in close secrecy,
Even to Madeline's chamber, and there hide
Him in a closet, of such privacy
That he might see her beauty unespied,
And win perhaps that night a peerless bride,
While legion'd faeries pac'd the coverlet,
And pale enchantment held her sleepy-eyed.
Never on such a night have lovers met,
Since Merlin paid his Demon all the
     monstrous debt.

20

"It shall be as thou wishest," said the Dame:
"All cates and dainties shall be stored there
Quickly on this feast-night: by the tambour frame
Her own lute thou wilt see: no time to spare,
For I am slow and feeble, and scarce dare
On such a catering trust my dizzy head.
Wait here, my child, with patience; kneel in prayer
The while: Ah! thou must needs the lady wed,
Or may I never leave my grave among the dead."

21

So saying, she hobbled off with busy fear.
The lover's endless minutes slowly pass'd;
The dame return'd, and whisper'd in his ear
To follow her; with aged eyes aghast
From fright of dim espial. Safe at last,
Through many a dusky gallery, they gain
The maiden's chamber, silken, hush'd, and chaste;
Where Porphyro took covert, pleas'd amain.
His poor guide hurried back with agues in her
        brain.

22

Her falt'ring hand upon the balustrade,
Old Angela was feeling for the stair,
When Madeline, St. Agnes' charmed maid,
Rose, like a mission'd spirit, unaware:
With silver taper's light, and pious care,
She turn'd, and down the aged gossip led
To a safe level matting. Now prepare,
Young Porphyro, for gazing on that bed;
She comes, she comes again, like ring-dove fray'd
        and fled.

23

Out went the taper as she hurried in;
Its little smoke, in pallid moonshine, died:
She clos'd the door, she panted, all akin
To spirits of the air, and visions wide:

No uttered syllable, or, woe betide!
But to her heart, her heart was voluble,
Paining with eloquence her balmy side;
As though a tongueless nightingale should swell
Her throat in vain, and die, heart-stifled, in
       her dell.

24

A casement high and triple-arch'd there was,
All garlanded with carven imag'ries
Of fruits, and flowers, and bunches of knot-grass,
And diamonded with panes of quaint device,
Innumerable of stains and splendid dyes,
As are the tiger-moth's deep-damask'd wings;
And in the midst, 'mong thousand heraldries,
And twilight saints, and dim emblazonings,
A shielded scutcheon blush'd with blood of queens
       and kings.

25

Full on this casement shone the wintry moon,
And threw warm gules on Madeline's fair breast,
As down she knelt for heaven's grace and boon;
Rose-bloom fell on her hands, together prest,
And on her silver cross soft amethyst,
And on her hair a glory, like a saint:
She seem'd a splendid angel, newly drest,
Save wings, for heaven:—Porphyro grew faint:
She knelt, so pure a thing, so free from mortal taint.

26

Anon his heart revives: her vespers done,
Of all its wreathed pearls her hair she frees;
Unclasps her warmed jewels one by one;
Loosens her fragrant bodice; by degrees
Her rich attire creeps rustling to her knees:
Half-hidden, like a mermaid in sea-weed,
Pensive awhile she dreams awake, and sees,
In fancy, fair St. Agnes in her bed,
But dares not look behind, or all the charm is fled.

27

Soon, trembling in her soft and chilly nest,
In sort of wakeful swoon, perplex'd she lay,
Until the poppied warmth of sleep oppress'd
Her soothed limbs, and soul fatigued away;
Flown, like a thought, until the morrow-day;
Blissfully haven'd both from joy and pain;
Clasp'd like a missal where swart Paynims pray;
Blinded alike from sunshine and from rain,
As though a rose should shut, and be a bud again.

28

Stol'n to this paradise, and so entranced,
Porphyro gazed upon her empty dress,
And listen'd to her breathing, if it chanced
To wake into a slumberous tenderness;
Which when he heard, that minute did he bless,
And breath'd himself: then from the closet crept,
Noiseless as fear in a wide wilderness,

And over the hush'd carpet, silent, stept,
And 'tween the curtains peep'd, where, lo!—how
        fast she slept.

29

Then by the bed-side, where the faded moon
Made a dim, silver twilight, soft he set
A table, and, half anguish'd, threw thereon
A cloth of woven crimson, gold, and jet:—
O for some drowsy Morphean amulet!
The boisterous, midnight, festive clarion,
The kettle-drum, and far-heard clarionet,
Affray his ears, though but in dying tone:—
The hall door shuts again, and all the noise is gone.

30

And still she slept an azure-lidded sleep,
In blanched linen, smooth, and lavender'd,
While he from forth the closet brought a heap
Of candied apple, quince, and plum, and gourd;
With jellies soother than the creamy curd,
And lucent syrops, tinct with cinnamon;
Manna and dates, in argosy transferr'd
From Fez; and spiced dainties, every one,
From silken Samarcand to cedar'd Lebanon.

31

These delicates he heap'd with glowing hand
On golden dishes and in baskets bright
Of wreathed silver: sumptuous they stand

In the retired quiet of the night,
Filling the chilly room with perfume light.—
"And now, my love, my seraph fair, awake!
Thou art my heaven, and I thine eremite:
Open thine eyes, for meek St. Agnes' sake,
Or I shall drowse beside thee, so my soul
      doth ache."

32

Thus whispering, his warm, unnerved arm
Sank in her pillow. Shaded was her dream
By the dusk curtains:—'twas a midnight charm
Impossible to melt as iced stream:
The lustrous salvers in the moonlight gleam;
Broad golden fringe upon the carpet lies:
It seem'd he never, never could redeem
From such a stedfast spell his lady's eyes;
So mus'd awhile, entoil'd in woofed phantasies.

33

Awakening up, he took her hollow lute,—
Tumultuous,—and, in chords that tenderest be,
He play'd an ancient ditty, long since mute,
In Provence call'd, "La belle dame sans mercy":
Close to her ear touching the melody;—
Wherewith disturb'd, she utter'd a soft moan:
He ceased—she panted quick—and suddenly
Her blue affrayed eyes wide open shone:
Upon his knees he sank, pale as smooth-sculptured
      stone.

34

Her eyes were open, but she still beheld,
Now wide awake, the vision of her sleep:
There was a painful change, that nigh expell'd
The blisses of her dream so pure and deep:
At which fair Madeline began to weep,
And moan forth witless words with many a sigh;
While still her gaze on Porphyro would keep;
Who knelt, with joined hands and piteous eye,
Fearing to move or speak, she look'd so dreamingly.

35

"Ah, Porphyro!" said she, "but even now
Thy voice was at sweet tremble in mine ear,
Made tuneable with every sweetest vow;
And those sad eyes were spiritual and clear:
How chang'd thou art! how pallid, chill, and drear!
Give me that voice again, my Porphyro,
Those looks immortal, those complainings dear!
Oh leave me not in this eternal woe,
For if thou diest, my love, I know not where to go."

36

Beyond a mortal man impassion'd far
At these voluptuous accents, he arose,
Ethereal, flush'd, and like a throbbing star
Seen mid the sapphire heaven's deep repose;
Into her dream he melted, as the rose
Blendeth its odour with the violet, —
Solution sweet: meantime the frost-wind blows

Like Love's alarum pattering the sharp sleet
Against the window-panes; St. Agnes' moon
      hath set.

37

'Tis dark: quick pattereth the flaw-blown sleet:
"This is no dream, my bride, my Madeline!"
'Tis dark: the iced gusts still rave and beat:
"No dream, alas! alas! and woe is mine!
Porphyro will leave me here to fade and pine.—
Cruel! what traitor could thee hither bring?
I curse not, for my heart is lost in thine,
Though thou forsakest a deceived thing—
A dove forlorn and lost with sick unpruned wing."

38

"My Madeline! sweet dreamer! lovely bride!
Say, may I be for aye thy vassal blest?
Thy beauty's shield, heart-shap'd and vermeil
      dyed?
Ah, silver shrine, here will I take my rest
After so many hours of toil and quest,
A famish'd pilgrim,—saved by miracle.
Though I have found, I will not rob thy nest
Saving of thy sweet self; if thou think'st well
To trust, fair Madeline, to no rude infidel.

39

"Hark! 'tis an elfin-storm from faery land,
Of haggard seeming, but a boon indeed:

Arise — arise! the morning is at hand; —
The bloated wassaillers will never heed: —
Let us away, my love, with happy speed;
There are no ears to hear, or eyes to see, —
Drown'd all in Rhenish and the sleepy mead:
Awake! arise! my love, and fearless be,
For o'er the southern moors I have a home
　　　　for thee."

40

She hurried at his words, beset with fears,
For there were sleeping dragons all around,
At glaring watch, perhaps, with ready spears —
Down the wide stairs a darkling way they found. —
In all the house was heard no human sound.
A chain-droop'd lamp was flickering by each door;
The arras, rich with horseman, hawk, and hound,
Flutter'd in the besieging wind's uproar;
And the long carpets rose along the gusty floor.

41

They glide, like phantoms, into the wide hall;
Like phantoms, to the iron porch, they glide;
Where lay the Porter, in uneasy sprawl,
With a huge empty flaggon by his side:
The wakeful bloodhound rose, and shook his hide,
But his sagacious eye an inmate owns:
By one, and one, the bolts full easy slide: —
The chains lie silent on the footworn stones; —
The key turns, and the door upon its hinges groans.

And they are gone: ay, ages long ago
These lovers fled away into the storm.
That night the Baron dreamt of many a woe,
And all his warrior-guests, with shade and form
Of witch, and demon, and large coffin-worm,
Were long be-nightmar'd. Angela the old
Died palsy-twitch'd, with meagre face deform;
The Beadsman, after thousand aves told,
For aye unsought for slept among his ashes cold.

The Eve of St. Mark

Upon a Sabbath day it fell;
Twice holy was the Sabbath bell,
That call'd the folk to evening prayer.
The city streets were clean and fair
From wholesome drench of April rains,
And on the western window panes
The chilly sunset faintly told
Of unmatur'd green vallies cold,
Of the green thorny bloomless hedge,
Of rivers new with springtide sedge,
Of primroses by shelter'd rills,
And daisies on the aguish hills.
Twice holy was the Sabbath bell:
The silent streets were crowded well
With staid and pious companies,
Warm from their fireside orat'ries,

And moving with demurest air
To even song and vesper prayer.
Each arched porch and entry low
Was fill'd with patient folk and slow,
With whispers hush and shuffling feet,
While play'd the organs loud and sweet.

The bells had ceas'd, the prayers begun,
And Bertha had not yet half done
A curious volume, patch'd and torn,
That all day long, from earliest morn,
Had taken captive her two eyes
Among its golden broideries;
Perplex'd her with a thousand things—
The stars of heaven, and angels' wings,
Martyrs in a fiery blaze,
Azure saints mid silver rays,
Aaron's breastplate, and the seven
Candlesticks John saw in heaven,
The winged Lion of St. Mark,
And the Covenantal Ark,
With its many mysteries,
Cherubim and golden mice.

Bertha was a maiden fair
Dwelling in the old Minster Square;
From her fireside she could see
Sidelong its rich antiquity,
Far as the bishop's garden wall,
Where sycamores and elm trees tall,

Full leav'd, the forest had outstript,
By no sharp north wind ever nipt,
So shelter'd by the mighty pile.
Bertha arose and read awhile,
With forehead 'gainst the window pane;
Again she tried, and then again,
Until the dusk eve left her dark
Upon the legend of St. Mark.
From pleated lawn-frill fine and thin
She lifted up her soft warm chin,
With aching neck and swimming eyes,
And dazed with saintly imageries.

All was gloom, and silent all,
Save now and then the still footfall
Of one returning townwards late,
Past the echoing minster gate.
The clamorous daws, that all the day
Above tree tops and towers play,
Pair by pair had gone to rest,
Each in its ancient belfry nest,
Where asleep they fall betimes
To music of the drowsy chimes.

All was silent, all was gloom,
Abroad and in the homely room;
Down she sat, poor cheated soul,
And struck a lamp from the dismal coal,
Leaned forward, with bright drooping hair,
And slant book full against the glare.

Her shadow in uneasy guise
Hover'd about, a giant size,
On ceiling beam and old oak chair,
The parrot's cage and pannel square,
And the warm angled winter screen,
On which were many monsters seen,
Call'd doves of Siam, Lima mice,
And legless birds of paradise,
Macaw, and tender av'davat,
And silken furr'd Angora cat.
Untired she read; her shadow still
Glower'd about as it would fill
The room with wildest forms and shades,
As though some ghostly queens of spades
Had come to mock behind her back,
And dance, and ruffle their garments black.
Untir'd she read the legend page
Of holy Mark from youth to age;
On land, on seas, in pagan-chains,
Rejoicing for his many pains.
Sometimes the learned eremite,
With golden star, or dagger bright,
Referr'd to pious poesies
Written in smallest crow-quill size
Beneath the text; and thus the rhyme
Was parcel'd out from time to time:
— "Als writith he of swevenis
Men han beforne they wake in bliss,
Whanne thate hir friendes thinke hem bound
In crimpid shroude farre under grounde;

And how a litling child mote be
A saint er its nativitie,
Gif thate the modre (God her blesse)
Kepen in solitarinesse,
And kissen devoute the holy croce.
Of Goddis love and Sathan's force
He writith; and thinges many mo:
Of swiche thinges I may not shew;
Bot I must tellen verilie
Somdel of Saintè Cicilie;
And chieflie whate he auctorethe
Of Saintè Markis life and dethe."

At length her constant eyelids come
Upon the fervent martyrdom;
Then lastly to his holy shrine,
Exalt amid the tapers' shine
At Venice

Why did I laugh tonight? No voice will tell

Why did I laugh tonight? No voice will tell:
No god, no demon of severe response,
Deigns to reply from heaven or from hell.
Then to my human heart I turn at once—
Heart! thou and I are here sad and alone;
Say, wherefore did I laugh? O mortal pain!
O darkness! darkness! ever must I moan,
To question heaven and hell and heart in vain!

Why did I laugh? I know this being's lease—
    My fancy to its utmost blisses spreads:
Yet could I on this very midnight ceasè,
    And the world's gaudy ensigns see in shreds.
Verse, fame, and beauty are intense indeed,
But death intenser—death is life's high meed.

Bright star, would I were stedfast as thou art

Bright star, would I were stedfast as thou art—
    Not in lone splendour hung aloft the night,
And watching, with eternal lids apart,
    Like nature's patient, sleepless eremite,
The moving waters at their priestlike task
    Of pure ablution round earth's human shores,
Or gazing on the new soft-fallen mask
    Of snow upon the mountains and the moors;
No—yet still stedfast, still unchangeable,
    Pillow'd upon my fair love's ripening breast,
To feel for ever its soft swell and fall,
    Awake for ever in a sweet unrest,
Still, still to hear her tender-taken breath,
And so live ever—or else swoon to death.

BOOK I

Deep in the shady sadness of a vale
Far sunken from the healthy breath of morn,
Far from the fiery noon, and eve's one star,
Sat grey-hair'd Saturn, quiet as a stone,
Still as the silence round about his lair;
Forest on forest hung above his head
Like cloud on cloud. No stir of air was there,
Not so much life as on a summer's day
Robs not one light seed from the feather'd grass,
But where the dead leaf fell, there did it rest.
A stream went voiceless by, still deadened more
By reason of his fallen divinity
Spreading a shade: the Naiad 'mid her reeds
Press'd her cold finger closer to her lips.

Along the margin-sand large foot-marks went,
No further than to where his feet had stray'd,
And slept there since. Upon the sodden ground
His old right hand lay nerveless, listless, dead,
Unsceptred; and his realmless eyes were closed;
While his bow'd head seem'd list'ning to the Earth,
His ancient mother, for some comfort yet.

It seem'd no force could wake him from his place;
But there came one, who with a kindred hand
Touch'd his wide shoulders, after bending low
With reverence, though to one who knew it not.

She was a Goddess of the infant world;
By her in stature the tall Amazon
Had stood a pigmy's height: she would have ta'en
Achilles by the hair and bent his neck;
Or with a finger stay'd Ixion's wheel.
Her face was large as that of Memphian sphinx,
Pedestal'd haply in a palace court,
When sages look'd to Egypt for their lore.
But oh! how unlike marble was that face:
How beautiful, if sorrow had not made
Sorrow more beautiful than Beauty's self.
There was a listening fear in her regard,
As if calamity had but begun;
As if the vanward clouds of evil days
Had spent their malice, and the sullen rear
Was with its stored thunder labouring up.
One hand she press'd upon that aching spot
Where beats the human heart, as if just there,
Though an immortal, she felt cruel pain:
The other upon Saturn's bended neck
She laid, and to the level of his ear
Leaning with parted lips, some words she spake
In solemn tenour and deep organ tone:
Some mourning words, which in our feeble tongue
Would come in these like accents; O how frail
To that large utterance of the early Gods!
"Saturn, look up!—though wherefore, poor
          old King?
I have no comfort for thee, no not one:
I cannot say, 'O wherefore sleepest thou?'

For heaven is parted from thee, and the earth
Knows thee not, thus afflicted, for a God;
And ocean too, with all its solemn noise,
Has from thy sceptre pass'd; and all the air
Is emptied of thine hoary majesty.
Thy thunder, conscious of the new command,
Rumbles reluctant o'er our fallen house;
And thy sharp lightning in unpractised hands
Scorches and burns our once serene domain.
O aching time! O moments big as years!
All as ye pass swell out the monstrous truth,
And press it so upon our weary griefs
That unbelief has not a space to breathe.
Saturn, sleep on:—O thoughtless, why did I
Thus violate thy slumbrous solitude?
Why should I ope thy melancholy eyes?
Saturn, sleep on! while at thy feet I weep."

As when, upon a tranced summer-night,
Those green-rob'd senators of mighty woods,
Tall oaks, branch-charmed by the earnest stars,
Dream, and so dream all night without a stir,
Save from one gradual solitary gust
Which comes upon the silence, and dies off,
As if the ebbing air had but one wave;
So came these words and went; the while in tears
She touch'd her fair large forehead to the ground,
Just where her falling hair might be outspread,
A soft and silken mat for Saturn's feet.
One moon, with alteration slow, had shed

Her silver seasons four upon the night,
And still these two were postured motionless,
Like natural sculpture in cathedral cavern;
The frozen God still couchant on the earth,
And the sad Goddess weeping at his feet:
Until at length old Saturn lifted up
His faded eyes, and saw his kingdom gone,
And all the gloom and sorrow of the place,
And that fair kneeling Goddess; and then spake,
As with a palsied tongue, and while his beard
Shook horrid with such aspen-malady:
"O tender spouse of gold Hyperion,
Thea, I feel thee ere I see thy face;
Look up, and let me see our doom in it;
Look up, and tell me if this feeble shape
Is Saturn's; tell me, if thou hear'st the voice
Of Saturn; tell me, if this wrinkling brow,
Naked and bare of its great diadem,
Peers like the front of Saturn. Who had power
To make me desolate? whence came the strength?
How was it nurtur'd to such bursting forth,
While Fate seem'd strangled in my nervous grasp?
But it is so; and I am smother'd up,
And buried from all godlike exercise
Of influence benign on planets pale,
Of admonitions to the winds and seas,
Of peaceful sway above man's harvesting,
And all those acts which Deity supreme
Doth ease its heart of love in. — I am gone
Away from my own bosom: I have left

My strong identity, my real self,
Somewhere between the throne, and where I sit
Here on this spot of earth. Search, Thea, search!
Open thine eyes eterne, and sphere them round
Upon all space: space starr'd, and lorn of light;
Space region'd with life-air; and barren void;
Spaces of fire, and all the yawn of hell. —
Search, Thea, search! and tell me, if thou seest
A certain shape or shadow, making way
With wings or chariot fierce to repossess
A heaven he lost erewhile: it must—it must
Be of ripe progress—Saturn must be King.
Yes, there must be a golden victory;
There must be Gods thrown down, and trumpets
        blown
Of triumph calm, and hymns of festival
Upon the gold clouds metropolitan,
Voices of soft proclaim, and silver stir
Of strings in hollow shells; and there shall be
Beautiful things made new, for the surprise
Of the sky-children; I will give command:
Thea! Thea! Thea! where is Saturn?"

  This passion lifted him upon his feet,
And made his hands to struggle in the air,
His Druid locks to shake and ooze with sweat,
His eyes to fever out, his voice to cease.
He stood, and heard not Thea's sobbing deep;
A little time, and then again he snatch'd
Utterance thus. — "But cannot I create?

Cannot I form? Cannot I fashion forth
Another world, another universe,
To overbear and crumble this to nought?
Where is another Chaos? Where?"—That word
Found way unto Olympus, and made quake
The rebel three.—Thea was startled up,
And in her bearing was a sort of hope,
As thus she quick-voic'd spake, yet full of awe.

"This cheers our fallen house: come to our friends,
O Saturn! come away, and give them heart;
I know the covert, for thence came I hither."
Thus brief; then with beseeching eyes she went
With backward footing through the shade a space:
He follow'd, and she turn'd to lead the way
Through aged boughs, that yielded like the mist
Which eagles cleave upmounting from their nest.

Meanwhile in other realms big tears were shed,
More sorrow like to this, and such like woe,
Too huge for mortal tongue or pen of scribe:
The Titans fierce, self-hid, or prison-bound,
Groan'd for the old allegiance once more,
And listen'd in sharp pain for Saturn's voice.
But one of the whole mammoth-brood still kept
His sov'reignty, and rule, and majesty;—
Blazing Hyperion on his orbed fire
Still sat, still snuff'd the incense, teeming up
From man to the sun's God; yet unsecure:
For as among us mortals omens drear

Fright and perplex, so also shuddered he—
Not at dog's howl, or gloom-bird's hated screech,
Or the familiar visiting of one
Upon the first toll of his passing-bell,
Or prophesyings of the midnight lamp;
But horrors, portion'd to a giant nerve,
Oft made Hyperion ache. His palace bright,
Bastion'd with pyramids of glowing gold,
And touch'd with shade of bronzed obelisks,
Glar'd a blood-red through all its thousand courts,
Arches, and domes, and fiery galleries;
And all its curtains of Aurorian clouds
Flush'd angerly: while sometimes eagle's wings,
Unseen before by Gods or wondering men,
Darken'd the place; and neighing steeds were
        heard,
Not heard before by Gods or wondering men.
Also, when he would taste the spicy wreaths
Of incense, breath'd aloft from sacred hills,
Instead of sweets, his ample palate took
Savour of poisonous brass and metal sick:
And so, when harbour'd in the sleepy west,
After the full completion of fair day,—
For rest divine upon exalted couch
And slumber in the arms of melody,
He pac'd away the pleasant hours of ease
With stride colossal, on from hall to hall;
While far within each aisle and deep recess,
His winged minions in close clusters stood,
Amaz'd and full of fear; like anxious men

Who on wide plains gather in panting troops,
When earthquakes jar their battlements and towers.
Even now, while Saturn, rous'd from icy trance,
Went step for step with Thea through the woods,
Hyperion, leaving twilight in the rear,
Came slope upon the threshold of the west;
Then, as was wont, his palace-door flew ope
In smoothest silence, save what solemn tubes,
Blown by the serious Zephyrs, gave of sweet
And wandering sounds, slow-breathed melodies;
And like a rose in vermeil tint and shape,
In fragrance soft, and coolness to the eye,
That inlet to severe magnificence
Stood full blown, for the God to enter in.

He enter'd, but he enter'd full of wrath;
His flaming robes stream'd out beyond his heels,
And gave a roar, as if of earthly fire,
That scar'd away the meek ethereal Hours
And made their dove-wings tremble. On he flared,
From stately nave to nave, from vault to vault,
Through bowers of fragrant and enwreathed light,
And diamond-paved lustrous long arcades,
Until he reach'd the great main cupola;
There standing fierce beneath, he stampt his foot,
And from the basements deep to the high towers
Jarr'd his own golden region; and before
The quavering thunder thereupon had ceas'd,
His voice leapt out, despite of godlike curb,
To this result: "O dreams of day and night!

O monstrous forms! O effigies of pain!
O spectres busy in a cold, cold gloom!
O lank-eared Phantoms of black-weeded pools!
Why do I know ye? why have I seen ye? why
Is my eternal essence thus distraught
To see and to behold these horrors new?
Saturn is fallen, am I too to fall?
Am I to leave this haven of my rest,
This cradle of my glory, this soft clime,
This calm luxuriance of blissful light,
These crystalline pavilions, and pure fanes,
Of all my lucent empire? It is left
Deserted, void, nor any haunt of mine.
The blaze, the splendour, and the symmetry,
I cannot see—but darkness, death and darkness.
Even here, into my centre of repose,
The shady visions come to domineer,
Insult, and blind, and stifle up my pomp.—
Fall!—No, by Tellus and her briny robes!
Over the fiery frontier of my realms
I will advance a terrible right arm
Shall scare that infant thunderer, rebel Jove,
And bid old Saturn take his throne again."—
He spake, and ceas'd, the while a heavier threat
Held struggle with his throat but came not forth;
For as in theatres of crowded men
Hubbub increases more they call out "Hush!"
So at Hyperion's words the Phantoms pale
Bestirr'd themselves, thrice horrible and cold;
And from the mirror'd level where he stood

A mist arose, as from a scummy marsh.
At this, through all his bulk an agony
Crept gradual, from the feet unto the crown,
Like a lithe serpent vast and muscular
Making slow way, with head and neck convuls'd
From over-strained might. Releas'd, he fled
To the eastern gates, and full six dewy hours
Before the dawn in season due should blush,
He breath'd fierce breath against the sleepy portals,
Clear'd them of heavy vapours, burst them wide
Suddenly on the ocean's chilly streams.
The planet orb of fire, whereon he rode
Each day from east to west the heavens through,
Spun round in sable curtaining of clouds;
Not therefore veiled quite, blindfold, and hid,
But ever and anon the glancing spheres,
Circles, and arcs, and broad-belting colure,
Glow'd through, and wrought upon the
          muffling dark
Sweet-shaped lightnings from the nadir deep
Up to the zenith,—hieroglyphics old,
Which sages and keen-eyed astrologers
Then living on the earth, with labouring thought
Won from the gaze of many centuries:
Now lost, save what we find on remnants huge
Of stone, or marble swart; their import gone,
Their wisdom long since fled.—Two wings
          this orb
Possess'd for glory, two fair argent wings,
Ever exalted at the God's approach:

And now, from forth the gloom their plumes
    immense
Rose, one by one, till all outspreaded were;
While still the dazzling globe maintain'd eclipse,
Awaiting for Hyperion's command.
Fain would he have commanded, fain took throne
And bid the day begin, if but for change.
He might not:—No, though a primeval God:
The sacred seasons might not be disturb'd.
Therefore the operations of the dawn
Stay'd in their birth, even as here 'tis told.
Those silver wings expanded sisterly,
Eager to sail their orb; the porches wide
Open'd upon the dusk demesnes of night;
And the bright Titan, phrenzied with new woes,
Unus'd to bend, by hard compulsion bent
His spirit to the sorrow of the time;
And all along a dismal rack of clouds,
Upon the boundaries of day and night,
He stretch'd himself in grief and radiance faint.
There as he lay, the heaven with its stars
Look'd down on him with pity, and the voice
Of Cœlus, from the universal space,
Thus whisper'd low and solemn in his ear.
"O brightest of my children dear, earth-born
And sky-engendered, Son of Mysteries
All unrevealed even to the powers
Which met at thy creating; at whose joys
And palpitations sweet, and pleasures soft,
I, Cœlus, wonder, how they came and whence;

And at the fruits thereof what shapes they be,
Distinct, and visible; symbols divine,
Manifestations of that beauteous life
Diffus'd unseen throughout eternal space:
Of these new-form'd art thou, oh brightest child!
Of these, thy brethren and the Goddesses!
There is sad feud among ye, and rebellion
Of son against his sire. I saw him fall,
I saw my first-born tumbled from his throne!
To me his arms were spread, to me his voice
Found way from forth the thunders round his head!
Pale wox I, and in vapours hid my face.
Art thou, too, near such doom? vague fear there is:
For I have seen my sons most unlike Gods.
Divine ye were created, and divine
In sad demeanour, solemn, undisturb'd,
Unruffled, like high Gods, ye liv'd and ruled:
Now I behold in you fear, hope, and wrath;
Actions of rage and passion; even as
I see them, on the mortal world beneath,
In men who die.—This is the grief, O Son!
Sad sign of ruin, sudden dismay, and fall!
Yet do thou strive; as thou art capable,
As thou canst move about, an evident God;
And canst oppose to each malignant hour
Ethereal presence:—I am but a voice;
My life is but the life of winds and tides,
No more than winds and tides can I avail:—
But thou canst.—Be thou therefore in the van
Of circumstance; yea, seize the arrow's barb

Before the tense string murmur.—To the earth!
For there thou wilt find Saturn, and his woes.
Meantime I will keep watch on thy bright sun,
And of thy seasons be a careful nurse."—
Ere half this region-whisper had come down,
Hyperion arose, and on the stars
Lifted his curved lids, and kept them wide
Until it ceas'd; and still he kept them wide:
And still they were the same bright, patient stars.
Then with a slow incline of his broad breast,
Like to a diver in the pearly seas,
Forward he stoop'd over the airy shore,
And plung'd all noiseless into the deep night.

BOOK II

Just at the self-same beat of Time's wide wings
Hyperion slid into the rustled air,
And Saturn gain'd with Thea that sad place
Where Cybele and the bruised Titans mourn'd.
It was a den where no insulting light
Could glimmer on their tears; where their
       own groans
They felt, but heard not, for the solid roar
Of thunderous waterfalls and torrents hoarse,
Pouring a constant bulk, uncertain where.
Crag jutting forth to crag, and rocks that seem'd
Ever as if just rising from a sleep,
Forehead to forehead held their monstrous horns;
And thus in thousand hugest phantasies
Made a fit roofing to this nest of woe.

Instead of thrones, hard flint they sat upon,
Couches of rugged stone, and slaty ridge
Stubborn'd with iron. All were not assembled:
Some chain'd in torture, and some wandering.
Cœus, and Gyges, and Briareüs,
Typhon, and Dolor, and Porphyrion,
With many more, the brawniest in assault,
Were pent in regions of laborious breath;
Dungeon'd in opaque element, to keep
Their clenched teeth still clench'd, and all
            their limbs
Lock'd up like veins of metal, crampt and screw'd;
Without a motion, save of their big hearts
Heaving in pain, and horribly convuls'd
With sanguine feverous boiling gurge of pulse.
Mnemosyne was straying in the world;
Far from her moon had Phœbe wandered;
And many else were free to roam abroad,
But for the main, here found they covert drear.
Scarce images of life, one here, one there,
Lay vast and edgeways; like a dismal cirque
Of Druid stones, upon a forlorn moor,
When the chill rain begins at shut of eve,
In dull November, and their chancel vault,
The heaven itself, is blinded throughout night.
Each one kept shroud, nor to his neighbour gave
Or word, or look, or action of despair.
Creüs was one; his ponderous iron mace
Lay by him, and a shatter'd rib of rock
Told of his rage, ere he thus sank and pined.

Iäpetus another; in his grasp,
A serpent's plashy neck; its barbed tongue
Squeez'd from the gorge, and all its uncurl'd length
Dead; and because the creature could not spit
Its poison in the eyes of conquering Jove.
Next Cottus: prone he lay, chin uppermost,
As though in pain; for still upon the flint
He ground severe his skull, with open mouth
And eyes at horrid working. Nearest him
Asia, born of most enormous Caf,
Who cost her mother Tellus keener pangs,
Though feminine, than any of her sons:
More thought than woe was in her dusky face,
For she was prophesying of her glory;
And in her wide imagination stood
Palm-shaded temples, and high rival fanes,
By Oxus or in Ganges' sacred isles.
Even as Hope upon her anchor leans,
So leant she, not so fair, upon a tusk
Shed from the broadest of her elephants.
Above her, on a crag's uneasy shelve,
Upon his elbow rais'd, all prostrate else,
Shadow'd Enceladus; once tame and mild
As grazing ox unworried in the meads;
Now tiger-passion'd, lion-thoughted, wroth,
He meditated, plotted, and even now
Was hurling mountains in that second war,
Not long delay'd, that scar'd the younger Gods
To hide themselves in forms of beast and bird.

Not far hence Atlas; and beside him prone
Phorcus, the sire of Gorgons. Neighbour'd close
Oceanus, and Tethys, in whose lap
Sobb'd Clymene among her tangled hair.
In midst of all lay Themis, at the feet
Of Ops the queen all clouded round from sight;
No shape distinguishable, more than when
Thick night confounds the pine-tops with
      the clouds:
And many else whose names may not be told.
For when the Muse's wings are air-ward spread,
Who shall delay her flight? And she must chaunt
Of Saturn, and his guide, who now had climb'd
With damp and slippery footing from a depth
More horrid still. Above a sombre cliff
Their heads appear'd, and up their stature grew
Till on the level height their steps found ease:
Then Thea spread abroad her trembling arms
Upon the precincts of this nest of pain,
And sidelong fix'd her eye on Saturn's face:
There saw she direst strife; the supreme God
At war with all the frailty of grief,
Of rage, of fear, anxiety, revenge,
Remorse, spleen, hope, but most of all despair.
Against these plagues he strove in vain; for Fate
Had pour'd a mortal oil upon his head,
A disanointing poison: so that Thea,
Affrighted, kept her still, and let him pass
First onwards in, among the fallen tribe.

As with us mortal men, the laden heart
Is persecuted more, and fever'd more,
When it is nighing to the mournful house
Where other hearts are sick of the same bruise;
So Saturn, as he walk'd into the midst,
Felt faint, and would have sunk among the rest,
But that he met Enceladus's eye,
Whose mightiness, and awe of him, at once
Came like an inspiration; and he shouted,
"Titans, behold your God!" at which some groan'd;
Some started on their feet; some also shouted;
Some wept, some wail'd, all bow'd with reverence;
And Ops, uplifting her black folded veil,
Show'd her pale cheeks, and all her forehead wan,
Her eye-brows thin and jet, and hollow eyes.
There is a roaring in the bleak-grown pines
When Winter lifts his voice; there is a noise
Among immortals when a God gives sign,
With hushing finger, how he means to load
His tongue with the full weight of utterless thought,
With thunder, and with music, and with pomp:
Such noise is like the roar of bleak-grown pines;
Which, when it ceases in this mountain'd world,
No other sound succeeds; but ceasing here,
Among these fallen, Saturn's voice therefrom
Grew up like organ, that begins anew
Its strain, when other harmonies, stopt short,
Leave the dinn'd air vibrating silverly.
Thus grew it up—"Not in my own sad breast,
Which is its own great judge and searcher out,

Can I find reason why ye should be thus:
Not in the legends of the first of days,
Studied from that old spirit-leaved book
Which starry Uranus with finger bright
Sav'd from the shores of darkness, when the waves
Low-ebb'd still hid it up in shallow gloom;—
And the which book ye know I ever kept
For my firm-based footstool:—Ah, infirm!
Not there, nor in sign, symbol, or portent
Of element, earth, water, air, and fire,—
At war, at peace, or inter-quarreling
One against one, or two, or three, or all
Each several one against the other three,
As fire with air loud warring when rain-floods
Drown both, and press them both against
        earth's face,
Where, finding sulphur, a quadruple wrath
Unhinges the poor world;—not in that strife,
Wherefrom I take strange lore, and read it deep,
Can I find reason why ye should be thus:
No, no-where can unriddle, though I search,
And pore on Nature's universal scroll
Even to swooning, why ye, Divinities,
The first-born of all shap'd and palpable Gods,
Should cower beneath what, in comparison,
Is untremendous might. Yet ye are here,
O'erwhelm'd, and spurn'd, and batter'd, ye
        are here!
O Titans, shall I say 'Arise!'—Ye groan:
Shall I say 'Crouch!'—Ye groan. What can I then?

O Heaven wide! O unseen parent dear!
What can I? Tell me, all ye brethren Gods,
How we can war, how engine our great wrath!
O speak your counsel now, for Saturn's ear
Is all a-hunger'd. Thou, Oceanus,
Ponderest high and deep; and in thy face
I see, astonied, that severe content
Which comes of thought and musing: give us help!"

So ended Saturn; and the God of the Sea,
Sophist and sage, from no Athenian grove,
But cogitation in his watery shades,
Arose, with locks not oozy, and began,
In murmurs, which his first-endeavouring tongue
Caught infant-like from the far-foamed sands.
"O ye, whom wrath consumes! who, passion-stung,
Writhe at defeat, and nurse your agonies!
Shut up your senses, stifle up your ears,
My voice is not a bellows unto ire.
Yet listen, ye who will, whilst I bring proof
How ye, perforce, must be content to stoop:
And in the proof much comfort will I give,
If ye will take that comfort in its truth.
We fall by course of Nature's law, not force
Of thunder, or of Jove. Great Saturn, thou
Hast sifted well the atom-universe;
But for this reason, that thou art the King,
And only blind from sheer supremacy,
One avenue was shaded from thine eyes,
Through which I wandered to eternal truth.

And first, as thou wast not the first of powers,
So art thou not the last; it cannot be:
Thou art not the beginning nor the end.
From Chaos and parental Darkness came
Light, the first fruits of that intestine broil,
That sullen ferment, which for wondrous ends
Was ripening in itself. The ripe hour came,
And with it Light, and Light, engendering
Upon its own producer, forthwith touch'd
The whole enormous matter into life.
Upon that very hour, our parentage,
The Heavens and the Earth, were manifest:
Then thou first-born, and we the giant-race,
Found ourselves ruling new and beauteous realms.
Now comes the pain of truth, to whom 'tis pain;
O folly! for to bear all naked truths,
And to envisage circumstance, all calm,
That is the top of sovereignty. Mark well!
As Heaven and Earth are fairer, fairer far
Than Chaos and blank Darkness, though once
                    chiefs;
And as we show beyond that Heaven and Earth
In form and shape compact and beautiful,
In will, in action free, companionship,
And thousand other signs of purer life;
So on our heels a fresh perfection treads,
A power more strong in beauty, born of us
And fated to excel us, as we pass
In glory that old Darkness: nor are we
Thereby more conquer'd, than by us the rule

Of shapeless Chaos. Say, doth the dull soil
Quarrel with the proud forests it hath fed,
And feedeth still, more comely than itself?
Can it deny the chiefdom of green groves?
Or shall the tree be envious of the dove
Because it cooeth, and hath snowy wings
To wander wherewithal and find its joys?
We are such forest-trees, and our fair boughs
Have bred forth, not pale solitary doves,
But eagles golden-feather'd, who do tower
Above us in their beauty, and must reign
In right thereof; for 'tis the eternal law
That first in beauty should be first in might:
Yea, by that law, another race may drive
Our conquerors to mourn as we do now.
Have ye beheld the young God of the Seas,
My dispossessor? Have ye seen his face?
Have ye beheld his chariot, foam'd along
By noble winged creatures he hath made?
I saw him on the calmed waters scud,
With such a glow of beauty in his eyes,
That it enforc'd me to bid sad farewell
To all my empire: farewell sad I took,
And hither came, to see how dolorous fate
Had wrought upon ye; and how I might best
Give consolation in this woe extreme.
Receive the truth, and let it be your balm."

Whether through poz'd conviction, or disdain,
They guarded silence, when Oceanus

Left murmuring, what deepest thought can tell?
But so it was, none answer'd for a space,
Save one whom none regarded, Clymene;
And yet she answer'd not, only complain'd,
With hectic lips, and eyes up-looking mild,
Thus wording timidly among the fierce:
"O Father, I am here the simplest voice,
And all my knowledge is that joy is gone,
And this thing woe crept in among our hearts,
There to remain for ever, as I fear:
I would not bode of evil, if I thought
So weak a creature could turn off the help
Which by just right should come of mighty Gods;
Yet let me tell my sorrow, let me tell
Of what I heard, and how it made me weep,
And know that we had parted from all hope.
I stood upon a shore, a pleasant shore,
Where a sweet clime was breathed from a land
Of fragrance, quietness, and trees, and flowers.
Full of calm joy it was, as I of grief;
Too full of joy and soft delicious warmth;
So that I felt a movement in my heart
To chide, and to reproach that solitude
With songs of misery, music of our woes;
And sat me down, and took a mouthed shell
And murmur'd into it, and made melody—
O melody no more! for while I sang,
And with poor skill let pass into the breeze
The dull shell's echo, from a bowery strand
Just opposite, an island of the sea,

There came enchantment with the shifting wind,
That did both drown and keep alive my ears.
I threw my shell away upon the sand,
And a wave fill'd it, as my sense was fill'd
With that new blissful golden melody.
A living death was in each gush of sounds,
Each family of rapturous hurried notes,
That fell, one after one, yet all at once,
Like pearl beads dropping sudden from
            their string:
And then another, then another strain,
Each like a dove leaving its olive perch,
With music wing'd instead of silent plumes,
To hover round my head, and make me sick
Of joy and grief at once. Grief overcame,
And I was stopping up my frantic ears,
When, past all hindrance of my trembling hands,
A voice came sweeter, sweeter than all tune,
And still it cried, 'Apollo! young Apollo!
The morning-bright Apollo! young Apollo!'
I fled, it follow'd me, and cried 'Apollo!'
O Father, and O Brethren, had ye felt
Those pains of mine; O Saturn, hadst thou felt,
Ye would not call this too indulged tongue
Presumptuous, in thus venturing to be heard."

So far her voice flow'd on, like timorous brook
That, lingering along a pebbled coast,
Doth fear to meet the sea: but sea it met,

And shudder'd; for the overwhelming voice
Of huge Enceladus swallow'd it in wrath:
The ponderous syllables, like sullen waves
In the half-glutted hollows of reef-rocks,
Came booming thus, while still upon his arm
He lean'd; not rising, from supreme contempt.
"Or shall we listen to the over-wise,
Or to the over-foolish, Giant-Gods?
Not thunderbolt on thunderbolt, till all
That rebel Jove's whole armoury were spent,
Not world on world upon these shoulders piled,
Could agonize me more than baby-words
In midst of this dethronement horrible.
Speak! roar! shout! yell! ye sleepy Titans all.
Do ye forget the blows, the buffets vile?
Are ye not smitten by a youngling arm?
Dost thou forget, sham Monarch of the Waves,
Thy scalding in the seas? What, have I rous'd
Your spleens with so few simple words as these?
O joy! for now I see ye are not lost:
O joy! for now I see a thousand eyes
Wide glaring for revenge!"—As this he said,
He lifted up his stature vast, and stood,
Still without intermission speaking thus:
"Now ye are flames, I'll tell you how to burn,
And purge the ether of our enemies;
How to feed fierce the crooked stings of fire,
And singe away the swollen clouds of Jove,
Stifling that puny essence in its tent.

O let him feel the evil he hath done;
For though I scorn Oceanus's lore,
Much pain have I for more than loss of realms:
The days of peace and slumberous calm are fled;
Those days, all innocent of scathing war,
When all the fair Existences of heaven
Came open-eyed to guess what we would speak:—
That was before our brows were taught to frown,
Before our lips knew else but solemn sounds;
That was before we knew the winged thing,
Victory, might be lost, or might be won.
And be ye mindful that Hyperion,
Our brightest brother, still is undisgraced—
Hyperion, lo! his radiance is here!"

   All eyes were on Enceladus's face,
And they beheld, while still Hyperion's name
Flew from his lips up to the vaulted rocks,
A pallid gleam across his features stern:
Not savage, for he saw full many a God
Wroth as himself. He look'd upon them all,
And in each face he saw a gleam of light,
But splendider in Saturn's, whose hoar locks
Shone like the bubbling foam about a keel
When the prow sweeps into a midnight cove.
In pale and silver silence they remain'd,
Till suddenly a splendour, like the morn,
Pervaded all the beetling gloomy steeps,
All the sad spaces of oblivion,

And every gulf, and every chasm old,
And every height, and every sullen depth,
Voiceless, or hoarse with loud tormented streams:
And all the everlasting cataracts,
And all the headlong torrents far and near,
Mantled before in darkness and huge shade,
Now saw the light and made it terrible.
It was Hyperion:—a granite peak
His bright feet touch'd, and there he stay'd to view
The misery his brilliance had betray'd
To the most hateful seeing of itself.
Golden his hair of short Numidian curl,
Regal his shape majestic, a vast shade
In midst of his own brightness, like the bulk
Of Memnon's image at the set of sun
To one who travels from the dusking east:
Sighs, too, as mournful as that Memnon's harp
He utter'd, while his hands contemplative
He press'd together, and in silence stood.
Despondence seiz'd again the fallen Gods
At sight of the dejected King of Day,
And many hid their faces from the light:
But fierce Enceladus sent forth his eyes
Among the brotherhood; and, at their glare,
Uprose Iäpetus, and Creüs too,
And Phorcus, sea-born, and together strode
To where he towered on his eminence.
There those four shouted forth old Saturn's
        name;

Hyperion from the peak loud answered, "Saturn!"
Saturn sat near the Mother of the Gods,
In whose face was no joy, though all the Gods
Gave from their hollow throats the name of
   "Saturn!"

BOOK III

Thus in alternate uproar and sad peace,
Amazed were those Titans utterly.
O leave them, Muse! O leave them to their woes;
For thou art weak to sing such tumults dire:
A solitary sorrow best befits
Thy lips, and antheming a lonely grief.
Leave them, O Muse! for thou anon wilt find
Many a fallen old Divinity
Wandering in vain about bewildered shores.
Meantime touch piously the Delphic harp,
And not a wind of heaven but will breathe
In aid soft warble from the Dorian flute;
For lo! 'tis for the Father of all verse.
Flush every thing that hath a vermeil hue,
Let the rose glow intense and warm the air,
And let the clouds of even and of morn
Float in voluptuous fleeces o'er the hills;
Let the red wine within the goblet boil,
Cold as a bubbling well; let faint-lipp'd shells,
On sands, or in great deeps, vermilion turn
Through all their labyrinths; and let the maid
Blush keenly, as with some warm kiss surpris'd.
Chief isle of the embowered Cyclades,

Rejoice, O Delos, with thine olives green,
And poplars, and lawn-shading palms, and beech,
In which the Zephyr breathes the loudest song,
And hazels thick, dark-stemm'd beneath
            the shade:
Apollo is once more the golden theme!
Where was he, when the Giant of the Sun
Stood bright, amid the sorrow of his peers?
Together had he left his mother fair
And his twin-sister sleeping in their bower,
And in the morning twilight wandered forth
Beside the osiers of a rivulet,
Full ankle-deep in lilies of the vale.
The nightingale had ceas'd, and a few stars
Were lingering in the heavens, while the thrush
Began calm-throated. Throughout all the isle
There was no covert, no retired cave
Unhaunted by the murmurous noise of waves,
Though scarcely heard in many a green recess.
He listen'd, and he wept, and his bright tears
Went trickling down the golden bow he held.
Thus with half-shut suffused eyes he stood,
While from beneath some cumbrous boughs
            hard by
With solemn step an awful Goddess came,
And there was purport in her looks for him,
Which he with eager guess began to read
Perplex'd, the while melodiously he said:
"How cam'st thou over the unfooted sea?
Or hath that antique mien and robed form

Mov'd in these vales invisible till now?
Sure I have heard those vestments sweeping o'er
The fallen leaves, when I have sat alone
In cool mid-forest. Surely I have traced
The rustle of those ample skirts about
These grassy solitudes, and seen the flowers
Lift up their heads, as still the whisper pass'd.
Goddess! I have beheld those eyes before,
And their eternal calm, and all that face,
Or I have dream'd."—"Yes," said the supreme
         shape,
"Thou hast dream'd of me; and awaking up
Didst find a lyre all golden by thy side,
Whose strings touch'd by thy fingers, all the vast
Unwearied ear of the whole universe
Listen'd in pain and pleasure at the birth
Of such new tuneful wonder. Is't not strange
That thou shouldst weep, so gifted? Tell me, youth,
What sorrow thou canst feel; for I am sad
When thou dost shed a tear: explain thy griefs
To one who in this lonely isle hath been
The watcher of thy sleep and hours of life,
From the young day when first thy infant hand
Pluck'd witless the weak flowers, till thine arm
Could bend that bow heroic to all times.
Show thy heart's secret to an ancient Power
Who hath forsaken old and sacred thrones
For prophecies of thee, and for the sake
Of loveliness new born."—Apollo then,

With sudden scrutiny and gloomless eyes,
Thus answer'd, while his white melodious throat
Throbb'd with the syllables. — "Mnemosyne!
Thy name is on my tongue, I know not how;
Why should I tell thee what thou so well seest?
Why should I strive to show what from thy lips
Would come no mystery? For me, dark, dark,
And painful vile oblivion seals my eyes:
I strive to search wherefore I am so sad,
Until a melancholy numbs my limbs;
And then upon the grass I sit, and moan,
Like one who once had wings. — O why should I
Feel curs'd and thwarted, when the liegeless air
Yields to my step aspirant? why should I
Spurn the green turf as hateful to my feet?
Goddess benign, point forth some unknown
       thing:
Are there not other regions than this isle?
What are the stars? There is the sun, the sun!
And the most patient brilliance of the moon!
And stars by thousands! Point me out the way
To any one particular beauteous star,
And I will flit into it with my lyre,
And make its silvery splendour pant with bliss.
I have heard the cloudy thunder: Where
       is power?
Whose hand, whose essence, what divinity
Makes this alarum in the elements,
While I here idle listen on the shores

In fearless yet in aching ignorance?
O tell me, lonely Goddess, by thy harp,
That waileth every morn and eventide,
Tell me why thus I rave, about these groves!
Mute thou remainest—mute! yet I can read
A wondrous lesson in thy silent face:
Knowledge enormous makes a God of me.
Names, deeds, grey legends, dire events,
       rebellions,
Majesties, sovran voices, agonies,
Creations and destroyings, all at once
Pour into the wide hollows of my brain,
And deify me, as if some blithe wine
Or bright elixir peerless I had drunk,
And so become immortal."—Thus the God,
While his enkindled eyes, with level glance
Beneath his white soft temples, stedfast kept
Trembling with light upon Mnemosyne.
Soon wild commotions shook him, and
       made flush
All the immortal fairness of his limbs;
Most like the struggle at the gate of death;
Or liker still to one who should take leave
Of pale immortal death, and with a pang
As hot as death's is chill, with fierce convulse
Die into life: so young Apollo anguish'd:
His very hair, his golden tresses famed,
Kept undulation round his eager neck.
During the pain Mnemosyne upheld
Her arms as one who prophesied.—At length

Apollo shriek'd;—and lo! from all his limbs
Celestial . . . .

. . . .

La Belle Dame sans Merci: A Ballad

1

O what can ail thee, knight at arms,
  Alone and palely loitering?
The sedge has wither'd from the lake,
  And no birds sing.

2

O what can ail thee, knight at arms,
  So haggard and so woe-begone?
The squirrel's granary is full,
  And the harvest's done.

3

I see a lily on thy brow
  With anguish moist and fever dew,
And on thy cheeks a fading rose
  Fast withereth too.

4

I met a lady in the meads,
  Full beautiful, a fairy's child;
Her hair was long, her foot was light,
  And her eyes were wild.

5

I made a garland for her head,
  And bracelets too, and fragrant zone;
She look'd at me as she did love,
  And made sweet moan.

6

I set her on my pacing steed,
  And nothing else saw all day long,
For sidelong would she bend, and sing
  A fairy's song.

7

She found me roots of relish sweet,
  And honey wild, and manna dew,
And sure in language strange she said —
  I love thee true.

8

She took me to her elfin grot,
  And there she wept, and sigh'd full sore,
And there I shut her wild wild eyes
  With kisses four.

9

And there she lulled me asleep.
  And there I dream'd — Ah! woe betide!
The latest dream I ever dream'd
  On the cold hill's side.

10

I saw pale kings, and princes too,
  Pale warriors, death pale were they all;
They cried—"La belle dame sans merci
   Hath thee in thrall!"

11

I saw their starv'd lips in the gloam
  With horrid warning gaped wide,
And I awoke and found me here
   On the cold hill's side.

12

And this is why I sojourn here,
  Alone and palely loitering,
Though the sedge is wither'd from the lake,
   And no birds sing.

Sonnet to Sleep

O soft embalmer of the still midnight,
  Shutting with careful fingers and benign
Our gloom-pleas'd eyes, embower'd from the light,
  Enshaded in forgetfulness divine:
O soothest Sleep! if so it please thee, close,
  In midst of this thine hymn, my willing eyes,
Or wait the Amen ere thy poppy throws
  Around my bed its lulling charities.

Then save me or the passed day will shine
  Upon my pillow, breeding many woes;
Save me from curious conscience, that still hoards
  Its strength for darkness, burrowing like the
                mole;
Turn the key deftly in the oiled wards,
  And seal the hushed casket of my soul.

Ode to Psyche

O Goddess! hear these tuneless numbers, wrung
  By sweet enforcement and remembrance dear,
And pardon that thy secrets should be sung
  Even into thine own soft-conched ear:
Surely I dreamt to-day, or did I see
  The winged Psyche with awaken'd eyes?
I wander'd in a forest thoughtlessly,
  And, on the sudden, fainting with surprise,
Saw two fair creatures, couched side by side
  In deepest grass, beneath the whisp'ring roof
  Of leaves and trembled blossoms, where there ran
      A brooklet, scarce espied:
'Mid hush'd, cool-rooted flowers, fragrant-eyed,
  Blue, silver-white, and budded Tyrian,
They lay calm-breathing on the bedded grass;
  Their arms embraced, and their pinions too;
  Their lips touch'd not, but had not bade adieu,
As if disjoined by soft-handed slumber,
And ready still past kisses to outnumber

At tender eye-dawn of aurorean love:
    The winged boy I knew;
But who wast thou, O happy, happy dove?
    His Psyche true!

O latest born and loveliest vision far
  Of all Olympus' faded hierarchy!
Fairer than Phœbe's sapphire-region'd star,
  Or Vesper, amorous glow-worm of the sky;
Fairer than these, though temple thou hast none,
    Nor altar heap'd with flowers;
Nor virgin-choir to make delicious moan
    Upon the midnight hours;
No voice, no lute, no pipe, no incense sweet
  From chain-swung censer teeming;
No shrine, no grove, no oracle, no heat
  Of pale-mouth'd prophet dreaming.

O brightest! though too late for antique vows,
  Too, too late for the fond believing lyre,
When holy were the haunted forest boughs,
  Holy the air, the water, and the fire;
Yet even in these days so far retir'd
  From happy pieties, thy lucent fans,
  Fluttering among the faint Olympians,
I see, and sing, by my own eyes inspired.
So let me be thy choir, and make a moan
    Upon the midnight hours;
Thy voice, thy lute, thy pipe, thy incense sweet
  From swinged censer teeming;

Thy shrine, thy grove, thy oracle, thy heat
　　Of pale-mouth'd prophet dreaming.

Yes, I will be thy priest, and build a fane
　　In some untrodden region of my mind,
Where branched thoughts, new grown with
　　　　　pleasant pain,
　　Instead of pines shall murmur in the wind:
Far, far around shall those dark cluster'd trees
　　Fledge the wild-ridged mountains steep by steep;
And there by zephyrs, streams, and birds, and bees,
　　The moss-lain Dryads shall be lull'd to sleep;
And in the midst of this wide quietness
A rosy sanctuary will I dress
With the wreath'd trellis of a working brain,
　　With buds, and bells, and stars without a name,
With all the gardener Fancy e'er could feign,
　　Who breeding flowers, will never breed the same:
And there shall be for thee all soft delight
　　That shadowy thought can win,
A bright torch, and a casement ope at night,
　　To let the warm Love in!

Ode to a Nightingale

1

My heart aches, and a drowsy numbness pains
　　My sense, as though of hemlock I had drunk,

Or emptied some dull opiate to the drains
  One minute past, and Lethe-wards had sunk:
'Tis not through envy of thy happy lot,
  But being too happy in thine happiness,—
    That thou, light-winged Dryad of the trees,
      In some melodious plot
Of beechen green, and shadows numberless,
  Singest of summer in full-throated ease.

2

O for a draught of vintage! that hath been
  Cool'd a long age in the deep-delved earth,
Tasting of Flora and the country green,
  Dance, and Provençal song, and sunburnt mirth!
O for a beaker full of the warm South,
  Full of the true, the blushful Hippocrene,
    With beaded bubbles winking at the brim,
      And purple-stained mouth;
That I might drink, and leave the world unseen,
  And with thee fade away into the forest dim:

3

Fade far away, dissolve, and quite forget
  What thou among the leaves hast never known,
The weariness, the fever, and the fret
  Here, where men sit and hear each other groan;
Where palsy shakes a few, sad, last grey hairs,
  Where youth grows pale, and spectre-thin,
      and dies;

Where but to think is to be full of sorrow
  And leaden-eyed despairs,
Where Beauty cannot keep her lustrous eyes,
  Or new Love pine at them beyond to-morrow.

4

Away! away! for I will fly to thee,
  Not charioted by Bacchus and his pards,
But on the viewless wings of Poesy,
  Though the dull brain perplexes and retards;
Already with thee! tender is the night,
  And haply the Queen-Moon is on her throne,
    Cluster'd around by all her starry Fays;
      But here there is no light,
  Save what from heaven is with the breezes blown
    Through verdurous glooms and winding
      mossy ways.

5

I cannot see what flowers are at my feet,
  Nor what soft incense hangs upon the boughs,
But, in embalmed darkness, guess each sweet
  Wherewith the seasonable month endows
The grass, the thicket, and the fruit-tree wild;
  White hawthorn, and the pastoral eglantine;
    Fast fading violets cover'd up in leaves;
      And mid-May's eldest child,
  The coming musk-rose, full of dewy wine,
    The murmurous haunt of flies on summer eves.

6

Darkling I listen; and, for many a time
　I have been half in love with easeful Death,
Call'd him soft names in many a mused rhyme,
　To take into the air my quiet breath;
Now more than ever seems it rich to die,
　To cease upon the midnight with no pain,
　　While thou art pouring forth thy soul abroad
　　　　In such an ecstasy!
　Still wouldst thou sing, and I have ears in
　　　　vain —
　　To thy high requiem become a sod.

7

Thou wast not born for death, immortal Bird!
　No hungry generations tread thee down;
The voice I hear this passing night was heard
　In ancient days by emperor and clown:
Perhaps the self-same song that found a path
　Through the sad heart of Ruth, when, sick
　　　　for home,
　　She stood in tears amid the alien corn;
　　　　The same that oft-times hath
　Charm'd magic casements, opening on the foam
　Of perilous seas, in faery lands forlorn.

8

Forlorn! the very word is like a bell
　To toll me back from thee to my sole self!

Adieu! the fancy cannot cheat so well
  As she is fam'd to do, deceiving elf.
Adieu! adieu! thy plaintive anthem fades
    Past the near meadows, over the still stream,
      Up the hill-side; and now 'tis buried deep
        In the next valley-glades:
    Was it a vision, or a waking dream?
    Fled is that music:—Do I wake or sleep?

Ode on a Grecian Urn

1

Thou still unravish'd bride of quietness,
  Thou foster-child of silence and slow time,
Sylvan historian, who canst thus express
  A flowery tale more sweetly than our rhyme:
What leaf-fring'd legend haunts about thy shape
    Of deities or mortals, or of both
      In Tempe or the dales of Arcady?
    What men or gods are these? What maidens loth?
What mad pursuit? What struggle to escape?
    What pipes and timbrels? What wild ecstasy?

2

Heard melodies are sweet, but those unheard
  Are sweeter; therefore, ye soft pipes, play on;
Not to the sensual ear, but, more endear'd,
    Pipe to the spirit ditties of no tone:
Fair youth, beneath the trees, thou canst not leave

Thy song, nor ever can those trees be bare;
  Bold lover, never, never canst thou kiss,
Though winning near the goal—yet, do not
      grieve;
  She cannot fade, though thou hast not thy bliss,
For ever wilt thou love, and she be fair!

3

Ah, happy, happy boughs! that cannot shed
  Your leaves, nor ever bid the spring adieu;
And, happy melodist, unwearied,
  For ever piping songs for ever new;
More happy love! more happy, happy love!
  For ever warm and still to be enjoy'd,
    For ever panting, and for ever young;
All breathing human passion far above,
  That leaves a heart high-sorrowful and cloy'd,
    A burning forehead, and a parching tongue.

4

Who are these coming to the sacrifice?
  To what green altar, O mysterious priest,
Lead'st thou that heifer lowing at the skies,
  And all her silken flanks with garlands drest?
What little town by river or sea shore,
  Or mountain-built with peaceful citadel,
    Is emptied of this folk, this pious morn?
And, little town, thy streets for evermore
  Will silent be; and not a soul to tell
    Why thou art desolate, can e'er return.

5

O Attic shape! Fair attitude! with brede
  Of marble men and maidens overwrought,
With forest branches and the trodden weed;
  Thou, silent form, dost tease us out of thought
As doth eternity: Cold Pastoral!
  When old age shall this generation waste,
    Thou shalt remain, in midst of other woe
    Than ours, a friend to man, to whom thou say'st,
  "Beauty is truth, truth beauty," — that is all
    Ye know on earth, and all ye need to know.

Ode on Melancholy

1

No, no, go not to Lethe, neither twist
  Wolf's-bane, tight-rooted, for its poisonous wine;
Nor suffer thy pale forehead to be kiss'd
  By nightshade, ruby grape of Proserpine;
Make not your rosary of yew-berries,
  Nor let the beetle, nor the death-moth be
    Your mournful Psyche, nor the downy owl
A partner in your sorrow's mysteries;
  For shade to shade will come too drowsily,
    And drown the wakeful anguish of the soul.

2

But when the melancholy fit shall fall
  Sudden from heaven like a weeping cloud,

That fosters the droop-headed flowers all,
  And hides the green hill in an April shroud;
Then glut thy sorrow on a morning rose,
  Or on the rainbow of the salt sand-wave,
    Or on the wealth of globed peonies;
Or if thy mistress some rich anger shows,
  Emprison her soft hand, and let her rave,
    And feed deep, deep upon her peerless eyes.

3

She dwells with Beauty—Beauty that must die;
  And Joy, whose hand is ever at his lips
Bidding adieu; and aching Pleasure nigh,
  Turning to poison while the bee-mouth sips:
Ay, in the very temple of Delight
  Veil'd Melancholy has her sovran shrine,
    Though seen of none save him whose strenuous
      tongue
Can burst Joy's grape against his palate fine;
His soul shall taste the sadness of her might,
  And be among her cloudy trophies hung.

Ode on Indolence

"They toil not, neither do they spin."

1

One morn before me were three figures seen,
  With bowed necks, and joined hands,
    side-faced;

And one behind the other stepp'd serene,
  In placid sandals, and in white robes graced:
They pass'd, like figures on a marble urn,
  When shifted round to see the other side;
    They came again; as when the urn once more
Is shifted round, the first seen shades return;
  And they were strange to me, as may betide
    With vases, to one deep in Phidian lore.

2

How is it, shadows, that I knew ye not?
  How came ye muffled in so hush a masque?
Was it a silent deep-disguised plot
  To steal away, and leave without a task
My idle days? Ripe was the drowsy hour;
  The blissful cloud of summer-indolence
    Benumb'd my eyes; my pulse grew less and less;
Pain had no sting, and pleasure's wreath no
        flower.
  O, why did ye not melt, and leave my sense
    Unhaunted quite of all but — nothingness?

3

A third time pass'd they by, and, passing, turn'd
  Each one the face a moment whiles to me;
Then faded, and to follow them I burn'd
  And ached for wings, because I knew the three:
The first was a fair maid, and Love her name;
  The second was Ambition, pale of cheek,
    And ever watchful with fatigued eye;

The last, whom I love more, the more of blame
  Is heap'd upon her, maiden most unmeek, —
    I knew to be my demon Poesy.

4

They faded, and, forsooth! I wanted wings:
  O folly! What is Love? and where is it?
And for that poor Ambition — it springs
  From a man's little heart's short fever-fit;
For Poesy! — no, — she has not a joy, —
  At least for me, — so sweet as drowsy noons,
    And evenings steep'd in honied indolence;
O, for an age so shelter'd from annoy,
  That I may never know how change the moons,
    Or hear the voice of busy common-sense!

5

A third time came they by; — alas! wherefore?
  My sleep had been embroider'd with dim dreams;
My soul had been a lawn besprinkled o'er
  With flowers, and stirring shades, and baffled
        beams:
The morn was clouded, but no shower fell,
  Though in her lids hung the sweet tears of May;
    The open casement press'd a new-leaved vine,
  Let in the budding warmth and throstle's lay;
O shadows! 'twas a time to bid farewell!
  Upon your skirts had fallen no tears of mine.

So, ye three ghosts, adieu! Ye cannot raise
  My head cool-bedded in the flowery grass;
For I would not be dieted with praise,
  A pet-lamb in a sentimental farce!
Fade softly from my eyes, and be once more
  In masque-like figures on the dreamy urn;
    Farewell! I yet have visions for the night,
And for the day faint visions there is store;
    Vanish, ye phantoms, from my idle spright,
    Into the clouds, and never more return!

Lamia

PART I

Upon a time, before the faery broods
Drove Nymph and Satyr from the prosperous
        woods,
Before King Oberon's bright diadem,
Sceptre, and mantle, clasp'd with dewy gem,
Frighted away the Dryads and the Fauns
From rushes green, and brakes, and cowslip'd lawns,
The ever-smitten Hermes empty left
His golden throne, bent warm on amorous theft:
From high Olympus had he stolen light,
On this side of Jove's clouds, to escape the sight
Of his great summoner, and made retreat
Into a forest on the shores of Crete.

For somewhere in that sacred island dwelt
A nymph, to whom all hoofed Satyrs knelt;
At whose white feet the languid Tritons poured
Pearls, while on land they wither'd and adored.
Fast by the springs where she to bathe was wont,
And in those meads where sometime she might
        haunt,
Were strewn rich gifts, unknown to any Muse,
Though Fancy's casket were unlock'd to choose.
Ah, what a world of love was at her feet!
So Hermes thought, and a celestial heat
Burnt from his winged heels to either ear,
That from a whiteness, as the lily clear,
Blush'd into roses 'mid his golden hair,
Fallen in jealous curls about his shoulders bare.

  From vale to vale, from wood to wood, he flew,
Breathing upon the flowers his passion new,
And wound with many a river to its head,
To find where this sweet nymph prepar'd her
        secret bed:
In vain; the sweet nymph might nowhere be found,
And so he rested, on the lonely ground,
Pensive, and full of painful jealousies
Of the Wood-Gods, and even the very trees.
There as he stood, he heard a mournful voice,
Such as once heard, in gentle heart, destroys
All pain but pity: thus the lone voice spake:
"When from this wreathed tomb shall I awake!

When move in a sweet body fit for life,
And love, and pleasure, and the ruddy strife
Of hearts and lips! Ah, miserable me!"
The God, dove-footed, glided silently
Round bush and tree, soft-brushing, in his speed,
The taller grasses and full-flowering weed,
Until he found a palpitating snake,
Bright, and cirque-couchant in a dusky brake.

  She was a gordian shape of dazzling hue,
Vermilion-spotted, golden, green, and blue;
Striped like a zebra, freckled like a pard,
Eyed like a peacock, and all crimson barr'd;
And full of silver moons, that, as she breathed,
Dissolv'd, or brighter shone, or interwreathed
Their lustres with the gloomier tapestries —
So rainbow-sided, touch'd with miseries,
She seem'd, at once, some penanced lady elf,
Some demon's mistress, or the demon's self.
Upon her crest she wore a wannish fire
Sprinkled with stars, like Ariadne's tiar:
Her head was serpent, but ah, bitter sweet!
She had a woman's mouth with all its pearls
       complete:
And for her eyes: what could such eyes do there
But weep, and weep, that they were born so fair?
As Proserpine still weeps for her Sicilian air.
Her throat was serpent, but the words she spake
Came, as through bubbling honey, for Love's sake,

And thus; while Hermes on his pinions lay,
Like a stoop'd falcon ere he takes his prey.

"Fair Hermes, crown'd with feathers, fluttering
      light,
I had a splendid dream of thee last night:
I saw thee sitting, on a throne of gold,
Among the Gods, upon Olympus old,
The only sad one; for thou didst not hear
The soft, lute-finger'd Muses chaunting clear,
Nor even Apollo when he sang alone,
Deaf to his throbbing throat's long, long melodious
      moan.
I dreamt I saw thee, robed in purple flakes,
Break amorous through the clouds, as morning
      breaks,
And, swiftly as a bright Phœbean dart,
Strike for the Cretan isle; and here thou art!
Too gentle Hermes, hast thou found the maid?"
Whereat the star of Lethe not delay'd
His rosy eloquence, and thus inquired:
"Thou smooth-lipp'd serpent, surely high inspired!
Thou beauteous wreath, with melancholy eyes,
Possess whatever bliss thou canst devise,
Telling me only where my nymph is fled,—
Where she doth breathe!" "Bright planet, thou
      hast said,"
Return'd the snake, "but seal with oaths, fair God!"
"I swear," said Hermes, "by my serpent rod,

And by thine eyes, and by thy starry crown!"
Light flew his earnest words, among the blossoms
       blown.
Then thus again the brilliance feminine:
"Too frail of heart! for this lost nymph of thine,
Free as the air, invisibly, she strays
About these thornless wilds; her pleasant days
She tastes unseen; unseen her nimble feet
Leave traces in the grass and flowers sweet;
From weary tendrils, and bow'd branches green,
She plucks the fruit unseen, she bathes unseen:
And by my power is her beauty veil'd
To keep it unaffronted, unassail'd
By the love-glances of unlovely eyes,
Of Satyrs, Fauns, and blear'd Silenus' sighs.
Pale grew her immortality, for woe
Of all these lovers, and she grieved so
I took compassion on her, bade her steep
Her hair in weird syrops, that would keep
Her loveliness invisible, yet free
To wander as she loves, in liberty.
Thou shalt behold her, Hermes, thou alone,
If thou wilt, as thou swearest, grant my boon!"
Then, once again, the charmed God began
An oath, and through the serpent's ears it ran
Warm, tremulous, devout, psalterian.
Ravish'd, she lifted her Circean head,
Blush'd a live damask, and swift-lisping said,
"I was a woman, let me have once more
A woman's shape, and charming as before.

I love a youth of Corinth — O the bliss!
Give me my woman's form, and place me where
        he is.
Stoop, Hermes, let me breathe upon thy brow,
And thou shalt see thy sweet nymph even now."
The God on half-shut feathers sank serene,
She breath'd upon his eyes, and swift was seen
Of both the guarded nymph near-smiling on
        the green.
It was no dream; or say a dream it was,
Real are the dreams of Gods, and smoothly
        pass
Their pleasures in a long immortal dream.
One warm, flush'd moment, hovering, it
        might seem
Dash'd by the wood-nymph's beauty, so he
        burn'd;
Then, lighting on the printless verdure, turn'd
To the swoon'd serpent, and with languid arm,
Delicate, put to proof the lythe Caducean charm.
So done, upon the nymph his eyes he bent
Full of adoring tears and blandishment,
And towards her stept: she, like a moon in wane,
Faded before him, cower'd, nor could restrain
Her fearful sobs, self-folding like a flower
That faints into itself at evening hour:
But the God fostering her chilled hand,
She felt the warmth, her eyelids open'd bland,
And, like new flowers at morning song of bees,
Bloom'd, and gave up her honey to the lees.

Into the green-recessed woods they flew;
Nor grew they pale, as mortal lovers do.

Left to herself, the serpent now began
To change; her elfin blood in madness ran,
Her mouth foam'd, and the grass, therewith
        besprent,
Wither'd at dew so sweet and virulent;
Her eyes in torture fix'd, and anguish drear,
Hot, glaz'd, and wide, with lid-lashes all sear,
Flash'd phosphor and sharp sparks, without one
        cooling tear.
The colours all inflam'd throughout her train,
She writh'd about, convuls'd with scarlet pain:
A deep volcanian yellow took the place
Of all her milder-mooned body's grace;
And, as the lava ravishes the mead,
Spoilt all her silver mail, and golden brede;
Made gloom of all her frecklings, streaks
        and bars,
Eclips'd her crescents, and lick'd up her stars:
So that, in moments few, she was undrest
Of all her sapphires, greens, and amethyst,
And rubious-argent: of all these bereft,
Nothing but pain and ugliness were left.
Still shone her crown; that vanish'd, also she
Melted and disappear'd as suddenly;
And in the air, her new voice luting soft,
Cried, "Lycius! gentle Lycius!"—Borne aloft

With the bright mists about the mountains hoar
These words dissolv'd: Crete's forests heard
      no more.

  Whither fled Lamia, now a lady bright,
A full-born beauty new and exquisite?
She fled into that valley they pass o'er
Who go to Corinth from Cenchreas' shore;
And rested at the foot of those wild hills,
The rugged founts of the Peræan rills,
And of that other ridge whose barren back
Stretches, with all its mist and cloudy rack,
South-westward to Cleone. There she stood
About a young bird's flutter from a wood,
Fair, on a sloping green of mossy tread,
By a clear pool, wherein she passioned
To see herself escap'd from so sore ills,
While her robes flaunted with the daffodils.

  Ah, happy Lycius!—for she was a maid
More beautiful than ever twisted braid,
Or sigh'd, or blush'd, or on spring-flowered lea
Spread a green kirtle to the minstrelsy:
A virgin purest lipp'd, yet in the lore
Of love deep learned to the red heart's core:
Not one hour old, yet of sciential brain
To unperplex bliss from its neighbour pain;
Define their pettish limits, and estrange
Their points of contact, and swift counterchange;

Intrigue with the specious chaos, and dispart
Its most ambiguous atoms with sure art;
As though in Cupid's college she had spent
Sweet days a lovely graduate, still unshent,
And kept his rosy terms in idle languishment.

Why this fair creature chose so fairily
By the wayside to linger, we shall see;
But first 'tis fit to tell how she could muse
And dream, when in the serpent prison-house,
Of all she list, strange or magnificent:
How, ever, where she will'd, her spirit went;
Whether to faint Elysium, or where
Down through tress-lifting waves the Nereids fair
Wind into Thetis' bower by many a pearly stair;
Or where God Bacchus drains his cups divine,
Stretch'd out, at ease, beneath a glutinous pine;
Or where in Pluto's gardens palatine
Mulciber's columns gleam in far piazzian line.
And sometimes into cities she would send
Her dream, with feast and rioting to blend;
And once, while among mortals dreaming thus,
She saw the young Corinthian Lycius
Charioting foremost in the envious race,
Like a young Jove with calm uneager face,
And fell into a swooning love of him.
Now on the moth-time of that evening dim
He would return that way, as well she knew,
To Corinth from the shore; for freshly blew

The eastern soft wind, and his galley now
Grated the quaystones with her brazen prow
In port Cenchreas, from Egina isle
Fresh anchor'd; whither he had been awhile
To sacrifice to Jove, whose temple there
Waits with high marble doors for blood and
          incense rare.
Jove heard his vows, and better'd his desire;
For by some freakful chance he made retire
From his companions, and set forth to walk,
Perhaps grown wearied of their Corinth talk:
Over the solitary hills he fared,
Thoughtless at first, but ere eve's star appeared
His phantasy was lost, where reason fades,
In the calm'd twilight of Platonic shades.
Lamia beheld him coming, near, more near—
Close to her passing, in indifference drear,
His silent sandals swept the mossy green;
So neighbour'd to him, and yet so unseen
She stood: he pass'd, shut up in mysteries,
His mind wrapp'd like his mantle, while her eyes
Follow'd his steps, and her neck regal white
Turn'd—syllabling thus, "Ah, Lycius bright,
And will you leave me on the hills alone?
Lycius, look back! and be some pity shown."
He did; not with cold wonder fearingly,
But Orpheus-like at an Eurydice;
For so delicious were the words she sung,
It seem'd he had lov'd them a whole summer long:

And soon his eyes had drunk her beauty up,
Leaving no drop in the bewildering cup,
And still the cup was full,—while he, afraid
Lest she should vanish ere his lip had paid
Due adoration, thus began to adore;
Her soft look growing coy, she saw his chain so sure:
"Leave thee alone! Look back! Ah, Goddess, see
Whether my eyes can ever turn from thee!
For pity do not this sad heart belie—
Even so thou vanishest so I shall die.
Stay! though a Naiad of the rivers, stay!
To thy far wishes will thy streams obey:
Stay! though the greenest woods be thy domain,
Alone they can drink up the morning rain:
Though a descended Pleiad, will not one
Of thine harmonious sisters keep in tune
Thy spheres, and as thy silver proxy shine?
So sweetly to these ravish'd ears of mine
Came thy sweet greeting, that if thou shouldst fade
Thy memory will waste me to a shade:—
For pity do not melt!"—"If I should stay,"
Said Lamia, "here, upon this floor of clay,
And pain my steps upon these flowers too rough,
What canst thou say or do of charm enough
To dull the nice remembrance of my home?
Thou canst not ask me with thee here to roam
Over these hills and vales, where no joy is,—
Empty of immortality and bliss!
Thou art a scholar, Lycius, and must know
That finer spirits cannot breathe below

In human climes, and live: Alas! poor youth,
What taste of purer air hast thou to soothe
My essence? What serener palaces,
Where I may all my many senses please,
And by mysterious sleights a hundred thirsts
              appease?
It cannot be—Adieu!" So said, she rose
Tiptoe with white arms spread. He, sick to lose
The amorous promise of her lone complain,
Swoon'd, murmuring of love, and pale with pain.
The cruel lady, without any show
Of sorrow for her tender favourite's woe,
But rather, if her eyes could brighter be,
With brighter eyes and slow amenity,
Put her new lips to his, and gave afresh
The life she had so tangled in her mesh:
And as he from one trance was wakening
Into another, she began to sing,
Happy in beauty, life, and love, and every thing,
A song of love, too sweet for earthly lyres,
While, like held breath, the stars drew in their
              panting fires.
And then she whisper'd in such trembling tone,
As those who, safe together met alone
For the first time through many anguish'd days,
Use other speech than looks; bidding him raise
His drooping head, and clear his soul of doubt,
For that she was a woman, and without
Any more subtle fluid in her veins
Than throbbing blood, and that the self-same pains

Inhabited her frail-strung heart as his.
And next she wonder'd how his eyes could miss
Her face so long in Corinth, where, she said,
She dwelt but half retir'd, and there had led
Days happy as the gold coin could invent
Without the aid of love; yet in content
Till she saw him, as once she pass'd him by,
Where 'gainst a column he leant thoughtfully
At Venus' temple porch, 'mid baskets heap'd
Of amorous herbs and flowers, newly reap'd
Late on that eve, as 'twas the night before
The Adonian feast; whereof she saw no more,
But wept alone those days, for why should she
          adore?
Lycius from death awoke into amaze,
To see her still, and singing so sweet lays;
Then from amaze into delight he fell
To hear her whisper woman's lore so well;
And every word she spake entic'd him on
To unperplex'd delight and pleasure known.
Let the mad poets say whate'er they please
Of the sweets of Faeries, Peris, Goddesses,
There is not such a treat among them all,
Haunters of cavern, lake, and waterfall,
As a real woman, lineal indeed
From Pyrrha's pebbles or old Adam's seed.
Thus gentle Lamia judg'd, and judg'd aright,
That Lycius could not love in half a fright,
So threw the goddess off, and won his heart

More pleasantly by playing woman's part,
With no more awe than what her beauty gave,
That, while it smote, still guaranteed to save.
Lycius to all made eloquent reply,
Marrying to every word a twinborn sigh;
And last, pointing to Corinth, ask'd her sweet,
If 'twas too far that night for her soft feet.
The way was short, for Lamia's eagerness
Made, by a spell, the triple league decrease
To a few paces; not at all surmised
By blinded Lycius, so in her comprised.
They pass'd the city gates, he knew not how,
So noiseless, and he never thought to know.

  As men talk in a dream, so Corinth all,
Throughout her palaces imperial,
And all her populous streets and temples lewd,
Mutter'd, like tempest in the distance brew'd,
To the wide-spreaded night above her towers.
Men, women, rich and poor, in the cool hours,
Shuffled their sandals o'er the pavement white,
Companion'd or alone; while many a light
Flared, here and there, from wealthy festivals,
And threw their moving shadows on the walls,
Or found them cluster'd in the corniced shade
Of some arch'd temple door, or dusky colonnade.

  Muffling his face, of greeting friends in fear,
Her fingers he press'd hard, as one came near

With curl'd grey beard, sharp eyes, and smooth
        bald crown,
Slow-stepp'd, and robed in philosophic gown:
Lycius shrank closer, as they met and past,
Into his mantle, adding wings to haste,
While hurried Lamia trembled: "Ah," said he,
"Why do you shudder, love, so ruefully?
Why does your tender palm dissolve in dew?"—
"I'm wearied," said fair Lamia: "tell me who
Is that old man? I cannot bring to mind
His features:—Lycius! wherefore did you blind
Yourself from his quick eyes?" Lycius replied,
" 'Tis Apollonius sage, my trusty guide
And good instructor; but to-night he seems
The ghost of folly haunting my sweet dreams."

  While yet he spake they had arrived before
A pillar'd porch, with lofty portal door,
Where hung a silver lamp, whose phosphor glow
Reflected in the slabbed steps below,
Mild as a star in water; for so new,
And so unsullied was the marble hue,
So through the crystal polish, liquid fine,
Ran the dark veins, that none but feet divine
Could e'er have touch'd there. Sounds Æolian
Breath'd from the hinges, as the ample span
Of the wide doors disclos'd a place unknown
Some time to any, but those two alone,
And a few Persian mutes, who that same year
Were seen about the markets: none knew where

They could inhabit; the most curious
Were foil'd, who watch'd to trace them to their
            house:
And but the flitter-winged verse must tell,
For truth's sake, what woe afterwards befell,
'Twould humour many a heart to leave them thus,
Shut from the busy world of more incredulous.

PART II

Love in a hut, with water and a crust,
Is—Love, forgive us!—cinders, ashes, dust;
Love in a palace is perhaps at last
More grievous torment than a hermit's fast:—
That is a doubtful tale from faery land,
Hard for the non-elect to understand.
Had Lycius liv'd to hand his story down,
He might have given the moral a fresh frown,
Or clench'd it quite: but too short was their bliss
To breed distrust and hate, that make the soft
            voice hiss.
Besides, there, nightly, with terrific glare,
Love, jealous grown of so complete a pair,
Hover'd and buzz'd his wings, with fearful roar,
Above the lintel of their chamber door,
And down the passage cast a glow upon the floor.

  For all this came a ruin: side by side
They were enthroned, in the even tide,
Upon a couch, near to a curtaining
Whose airy texture, from a golden string,

Floated into the room, and let appear
Unveil'd the summer heaven, blue and clear,
Betwixt two marble shafts:—there they reposed,
Where use had made it sweet, with eyelids closed,
Saving a tythe which love still open kept,
That they might see each other while they
       almost slept;
When from the slope side of a suburb hill,
Deafening the swallow's twitter, came a thrill
Of trumpets—Lycius started—the sounds fled,
But left a thought, a buzzing in his head.
For the first time, since first he harbour'd in
That purple-lined palace of sweet sin,
His spirit pass'd beyond its golden bourn
Into the noisy world almost forsworn.
The lady, ever watchful, penetrant,
Saw this with pain, so arguing a want
Of something more, more than her empery
Of joys; and she began to moan and sigh
Because he mused beyond her, knowing well
That but a moment's thought is passion's
       passing bell.
"Why do you sigh, fair creature?" whisper'd he:
"Why do you think?" return'd she tenderly:
"You have deserted me;—where am I now?
Not in your heart while care weighs on your brow:
No, no, you have dismiss'd me; and I go
From your breast houseless: ay, it must be so."
He answer'd, bending to her open eyes,

Where he was mirror'd small in paradise,
"My silver planet, both of eve and morn!
Why will you plead yourself so sad forlorn,
While I am striving how to fill my heart
With deeper crimson, and a double smart?
How to entangle, trammel up and snare
Your soul in mine, and labyrinth you there
Like the hid scent in an unbudded rose?
Ay, a sweet kiss—you see your mighty woes.
My thoughts! shall I unveil them? Listen then!
What mortal hath a prize, that other men
May be confounded and abash'd withal,
But lets it sometimes pace abroad majestical,
And triumph, as in thee I should rejoice
Amid the hoarse alarm of Corinth's voice.
Let my foes choke, and my friends shout afar,
While through the thronged streets your bridal car
Wheels round its dazzling spokes."—The lady's
        cheek
Trembled; she nothing said, but, pale and meek,
Arose and knelt before him, wept a rain
Of sorrows at his words; at last with pain
Beseeching him, the while his hand she wrung,
To change his purpose. He thereat was stung,
Perverse, with stronger fancy to reclaim
Her wild and timid nature to his aim:
Besides, for all his love, in self despite,
Against his better self, he took delight
Luxurious in her sorrows, soft and new.

His passion, cruel grown, took on a hue
Fierce and sanguineous as 'twas possible
In one whose brow had no dark veins to swell.
Fine was the mitigated fury, like
Apollo's presence when in act to strike
The serpent—Ha, the serpent! certes, she
Was none. She burnt, she lov'd the tyranny,
And, all subdued, consented to the hour
When to the bridal he should lead his paramour.
Whispering in midnight silence, said the youth,
"Sure some sweet name thou hast, though, by
          my truth,
I have not ask'd it, ever thinking thee
Not mortal, but of heavenly progeny,
As still I do. Hast any mortal name,
Fit appellation for this dazzling frame?
Or friends or kinsfolk on the citied earth,
To share our marriage feast and nuptial mirth?"
"I have no friends," said Lamia, "no, not one;
My presence in wide Corinth hardly known:
My parents' bones are in their dusty urns
Sepulchred, where no kindled incense burns,
Seeing all their luckless race are dead, save me,
And I neglect the holy rite for thee.
Even as you list invite your many guests;
But if, as now it seems, your vision rests
With any pleasure on me, do not bid
Old Apollonius—from him keep me hid."
Lycius, perplex'd at words so blind and blank,
Made close inquiry; from whose touch she shrank,

Feigning a sleep; and he to the dull shade
Of deep sleep in a moment was betray'd.
  It was the custom then to bring away
The bride from home at blushing shut of day,
Veil'd, in a chariot, heralded along
By strewn flowers, torches, and a marriage song,
With other pageants: but this fair unknown
Had not a friend. So being left alone,
(Lycius was gone to summon all his kin)
And knowing surely she could never win
His foolish heart from its mad pompousness,
She set herself, high-thoughted, how to dress
The misery in fit magnificence.
She did so, but 'tis doubtful how and whence
Came, and who were her subtle servitors.
About the halls, and to and from the doors,
There was a noise of wings, till in short space
The glowing banquet-room shone with wide-arched
        grace.
A haunting music, sole perhaps and lone
Supportress of the faery-roof, made moan
Throughout, as fearful the whole charm might fade.
Fresh carved cedar, mimicking a glade
Of palm and plantain, met from either side,
High in the midst, in honour of the bride:
Two palms and then two plantains, and so on,
From either side their stems branch'd one to one
All down the aisled place; and beneath all
There ran a stream of lamps straight on from wall
        to wall.

So canopied, lay an untasted feast
Teeming with odours. Lamia, regal drest,
Silently paced about, and as she went,
In pale contented sort of discontent,
Mission'd her viewless servants to enrich
The fretted splendour of each nook and niche.
Between the tree-stems, marbled plain at first,
Came jasper pannels; then, anon, there burst
Forth creeping imagery of slighter trees,
And with the larger wove in small intricacies.
Approving all, she faded at self-will,
And shut the chamber up, close, hush'd and still,
Complete and ready for the revels rude,
When dreadful guests would come to spoil her
                    solitude.

  The day appear'd, and all the gossip rout.
O senseless Lycius! Madman! wherefore flout
The silent-blessing fate, warm cloister'd hours,
And show to common eyes these secret bowers?
The herd approach'd; each guest, with busy brain,
Arriving at the portal, gaz'd amain,
And enter'd marveling: for they knew the street,
Remember'd it from childhood all complete
Without a gap, yet ne'er before had seen
That royal porch, that high-built fair demesne;
So in they hurried all, maz'd, curious and keen:
Save one, who look'd thereon with eye severe,
And with calm-planted steps walk'd in austere;

'Twas Apollonius: something too he laugh'd,
As though some knotty problem, that had daft
His patient thought, and now begun to thaw,
And solve and melt:—'twas just as he foresaw.

  He met within the murmurous vestibule
His young disciple. "'Tis no common rule,
Lycius," said he, "for uninvited guest
To force himself upon you, and infest
With an unbidden presence the bright throng
Of younger friends; yet must I do this wrong,
And you forgive me." Lycius blush'd, and led
The old man through the inner doors
              broad-spread;
With reconciling words and courteous mien
Turning into sweet milk the sophist's spleen.

  Of wealthy lustre was the banquet-room,
Fill'd with pervading brilliance and perfume:
Before each lucid pannel fuming stood
A censer fed with myrrh and spiced wood,
Each by a sacred tripod held aloft,
Whose slender feet wide-swerv'd upon the soft
Wool-woofed carpets: fifty wreaths of smoke
From fifty censers their light voyage took
To the high roof, still mimick'd as they rose
Along the mirror'd walls by twin-clouds odorous.
Twelve sphered tables, by silk seats insphered,
High as the level of a man's breast rear'd

On libbard's paws, upheld the heavy gold
Of cups and goblets, and the store thrice told
Of Ceres' horn, and, in huge vessels, wine
Come from the gloomy tun with merry shine.
Thus loaded with a feast the tables stood,
Each shrining in the midst the image of a God.

When in an antechamber every guest
Had felt the cold full sponge to pleasure press'd,
By minist'ring slaves, upon his hands and feet,
And fragrant oils with ceremony meet
Pour'd on his hair, they all mov'd to the feast
In white robes, and themselves in order placed
Around the silken couches, wondering
      Whence all this mighty cost and blaze of wealth
          could spring.

Soft went the music the soft air along,
While fluent Greek a vowel'd undersong
Kept up among the guests, discoursing low
At first, for scarcely was the wine at flow;
But when the happy vintage touch'd their brains,
Louder they talk, and louder come the strains
Of powerful instruments:— the gorgeous dyes,
The space, the splendour of the draperies,
The roof of awful richness, nectarous cheer,
Beautiful slaves, and Lamia's self, appear,
Now, when the wine has done its rosy deed,
And every soul from human trammels freed,

No more so strange; for merry wine, sweet wine,
Will make Elysian shades not too fair, too divine.

Soon was God Bacchus at meridian height;
Flush'd were their cheeks, and bright eyes double
            bright:
Garlands of every green, and every scent
From vales deflower'd, or forest-trees branch-rent,
In baskets of bright osier'd gold were brought
High as the handles heap'd, to suit the thought
Of every guest; that each, as he did please,
Might fancy-fit his brows, silk-pillow'd at his ease.

What wreath for Lamia? What for Lycius?
What for the sage, old Apollonius?
Upon her aching forehead be there hung
The leaves of willow and of adder's tongue;
And for the youth, quick, let us strip for him
The thyrsus, that his watching eyes may swim
Into forgetfulness; and, for the sage,
Let spear-grass and the spiteful thistle wage
War on his temples. Do not all charms fly
At the mere touch of cold philosophy?
There was an awful rainbow once in heaven:
We know her woof, her texture; she is given
In the dull catalogue of common things.
Philosophy will clip an Angel's wings,
Conquer all mysteries by rule and line,
Empty the haunted air, and gnomed mine —

Unweave a rainbow, as it erewhile made
The tender-person'd Lamia melt into a shade.

By her glad Lycius sitting, in chief place,
Scarce saw in all the room another face,
Till, checking his love trance, a cup he took
Full brimm'd, and opposite sent forth a look
'Cross the broad table, to beseech a glance
From his old teacher's wrinkled countenance,
And pledge him. The bald-head philosopher
Had fix'd his eye, without a twinkle or stir
Full on the alarmed beauty of the bride,
Brow-beating her fair form, and troubling her
        sweet pride.
Lycius then press'd her hand, with devout touch,
As pale it lay upon the rosy couch:
'Twas icy, and the cold ran through his veins;
Then sudden it grew hot, and all the pains
Of an unnatural heat shot to his heart.
"Lamia, what means this? Wherefore dost thou
        start?
Know'st thou that man?" Poor Lamia answer'd not.
He gaz'd into her eyes, and not a jot
Own'd they the lovelorn piteous appeal:
More, more he gaz'd: his human senses reel:
Some hungry spell that loveliness absorbs;
There was no recognition in those orbs.
"Lamia!" he cried—and no soft-toned reply.
The many heard, and the loud revelry
Grew hush; the stately music no more breathes;

The myrtle sicken'd in a thousand wreaths.
By faint degrees, voice, lute, and pleasure ceased;
A deadly silence step by step increased,
Until it seem'd a horrid presence there,
And not a man but felt the terror in his hair.
"Lamia!" he shriek'd; and nothing but the shriek
With its sad echo did the silence break.
"Begone, foul dream!" he cried, gazing again
In the bride's face, where now no azure vein
Wander'd on fair-spaced temples; no soft bloom
Misted the cheek; no passion to illume
The deep-recessed vision:—all was blight;
Lamia, no longer fair, there sat a deadly white.
"Shut, shut those juggling eyes, thou ruthless man!
Turn them aside, wretch! or the righteous ban
Of all the Gods, whose dreadful images
Here represent their shadowy presences,
May pierce them on the sudden with the thorn
Of painful blindness; leaving thee forlorn,
In trembling dotage to the feeblest fright
Of conscience, for their long offended might,
For all thine impious proud-heart sophistries,
Unlawful magic, and enticing lies.
Corinthians! look upon that grey-beard wretch!
Mark how, possess'd, his lashless eyelids stretch
Around his demon eyes! Corinthians, see!
My sweet bride withers at their potency."
"Fool!" said the sophist, in an under-tone
Gruff with contempt; which a death-nighting moan
From Lycius answer'd, as heart-struck and lost,

He sank supine beside the aching ghost.
"Fool! Fool!" repeated he, while his eyes still
Relented not, nor mov'd; "from every ill
Of life have I preserv'd thee to this day,
And shall I see thee made a serpent's prey?"
Then Lamia breath'd death breath;
       the sophist's eye,
Like a sharp spear, went through her utterly,
Keen, cruel, perceant, stinging: she, as well
As her weak hand could any meaning tell,
Motion'd him to be silent; vainly so,
He look'd and look'd again a level — No!
"A Serpent!" echoed he; no sooner said,
Than with a frightful scream she vanished:
And Lycius' arms were empty of delight,
As were his limbs of life, from that same night.
On the high couch he lay! — his friends came
       round —
Supported him — no pulse, or breath they found,
And, in its marriage robe, the heavy body wound.

To Autumn

1

Season of mists and mellow fruitfulness,
  Close bosom-friend of the maturing sun;
Conspiring with him how to load and bless
  With fruit the vines that round the thatch-eves run;

To bend with apples the moss'd cottage-trees,
  And fill all fruit with ripeness to the core;
    To swell the gourd, and plump the hazel shells
  With a sweet kernel; to set budding more,
And still more, later flowers for the bees,
Until they think warm days will never cease,
    For summer has o'er-brimm'd their clammy cells.

2

Who hath not seen thee oft amid thy store?
  Sometimes whoever seeks abroad may find
Thee sitting careless on a granary floor,
  Thy hair soft-lifted by the winnowing wind;
Or on a half-reap'd furrow sound asleep,
  Drows'd with the fume of poppies, while thy hook
    Spares the next swath and all its twined flowers:
And sometimes like a gleaner thou dost keep
  Steady thy laden head across a brook;
  Or by a cyder-press, with patient look,
    Thou watchest the last oozings hours by hours.

3

Where are the songs of spring? Ay, where are they?
  Think not of them, thou hast thy music too,—
While barred clouds bloom the soft-dying day,
  And touch the stubble-plains with rosy hue;
Then in a wailful choir the small gnats mourn
  Among the river sallows, borne aloft
    Or sinking as the light wind lives or dies;

And full-grown lambs loud bleat from hilly bourn;
Hedge-crickets sing; and now with treble soft
The red-breast whistles from a garden-croft;
And gathering swallows twitter in the skies.

The Fall of Hyperion: A Dream

CANTO I

Fanatics have their dreams, wherewith they weave
A paradise for a sect; the savage too
From forth the loftiest fashion of his sleep
Guesses at heaven: pity these have not
Trac'd upon vellum or wild Indian leaf
The shadows of melodious utterance.
But bare of laurel they live, dream, and die;
For Poesy alone can tell her dreams,
With the fine spell of words alone can save
Imagination from the sable charm
And dumb enchantment. Who alive can say
"Thou art no poet; may'st not tell thy dreams"?
Since every man whose soul is not a clod
Hath visions, and would speak, if he had lov'd
And been well nurtured in his mother tongue.
Whether the dream now purposed to rehearse
Be poet's or fanatic's will be known
When this warm scribe my hand is in the grave.

Methought I stood where trees of every clime,
Palm, myrtle, oak, and sycamore, and beech,

With plantane, and spice blossoms, made a
        screen;
In neighbourhood of fountains, by the noise
Soft showering in mine ears, and, by the touch
Of scent, not far from roses. Turning round,
I saw an arbour with a drooping roof
Of trellis vines, and bells, and larger blooms,
Like floral-censers swinging light in air;
Before its wreathed doorway, on a mound
Of moss, was spread a feast of summer fruits,
Which, nearer seen, seem'd refuse of a meal
By angel tasted, or our mother Eve;
For empty shells were scattered on the grass,
And grape stalks but half bare, and remnants more
Sweet smelling, whose pure kinds I could not know.
Still was more plenty than the fabled horn
Thrice emptied could pour forth, at banqueting
For Proserpine return'd to her own fields,
Where the white heifers low. And appetite
More yearning than on earth I ever felt
Growing within, I ate deliciously;
And, after not long, thirsted, for thereby
Stood a cool vessel of transparent juice,
Sipp'd by the wander'd bee, the which I took,
And, pledging all the mortals of the world,
And all the dead whose names are in our lips,
Drank. That full draught is parent of my theme.
No Asian poppy, nor elixir fine
Of the soon fading jealous caliphat;
No poison gender'd in close monkish cell

To thin the scarlet conclave of old men,
Could so have rapt unwilling life away.
Among the fragrant husks and berries crush'd,
Upon the grass I struggled hard against
The domineering potion; but in vain:
The cloudy swoon came on, and down I sunk
Like a Silenus on an antique vase.
How long I slumber'd 'tis a chance to guess.
When sense of life return'd, I started up
As if with wings; but the fair trees were gone,
The mossy mound and arbour were no more;
I look'd around upon the carved sides
Of an old sanctuary with roof august,
Builded so high, it seem'd that filmed clouds
Might spread beneath, as o'er the stars of heaven;
So old the place was, I remembered none
The like upon the earth; what I had seen
Of grey cathedrals, buttress'd walls, rent towers,
The superannuations of sunk realms,
Or nature's rocks toil'd hard in waves and winds,
Seem'd but the faulture of decrepit things
To that eternal domed monument.
Upon the marble at my feet there lay
Store of strange vessels, and large draperies,
Which needs had been of dyed asbestos wove,
Or in that place the moth could not corrupt,
So white the linen; so, in some, distinct
Ran imageries from a sombre loom.
All in a mingled heap confus'd there lay

Robes, golden tongs, censer, and chafing dish,
Girdles, and chains, and holy jewelries.

  Turning from these with awe, once more I rais'd
My eyes to fathom the space every way;
The embossed roof, the silent massy range
Of columns north and south, ending in mist
Of nothing, then to eastward, where black gates
Were shut against the sunrise evermore.
Then to the west I look'd, and saw far off
An image, huge of feature as a cloud,
At level of whose feet an altar slept,
To be approach'd on either side by steps,
And marble balustrade, and patient travail
To count with toil the innumerable degrees.
Towards the altar sober-pac'd I went,
Repressing haste, as too unholy there;
And, coming nearer, saw beside the shrine
One minist'ring; and there arose a flame.
When in mid-May the sickening east wind
Shifts sudden to the south, the small warm rain
Melts out the frozen incense from all flowers,
And fills the air with so much pleasant health
That even the dying man forgets his shroud;
Even so that lofty sacrificial fire,
Sending forth Maian incense, spread around
Forgetfulness of every thing but bliss,
And clouded all the altar with soft smoke,
From whose white fragrant curtains thus I heard

Language pronounc'd. "If thou canst not ascend
These steps, die on that marble where thou art.
Thy flesh, near cousin to the common dust,
Will parch for lack of nutriment—thy bones
Will wither in few years, and vanish so
That not the quickest eye could find a grain
Of what thou now art on that pavement cold.
The sands of thy short life are spent this hour,
And no hand in the universe can turn
Thy hour glass, if these gummed leaves be burnt
Ere thou canst mount up these immortal steps."
I heard, I look'd: two senses both at once
So fine, so subtle, felt the tyranny
Of that fierce threat, and the hard task proposed.
Prodigious seem'd the toil; the leaves were yet
Burning,—when suddenly a palsied chill
Struck from the paved level up my limbs,
And was ascending quick to put cold grasp
Upon those streams that pulse beside the throat:
I shriek'd; and the sharp anguish of my shriek
Stung my own ears—I strove hard to escape
The numbness; strove to gain the lowest step.
Slow, heavy, deadly was my pace: the cold
Grew stifling, suffocating, at the heart;
And when I clasp'd my hands I felt them not.
One minute before death, my iced foot touch'd
The lowest stair; and as it touch'd, life seem'd
To pour in at the toes: I mounted up,
As once fair angels on a ladder flew
From the green turf to heaven.—"Holy Power,"

Cried I, approaching near the horned shrine,
"What am I that should so be sav'd from death?
What am I that another death come not
To choke my utterance sacrilegious here?"
Then said the veiled shadow—"Thou hast felt
What 'tis to die and live again before
Thy fated hour. That thou hadst power to do so
Is thy own safety; thou hast dated on
Thy doom."—"High Prophetess," said I, "purge off
Benign, if so it please thee, my mind's film."
"None can usurp this height," return'd that shade,
"But those to whom the miseries of the world
Are misery, and will not let them rest.
All else who find a haven in the world,
Where they may thoughtless sleep away their days,
If by a chance into this fane they come,
Rot on the pavement where thou rotted'st half."—
"Are there not thousands in the world," said I,
Encourag'd by the sooth voice of the shade,
"Who love their fellows even to the death;
Who feel the giant agony of the world;
And more, like slaves to poor humanity,
Labour for mortal good? I sure should see
Other men here: but I am here alone."
"They whom thou spak'st of are no vision'ries,"
Rejoin'd that voice—"They are no dreamers weak,
They seek no wonder but the human face;
No music but a happy-noted voice—
They come not here, they have no thought to
        come—

And thou art here, for thou art less than they.
What benefit canst thou do, or all thy tribe,
To the great world? Thou art a dreaming thing;
A fever of thyself—think of the earth;
What bliss even in hope is there for thee?
What haven? Every creature hath its home;
Every sole man hath days of joy and pain,
Whether his labours be sublime or low—
The pain alone; the joy alone; distinct:
Only the dreamer venoms all his days,
Bearing more woe than all his sins deserve.
Therefore, that happiness be somewhat
        shar'd,
Such things as thou art are admitted oft
Into like gardens thou didst pass erewhile,
And suffer'd in these temples; for that cause
Thou standest safe beneath this statue's knees."
"That I am favour'd for unworthiness,
By such propitious parley medicin'd
In sickness not ignoble, I rejoice,
Aye, and could weep for love of such award."
So answer'd I, continuing, "If it please,
Majestic shadow, tell me: sure not all
Those melodies sung into the world's ear
Are useless: sure a poet is a sage;
A humanist, physician to all men.
That I am none I feel, as vultures feel
They are no birds when eagles are abroad.
What am I then? Thou spakest of my tribe:

What tribe?"—The tall shade veil'd in drooping
      white
Then spake, so much more earnest, that the breath
Mov'd the thin linen folds that drooping hung
About a golden censer from the hand
Pendent.—"Art thou not of the dreamer tribe?
The poet and the dreamer are distinct,
Diverse, sheer opposite, antipodes.
The one pours out a balm upon the world,
The other vexes it." Then shouted I
Spite of myself, and with a Pythia's spleen,
"Apollo! faded, far flown Apollo!
Where is thy misty pestilence to creep
Into the dwellings, through the door crannies,
Of all mock lyrists, large self worshipers,
And careless hectorers in proud bad verse.
Though I breathe death with them it will be life
To see them sprawl before me into graves.
Majestic shadow, tell me where I am:
Whose altar this; for whom this incense curls:
What image this, whose face I cannot see,
For the broad marble knees; and who thou art,
Of accent feminine, so courteous."
Then the tall shade in drooping linens veil'd
Spake out, so much more earnest, that her breath
Stirr'd the thin folds of gauze that drooping hung
About a golden censer from her hand
Pendent; and by her voice I knew she shed
Long treasured tears. "This temple sad and lone

Is all spar'd from the thunder of a war
Foughten long since by giant hierarchy
Against rebellion: this old image here,
Whose carved features wrinkled as he fell,
Is Saturn's; I, Moneta, left supreme
Sole priestess of his desolation."—
I had no words to answer; for my tongue,
Useless, could find about its roofed home
No syllable of a fit majesty
To make rejoinder to Moneta's mourn.
There was a silence while the altar's blaze
Was fainting for sweet food: I look'd thereon
And on the paved floor, where nigh were pil'd
Faggots of cinnamon, and many heaps
Of other crisped spice-wood—then again
I look'd upon the altar and its horns
Whiten'd with ashes, and its lang'rous flame,
And then upon the offerings again;
And so by turns—till sad Moneta cried,
"The sacrifice is done, but not the less
Will I be kind to thee for thy good will.
My power, which to me is still a curse,
Shall be to thee a wonder; for the scenes
Still swooning vivid through my globed brain
With an electral changing misery
Thou shalt with those dull mortal eyes behold,
Free from all pain, if wonder pain thee not."
As near as an immortal's sphered words
Could to a mother's soften, were these last:
But yet I had a terror of her robes,

And chiefly of the veils, that from her brow
Hung pale, and curtain'd her in mysteries
That made my heart too small to hold its blood.
This saw that Goddess, and with sacred hand
Parted the veils. Then saw I a wan face,
Not pin'd by human sorrows, but bright blanch'd
By an immortal sickness which kills not;
It works a constant change, which happy death
Can put no end to; deathwards progressing
To no death was that visage; it had pass'd
The lily and the snow; and beyond these
I must not think now, though I saw that face—
But for her eyes I should have fled away.
They held me back, with a benignant light,
Soft mitigated by divinest lids
Half closed, and visionless entire they seem'd
Of all external things—they saw me not,
But in blank splendour beam'd like the mild moon,
Who comforts those she sees not, who knows not
What eyes are upward cast. As I had found
A grain of gold upon a mountain's side,
And twing'd with avarice strain'd out my eyes
To search its sullen entrails rich with ore,
So at the view of sad Moneta's brow,
I ached to see what things the hollow brain
Behind enwombed: what high tragedy
In the dark secret chambers of her skull
Was acting, that could give so dread a stress
To her cold lips, and fill with such a light
Her planetary eyes; and touch her voice

With such a sorrow. "Shade of Memory!"
Cried I, with act adorant at her feet,
"By all the gloom hung round thy fallen house,
By this last temple, by the golden age,
By great Apollo, thy dear foster child,
And by thy self, forlorn divinity,
The pale Omega of a wither'd race,
Let me behold, according as thou said'st,
What in thy brain so ferments to and fro."—
No sooner had this conjuration pass'd
My devout lips, than side by side we stood,
(Like a stunt bramble by a solemn pine)
Deep in the shady sadness of a vale,
Far sunken from the healthy breath of morn,
Far from the fiery noon, and eve's one star.
Onward I look'd beneath the gloomy boughs,
And saw, what first I thought an image huge,
Like to the image pedestal'd so high
In Saturn's temple. Then Moneta's voice
Came brief upon mine ear,— "So Saturn sat
When he had lost his realms."—Whereon
        there grew
A power within me of enormous ken,
To see as a God sees, and take the depth
Of things as nimbly as the outward eye
Can size and shape pervade. The lofty theme
At those few words hung vast before my mind,
With half unravel'd web. I set myself
Upon an eagle's watch, that I might see,

And seeing ne'er forget. No stir of life
Was in this shrouded vale, not so much air
As in the zoning of a summer's day
Robs not one light seed from the feather'd grass,
But where the dead leaf fell there did it rest:
A stream went voiceless by, still deaden'd more
By reason of the fallen divinity
Spreading more shade: the Naiad mid her reeds
Press'd her cold finger closer to her lips.
Along the margin sand large footmarks went
No farther than to where old Saturn's feet
Had rested, and there slept, how long a sleep!
Degraded, cold, upon the sodden ground
His old right hand lay nerveless, listless, dead,
Unsceptred; and his realmless eyes were clos'd,
While his bow'd head seem'd listening to
      the Earth,
His antient mother, for some comfort yet.

  It seem'd no force could wake him from his
      place;
But there came one who with a kindred hand
Touch'd his wide shoulders, after bending low
With reverence, though to one who knew it not.
Then came the griev'd voice of Mnemosyne,
And griev'd I hearken'd. "That divinity
Whom thou saw'st step from yon forlornest wood,
And with slow pace approach our fallen King,
Is Thea, softest-natur'd of our brood."

I mark'd the goddess in fair statuary
Surpassing wan Moneta by the head,
And in her sorrow nearer woman's tears.
There was a listening fear in her regard,
As if calamity had but begun;
As if the vanward clouds of evil days
Had spent their malice, and the sullen rear
Was with its stored thunder labouring up.
One hand she press'd upon that aching spot
Where beats the human heart; as if just there,
Though an immortal, she felt cruel pain;
The other upon Saturn's bended neck
She laid, and to the level of his hollow ear
Leaning, with parted lips, some words she spake
In solemn tenour and deep organ tune;
Some mourning words, which in our feeble tongue
Would come in this-like accenting; how frail
To that large utterance of the early Gods!—
"Saturn! look up—and for what, poor lost King?
I have no comfort for thee, no—not one:
I cannot cry, *Wherefore thus sleepest thou?*
For heaven is parted from thee, and the earth
Knows thee not, so afflicted, for a God;
And ocean too, with all its solemn noise,
Has from thy sceptre pass'd, and all the air
Is emptied of thine hoary majesty.
Thy thunder, captious at the new command,
Rumbles reluctant o'er our fallen house;
And thy sharp lightning in unpractised hands

Scorches and burns our once serene domain.
With such remorseless speed still come new woes
That unbelief has not a space to breathe.
Saturn, sleep on:—Me thoughtless, why should I
Thus violate thy slumbrous solitude?
Why should I ope thy melancholy eyes?
Saturn, sleep on, while at thy feet I weep."

  As when, upon a tranced summer night,
Forests, branch-charmed by the earnest stars,
Dream, and so dream all night, without a noise,
Save from one gradual solitary gust,
Swelling upon the silence; dying off;
As if the ebbing air had but one wave;
So came these words, and went; the while in tears
She press'd her fair large forehead to the earth,
Just where her fallen hair might spread in curls,
A soft and silken mat for Saturn's feet.
Long, long, those two were postured motionless,
Like sculpture builded up upon the grave
Of their own power. A long awful time
I look'd upon them; still they were the same;
The frozen God still bending to the earth,
And the sad Goddess weeping at his feet;
Moneta silent. Without stay or prop
But my own weak mortality, I bore
The load of this eternal quietude,
The unchanging gloom, and the three fixed
          shapes

Ponderous upon my senses a whole moon.
For by my burning brain I measured sure
Her silver seasons shedded on the night,
And every day by day methought I grew
More gaunt and ghostly. Oftentimes I pray'd
Intense, that death would take me from the vale
And all its burthens. Gasping with despair
Of change, hour after hour I curs'd myself:
Until old Saturn rais'd his faded eyes,
And look'd around, and saw his kingdom gone,
And all the gloom and sorrow of the place,
And that fair kneeling Goddess at his feet.
As the moist scent of flowers, and grass, and leaves
Fills forest dells with a pervading air
Known to the woodland nostril, so the words
Of Saturn fill'd the mossy glooms around,
Even to the hollows of time-eaten oaks,
And to the windings in the foxes' hole,
With sad low tones, while thus he spake, and sent
Strange musings to the solitary Pan.

"Moan, brethren, moan; for we are swallow'd up
And buried from all godlike exercise
Of influence benign on planets pale,
And peaceful sway above man's harvesting,
And all those acts which deity supreme
Doth ease its heart of love in. Moan and wail.
Moan, brethren, moan; for lo! the rebel spheres
Spin round, the stars their antient courses keep,
Clouds still with shadowy moisture haunt the earth,

Still suck their fill of light from sun and moon,
Still buds the tree, and still the sea-shores murmur.
There is no death in all the universe,
No smell of death.—There shall be death.—
        Moan, moan,
Moan, Cybele, moan, for thy pernicious babes
Have chang'd a God into a shaking palsy.
Moan, brethren, moan; for I have no strength left,
Weak as the reed—weak—feeble as my voice—
O, O, the pain, the pain of feebleness.
Moan, moan; for still I thaw—or give me help:
Throw down those imps and give me victory.
Let me hear other groans, and trumpets blown
Of triumph calm, and hymns of festival
From the gold peaks of heaven's high piled
        clouds;
Voices of soft proclaim, and silver stir
Of strings in hollow shells; and let there be
Beautiful things made new for the surprise
Of the sky children."—So he feebly ceas'd,
With such a poor and sickly sounding pause,
Methought I heard some old man of the earth
Bewailing earthly loss; nor could my eyes
And ears act with that pleasant unison of sense
Which marries sweet sound with the grace of form,
And dolorous accent from a tragic harp
With large limb'd visions. More I scrutinized:
Still fix'd he sat beneath the sable trees,
Whose arms spread straggling in wild serpent forms,
With leaves all hush'd: his awful presence there

(Now all was silent) gave a deadly lie
To what I erewhile heard: only his lips
Trembled amid the white curls of his beard.
They told the truth, though, round, the snowy locks
Hung nobly, as upon the face of heaven
A midday fleece of clouds. Thea arose
And stretch'd her white arm through the hollow
        dark,
Pointing some whither: whereat he too rose
Like a vast giant seen by men at sea
To grow pale from the waves at dull midnight.
They melted from my sight into the woods:
Ere I could turn, Moneta cried—"These twain
Are speeding to the families of grief,
Where roof'd in by black rocks they waste in pain
And darkness for no hope."—And she spake on,
As ye may read who can unwearied pass
Onward from the antechamber of this dream,
Where even at the open doors awhile
I must delay, and glean my memory
Of her high phrase: perhaps no further dare.

CANTO II

"Mortal, that thou may'st understand aright,
I humanize my sayings to thine ear,
Making comparisons of earthly things;
Or thou might'st better listen to the wind,
Whose language is to thee a barren noise,
Though it blows legend-laden through the trees.

In melancholy realms big tears are shed,
More sorrow like to this, and such-like woe,
Too huge for mortal tongue, or pen of scribe.
The Titans fierce, self-hid, or prison-bound,
Groan for the old allegiance once more,
Listening in their doom for Saturn's voice.
But one of our whole eagle-brood still keeps
His sov'reignty, and rule, and majesty;
Blazing Hyperion on his orbed fire
Still sits, still snuffs the incense teeming up
From man to the Sun's God: yet unsecure;
For as upon the earth dire prodigies
Fright and perplex, so also shudders he:
Nor at dog's howl, or gloom-bird's even screech,
Or the familiar visitings of one
Upon the first toll of his passing bell:
But horrors portion'd to a giant nerve
Make great Hyperion ache. His palace bright,
Bastion'd with pyramids of glowing gold,
And touch'd with shade of bronzed obelisks,
Glares a blood red through all the thousand
                    courts,
Arches, and domes, and fiery galleries:
And all its curtains of Aurorian clouds
Flush angerly: when he would taste the wreaths
Of incense breath'd aloft from sacred hills,
Instead of sweets, his ample palate takes
Savour of poisonous brass and metals sick.
Wherefore when harbour'd in the sleepy west,

After the full completion of fair day,
For rest divine upon exalted couch
And slumber in the arms of melody,
He paces through the pleasant hours of ease,
With strides colossal, on from hall to hall;
While, far within each aisle and deep recess,
His winged minions in close clusters stand
Amaz'd, and full of fear; like anxious men
Who on a wide plain gather in sad troops,
When earthquakes jar their battlements and
       towers.
Even now, while Saturn, rous'd from icy trance,
Goes, step for step, with Thea from yon woods,
Hyperion, leaving twilight in the rear,
Is sloping to the threshold of the west.
Thither we tend."—Now in clear light I stood,
Reliev'd from the dusk vale. Mnemosyne
Was sitting on a square edg'd polish'd stone,
That in its lucid depth reflected pure
Her priestess-garments. My quick eyes ran on
From stately nave to nave, from vault to vault,
Through bowers of fragrant and enwreathed light,
And diamond paved lustrous long arcades.
Anon rush'd by the bright Hyperion;
His flaming robes stream'd out beyond his heels,
And gave a roar, as if of earthly fire,
That scar'd away the meek ethereal hours
And made their dove-wings tremble: on he
       flared

. . . .

This living hand, now warm and capable

This living hand, now warm and capable
Of earnest grasping, would, if it were cold
And in the icy silence of the tomb,
So haunt thy days and chill thy dreaming nights
That thou would wish thine own heart dry of blood,
So in my veins red life might stream again,
And thou be conscience-calm'd. See, here it is—
I hold it towards you.

PHILIP LEVINE is the author of sixteen books of poetry, including *The Simple Truth* (1994), which won the Pulitzer Prize; *What Work Is* (1991), which won the National Book Award; *Ashes: Poems New and Old* (1979), which received the National Book Critics Circle Award and the first American Book Award for Poetry; and *7 Years From Somewhere* (1979), which won the National Book Critics Circle Award. For two years he served as chair of the Literature Panel of the National Endowment for the Arts, and he was elected a Chancellor of The Academy of American Poets in 2000. Philip Levine lives in New York City and Fresno, California, and teaches at New York University.